NORTHERN HONSHU
Pages 254–273

HOKKAIDO
Pages 274–285

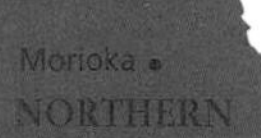

KYOTO CITY
Pages 148–179

CENTRAL HONSHU
Pages 122–147

TOKYO AREA BY AREA
Pages 56–107; for Street Finder map, see pages 108–117

CENTRAL TOKYO
Pages 60–71

NORTHERN TOKYO
Pages 72–83

WESTERN TOKYO
Pages 84–95

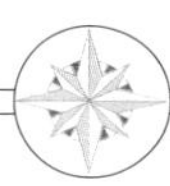

EYEWITNESS *TRAVEL GUIDES*

JAPAN

DK EYEWITNESS *TRAVEL GUIDES*

JAPAN

DORLING KINDERSLEY

LONDON • NEW YORK • SYDNEY • DELHI

PARIS • MUNICH • JOHANNESBURG

www.dk.com

A DORLING KINDERSLEY BOOK

www.dk.com

Produced by Blue Island Publishing Limited
London, England
EDITORIAL DIRECTOR Rosalyn Thiro
ART DIRECTOR Stephen Bere
SENIOR EDITOR Jane Simmonds
US EDITOR Mary Sutherland
ART EDITORS Tessa Bindloss, Ian Midson
PICTURE RESEARCHER Ellen Root

Dorling Kindersley Limited
MAP CO-ORDINATOR Dave Pugh
DTP DESIGNER Lee Redmond

CONTRIBUTORS
John Benson, Mark Brazil, Jon Burbank, Angela Jeffs, Emi Kazuko, Stephen Mansfield, Bill Marsh, Catherine Rubinstein, Jacqueline Ruyak

RESEARCHER
Mayumi Hayashi

MAPS
Era-Maptech Ltd

PHOTOGRAPHERS
Demetrio Carrasco, Clive Streeter, Linda Whitwam, Peter Wilson

ILLUSTRATORS
Richard Bonson, Gary Cross, Richard Draper, Paul Guest, Claire Littlejohn, Maltings Partnership, Mel Pickering, John Woodcock

Reproduced by Colourscan (Singapore)
Printed and bound in China by L. Rex Printing Co., Ltd

First published in Great Britain in 2000
by Dorling Kindersley Limited
9 Henrietta Street, London WC2E 8PS

A CIP CATALOGUE RECORD IS AVAILABLE FROM THE BRITISH LIBRARY.

ISBN 0 7513 2729 8

Throughout this book, floors are referred to in accordance with US usage, ie the "first floor" is at ground level.

This DK Eyewitness Travel Guide is updated annually.
In addition, regular updates and information on current events *in Tokyo* are available on this Guide's own website at:
www.dk.com/travel

We value the views and suggestions of our readers very highly. Please write to: Senior Managing Editor, DK Eyewitness Travel Guides, Dorling Kindersley, 9 Henrietta Street, London WC2E 8PS. Or contact us via: travelguides@dk.com.

Even though every effort has been made to ensure that this book is as up-to-date as possible at the time of going to press, some details are liable to change. The publishers cannot accept responsibility for any consequences arising from the use of this book.

◁ **Student monks at Mount Koya, Western Honshu**

Matsumoto Castle in the Japan Alps

CONTENTS

HOW TO USE THIS GUIDE *6*

INTRODUCING JAPAN

PUTTING JAPAN ON THE MAP *10*

Wall hanging of a geisha in a museum in Takayama

A PORTRAIT OF JAPAN *12*

JAPAN THROUGH THE YEAR *40*

THE HISTORY OF JAPAN *46*

Tokyo Area by Area

Tokyo at a Glance *58*

Central Tokyo *60*

Northern Tokyo *72*

Western Tokyo *84*

Farther Afield *96*

Shopping in Tokyo *100*

Entertainment in Tokyo *104*

Tokyo Street Finder *108*

Neon lights in the Roppongi district of Western Tokyo

Japan Region by Region

Japan at a Glance *120*

Central Honshu *122*

Kyoto City *148*

Western Honshu *180*

Shikoku *214*

Kyushu *224*

Okinawa *244*

Northern Honshu *254*

Hokkaido *274*

Imperial figure at Yomeimon Gate, Tosho-gu Shrine, Nikko

Travelers' Needs

Where to Stay *288*

Where to Eat *308*

Shopping in Japan *340*

Makunouchi bento, a classic meal-in-a-box

Onsen *346*

Theme Parks *348*

Sports and Outdoor Activities *350*

Special Interests *354*

Survival Guide

Practical Information *360*

Travel Information *378*

Index *386*

Further Reading *401*

Phrase Book *404*

Todai-ji Temple, Nara

How to Use this Guide

THIS GUIDE helps you to get the most from your visit to Japan. It provides detailed practical information and expert recommendations. *Introducing Japan* maps the country and sets it in its historical and cultural context. Tokyo and the eight regional sections describe important sights, using maps, photographs, and illustrations. Restaurant and hotel recommendations can be found in *Travelers' Needs*, together with general advice about accommodations and Japanese food. The *Survival Guide* has tips on everything from transportation to etiquette.

Tokyo

This city is divided into areas, each with its own chapter. The *Farther Afield* section covers peripheral sights. All sights are numbered and plotted on the chapter's area map. The information for each sight follows the map's numerical order, making sights easy to locate within the chapter.

All pages relating to Tokyo have red thumb tabs.

A locator map shows where you are in relation to other areas of the city.

1 Area Map
For easy reference, sights are numbered and located on a map. City center sights are also marked on the Street Finder *on pages 108–117.*

Sights at a Glance lists the chapter's sights by category, such as Notable Districts, Historic Buildings, Modern Architecture, Parks and Gardens, and Markets.

2 Street-by-Street Map
This gives a bird's-eye view of the key areas in each chapter.

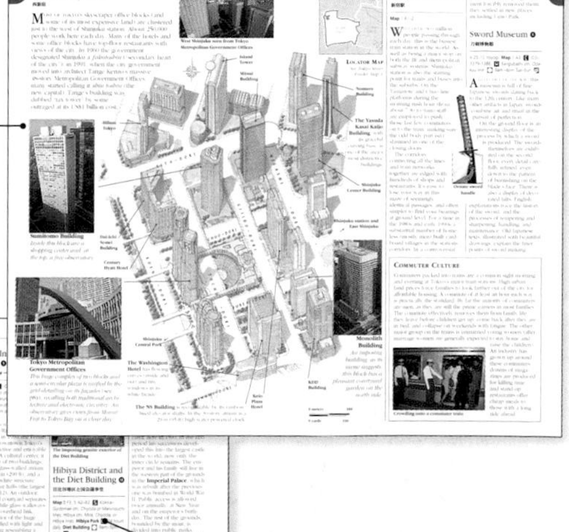

3 Detailed Information
The top sights in Tokyo are described individually. Telephone numbers and public transportation links are given, along with other practical information. The key to the symbols is on the back flap of the book.

JAPAN REGION BY REGION
Following the Tokyo chapter, the country has been divided into eight regions, each of which has a separate chapter, including Kyoto City. The most interesting towns and other places to visit are numbered on a map at the beginning of each chapter.

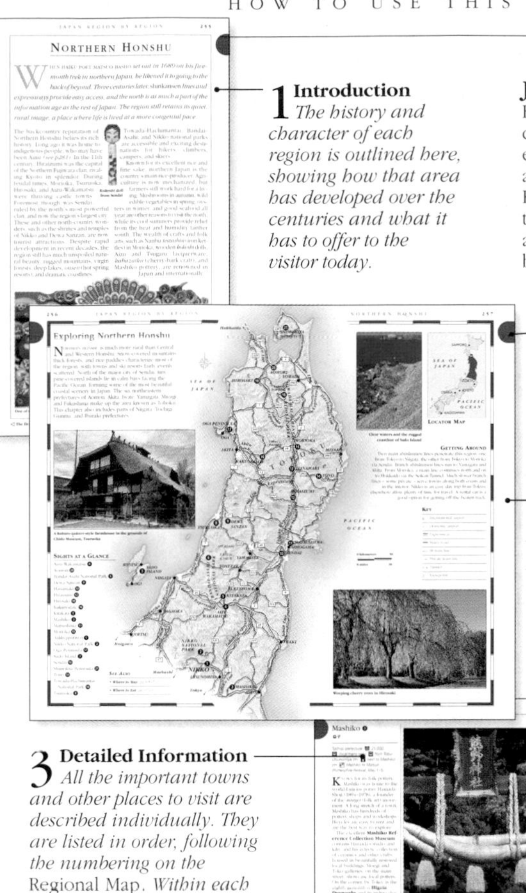

1 Introduction
The history and character of each region is outlined here, showing how that area has developed over the centuries and what it has to offer to the visitor today.

Each region of Japan can be quickly identified by its color coding, shown on the front flap of the book.

2 Regional Map
This shows the road and rail network and gives an overview of the whole region. All the best sights to visit are numbered. There are also useful tips on getting to, and around, the region by public transportation.

3 Detailed Information
All the important towns and other places to visit are described individually. They are listed in order, following the numbering on the Regional Map. *Within each town or city, there is detailed information on important buildings and other sights.*

Stars indicate the highlights and most important features of Japan's top sights.

Story boxes explore related topics.

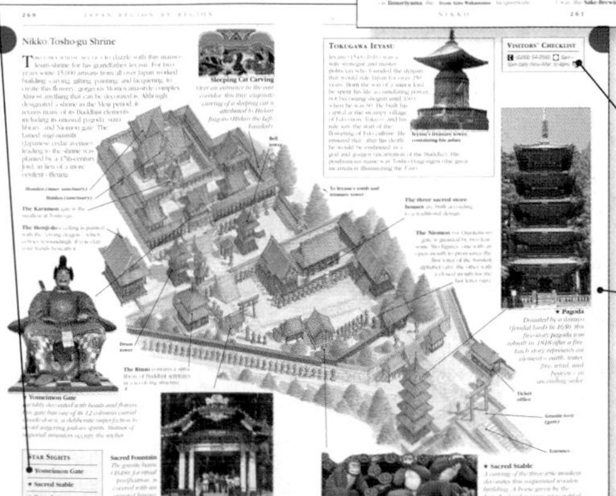

For all top sights, a Visitors' Checklist provides the practical information you need to plan your visit.

4 Japan's Top Sights
These are given two or more full pages. Three-dimensional illustrations reveal the layouts and interiors of historic monuments. Interesting districts are given street-by-street maps from a bird's eye view.

INTRODUCING JAPAN

PUTTING JAPAN ON THE MAP 10-11

A PORTRAIT OF JAPAN 12-39

JAPAN THROUGH THE YEAR 40-45

THE HISTORY OF JAPAN 46-55

Putting Japan on the Map

JAPAN IS MADE UP of four main islands – Honshu, Hokkaido, Kyushu, and Shikoku – and several thousand smaller ones, lying to the east of mainland Asia, in the northwest of the Pacific Ocean. The archipelago curves across 3,000 km (1,900 miles) between Russia's Sakhalin Island and Taiwan.

◁ **"Brocade sash" bridge, Iwakuni**

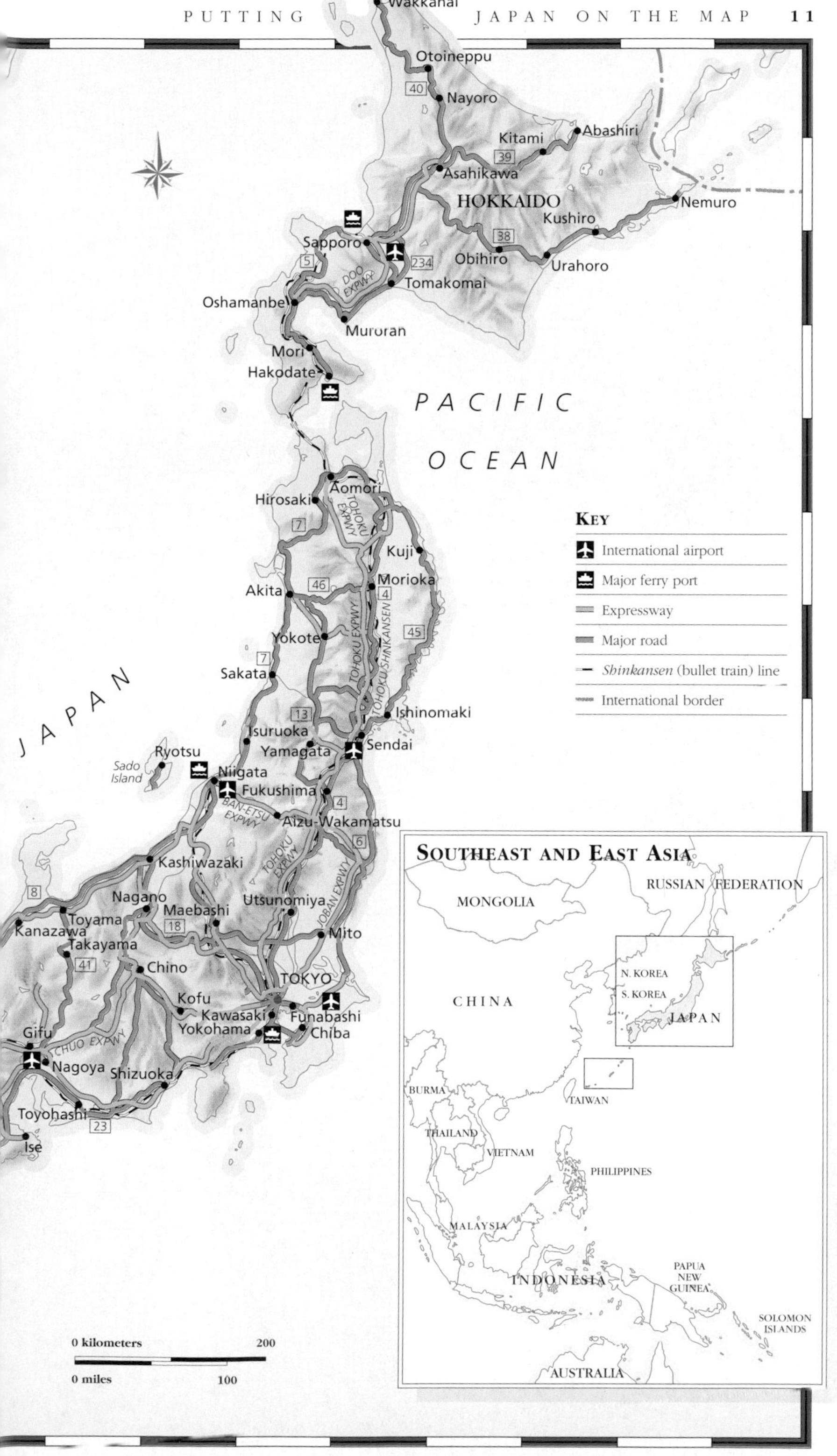
Wakkanai
Otoineppu
Nayoro
Kitami
Abashiri
Asahikawa
HOKKAIDO
Nemuro
Kushiro
Sapporo
Obihiro
Urahoro
DOO EXPWY
Tomakomai
Oshamanbe
Muroran
Mori
Hakodate
PACIFIC OCEAN
Aomori
Hirosaki
TOHOKU EXPWY
KEY
International airport
Major ferry port
Expressway
Major road
Shinkansen (bullet train) line
International border
Kuji
Morioka
Akita
TOHOKU EXPWY
TOHOKU SHINKANSEN
Yokote
Sakata
Ishinomaki
JAPAN
Tsuruoka
Yamagata
Sendai
Ryotsu
Sado Island
Niigata
Fukushima
BAN-ETSU EXPWY
Aizu-Wakamatsu
Kashiwazaki
TOHOKU EXPWY
JOBAN EXPWY
Nagano
Utsunomiya
Maebashi
Toyama
Kanazawa
Mito
Takayama
Chino
TOKYO
Kofu
Kawasaki
Funabashi
Yokohama
Chiba
Gifu
CHUO EXPWY
Nagoya
Shizuoka
Toyohashi
Ise
0 kilometers 200
0 miles 100
SOUTHEAST AND EAST ASIA
RUSSIAN FEDERATION
MONGOLIA
N. KOREA
S. KOREA
CHINA
JAPAN
BURMA
TAIWAN
THAILAND
VIETNAM
PHILIPPINES
MALAYSIA
INDONESIA
PAPUA NEW GUINEA
SOLOMON ISLANDS
AUSTRALIA

A Portrait of Japan

FEW PEOPLE IN THE MODERN WORLD *are not affected in some way by the ideas, culture, and economy of Japan, yet this country remains for many an enigma, an unsolved riddle. Westernized, but different from any Western country, part of Asia, but clearly unlike any other Asian society, Japan is a uniquely adaptable place where tradition and modernity are part of one continuum.*

With over 3,000 islands lying along the Pacific Ring of Fire, the Japanese archipelago is prone to frequent earthquakes and has 60 active volcanoes. Much of the country is mountainous, while cities consume large areas of flat land and coastal plain. The Tokyo–Yokohama area is the largest urban concentration in the world, and 70 percent of Japan's 125 million people live along the Pacific coast stretch between Tokyo and Kyushu.

The remaining slivers of cultivable land are farmed to yield maximum crops. Generous amounts of rainfall, melting snowcaps, and deep lakes enable rice to be cultivated in near-perfect conditions.

Fashionable teenager in Tokyo

Each spring, the Japanese are reminded of their country's geographical diversity as the media enthusiastically tracks the progress of the *sakura zensen*, the "cherry-blossom front," as it advances from the subtropical islands of Okinawa to the northernmost island of Hokkaido.

The Japanese regard themselves as a racially integrated tribe, though different dialects and physical features distinguish the people of one region from another. Moreover, there are many minority peoples in Japan, from the indigenous Ainu to Okinawans, and an admixture of Koreans, Chinese, and, more recently, Southeast Asians and Westerners who have made Japan their home.

Buddhist monks gathered for a ceremony in the ancient capital of Nara

◁ **Soft colors of an old temple garden given over to moss, one of many tranquil corners in Kyoto**

Planting rice in flooded paddy fields, Fushimi

A Land of Contradictions

Appearances are often deceptive in Japan, obliging foreign visitors to keep adjusting their perceptions of the country. An exit at a large train station, for example, might deliver you to street level or just as likely funnel you through a modern, high-rise department store. Here, among familiar shops, you might discover a whole floor of restaurants, some with rustic, *tatami*-mat floors and open charcoal braziers, others with displays of plastic food in the window. Closer inspection might reveal a fortune-teller's stall set up outside a software store, a moxibustion clinic next to a fast-food outlet, or a rooftop shrine to the fox-god Inari by the store's Astroturf mini-golf course.

Priest at Senso-ji, Tokyo

In this country of cherry blossoms and capsule hotels, of Buddhist monks and tattooed gangsters, the visitor finds that rock music, avant-garde theater, and abstract painting are as popular as flower arranging, Noh drama, or the tea ceremony. The Grand Shrine at Ise, torn down and rebuilt every 20 years in identical design and materials, exists not to replace tradition but to preserve and renew it – the ultimate illustration of the Japanese belief in the transience of the material world. Nature, too, retains its key role in the national consciousness, in cities and rural areas alike, often ritualized in the annual cycle of *matsuri* (festivals). Wherever one looks, a stimulating fusion of East and West reveals itself: Zen priests on Hondas; the *salaryman* bowing deeply to a client on his cell phone; neon signs written in Japanese ideograms; ice-cream flavors that include red-bean paste and green tea. In one of the world's most energetic and industrialized nations, there are moments of carefully arranged beauty too, even tranquillity, with people who still find the time to contemplate the crack or glaze of a tea bowl, and burn incense for the dead.

Woman on a scooter passing a monk with his begging bowl, Kyoto

Businessmen bowing, Osaka

Society, Values, and Beliefs

Although modern Japanese society developed from a feudal system, Japan today is astonishingly egalitarian. Hereditary titles were abolished along with the aristocracy after World War II, and members of the imperial family, the world's longest unbroken line of monarchs, now marry commoners. Class is defined by education and job status. The people employed by the top government ministries, large corporations, and other prestigious companies are Japan's true elite today.

Burning incense and praying, Nagano

The Japanese have a practical, syncretic, and polytheistic approach to religion, often perplexing to outsiders. Religion is essentially an instrument for petitioning the gods to grant such requests as success in business or a school entrance exam, recovery from illness, or an uncomplicated birth. It is common in Japanese homes to find both Buddhist and Shinto altars. Confucianism is sometimes called Japan's unofficial, third religion after Buddhism and Shinto. More moral code and tool for social organization than religion proper, it has had a profound influence on Japanese thought since its introduction in the 6th century.

These beliefs, alongside family values and devotion to hard work, combined with a submission to the consensus of the group rather than the individual, have long been major binding elements in Japanese society. Most women regard child-rearing as their main objective. Men aim to climb the corporate ladder, seeing their work as integral to their identity, and many will socialize exclusively with their work colleagues.

Faultlines, however, are appearing in this monolithic structure, as younger voices question the benefits and value of self-sacrifice. A life outside the group, or in smaller, more intimate, groups, has increasing appeal. Young couples now prefer to live apart from their parents, and men are gradually disengaging themselves from a practice of after-hours socializing, in order to spend more time with their family. The steady increase in the divorce rate and the larger number of women who remain unmarried are other indications of changes taking place. The latter is often a decision on the part of Japanese women who cannot find partners with the right credentials. Thus, what might appear to be a contemporary Western-driven tendency, or an expression of feminist awareness, is a reflection, to some degree, of orthodoxy.

Lion mask to ward off evil spirits, Takayama

Japan's declining birthrate, now fewer than 1.5 births per family, is not enough to sustain current population levels, and the specter of an aging, more state-dependent population, looms. This is not just a result of women choosing not to marry. Cramped living conditions and the need for parents to provide offspring with a first-rate, costly education are among other factors.

Visitors dwarfed by the Great Buddha statue at Kamakura

The landmark Studio Alta screen and neon-lit streets of East Shinjuku, Tokyo

Politics and the Economy

Through much of Japan's history, parallel with the institutions and prevailing ideologies of the day, there has been a distinction between power and office. The emperor had little power from the 12th century onward, being essentially a puppet under first the regents, then the shoguns, and, later, the military government before and during World War II. This distinction persists today in the relationship between bureaucrats, who are given enormous power to oversee the economy, and politicians, who merely co-opt, accommodate, or head off the opposition groups.

Car on display in Toyota showroom

The existence of widespread political corruption was revealed in 1983 with the exposure of a scandal in which a former Prime Minister, Kakuei Tanaka, was implicated. Pressure then mounted on Japan's conservative regime. Contentious economic stimulus packages, an unpopular consumption tax, and more scandals connected to corruption, fund raising, and graft, further tarnished the party's image for consistency and reliability. The Liberal Democratic Party (LDP) eventually lost its 38-year long grip on power in 1993, ending almost four decades of political hegemony. The government was forced into potentially unstable coalition arrangements.

In the 1980s the yen soared against the dollar, and Japanese companies made the headlines by buying up American film studios and over-priced works of art. Japanese tourists, long used to sightseeing in their own country, began to travel abroad in unprecedented numbers. Land prices in Japan, foreigners were confidently told, would continue to rise because "Japan was different from other countries." However, friction over a massive trade surplus with America, growing criticism of Japan's "checkbook diplomacy," and the recession that struck in 1992, bursting its "bubble" economy, have been sobering. Despite the hardships suffered by the unemployed and those

Door attendants at Gucci emporium, Tokyo

forced into early retirement, and the increase in homeless people evident in big cities like Tokyo and Osaka, the 90s recession brought back a degree of sanity that was missing during the decades of uninterrupted growth. It also prompted the Japanese government to make moves toward long overdue economic reform and a greater opening of its markets to international trade.

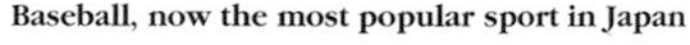

Baseball, now the most popular sport in Japan

Leisure and the Art of Living

The Japanese take their sports and leisure activities almost as seriously as their work. Traditional sports, in particular, often embody some underlying cultural, spiritual, or aesthetic principle, so that there is not only the method but "the way." This applies especially to ancient disciplines like kyudo (archery), kendo, karate, and aikido. Sumo, the national sport of Japan, originated as an oracular ritual linked to prayers for a bountiful harvest. Having a similar appeal to sports audiences as Kabuki dramas do to theater-goers, sumo ranks many non-Japanese among its fans. Japan gained many soccer fans after the creation of the J-League in 1993 and its selection, along with Korea, as co-host for the 2002 World Cup. Professional baseball attracts an even larger and more devoted following.

Sumo wrestler preparing for a bout

Traditional leisure activities, such as the pleasures of summer fireworks, and seasonal maple, moon, and snow viewing, are much celebrated in literature and art, in the poetry, diaries, and early novels of the Heian period, and in the screen painting and *ukiyo-e* woodblock prints of the Edo era.

Visits by geisha and their patrons to discreet hot springs in the mountains are the material for some atmospheric novels by writers such as the Nobel laureate Kawabata Yasunari (1899–1972).

Nature and aesthetics fuse in the national appreciation for cherry blossoms, a passion that both charms and perplexes the visitor. *Hanami* (cherry blossom) parties are held throughout the country. Because competition for the best viewing sites can be fierce, company bosses often send their younger scions ahead to claim a good patch under the trees. The cherry, as the Japanese see it, is a felicitous symbol but also a poignant reminder of the evanescent beauty of this floating world. Few nations have extracted so much refined pleasure and sadness from the contemplation of a flower.

The Japanese hunger for innovation and advancement has not devoured their spiritual heritage or the natural grace extended toward visitors. Most travelers return home with the impression, in fact, of an unfailingly generous and hospitable people, for whom politeness and consideration toward a guest are second nature.

Kabuki performance, a traditional entertainment

The Landscape of Japan

Japan lies on the intersection of four plates and is the world's most geologically active zone. The islands themselves were pushed up from the ocean floor by earth movements. Evidence of this activity can be seen in the sharply defined mountain ranges rising from the plains, in smoking volcanoes, and in hot mineral waters that well up from the ground. The Japanese take earthquakes, volcanoes, tsunamis, and typhoons in their stride, building and rebuilding their towns wherever they can find flat land. Modern cityscapes *(see pp20–21)* contrast greatly with the seasonal beauty of the relatively undeveloped mountainous interior, and the national parks, the largest of which are in Hokkaido.

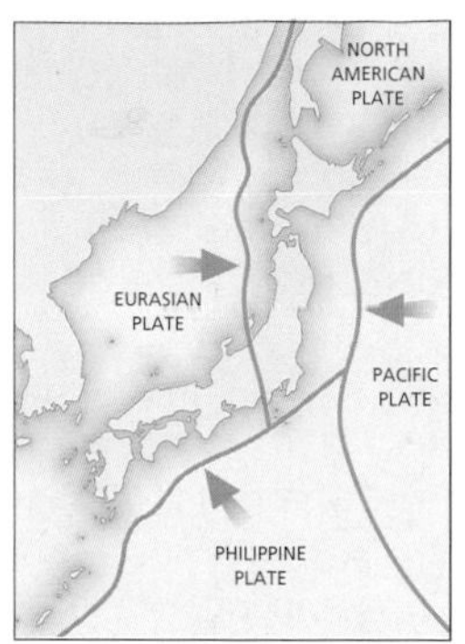

***Plate movements**, as shown, force the sea-bed to be pushed underneath the lighter rocks of the Japanese archipelago. This causes nearly a thousand obvious earthquakes each year in Japan.*

***Maple, birch, cypress, and cedar trees** are among the most common woodland mixes on the hillsides, creating stunning fiery colors in the fall.*

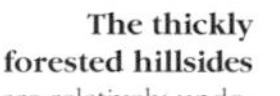

The thickly forested hillsides are relatively undeveloped, though some remote peaks are used as the isolated setting for hill shrines and temples.

Typical View of the Land

This idealized representation shows the typical landscape features of central Japan. The plains next to the sea are densely populated, while farther inland thickly forested hillsides rise up steeply to snow-covered mountain peaks and the craters of both dormant and active volcanoes.

Freshwater lakes such as Lake Biwa in Western Honshu *(see p206)* are utilized for industry, irrigation, and recreation.

Faultlines run beneath the sea and land, showing up in some places as a rift in the landscape.

***Bamboo groves** are found in the tropical and temperate zones of Japan. The fast-growing plant is both a foodstuff and building material.*

***Paddy fields** may not be associated with Japan as much as they are with other parts of Asia; nonetheless rice-growing occupies a major part of the cultivable landscape. In suburban areas, small rice plots often take the place of gardens.*

Japan's 60 or so active volcanoes *are scattered along a line through the main islands. Many of these, such as Sakurajima* (see p243)*, smoke and steam constantly. Explosive eruptions of lava and pyroclastic rock-flows take place every few years.*

Sulfur vents *are found in volcanic regions, staining the rocks yellow in such places as Hokkaido's Akan National Park* (see p281) *and releasing noxious fumes at Mount Aso* (see pp238–9) *and other craters.*

Dormant crater

Fruit and vegetable farming takes up what slivers of cultivable land are left after rice farming, but Japan is forced to import about half its food.

The high, snow-covered mountain areas, such as the Japan Alps near Matsumoto *(see p145)* and parts of Northern Honshu and Hokkaido, have been developed as skiing resorts.

Rising from the plain is the near-perfect cone of a dormant volcano, the supreme example of which is Mount Fuji *(see pp134–5).*

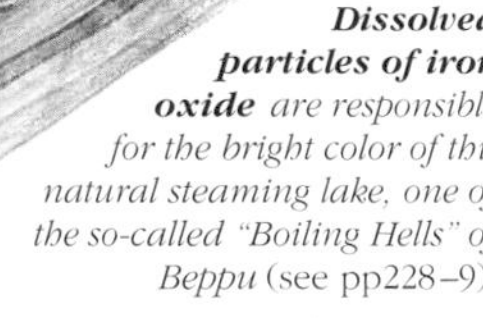

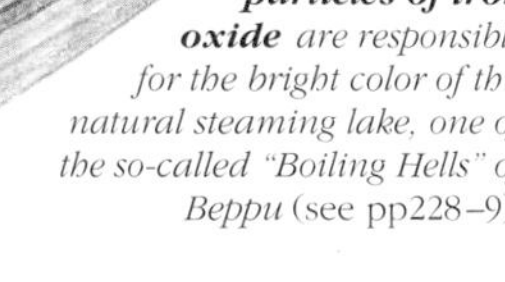

Dissolved particles of iron oxide *are responsible for the bright color of this natural steaming lake, one of the so-called "Boiling Hells" of Beppu* (see pp228–9).

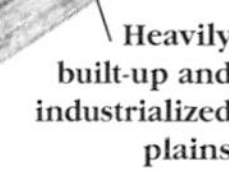

Heavily built-up and industrialized plains

Most of the major Japanese cities*, such as Tokyo, Osaka, and Kobe, are working ports. Land suitable for building is at such a premium that artificial peninsulas and islands have been constructed.*

Natural Hot Springs

Geothermal activity at thousands of sites in Japan has created natural hot springs either at ground level or just below the surface. The mineral content of the waters varies; some are declared to have therapeutic benefits for humans, especially for diseases of the nervous system and intestines. The Japanese have bathed in the springs for centuries and have also used them for purification rituals. Many have been developed as spas, or *onsen (see pp346–7)*; the Dogo Onsen in Matsuyama is over a thousand years old *(see p220)*. The water of some springs must be cooled before it is suitable for bathing.

Monkeys bathing in the geothermal waters of Jigokudani *(see p145)*

Modern Japan

PERHAPS NOWHERE ELSE does the modern world of high technology and constant change show itself more poignantly than in Japan. For some people, modern Japan is an anathema, a kitsch distillation of the Western world that destroys traditional culture. Others embrace the nation's fascination with invention and image, and praise it for often leading the West. Few urban buildings are more than 25 years old, and consumer trends may change in a matter of weeks in this economic powerhouse. In some ways, though, the liking for change is a manifestation of ancient religious concepts *(see pp22–5)* that emphasize the importance of impermanence and renewal.

The Japanese automobile industry *manufactures about ten million vehicles each year. In a land where space is at a premium, the small car is king.*

A forest of neon *characterizes the shopping and entertainment districts of cities that strive to be modern, such as Tokyo, Osaka, and here in Fukuoka. Vast television screens and public announcements over loudspeakers add to the audio-visual tumult.*

Tange Kenzo's earthquake-proof Metropolitan Offices *(see p88)* are praised by some and villified by others.

The Yamanote train line connects Tokyo's main districts in a loop.

Department stores are accessed directly from the world's busiest train station.

The Sony Corporation *has grown from 20 employees in 1946 to an electronics empire with assets of $52 billion. The Sony Showroom* (see p62) *displays the latest inventions before they reach the shops.*

HIGH-TECH TOYS AND GAMES

Japan has been at the forefront of high-tech toys and games since the late 1970s, when Taito invented the video arcade game *Space Invaders*, followed by Namco's *Pacman*. In 1983 came Nintendo's home computer for games software. *Super Mario* was issued in 1985. Nintendo's handheld *GameBoy* then enabled a range of games to be played on the move. Stars of the late 1990s included the pocket virtual pet *Tamagotchi* and collectible *Pokémon* characters.

Tamagotchis for sale in Harajuku

Robot (robotto) *technology was exported to Japan from the US in 1967. Today, about half of the world's robots are found in Japan, used widely in industry. Some are delightfully zoomorphic.*

***The oxygen bar**, in which customers inhale pure or scented oxygen for health and relaxation instead of imbibing alcohol, originated in Japan and is becoming popular in other countries.*

Mount Fuji **The Greater Tokyo conurbation**

Modern Cityscapes

Shinjuku district in Tokyo, shown here *(see also pp86–9)*, epitomizes the modern Japanese urban labyrinth. Buildings are constructed wherever land becomes available, using such materials as aluminum, steel, and concrete. Increasingly, flexible-frame technologies are used to withstand powerful earthquakes.

Manga *("comic pictures") are immensely popular in Japan, especially the genre of narrative comics called* gekiga, *which emerged in the 1960s. The content is diverse – politics, baseball, romance, martial arts, and pornography are all popular.*

Modern Architecture

An eclectic mix of contemporary building styles can be seen in Japan. Tange Kenzo (1913–), who built the Olympic Stadiums in 1964 *(see pp90–91)*, still casts a shadow over younger designers. Foreign practitioners, too, have been influential.

***Osaka's Umeda Sky Building** (completed 1993) was inspired by the 1960s' dream of a "city in the air." Hara Hiroshi's twin towers are linked by the Floating Garden Observatory, which hovers above the city* (see p196).

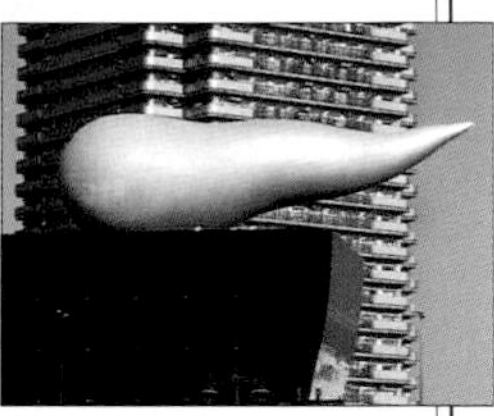

***An amusing, almost cartoon-like building**, the Super Dry Hall was built in 1989 by French designer Philippe Starcke for the Asahi beer company, near the Sumida River in the Asakusa district of Tokyo. International architects have designed some of their most ambitious projects in Tokyo.*

***A modern house**, designed by Ando Tadao (1941–), allows light to seep through in unusual ways, such as through glass slots between ceiling and walls. One of the foremost contemporary Japanese architects, Ando's works include the Himeji City Museum of Literature* (see p203).

The Tokyo International Forum (see p67) *is a shiplike structure built by the South American architect Rafael Viñoly in 1996. Its glass-walled atrium, supported by elegant columns and bars, is widely considered to be a masterpiece of engineering.*

Shinto: the Native Religion

SHINTO IS JAPAN'S OLDEST religion, the "way of the gods." Its core concept is that deities, *kami*, preside over all things in nature, be they living, dead, or inanimate. There are lesser and greater *kami*, worshiped at thousands of shrines *(jinja)* erected on hills and along waysides. From ancient times the emperor's rule was sanctioned by the authority of the greatest gods, said to be his ancestors. Shinto was the state religion from the 1870s to 1940s. Today, few Japanese are purely Shintoists, but most will observe Shinto rituals alongside Buddhist practices. Many Japanese habits, such as an emphasis on purification and an austere aesthetic, are derived at least in part from Shinto.

***The* torii** *is the most recognizable icon of Shinto. These gateways mark the entrance to the sacred precincts of a shrine. Many are made of vermilion-painted wood; some are constructed in stone, even concrete. All have two rails at the top.*

***The* shimenawa** *is a rope made of twisted rice straw. It is hung over entrances within shrine precincts to separate sacred and secular places. It is also set above doors of houses to ward off evil and sickness. Izumo Taisha* (see p207) *has many examples of* shimenawa, *some of them immense.*

Miscanthus grass thatch

The treasuries, to the west and east of the main structure, house ceremonial regalia, silks, and paper.

ISE INNER GRAND SHRINE

The home of the spirits of all past emperors, the Grand Shrine at Ise *(see p192)* is the most venerated Shinto site. The inner shrine shown here is dedicated to Amaterasu, the sun goddess, and is said to house her mirror, an imperial sacred treasure. It is not open to the public. The complex is completely rebuilt every 20 years, most recently in 1993, following a tradition begun in AD 690.

Inari shrines, *identifiable by the bibbed stone foxes standing guard within them, are dedicated to the* kami *of cereal crops. The head Inari shrine is at Fushimi* (see p173), *just south of Kyoto, and 30,000 others are scattered throughout the country.*

***The Shinto priesthood* (kannushi)** *tended to be transmitted through families, and important families* (shake) *are still connected with some shrines. The* kannushi, *who usually wear white and orange robes, perform purification ceremonies and other rituals.*

In the main sanctuary (honden) *of a shrine is an object* (shintai) *believed to be the abode of the* kami *to whom the shrine is dedicated. Usually only the head priests enter the* honden; *the hall for worship* (haiden) *is often separate.*

Worshipers *stand in front of the* haiden *hall, pull on a bell rope, toss money into a box, clap three times to summon the resident* kami, *then stand in silent prayer for a few moments.*

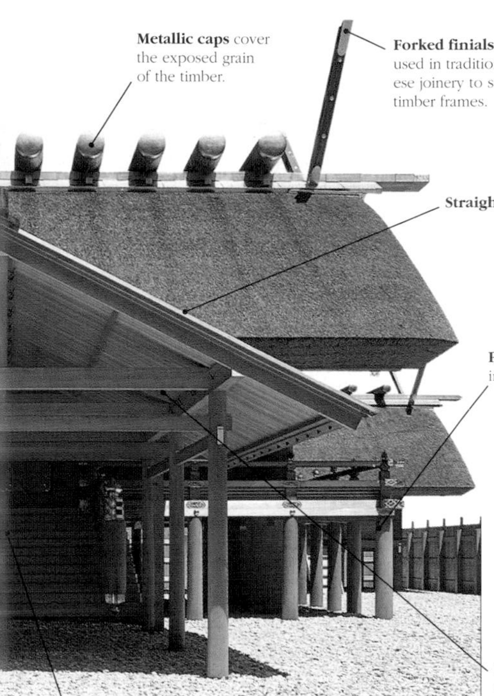

Metallic caps cover the exposed grain of the timber.

Forked finials, *chigi*, are used in traditional Japanese joinery to secure timber frames.

Straight roofline

Posts are set directly into the ground.

Ise Shrine has its own style of architecture, called *yuitsu shimmei-zukuri*, which has been imitated at just a handful of other shrines.

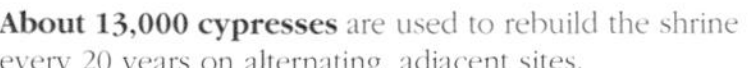

About 13,000 cypresses are used to rebuild the shrine every 20 years on alternating, adjacent sites.

Fertility *is a major concern of Shinto. Some shrines have statues depicting phalluses, lovemaking, childbirth, or milk-engorged breasts. Couples will ask the spirits for conception and good health for mother and child.*

Charms and Votive Tablets

Good-luck charms, called *omamori*, are sold at shrines across Japan. Common themes relate to fertility, luck in examinations, general health, or safety while driving. The charm itself might be written on a piece of paper or thin wooden board and tucked into a cloth bag, which can be worn next to the body or placed somewhere relevant. (Do not open the bag to read the charm or it will not work.) Prayers or wishes can also be written on *ema* boards and hung at the shrine.

***Ema* boards wishing for success in examinations**

Charms for conception, safe childbirth, and safety while driving

Buddhism in Japan

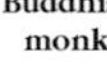

Buddhist monk

BUDDHISM, founded in India, arrived in Japan via China and Korea in the 6th century AD. Different sects *(see p269)* evolved and were adopted over the centuries. The new religion sometimes had an uneasy relationship with Shinto, despite incorporating parts of the native belief system. Buddhism lost official support in 1868 but has flowered again since World War II. The complex cosmological beliefs and morality of Buddhism permeate modern Japanese life, especially in the emphasis on mental control found in Zen Buddhism.

Prince Shotoku *(573–621) promoted Buddhism in its early days in Japan* (see p190).

Senso-ji temple (see pp82–3) *is the site of some of Tokyo's main festivals* (see pp38–43). *Buddhist festivals honor events in the Buddha's life and the return of dead spirits to Earth* (bon). *They often incorporate Shinto elements.*

Worshipers remove their shoes and kneel before the altar in silent contemplation and prayer.

Memorial stones *are erected in cemeteries attached to temples. Called* gorin-to, *many are made up of five different-shaped stones. Plain, box-shaped ones are called* sotoba.

Pagodas, *found in some temple complexes, house relics of the Buddha, such as fragments of bone. The relic is usually placed at the base of the central pillar, hidden from view. Three- or five-story* (see p190) *pagodas are common, but access to the upper stories is rarely permitted.*

Jizo Statues

Red-bibbed statues of Jizo are found at thousands of temples and along waysides in Japan. Jizo is the guardian *bosatsu* of those who suffer, especially sickly children and pregnant women. Children who have died young, including babies who have been miscarried or aborted, are helped into the next world by Jizo. He is often shown holding a staff in one hand and a jewel talisman in the other. The red bibs are placed on the statues by bereaved mothers and other sufferers.

Jizo, Toji Temple, Kyoto

Jizo and babies, Uwajima, Shikoku

Pilgrimages to Buddhist sites *are very popular. Pilgrims, typically dressed in white, walk from site to site, sometimes making epic journeys of many weeks' duration, such as for Shikoku's 88-Temple Pilgrimage* (see pp222–3).

The semi-enclosed area at the front of the platform has a burner for incense offerings. Beyond is a type of tabernacle containing a sacred object *(honzon)*, hidden from view.

The Asuka Plain *of Western Honshu was the site of the earliest Buddhist worship in Japan* (see p191). *This bronze image of the Buddha dates from 609.*

Tatami **mats** line the floor of the *hondo*. The Zen temple *hondo* is characterized by its relative starkness and lack of ornamentation.

THE BUDDHIST TEMPLE IN JAPAN

Buddhist sites, identifiable by the suffixes *-ji* and *-dera*, are usually translated as "temples" (whereas Shinto sites are "shrines"). The temple complex includes a main hall *(hondo)*, shown here, maybe a pagoda, cemetery, buildings used by monks, and often a small Shinto shrine as well. The layout of a typical Zen Buddhist temple is shown on page 131.

Meditation *is a cornerstone of Buddhism: clearing the mind of cluttered thoughts is the road to Enlightenment. In* zazen *sitting meditation, photographed here in about 1950, a nun uses a* keisaku *stick to slap meditators who seem to be losing their alertness.*

GLOSSARY

Amida

Amida The Buddha of Infinite Light, as venerated by the Pure Land sect.
Bosatsu Japanese word for *bodhisattva*, a figure that has attained Enlightenment and helps others.
Buddha Usually means the historical Buddha, who was born in India in 563 BC.
Butsudan Altar in house.
Enlightenment An expansion of mind as achieved by *bosatsu.*
Hondo Main hall of temple.
Honzon Principal object of worship in main hall.
Jizo A popular *bosatsu*.
Juzu Buddhist rosary.
Kaimyo Buddhist name awarded posthumously.
Kannon The goddess of mercy. Sometimes has 1,000 arms (Senju Kannon).
Karesansui A rock and sand garden inspired by Zen Buddhism and Chinese landscape painting.
Keisaku Stick used to slap shoulders during meditation.
Mahayana Major branch of Buddhism, emphasizing the importance of *bosatsu*. Practiced in Tibet, China, Korea, and Japan.

Kannon

Myoo Deified king of light.
Nio Temple gate guardians (Brahma and Indra in India).
Nirvana Release from the cycle of rebirth and suffering.
Nyorai Epithet for the Buddha.
Pure Land Western Paradise of the Amida Buddha.
Sanmon Free-standing gateway to a temple complex.
Satori Sudden Enlightenment in Zen Buddhism.
Shingon Very popular Buddhist sect *(see p269)*.
Takuhatsu The monks' practice of begging.
Tembu Type of heavenly being.
Tendai Major Buddhist sect *(see p269)*.
Zazen Sitting meditation, popular in Zen.
Zen Major school of Buddhism *(see p269)*.

Tembu

Japanese Gardens

Originating around early Shinto shrines, Japanese gardens have been influenced by the Shinto love of nature and the Buddhist ideal of paradise. Although classic Japanese gardens can be roughly divided into four types – paradise gardens, dry-landscape gardens, stroll gardens, and tea gardens – they share many components and principles, and have continued evolving through the centuries. The common aim was to create a microcosm: stones, water, bridges, and other elements were combined to form an idealized and symbolic miniature landscape. Paradise and dry-landscape gardens were designed to be viewed from a single point or side, while stroll gardens and tea gardens were made to be walked through.

***Modern gardens** in Japan have altered as architectural styles have changed, but many still use traditional components, such as water, stones, and gravel, in a less sinuous, more geometric way than in the past.*

Paradise Garden

Motsu-ji garden in Hiraizumi *(see p270)* is a beautifully preserved example of a paradise garden, designed to evoke the Pure Land, or Buddhist paradise. Use is made of "borrowed landscape" – trees or mountains outside the garden that appear to be part of it. Stones are arranged to create islands and rocky shores.

Dry-Landscape Garden

Attached to Zen Buddhist temples, these gardens of carefully chosen stones grouped amid an expanse of raked gravel provide an object for meditation. A classic dry-landscape garden is at Ryoan-ji temple, Kyoto *(see p168)*, where the plain, earthen walls enhance the abstract arrangement of the stones.

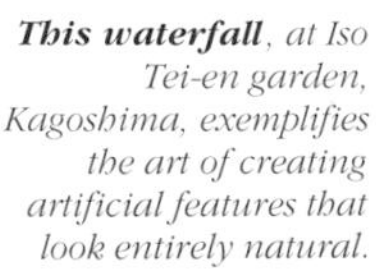

***This waterfall**, at Iso Tei-en garden, Kagoshima, exemplifies the art of creating artificial features that look entirely natural.*

***This sand mound,** like a flattened Mount Fuji, is at Ginkaku-ji temple in Kyoto. The raked sand around it resembles a silver sea by moonlight.*

***The Phoenix Hall** at Byodo-in near Kyoto houses an Amida Buddha* (see p25). *The building is reflected in the pond in front, which represents the Western Ocean.*

***The "Treasure Ship" stone** at Daisen-in, Kyoto* (see p167), *is one of Japan's most famous stones. Individual stones are not intended as symbols, but this is said to suggest a junk traveling through waves.*

Seasons in a Japanese Garden

The Japanese awareness of the seasons is an integral part of their garden design. A careful balance of shrubs and trees is one of the essential ingredients for a harmonious garden. Evergreen trees and bamboos are often planted for year-round greenery; deciduous trees are chosen for their shape when bare as well as when clothed with foliage to ensure year-round interest. In tea gardens, where every detail is symbolic, fallen blossoms or leaves may be arranged by the path to suggest the season. Some gardens are planned for a spectacular effect in one season; many are best visited in spring or fall.

Contrasting maple leaves in fall at Tenryu-ji, Kyoto

Winter in a Kyoto temple garden

Stroll Garden

The views in a stroll garden change with virtually every step, with vistas concealed and revealed. These gardens were popular in the Edo period when they were made by *daimyo* (feudal lords). Kenroku-en in Kanazawa *(see p142)* included four ponds and uses "borrowed landscape" skillfully.

Murin-an garden *in Kyoto is a small stroll garden, designed to look highly naturalistic. A meandering stream, pond, and overhanging trees create a quiet and secluded enviroment through which to walk.*

Pruning *is prized as an art, bringing out the inherent qualities of a tree. A beautifully pruned tree often forms a focal point in a stroll garden.*

Tea Garden

Dating from the Momoyama period (1568–1600), a tea garden consists of a short path, with trimmed plants on either side, leading to a teahouse. The path links the real world to the world of the tea ceremony *(see p163)*. In keeping with the simple ceremony, this Kyoto garden has rustic posts and a bamboo fence.

Stone basins *were at first purely functional, for washing hands and mouth, but then came to symbolize purification before the ceremony.*

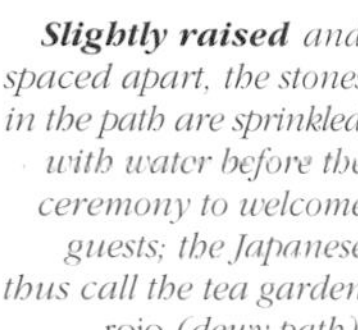

Slightly raised *and spaced apart, the stones in the path are sprinkled with water before the ceremony to welcome guests; the Japanese thus call the tea garden* rojo *(dewy path).*

Traditional Japanese Houses

Known as *minka* or "commoners' houses," traditional dwellings vary widely in their layout and appearance from region to region, often in response to local weather conditions. Made largely of wood and paper, they were designed to be adaptable in their use of the interior space. Although *minka* in their original form are rarely occupied today, partly due to a move toward Western domestic architecture, partly through destruction (often by fire), they can still be seen around Japan and are sometimes open as museums. The way of organizing the living space is, however, still widely used, even in modern, Western-style houses.

Town houses *such as these in the Gion area of Kyoto are known as* machiya *and are the urban equivalent of* minka. *The layout differs as the width of the frontage is limited.*

***The* irori** *(hearth) forms the heart of the house, often kept burning as the main source of heat. It is also sometimes used for cooking. In* minka *the hearth is usually sunk into a wooden floor; a* tatami *surrounding indicates a wealthy household.*

The *doma* (area with a packed-earth floor) lies just behind the entrance. Here people take off their shoes before stepping up to the wooden surface.

The main entrance to the *minka* is through sliding doors.

***The* engawa** *is a space outside, like a veranda, covered with a sloping roof. It may be enclosed by heavy wooden doors, or opened to allow air to circulate. This entrance is mainly used by visitors, who will stand on the stone step to remove their shoes.*

Types of Roof

Traditionally a *minka* roof is thatched, often with miscanthus reed, though the material varies according to what is available locally. Tiled roofs are also widespread as they are simpler to construct and fire-resistant; the ends of tiles may be decorated with an image, such as a devil, to protect the house. Shingles are also used, sometimes weighted down by stones. Roof shapes vary widely in design and complexity.

An intricate, gabled roof with decorated tile ends

A semi-gabled thatched roof of a *kabuto-zukuri* house

A thatcher at work replacing worn thatch

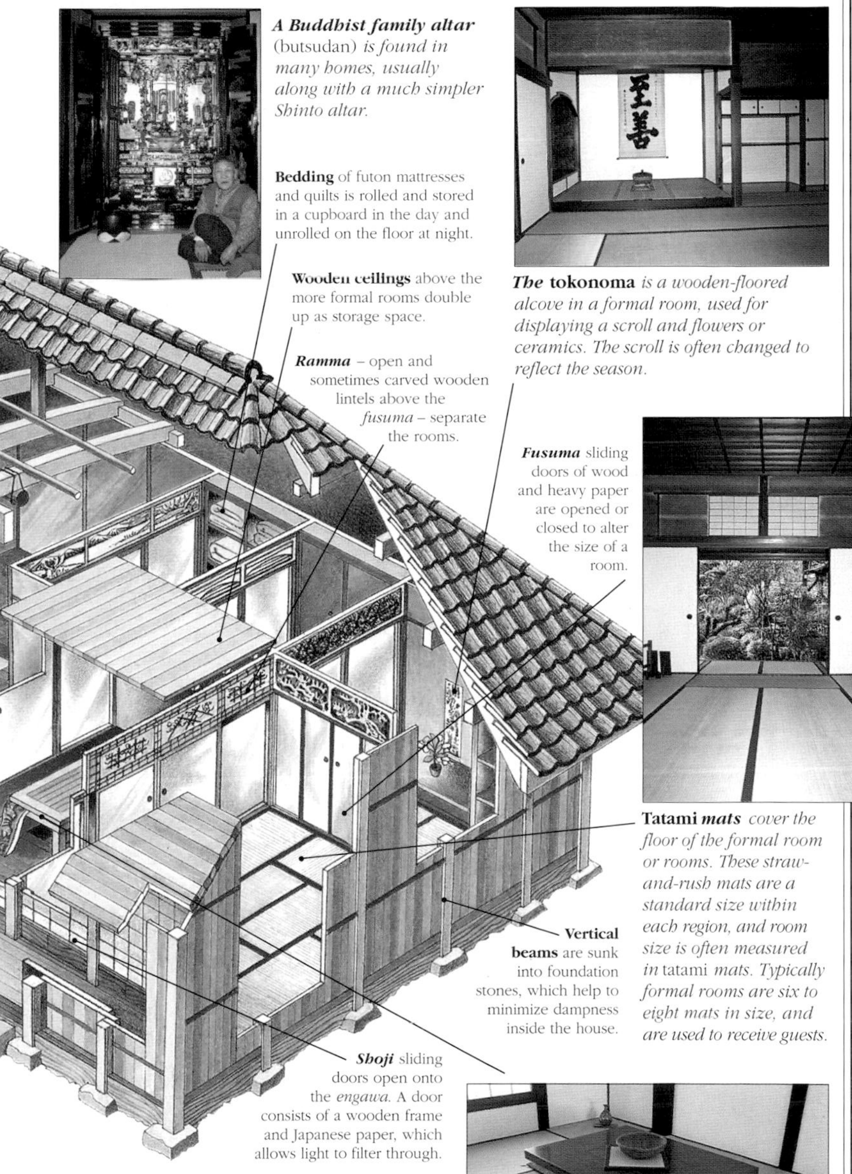

A Buddhist family altar (butsudan) *is found in many homes, usually along with a much simpler Shinto altar.*

Bedding of futon mattresses and quilts is rolled and stored in a cupboard in the day and unrolled on the floor at night.

Wooden ceilings above the more formal rooms double up as storage space.

Ramma – open and sometimes carved wooden lintels above the *fusuma* – separate the rooms.

***The* tokonoma** *is a wooden-floored alcove in a formal room, used for displaying a scroll and flowers or ceramics. The scroll is often changed to reflect the season.*

Fusuma sliding doors of wood and heavy paper are opened or closed to alter the size of a room.

Tatami *mats* *cover the floor of the formal room or rooms. These straw-and-rush mats are a standard size within each region, and room size is often measured in* tatami *mats. Typically formal rooms are six to eight mats in size, and are used to receive guests.*

Vertical beams are sunk into foundation stones, which help to minimize dampness inside the house.

Shoji sliding doors open onto the *engawa*. A door consists of a wooden frame and Japanese paper, which allows light to filter through.

A One-Story Minka

This illustration shows features of the layout of a *minka*. The toilet and washing facilities were usually located outside the main house. The main variations on this basic design include the *gassho-zukuri* house *(see p141)*, the L-shaped *magariya*, used to house horses as well as people (found mainly in Iwate prefecture, Northern Honshu), and the *kabuto-zukuri* house, designed to allow in more light and air (found in Yamagata prefecture, Northern Honshu).

A kotatsu *is a heater combined with a low table. The heater (traditionally charcoal, now electric) may be situated under the frame, or inside a pit sunk into the floor. A futon is draped under the tabletop for extra warmth in winter. Individuals kneel on cushions or rest their feet in the pit.*

Sumo and the Martial Arts

A karate kick

NOW MORE OF A PROFESSIONAL SPORT than a martial art, sumo can trace its origins back 2,000 years to Shinto harvest rites, and strong links with Shinto remain in many sumo rituals. There are six sumo tournaments in Japan every year *(see p350)*, broadcast live on TV and followed enthusiastically. Training is a way of life *(see p98)* for sumo wrestlers, and if a tournament is not on, it may be possible to watch practice sessions *(see pp106–7)*. Martial arts are known as *budo*, or the "martial way." They aim to cultivate balance, control, speed, and accuracy in a spiritual, mental, and physical sense. Kendo and kyudo, the least changed since the days of the samurai, are seen as the purest of the martial arts.

Sumo wrestlers *were a highly popular subject for Edo-period woodblock prints.*

Throwing salt *to purify the ring and the fight to come is part of a complex pre-match ritual that the wrestlers undertake. They also stamp, clap, and raise their hands before crouching down in front of their opponent ready to start.*

The *gyoji* (referee) wears traditional court costume and uses a fan to signal when to begin.

Grand champions (yokozuna) *perform pre-match rituals wearing a richly decorated ceremonial apron and a white hemp-rope belt hung with folded paper (as seen at Shinto shrines). This champion is performing* shiko, *lifting his leg and stamping his foot to banish evil spirits and intimidate his opponents.*

SUMO WRESTLING

Despite their size – there are no weight restrictions – sumo wrestlers *(rikishi)* move quickly and with agility, and so matches are often short (10 seconds or so). The loser is the first to touch the ground with any part of his body, except the soles of his feet, or to step out of, or be pushed from, the ring. The referee *(gyoji)* declares the winner.

A referee pours an offering *of sake onto the ring as part of the dedication ceremony before a tournament. The ring is a platform of clay edged by a square of sunken rice-straw bales, with an inner ring (where the match is fought) also marked by sunken bales.*

***Banners** announce a sumo tournament – here at the National Sumo Stadium in Tokyo* (see p98)*. Each tournament lasts 15 days. The lower-ranking wrestlers fight early in the day, while higher-ranking ones appear from mid-afternoon onward.*

The wrestlers' hair is oiled and fastened into a topknot *(mage)*.

Only 48 winning techniques are commonly used, but many more have been identified.

A loincloth *(mawashi)* is worn for bouts, along with a thin belt *(sagari)* hung with threads similar to those seen at Shinto shrines.

***The ring stands** under a suspended roof resembling that of a Shinto shrine. A different-colored tassel hangs from each corner of the roof, representing the four seasons.*

Martial Arts

Originally developed as arts of war by the samurai, the martial arts have evolved into forms of austere discipline *(shugyo)* aimed at spiritual improvement; some are also competitive sports. The modern forms of kendo and kyudo trace their origins to methods practiced in Japanese antiquity.

***Kendo** means the "way of the sword." Originating from samurai fencing, kendo now uses bamboo swords. Contestants wear extensive padding and protection. In a match, points are gained for hitting the head, torso, forearm, or throat.*

***Kyudo**, or the "way of the bow," has close associations with Zen Buddhism. Although accuracy in hitting a target is important, the emphasis is also on concentration of mind and body.*

***Judo** developed from jujitsu. A system of self-defense, it is well established as a sport in which throwing and grappling techniques are used to subdue an opponent.*

***Karate** ("empty hand") reached Japan in 1922 from Okinawa. A form of self-defense as well as spiritual and physical training, it has become a sport, consisting of explosive yet controlled kicks, punches, or strikes, and blocking moves.*

***Aikido** – the "way of harmonious spirit" – uses an opponent's strength and speed against them. Training unites spiritual awareness and physical flexibility.*

Japanese Traditional Theater

FOUR MAJOR TYPES of traditional theater are still performed regularly in Japan: Noh, Kyogen, Kabuki, and Bunraku *(see p104 and p178)*. Originating in Shinto rites, Noh was first performed by Kan'ami Kiyotsugu (1333–84) and developed by his son Zeami. Adopted by the *daimyo* (feudal lords), Noh became more ritualistic and ceremonial. Gradually its farcical elements were confined to a separate form, Kyogen. By the 17th century, people wanted a more comprehensible and entertaining form of drama, and Kabuki evolved from Noh, starting in Kyoto. A form of puppet theater, Bunraku, like Kabuki, was aimed at the general populace.

A Noh play *is being performed for the imperial household in this 1863 woodblock print by Taiso Yoshitoshi.*

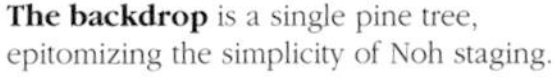

The backdrop is a single pine tree, epitomizing the simplicity of Noh staging.

Noh actors are all men. Female characters are represented by male actors in a variety of masks.

Musicians playing traditional drums and flutes sit at the back of the stage and accompany the actors.

The chorus of six to eight men sit to one side and comment on the action.

NOH

An austere, restrained, and powerful theatrical form, Noh is performed on a bare, three-sided cypress-wood stage roofed like a shrine, with an entrance ramp to one side. One or two masked characters appear at a time. Their slow, choreographed actions *(kata)* are performed to music.

Kyogen *evolved from comic interludes devised as relief from the demanding nature of Noh. A down-to-earth, colloquial form, its characters highlight human foibles and frailties. Masks are rarely used, and costumes are plain. The actors wear distinctive yellow* tabi *socks.*

Noh costumes *are usually richly decorated and heavy. Many layers are worn to make the actors seem larger and more imposing.*

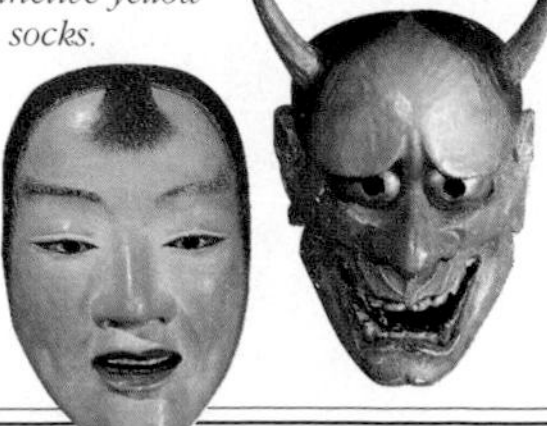

Noh masks *are worn by the leading characters; the greatest masks are classified as National Treasures. The mask on the right represents a samurai, and on the far right, a demon.*

***Kabuki actors** were popular subjects for Edo-era woodblock prints. The tradition can still be seen in this modern poster advertising a Kabuki play.*

Bunraku

Bunraku puppets are about 1.2 m (4 ft) tall with carved wooden heads, movable hands, and elaborate costumes. The main puppeteer wears traditional formal dress; his two assistants, one on each side, are clothed in black. *Shamisen* music accompanies the action, and a narrator both tells the story and speaks all the parts. Many Kabuki plays were originally written for puppets; Bunraku has in turn borrowed a number of Kabuki dramas.

Bunraku puppet with his manipulator

Stage right is where less important characters are usually located.

Costumes and wigs are highly elaborate, indicating the status and personality of each character.

The pine trees on Kabuki stage backdrops are a reference to its evolution from Noh.

Kabuki

Kabuki is flamboyant and colorful with a large stage and cast. The major actors are stars, often from famous acting dynasties. Elaborate make-up replaced Noh masks, and a curtain allowed set changes. The musicians and chorus sit behind screens on either side or on stage.

Stage sets often incorporate special effects including trapdoors, revolving sections, and overhead cables for flying.

Stage left is usually occupied by characters of high rank or importance.

***Aragoto,** or "rough-style" acting, is used in certain plays by male characters who move in exaggerated, choreographed ways and wear stylized makeup. Eye and facial movements are crucial to an actor's success.*

***The** **hanamichi** (flower path) is a raised walkway running from stage right through the audience and is used for dramatic entrances and exits.*

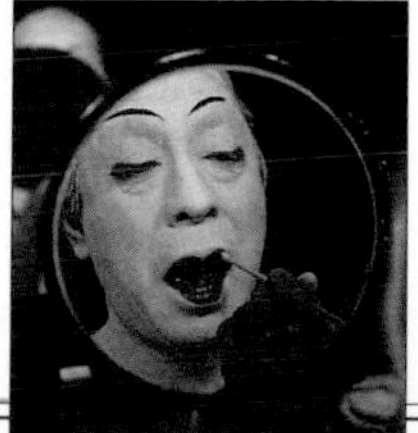

***Although Kabuki** was founded by a woman, Izumo no Okuni, female actors were soon banned as immoral. All actors are now male, and female roles are played by highly skilled* onnagata.

Traditional Arts and Crafts

Wood *netsuke*, used to secure a cord

In Japan there is no rigid distinction between arts and crafts; both have a long, distinguished history and are equally prized. Many techniques came to Japan from the Asian continent, especially China and Korea, and have since evolved and been refined. Early arts and crafts were dominated by Buddhist influences, but from medieval times onward they became increasingly secular and decorative. Today traditional arts and crafts are thriving, with thousands of practitioners making a living from their work. Artisans can be seen at work in many areas.

Metalwork *includes items such as samurai swords, temple bells, and tea kettles. This tea kettle is from Morioka* (see p271).

Calligraphy

Known as *shodo*, the way of writing, the art of calligraphy was introduced to Japan along with the Chinese writing system in the 5th century and came to be considered as an essential accomplishment for the cultured person. Traditional writing implements consist of a brush, ink, an inkstone, and a water vessel. Buddhist monks have often led the development of styles through the centuries. Modern calligraphy has been influenced by Western Minimalist and Abstract art.

A 17th-century example of calligraphy

Calligraphy today, still using traditional methods

Painting

Early paintings include religious mandalas, and scrolls illustrating works such as the *Tale of Genji (see p48)*. Ink painting thrived in the 14th century; its most famous practitioner was the Zen monk Sesshu (1420–1506). The Kano School *(see p155)* was most noted for its screens. *Ukiyo-e* woodblock prints *(see p81)* predominated in the Edo period. Modern painting in Japan is inspired by Western and traditional sources.

Screen by Shibata Zeshin (1807–91) depicting the four elegant pastimes of painting, music, the game of Go, and calligraphy

Potter at work in Kanazawa, Central Honshu

Ceramics

Ceramics up to 12,000 years old have been found in Japan. Myriad styles have developed in different areas, fueled by the central role of ceramics in the tea ceremony and cuisine. Kyushu is renowned for its porcelain and stoneware *(see p233)*; Hagi *(see pp212–13)* and Inbe *(see p204)* produce stoneware for the tea ceremony; Mashiko *(see p266)* is known for its folk pottery and as the birthplace of 20th-century potter Hamada Shoji.

Bowl from Naha, Okinawa

19th-century vase from Kyushu

TEXTILES

Sophisticated methods of dyeing, weaving, and hand decoration have developed in Japan, resulting in an astonishing range of textiles. Relatively isolated islands and areas evolved their own techniques; for example, the Okinawans use the *kasuri* method to tie-dye threads before weaving. *Yuzen*-dyeing in Kanazawa *(see p142)* uses a paste for resist-dyeing to create complex and colorful designs, often using natural vegetable dyes. Indigo *(ai)* was the most popular dye, though it has largely been replaced by synthetic alternatives. Modern designers such as Issey Miyake continue to experiment boldly with fabrics.

Dyeing *bashofu* fabric in Kijoka village, Okinawa *(see p251)*

Complex design of samurai woven into silk

Hand-painting dyes onto fabric, part of the resist-dyeing process

WOODCRAFT, BAMBOO, AND LACQUERWARE

The Japanese admire the grain and color of wood as much as the artifacts that are created from it. Traditional buildings have been made from wood for centuries; some are still in existence as a testament to their makers' craftsmanship. On a smaller scale there are exquisite wooden statues, along with wooden vessels and utensils, and traditional dolls *(see p271)*. To produce lacquerware, for which Japan is famed worldwide, the wood is coated with many layers of lacquer (derived from tree sap) and burnished to a smooth, lustrous finish. Bamboo, being strong and flexible, is used for umbrellas, toys, and baskets.

An 18th-century wooden carving of Amida Buddha

Laquerware box from Aizu-Wakamatsu

Bamboo craftsman at work

Demonstrating the art of *ikebana*, or flower arranging

IKEBANA AND BONSAI

Ikebana is also known as *kado*, or the "way of flowers," and originated from early Buddhist flower offerings. The tea ceremony required simple arrangements of flowers, while more avant-garde creations have been popular since the late 19th century. Today there are about 3,000 *ikebana* schools in Japan. Bonsai came from China and involves growing and training trees in miniature form; prize specimens are valuable heirlooms. Both *ikebana* arrangements and bonsai may be displayed in the *tokonoma (see p29)* of a traditional house.

An evergreen bonsai tree

Japanese Traditional Dress

ALTHOUGH MOST JAPANESE now wear Western-style clothes *(yofuku)*, it is not unusual to glimpse a kimono-clad woman in the street or a man relaxing in a lightweight summer kimono *(yukata)*. Kimonos are wraparound garments worn by men and women, usually on formal occasions and at festivals. Some people change into a cotton kimono to relax in the evenings. A good kimono can last for years, even generations – it is made to a standard pattern, rather than to fit the wearer; the fitting is done when dressing. The left side of the garment is always wrapped over the right; the opposite is done only when dressing the dead.

Kimono style *for women and men has changed little since the Edo period.*

A new*, formal kimono can cost tens of thousands of yen, but these garments become family heirlooms. Before cleaning, they are taken apart along the seams; for storage they are folded and wrapped in paper.*

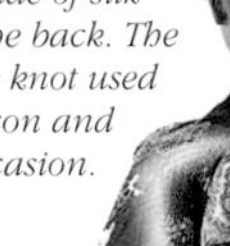

***The* obi** *sash is usually made of silk and tied tightly at the back. The quality of material and the knot used vary according to the season and formality of the occasion.*

The *haneri* is a replaceable neckband, just visible under the kimono.

A length of silk known as the *obiage* holds the *obi* in place.

The *obi* is a sash up to 4 m (13 ft) long.

The *obijime* decorative cord further secures the *obi*.

A tuck, or *ohashiori*, at the waist adjusts the length of a kimono.

Tabi socks have a split between the big and second toes.

Zori sandals usually have wedge soles.

Yukata *are unlined cotton kimonos worn by men and women, often at summer festivals or hot-spring resorts.*

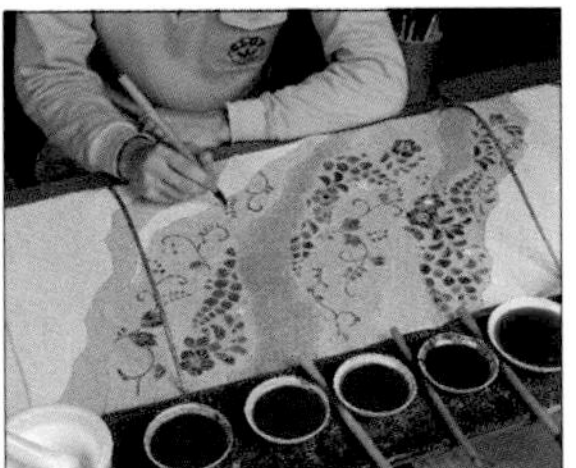

The sumptuous fabric *used for women's kimonos is often hand-painted, woven, or dyed using one of the many traditional Japanese techniques to produce a complex design.*

WOMAN'S KIMONO

This woman is wearing a *furisode*, a formal kimono with long, flowing sleeves. These are traditionally worn by young, unmarried women on special occasions, such as Coming-of-Age Day on January 15, and are often made of brightly colored and extravagantly patterned materials.

Women's hairstyles *grew increasingly elaborate in the Edo period, reflecting a woman's age and social and marital status. Today, women wear traditional styles only on formal occasions.*

Handpainted fan

Comb and hair pin

Fans*, usually bamboo covered with hand-painted paper, are traditional accessories carried by women and men. Combs and hairpins may be tortoiseshell, lacquer, or ivory, and are often exquisitely decorated.*

The family crest is known as the *mon*.

The *montsuki* is a formal kimono (which can be worn by men or women) bearing a crest.

The *haori* is an outer coat worn over the kimono.

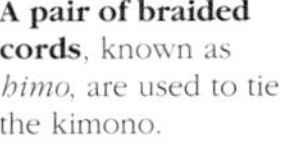

A pair of braided cords, known as *himo*, are used to tie the kimono.

Hakama are loose trousers, similar to culottes, which are worn over the kimono.

Men's sandals are known as *setta* and have a surface similar to *tatami* mats. The soles are made of leather.

At a traditional wedding*, or* tomesode*, the man wears a formal kimono, while the woman wears a white kimono, known as* shiromuku*, and a special headdress.*

Children wear *miniature versions – often rented – of the adult kimonos on formal occasions, and especially at the Shichi-go-san (Seven-Five-Three) Festival in November* (see p42).

Man's Kimono

Formal clothing for a man consists of a black silk kimono; a man's kimono is shorter than a woman's, allowing greater freedom of movement. Over the top go ankle-length *hakama* and a long, loose jacket or *haori*, plain apart from the family crest embroidered in white.

Traditional Shoes

Geta **wooden clogs**

Since the Nara and Heian periods (from the 8th century on), the Japanese have worn variations on thonged rush or leather sandals *(zori)* and wooden clogs *(geta)*. Both are highly practical for slipping on and off when entering and leaving houses. *Zori* are still worn with formal kimonos, and *geta* with *yukata*. *Geta* often tended to be raised off the ground to prevent the wearer's feet from becoming muddy; in the late 17th century the fashion for courtesans was for 30-cm (12-in) high soles, almost impossible to walk in. *Tabi* split socks are worn with both types of shoes.

Making wooden clogs

Japan's Festivals: Matsuri

Matsuri means both festival and worship, indicating the Shinto origins of Japanese festivals. Some are nationwide, others are local to individual temples and shrines. Matsuri are a link between the human and the divine, often marking stages in the rice-growing cycle (mainly planting and harvest) or historical events. The aim of the matsuri is to preserve the goodwill of the deities *(kami)*. All matsuri follow a basic form: purification (often by water or fire); then offerings; then a procession in which the *kami* is invoked at the shrine and escorted in a portable shrine *(mikoshi)* to a temporary dwelling where there is entertainment such as dancing or archery. The *kami* is then taken back to the shrine.

***The basic form** of matsuri has changed little over the centuries. This print shows an 18th-century religious festival with men carrying a* mikoshi.

***Omizu-tori** has been celebrated at Todai-ji temple, Nara* (see pp184–7), *since the 8th century to signal the advent of spring. Water is drawn from a sacred well and purified with fire from huge torches.*

The *mikoshi* is a colorful, ornate portable shrine in which the *kami* rides en route from and to the shrine.

***Takayama Matsuri** takes place in spring and fall. Spectacular floats are escorted from the Hie Shrine through the town by people dressed in Edo-period costumes. The aim is to placate the* kami *of plague.*

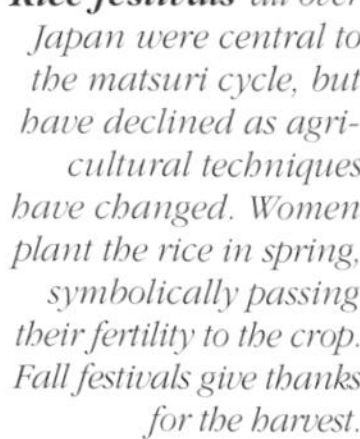

***Rice festivals** all over Japan were central to the matsuri cycle, but have declined as agricultural techniques have changed. Women plant the rice in spring, symbolically passing their fertility to the crop. Fall festivals give thanks for the harvest.*

***Aoi Matsuri**, or the Hollyhock Festival, in Kyoto, originated in the 6th century. Participants in Heian-period costume parade from the Imperial Palace to Shimogamo and Kamigamo shrines, re-creating the journey of imperial messengers who were sent to placate the gods.*

***Nebuta Matsuri**, held in Aomori in August, is one of Japan's most spectacular festivals, featuring huge paper lanterns. At the end they are carried off to sea as a symbol of casting away anything that might interfere with the harvest.*

***Bon,** the Buddhist Festival of the Dead, takes place in mid-July or mid-August. Ancestors are welcomed back to the world of the living and then bid farewell again. Bon Odori, hypnotic outdoor dancing, takes place.*

Participants are dressed in short kimonos known as *happi*, and headbands, or *hachimaki*.

The bearers of the *mikoshi* tend to take it on a boisterous ride as the gods are said to enjoy revelry.

Kanda Matsuri, Tokyo

Held in May in alternate years, this festival is one of Tokyo's largest. Numerous floats and portable shrines are paraded through the streets of Tokyo to placate the gods of Kanda Myojin Shrine *(see p69)*. In addition to communicating with the gods, the festival encourages a sense of community.

***Tanabata Matsuri** in July is known as the Weaver, or Star, Festival. Based on a Chinese legend, it is said to be the only day when the two stars Vega (the weaver) and Altair (the herdsman) can meet as lovers across the Milky Way. People write down wishes and poems and hang them on bamboo poles.*

***Jidai Matsuri**, or the Festival of the Ages, is a relatively new matsuri. It was initiated in 1895 to commemorate Kyoto's long history. Dressed in historical costumes dating from the 8th century onward, people parade from the Imperial Palace to the Heian Shrine.*

***Equestrian archery** is a traditional test of martial skills at matsuri. Archery contests take place at Hachiman shrines as offerings to the god of war; the best-known is at Kamakura's Hachiman-gu Shrine* (see p128).

Japan Through the Year

THE YEAR in Japan revolves through five seasons: spring, rainy season, summer, fall, and winter. Though less reliable than in the past, perhaps due to global warming, the seasons are still clearly discernable and dictate many of the traditional, agricultural-based *matsuri*, or festivals. The country follows two calendars: the contemporary Gregorian, and to a lesser degree the ancient Chinese lunar system. Because Japan also has two main religions, Shinto and Buddhism, there are double the number of festivals found in most countries. In fact, the days, weeks, and months are marked by so many festive occasions and national holidays that the year speeds past in a colorful procession of official observations, historic commemorations, sacred rites, and wild celebration.

Puppet from a Takayama festival float

Cherry blossom along the Philosopher's Walk, Kyoto

Spring

ALTHOUGH SPRING does not officially begin until the cherry trees bloom in early to mid-April, this is the time the elements begin to warm and thaw. Cherry-blossom parties take place throughout the country. In Golden Week (April 29 – May 5) and adjacent weekends many Japanese take the time off to travel.

March

Omizu-tori *(Water-Drawing Festival, Mar 1–14)*, Nara. At Todai-ji temple, water is ritually drawn to the sound of ancient sacred music at 2am on the 13th day *(see p38)*.
Hina Matsuri *(Doll Festival, Mar 3)*. Throughout Japan, dolls in Heian-period imperial costumes are displayed in homes with daughters.
Kasuga Shrine Festival *(Mar 13)*, Nara. Shrine maidens perform a 1,100-year-old dance.

April

Hana Matsuri *(Buddha's Birthday, Apr 8)*. Celebrated at temples nationwide. Sweet tea is poured over a small image of the Buddha to signify devotion.
Takayama Matsuri *(Apr 14–15)*, Gifu prefecture. A festival at Takayama's Hie Shrine, famed for its procession of richly decorated floats *(see p38)*.
Yayoi Matsuri *(Apr 16–17)*, Nikko, Tochigi prefecture. A festival at Futara-san Shrine including colorful floats.

May

Hakata Dontaku Matsuri *(May 3–4)*, Fukuoka. Costumed citizens escort legendary gods on horseback.
Hamamatsu Matsuri *(Kite-Flying Festival, May 3–5)*, Hamamatsu, Shizuoka prefecture. Amazing kites are flown.
Kanda Matsuri *(Sat & Sun before May 15, alternate years; next in 2001)*, Tokyo. Portable shrines are paraded in the neighborhood around Kanda Myojin Shrine; there is also a gala tea ceremony *(see pp38–9)*.
Aoi Matsuri *(Hollyhock Festival, May 15)*, Kyoto. Magnificent pageantry at the Shimogamo and Kamigamo shrines, reproducing past imperial processions *(see p38)*.
Cormorant Fishing *(May 11–Oct 15)*, Nagara River, Gifu city. Start of the season of nighttime torchlit fishing with trained birds.

Seasonal vegetables on sale in Naha, Okinawa

Cormorant fishing in Nagara River, Gifu, between May and October

Tosho-gu Grand Festival *(May 17–18)*, Nikko, Tochigi prefecture. As the highlight, 1,000 men in samurai armor escort three *mikoshi* (portable shrines) through the local streets.
Sanja Matsuri *(3rd Fri–Sun in May)*, Tokyo. Locals parade *mikoshi* through the streets near the shrine of Asakusa Jinja, accompanied by music. Can be quite wild.
Mifune Matsuri *(3rd Sun in May)*, Kyoto. An ancient boat festival charmingly re-enacted on the Oi River.

Rainy Season

From the pleasant climate of late spring, skies cloud and there are torrential downpours which are often the cause of landslides and flooding. A blanket of humidity envelops the landscape. Only Hokkaido, being so far north, manages to steer clear of such discomfort. The rest of Japan finds beauty in viewing hydrangeas and other flowers through the mists of mid-June to mid-July.

June

Sanno Matsuri *(Jun 10–16)*, Tokyo. Portable shrines are carried around Hie Shrine in the Akasaka area.
Rice-Planting Festival *(Jun 14)*, southern Osaka. Girls wearing traditional farmers' costumes ceremonially plant rice in the Sumiyoshi Shrine's fields, praying for a good harvest *(see p38)*.
Chagu-chagu Umakko *(Horse Festival, Jun 15)*, Morioka, Iwate prefecture. Decorated horses parade to Hachiman Shrine.

Summer

Technically summer begins in mid-July, as soon as the last clouds of the rainy season have left the sky. The heat and humidity continue to rise, mountains "open" for the season, and in mid-July, as soon as schools break for the vacations, the sea also "opens" for swimming. The air vibrates with the sound of insects; the rice grows fast; and people do what they can to keep cool. Even as the overheated landscape begins to sigh with exhaustion, frenzied summer celebrations break out, including spectacular firework displays that light up the night skies.

July

Yamagasa Matsuri *(Jul 1–15)*, Fukuoka. Climaxes with a race of giant floats over 5 km (3 miles).
Tanabata Matsuri *(Star Festival, Jul 7)*. Celebrated nationwide to mark a Chinese legend *(see p39)*. Stems of bamboo are decorated with paper streamers inscribed with poems. The week-long Hiratsuka Tanabata in Kanagawa prefecture features Disney-style mechanical exhibits in competition.
Bon *(Jul 13–16; held in Aug in most areas)*. See under August, page 42.
Nachi no Hi-Matsuri *(Fire Festival, Jul 14)*, Nachi-Katsura, Wakayama prefecture. At Nachi Shrine, 12 massive torches are set alight and carried by priests in white robes.
Gion Matsuri *(Jul, esp 17 and 24)*, Kyoto. The city's biggest festival, dating from the 9th century, when the people were seeking the protection of the gods from a deadly pestilence that was ravaging the local population. The streets are especially crowded for the parade of fabulous ancient floats on the 17th.
Kangensai Music Festival *(mid-Jul)*, Miyajima, Hiroshima prefecture. Classical court music and dance performed on beautifully decorated boats at Itsukushima Shrine.
Tenjin Matsuri *(Jul 24–25)*, Osaka. Celebrated at Tenman-gu Shrine. A flotilla of boats carries portable shrines down the Dojima River accompanied by the sound of drumbeats.
Hanabi Taikai *(last Sat in Jul)*, Tokyo. Spectacular fireworks on the Sumida River near Asakusa; a revival of Edo-era celebrations.

Carrying torches at Nachi no Hi-Matsuri

Fall colors at Sounkyo Gorge in central Hokkaido

August

Neputa Matsuri *(Aug 1–7)*, Hirosaki, and **Nebuta Matsuri** *(Aug 2–7)*, Aomori. These festivals are so spectacular they are televised. Massive illuminated and painted papier mâché figures are paraded on floats *(see p39)*.
Kanto Matsuri *(Aug 4–7)*, Akita. Men compete in balancing huge poles hung with lanterns on their shoulders, foreheads, chins, and hips.
Sendai Tanabata *(on the original date of the old calendar: Aug 6–8)*, Sendai, Miyagi prefecture. In Sendai's traditional version of the festival celebrated in July elsewhere, streets are decorated with colored paper streamers and hanging banners.
Awa-Odori *(Aug 12–15)*, Tokushima, Shikoku. The whole city sings and dances for four days and nights; the festival originally commemorated the building of the castle here in 1587.

Girls holding bamboo decorated with paper strips, Sendai Tanabata

Bon *(Festival of the Dead, Aug 13–16)*. Religious rites in connection with the Buddhist belief that spirits return to this world to visit loved ones in summer. A big family holiday, with everyone visiting, cleaning, and decorating tombs. Communal Bon Odori dance parties are held most evenings *(see p39)*.
Daimonji Bonfire *(Aug 16)*, Kyoto. Five large bonfires on the hills surrounding the city burn to mark the end of Bon, followed by dancing.

September

Hachiman-gu Festival *(Sep 14–16)*, Kamakura. A procession of floats and horseback archery at the Hachiman-gu Shrine invariably draw a big crowd *(see p39)*.

Fall

Although the children are back at school and the sea is once again "closed," the heat goes on. Now is the time to start thinking about harvesting the rice. Apples flood the shops, leaves start to fall, and snow will soon begin in the north.

October

Kunchi Matsuri *(Oct 7–9)*, Nagasaki. A dragon dance of Chinese origin winds between floats with umbrella-shaped decorations at Suwa Shrine.
Takayama Matsuri *(Oct 9–10)*, Gifu prefecture. Held at Takayama's Hachiman-gu Shrine, this harvest festival is most memorable for a procession with ornate floats.
Kenka Matsuri *(Oct 14–15)*, Himeji, Hyogo prefecture. At Matsubara Shrine, nearly naked youths carrying *mikoshi* challenge each others' skills in balancing.
Doburoku Matsuri *(Oct 14–19)*, Shirakawa-go, Gifu prefecture. A harvest festival with dancing and drinking.
Nagoya Festival *(Fri–Sun in mid-Oct)*. Long procession in Nagoya City with impersonations of historical characters.
Tosho-gu Fall Festival *(Oct 17)*, Nikko, Tochigi prefecture. Armor-clad samurai escort a portable shrine.
Jidai Matsuri *(Festival of the Ages, Oct 22)*, Kyoto. One of the city's big three festivals. Citizens in colorful costumes re-create 1,200 years of the city's history at Heian Shrine *(see p39)*.
Kurama Matsuri *(Fire Festival, Oct 22)*, Kyoto. Torches lining the route to Yuki Shrine, Kurama, are set alight, and children march through them holding more torches.

November

Karatsu Kunshi *(Nov 2–4)*, Kyushu. Celebrated at Karatsu Shrine and known for its colorful parade of floats.
Daimyo Gyoretsu *(Nov 3)*, Hakone. A re-enactment of a feudal lord's procession along the old Tokaido road between Edo and Kyoto.
Tori-no-ichi *(Rake Fair, mid-Nov)*, Tokyo. Stalls at the Otori Shrine near Asakusa sell ornately decorated rakes *(kumade)* for raking in the money next year.
Shichi-go-san *(Seven-Five-Three Children's Festival, Nov 15)*. Parents take children of

these ages to shrines in appreciation of their health and to pray for further blessings. Wonderful photo opportunities of kimono-clad kids.

Winter

The cold season begins in Hokkaido, Northern Honshu, and to the west of the Japan Alps in late fall, with the first snows. By contrast, the east coast – including Tokyo – rarely experiences more than a few days of snow a year. Down south, Kyushu remains quite dry and warm through the winter; Okinawa even more so. The period around New Year is one of the year's peak travel times.

December

On Matsuri *(Dec 15–18)*, Nara. Celebrated at Kasuga Shrine. A procession of courtiers, retainers, and wrestlers of ancient times.
Hagoita-Ichi *(Battledore Fair, Dec 17–19)*, Tokyo. Ornately decorated battledores are sold in the precincts of Senso-ji Temple.
Namahage *(Dec 31)*, Oga, Akita prefecture. Grotesquely masked men visit households with children, scaring them into being good.
Okera Mairi Ceremony *(Dec 31)*, Kyoto. A sacred fire is lit at Yasaka Shrine; people each take some embers home to start their own fires of the new year.

January

New Year's Day *(Jan 1)*. Japan's most important religious festival. Most people eat *soba* noodles the night before to bring long life. Witnessing the first sunrise is considered very lucky. The first few days are family-oriented, with visits to temples and shrines to buy lucky talismans for the year ahead.

Tokyo fireman at the Dezomeshiki, or New Year's Parade

Dezomeshiki *(New Year's Parade, Jan 6)*, Tokyo. Dazzling display by downtown Tokyo firemen in traditional uniforms, performing acrobatic tricks on top of bamboo ladders.
Usokae *(Bullfinch Exchange, Jan 7)*, Dazaifu, Fukuoka prefecture. Festival of Dazaifu Tenman-gu Shrine.
Toka Ebisu Festival *(Jan 9–11)*, Osaka. Celebrated at Imamiya Shrine. Ebisu is worshiped by those who pray for good commercial fortune in the year ahead.
Yamayaki *(Grass Fire Festival, Jan 15)*, Nara. Old grass is burned on Mount Wakakusa-yama to initiate new growth.

One of the snow carvings at Yuki Matsuri, Sapporo

February

Setsubun *(Bean-throwing Festival, Feb 3 or 4)*. Nationwide. Celebrities at major temples throw dried soy beans into crowds of onlookers, symbolizing casting out bad spirits.
Lantern Festival *(Feb 3 or 4)*, Nara. Some 3,000 candle-lit lanterns attract huge crowds to the Kasuga Shrine.
Yuki Matsuri *(Snow Festival, early Feb)*, Sapporo, Hokkaido. Vast, intricate sculptures carved from snow and ice fill Odori Park.
Saidai-ji Eyo Matsuri *(Naked Festival, 3rd Sat in Feb)*, Saidai-ji, Okayama prefecture. Celebrated at Saida-ji Temple. Young male devotees wearing *fundoshi* (loin cloths) jostle for a pair of sacred wands thrown into the darkness by priests.

Public Holidays

If a public holiday falls on a Sunday, the following Monday is also a public holiday.

New Year's Day (Jan 1)
Coming-of-Age Day (Jan 15)
National Foundation Day (Feb 11)
Vernal Equinox Day (Mar 21)
Greenery Day (Apr 29)
Constitution Memorial Day (May 3)
Children's Day (May 5)
Maritime Day (Jul 20)
Respect for the Aged Day (Sep 15)
Fall Equinox Day (Sep 23)
Health-Sports Day (2nd Mon in Oct)
Culture Day (Nov 3)
Labor Thanksgiving Day (Nov 23)
Emperor's Birthday (Dec 23)

The Climate of Japan

JAPAN'S CLIMATE varies primarily with latitude, from cool, temperate Hokkaido to subtropical Okinawa. Most of the country is warm, temperate, and rainy; temperatures are cooler year-round in the mountains. The other key distinction is between the Pacific and Japan Sea coasts. Both have a lot of rain in June and July. The Pacific coast also has heavy rainfall and typhoons in September but is sunny in winter, while the Japan Sea coast has long spells of rain and snow in winter.

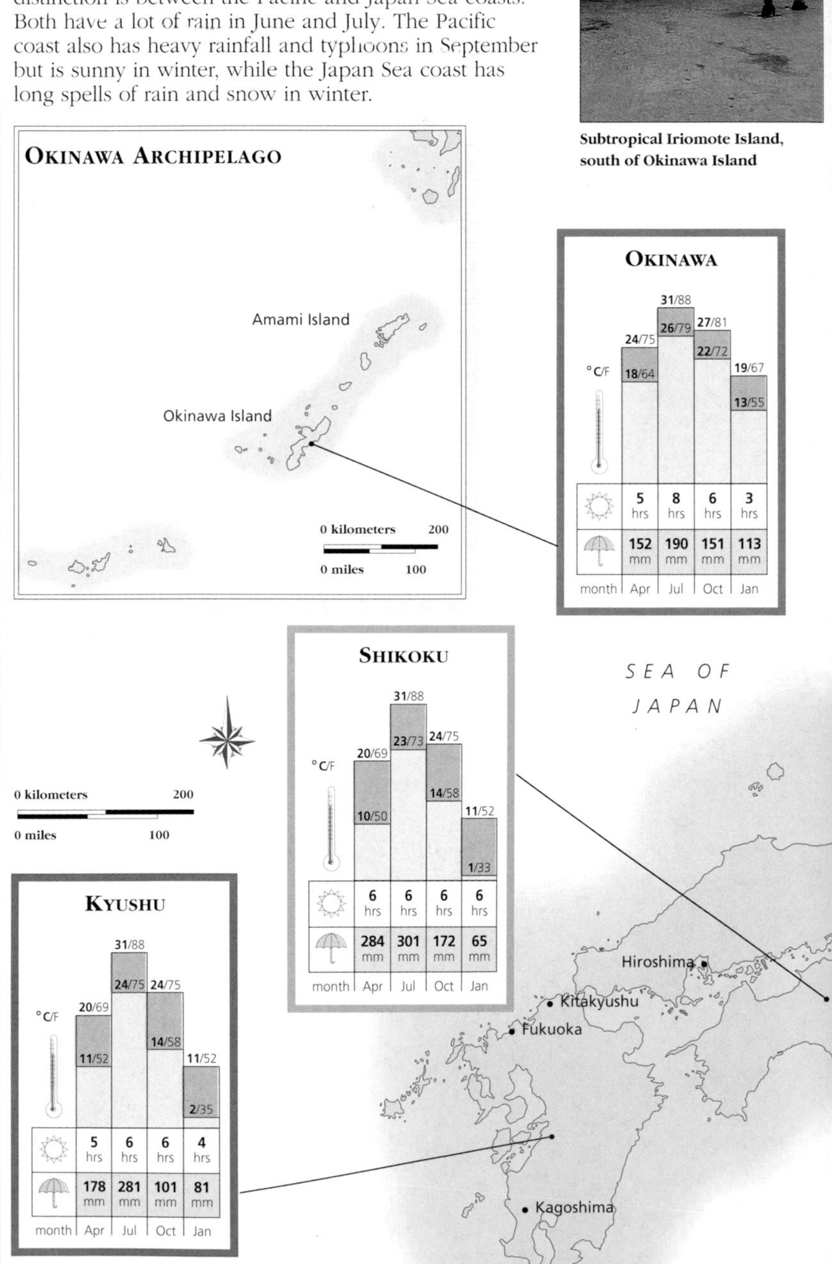

Subtropical Iriomote Island, south of Okinawa Island

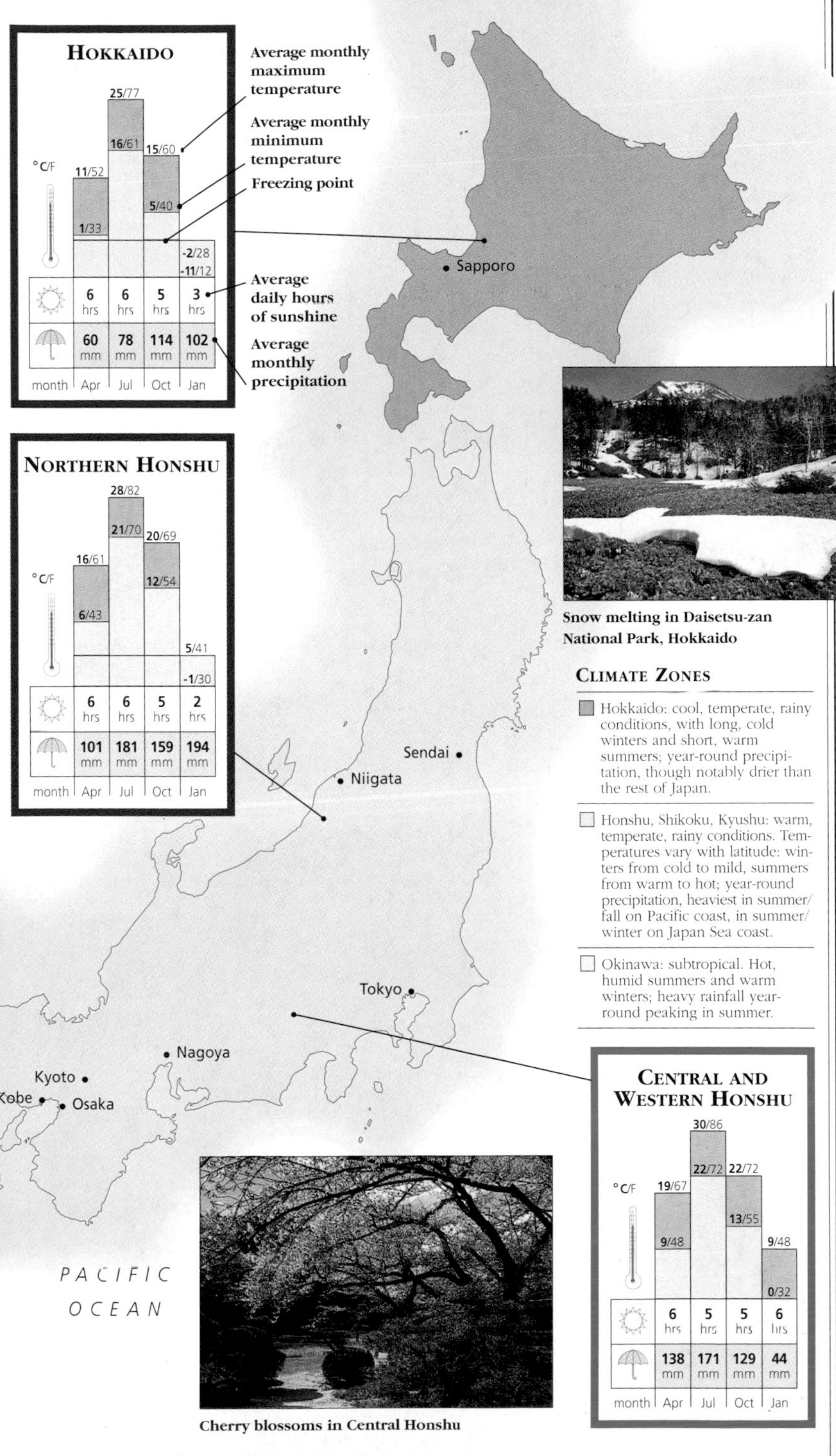

Snow melting in Daisetsu-zan National Park, Hokkaido

Cherry blossoms in Central Honshu

CLIMATE ZONES

- Hokkaido: cool, temperate, rainy conditions, with long, cold winters and short, warm summers; year-round precipitation, though notably drier than the rest of Japan.
- Honshu, Shikoku, Kyushu: warm, temperate, rainy conditions. Temperatures vary with latitude: winters from cold to mild, summers from warm to hot; year-round precipitation, heaviest in summer/fall on Pacific coast, in summer/winter on Japan Sea coast.
- Okinawa: subtropical. Hot, humid summers and warm winters; heavy rainfall year-round peaking in summer.

The History of Japan

From the origins of the Japanese race to its military behavior in World War II, Japan's history is still subject to conjecture. What is indisputable is that the people of this archipelago were able to avail themselves of the fruits of continental civilization even as their isolation protected them from attack. As a result, Japan has one of the most distinct of all the many Chinese-influenced cultures in Asia.

During glacial epochs when the sea level was low, Japan's first inhabitants may have reached the archipelago overland from Sakhalin and Siberia, China and Korea, or the Okinawa islands. Crude stone tools found at sites in Aichi and Tochigi prefectures may date back 40,000 years.

Recent discoveries posit the emergence of the hunting and gathering society known as Jomon around 14,500 BC. Jomon pottery is among the world's oldest and includes vessels and figurines, particularly of women. Mounds of shells and other evidence indicate that the diet included fish, shellfish, deer, wild pigs, and wild plants and seeds. In the Kanto Plain (near Tokyo), the Jomon culture in its later stages included village-like groupings.

Clay figurine from the Kofun period

Rice agriculture and bronze, iron, and other crafts are believed to have reached Kyushu island via Korea during the Yayoi period. The Yayoi people spread from Kyushu to Honshu and Shikoku over time, pushing the earlier inhabitants north. Chinese histories record a visit by an envoy of Himiko, queen of Yamatai, to the Chinese kingdom of Wei in 239, but Yamatai's location is still open to debate. Aristocratic orders emerged, including that of the emperor (a line unbroken to the present day), said to be descended from the sun goddess Amaterasu. Figures of high rank were buried in *kofun* (tumuli), along with clay sculptures, armor, mirrors, and jewelry.

By the late 6th century, tribes that had migrated to the fertile lands of Yamato *(see p181)* were engaged in a power struggle over the introduction of Buddhism. Prince Shotoku, appointed regent by Empress Suiko in 593, helped seal victory for the pro-Buddhist camp. The temple Horyu-ji *(see p190)* was completed in 607.

In 701, the Taiho code, a penal and administrative system based on the Chinese model, was in place. The temples of Nara *(see pp184–9)*, which became the capital in 710, epitomize this Chinese influence and are some of the best intact examples of their kind. With the completion of the *Man'yoshu*, the earliest known Japanese poetry, in 759, the culture began to establish a clear voice of its own.

Periods at a Glance

Jomon	14,500–300 BC
Yayoi	300 BC–AD 300
Kofun/Asuka	300–710
Hakuho	645–710
Nara	710–794
Heian	794–1185
Kamakura	1185–1333
Muromachi	1333–1568
Momoyama	1568–1600
Tokugawa (Edo)	1600–1868
Meiji	1868–1912
Taisho	1912–1926
Showa	1926–1989
Heisei	1989–present

Timeline

300 BC–AD 300 Continental methods of farming, metalworking, pottery, and other skills reach southwestern Japan via Korea, and spread through islands

710 Heijo-kyo (Nara) made capital

701 Taiho code put in place, the basis of the first Japanese legal system

AD 1 | 200 | 400 | 600

Yayoi earthenware

239 Himiko, queen of Yamatai, sends envoy to kingdom of Wei in China

587 Power struggle over introduction of Buddhism from China

712 *Kojiki* completed, Japan's oldest historical account

◁ **Detail from a 16th-century screen painting, showing customs month-by-month in the Momoyama period**

Court Life and the Tale of Genji

Court life in Kyoto focused on romance, aesthetic pursuits, and fastidious observation of precedent and ritual, as documented in the *Pillow Book* of court lady Sei Shonagon in the late 10th century. The *Tale of Genji*, written in the early 11th century by Sei Shonagon's rival, Murasaki Shikibu, a court lady of the Fujiwara clan, is possibly the world's oldest novel. It depicts the loves and sorrows of a fictitious prince, Genji, and, after he dies, the amorous pursuits of a man whom Genji mistakenly thought was his son. The story has been illustrated in countless scrolls and other media.

***Tale of Genji* scroll**

Heian Period

The powerful Fujiwara family and Emperor Kammu built a new capital, Heian-kyo, now Kyoto *(see pp148–73)*, in 794. The new system, also based on Chinese models, held that the land and people were ultimately the property of the emperor. Tax-exempt status was granted to Buddhist institutions, large landholders, and settlers who would expand the state's frontiers. Meanwhile, the Fujiwara clan gained influence by acting as regents, and intermarriage with the imperial family. A pattern emerged in which emperors would abdicate, name a younger successor, enter a monastery, then exercise power from behind the scenes.

Buddhism's influence continued as proponents such as Saicho adapted it, launching the Tendai, Shingon, and Pure-Land schools *(see p269)*. Powerful temples like Enryaku-ji *(see p172–3)* grew militant in faceoffs with other temples and the government, creating armies of warrior-monks.

Wooden statue of Minamoto no Yoritomo

Ironically, Buddhism's abhorrence of killing fed the nobility's contempt for the farmer-warriors – the early samurai *(see pp50–51)* – on the frontier, who battled the indigenous Ainu people *(see p281)* and each other. After 1100, the court could no longer control infighting, and tensions rose between two clans of farmer-warriors from the northeast: the Taira and the Minamoto. By 1160, ruthless Taira no Kiyomori was the most powerful man in Japan. But the Minamoto, led by the brothers Yoshitsune and Yoritomo, fought back to defeat the Taira and establish the first military shogunate at Kamakura *(see pp128–31)* in 1185.

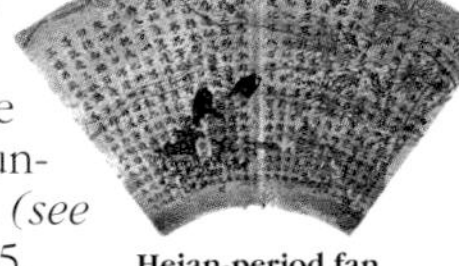

Heian-period fan

Kamakura Shogunate

Deliberately basing his government far from the imperial court in the village of Kamakura, Minamoto no Yoritomo carefully crafted a system that benefited his *bushi* (warrior) peers and brought 150 years of relative peace and stability. Yoritomo's direct heirs were shoguns only in name, however, as they were dominated by hereditary regents from the military Hojo family of Kamakura. The Hojo assumed the prerogatives of power while granting the imperial institution and nobility the privilege of signing off on policy.

Timeline

794 Heian-kyo (Kyoto) becomes capital, which it remains until 1868

800

801 Warriors sent to Northern Honshu to battle Ezo tribes

823 Kukai, leading proponent of Shingon Buddhism, appointed head of Toji temple

866 First Fujiwara regent assumes post

900

940 First uprising by a warrior member of the Taira clan

Toji temple

985 Genshin writes tract promoting Pure-Land Buddhism

1000

c.1000 *Tale of Genji* written by court lady Murasaki Shikibu

1087 Emperor Shirakawa abdicates and becomes first cloistered emperor

1100

Portuguese in Kyushu – the "Southern Barbarians" who introduced firearms and Christianity to Japan

The *Tale of the Heike*, a chronicle of the war between the Taira and Minamoto clans, was first recited to lute accompaniment at this time. Temples and works of art were created in Kamakura, reflecting Yoritomo's warrior ideals of stoicism, self discipline, frugality, and loyalty. Zen Buddhism as imported from China was popular with the samurai, while the Pure-Land, True-Pure-Land, and Nichiren Buddhist sects promoted salvation to the common people.

Mongol invasions were repelled twice in the 13th century, but weakened the resources and command of Kamakura. The end came in 1333, when the Ashikaga clan, led by Takauji, toppled the Kamakura shogunate. However, the power systems instigated by Yoritomo and the Hojo influenced Japanese life for five more centuries.

Muromachi-period sword guard

Muromachi Shogunate

With military power back with the imperial court in Kyoto, arts such as Noh drama and the tea ceremony flowered under the patronage of Shogun Ashikaga Yoshimasa. However, a succession dispute split the court into southern and northern factions. With leaders engaged in power struggles, chaos and famine were common. The nadir was reached during the Onin War (1467–77), when arson and looting destroyed much of Kyoto.

The Muromachi period, named for the Kyoto district where the Ashikagas built their palace, was a time of craven ambition that unleashed every class in society to vie for advantage. Warfare, once the exclusive business of samurai, now involved armies of footsoldiers *(ashigaru)* recruited from the peasantry, who could hope for promotion based on success in the battlefields.

In 1542 a trio of Portuguese from a shipwrecked junk emerged in Tanegashima, an island off Kyushu, and introduced firearms to Japan. Francis Xavier, a founding member of the Society of Jesus, established a Jesuit mission at Kagoshima in 1549. The contact with Europeans further destabilized the political situation and set the stage for the first of the great unifiers, Oda Nobunaga, who entered Kyoto in 1568.

1180–85 Minamoto clan defeats the Taira and establishes Kamakura shogunate

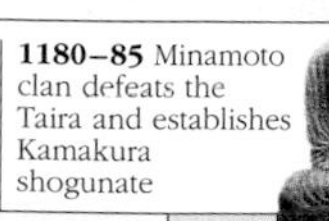

Great Buddha image at Kamakura

c. 1400 Zeami performing Noh dramas and writing

1467 Devastating Onin War begins. Vast sections of Kyoto are burned over the next decade

1200 | 1300 | 1400 | 1500

1160 Ascendant Taira clan under Taira no Kiyomori suppresses its rivals, the Minamoto, and dominates court life

1281 Second Mongol invasion

1274 First Mongol invasion

1242 Emperor Shijo dies without naming heir, setting off succession dispute

1560–80 Oda Nobunaga victorious in battles for hegemony of Japan

1428 Peasant uprising in Kyoto

1401 Formal relations with China reestablished

The Samurai

The samurai, also known as *bushi*, emerged in the 9th century when the emperor's court in Kyoto, disdaining warfare, delegated the overseeing and defense of far-flung holdings to constables and local farmer-warriors. Affiliated to *daimyo* (lords of noble descent), the samurai formed their own hereditary clans over time and became more powerful than the emperor; from their ranks emerged the shogunates (military dictatorships) of the 12th–19th centuries. Strict codes of loyalty and behavior, called *bushido* ("way of the warrior"), were inspired in part by Zen Buddhism and included ritualized acts of suicide *(seppuku)* to prove honor.

***Castle towns** were built in strategic positions by powerful samurai. The most distinctive castles, such as at Himeji* (see pp200–203) *and Osaka, date from the 16th century.*

Seppuku, *also known less formally as harakiri, was the honorable method of suicide, whereby the samurai would disembowel himself in front of witnesses.*

On the wet and windy night of October 20, the armies massed in the hills around Sekigahara. At 8am the following morning, 100,000 samurai went to war.

Most military archers were mounted on horseback.

Battle of Sekigahara

After Toyotomi Hideyoshi died, *daimyo* from eastern and western Japan fell into dispute and sent their samurai, led by Tokugawa Ieyasu and Ishida Mitsunari, to battle. Ieyasu won the battle, in a valley in Central Honshu on October 21, 1600, and subsequently founded the Tokugawa shogunate.

***Oda Nobunaga** (1534–82) was the first of the "Three Heroes" of samurai history, who between them unified most of Japan. The other two were Toyotomi Hideyoshi (1537–98) and Tokugawa Ieyasu (1543–1616).*

***Saigo Takamori** (1827–77) was one of the last samurai. After helping to overthrow the Tokugawa shogunate and leading the Satsuma Rebellion he committed suicide.*

***The** **daimyo** were the hereditary, landholding lords of the feudal era, to whom most samurai swore their allegience. Under the Tokugawa shogunate the* daimyo *were forced to journey to Edo every two years with all their people.*

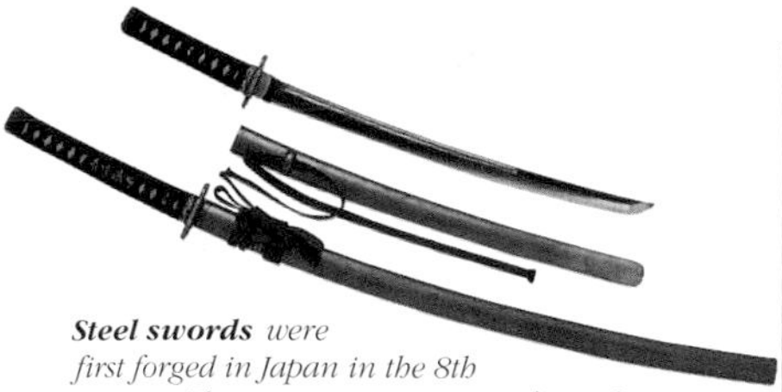

***Steel swords** were first forged in Japan in the 8th century. The samurai wore pairs of swords, long and short, from 1600. They were banned after the Meiji Restoration of 1868.*

Every warrior took a musket, spear, or bow into battle, as well as a sword.

Long vertical banners *(nobori)* were hung on poles to identify different military families and groups of warriors.

Heads were collected in the thousands and set by roadsides.

Samurai Battledress

The samurai developed remarkably ornate and colorful armor from the 9th century on. The earliest style, *oyoroi*, was designed for archers on horseback. In the Muromachi period it was superseded by lighter armor, *domaru*, worn by foot soldiers, and later a style called *tosei gusoku*, shown here, which helped protect against firearms.

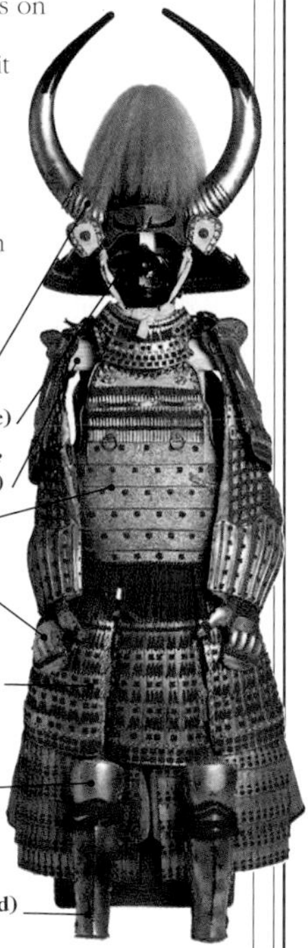

Kabuto **(helmet)**

Mempo **(face defense)**

Sode **(shoulder defense)**

Do **(cuirass)**

Kote **(arm defense)**

Kusazuri **(upper thigh defense)**

Haidate **(lower thigh defense)**

Suneate **(shin guard)**

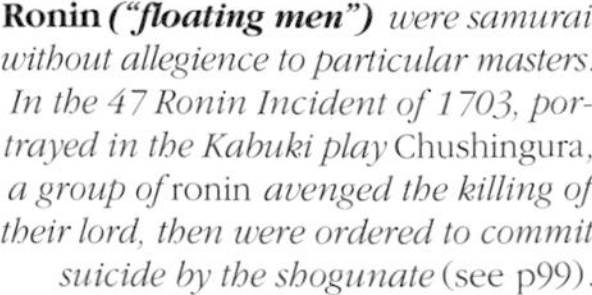

Ronin *("floating men")* *were samurai without allegience to particular masters. In the 47 Ronin Incident of 1703, portrayed in the Kabuki play* Chushingura, *a group of* ronin *avenged the killing of their lord, then were ordered to commit suicide by the shogunate* (see p99).

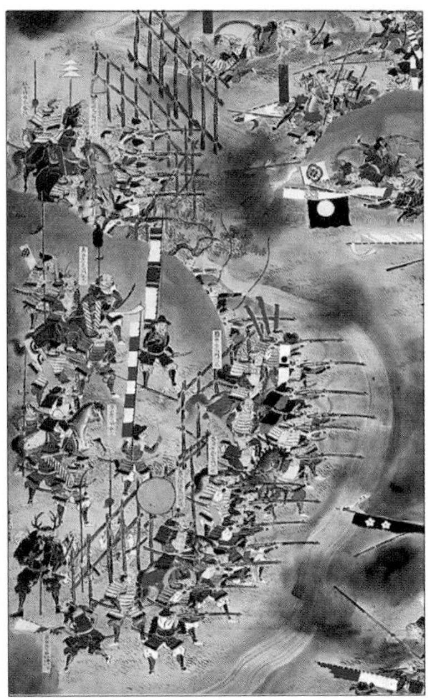

Screen depicting the Battle of Nagashino in 1575, won by Oda Nobunaga's 3,000 musketeers

Momoyama Period

After Japan had been racked by over a century of debilitating, inconclusive warfare, Oda Nobunaga, who rose through military ranks in the provinces, set out to unify the nation under his rule. From 1568–76 Nobunaga defeated rival warlord Asai Nagamasa; burned down Enryaku-ji, where militant monks had long challenged the court and their Buddhist rivals; drove Ashikaga Yoshiaki into exile; and deployed 3,000 musketeers to massacre the Takeda forces at the Battle of Nagashino. In 1580, in his last great military exploit, Nobunaga obtained the surrender of Ishiyama Hongan-ji, a nearly impregnable temple fortress in what is now central Osaka. Surrounded by moats and walls, the temple had been the power base of the Buddhist True-Pure-Land sect.

Momoyama-period detail at Nishi Hongan-ji, Kyoto

By 1582, when he was forced to commit suicide by a treasonous vassal, Nobunaga was in control of 30 of Japan's 68 provinces. Nobunaga's deputy, a warrior of humble birth named Toyotomi Hideyoshi, promptly avenged his lord and continued the work of unification, launching epic campaigns that brought Shikoku (1585), Kyushu (1587), the Kanto region (1590), and Northern Honshu (1591) under his control. He followed up by destroying many of the castles and forts belonging to potential rivals, confiscating weapons belonging to peasants, and devising a system in which peasants held their own small plots and paid a fixed tax directly to the central government.

In his later years, Hideyoshi ordered two unsuccessful invasions of Korea and persecuted the Portuguese missionaries and their Japanese converts *(see p234)*. Like Oda Nobunaga, however, Hideyoshi never actually claimed the title of shogun but became obsessed with ensuring the perpetuation of his line after his death. Two years after his death in 1598, however, dissension among his retainers led to the Battle of Sekigahara *(see pp50–51)*, in which Tokugawa Ieyasu emerged victorious.

The Tokugawa Shogunate

Named shogun by the emperor in 1603, Ieyasu split the population into rigidly defined hereditary classes. To end turf wars, samurai were forbidden to own

Timeline

1590 Hideyoshi controls all Japan

1597 Violent persecution of Christians in Nagasaki

1600

Osaka Castle

1600 Tokugawa Ieyasu wins battle of Sekigahara, achieves hegemony over Japan

1614 Christianity banned

1615 Siege of Osaka Castle

1625

1635 All foreign commerce confined to artificial island of Dejima in Nagasaki Bay. From 1641, only Dutch and Chinese allowed access

1650

1657 Meireki fire in Edo kills over 100,000

1675

Basho

1689 Haiku poet Basho departs on his journey to the north

1700

1703 Suicide of the 47 Ronin *(see p51)*

1707 Last eruption of Mount Fuji

land and could reside only within certain quarters of castle towns. Farmers were allotted small plots, which they were obliged to cultivate. Artisans formed the next class, merchants the bottom. Movement between regions was strictly regulated, and families or whole villages could be punished for crimes by their kin or neighbors.

The *daimyo* or lords who governed regions were subject to Tokugawa authority and shuffled to different regions if their service was not approved. After 1635, the *daimyo* and their samurai retinue were forced to reside every other year in the city of Edo (Tokyo), the new seat of the shogunate.

Fireman official's garment in Edo

Isolation and the Rise of Edo

William Adams, an Englishman who reached Japan on a Dutch ship in 1600, served Ieyasu in various capacities over the next two decades (as portrayed in James Clavell's 1976 book *Shogun*). During this time, the English, Dutch, Portuguese, Spanish, and New World governments made overtures to the shogunate on trade. However, the increasingly xenophobic Tokugawa regime restricted all foreign shipping to Nagasaki from 1635; only Chinese and Dutch traders were allowed from 1641. This heralded 200 years of isolation from the rest of the world. Persecution of Christians intensified.

While Kyoto remained the official capital through the Tokugawa period, Edo eclipsed it in size and was probably the largest city in the world by around 1700. Edo also hosted an explosion of arts such as Kabuki and Bunraku theater *(see pp32–3)* and the *ukiyo-e* works *(see p81)* of Utamaro, Sharaku, Hokusai, and Hiroshige. Patrons included the merchant class and samurai.

In 1853 Commodore Matthew Perry steamed into Edo Bay leading a fleet of nine US vessels to challenge Japan's refusal to enter into international relations. Weakened by unrest from within its own and other ranks, the shogunate could only accede to Perry's demands. Samurai from the Satsuma, Choshu, and Tosa domains in Kyushu, Western Honshu, and Shikoku became the driving force behind a successful restoration of imperial power and a reorganization of the government carried out in 1868.

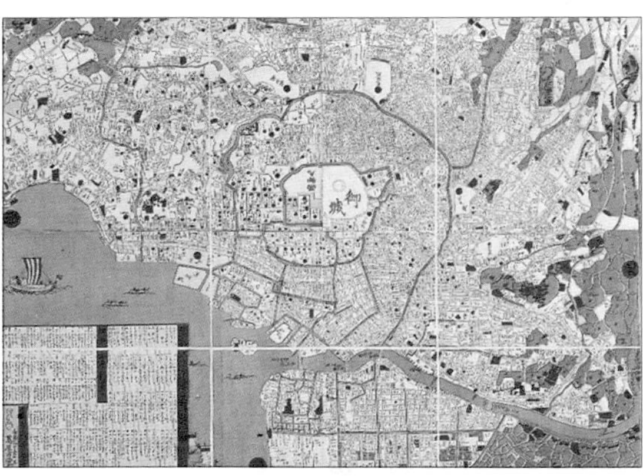

Early map of Edo, which outgrew Kyoto under the Tokugawa shogunate

1723 Love suicides *(joshi)*, spurred by rigid customs and hierachy during the Edo period, reach a peak

1725

1748 Kabuki drama *Chushingura* debuts, based on suicide by 47 Ronin

1750

1775

1782 Tenmei Famine claims as many as 900,000 lives

1800

A Hokusai view of Mount Fuji

1825

1831 Hokusai's *Thirty-Six Views of Mount Fuji* published

1853 Commodore Matthew Perry anchors in Edo Bay; Kanagawa Treaty between US and Japan signed

Woodblock print of Sino-Japanese War of 1894–5

Meiji Restoration

Emperor Meiji (1852–1912) was 16 when the restoration of imperial rule was declared on January 3, 1868. Tokyo was swiftly made the new capital.

A new centralized system pressed for changes that would render Japan capable of competing with the West. Military conscription and the elimination of the hereditary samurai class were undertaken to create a modern fighting force, provoking furious resistance from samurai in 1874–6. *Daimyo* domains were gradually transformed into prefectures, although *daimyo* and court nobles lingered in the form of a new class called *kazoku*. Universal literacy became a goal. By 1884, tax and banking reforms, and an industrial strategy aimed at exports were underway. The Meiji Constitution of 1889, promulgated by the emperor, allowed the military direct access to the throne while creating a house of peers and a lower house.

Women in traditional Japanese and 1920s Western dress

Following disputes over control of the Korean peninsula, the Sino-Japanese War of 1894–5 ended with Japan's victory over China, but showed that greater military strength would be needed for the nation to contend as an imperial power equal with the West.

By the turn of the century, the transformation to an industrial economy, with textiles the chief export, was well underway. A second imperialist conflict, the Russo-Japanese war of 1904–5, ended with Japan aggrandizing its claims to Korea, which was annexed in 1910, and southern Manchuria.

During the final decade of Meiji's reign, the home ministry stressed reverence for the emperor, the family, the Shinto religion, and military and national heroes. Suppression of groups seen as enemies of the state became the government's prerogative.

War with China and World War II

The attempt to transform Japan from a feudal to a modern industrial state caused severe dislocation. By 1929, when the stock market collapsed, resentment against those who had prospered from exports intensified. Young officers, chafing to restore national pride, began assassinating rich moderates, while militarists and oligarchs in the government believed that seizing land from China and Russia would secure raw materials and improve national security. At the same time, a Pan-Asianist movement, which saw Japan on a mission to lead Asia out of servility, construed the Chinese resistance to Japanese domination as an insult. By 1937, the country was embroiled in an unwinnable war with China that further estranged it from the rest of the world.

Timeline

1865 · 1880 · 1895 · 1910 · 1925

1868 Meiji Restoration; Edo is renamed Tokyo and made capital

1869 Colonization of Hokkaido begins

1889 Imperial constitution promulgated

1890 Imperial Diet convenes for first time

Diet Building

1894 Sino-Japanese war begins

1895 China cedes territory to Japan, ending war. Russia, France, and Germany force Japan to relinquish the territory

1904 Russo-Japanese war begins

1905 Treaty of Portsmouth ends war. Korea becomes a Japanese protectorate

1910 Korea becomes Japanese colony

1923 Great Kanto Earthquake

1932 In the May 15 incident, young naval officers assassinate prime minister and attempt coup

1933 Japan withdraws from League of Nations

Aftermath of the bombing of Tokyo in 1945

When the US cut off Japanese access to oil, Tokyo made the desperate decision to seize Pacific territory in a sneak attack on Pearl Harbor, Hawaii, in December 1941. A few months later, Japan took Southeast Asia.

By 1944, American bombers were decimating Japanese cities, but the Japanese army was determined not to surrender unconditionally, opting instead for a suicidal defensive strategy. In August 1945, the US dropped atomic bombs on Hiroshima and Nagasaki, and the Soviet Union entered the war in the Pacific. Emperor Hirohito ordered the cabinet to sue for peace.

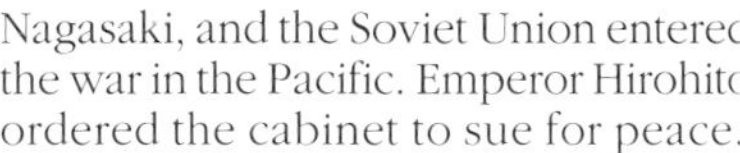

Akihito, who was made emperor in 1989

Japan Since 1945

Although World War II ended in disaster, the experience mobilized the Japanese people toward instinctive self-discipline and cooperation. The Allied Occupation force under General Douglas MacArthur began arriving as millions of homeless Japanese returned to bombed-out cities. The emperor renounced his divine status; land reform was promptly implemented; and war-crimes trials were soon underway. Against the backdrop of escalating Cold War tensions, the reformist ardor of the occupation leadership soon cooled; a general strike was canceled and communists were purged from government jobs.

By 1952, when the occupation ended, the neighboring war in Korea had turned into a boon for the Japanese economy. Industrial production surged as the average household set its sights on obtaining a washing machine, refrigerator, and television.

In 1960, massive protests against the ratification of the US-Japan Security Treaty rocked Japan, leading to the cancellation of a visit by President Eisenhower. The prime minister resigned. His successors concentrated on economic growth, promising to double incomes. By the time of the Tokyo Olympics in 1964, annual growth was around ten percent and rising.

Prosperity based on exports like electronic equipment, automobiles, and sophisticated technological products has since made Japan one of the world's richest nations and also helped keep the Liberal Democratic Party the dominant force in politics since its creation in 1955. The recession of the 1990s, however, along with significant changes in traditional roles in society *(see p15)*, has created a climate for further change.

High-tech games in Roppongi, Tokyo

1937 Sino-Japanese war of 1937–45 begins; 140,000 Chinese massacred in Nanjing

1945 Atomic bombs dropped on Hiroshima and Nagasaki; Japan surrenders

1995 Great Hanshin Earthquake in Kobe; fanatical cult releases sarin gas on Tokyo Subway

1997 Economic recession in Southeast Asia, spreading to Japan

1940 | 1955 | 1970 | 1985 | 2000

Prayers of a soldier

1941 Japan enters World War II

1964 Tokyo Olympics; first "bullet train"; government begins to promote computer industry

1989 Emperor Hirohito (Showa) dies; Akihito is new emperor

Shinkansen *("bullet train")*

TDK
acom
カードは
メガネ
メガネドラッグ
PUB
アコム
洋装服飾
芸材料
オカダヤ
東京電話
お申込は0120-719-019

Tokyo Area by Area

Tokyo at a Glance 58-59
Central Tokyo 60-71
Northern Tokyo 72-83
Western Tokyo 84-95
Farther Afield 96-99
Shopping in Tokyo 100-103
Entertainment in Tokyo 104-107
Tokyo Street Finder 108-117

Tokyo at a Glance

Japan's capital is situated on the banks of the Sumida River, by Tokyo Bay. As the fishing village of Edo it became the shogunate's center of power in 1590. The Shitamachi (low city) of merchants and artisans served the political and intellectual elite in the Yamanote (high city) on the hills to the west. Renamed Tokyo and made capital in 1868, the city was devastated by the Great Kanto Earthquake of 1923, followed by World War II bombing. It has since reinvented itself as one of the world's most modern, exciting, and energizing cities. Transportation is efficient: the easy-to-use Yamanote JR line circles the city, subway lines crisscross the center (*see* Back End Paper), and *shinkansen* lines link it with the rest of the country. It can be difficult to find individual buildings by their addresses *(see pp376–7)*. The Tokyo Street Finder *(see pp108–17)* locates all the sights, restaurants, and hotels mentioned in this guide.

Locator Map

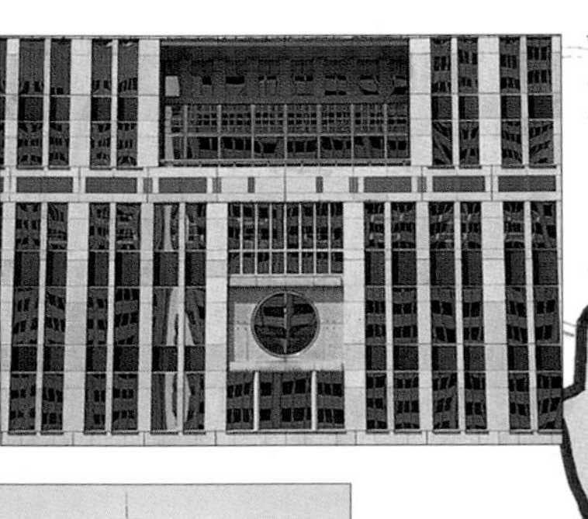

West Shinjuku (see pp88–9) *is an area of soaring skyscrapers, providing a visible manifestation of the corporate wealth of Tokyo. The most impressive buildings are the Tokyo Metropolitan Government Offices, designed by Tange Kenzo.*

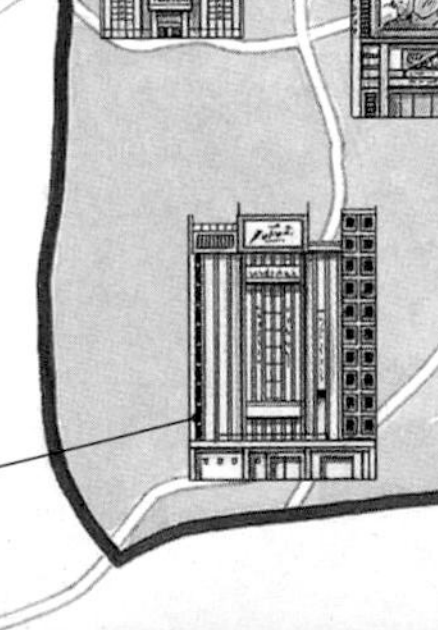

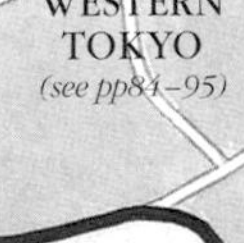

Shibuya (see pp92–3) *is a mixture of large department stores and smaller shops, all catering to young consumers. Adjacent to Shibuya are the equally fashion-oriented areas of Harajuku and Minami-Aoyama.*

East Shinjuku (see pp86–7) *comes alive when West Shinjuku shuts down. It encompasses a red-light area, countless bars, and various forms of entertainment from movies to* pachinko *parlors.*

◁ **The neon lights and busy streets of East Shinjuku**

VISITORS' CHECKLIST

11,950,000. Narita 60 km (37 miles) NE, Haneda 20 km (12 miles) S. Tokyo International Forum: (03) 3201-3331; Narita airport: (0476) 34-6251. Kanda Matsuri (Sat & Sun before May 15, alternate years), Sanja Matsuri (3rd Fri–Sun in May), Sanno Matsuri (Jun 10–16).

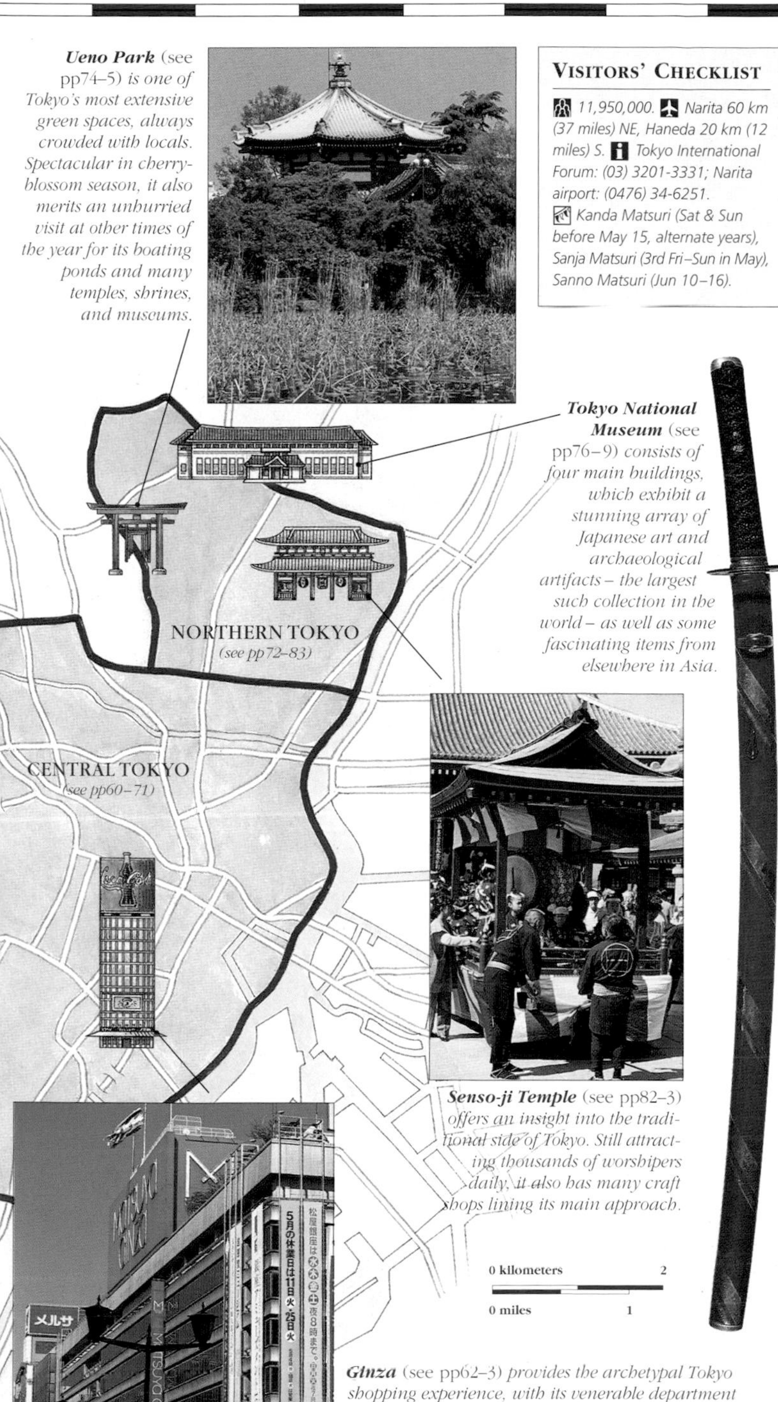

Ueno Park (see pp74–5) *is one of Tokyo's most extensive green spaces, always crowded with locals. Spectacular in cherry-blossom season, it also merits an unhurried visit at other times of the year for its boating ponds and many temples, shrines, and museums.*

Tokyo National Museum (see pp76–9) *consists of four main buildings, which exhibit a stunning array of Japanese art and archaeological artifacts – the largest such collection in the world – as well as some fascinating items from elsewhere in Asia.*

Senso-ji Temple (see pp82–3) *offers an insight into the traditional side of Tokyo. Still attracting thousands of worshipers daily, it also has many craft shops lining its main approach.*

Ginza (see pp62–3) *provides the archetypal Tokyo shopping experience, with its venerable department stores and small, exclusive shops, which have been joined by various international designer boutiques. Some excellent restaurants are also located here.*

Coca-Cola
KYOCERA
京セラ
鳩居堂
San-ai
Siena
TRY VERNAL
0120-800-777
TWININGS
STAFF SERVICE
0120-022-022
スタッフサービス
DressBlack

Central Tokyo

Situated to the north and west of the Sumida River, this area has been at the heart of Tokyo since the first shogun, Ieyasu, built his castle and capitol where the Imperial Palace still stands today. Destroyed by a series of disasters, including the Great Kanto Earthquake of 1923 and the Allied bombing in World War II, the area has reinvented itself several times over. Ginza and Nihonbashi were commercial centers and are still thriving and prosperous, offering a mix of huge department stores and well-heeled, side-street boutiques. For more down-to-earth shopping, there's the Jinbocho area for books, Akihabara for discount electronics and software, and the early-morning Tsukiji Fish Market. Central Tokyo's continuing political importance is evident in the Hibiya and Marunouchi districts, and the area is also home to two very different shrines: Kanda and Yasukuni. A selection of green spaces provides a respite from the frenetic bustle elsewhere.

A kimono-clad woman at Kanda Myojin Shrine

Sights at a Glance

Notable Districts
Akihabara Electronics District 17
Ginza see pp62–3 1
Hibiya District 10
Jinbocho Booksellers' District 14
Marunouchi District 8
Nihonbashi District 7

Historic Buildings
Diet Building 10
Imperial Palace 11
Kabuki-za Theater 2

Shrines
Kanda Myojin Shrine 16
Yasukuni Shrine 13

Modern Architecture
Tokyo International Forum 9
Tokyo Tower 6

Parks and Gardens
Hama Detached Palace Garden 4
Kitanomaru Park 12
Koishikawa Korakuen Garden 15
Shiba Park 6

Market
Tsukiji Fish Market 3

River Trip
Sumida River Trip 5

Key

Street-by-Street map *pp62–3*
Subway station
Train station
Long-distance bus station
Tourist information

Getting There

The best ways to get around are by Yamanote line or subway, or, for smaller distances, on foot. The Yamanote line stops at Akihabara, Kanda, Tokyo, and Shinbashi stations, while a number of subway lines crisscross the area.

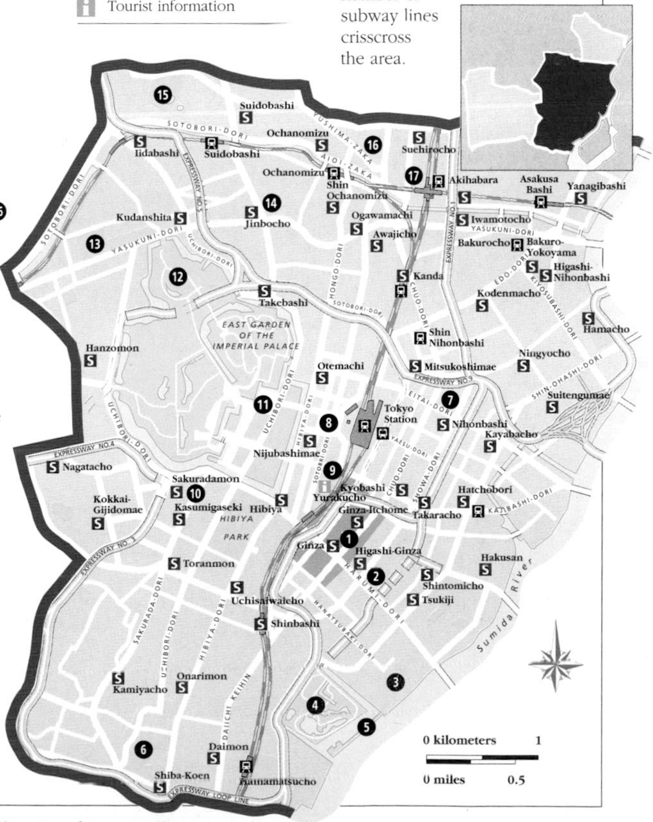

◁ **The San'ai Building at Ginza Yon-chome crossing**

Street-by-Street: Ginza ❶

銀座

When Ieyasu moved his military capital to Edo in 1590, Ginza was all swamp and marshland. Once filled in, the area attracted tradesmen and merchants. The silver mint that provided Ginza's name, "silver place," was built in 1612. In 1872 fire destroyed everything and, with the Meiji Restoration in full swing, the government ordered English architect Thomas Waters to rebuild the area in red brick. From then on it was the focus for Western influences and all things modern, and is still one of Tokyo's great centers. Tiny shops selling traditional crafts mix with galleries, landmark department stores, and the ultra-modern Sony showroom for an unrivaled shopping experience.

Takarazuka Theater
Here the all-female Takarazuka troupe stage extravagant productions in Japanese of Western musicals (see p107).

Shoppers at the Ginza Yon-chome crossing

Hankyu and Seibu department stores focus on fashions, with a mix of Japanese and international labels.

Gallery Center Building
On the second floor of this modern building are a number of exclusive galleries showcasing Japanese and Western art. On the fifth is an auction house, and the sixth has the Youkyo Art Hall, with exhibits by artists working in different media.

HARUMI-DORI

SOTOBORI-DORI

NAMIKI-DORI

MIYUKI-DORI

Ginza Noh Theater

Sony Showroom
Sony's latest technology and gadgets are on display on several floors here, and many can be tried out.

Fugetsudo is a traditional sweet and savory cracker shop.

The Asahi Building contains a traditional kimono shop, silversmiths, and several boutiques.

Tachikichi ceramics shop sells exquisite and unique handmade items in traditional and modern styles.

Key

- – – Suggested walk route
- Train line

Printemps is a branch of the French department store. Parisian influence came to Ginza in the 1930s and can also be seen in the nearby French cafés and boutiques.

Wako Department Store
Opposite the San'ai Building, this enduring landmark was originally built in 1894. Its clocktower is a popular symbol of Ginza, and the window displays are always entertaining

LOCATOR MAP
See Tokyo Street Finder map 5

Matsuya department store is another huge store stocking everything from food to bonsai. Restaurant City offers a large range of cuisines.

SOTOBORI-DORI

Nihonbashi

NAMIKI-DORI

CHUO-DORI

Mikimoto
Visit the glittering interior of this shop, the original producer of cultured pearls.

Mitsukoshi Department Store
This classic Tokyo store retains an aura of glamour – some people still dress up to shop here. Don't miss the particularly sumptuous kimono department.

Kabuki-za Theater *(see p64)*

Ginza Yon-chome crossing, one of the busiest in the world, is Ginza's main intersection.

Jena bookstore has a good selection of foreign-language books, including plenty on Japan, on the top floor.

San'ai Building
Made of glass, this building is at its best at dusk when the lights and neon signs inside shine through the glass, creating a magical effect.

0 meters 100

0 yards 100

The curved gable at the front of the Kabuki-za Theater

Kabuki-za Theater ❷

歌舞伎座

Map 5 C3. 4-12-15 Ginza. ☎ *(03) 3541-3131.* **S** *Higashi-Ginza stn, Toei Asakusa & Hibiya lines.*

TOKYO'S PRINCIPAL theater for Kabuki *(see p33)* opened in 1889 during the reign of Emperor Meiji and was a part of Kabuki's shift from daytime entertainment for the Shitamachi masses in Asakusa to a more highbrow (and high-priced) art form.

The dramatic building is one of the oldest surviving examples of the use of Western building materials and techniques in traditional Japanese styles. Its curved front gable was added in 1925 after earthquake damage in 1923. Almost destroyed by the Allied bombing of 1945, the theater was rebuilt in 1951. Performances take place most days *(see p104).*

Tsukiji Fish Market ❸

築地中央卸売市場

Map 5 C4. **S** *Tsukiji stn, Hibiya line.* *5am–noon Mon–Sat.*

A VISIT to this bustling fish market, officially Tokyo Central Wholesale Market, is an experience unique to Tokyo. It moved to this location from Nihonbashi after the 1923 earthquake and its subsequent fires destroyed the old one.

Every morning except Sunday, auctions are held from about 5am to 10am (the busiest time is 5am to 8am). During this time 15,000 restaurateurs and food sellers from all over the city buy 450 types of sea produce from about 1,700 stalls. The market itself is a huge hangar filled with a maze of tiny stalls, each crammed with fish still dripping sea water. The best way to see it is simply to plunge in. In spite of the frantic pace most people are quite friendly and tolerant of casual visitors. On the same site is a large wholesale vegetable market.

A small bridge marks the entrance to the market. Just before the bridge is **Namiyoke Inari Jinja** (Wave-repelling Fox shrine), where fishermen and traders come to pray for safety and prosperity. Opposite is a street lined with shops selling everything from dried tuna to porcelain dishes. In the alleys to the right are more shops and stalls where excellent and cheap sushi, tempura, even curry, are sold.

When leaving the market, turn left before the bridge for a line of shops and small restaurants. The river wharf where boats unload is over the bridge to the left.

A box of fish from Tsukiji market

TUNA FISH SUPPLIES

Tsukiji market specializes in huge slabs of *maguro* (tuna) from as far away as New Zealand and the North Atlantic. Japan consumes about 30 percent of the annual global 1.7 million ton tuna catch, and eats 80 percent of its tuna raw, as sashimi, requiring the best cuts of the best fish. Suppliers can demand top prices, typically 10–20 times that of the lower-grade tuna used for canning. The Pacific Ocean's South Blue Fin tuna, a favorite for sashimi, is endangered. The catch is managed and tuna numbers currently seem to be stable, although that may be due to economic recession. If the Japanese economy starts to grow again, South Blue Fin stocks could once again be put under extreme pressure.

Rows of frozen tuna at Tsukiji fish market

Hama Detached Palace Garden ❹

浜離宮庭園

Map 5 B4. ☎ *(03) 3541-0200.* **S** *Tsukiji stn, Hibiya line; Shinbashi stn, Ginza & Toei Asakusa lines.* *Shinbashi stn, Yamanote line.* *see Sumida River Trip.* *9am–5pm. (Last adm 30 mins before closing.)*

SITUATED where the Sumida River empties into Tokyo Bay, this 25-hectare (62-acre) garden was built in 1654 as a retreat for the shogun's family, who also hunted duck here. America's President Ulysses S. Grant stayed in a villa in the gardens during his visit in 1879 and sipped green tea with Emperor Meiji in Nakajima teahouse.

The garden grounds surrounding the duck ponds are still a pleasant, uncrowded place to stroll and sit. All of the original teahouses and villas, trees, and vegetation burned down after a bombing raid on November 29, 1944. **Nakajima teahouse** has been faithfully rebuilt, appearing to float over the large pond. Green tea and Japanese sweets are available here.

Nakajima teahouse in Hama Detached Palace Garden

Sumida River Trip ❺

隅田川の屋形船

Map 5 C4, 4 F3. *about every 40 mins; from Hama Detached Palace Garden 10:25am–4:05pm (Sat, Sun & public hols: from 10:15am); from Asakusa 9:50am–6:15pm (Sat, Sun & public hols: 9:40am–6:55pm; Jul 9–Sep 23: to 7:35pm).*

TOKYO WAS ONCE a city that lived by its rivers and canals. During the Edo period almost all commerce came to the capital on waterways. As wheeled transport, particularly rail, grew, the rivers and canals declined. In recent years, the city's main river, the Sumida, has been cleaned up to an extent, and river traffic is on the increase again. A little-seen view of Tokyo is available on the river trip from Hama Detached Palace Garden to Asakusa in Northern Tokyo.

The boat squeezes though a gate in the sea wall into the open water where the river meets the salt water of Tokyo Bay. **Hinode Pier** is the first stop – it is also possible to start from here, and to take a number of other trips around Tokyo Bay. From Hinode the boat starts back up the river, passing first between Tsukiji and **Tsukuda island**, which escaped the worst of the World War II bombing and remains a center of old Edo culture. The boat passes under 12 bridges, each painted a different color. It is still possible to glimpse people in the narrow parks that line most of the banks beyond the sea walls. Near Asakusa are long, low boats that take out groups for lantern-lit evening cruises.

Shiba Park and Tokyo Tower ❻

芝公園と東京タワー

Map 5 A4, 2 F5. *Shiba-Koen stn, Toei Mita line.* **Tokyo Tower** *Onarimon stn, Toei Mita line.* *(03) 3433-5111.* *Mar 16–Jul 31 & Sep 1–Nov 15: 9am–8pm daily; Aug 1–31: 9am–9pm daily; Nov 16–Mar 15: 9am–7pm daily.* *(extra for higher viewpoint).*

SHIBA PARK is a rather fragmented green space. A large part of it is a golf driving range, but a portion in the east is pleasantly landscaped with woods and a water course. The park used to be the Tokugawa family's graveyard. At its center is **Zojo-ji**, the family temple of the Tokugawas. It was founded in 1393 and Ieyasu moved it here in 1598 to protect his new capital spiritually from a south-easterly direction. The present-day building dates from 1974; nearby are the rebuilt Daimon (big gate) and the Sanmon (great gate, 1622).

The soaring Tokyo Tower, the city's highest viewpoint

To the west of the park is **Tokyo Tower**. Completed in 1958, at 333 m (1,093 ft) tall, it is higher than the Eiffel Tower in Paris, on which it is based. The ground floor has an aquarium and elevators to the observation deck. Other floors house amusements. You can visit two viewpoints – the main one at 150 m (492 ft) and a higher one at 250 m (820 ft), with more spectacular views. Be sure to go on a clear day.

Tokyo's skyline from the vantage point of the Sumida River

View of Mitsukoshi's central hall in Nihonbashi

Nihonbashi District 7

日本橋地区

Map 5 C1–2, 6 D1. *Tokyo stn, Marunouchi line; Nihonbashi stn, Ginza, Tozai & Toei Asakusa lines; Mitsukoshimae stn, Ginza & Hanzomon lines.* *Tokyo stn, many lines.* **Tokyo Stock Exchange** *(03) 3665-1881.* *9–11am, 1–4pm Mon–Fri.* **Bridgestone Museum of Art** *(03) 3563-0241.* *10am–5:30pm Tue–Sun.*

Nihonbashi was the mercantile and entrepreneurial center of Edo and Meiji Tokyo. Its name means "Japan's bridge" after the bridge over the Nihonbashi River that marked the start of the five major highways of the Edo period. After the destruction of the 1923 earthquake, shops, businesses, and banks started relocating to Marunouchi and Ginza; even the fish market moved to Tsukiji.

Although the area never regained its original importance, it is still a thriving commercial center, with dozens of bank headquarters as well as huge department stores and smaller traditional shops. **Mitsukoshi** has its main store here, on Mitsukoshimae. It started as a kimono shop in 1673. Head for the basement food market with its free samples, and the sixth-floor bargain counters where you can jostle with Tokyo's thrifty elite.

To the west of Mitsukoshi, the **Bank of Japan**, built in 1896 and modeled on the Neo-Classical Berlin National Bank, was the first Western-style building designed by a Japanese architect, Tatsuno Kingo.

On the north bank of Nihonbashi River, just before **Nihonbashi bridge**, is the bronze marker from which distances to and from Tokyo are still measured. The bridge here today dates from 1911.

On the south bank of the river, east of the bridge, is the **Tokyo Stock Exchange**, which lists around 2,500 companies, making it one of the world's top five. During the "bubble" economy of 1980s, it was possible to watch the frenetic hand signals of the traders. In 1999 trading was completely computerized, but this is still a great place to see how important commerce remains in Tokyo. The visitors' observation deck overlooks the trading floor and has some interesting exhibits comparing stock markets worldwide, with French and English explanations.

A robot trader exhibit, Tokyo Stock Exchange

To the south of Nihonbashi bridge, along Chuo-dori, the **Bridgestone Museum of Art** holds one of Japan's best collections of Western art, including works by Manet, Picasso, Rouault, and Brancusi, and Western-style paintings by Japanese artists.

Marunouchi District 8

丸の内地区

Map 5 B1–2. *Tokyo stn, Marunouchi line.* *Tokyo stn, many lines.*

This district lies to the south and west of Tokyo Station. During the Edo era, it earned the name "Gambler's Meadow" as its isolation made it an ideal place to gamble secretly. In the Meiji period the army used it, selling it in 1890 to Mitsubishi. Many laughed at Mitsubishi's apparent folly in buying a barren wasteland. The arrival of the railway increased Marunouchi's desirability as a business site, and firms from elsewhere in the city moved here after the 1923 earthquake.

Tokyo Station, designed by Tatsuno Kingo and completed in 1914, is a brick building based on the design of Amsterdam station. Its handsome dome was terribly damaged in the 1945 air raids and subsequently replaced by the polyhedron there today.

Tokyo Station's Western-style façade

A short walk west of the station up Miyuki-dori and over the moat via the gently arched Wadakura bridge leads to the **Wadakura Fountain Park**, which contains some interesting water features. Returning over the Wadakura bridge, cross Hibiya-dori and turn right. After about 500 m (550 yds) is the **Meiji Seimei Building** (1934), with its huge Corinthian columns. Hiroshige, the woodblock print artist, was born on this site in 1797. Beyond is the **Imperial Theater**, where Broadway musicals and Japanese popular dramas are performed.

Tokyo International Forum ❾

東京国際フォーラム

Map 5 B2. *Yurakucho stn, Yurakucho line; Tokyo stn, Marunouchi line.* *Tokyo and Yurakucho stns, many lines.* *(03) 3201-3331* *8am–11pm daily.*

DESIGNED BY the American-based Rafael Viñoly, and completed in 1996, the Forum is one of downtown Tokyo's most distinctive and enjoyable buildings *(see p21)*. A cultural center, it is made up of two buildings: a curved, glass atrium soaring 60 m (200 ft), and a cube-like, white structure housing four halls (the largest seating 5,012). A tree-shaded courtyard separates the two, while glass walkways provide an overhead link.

The interior of the huge atrium is filled with light and has a ceiling resembling a ship's hull. Inside the Forum are a number of shops, cafés, and restaurants, plus Tokyo's main **Tourist Information Center**, all supported by state-of-the-art facilities.

The airy glass-and-metal interior of the Tokyo International Forum

The imposing granite exterior of the Diet Building

Hibiya District and the Diet Building ❿

日比谷地区と国会議事堂

Map 2 F3, 5 A2, 5 B2. *Kokkai-Gijidomae stn, Chiyoda & Marunouchi lines; Hibiya stn, Toei Mita, Chiyoda & Hibiya lines.* **Hibiya Park** *24 hours daily.* **Diet Building** *9am–5pm daily.* *(compulsory, by reservation)*

CENTRAL TOKYO'S only large, Western-style park, Hibiya Park is the focus of Hibiya district. Its location, east of the political centers of Kasumigaseki and the Diet Building, makes it a favorite gathering place for protests, especially on May Day. The large bandstand is occasionally used for concerts.

Completed in 1936, the **Diet Building** houses the legislature of the Japanese government, originally established as the Imperial Diet in the Meiji era. Tours (in Japanese only) cover the well-worn inside, including the diet chamber, where you can see the deliberations of diet members. You can also glimpse extravagantly decorated rooms, used by the emperor for official functions.

Imperial Palace ⓫

皇居

Map 3 A5, 3 B5, 5 A1, 5 B1. *Otemachi stn, Tozai, Hanzomon, Marunouchi, Chiyoda & Toei Mita lines.* **Imperial Palace** *Jan 2, Dec 23.* **East Garden of the Imperial Palace** *(03) 3213-2050.* *9am–4pm Tue–Thu, Sat, Sun (Nov–Feb: to 3:30pm).*

IEYASU, THE FIRST Tokugawa shogun, started building his castle here in 1590. In the Edo period his successors made this into the world's largest castle; only the inner circle remains. The emperor and his family still live in the western part of the grounds in the **Imperial Palace**, rebuilt after the previous one was bombed in World War II. Public access is allowed twice a year: at New Year and on the emperor's birthday. The rest of the grounds, bounded by the moat, is divided into public parks.

The most famous landmark is the **Nijubashi,** a double-arched stone bridge, east of the palace. Completed in 1888, it was the palace's main entrance. The huge **Otemon** (Big Hand Gate), rebuilt in 1967, was the main gate before Nijubashi was built. Now it is the entrance to the **East Garden of the Imperial Palace**. Just inside is **Sannomaru Shozokan**, a collection of art and artifacts of the Showa Emperor. Beyond is the Edo-era **Hyakunin Basho**, where 100 samurai lived while standing guard in shifts. Behind is the **Honmaru**, the castle's main keep, now just massive stone walls with good views from the top. To the east of the Honmaru is the restful **Ninomaru** garden, landscaped by shogun Iemitsu in 1630.

A glimpse of the Imperial Palace over Nijubashi

Tokyo-ites enjoying a summer picnic in Kitanomaru Park

Kitanomaru Park ⓬

北の丸公園

Map 3 A5. **S** *Kudanshita stn, Hanzomon, Toei Shinjuku & Tozai lines; Takebashi stn, Tozai line.* **National Museum of Modern Art** ● *for renovation until fall 2001.* **Crafts Gallery** *(03) 3211-7781.* *10am–5pm Tue–Sun.* **Science and Technology Museum** *(03) 3212-8544.* *9:30am–4:50pm daily.*

Lying to the north of the Imperial Palace, Kitanomaru Park is reached through the massive **Tayasumon** (gate). A former ground for the Imperial Palace Guard, the area became a park in 1969. Before entering, walk past with Tayasumon on the left to reach **Chidorigafuchi** (the west moat), one of Tokyo's most beautiful cherry-blossom viewing spots. Row boats can be rented here.

Within Kitanomaru's pleasant grounds are a number of buildings. Near Tayasumon is the **Nippon Budokan** *(see p353)*. Built for the 1964 Olympics martial arts competition, it is now used mostly for rock concerts. A short walk farther on is the **Science and Technology Museum**. Some of the interactive exhibits are fun, including some virtual bike rides and electricity demonstrations, though all explanations are in Japanese.

Five minutes beyond, over a main road and left down the hill, is the **National Museum of Modern Art**. The permanent collection comprises Japanese works from the 1868 Meiji Restoration to the present day; visiting exhibits are often excellent. Nearby is the National Museum of Modern Art's **Crafts Gallery**. Inside this 1910 Neo-Gothic brick building is an exquisite collection of modern workings of traditional Japanese crafts including pottery, lacquerware, and damascene (etched metal artifacts). Some pieces are for sale.

Yasukuni Shrine ⓭

靖国神社

Map 2 F1. *(03) 3261-8326.* **S** *Kudanshita stn, Hanzomon, Tozai & Toei Shinjuku lines.* *24 hours daily.* **Yushukan** *9am–5pm daily.*

The 2.5 million Japanese, soldiers and civilians, who have died in war since the Meiji Restoration are enshrined at Yasukuni Jinja (Shrine of Peace for the Nation), which was dedicated in 1879. Its history makes it a sobering, sometimes disturbing place to visit.

Until the end of World War II Shinto was the official state religion, and the ashes of all who died in war were brought here regardless of the families' wishes. Unsettling for some of Japan's neighbors, the planners and leaders of World War II and the colonization of China and Korea are also enshrined here, including the wartime prime minister, Tojo Hideki, and eight other Class-A war criminals. Visits by cabinet ministers, even though they are said to be in a private capacity, are still controversial.

Beside the shrine is the **Yushukan**, a museum dedicated to the war dead. Many exhibits put a human face on Japan at war: under a photo of a smiling young officer is a copy of his last letter home, and there are mementos of a nurse who died from overwork. Still, romanticized paintings of Japanese soldiers in Manchuria and displays of guns, planes, and even a locomotive from the Thai-Burma Railway may be troubling to some.

Jinbocho Booksellers' District ⓮

神保町古本屋街

Map 3 B4–5. **S** *Jinbocho stn, Toei Mita, Hanzomon & Toei Shinjuku lines.*

Three of Japan's great universities, Meiji, Chuo, and Nihon, started out in this area in the 1870s and 1880s, and soon booksellers sprang up selling both new and used books. At one time 50 percent of Japan's publishers were based here. Although only Meiji University is still here, dozens of bookshops, several selling *ukiyo-e* prints, remain, all clustered around the junction of Yasukuni-dori and Hakusan-dori. For English books on Oriental subjects try **Kitazawa Books** or **Issei-do**; for *ukiyo-e* prints, visit **Oya Shobo** – all are on the south side of Yasukuni-dori, walking away from Hakusan-dori.

Browsing in one of Jinbocho's bookshops

The change in the economic status (and priorities) of students is evident here. Shops selling surf- or snowboards are everywhere. Music shops selling electric guitars seem as numerous as the bookshops.

Tsutenkyo bridge in Koshikawa Korakuen Garden

Koishikawa Korakuen Garden ⓯

小石川後楽園

Map 3 A3–4. *(03) 3811-3015.* *Korakuen stn, Marunouchi & Namboku lines.* *9am–5pm daily.*

KORAKUEN, meaning "garden of pleasure last," is one of Tokyo's best traditional stroll gardens, a delightful place to spend a few restful hours. The name Korakuen comes from the Chinese poem *Yueyang Castle* by Fan Zhongyan: "Be the first to take the world's trouble to heart, be the last to enjoy the world's pleasure."

Construction of the garden started in 1629 and finished 30 years later. Once four times its present size of almost 8 hectares (20 acres), it belonged to the Mito branch of the Tokugawa family. An exiled Chinese Scholar, Zhu Shun Shui, helped design the garden including the **Engetsukyo** (full-moon) **bridge**, a stone arch with a reflection resembling a full moon. **Tsukenkyo bridge**, a copy of a bridge in Kyoto, is striking for the contrast between the vermilion of the bridge with the surrounding deep green forest.

The garden represents larger landscapes in miniature. Rozan, a famous Chinese sightseeing mountain, and Japan's Kiso River are two famous geographic features recreated here. In the middle of the large pond is **Horai island**, a beautiful composition of stone and pine trees.

Kanda Myojin Shrine ⓰

神田明神

Map 3 C4. *(03) 3254-0753.* *Ochanomizu stn, Marunouchi line.* *Ochanomizu stn, Chuo & Sobu lines.* *24 hours daily.* **Museum** *10am–4pm Tue, Thu, Sat & Sun.* *Kanda Matsuri (mid-May alternate years; next in 2001).*

MYOJIN IS MORE than 1,200 years old, although the present structure is a reproduction built after the 1923 earthquake. The gate's guardian figures are two beautifully dressed, tight-lipped archers: Udaijin on the right and Sadaijin on the left. Just inside the compound on the left is a large stone statue of Daikoku, one of the *shichi-fuku-jin* (seven lucky gods). Here, as always, he is sitting on top of two huge rice bales.

Lions on the gate to Kanda Myojin Shrine

The vermilion shrine itself and its beautiful interior, all lacquer and gold and ornate Chinese-style decoration, are very impressive. Early morning is the best time to glimpse the Shinto priests performing rituals. The Kanda Matsuri *(see pp38–9)* is one of the greatest and grandest of Tokyo's festivals – come early and be prepared for crowds.

Behind the main shrine is a **museum** containing relics from the long history of Myojin. There are also several small shrines, hemmed in by the surrounding office blocks.

Akihabara Electronics District ⓱

秋葉原電気店街

Map 3 C4. *Akihabara stn, Hibiya line.* *Akihabara stn, Yamanote, Chuo & Sobu lines.*

AKIHABARA electronics district surrounds Akihabara station. Directly under the station is a bazaar of tiny shops along narrow aisles selling any electronic device, simple or complex, from Christmas-tree lights to the latest chip. The market grew out of the ruins of World War II when the Japanese army had surplus equipment they wanted to dispose of. Students from the nearby universities, who desperately needed money, bought the surplus army parts and made radios – status symbols and much in demand – to sell on roadsides or in tiny shops here. Akihabara and electronics have been synonymous ever since. Later as the economy improved, the focus changed to televisions, washing machines, and refrigerators. You can still see these, dozens at a time, on display, but increasingly the emphasis is on computers, cell phones, and video games.

Brand-name goods are available at a three to ten percent discount – sometimes more. On Chuo-dori, **Laox** *(see p103)* is a famous source of tax-free goods for tourists.

Colorful shop fronts and advertisements in Akihabara district

Bustling electronics shops and stalls under the tracks at Akihabara ▷

103-379
パソコン
モバイル
nasonic
Let's note
ルで差がつく

JR
RADIO
テレビ
激安
ビデオ
2階
激安
パソコン
激安
ビデオ・テレビ
激安
エアコン
激
テレビ
激安
ビデオ
テレビ
加盟店で
安心な
お買い物

NORTHERN TOKYO

THE NORTHERN DISTRICTS of Ueno and Asakusa contain what remains of Tokyo's old Shitamachi (low city). Once the heart and soul of Edo culture *(see p53)*, Shitamachi became the subject of countless *ukiyo-e* woodblock prints *(see p81)*. Merchants and artisans thrived here, as did Kabuki theater *(see p33)* and the Yoshiwara pleasure district near Asakusa. The last great battle in Japan took place in Ueno in 1868 when the Emperor Meiji's forces defeated the Tokugawa shogunate. Ueno and Asakusa are the best parts of Tokyo for just strolling and observing. Life in Asakusa still revolves around the bustling Senso-ji Temple, its main approach packed with shops. Ueno is dominated by its huge park containing the National and Shitamachi Museums, among others. It is still possible to find pockets of narrow streets lined with tightly packed homes, especially in the Yanaka area, which escaped destruction by war and earthquake. Shopping is a pleasure in Northern Tokyo: as well as the traditional arts and crafts shops near Senso-ji Temple, there are specialists in plastic food in Kappabashi-dori, religious goods in neighboring Inaricho, and electronic items at Ameyoko Market.

In festival costume at Senso-ji Temple

SIGHTS AT A GLANCE

Temples

Senso-ji Temple pp82–3 7

Parks and Gardens

Ueno Park pp74–5 1

Notable Districts

Inaricho District and Kappabashi-dori 6

Yanaka District 4

Museums

Shitamachi Museum 3

Tokyo National Museum pp76–9 2

Markets

Ameyoko Market 5

KEY

S Subway station

Train station

Tourist information

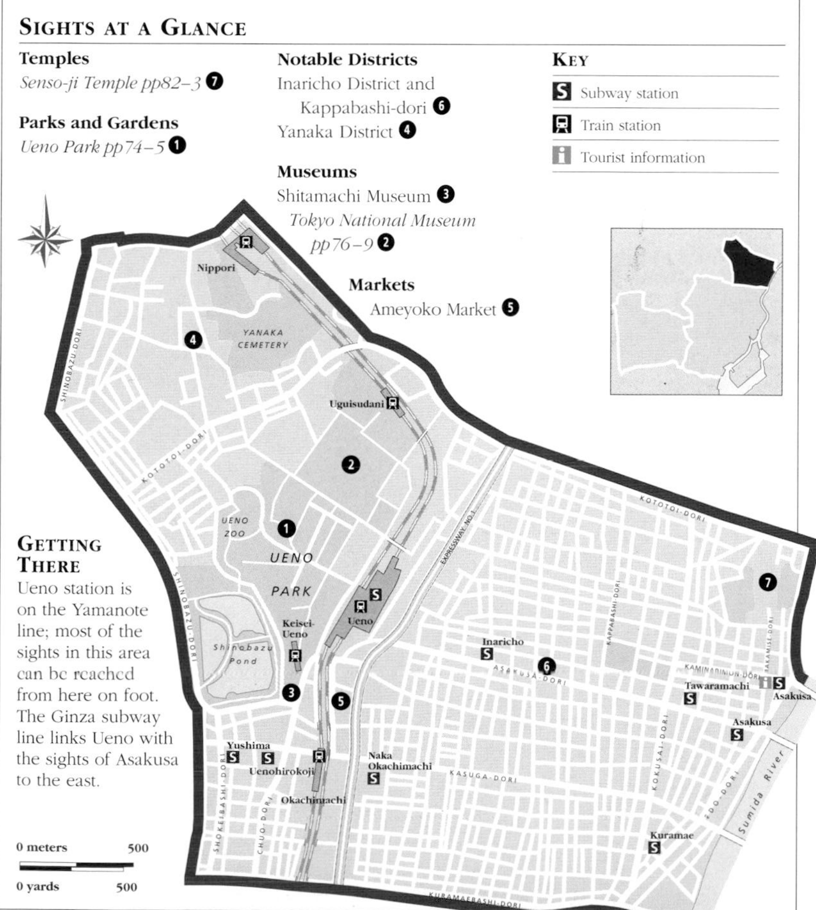

GETTING THERE

Ueno station is on the Yamanote line; most of the sights in this area can be reached from here on foot. The Ginza subway line links Ueno with the sights of Asakusa to the east.

◁ **Detail of a kimono from a Noh play in the Tokyo National Museum**

Ueno Park ❶

上野公園

IEYASU, the first Tokugawa shogun, built the Kanei-ji temple and subtemples here in the 17th century to negate evil spirits that might threaten from the northeast. Judging by how long the Tokugawas lasted, it was a wise move. In 1873, five years after the Battle of Ueno, when the last supporters of the shogun were crushed by Imperial forces, the government designated Ueno a public park. A favorite since its earliest days, the park has figured in many popular woodblock prints and short stories. The Shinobazu pond (actually three ponds) is an annual stop for thousands of migrating birds. Several museums and temples are dotted around the park, and Japan's oldest and best zoo is here.

Boating on the Shinobazu pond

The Tokyo Metropolitan Art Museum, in a modern red-brick building, has a large collection of contemporary Japanese art, plus special exhibitions.

★ Pagoda

This landmark five-story pagoda dates from the 17th century and is a survivor from the original Kanei-ji temple complex. Today it stands in the grounds of Ueno Zoo, a popular destination for Japanese schoolchildren, among others, due to its giant pandas.

★ Tosho-gu Shrine

This ornate complex of halls is one of Tokyo's few remaining Edo-era structures. Ieyasu was enshrined here and later reburied at Nikko (see pp258–65).

The Great Buddhist Pagoda was built in 1967. A Buddha statue formerly stood on the site; only its head remains.

The Gojo shrine is reached through a series of red *torii* (gates). Inside, red-bibbed Inari fox statues stand in an atmospheric grotto.

Shitamachi Museum *(see p80)*

KEY

Tourist information

STAR SIGHTS

- **★ Tokyo National Museum**
- **★ Tosho-gu Shrine**
- **★ Pagoda**

★ **Tokyo National Museum** *(see pp76–9)*

(see pp76–9)

National Science Museum
A steam engine and life-sized blue whale model mark this museum's entrance. Inside are exhibits on natural history, science, and technology.

National Museum of Western Art
Rodin's massive Gate of Hell *stands outside this building by Le Corbusier. On display are various Impressionist works, plus paintings by Rubens, Pollock, and others.*

The main walkway is lined with hundreds of cherry trees. Boisterous *hanami* (blossom-viewing) parties are held here each spring.

The Tomb of the Shogi Tai is a small, leafy area containing two tombstones to the many samurai who died in the 1868 Battle of Ueno.

Saigo Takamori Statue
The leader of the victorious Meiji forces, Saigo subsequently instigated the Satsuma rebellion against the emperor in 1877, but killed himself when it failed. He was posthumously pardoned, and this statue was erected in 1899.

Kiyo-mizu Hall
Part of the original Kanei-ji temple, this dates from 1631 and is dedicated to Senju (1,000-armed) Kannon. Kosodate Kannon, the bosatsu *of conception, is also here, surrounded by numerous offerings of dolls.*

Visitors' Checklist

Map 3 C2–3, 4 D2. *Ueno stn, Hibiya & Ginza lines. Ueno & Uguisudani stns, many lines. (03) 5685-1181.* **Ueno Zoo** *9:30am–4pm Tue–Sun.* **Tokyo Metropolitan Art Museum & National Science Museum** *9am–4:30pm Tue–Sun.* **National Museum of Western Art** *9:30am–4:30pm Tue–Sun.*

Tokyo National Museum ❷

東京国立博物館

The group of buildings that makes up the Tokyo National Museum is in a compound in the north-east corner of Ueno Park; tickets to all buildings are available at the entrance gate. The Honkan is the main building. To its east is the Toyokan (see p78). The 1908 Beaux-Arts Hyokeikan currently stands empty. Behind it is the Gallery of Horyu-ji Treasures, containing stunning objects from Nara's Horyu-ji temple, and the Heiseikan (see p79). More than 89,000 items make up the total collection – the best assembly of Japanese art in the world. Displays are changed regularly, about every two or three months.

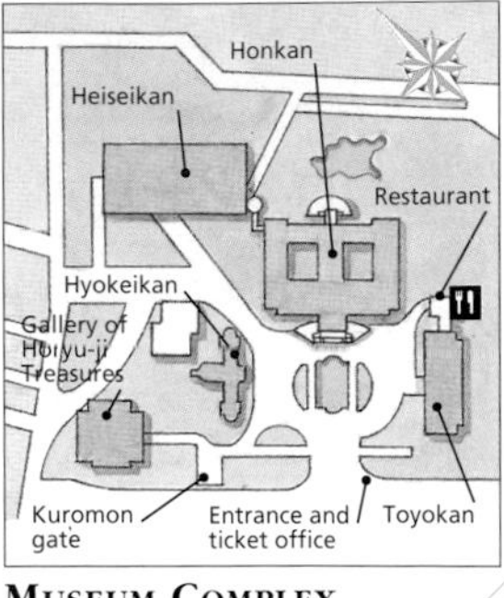

Museum Complex Locator Map

★ Sculpture
This serene, wooden 12th-century sculpture of the Juichimen Kannon Bosatsu (11-faced goddess of mercy) is about 3 m (10 ft) high. Mainly Buddhist, the pieces in the sculpture collection range from miniature to monumental.

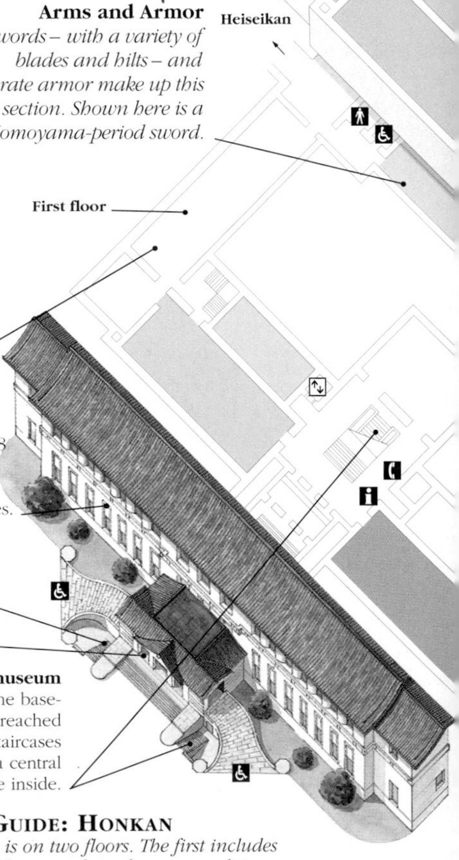

Arms and Armor
Swords – with a variety of blades and hilts – and elaborate armor make up this section. Shown here is a Momoyama-period sword.

Heiseikan

First floor

This building dates from 1938 and combines Japanese and Western features.

Steps down to museum shop

Entrance

The museum shop in the basement can be reached via twin staircases outside and a central one inside.

Key to Floor Plan

- Metalwork
- Ainu and Ryukyu materials
- Ceramics
- Textiles
- Arms and armor
- Sculpture
- Calligraphy
- Paintings and prints
- Lacquerware
- Temporary exhibitions
- Non-exhibition space

Star Collections

- ★ **Textiles**
- ★ **Lacquerware**
- ★ **Sculpture**

Gallery Guide: Honkan
The collection is on two floors. The first includes ceramics, textiles, swords and armor, sculpture, masks, and metalwork; on the second are paintings, screens, woodblock prints, lacquerware, calligraphy, and modern Western-style and Japanese paintings. A guide brochure to the whole complex is available at the counter inside the entrance.

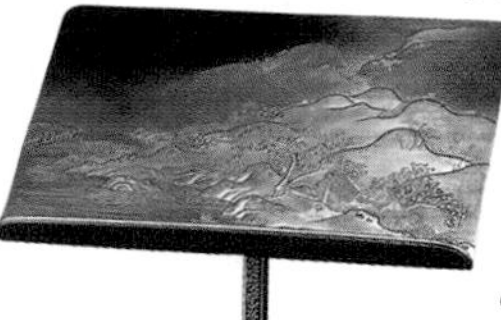

★ Lacquerware

This 18th-century reading stand in the lacquerware collection has a maki-e *design of cherry trees. The* maki *technique requires painting the design then sprinkling gold or silver dust onto the wet lacquer.*

VISITORS' CHECKLIST

Map 3 C2, 4 D2. *(03) 3822-1111.* *Ueno stn, Hibiya & Ginza lines.* *Ueno stn, many lines; Uguisudani stn, Yamanote line.* *9:30am–5pm Tue–Sun (Apr 1–Sep 30: 8pm Fri).*

Paintings and Prints

This collection includes scrolls, woodblock prints, and screens. This 16th-century gold screen is illustrated with a procession of noblemen, a scene from the Tale of Genji *(see p48).*

Second floor

★ Textiles

One of the exquisite kimonos that forms part of the textile collection, this dates from the 16th century when it was used in a Noh play (see p32). *It depicts lilies and court vehicles.*

GALLERY OF HORYU-JI TREASURES

When the estates of the Horyu-ji temple *(see p190)* in Nara were seized as part of the Meiji reforms, the impoverished temple gave a number of its treasures to the imperial family in exchange for money to finance its repairs. Over 300 of those priceless treasures are housed in this modern gallery, including rare and early Buddhist statues, masks used for Gigaku dances, and beautifully painted screens.

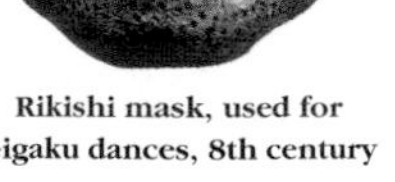

Rikishi mask, used for Gigaku dances, 8th century

7th-century gilt-bronze Kannon statue

Ceramics

One of the highlights of the museum's ceramics collection is this 17th-century tea-leaf jar which depicts a craggy plum tree, its branches covered in blossom, rising up amid swirling gold clouds.

Tokyo National Museum: Toyokan

Opened in 1968, the Toyokan has an excellent and eclectic collection of non-Japanese Eastern art, including textiles, sculpture, and ceramics. Many of the exhibits are from China and Korea – a result of their long ties with Japan. The slightly confusing layout of the three floors is in a rough spiral; a well-marked route takes visitors from the sculpture on the first floor up to the Korean collection at the top.

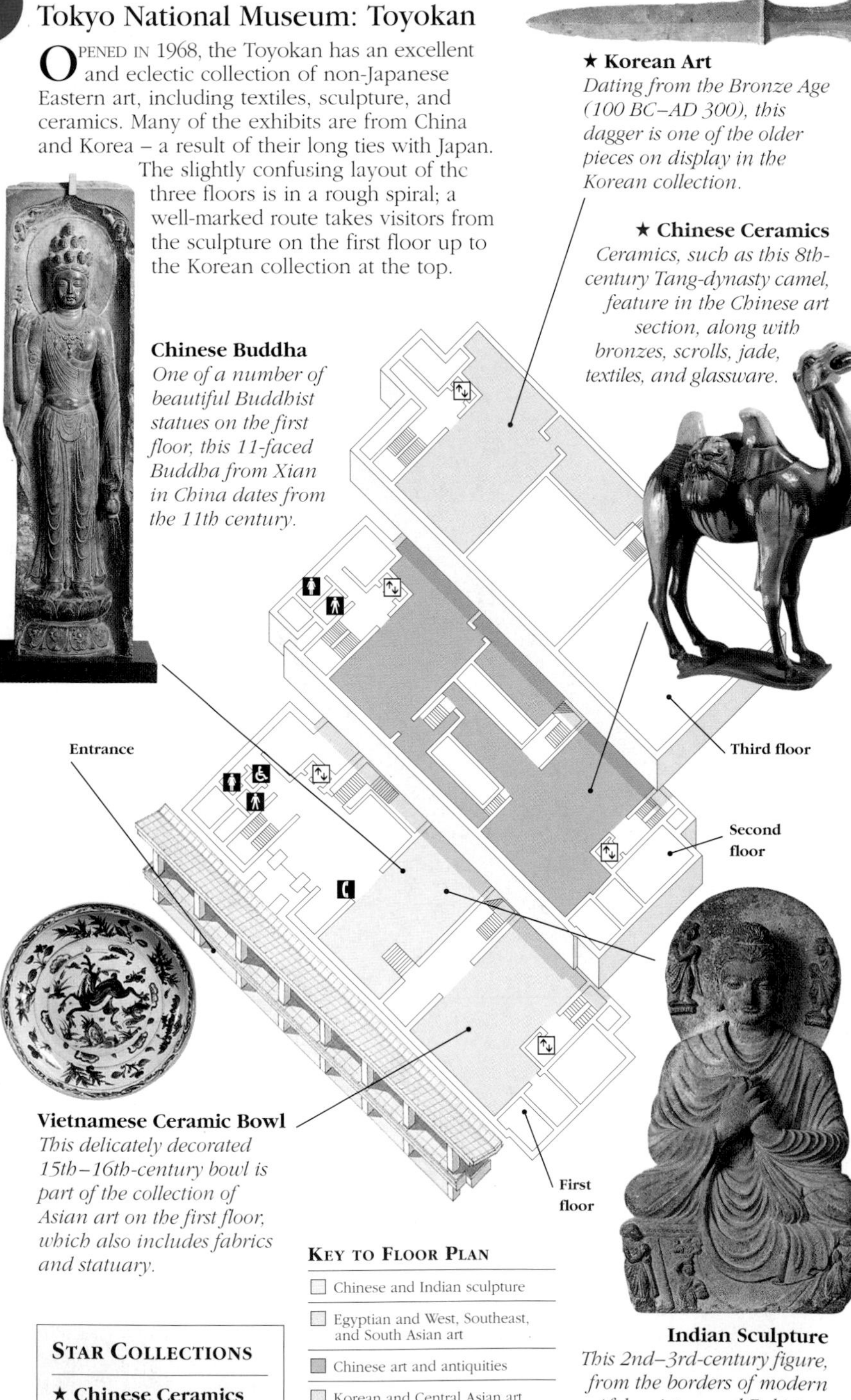

★ Korean Art
Dating from the Bronze Age (100 BC–AD 300), this dagger is one of the older pieces on display in the Korean collection.

★ Chinese Ceramics
Ceramics, such as this 8th-century Tang-dynasty camel, feature in the Chinese art section, along with bronzes, scrolls, jade, textiles, and glassware.

Chinese Buddha
One of a number of beautiful Buddhist statues on the first floor, this 11-faced Buddha from Xian in China dates from the 11th century.

Vietnamese Ceramic Bowl
This delicately decorated 15th–16th-century bowl is part of the collection of Asian art on the first floor, which also includes fabrics and statuary.

Indian Sculpture
This 2nd–3rd-century figure, from the borders of modern Afghanistan and Pakistan, is grouped with the Indian sculptures on the first floor.

Key to Floor Plan

- Chinese and Indian sculpture
- Egyptian and West, Southeast, and South Asian art
- Chinese art and antiquities
- Korean and Central Asian art and antiquities
- Non-exhibition space

Star Collections

- ★ Chinese Ceramics
- ★ Korean Art

Tokyo National Museum: Heiseikan

THE HEISEIKAN opened in 1999 and was purpose-built to house major temporary exhibitions and a superb collection of Japanese archaeological artifacts. Its modern facilities do full justice to the fascinating displays. The first floor houses the Japanese archaeology gallery, with items from 10,000–7,000 BC onward. The temporary exhibitions on the second floor are of mainly – but not only – Japanese art. Captions are in English and Japanese.

Key to Floor Plan

- Archaeological exhibits
- Temporary exhibitions
- Non-exhibition space

★ Haniwa Horse
Haniwa literally means "clay ring", and is used to describe earthenware sculptures that were made for 4th–7th-century tombs and were thought to protect the dead. Many forms have been found, including horses and other animals.

★ Haniwa Male Figure
This haniwa *is dressed as a warrior. Other human figures that have survived include singers, dancers, and farmers.*

First floor

Second floor

Entrance

Honkan

Star Collections

- ★ Haniwa Sculptures
- ★ Jomon Figures

Fukabochitadoki Bowl
This large cooking pot is a fine example of Jomon pottery, which is among the oldest in the world. The curved, deep sides allowed the fire to be built up around it, while the flattened base ensured it could be balanced when in the hearth.

★ Jomon Figures
The prehistoric Jomon period (14,500–300BC) is thought to have produced Japan's first pottery, known as dogu. *This figurine is one of several female figures characterized by bulging eyes.*

Shitamachi Museum ❸

下町民俗資料館

2-1 Ueno-koen, Taito-ku. **Map** 3 C3. *(03) 3823-7451.* *Ueno stn, Hibiya & Ginza lines.* *Keisei-Ueno stn, Keisei line; Ueno stn, many lines.* *9:30am–4pm Tue–Sun.*

DEDICATED to preserving the spirit and artifacts of Shitamachi *(see p73)*, this museum is both fascinating and fun. On the first floor are re-creations of Edo-era shops such as a candy store and a coppersmith's. Second-floor exhibits include traditional toys (which can be handled), tools, and photographs. All the exhibits, amounting to over 50,000 items, were donated by Shitamachi residents.

Meiji-period doll, Shitamachi Museum

Yanaka District ❹

谷中地区

Map 3 C1. *Nippori stn, many lines.* **Asakura Museum** *(03) 3821-4549.* *9:30am–4:15pm Tue–Thu, Sat–Sun. (Last adm 30 mins before closing.)* **Daimyo Clock Museum** *(03) 3821-6913.* *Jan 15–Jun 30, Oct 1–Dec 24: 10am–4pm Tue–Sun.*

THIS QUIET AREA is rewarding to wander through because it survived the 1923 earthquake and bombing of World War II. It preserves something of the feel of old Shitamachi with tightly packed houses in narrow alleys, and traditional food stalls selling rice crackers and old-fashioned candy. The large **Yanaka cemetery** is a must-see in cherry-blossom season. Inside is **Tenno-ji**, a temple with a large bronze Buddha dating from 1690. Nearby are tea shops and florists. To the west of Tenno-ji is the **Asakura Museum**, home of sculptor Asakura Fumio (1883–1964). On the second floor is a delightful room full of his small statues of one of his favorite subjects – cats – but the garden is the real highlight with a traditional composition of water and stone.

Sansaki-dori, the area's main street, has some traditional shops, and the temple of **Kanchan-in** here holds an archery school on Saturdays. The understated **Daimyo Clock Museum** has 100 Edo-era clocks lovingly presented.

Some of the surviving old houses in Yanaka district

Ameyoko Market ❺

アメ横

Map 3 C3. *Ueno stn, Hibiya & Ginza lines.* *Okachimachi stn, Yamanote line; Ueno stn, many lines.*

ONE OF THE GREAT bazaars in Asia, Ameyoko is a place where anything is available, almost always at a discount. In Edo times this was the place to come and buy *ame* (candy). After World War II black-market goods, such as liquor, cigarettes, chocolates, and nylons from the American military store, started appearing here, and *ame* acquired its second meaning as an abbreviation for American (*yoko* means alley). An area of tiny shops packed under the elevated train tracks, Ameyoko is no longer a black market but is still is the place for bargain foreign brands, including Chanel, Nike, and Rolex. Clothes and accessories are concentrated under the tracks, while foods, including a huge range of fish, line the street that follows the tracks.

Shopping for a bargain at Ameyoko Market

Inaricho District and Kappabashi-dori ❻

稲荷町地区とかっぱ橋通り

Map 4 D3, 4 E2–3. *Inaricho & Tawaramachi stns, Ginza line.*

INARICHO is the Tokyo headquarters for wholesale religious goods. Small wooden boxes to hold Buddhas and family photos, paper lanterns, bouquets of brass flowers *(jouka)*, Shinto household shrines, and even prayer beads can be found here. Most of the shops lie on the south side of Asakusa-dori, in the stretch between between Inaricho and Tawaramachi stations.

Kappabashi-dori, named after the mythical water imps *(kappa)* who supposedly helped built a bridge *(bashi)* here, is Tokyo's center for kitchenware and the source of the plastic food displayed in almost every restaurant window. Although the "food" is for sale, prices are much higher than for the real thing.

The Floating World of Ukiyo-e

In the Edo period, woodblock prints, called *ukiyo-e*, or pictures of the pleasure-seeking "floating world," became the most popular pictorial art of Japan. They had a profound influence on artists such as Matisse and Van Gogh. Although today they are credited to individual artists, they were in fact a cooperative effort between the publisher, responsible for financing and distributing the work; the artist, who produced a fine line drawing; the carver, who pasted the drawings onto blocks of wood and carved away what was not to appear on the print, making one block for each color; and the printer, who inked the wooden blocks and pressed them onto the paper – one for each color, starting with the lightest. Editions were limited to 100–200 copies. The first artist known by name was Moronobu, who died in 1694. The golden age of *ukiyo-e* lasted from about 1790 to the 1850s. Beautiful women, Kabuki actors, scenes from Japan, including Shitamachi, and the supernatural were recurring themes.

Two Kabuki actors by Sharaku

A full-color *calendar of beautiful women published by Suzuki Harunobu in 1765 marked a transition from the earlier black-and-white techniques. Highly popular (and a moneymaker), the calendar's success attracted both financiers and artists to the medium.*

After *Harunobu's calendar, depictions of women were individualized and eroticized by artists such as Kitagawa Utamaro and Torii Kiyonaga. This print is by Utamaro.*

Landscape *prints were dominated by Hokusai (1760–1849) and his younger rival Hiroshige (1797–1858). This print is from the latter's* Fifty-Three Stations of the Tokaido.

Ghosts and goblins *were a favorite theme, especially in summer (to be scared was thought to be cooling). Utagawa Kuniyoshi (whose print is shown here), Taiso Yoshitoshi, and Kobayashi Kiyochika were masters of the genre, which marked the end of* ukiyo-e *'s golden age.*

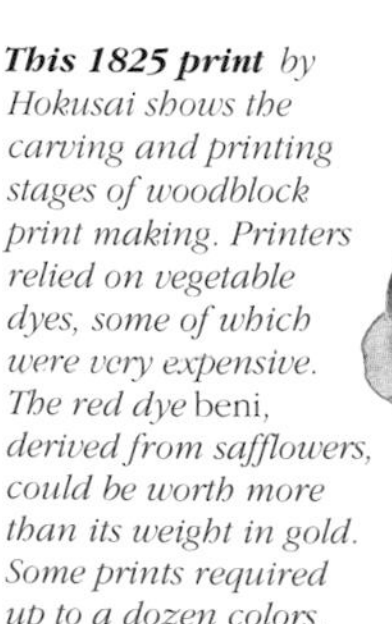

This 1825 print *by Hokusai shows the carving and printing stages of woodblock print making. Printers relied on vegetable dyes, some of which were very expensive. The red dye* beni, *derived from safflowers, could be worth more than its weight in gold. Some prints required up to a dozen colors.*

Senso-ji Temple 7

浅草寺

Stroking the Nadi Botokesan Buddha

Popularly known as Asakusa Kannon, this is Tokyo's most sacred and spectacular temple. In AD 628, two fishermen fished a small gold statue of Kannon, the Buddhist goddess of mercy, from the Sumida River. Their master built a shrine to Kannon, then in 645, the holy man Shokai built a temple to her. Its fame, wealth, and size grew until Tokugawa Ieyasu bestowed upon it a large stipend of land. The Yoshiwara pleasure quarter moved nearby in 1657 only increasing its popularity. The temple survived the 1923 earthquake but not World War II bombing. Its main buildings are therefore relatively new, but follow the Edo-era layout. While these buildings are impressive, it is the people following their daily rituals that make this place so special.

Awashima Hall is dedicated to a deity who looks after women.

Five-Story Pagoda
This replica of the original was constructed in 1973.

The garden of Dembo-in (abbot's residence) is a tranquil stroll garden designed by Kobori Enshu in the early 1600s. It is a masterly arrangement of woods, bamboo groves, lawns, and water.

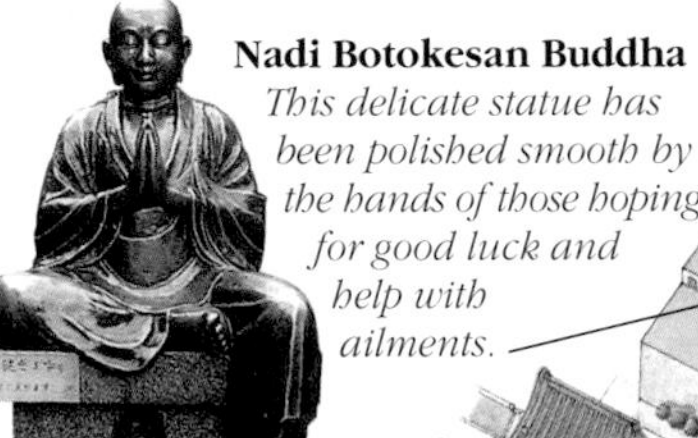

Nadi Botokesan Buddha
This delicate statue has been polished smooth by the hands of those hoping for good luck and help with ailments.

Entrance to Dembo-in garden

★ Nakamise-dori
This street is a treasure trove of traditional wares, including specialists in obi *sashes, haircombs, fans, dolls, and kimonos.*

For more details about individual shops here, see pages 100–102

Kaminarimon Gate
"Thunder Gate" burned down in 1865 and was not rebuilt until 1960. The guardian statues of Fujin (right) and Raijin (left) have old heads and new bodies.

To Asakusa stations and tourist information office

This hexagonal temple is a rare survivor from the 15th or 16th century.

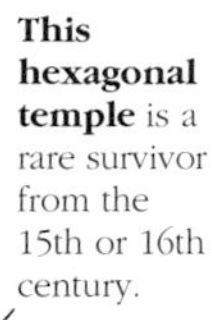

★ Main Hall
Inside the hall (1958) the gold-plated main shrine houses the original Kannon image. Worshipers come to pay their respects by throwing coins and lighting candles.

Yagodo Hall houses eight fairly recent Buddha statues.

Visitors' Checklist

Map 4 E2, 4 F2–3. *(03) 3842-0181.* *Asakusa stn, Ginza & Toei-Asakusa lines.* *Tobu-Asakusa stn, Tobu-Isesaki line.* **Temple** *6am–5pm daily (Oct–Mar: from 6:30am).* **Dembo-in garden** *9am–3pm Mon–Sat (by permission only).* **Nakamise-dori** *9.30am–7pm daily.* *Sanja Matsuri (3rd Fri–Sun in May), Hagoita-Ichi (Battledore Fair, Dec 17–19).*

Asakusa Jinja, built in 1649, is a shrine dedicated to the men who found the Kannon statue.

★ Main Hall
Several large paintings hang inside the main hall. The painting of angels with lotus flowers is a 20th-century work by Domoto Insho.

Niten-mon Gate was built in 1618 and is the oldest structure on the site.

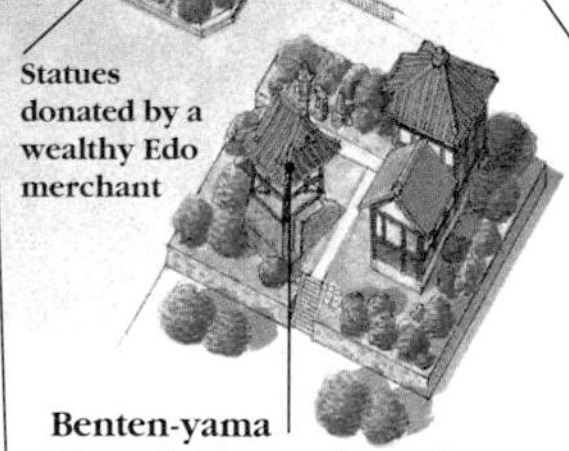

Statues donated by a wealthy Edo merchant

Benten-yama Shoro belfry stands amid a group of temple buildings. The bell used to ring on the hour in Edo.

Incense Burner
One of the temple's focal points, this incense burner (joukoro) is constantly surrounded by people wafting the smoke over them to keep them healthy.

Hozo-mon Gate
Built in 1964 of reinforced concrete, this two-story gate has a treasure house upstairs holding a number of 14th-century Chinese sutras.

Star Sights

★ **Nakamise-dori**

★ **Main Hall**

WESTERN TOKYO

SHINJUKU AND SHIBUYA, the dual centers of Western Tokyo, three stops apart on the Yamanote line, started to boom only after the 1923 earthquake. This part of the city is new Tokyo – all vitality and energy, fast-paced, constantly changing, and challenging the more traditional pleasures of Central and Northern Tokyo. Modern architectural landmarks are dotted around, from the Olympic Stadiums of Yoyogi Park to the magnificent twin-towered home for the city government in West Shinjuku. Shibuya, along with neighboring Harajuku and Minami-Aoyama, is the epicenter of both young and haute-couture Japanese fashon. Nightlife is also in plentiful supply with Roppongi's cosmopolitan clubs, bars, and music venues, and the neon lights and *pachinko* parlors of East Shinjuku. In these overwhelmingly modern surroundings, historical sights are few and far between but include the popular Meiji Shrine and the nearby Sword Museum.

All dressed up in Harajuku

SIGHTS AT A GLANCE

Notable Districts

Akasaka District ⓫
East Shinjuku pp86–7 ❶
Harajuku District ❼
Minami-Aoyama District ❾
Roppongi District ❿
Shibuya pp92–3 ❽
West Shinjuku pp88–9 ❷

Shrines

Meiji Shrine ❺

Museums

Sword Museum ❹

Stations

Shinjuku Station ❸

Parks

Yoyogi Park ❻

GETTING THERE

Shinjuku, Shibuya, Harajuku, and Yoyogi are all on the Yamanote line. The Ginza and Hanzomon subway lines stop in or near Harajuku, Minami-Aoyama, and Akasaka, and the Hibiya line serves Roppongi.

KEY

- Street-by-Street map *pp86–7*
- Street-by-Street map *p88*
- Street-by-Street map *pp92–3*
- Subway station
- Train station
- Long-distance bus station

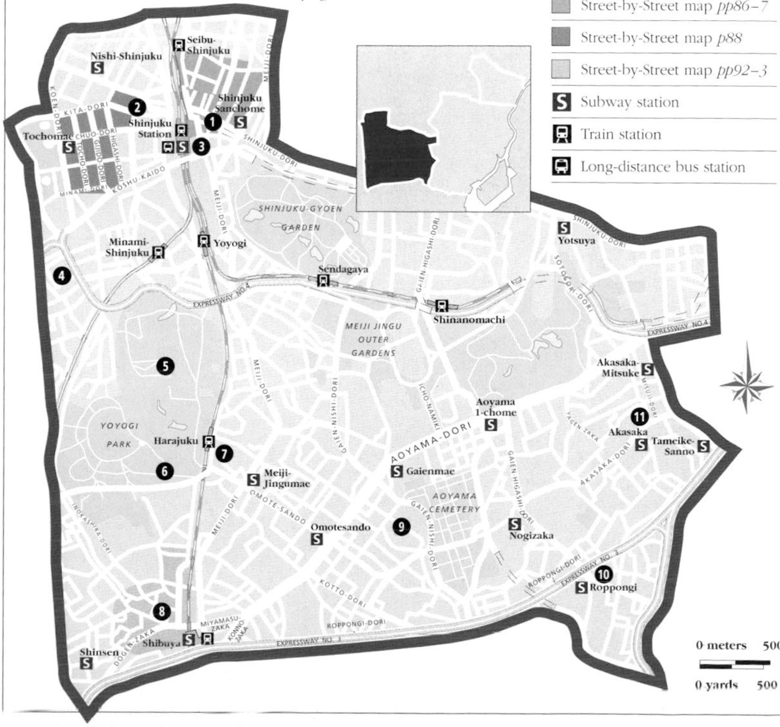

0 meters 500
0 yards 500

◁ **Tange Kenzo's landmark Tokyo Metropolitan Government Offices in West Shinjuku**

Street-by-Street: East Shinjuku ❶

東新宿

Façade of the Excelsior café

EAST SHINJUKU is where Tokyo plays. The area has been a nightlife center from Edo times on, when it was the first night stop on the old Tokaido road to Kyoto. Since Shinjuku station opened in the 1880s, entertainments have been targeted at commuters (mainly men) en route back to the suburbs. Amusements are focused in the tiny bars of Golden Gai, and in the red-light district of Kabukicho. Daytime attractions include several art galleries, a tranquil shrine, and some of Tokyo's best department stores. A late-afternoon stroll as the neon starts to light up will take in both sides of this fascinating, bustling area.

The Koma Theater specializes in Japanese historical melodramas.

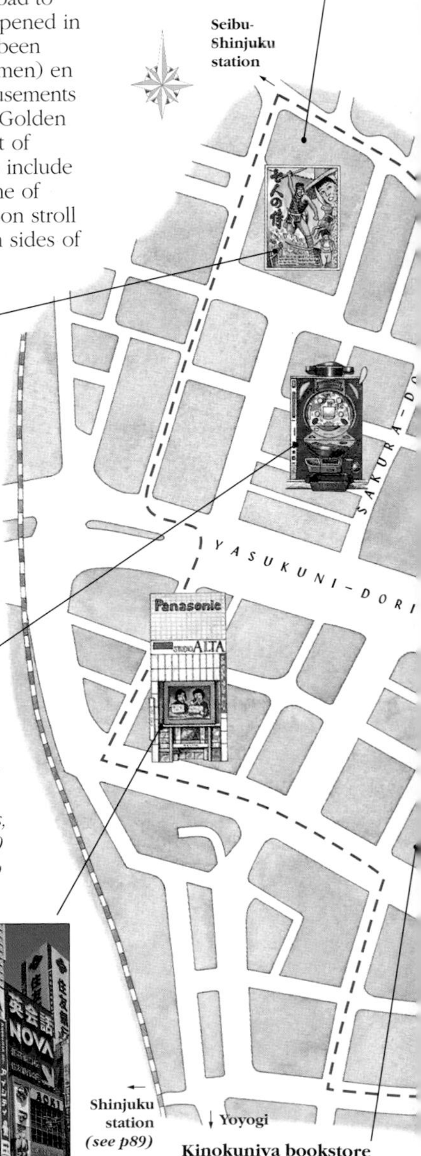

Seibu-Shinjuku station

Movie Houses
This corner of Kabukicho is dominated by cinemas, many showing the latest blockbusters.

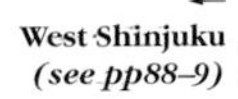
← West Shinjuku *(see pp88–9)*

YASUKUNI-DORI

SAKURA-DORI

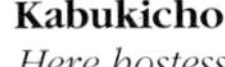

Kabukicho
Here hostess bars and pachinko parlors (see p93) *flourish alongside cafés and restaurants. In this area of contrasts, prices range from ¥500 for a bowl of noodles to ¥10,000 for a drink.*

Studio Alta
Instantly recognizable by its huge TV screen, Studio Alta stands opposite the crossing from Shinjuku station and is a favorite place for meeting up or just hanging out.

← Shinjuku station *(see p89)*

↓ Yoyogi

Kinokuniya bookstore has one of Tokyo's best selections of foreign books.

KEY

- - - Suggested walk route

Train line

Golden Gai
Viewed in the daytime these scruffy alleys look anything but golden. Most of the bars here are just wide enough for a bar, a counter, and a row of stools. Each has a set of regulars – from writers to bikers – but few welcome strangers inside.

LOCATOR MAP
See Tokyo Street Finder Map 1

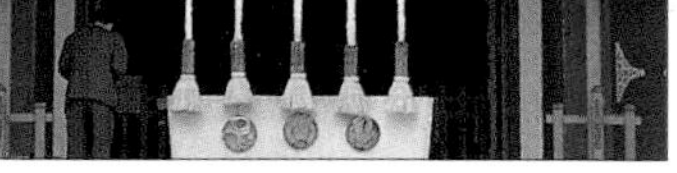

Hanazono Shrine
This Shinto shrine, founded in the mid-17th century, is a calm and surprising oasis among the concrete towers. In the tree-filled compound are a reconstructed traditional vermilion-and-white building and several Inari fox statues.

0 meters 100
0 yards 100

Isetan Department Store
Top Japanese and Western designer boutiques make this stylish store a favorite with Tokyo's affluent young. The food hall in the basement is also worth a visit. Behind the main store, the Isetan Art Museum has interesting special exhibitions.

The Excelsior café is a convenient coffee stop next to a kimono store.

West Shinjuku ❷

西新宿

Most of Tokyo's skyscraper office blocks (and some of its most expensive land) are clustered just to the west of Shinjuku station. About 250,000 people work here each day. Many of the hotels and some office blocks have top-floor restaurants with views of the city. In 1960 the government designated Shinjuku a *fukutoshin* ("secondary heart of the city"); in 1991, when the city government moved into architect Tange Kenzo's massive 48-story Metropolitan Government Offices, many started calling it *shin toshin* (the new capital). Tange's building was dubbed "tax tower" by some outraged at its US$1 billion cost.

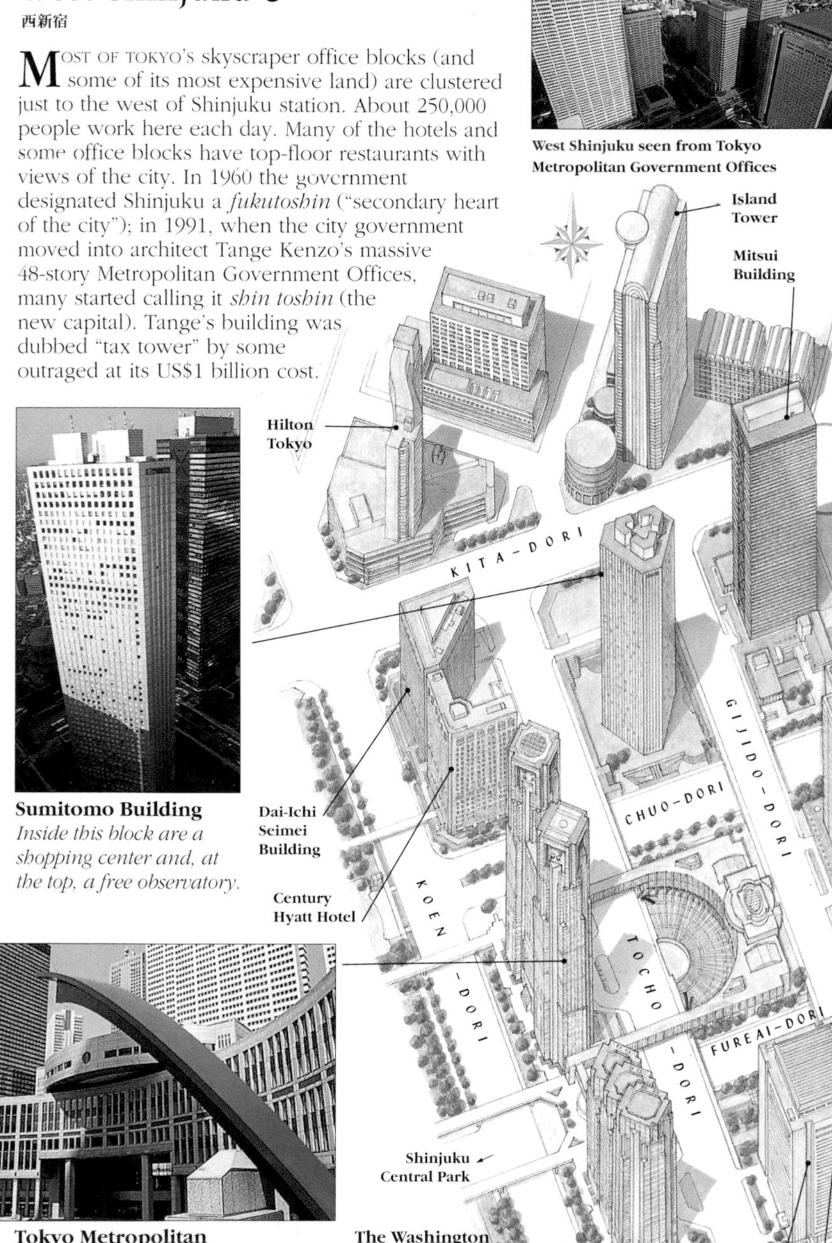

West Shinjuku seen from Tokyo Metropolitan Government Offices

Sumitomo Building
Inside this block are a shopping center and, at the top, a free observatory.

Tokyo Metropolitan Government Offices
This huge complex of two blocks and a semi-circular plaza is unified by the grid-detailing on its façades (see p84), *recalling both traditional architecture and electronic circuitry. An observatory gives views from Mount Fuji to Tokyo Bay on a clear day.*

The Washington Hotel has flowing curves (inside and out) and tiny windows in its white façade.

The NS Building is recognizable by its rainbow-hued elevator shafts. In the 30-story atrium is a 29-m (95-ft) high water-powered clock.

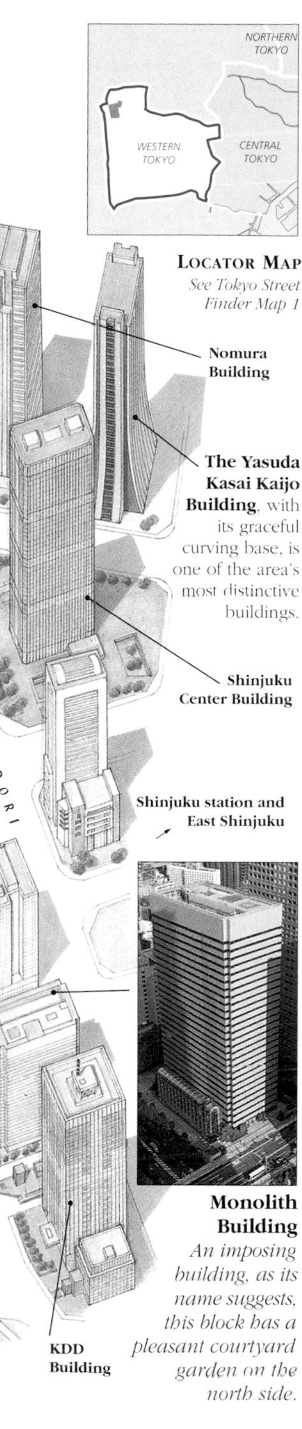

LOCATOR MAP
See Tokyo Street Finder Map 1

The Yasuda Kasai Kaijo Building, with its graceful curving base, is one of the area's most distinctive buildings.

Shinjuku station and East Shinjuku

Monolith Building
An imposing building, as its name suggests, this block has a pleasant courtyard garden on the north side.

KDD Building

Shinjuku Station ❸

新宿駅

Map 1 B1–2.

WITH OVER TWO million people passing through each day, this is the busiest train station in the world. As well as being a major stop on both the JR and metropolitan subway systems, Shinjuku station is also the starting point for trains and buses into the suburbs. On the Yamanote and Chuo line platforms during the morning rush hour (from about 7:30 to 9am) staff are employed to push those last few commuters on to the train, making sure the odd body part isn't slammed in one of the closing doors.

The corridors connecting all the lines and train networks together are edged with hundreds of shops and restaurants. It's easy to lose your way in this maze of seemingly identical passages, and often simpler to find your bearings at ground level. For a time in the 1980s and early 1990s a substantial number of homeless (mostly men) built cardboard villages in the stations corridors. In a controversial move, the municipal government forcibly removed them; they settled in new places, including Ueno Park.

Sword Museum ❹

刀剣博物館

4-25-10 Yoyogi. **Map** 1 A3. *(03) 3379-1386.* *Sangubashi stn, Odakyu line.* *9am–4pm Tue–Sun.*

A LITTLE OUT OF THE WAY, this museum is full of fine Japanese swords dating back to the 12th century. Like many other artifacts in Japan, swords combine art and ritual in the pursuit of perfection.

On the first floor is an interesting display of the process by which a sword is produced. The swords themselves are exhibited on the second floor, every detail carefully refined, even down to the pattern of burnishing on the blade's face. There is also a display of decorated hilts. English explanations trace the history of the sword, and the processes of tempering and sharpening, handling, and maintenance. Old Japanese texts, illustrated with beautiful drawings, explain the finer points of sword-making.

Ornate sword handle

COMMUTER CULTURE

Commuters packed into trains are a common sight morning and evening at Tokyo's major train stations. High urban land prices force families to look farther out of the city for affordable housing. A commute of at least an hour each way is practically the standard. By far the majority of commuters are men, as they are still the prime earners in most families. The commute effectively removes them from family life: they leave before children get up, come back after they are in bed, and collapse on weekends with fatigue. The other major group on the trains is unmarried young women (after marriage women are generally expected to stay home and raise the children). An industry has grown up around these commuters: dozens of magazines are produced for killing time, and stand-up restaurants offer cheap meals to those with a long ride ahead.

Crowding onto a commuter train

One of the many stalls selling good-luck charms at the Meiji Shrine

Meiji Shrine ❺

明治神宮

Map 1 B3. *(03) 3379-5511.* *Harajuku stn, Yamanote line.* **Meiji Treasure House and Annex** *Mar–May & Jul–Oct: 9am–4:30pm daily; Jun: 8am–5pm daily; Nov–Feb: 9am–4pm daily.* *3rd Fri of month.* **Nai-en garden** *daily (times vary).* *Spring Festival (May 3–5), Fall Festival (Nov 1–3).*

THE MOST IMPORTANT Shinto shrine in Tokyo, Meiji Jingu (imperial shrine) dates from 1920. The Emperor Meiji (who reigned 1868–1912) and his wife the Empress Shoken are enshrined here. A focal point for right-wing militarists during Japan's colonial expansion prior to World War II, the shrine was destroyed by Allied aerial bombardment in 1945 but rebuilt with private donations in 1958. During the New Year holidays it is the most heavily visited place in Japan, with over three million people worshiping here and buying good-luck charms for the year ahead.

A wide graveled road under a huge *torii* (gate) and shaded by cedars leads into the shrine grounds. On the right is an abandoned entrance to the JR Harajuku station. Just beyond is the small entrance still used by the emperor when he visits by train for official functions. Next on the right is a complex with a café and restaurant, and the **Meiji Treasure House Annex**. The annex holds changing exhibitions of the the royal couples' artifacts, including clothes, lacquerware, and furniture. Tickets bought here are also valid for the main Treasure House.

A left turn takes you under the massive **Otorii** (gate), built in 1975 of huge logs that came from a 1,500-year-old Japanese cypress on Mount Tandai in Taiwan. A short distance beyond the gate, on the left, is the entrance to the **Nai-en garden**, a favorite of the Meiji imperial couple. It is said that the Emperor Meiji designed it himself for his Empress. Inside there is a teahouse overlooking a pond stocked with water lilies and carp. To the right of the pond, a path leads to the beautiful **Minami-ike Shobuda** (iris garden), at its peak in June, and containing over 150 species.

Past the entrance to Nai-en, the road turns to the right and enters the **main shrine** area, set in the middle of a grove of cedars. Another large wooden *torii* leads to the outer gate (Minami Shinmon) through which is a spacious outer courtyard. A second gate (Gehaiden), straight ahead, separates the public from the inner courtyard and the shrine. The simple shrine buildings are made of unadorned aging wood in deep hues of brown; the roof is copper, now oxidized bright green. Gracefully curving, the roof is in the Shinto style of architecture known as *shimmei*, used for imperial shrines. Around the other three sides of the outer courtyard are booths selling charms and prophecies for the new year. Through a gateway to the right is the **Kaguraden**, a hall built in 1993 for sacred music and dance.

To reach the **Meiji Treasure House**, either return to the Otorii and turn left, following the signs, or walk through the woods to the left of the shrine. Lining the walls of the single high-vaulted room of the Treasure House are portraits of every emperor going back more than 1,000 years. The objects on display change regularly; watch for the gorgeous kimonos worn by the Emperor Meiji and the Empress for court functions.

Minami Shinmon gateway through a wooden *torii*, Meiji Shrine

Yoyogi Park ❻

代々木公園

Map 1 A4, 1 B4. *Harajuku stn, Yamanote line.*

TANGE KENZO's two **Olympic Stadiums**, the landmark structures in Yoyogi Park, were completed in 1964 for the Tokyo Olympics. They are still used for national and international sports competitions. The impressive curves of the shell-like structures are achieved with the use of steel suspension cables.

For almost three decades the park filled with a fantastic array of performers and bands every Sunday.

The main Olympic Stadium in Yoyogi Park

These events were stopped by the authorities in the mid-1990s, supposedly due to worries about the rise in criminal activities and maintaining public order. Sundays are still a good time to visit, though, as at the entrance to the park you can still see members of the *zoku* (tribes) who used to perform here, from punks, rockabillies, and goths to hippies and break-dancers.

Large advertising screens in Harajuku

Harajuku District 7

原宿地区

Map 1 B4, 1 C4. *Meiji-jingumae stn, Chiyoda line.* *Harajuku stn, Yamanote line.* **Ota Memorial Museum of Art** *(03) 3272-8600.* *10:30am–5pm Tue–Sun.*

HARAJUKU STATION was the main station for the 1964 Tokyo Olympic village; that concentration of international culture had a great impact on the area, attracting the young and innovative of Tokyo. Today Harajuku remains a center for fashion from high-end international showcases to bargain boutiques.

Takeshita-dori, a narrow alley between Meiji-dori and Harajuku station, is the place to find what's hot in teen fashion and culture. Sundays bring the biggest crowds. Prices range from cheap to outrageous, as do the fashions. Starting from the Harajuku station end, about 200 m (220 yards) down, a left turn leads up some stairs to the **Togo Shrine**, founded for Admiral Togo, the commander who defeated the Russian fleet at the straits of Tsushima in the 1904–5 war. Known as Nihon-kai Kaisen (the Battle of the Sea of Japan), it was a huge naval victory, the first of an Asian country over a Western one. Admiral Togo remains a hero in Japan, and his shrine has a beautiful garden and pond. An **antiques market** is held in the grounds of the shrine on the first, fourth, and fifth Sundays of the month.

Street performer in Harajuku

Back on Takeshita-dori, a short walk farther on is a right turn that leads about 30 m (33 yards) to a lifesized statue of Elvis Presley. It stands at the entrance to the **Rock and Roll Museum**, which is in fact a store filled with memorabilia for sale. The first floor is devoted to Elvis, the basement to the Rolling Stones and heavy metal.

Running parallel to, and south of, Takeshita-dori is the more sophisticated **Omote-sando**. With its wide, tree-shaded sidewalks and dozens of fashionable boutiques and sidewalk cafés, this is one of the best strolls in Tokyo. Walking from Harajuku station, just before the intersection with Meiji-dori, a small street off to the left leads to the **Ota Memorial Museum of Art**, which houses one of the best collections of *ukiyo-e* prints *(see p81)* in Japan, all labeled in both Japanese and English. A vivid image of a Kabuki actor portraying an *arogoto* (superhero) by Sharaku and a masterful program of a memorial Kabuki performance by Hiroshige are among many familiar works. There is a small restaurant and a shop selling prints and other *ukiyo-e* related souvenirs.

Just to the left down Meiji-dori is **LaForet**, a fashion mecca, with five floors of boutiques. Leading off Omote-sando, just before the pedestrian bridge, a narrow lane to the left is lined with boutiques of up-and-coming designers and gives a good idea of residential life in this upscale area. Over the pedestrian bridge to the right is the landmark **Hanae Mori Building**. Designed by Tange Kenzo in 1974, it resembles a stack of glass blocks. Hanae Mori was the first Japanese designer to open her own salon in Paris. Famous for incorporating butterflies in her designs, her empire takes in everything from haute-couture clothing to place mats. Just before the Hanae Mori Building is the vermilion-and-white **Oriental Bazaar**, a collection of shops full of real and fake antiques and good handicrafts, ideal for souvenir hunting *(see p103)*.

A group of teenagers, Harajuku

Street-by-Street: Shibuya ❽

渋谷

Sign for a *pachinko* parlor

SHIBUYA IS THE *sakariba* (party town) for Tokyo's youth. It has been so since the 1930s, when façades featured rockets streaking across the sky. Today this is the place to see the latest in fashion, food, music, and gadgets. Shibuya really started to grow after the 1964 Tokyo Olympics, and its continuing expansion has been spurred by the affluent youth of the world's second-biggest economy. The area, which lies to the northwest of Shibuya station and south of Yoyogi Park, is a mix of trendy boutiques, fashionable department stores, and record shops, plus a couple of interesting museums, and the Bunkamura cultural center. Adjoining this area is Dogen-zaka, a jumble of sloping streets and alleyways lined with nightclubs, bars, and love hotels *(see p289)*.

Visitors' Checklist

Shibuya stn, Hanzomon & Ginza lines. *Shibuya stn, Yamanote, Tokyu Shin-Tamagawa & Keio Inogashira lines.* **TEPCO Electric Energy Museum** *(03) 3477-1191.* *10am–6pm Thu–Tue.* *Thu if Wed is public hol.* **Tobacco and Salt Museum** *(03) 3476-2041.* *10am–5:30pm Tue–Sun.* *Tue if Mon is public hol.*

Center Gai
The focus for youth entertainment in Tokyo, Center Gai is lined with shops, pachinko *parlors, restaurants, and karaoke bars full of high-school and college-age kids.*

Bunkamura
This cultural center is a popular site for rock and classical concerts, and has movies, an art gallery, and a theater.

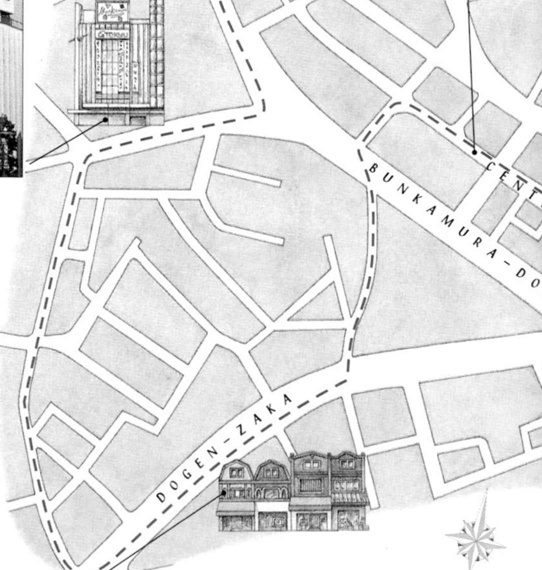

Tokyu Hands is a huge store full of housewares and handicrafts.

Dogen-zaka
Named after a bandit who retired here as a monk, this nighttime destination includes old houses, now art galleries.

Key

- - - Suggested walk route

Train line

This purple clock tower stands in front of the Shibuya Ward Office and is overlooked by Yoyogi Park and the NHK Studios.

The Tobacco and Salt Museum has excellent, well-laid-out exhibits explaining the history of tobacco and salt (both former government monopolies) in Japan.

Locator Map

See Tokyo Street Finder Map 1

Tower Records has a good stock of Japanese and international music CDs at prices among the best in Tokyo.

Yoyogi Park and Olympic stadiums

Harajuku

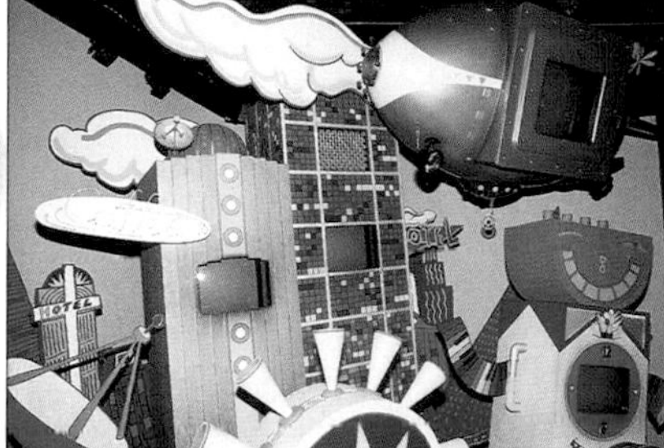

TEPCO Electric Energy Museum

Housed in a modern building with a distinctive dome, this fun museum is packed with interactive exhibits illustrating the uses of electricity.

The Humax Pavilion Building is one of the more fanciful buildings in the area, resembling a cartoon rocket.

Marui (Young) department store is a paradise for clothes – the place for fashionable under 25s.

Statue of Hachiko

Tokyo's favorite meeting place, this statue commemorates the dog who continued to wait for his master at the station every night for more than a decade after his death. The statue dates from 1936.

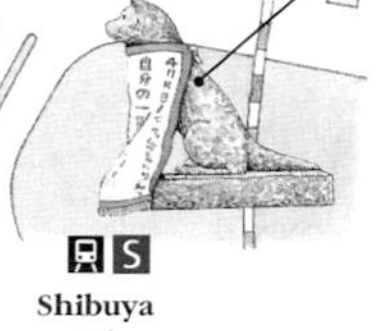

Shibuya station

0 meters 100

0 yards 100

Pachinko

Japan's most popular form of recreation, *pachinko* is similar to pinball, but without the flippers and requiring little skill. Players buy some steel balls to feed into the *pachinko* machine, winning more steel balls; these are traded in for a prize (gambling for money is illegal). The prize in turn can be exchanged for money, usually in a small shop nearby. Shibuya and Shinjuku have hundreds of *pachinko* parlors, but they are found all over Japan.

A typical *pachinko* machine

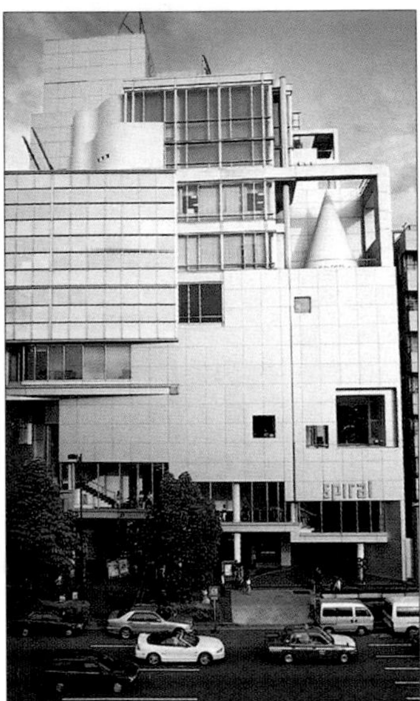

The Spiral Building, Minami-Aoyama

Minami-Aoyama District ❾

南青山地区

Map 1 C4–5, 2 D4–5. 🅢 *Gaienmae stn, Ginza line.* **Japan Traditional Craft Center** ☎ *(03) 3403-2460.* 🕐 *10am–6pm Fri–Wed.* **Museum of Contemporary Art** ☎ *(03) 3402-3001.* 🕐 *11am–7pm Tue–Sun (9pm Wed).* **Nezu Art Museum** ☎ *(03) 3272-8600.* 🕐 *9:30am–4pm Tue–Sun.* **National Children's Castle** ☎ *(03) 3797-5666.* 🕐 *12:30–5pm Tue–Fri, 10am–5pm Sat, Sun, public hols & school vacations.*

Favored by artists, writers, and young entrepreneurs, this district lies between the large Aoyama Cemetery and Shibuya. Aoyama-dori, the wide street at its heart, is a center for boutiques and upscale life. Omote-sando crosses it just about in the middle.

By the junction of Aoyama-dori with Gaien-Nishi-dori (a fashionable street nicknamed "Killer-dori"), look for the sign for Plaza 246. Just above is a small sign for the **Japan Traditional Craft Center** on the second floor, which stocks a huge collection of crafts, from lacquer and ceramics to handmade paper. The crafts are expensive but of excellent quality. From here, it is a short walk up Gaien-Nishi-dori to the **Museum of Contemporary Art** (Watari-um). Exhibits are by international and Japanese artists, and change regularly. The bookstore stocks an excellent range of art books.

Back on Aoyama-dori, turn left at the Omote-sando junction for the **Nezu Art Museum**, which houses Japanese, Chinese, and Korean art and is situated in landscaped gardens containing traditional tea houses. On Aoyama-dori, heading toward Shibuya, the next landmark is the white, geometric **Spiral Building**, which owes its name to the large, spiral ramp inside. Designed by Maki Fumihiko in 1985, and one of the most popular places in Minami-Aoyama, this building is the figurative definition of cool. There is nothing in it that can't be described as hip and trendy (*torendi* in Japanese), and that includes most of the people seen here. Attractions inside comprise a first-floor exhibition and performance space, the Spiral Hall (on the third floor), also used for a variery of exhibits and performances, an Italian café looking out onto a lush garden, a French restaurant, a stationery and housewares boutique, and a beauty salon.

Farther along, the **National Children's Castle** is marked by a large, moon-faced sculpture by Okamoto Taro in front. There are many activities for kids here, open to Japanese and non-Japanese speakers alike, including areas for free play with toys, computers, music and art classes, and even a child-friendly hotel.

Roppongi District ❿

六本木地区

Map 2 E5. 🅢 *Roppongi stn, Hibiya line.*

Roppongi is the music and club center of Tokyo. You can find just about any music you want here: jazz, blues, ska, hip-hop, classic disco, country and western, soul. This is also the place for big-name international restaurant chains such as the Hard Rock Café, Spago's, and Tony Roma's.

During the halcyon days of the "bubble" economy crowds of high-earners filled huge clubs in a hedonistic, disco version of the Roaring Twenties. Since the bubble burst in about 1990, there have been fewer people with the money to spend here, but the spirit lives on.

Almond (*Amando* in Japanese), at the intersection of Roppongi-dori and Gaien-

Nighttime scene in the district of Roppongi

Flamboyant entrance to a nightclub in Roppongi

Higashi-dori, is the main rendezvous spot in Roppongi. The area to the south is where a great deal of the action is. Clubs come in all shapes and sizes, some just wide enough for a counter and stools. Most will welcome you warmly, but check the prices of drinks as they vary hugely. To the west of Almond, along Roppongi-dori, is **Wave**, a music and video center guarded by a holographic Jizo (guardian figure). West of Almond is the **Square Building**, full of more clubs, including Birdland jazz club *(see p107)*.

Akasaka District ⓫

赤坂地区

Map 2 E3–4, 2 F3–4. **S** *Akasaka-Mitsuke stn, Ginza & Marunouchi lines; Nagatacho stn, Yurakucho, Namboku & Hanzomon lines.*
Suntory Museum of Art *(03) 3470-1073. 10am–5pm Tue–Sun (to 7pm Fri). Sanno Matsuri (Jun 10–16, Hie Jinja).*

With the Diet Building *(see p67)* and many government offices just to the east, Akasaka is a favorite place for politicians to socialize. Limousines carry dark-blue-suited men to the many exclusive establishments lining the streets here.

Opposite Akasaka-Mitsuke station is the **Suntory Museum of Art**, located in a single room on the 11th floor. It has an unrivaled collection of Edo-era screens, depicting scenes from the Edo court; one particularly fine example is *Namban* (Westerners in Japan). Traditional decorative arts are also well represented, with ceramics, lacquerware, and tea utensils.

About 200 m (220 yards) along Aoyama-dori from the Suntory Museum is the **Toyokawa Inari Shrine** (also called Myogon-ji). With its red lanterns and flags, and dozens of statues of foxes (the traditional messengers of Inari, a Shinto Rice deity), this is a pleasant place to linger.

Ironware kettle in the Suntory Museum of Art

Back past the Suntory Museum and over the moat, you will see on the right the gleaming white **Akasaka Prince Hotel** *(see p293)*, designed by Tange Kenzo. The open lobby has white marble floors and interior walls, while the exterior wall is glass. Past this hotel on the left is the huge, luxurious **Hotel New Otani**. On the 17th floor is the revolving Blue Sky restaurant, which serves Chinese, Japanese, and Italian food, and offers stunning views across central Tokyo and the Imperial Palace. In the grounds and open to all is the 400-year-old garden of Kato Kiyomasa, lord of Kyushu's Kumamoto area.

South of Akasaka-Mitsuke station is the shrine of **Hie Jinja**, with a history dating back to 830. Shogun Ietsuna moved it here in the 17th century to buffer his castle; the present-day buildings are all modern. Each year in mid-June the Sanno Matsuri is celebrated here with a grand procession of 50 *mikoshi* (portable shrines) and people in Heian-era costumes.

A *shinowa* circle, erected for good luck, at Hie Jinja in Akasaka

Youth Culture

In Japan youth sells, although, ironically, the average age of the population is one of the highest in the world. Youth is seen by most Japanese as the time when life can be lived according to personal choice, before adult responsibilities – in the form of jobs or parenthood – take over. Products from beer and cars to CDs and fashions are aimed at the youth market, and are rapidly adopted and then shed as individuals are attracted by the new and the desire to keep up with their peers. A stream of teenage *idoru* (idols) become wildly famous when they are young; if they are girls they tend to drop out in their early twenties to marry and have children, while boys may become talk-show hosts or game-show contestants.

A Tokyo teenager on her cell phone

Farther Afield

A SHORT DISTANCE from Tokyo city center are a number of interesting sights. The Japan Folk Craft Museum and Goto Art Museum are small gems in pleasant neighborhoods that give an idea of Tokyo life as well as its heritage; in contrast Ikebukuro, Daiba, and Ebisu are all modern urban centers in their own right. Ryogoku, the place for all things sumo, also has the Edo-Tokyo Museum. Rikugi-en, near Ikebukuro, is one of Edo's last great stroll gardens.

Back carrier, Japan Folk Craft Museum

SIGHTS AT A GLANCE

Arakawa Tram Line 4
Daiba 8
Ebisu District 10
Goto Art Museum 1
Ikebukuro District 5
Japan Folk Craft Museum 2
Rikugi-en Garden 6
Ryogoku District 7
Sengaku-ji Temple 9
Tokyo Opera City 3

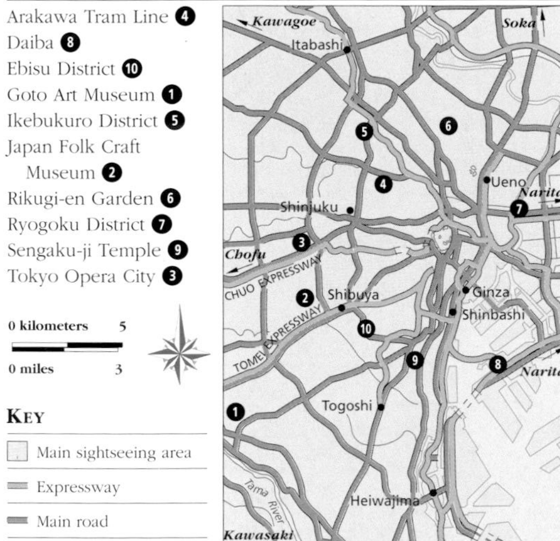

Goto Art Museum 1

五島美術館

3-9-25 Kaminoge, Setagaya-ku. *(03) 3703-0661. Tokyu Shin-Tamagawa line from Shibuya stn to Futako-Tamagawaen, then Tokyu Oimachi line to Kaminoge. 9:30am–4pm Tue–Sun. when exhibitions change.*

SET IN A PLEASANT hillside garden, this museum showcases the private collection of the late chairman of the Tokyu Corporation, Goto Keita. Avidly interested in Zen, he was originally attracted to Buddhist calligraphy, particularly that of 16th-century priests. His collection contains many examples of this work, called *bokuseki*. Also included are ceramics, calligraphy, paintings, and metalwork mirrors; items are changed several times a year. The museum's most famous works, however, are scenes from 12th-century scrolls of the *Tale of Genji*, painted by Fujiwara Takayoshi, which have been designated National Treasures. They are shown one week a year, usually in May.

Japan Folk Craft Museum 2

日本民芸館

4-3-33 Komaba, Meguro-ku. *(03) 3467-4527. Komaba-Todaimae stn, Keio Inokashira line. 10am–5pm Tue–Sun.*

KNOWN TO THE JAPANESE as Mingeikan, this small but excellent museum was founded by art historian Yanagi Muneyoshi. The criteria for inclusion in the museum are that the object should be the work of an anonymous maker, produced for daily use, and representative of the region from which it comes. The museum building, designed by Yanagi and completed in 1931, uses black tiles and white stucco outside.

On display are items ranging from woven baskets to ax sheaths, iron kettles, pottery, and kimonos; together they present a fascinating view of rural life. There are also special themed exhibits, such as 20th-century ceramics or Japanese textiles, and a room dedicated to Korean Yi-dynasty work. A small gift shop sells fine crafts and some books.

Tokyo Opera City 3

東京オペラシティー

3-20-2 Nishi-Shinjuku, Shinjuku-ku. *(03) 5353-0700. Hatsudai stn, Keio line.*

TOKYO'S NEWEST music and theater complex has two main halls, one primarily for Japanese classical music and theater, and a larger opera hall with a soaring vaulted roof. Performances are frequent – phone for details or pick up a leaflet from the foyer information counter.

There are 54 floors, mostly offices. On the first three are an art gallery, shops, and restaurants. The fourth has the **NTT Intercommunication Center**, with modern interactive art. The 53rd and 54th floors hold a dozen restaurants and bars with great city views.

Exhibit at the NTT Intercommunication Center, Tokyo Opera City

The aquarium at Sunshine City, Ikebukuro District

Arakawa Tram Line ❹

荒川都電

S Edogawabashi stn, Yarachuko line. **Sumida River trips** i (03) 5608-8869.

As recently as 1955, 600,000 people a day were riding the dozens of tram lines that crisscrossed the city. Now the 13 km (8 miles) of the Arakawa line are all that is left. The others were eliminated as old-fashioned in the modernization for the 1964 Olympics.

The Arakawa tram line runs from Waseda in the west to Minowabashi in the east and costs ¥160 for each trip, short or long. Near the Waseda end of the line is the quiet stroll garden of **Shin Edogawa**. There are few outstanding sights en route, but the pleasure of this tram ride lies in seeing a quieter, residential side to Tokyo. A short walk from Arakawa Yuenchimae stop, past tightly packed, tiny houses, leads to a modest amusement park, **Arakawa Yuen Park**; Sumida River tourboat trips leave from here. Opposite the Arakawa Nanachome stop is **Arakawa Nature Park**.

Ikebukuro District ❺

池袋地区

S Ikebukuro stn, Marunouchi & Yurachuko lines. Ikebukuro stn, Yamanote & many other lines.

With the second-busiest train station in Japan (after Shinjuku), Ikebukuro is a designated *fukutoshin* (sub-center) of Tokyo. By the station's south entrance is the flagship store of **Seibu**, perhaps the country's most innovative department store, with boutiques of up-and-coming designers, a 12th-floor art museum, and a large basement food market, where you can often try free samples. To the west of the station is the newer **Tobu** department store with an almost identical set-up.

The **Sunshine City** complex, including the **Sunshine 60** tower, is about 400 m (440 yards) east of the station. It is built on top of what was Sugamo Prison, where seven Class-A World War II war criminals, including the prime minister, Tojo Hideki, were convicted and hung. A huge Sunshine City sign points down an escalator; just before here, investigate the **Tokyu Hands** store for home furnishings and the latest kitchen gadgets. Down the escalator is **Amlux Toyota**, five stories packed with cars, where you can sit in any model Toyota makes. In Sunshine 60 there is also a planetarium, an aquarium, and a rooftop outdoor viewing platform.

Rikugi-en Garden ❻

六義園

S Komagome stn, Namboku line. Komagome stn, Yamanote line. (03) 3941-2222. 9am–5pm daily.

Yanagisawa Yoshiyasu, grand chamberlain of the fifth shogun, constructed this garden in seven years, starting in 1695. Yanagisawa had a well-earned reputation for debauchery, but he also managed to build this, one of the finest Edo-era stroll gardens. Iwasaki Yataro, Mitsubishi's founder, oversaw its Meiji-era renovation. The design recreates 88 landscapes in miniature from famous *waka* (31-syllable poems), so the view changes every few steps. Near the entrance is a weeping cherry that is beautiful all year. Numerous paths and seats offer opportunities to enjoy the views. Bush warblers and turtledoves are among the birds that can be seen here.

Manicured shrubs around the lake at Rikugi-en Garden

Living in Small Spaces

Land, and therefore housing, is very expensive in Japan. The average home costs 7–8 times the family's yearly income, and space is at a premium. A traditional design has closets for storing rolled-up futons; in the morning the bedding is swapped for a low table at which the family sits cross-legged to eat meals. More and more families are opting for a semi-Western style with raised beds, table, and chairs, resulting in homes being even more cramped.

Ryogoku District 7

両国地区

Map 4 E4–5. *Ryogoku stn, JR Sobu line.* **Sumo Museum** 1-3-28 Yokoami, Sumida-ku. *(03) 3622-0366.* *10am–4:30pm daily.* **Edo-Tokyo Museum** 1-4-1 Yokoami, Sumida-ku. *(03) 3626-9974.* *10am–5:30pm daily (7:30pm Thu & Fri).*

On the east bank of the Sumida River, Ryogoku was a great entertainment and commerce center in Edo's Shitamachi. These days it is a quiet place between the city center and the suburbs, but it still has its most famous residents: sumo wrestlers. Many *beya* (sumo stables) are here, and it is not unusual to see huge young men walking the streets in *yukata* (light cotton kimonos) and *geta* (wooden sandals), even in winter.

The **National Sumo Stadium** has been here since 1945; the current building dates from 1985. During a tournament *(see p106)* many of the wrestlers simply walk from their *beya* just down the street. Inside the stadium is a **Sumo Museum** lined with portraits of all the *yokozuna* (grand champions) dating back 200 years.

Beside the stadium is the huge **Edo-Tokyo Museum**, built to resemble an old style of elevated warehouse. One of Tokyo's most imaginative and interesting museums, its exhibition space is divided into two zones on two floors tracing life in Edo and then Tokyo, as Edo was renamed in 1868.

Life in a Sumo Stable

At the age of about 15 boys are accepted into a sumo *beya*. From that day they will probably not return home or see their parents for several years. Sumo society is supremely hierarchical, with newcomers serving senior wrestlers as well as cleaning and cooking for the entire *beya*. Their practices may start at 4am, with seniors starting about 6am. The day's single meal of *chanko-nabe*, a large stew, comes about noon with juniors getting what the seniors leave. That is followed by more work. The life is extremely grueling – it is a society and culture few foreigners have successfully entered.

Sumo wrestlers training in the early morning

The exhibits, some of which are interactive, appeal to both adults and children and have detailed explanations in Japanese and English.

The route around the museum starts by crossing a traditional arched wooden bridge, a replica of Nihonbashi *(see p66)*. There are life-sized reconstructed buildings including the façades of a Kabuki theater and a Meiji-era newspaper office. Marvelous scale-model dioramas, some of which are automated, show everything from the house of a *daimyo* (feudal lord) to a section of Shitamachi. Beside a scale model of Tokyo's first skyscraper is rubble from the 1923 earthquake that destroyed it. There is a rickshaw and Japan's first "light" automobile: a three-seater Subaru with a 360 cc engine. In the media section is a step-by-step example of how *ukiyo-e* woodblock prints *(see p81)* were produced. Models of the boats that once plied the Sumida River give some idea of just how important the river was to Edo life.

Image of a Kabuki actor, Edo-Tokyo Museum

Reconstruction of a Kabuki theater in Ryogoku's Edo-Tokyo Museum

Daiba 8

台場

Yurikamome monorail from Shinbashi stn; Rinkai Fukutoshin line to Tokyo Teleport. *approx 10am–6pm, every 40 mins.* **Museum of Maritime Sciences** *(03) 5500-1111.* *10am–4:30pm daily (5:30pm Sat, Sun, public hols & in summer).*

When the West started to force Japan to open up in the 1850s, the shogunate constructed a series of *daiba* (obstructions) across Tokyo harbor to keep the foreigners' powerful "black ships" out. Daiba (sometimes known as Odaiba), an island almost blocking the mouth of Tokyo Bay, takes its name from these. Neglected for years, it is now the closest thing in the city to a resort and, ironically, Western pop culture is rampant. The spectacular route to Daiba is via the Yurikamome monorail, which climbs a loop before joining Rainbow Bridge high over Tokyo Harbor. On Daiba the monorail is a convenient way to travel around, although most places are within a short walk of each other.

The first station, Odaiba-Kaihin-Koen, leads to Tokyo's only beach. Nearby is the **Daisan Daiba Historic Park**, which includes the remains of the shogun's original obstructions. A short walk west is **Tokyo Decks** with five floors of restaurants, boutiques, and shops plus **Joypolis**, a huge Sega center full of the latest electronic and virtual arcade games. In front of Decks is the station for water buses from Hinode Pier. Behind it is the headquarters of **Fuji TV**, a new Tokyo landmark. A pleasant, tree-filled waterfront park extends to the **Museum of Maritime Sciences** (accessible from Fune-no-Kagakukan station), shaped like a boat. Moored at the museum's dock are several ships to board.

At Aomi station is the **Palette Town** development, including Toyota's City Showcase, a large showroom displaying Toyota cars with state-of-the-art driving simulators, a test-drive course, and another track for trying out futuristic electric mini-cars. In the History Garage are cleverly displayed cars from the 1950s on. Nearby is Future World with a short virtual drive into the future. Right beside all this is a large Ferris wheel and a waterbus terminal.

The futuristic Fuji TV headquarters, Daiba

Part of the Ebisu Garden Place complex, Ebisu

Wanza Ariake building has shops and restaurants below and offices above; it's connected directly to Kokusai-Tenjijo Seimon station. On the other side of the station is **Tokyo Big Sight** (or Tokyo International Exhibition Hall).

The gate of Sengaku-ji Temple

Sengaku-ji Temple ❾

泉岳寺

Sengaku-ji stn, Toei Asakusa line. **Museum** *9am–4pm daily.*

THIS TEMPLE is the site of the climax of Japan's favorite tale of loyalty and revenge, retold in the play *Chushingura* and many movies *(see p51)*. Lord Asano was sentenced to death by *seppuku* (suicide by disembowelment) for drawing his sword when goaded by Lord Kira. Denied the right to seek revenge, 47 of Asano's retainers, led by Oishi Yuranosuke, plotted in secret. In 1703, they attacked Kira's house and beheaded him, presenting the head to Asano's grave at Sengaku-ji. They in turn were sentenced to *seppuku*, and are buried here.

Inside the temple gate and up the steps on the right is the well (now covered with wire) where the retainers washed Kira's head. Farther ahead on the right are the retainers' graves, still tended with flowers. Back at the base of the steps is an interesting **museum** with artifacts from the incident and statues of the 47.

Ebisu District ❿

恵比寿地区

Ebisu stn, Hibiya line. *Ebisu stn, Yamanote line.* **Tokyo Metropolitan Museum of Photography** *(03) 3280-0031.* *10am–5:30pm Tue–Sat (7:30pm Thu & Fri).* **Beer Museum Ebisu** *(03) 5423-7255.* *10am–5pm Tue–Sun. (Last adm 1 hr before closing.)*

THE COMPLETION in the mid-1990s of **Ebisu Garden Place**, a commercial and residential center, brought this area to life. The superb **Tokyo Metropolitan Museum of Photography**, to the right of the entrance, has a permanent collection of work by Japanese and foreign photographers, and excellent special exhibitions. In the heart of Ebisu Garden Place are a Mitsukoshi store, boutiques, two cinemas, a theater, and restaurants, including Taillevent Robuchon, a French restaurant that looks like a 19th-century chateau. The crowded central plaza is a great spot for people-watching. To the left of Mitsukoshi is the small **Beer Museum Ebisu** with exhibits and videos about beer worldwide and in Japan, and free samples.

Shopping in Tokyo

YOU CAN BUY almost anything you want in Tokyo, from a traditional *kokeshi* (cylindrical wooden doll) to a Chanel handbag or an up-to-the-minute computer game. Tokyo-ites love shopping and, budget permitting, the city is a paradise for browsing and buying, with its huge department stores, informal street markets, and fascinating one-of-a-kind shops. Although half the joy of shopping here is the amazing contrasts that can be found side-by-side, some areas do specialize in certain types of shops. Ginza is the place for traditional, upscale stores, while Shinjuku mixes huge arcades with electronics shops stacked high with the latest innovations. Harajuku and Minami-Aoyama are the areas for the funkiest fashions and designs; the older quarters around Ueno and Asakusa offer more traditional Japanese crafts. For general information on shopping in Japan, see pages 340–45.

***Kanzashi* hairpin, Nakamise-dori, Asakusa**

Department Stores

DEPARTMENT STORES grew out of Edo-period mercantile houses. Customers would sit on *tatami* mats and describe what they wanted, then staff would bring out the goods for their perusal. After the 1923 earthquake, newly built stores allowed customers inside with shoes on for the first time, revolutionizing shopping. Since the collapse of the "bubble" economy in about 1990, the opulence of Tokyo's department stores has been more muted, and prices lower, but they continue to offer a huge variety and immaculate service. Basements are usually supermarkets, where free samples are handed out. Top floors are often filled with restaurants, both Western and Japanese, plus an art gallery and sometimes a museum, too. Ginza's **Mitsukoshi** is perhaps Tokyo's most famous store; the main Mitsukoshi store is in nearby Nihonbashi, with other branches in Ikebukuro and Ebisu. In Ginza **Matsuya** is more informal and aimed at a younger, yuppie crowd. Shinjuku has never been famous for department stores, but the new **Takashimaya** with an IMAX theater on the 12th floor has been a big success. For a heavy dose of youth culture, try **Marui (Young)** in Shibuya.

Matsuya, one of Ginza's major department stores

If you have time for just one department store, visit the flagship **Seibu** store right over Ikebukuro station. Filled with hip designer boutiques as well as more established brand names, it elevates shopping to an art form. Also in Ikebukuro (and Shibuya, *see p92*) is **Tokyu Hands**, a cornucopia of housewares, which is always fun to browse through.

Shopping Arcades

LABYRINTHS of corridors lined with shops occupy major subway and train stations. They are good for window-shopping and sometimes for bargains, but are notoriously disorienting. **Tokyo station** is packed with shops and kiosks. In **Shinjuku station** underground passages run for hundreds of meters to the "Subnade" (underground shopping street) below Yasukuni-dori. Tokyo's **Yaesu underground** is also huge, starting below the Daimaru department store side. Daiba's **Tokyo Decks** *(see p99)* is five floors of shops and a promenade deck with restaurants and a game center. Nearby **Wanza Ariake** *(see p99)* is similar. The lower floors of **Tokyo Opera City** *(see p96)* also have restaurants and shops.

Crowds milling up and down Takeshita-dori in Harajuku

Markets

STREET MARKETS flourish outside many of the city's train stations. Tokyo's most famous station market is **Ameyoko** *(see p80)* under the tracks at Ueno station. **Takeshita-dori** in Harajuku *(see p91)* is full of shops for the young and fashion-conscious. The ultimate market experience is **Tsukiji Fish Market** *(see p64)*; the area to the east is full of small restaurants where piles of dishes crowd the sidewalk, and shops with pungent crates of *wasabi* horseradish and dried fish hanging from storefronts.

One of West Shinjuku's huge camera stores

Electronic Goods

The best place to buy electronic goods is Akihabara *(see p69)*. Computers, video games, and software fuel the economy here, but you can usually find just about anything. Prices in Japan are high, and even with the ten percent or so discount here, the cost is unlikely to be cheaper than elsewhere, though the selection is unmatched. Check that you are buying equipment that is compatible with voltage and systems back home *(see p363)*.

In Akihabara, **Laox** is a big favorite with tax-free shoppers; **Ishimaru** and **Yamagiwa** are two more huge electronic department stores. **Gateway Country** and **T-Zone** sell English-language computers and some English-language software. Bring your passport along and ask for the tax-free price.

Camera Equipment

The west side of Shinjuku is the main place to come for camera equipment. **Yodobashi Camera** and **Camera Doi** are two of the biggest stores here, with several floors of every brand and every type of equipment. Prices are high, although the margin is not as much as it once was, and you can be sure that the camera bought is genuine. The language of cameras is universal, and staff can usually help find anything. Ask for the duty-free price; you can even try and bargain a little, particularly if you pay cash.

Jewelry and Accessories

Pearls are the only form of jewelry native to Japan; all gem stones are either imported or synthetic. **Mikimoto** perfected the process and marketing of cultured pearls in 1893, and sells its jewelry in opulent surroundings. For a selection of silver and other types of jewelry, pay a visit to **Mori Silver** in the Oriental Bazaar (*see* "Clothing") and **Takane Jewelry**.

Japan's traditional jewelry for women was *kanzashi*, the hairpins worn in traditional hairstyles (with tortoise-shell combs). Nakamise-dori at Senso-ji Temple *(see pp82–3)* is the place to find these. **Sanoya** sells *kanzashi*, plus other jewelry, and nearby **Ginkado** sells *kanzashi*, costume swords, and fans. Next door is **Bunsendo**, also selling fans. The last maker of handmade wooden combs is **Jusanya** in Ueno.

An *obi* sash on a kimono

Clothing

A traditional Japanese kimono can be incredibly expensive but makes a unique and beautiful souvenir; one supplier is **Kodaimaru** at the Imperial Hotel. Used kimonos are usually a much more reasonable price and are usually in excellent condition: try the **Oriental Bazaar**, a complex of several shops on Omote-sando and **Hayashi Kimono** in Yurakucho. *Yukata* (cotton kimonos suitable for men and women) or *hapi* (cotton kimono-style short jackets) are affordable alternatives.

Mainstream men's and women's clothes tend to be conservative, though immaculately designed and cut. Many international designers have their own outlets or are stocked by the major stores.

Designers aiming primarily at the young are doing very inventive things with bold colors and unusual materials and cuts. **Seibu** department store in Ikebukuro is full of boutiques of new, innovative designers. Gaien-Nishi-dori in Minami-Aoyama *(see p94)* is packed with trendy boutiques, as is Omote-sando *(see p91)* and its side streets.

Japan's internationally famous designers have outlets around the city. **Issey Miyake** has boutiques in several department stores and a shop in Minami-Aoyama. **Comme des Garçons** has two shops; go to the main store for directions to the second. **Hanae Mori** has a shop in her own building in Harajuku.

Textiles

Silk, cotton, linen, hemp, and wool all feature in Japan's long and rich textile history. While some traditional techniques are fading, most are alive and well. Department stores are often the best places to find a range of textiles. **Matsuzakaya** (in Ginza) grew from a Nagoya kimono merchant and stocks bolts of kimono cloth made in Kyoto and textured *furoshiki* (square wrapping cloths). The **Tokyo National Museum shop** *(see pp76–9)* has a good selection of *furoshiki* and scarves made using traditional techniques. Also good is **Bengara** (*see* "Traditional Arts and Crafts"). **Miyashita Obi** on Nakamise-dori at Senso-ji Temple *(see pp82–3)* has wonderful *obi* sashes, used to wrap the waist of a kimono.

Traditional umbrellas for sale in Nakamise-dori, near Senso-ji Temple

Contemporary Art and Design

Galleries and showrooms come and go in Tokyo; check local sources of information *(see p104)* for the latest shows. The **Spiral Garden** in Minami-Aoyama's Spiral Building *(see p94)* usually has something interesting by Japanese artists. The shop on the second floor has a selection of contemporary housewares.

In Ginza you can find works by Japanese artists at **Galleria Grafica**, **Plus Minus Gallery**, and **Yosheido Gallery**. **Ginza Graphic Gallery** exhibits both Japanese and foreign works, while the **Ginza Art Space** stocks Japanese and international contemporary photography. In Shinjuku the **NTT Intercommunication Center** in Tokyo Opera City *(see p96)* features exhibits and installations using the latest technology. In the same building is the **Shinjuku Opera City Gallery** which displays Japanese painting, watercolors, and examples of graphic art of all types.

Excellent contemporary prints can be found at the **Tolman Collection** near the Tokyo Tower. For contemporary ceramics, try **Tachikichi** and **Koransha**, which are both in Ginza. Good sources of modern housewares are the department stores **Tokyu Hands** and **Matsuya**, which is also in Ginza.

Traditional Arts and Crafts

Crafts are thriving in Japan. Ceramics is by far the most active craft, and the average Japanese has a working knowledge of the distinct styles and techniques used in different areas of the country. The larger ceramic bowls used for *matcha* (a form of green tea) are striking in their simple, natural forms; good pieces will be firmly packed in a wooden box.

Ironware kettle, Japan Traditional Crafts Center

Lacquerware plates, trays, chopsticks, and bowls make excellent souvenirs that are light and easy to transport. The various forms of Japan's beautiful paper, *washi*, also make lightweight gifts; it can be bought as writing paper or in packs of square sheets for origami.

The **Japan Traditional Craft Center** in Minami-Aoyama is an excellent source of many of these crafts, as is **Maruzen** in Nihonbashi and **Takumi** in Ginza. **Itoya,** also in Ginza, is packed with crafts, especially *washi*; it also has brushes, ink, and inkstones for calligraphy. **Kurodaya**, at Senso-ji Temple *(see pp82–3)*, has been selling *washi* for over 140 years and stocks everything from modern stationery to traditional kites plus a wide selection of *chiyogami* (wrapping paper), and traditional masks and clay figurines. The **Japan Folk Craft Museum** *(see p96)* has a small, high-quality selection.

There is a whole tradition of dolls made for viewing in glass cases; these run into hundreds, even thousands, of dollars to buy. Two good suppliers are **Yoshitoku** and **Beishu**. The small figurines in **Sukeroku**, at the end of Senso-ji's Nakamise-dori are charming and easy to carry home.

Noren, the cloth curtains that hang over the entrances to many small shops and restaurants, are unique mementos. **Bengara** is the only shop to specialize in *noren*, with beautiful cotton and silk designs.

Woodblock prints are rarely bargains, but good prints are available at reasonable prices. In Jinbocho two famous shops are almost next to each other: **Oya Shobo** and **Hara Shobo**. For new prints of old woodblocks on *washi* **Isetatsu** in Yanaka is excellent; it also sells beautiful sheets of *chiyogami* from old designs.

Specialty Shops

There are all kinds of small niche shops filled with uniquely Japanese items. The following are all in Nakamise-dori at Senso-ji: **Sanbido** sells religious statues and beautiful dolls; **Nishijima Umbrellas** has traditional umbrellas; **Tokiwado** has been selling *kaminari okoshi* crackers – famous for crackling like a clap of thunder when bitten – for 200 years; **Nakatsuka** sells candies and sweet crackers.

Kappabashi-dori *(see p80)* is Tokyo's center for kitchenware and plastic food.

A traditional candy shop in Nakamise-dori, Senso-ji Temple

DIRECTORY

DEPARTMENT STORES

Marui (Young)
1-22-6 Jinnan, Shibuya.
Map 1 B5.
(03) 3464-0101.
Wed.

Matsuya
3-6-1 Ginza. **Map** 5 C2.
(03) 3567-1211.
Tue.

Mitsukoshi
1-4-1 Nihonbashi.
Map 5 C1.
(03) 3241-3311.
Mon.

Seibu
1-28-1 Minami-Ikebukuro.
(03) 3981-0111.
Tue.

Takashimaya
5-24-2 Sendagaya.
Map 1 B2.
(03) 5361-1111.
Wed.

Tokyu Hands
1-28-10 Higashi-Ikebukuro.
(03) 3980-6111.
2nd or 3rd Thu of month.

ELECTRONIC GOODS

Gateway Country
Suehiro Bldg, 5-1-2 Soto-Kanda. **Map** 3 C4.
(03) 3834-2001

Ishimaru
1-9-14 Soto-Kanda.
Map 3 C4.
(03) 3255-1500.

Laox
1-2-9 Soto-Kanda.
Map 3 C4.
(03) 3253-7111.

T-Zone
4-3-3 Soto-Kanda.
Map 3 C4.
(03) 3526-7711.

Yamagiwa
4-1-1 Soto-Kanda.
Map 3 C4.
(03) 3253-2111.

CAMERA EQUIPMENT

Camera Doi
1-15-4 Nishi-Shinjuku.
Map 1 B2.
(03) 3344-2310.

Yodobashi Camera
1-11-1 Nishi-Shinjuku.
Map 1 B2.
(03) 3346-1010.

JEWELRY AND ACCESSORIES

Jusanya
2-12-21 Ueno.
Map 3 C3.
(03) 3831-3238.
1st and 3rd Sun of month.

Mikimoto
4-5-5 Ginza.
Map 5 B2.
(03) 3535-4611.
Wed.

Takane Jewelry
1-7-23 Uchisawaicho.
Map 5 B3.
(03) 3591-2764.
Sun.

CLOTHING

Comme des Garçons
5-2-1 Minami-Aoyama.
Map 1 C5.
(03) 3406-3951.

Hanae Mori
3-6-1 Kita-Aoyama.
Map 1 C4.
(03) 3400-3301.

Hayashi Kimono
International Arcade,
2-1-1 Yurakucho.
Map 5 B2.
(03) 3591-9826.

Issey Miyake
3-18-11 Minami-Aoyama.
Map 1 C5.
(03) 3423-1407.

Kodaimaru
Imperial Hotel Arcade,
1-1-1 Uchisaiwaicho.
Map 5 B2.
(03) 3508 7697.

Oriental Bazaar
5-9-13 Jingumae.
Map 1 C4.
(03) 3400-3933.
Thu.

TEXTILES

Matsuzakaya
6-10-1 Ginza. **Map** 5 B2.
(03) 3572-1111.
Wed.

CONTEMPORARY ART AND DESIGN

Galleria Grafica
1F and 2F Ginza S2 Bldg,
6-13-4 Ginza.
Map 5 B3.
(03) 5550-1335.
Sun.

Ginza Art Space
B1 Ginza Bldg, 7-8-10 Ginza. **Map** 5 B3.
(03) 3571-7741.
only for exhibitions.

Ginza Graphic Gallery
DNP Ginza Bldg, 7-7-2 Ginza.
Map 5 B3.
(03) 3571-5206.
Sun.

Koransha
5-12-12 Ginza.
Map 5 B3.
(03) 3543-0951.
Sun.

Plus Minus Gallery
2F TEPCO Ginza-kan,
6-11-1 Ginza.
Map 5 B3.
(03) 3575-0456.
Wed.

Tachikichi
5-6-13 Ginza. **Map** 5 B3.
(03) 3573-1986.
Sun.

Tolman Collection
2-2-18 Shiba Daimon.
Map 5 A4.
(03) 3434-1300.
Tue.

Yosheido Gallery
5-5-15 Ginza. **Map** 5 B3.
(03) 3571-1312.
Sun

TRADITIONAL ARTS AND CRAFTS

Beishu
2-15-3 Yanagibashi, Taito-ku. **Map** 5 B3.
(03) 5823-2171.
Sat & Sun.

Bengara
2-35-11 Asakusa.
Map 4 F2.
(03) 3841-6613.
Thu.

Hara Shobo
2-3 Kanda-Jinbocho.
Map 3 B5.
(03) 3261-7444
Sun & Mon.

Isetatsu
2-18-9 Yanaka.
Map 3 B1.
(03) 3823-1453.

Itoya
2-7-15 Ginza. **Map** 5 C2.
(03) 3561-8311.

Japan Traditional Craft Center
Plaza 246, 3-1-1 Minami-Aoyama.
Map 1 C4.
(03) 3403-2460.
Thu.

Kurodaya
1-2-5 Asakusa.
Map 4 F3.
(03) 3844-7511
Mon.

Maruzen
2-3-10 Nihonbashi.
Map 5 C1.
(03) 3272-7211.
Sun.

Oya Shobo
1-1 Kanda-Jinbocho.
Map 3 B5.
(03) 3291-0062.
Sun.

Takumi
8-4-2 Ginza.
Map 5 B3.
(03) 3571-2017.
Sun.

Yoshitoku
1-9-14 Asakusabashi.
Map 4 D4.
(03) 3863-4419.

Entertainment in Tokyo

Tokyo is one of the liveliest places on the planet. Contrary to the popular image, the Japanese are not simply a nation of workaholics – they play hard, too. The young in particular are demanding more "lifestyle" time. Traditionally Japanese gather with like-minded friends at small establishments catering to their interests; as a result, thousands of entertainment venues fill the city. There's a mind-boggling range of live music from jazz and blues to pop and techno, and the classical music scene is also very active. Tokyo is the best place to see traditional drama and is well served by touring local and international theater groups. Sports fans can head for packed baseball and soccer games, or sample traditional martial arts including sumo, the national sport.

National Theater poster

Information Sources

A couple of monthly guides are indispensible for planning your entertainment. *Tokyo Journal* covers entertainment and the arts, and its restaurants section includes descriptions and maps, while *Tokyo Day and Night* gives practical listings of everything from theaters to churches and also includes useful maps. Saturday's *Japan Times* and Thursday's *Daily Yomiuri* also have good listings, as does *Tokyo Classified.* All are available in stores selling non-Japanese books, including **Kinokuniya**, **Tower Records**, **Maruzen**, and **Jena**. **Teletourist Service** provides round-the-clock taped information in English on current events in and around Tokyo. Your hotel may have information, and the **Tokyo TIC** in the Tokyo International Forum *(see p67)* is another good source.

Booking Tickets

Tickets can go very quickly, so make your decisions fast, be prepared for some disappointments, and have an alternative plan. For popular Japanese entertainment (such as Kabuki, Noh, sumo, or baseball) try to book via a travel agent before arriving.

In Tokyo three of the main ticket agencies are **Ticket Saison**, **Ticket PIA**, and **CN Playguide**. They can be hard to reach by phone, so it's often easier to book in person; a convenient office is **Ticket PIA** at Ginza's Sony Building *(see p62)*. Many department stores also have their own ticket offices. An alternative is to book directly by phoning the venue. They will hold the tickets, and you pay when you pick them up. Most agencies speak only Japanese, so try to have a Japanese-speaker help you.

Staff ready to help at Daimaru department store ticket office

Traditional Theater

Kabuki and Noh, the two main forms of traditional theater *(see pp32–3)*, are well represented in Tokyo. Many visitors find Noh heavy going due to the slow-paced action and dialogue in a foreign language (many Japanese have to rely on a libretto, too), but Noh can be exceptionally powerful. The **National Noh Theater** near Sendagaya JR station usually has weekend performances. Tickets vary from ¥2,800 to ¥5,600 for different performances. It is also possible to see plays at one of the capital's Noh schools, **Kanze Noh-gakudo**, for example. Noh can occasionally be seen as it was originally performed: on an outdoor stage in front of a temple illuminated by torchlight. Check the listings for information.

Kabuki is a flamboyant spectacle with rousing stories, elaborate sets, and amazing costumes. In 1986 Super Kabuki controversially combined avant-garde ideas and high-tech special effects with traditional Kabuki, changing the art form again. **Kabuki-za Theater** *(see p64)* is the main venue for Kabuki, with almost daily performances starting mid-morning and lasting three or more hours. It is also possible to buy a ticket to see just one act. Prices range from ¥2,400 to ¥16,000, or ¥900 for a one-act ticket. The **National Theater** has Kabuki performances in January, June, July, October, and November. Bunraku traditional puppet theater *(see p33)* is sometimes staged in the National Theater's Small Hall.

Kabuki in action at the Kabuki-za Theater

Movie poster in Shinjuku, one of Tokyo's centers for cinema

International and Contemporary Theater and Dance

THE THEATER SCENE encompasses everything from Shakespeare and Broadway musicals to modern dance. Venues are scattered throughout the city, though the main centers are in Shinjuku, Shibuya, and Marunouchi. Visiting national companies, professional troupes, and touring companies assure that the level of performance is high. Several very competitive amateur groups are also active.

A uniquely Japanese theater experience is Takarazuka, a troupe composed entirely of women, with their own **Takarazuka Theater** *(see p62)*. They perform adaptations in Japanese of Western musicals and are famed for their lavish productions and elaborate costumes.

Nihon Buyo Kyokai stages regular performances of traditional dance. Usually toward the end of May, the Azuma Odori, a lavish annual production of dance, drama, and music, brings the geisha community to the stage of the **Shinbashi Enbujo Theater**.

Buto is modern dance combined with performance art. Developed in the 1960s, the performances feature shaven-headed dancers, almost naked, painted with makeup. The slow, childish dance motions work to create beauty and release out of the self-imposed grotesqueness. With a number of Buto troupes, Tokyo is the best place to see it – check listings for small venues.

Cinema

MOVIE-GOING is not cheap in Japan, costing about ¥1,800 per person. On Cinema Day, usually the first of each month, tickets are reduced. American and European films usually reach Japan at least six months after release in their home countries. Non-Japanese films are usually shown in the original language with Japanese subtitles; an exception is children's films, which are usually dubbed into Japanese, with one showing a day in the original language.

In Shibuya, **Bunkamura** sometimes shows Japanese films with English subtitles and occasionally screens independent and European films. The centrally located **Hibiya Chanter** shows art-house and independent movies. For mainstream movies, there are six cinemas around the square in which the **Koma** cinema is situated, in Shinjuku's Kabukicho *(see p86)*. **Marunouchi Piccadilly** in the Mullion Building in Ginza has four screens; **Ebisu Garden Place** *(see p99)* has two. Fans of Japanese cinema should visit the superb **National Film Center**. The increasingly popular **Tokyo International Film Festival** is held every October/ November.

Live Music

THERE IS NO shortage of venues in which to hear live music in Tokyo. Many big acts, Japanese and foreign, appear at Shibuya's **Club Quattro**. **On Air East** and **On Air West** are two other good venues in Shibuya for techno and J-pop. In Shinjuku the **Liquid Room** is a trendy place to see a mix of bands. The **Akasaka Blitz** hosts J-pop groups and some foreign acts. The **Mandala Live House** has mostly Japanese bands.

For big-name jazz performers try the **Shinjuku Pit Inn** and the **Blue Note Tokyo**. **Birdland**, in Roppongi's Square Building, is one of Tokyo's longest-running jazz clubs. The **Blues Alley Japan** is a small club featuring blues, jazz, and rock. In Roppongi **Sweet Basil** offers a very eclectic mix of music.

The domestic and international classical music and opera scene in Tokyo is flourishing. **Tokyo Opera City** *(see p96)*, the nearby **New National Theater**, the **Suntory Hall**, the **NHK Hall**, and **Tokyo International Forum** *(see p67)* are all popular spots.

June and July see the **Tokyo Summer Festival** in various places; its classical, rock, folk, and jazz musicians from the world over draw thousands.

Roppongi District, a focus for music and clubs

Kendo training at a Tokyo *dojo*

Nightclubs

Tokyo's clubs are many and varied, and the club scene is very fluid; check listings for the latest information. There are several centers for nightclubs; Roppongi, the city's upscale playground, is the one of the best. The **Square Building** (*see* Birdland, under "Live Music") near Roppongi station is full of clubs from top to bottom. In the other direction, the **Pentax Gallery** is a complex housing clubs and restaurants. In Shinjuku the Hilton Tokyo has **Show Boat 5i**, which is always popular. The Ni-chome area of Shinjuku is home to some 250 gay clubs, as well as numerous pubs and bars.

Clubs with a show tend to start early, around 7–8pm; the last show ends in time for last trains, about 11–11:30pm. Smaller clubs start and end later, while dance clubs will warm up around 11pm and keep going all night. Expect a cover charge of ¥2,000–4,000, usually including one drink.

Sumo

Sumo tournaments, each lasting 15 days, are held in Tokyo in January, May (when the emperor attends), and September at the 10,000-seat **National Sumo Stadium** in Ryogoku *(see p98)*. Tournaments begin on a Sunday with each fighter wrestling once a day. Bouts start each day around 2:30pm with the lowest-ranking wrestlers and continue in ascending order with the top ranks wrestling from 5–6pm, ending with a bout involving the highest-ranked wrestler, usually a *yokozuna* (grand champion). The stadium fills up with spectators as the day goes on.

Wrestlers' banners outside the National Sumo Stadium, Ryogoku

Best views are on the north side. It is advisable to book tickets in advance from **Playguide**, **Ticket PIA** at the Sony Building, or any **Lawson's** convenience store. Easiest to get are midweek tickets in the first week of a tournament. If you cannot buy tickets via an agency, try asking your hotel to check for returns, or lining up at the stadium itself at about 8am on the day.

If you are not in Tokyo during a tournament, you may be able to watch the daily practice at a sumo stable, or *beya (see p98)*. Most are open to anyone who wants to watch, with a few basic rules: don't eat or use a camera flash, and be quiet. The closer a tournament is, the more likely you are to be politely turned away. The best time to view practice is 6–10am. Most of the *beya* are near Ryogoku station. Try **Kasugano Beya**, a tall new building with a green copper gable over the entrance, **Iztsu Beya**, or **Dewanoumi Beya**.

Other Martial Arts

Martial arts *(see p31)* are practiced in many places throughout Tokyo, but different establishments vary in their openness to non-Japanese as observers and participants. Contact **Tokyo TIC** for a list of *dojos* (practice halls) that allow spectators. To find out about participating in martial arts training, contact one of the national regulatory bodies *(see pp350–53)*.

Baseball Hall of Fame, Tokyo Dome

Baseball and Soccer

The Yomiuri Giants are Japan's most popular pro baseball team *(see p351)*. Their games in the **Tokyo Dome** are always sold out; book through an agent well in advance or try the **Tokyo Dome Service Counter** at Sogo's Yurakucho department store. The best place to enjoy a game is in the beautiful **Jingu Stadium**, home of the Swallows. Tickets are often available at **Ticket PIA** in Ginza's Sony Building

The J-League, Japan's professional soccer league, started in 1993 and has an up-and-down history of support. None of the teams calls Tokyo home, but the Kawasaki team, Verdy, and the Yokohama Marinos are close by. The **National Stadium** is used for many games. The **TIC** have information, and tickets are available at **Ticket PIA**.

Directory

Information Sources

Jena
5-6-1 Ginza.
Map 5 B2.
(03) 3571-2980.

Kinokuniya
3-17-7 Shinjuku.
Map 1 B1.
(03) 3354-0131.
www.kinokuniya.co.jp

Maruzen
2-3-10 Nihonbashi.
Map 5 C1.
(03) 3272-7211.
www.maruzen.co.jp

Teletourist Service
(03) 3201-2911.

Tower Records
1-22-14 Jinnan.
Map 1 B5.
(03) 3496-3661.

Booking Tickets

CN Playguide
(03) 5802-9999.

Ticket PIA
(03) 5237-9999.

Ticket Saison
(03) 3250-9999.

Traditional Theater

Kanze Noh-gakudo
1-16-4 Shoto.
Map 1 A5.
(03) 3469-5241.

National Noh Theater
4-18-1 Sendagaya.
Map 1 C3.
(03) 3423-1331.

National Theater
4-1 Hayabusa-cho.
Map 2 F3.
(03) 3265-7411.

International and Contemporary Theater and Dance

Nihon Buyo Kyokai
2-18-1 Kachidoki.
Map 6 D4.
(03) 3533-6455.

Shinbashi Enbujo Theater
6-18-2 Ginza.
Map 5 C3.
(03) 3541-2600.

Takarazuka Theater
3-8-3 Marunouchi.
Map 5 B2.
(03) 5251-2001.

Cinema

Bunkamura
2-24-1 Dogen-zaka, Shibuya-ku.
Map 1 A5.
(03) 3477 9111.

Hibiya Chanter
Hibiya Chanter Bldg, 1-2-2 Yurakucho.
Map 5 B2.
(03) 3591-1511.

Marunouchi Piccadilly
Mullion Bldg, 2-5-1 Yurakucho.
Map 5 B2.
(03) 3201-2881.

National Film Center
3-7-6 Kyobashi.
Map 5 C2.
(03) 3272-8600.

Tokyo International Film Festival
(03) 3563-6407.

Live Music

Akasaka Blitz
TBS Square, 5-3-6 Akasaka.
Map 2 E4.
(03) 3224-0567.

Birdland
B2 Square Bldg, 3-10-3 Roppongi.
Map 2 E5.
(03) 3478-3456.

Blue Note Tokyo
6-3-16 Minami-Aoyama.
Map 2 D5.
(03) 5485-0088.

Blues Alley Japan
B1 Meguro Station Hotel, 1-3-14 Meguro.
(03) 5496-4381

Club Quattro
4F Quattro Bldg, 32-13 Udagawa-cho.
Map 1 A5.
(03) 3477-8750.

Liquid Room
7F Shinjuku HUMAX Pavilion, 1-20-1 Kabukicho.
Map 1 B1.
(03) 3200-6831.

Mandala Live House
B1 MR Bldg, 3-2-2 Minami-Aoyama.
Map 1 C4.
(03) 5474-0411.

New National Theater
1-1-1 Honmachi, Shibuya-ku.
(03) 5352-5745.

NHK Hall
2-2-1 Jinnan.
Map 1 B4.
(03) 3465-1751.

On Air East
2-14-9 Dogen-zaka.
Map 1 A5.
(03) 3476-8686.

On Air West
2-3 Maruyamacho.
Map 1 A5.
(03) 5458-4646.

Shinjuku Pit Inn
B1 Accord Bldg, 2-12-4 Shinjuku.
Map 1 B1.
(03) 3354-2024.

Suntory Hall
1-13-1 Akasaka.
Map 2 E3.
(03) 3584 9999.

Sweet Basil
6-7-11 Roppongi.
Map 2 E5.
(03) 5474-0139.

Tokyo Summer Festival
(03) 3400-5052.

Nightclubs

Pentax Gallery
3-21-20 Nishi-Azabu, Minato-ku.
Map 2 D5.
(03) 3401-2186.

Show Boat 5i
B1 Hilton Tokyo, 6-6-2 Nishi-Shinjuku.
Map 1 A1.
(03) 3344-5111.

Sumo

Dewanoumi Beya
2-3-15 Ryogoku.
Map 4 E5.
(03) 3631-0090.

Iztsu Beya
2-2-7 Ryogoku.
Map 4 E5.
(03) 3633-8920.

Kasugano Beya
1-7-11 Ryogoku.
Map 4 E5.
(03) 3631-1871.

National Sumo Stadium
1-3-28 Yokoami.
Map 4 E4.
(03) 3623-5111.

Baseball and Soccer

Jingu Stadium
13 Kasumigaoka.
Map 2 D4.
(03) 3404-8999.

National Stadium
10 Kasumigaoka-machi.
Map 1 C3.
(03) 3403-1151.

Tokyo Dome
1-3-61 Koraku.
Map 3 A3.
(03) 5800-9999.

Tokyo Dome Service Counter
Sogo Dept Store, 1-11-1 Yurakucho.
Map 5 B2.
(03) 3213-4330.

Tokyo Street Finder

Tokyo is notoriously hard for visitors to find their way around, due to the scarcity of street names and complex numbering system for buildings *(see pp376–7)*. The Tokyo sights covered in this guide, plus Tokyo hotels *(see pp292–4)*, restaurants *(see pp324–7)*, and many of the city's key landmarks are plotted on the maps on the following pages. Transportation points are also marked, and indicated by the symbols listed in the key below. When map references are given, the first number tells you which Street Finder map to turn to, and the letter and number that follow refer to the grid reference on that map. The map below shows the area of Tokyo covered by the six Street Finder maps. The Street Finder index opposite lists street names, buildings, and stations. For a map of the Tokyo subway, see the Back Endpaper.

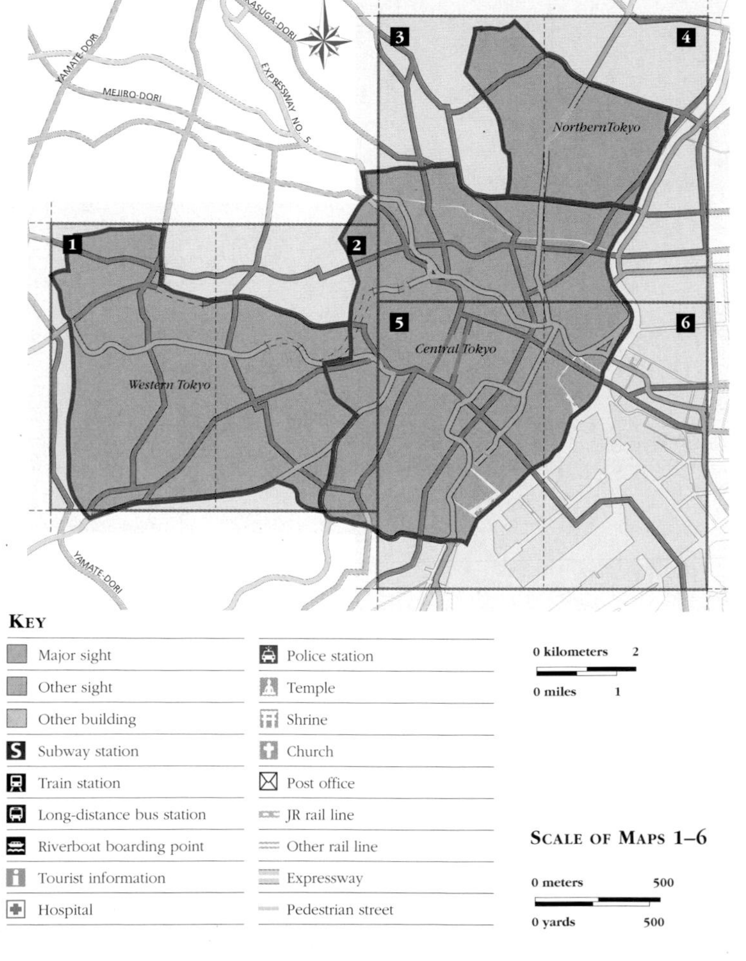

Key

Major sight	Police station
Other sight	Temple
Other building	Shrine
Subway station	Church
Train station	Post office
Long-distance bus station	JR rail line
Riverboat boarding point	Other rail line
Tourist information	Expressway
Hospital	Pedestrian street

0 kilometers 2

0 miles 1

Scale of Maps 1–6

0 meters 500

0 yards 500

A

Aioi-zaka 4 D4
Akasaka 2 E4
Akasaka Prince Hotel 2 F3
Akasaka Rikyu Restaurant 2 F4
Akasaka Subway Station 2 E4
Akasaka Tokyu Hotel 2 F3
Akasaka-dori 2 E4
Akasaka-Mitsuke Subway Station 2 F3
Akebonobashi Subway Station 2 D1
Akihabara Subway Station 4 D4
Akihabara Train Station 3 C4
Almond 2 E5
Ameyoko 3 C3
Ana Hotel Tokyo 2 F4
Aoyama 1-chome Subway Station 2 D4
Aoyama Cemetery 2 D4
Aoyama-dori 2 D4
Asahi Bank 5 B1
Asahi Breweries 4 F3
Asakura Museum 3 C1
Asakusa 4 E2
Asakusa Bashi Train Station 4 D4
Asakusa Subway Station 4 E3 & 4 F3
Asakusa-dori 4 D3
Asia Center of Japan 2 E4
Awajicho Subway Station 3 E5

B

Bakuro-Yokoyama Subway Station 4 D5
Bakurocho Train Station 4 D5
Bank of Japan 5 C1
Belle Vie Akasaka 2 E3
Benihana Restaurant 5 C1
Bridgestone Museum of Art 5 C2
Bunkamura 1 A5
Bunkamura-dori 1 A5
Bunkyo Ward Office 3 B3

C

Capitol Tokyo Hotel 2 F3
Capsule Hotel Fontaine Akasaka 2 E3
Capsule Hotel Riverside 4 F3
Center Gai 1 A5
Central Post Office 5 B1
Chanko Kawasaki Restaurant 4 E5
Chiyoda Ward Office 3 A5
Chuo Ward Office 5 C3
Chuo-dori 3 C4
continues 3 C5
continues 5 C1 & 5 C2
Chuo-dori, Shinjuku 1 A1

D

Daiichi Keihin 5 A5
Daimaru Department Store 5 C1
Daimon Subway Station 5 A4
Daimyo Clock Museum 3 B2
Diet Building 2 F3
Dogen-zaka 1 A5

E

East Garden of the Imperial Palace 3 A5
continues 5 A1
East Shinjuku 1 B1
Edo-dori 4 D5
Edo-Tokyo Museum 4 E4
Eitai-dori 5 C1
Embassy of Canada 2 E4
Embassy of Ireland 2 F2
Embassy of the UK 2 F2
Embassy of the United States 2 F4
Etchujima Train Station 6 E3
Expressway Loop Line 5 A5
Expressway No.1 3 C5
continues 5 B5
Expressway No.3 1 C5
continues 2 E5
Expressway No.4 1 B3
continues 2 F3
Expressway No.5 3 A4
Expressway No.6 4 E4
continues 4 F3
Expressway No.7 4 F5
Expressway No.9 5 C1
continues 6 E2 & 6 F3

F

Fairmont Hotel 3 A5
Fook Lammoon Restaurant 5 B3
Fureia-dori 1 A2
Futaba Restaurant 3 C3

G

Gaien-Higashi-dori 2 D1
Gaien-Nishi-dori 1 C4
Gaienmae Subway Station 2 D4
Gijido-dori 1 A2
Ginza 5 B3
Ginza Dai-Ichi Hotel 5 B3
Ginza Nikko Hotel 5 B3
Ginza Subway Station 5 B2
Ginza-Itchome Subway Station 5 C2

H

Hakusan Subway Station 3 A1
Hakusan-dori 3 A1
Hama Detached Palace Garden 5 B4
Hamacho Subway Station 4 E5
Hamamatsucho Train Station 5 B4
Hanae Mori Building 1 C4
Hanatsubaki-dori 5 B3
Hanzomon Subway Station 2 F2
Harajuku Train Station 1 B4
Harumi 6 D5
Harumi Futo Park 5 C5
Harumi-dori 5 B3
Hatchobori Subway Station 6 D2
Hatchobori Train Station 6 D2
Heisei-dori 5 C3
Hibiya 5 B2
Hibiya Chanter 5 B2
Hibiya Park 5 A2
Hibiya Subway Station 5 B2
Hibiya-dori 5 A5
Hie Shrine 2 F3
Higashi-dori 1 A2
Higashi-Ginza Subway Station 5 C3
Higashi-Nihonbashi Subway Station 4 D5
Hill-Top Hotel 3 B4
Hilton Tokyo 1 A1
Hinode Train Station 5 B5
Hishinuma Restaurant 5 A5
Hitotsugi-dori 2 E3
Hon-Komagome Subway Station 3 A1
Hongo 3 B3
Hongo 3-chome Subway Station 3 B3
Hongo-dori 3 A1
Honjo-Azumabashi Subway Station 4 F3
Horai-ya Restaurant 3 C3
Hotel Inter-Continental Tokyo Bay 5 B5
Hotel Kokusai Kanko 5 C1
Hotel New Otani 2 E3
Hotel Okura 2 F4
Hotel Okura Annex 2 F4
Hotel Parkside 3 C3
Hotel Yaesu-Ryumeikan 5 C1

I

IBM Japan 2 F5
Ichigaya Subway Station 2 E1
Ichigaya Train Station 2 E1
Icho-Namiki 2 D3
Iidabashi Subway Station 3 A4
Imperial Hotel 5 B2
Imperial Palace 5 A1
Imperial Palace Plaza 5 B1
Imperial Theater 5 B2
Inari-zaka 2 E4
Inaricho Subway Station 4 D3
Inokashira-dori 1 A4
Iriya Subway Station 4 D2
Iwamotocho Subway Station 4 D5

J

Japan Traditional Crafts Center 1 C4
Jiji Press 5 A2
Jinbocho 3 A4
Jinbocho Subway Station 3 B4
Jingu Stadium 2 D4
Jingumae 1 C4
John Kanaya Azabu Restaurant 2 E5

K

Kabuki-za Theater 5 C3
Kabukicho 1 B1
Kachidoki 5 C4
Kaede-dori 3 B4
Kaigan-dori 5 B5
Kaiseki Tsuijitome Restaurant 2 E3
Kaitenzushi Tsukiji Honten Restaurant 1 B5
Kajibashi-dori 6 D2
Kaminarimon-dori 4 E3
Kamiyacho Subway Station 2 F5
Kanda 3 B4
Kanda Myojin Shrine 3 C4
Kanda River 1 A1
Kanda Subway Station 3 C5
Kanda Train Station 3 C5
Kanda Yabu Soba Restaurant 3 C4
Kanetanaka An Restaurant 5 B3
Kappabashi-dori 4 E3
Kasuga Subway Station 3 A3
Kasuga-dori 3 A3
Kasumigaseki 5 A3
Kasumigaseki Subway Station 5 A2

Katsutaro Ryokan **3 C2**
Kayabacho Subway Station **6 D1**
Keio Hospital **2 D2**
Keisei-Ueno Train Station **3 C3**
Keiyo-dori **4 F5**
Ketel Restaurant **5 B3**
Kikukawa **6 F1**
Kikukawa Subway Station **4 F5**
Kikuya Ryokan **4 E2**
Kita-dori **1 A1**
Kitanomaru Park **3 A5**
Kiyo Sumi Gardens **6 E1**
Kiyosubashi-dori **4 D5**
continues **6 E1**
Kiyosumi-dori **4 F3**
continues **4 F4**
continues **6 F1** & **6 D4**
Kodenmacho Subway Station **4 D5**
Koen-dori **1 A1**
Koishikawa Botanical Garden **3 A2**
Koishikawa Korakuen Garden **3 A3**
Kojimachi Subway Station **2 F2**
Kojunsha-dori **5 B3**
Kokkai-dori **5 A2**
Kokkai-Gijidomae Subway Station **2 F3**
Kokusai-dori **4 E1**
continues **4 E3**
Kokusai-dori, Shinjuku **1 A2**
Koma **1 B1**
Komagata Dojo Restaurant **4 E3**
Komagome Hospital **3 A1**
Konno-zaka **1 B5**
Korakuen Subway Station **3 A3**
Koshu-Kaido **1 A2**
Kototoi-dori **3 B2**
Kotto-dori **1 C5**
Kudan Kaikan **3 A5**
Kudanshita Subway Station **3 A5**
Kuramae Subway Station **4 E4**
Kuramaebashi-dori **3 B4**
Kushinobo Restaurant **1 B1**
Kuyakushi-dori **1 B1**
Kyobashi Subway Station **5 C2**
Kyu-Kaigan-dori **5 A5**
Kyu-Shiba Rikyu Garden **5 B4**
Kyushu Jangara Ramen Restaurant **5 B3**

L

Les Cristallines Restaurant **1 C5**

M

Marunouchi **5 B2**
Marunouchi Hotel **5 B1**
Maruzen **5 C1**
Matsuzakaya Department Store **5 B3**
Medical School Hospital **3 B1**
Meidai-dori **3 B4**
Meiji Seimei **5 B2**
Meiji Shrine **1 B3**
Meiji Treasure House **1 B3**
Meiji-dori **1 B2**
continues **1 B3** & **1 B4**
Meiji-dori **4 F1**
Meiji-Jingumae Subway Station **1 B4**
Minami-Aoyama **1 C5**
Minami-dori **1 A2**
Minami-Shinjuku Train Station **1 B2**
Minato Ward Office **5 A4**
Minowa Subway Station **4 E1**
Misuji-dori **2 E3**
Mita Subway Station **5 A5**
Mitokaido **4 F3**
Mitsui Bussan **5 B1**
Mitsukoshimae Subway Station **5 C1**
Mitsume-dori **4 F4**
Miyagawa Honten Restaurant **5 C3**
Miyamasu-zaka **1 B5**
Momonjiya Restaurant **4 E5**
Monzen Nakacho Subway Station **6 E2**
Morishita Subway Station **6 F1**
Museum of Contemporary Art **1 C4**

N

Nagatacho Subway Station **2 F3**
Naka Okachimachi Subway Station **4 D3**
Nakamise-dori **4 F3**
Nakamura-ya Honten Restaurant **1 B1**
Nakasendo-dori **3 A1**
Namiyoke Inari Shrine **5 C3**
Naruto Restaurant **5 B3**
National Cancer Center **5 C3**
National Children's Castle **1 B5**
National Diet Library **2 F3**
National Museum of Modern Art **3 A5**
National Noh Theater **1 C3**
National Stadium **1 C3**
National Sumo Stadium **4 E4**
National Theater **2 F3**
New Shinbashi **5 B3**
Nezu Subway Station **3 B2**
NHK Broadcasting Station **1 A5**
Nichigu-dori **5 C1**
Nihon TV-dori **2 E2**
Nihon University **3 A4**
Nihonbashi **5 C1**
Nihonbashi Subway Station **5 C1**
Nijubashimae Subway Station **5 B1**
Ningyocho Subway Station **6 D1**
Ningyocho-dori **4 D5**
continues **6 D1**
Nippon Budokan **3 A5**
Nippon Oil **5 A3**
Nippon Press Center **5 A3**
Nippon TV **2 F2**
Nippori Train Station **3 C1**
Nishi-Shinjuku Subway Station **1 A1**
Nisseki-dori **2 D5**
Niwa Restaurant **3 C4**
Nodaiwa Restaurant **2 F5**
Nogi Jinja Shrine **2 E4**
Nogizaka Subway Station **2 D4**

O

Ochanomizu Subway Station **3 B4**
Ochanomizu Train Station **3 B4**
Ogawamachi Subway Station **3 C5**
Ogubashi-dori **3 C1**
Okachimachi Train Station **3 C3**
Olympic Stadiums **1 B4**
Ome-Kaido **1 A1**
Omote-sando **1 B4**
Omotesando Subway Station **1 C5**
Onarimon **5 A4**
Ota Memorial Museum of Art **1 D4**
Otakebashi-dori **4 D1**
Otako Restaurant **5 B2**
Otemachi Subway Station **5 B1**
Otemon **5 B1**

P

Palace Hotel **5 B1**
Park Hyatt Tokyo **1 A2**
Plaza-dori **1 A2**
President Hotel **2 D4**
Prime Minister's Offical Residence **2 F4**

R

Raku-tei Restaurant **2 F4**
Rice Terrace Restaurant **2 D5**
Roppongi **2 E5**
Roppongi Subway Station **2 E5**
Roppongi-dori **1 C5**
Ryogoku **4 E5**
Ryogoku Train Station **4 E5**
Ryokan Shigetsu **4 E3**

S

Sakura Ryokan **4 D2**
Sakura-dori **5 C1**
Sakurabashi-dori **5 C2**
Sakurada-bori **2 F2**
Sakurada-dori **2 F5**
continues **5 A3**
Sakuradamon **5 A2**
Sanai Building **5 B3**
Sangedatsu-mon **5 A4**
Sangubashi Train Station **1 A3**
Sanwa Bank **5 B1**
Sawanoya Ryokan **3 B2**
Science and Technology Museum **3 A5**
Seibu Department Store **1 B5**
Seibu-Shinjuku Train Station **1 B1**
Sendagaya **1 C3**
Sendagaya Train Station **1 C3**
Sendagi **3 B1**
Sendagi Subway Station **3 B1**
Sengoku Subway Station **3 A1**
Senkawa-dori **3 A2**
Senshu University **3 A4**
Senso-ji Temple **4 F2**
Shanpia Hotel Aoyama **1 B5**
Shiba **5 E5**
Shiba Park **5 E4**
Shiba-Koen Subway Station **5 A5**
Shibuya **1 B5**
Shibuya Subway Station **1 B5**
Shibuya Tobu Hotel **1 B5**
Shibuya Tokyu Hotel **1 B5**
Shibuya Train Station **1 B5**
Shibuya Ward Office **1 B5**
Shin-Nihonbashi Train Station **5 C1**

Shin-Ochanomizu Subway Station 3 B4
Shin-Ohashi-dori 4 F5
continues 6 D2
Shinanomachi Train Station 2 D3
Shinbashi 5 A4
Shinbashi Subway Station 5 B3
Shinbashi Train Station 5 B3
Shinichi-Kan Restaurant 1 B1
Shinjuku 1 A1
Shinjuku Central Park 1 A1
Shinjuku Gyoemmae Subway Station 1 C2
Shinjuku Sanchome Subway Station 1 B1
Shinjuku Subway Station 1 B1
Shinjuku Train Station 1 B1
Shinjuku Ward Office 1 B1
Shinjuku Washington Hotel 1 A2
Shinjuku-dori 1 B1
Shinjuku-Gyoen Garden 1 C2
Shinobazu-dori 3 B1
Shinsen Subway Station 1 A5
Shintomicho Subway Station 5 C3
Shitamachi Museum 3 C3
Shokeibashi-dori 3 C4
Shokuan-dori 1 C1
Shoto 1 A5
Showa-dori 5 E2
Shunko-Tei Restaurant 2 F4
Soto-bori 2 F1
Sotobori-dori 2 E3 & 2 F1
continues 3 A4 & 5 A3
Spiral Building 1 C5
St. Lukes Hospital 5 C3
Studio Alta 1 B1
Suehirocho Subway Station 3 C4
Suidobashi Train Station 3 A4
Suigetsu Hotel 3 C2
Suitengumae Subway Station 6 D1
Sumibiyaki Steak Hatlina Restaurant 2 F4
Sumida Park 4 F2
Sumida Ward Office 4 F3
Suntory Hall 2 F4
Suntory Museum of Art 2 E3
Supreme Court 2 F3
Sword Museum 1 A3

T

Taito Ward Office 4 D3
Takaracho Subway Station 5 C2
Takarazuka Theater 5 B2
Takashimaya Dept Store, Nihonbashi 5 C1
Takashimaya Dept Store, Shinjuku 1 B2
Takebashi Subway Station 3 B5
Takeshiba 5 B5
Takeshita-dori 1 B4
Tamachi Train Station 5 A5
Tameike-Sanno Subway Station 2 F4
Tanzo-bori 2 F2
Tawaramachi Subway Station 4 E3
Tayasumon 3 A5
TBS Broadcasting Center 2 E4
Ten-Ichi Restaurant 5 B3
Tenno-ji Temple 3 C1
TEPCO Electric Energy Museum 1 B5
Tobacco and Salt Museum 1 B5
Tobu Asakusa Train Station 4 F3
Tocho-dori 1 A2
Tochomae Subway Station 1 A2
Todaimae Subway Station 3 B2
Togo Shrine 1 B4
Togo-zaka 2 F2
Tokyo Department Store 5 C1
Tokyo Dome 3 A3
Tokyo Gas 5 E5
Tokyo International Forum 5 B2
Tokyo Medical College Hospital 1 A1
Tokyo Metropolitan Government Offices 1 A2
Tokyo Mitsubishi Bank 5 B2
Tokyo National Museum 4 D2
Tokyo Opera City 1 A2
Tokyo Prince Hotel 5 A4
Tokyo Railway Hospital 1 B2
Tokyo Station Hotel 5 B1
Tokyo Stock Exchange 6 D1
Tokyo Subway Station 5 C1
Tokyo Tower 2 F5
Tokyo Train Station 5 C1
Tokyo Women's Medical College Hospital 2 D1
Tokyu Hands 1 B5
Toranomon Aoyagi Restaurant 5 A3
Toranomon Hospital 2 A4
Toranomon Subway Station 5 A3
Toricho Restaurant 2 E5
Torigin Restaurant 5 B2
Toshiba Building 5 B5
Toyokawa Inari Shrine 2 E3
Toyomi-cho 5 C5
Toyosu 6 E5
Toyosu Park 6 E5
Toyosu Subway Station 6 F4
Tsukiji 5 C3
Tsukiji Edogin Restaurant 5 E3
Tsukiji Fish Market 5 C4
Tsukiji Hongan 5 C3
Tsukiji Subway Station 5 C3
Tsukiji Sushi-sei Restaurant 5 C3
Tsukishima 6 D3
Tsukishima Subway Station 6 D3
Tsunahachi Restaurant 1 B1
TV Asahi 2 F4
TV Asahi-dori 2 E5

U

Uchibori-dori 2 F2 & 2 F3
continues 3 A5 & 5 A2
continues 5 B1
Uchisaiwaicho Subway Station 5 A3
Ueno Park 3 C2
Ueno Subway Station 4 D2
Ueno Train Station 4 D2
Ueno Zoo 3 C2
Uenohirokoji Subway Station 3 C3
Uguisudani Train Station 4 D2
Umamichi-dori 4 E1
University of Tokyo 3 B3
Uosei Restaurant 4 E2
Ushigome Chuo-dori 2 E1

W

Waketokuyama Restaurant 2 D5
Wave Building 2 E5
West Shinjuku 1 A1
World Center 5 A4

Y

Yaesu Fujiya Hotel 5 C2
Yaesu-dori 5 C1
Yagen-zaka 2 E4
Yamate-dori 1 A4
Yanagibashi Subway Station 4 E4
Yanaka 3 C1
Yanaka Cemetery 3 C1
Yasukuni Shrine 2 F1
Yasukuni-dori 1 C1
continues 2 E1 & 3 A5
Yoshino-dori 4 F1
Yotsuya 3-chome Subway Station 2 D2
Yotsuya Subway Station 2 E2
Yotsuya Train Station 2 E2
Yoyogi 1 A2
Yoyogi Park 1 A4
Yoyogi Train Station 1 B2
Yoyogi-Hachiman Train Station 1 A4
Yoyogi-Koen Subway Station 1 A4
Yurakucho Train Station 5 B2
Yushima 3 B3
Yushima Subway Station 3 C3
Yushima-zaka 3 B4
Yushukan Museum 2 F1

Z

Zakuro Restaurant 5 B2
Zojo-ji Temple 5 A4

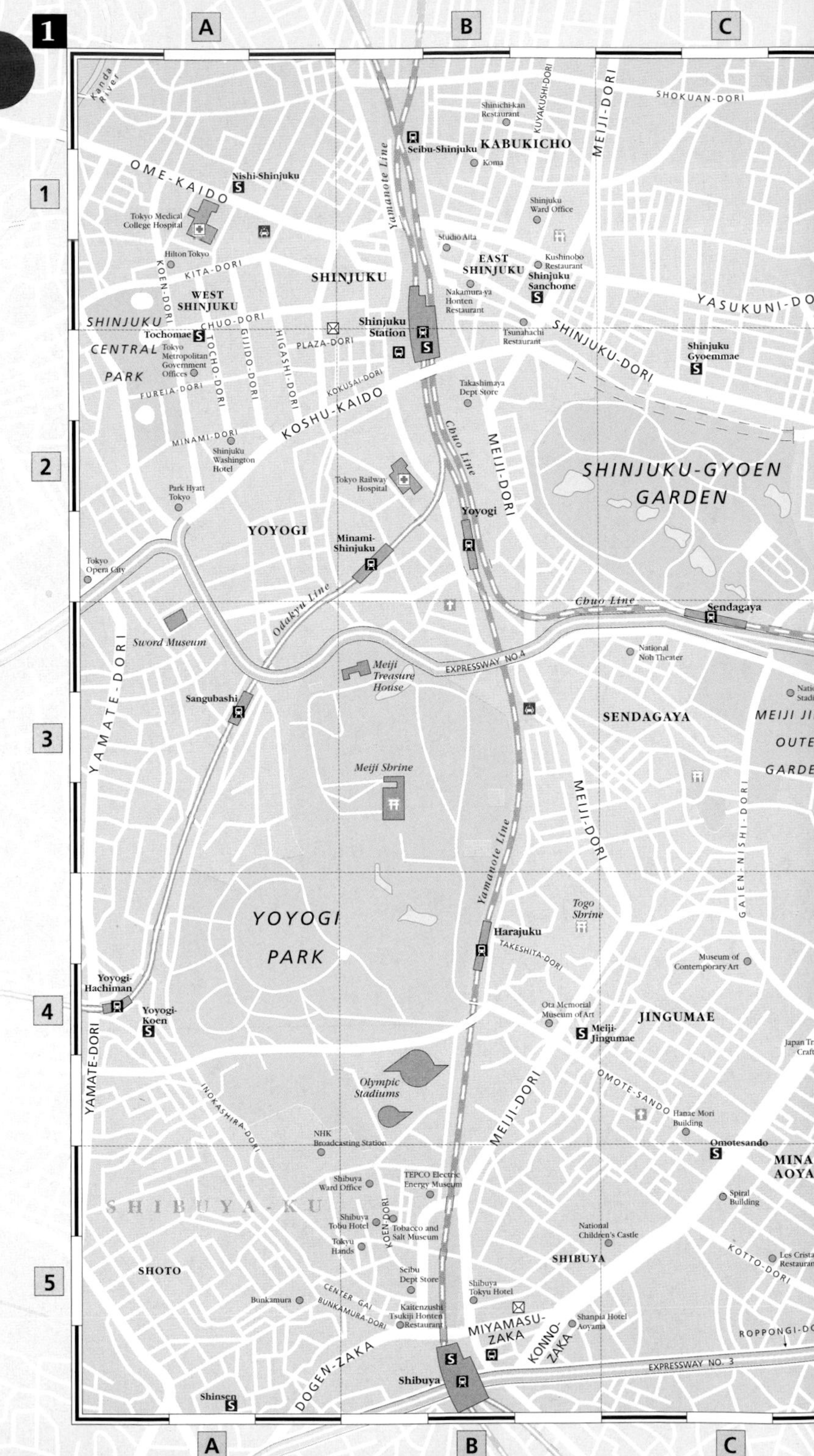
1
A
B
C
1
2
3
4
5
Kanda River
OME-KAIDO
Nishi-Shinjuku
Tokyo Medical College Hospital
Hilton Tokyo
KITA-DORI
KOEN-DORI
WEST SHINJUKU
SHINJUKU CENTRAL PARK
Tochomae
CHUO-DORI
Tokyo Metropolitan Government Offices
TOCHO-DORI
GIJIDO-DORI
HIGASHI-DORI
PLAZA-DORI
FUREIA-DORI
KOKUSAI-DORI
KOSHU-KAIDO
MINAMI-DORI
Shinjuku Washington Hotel
Park Hyatt Tokyo
Tokyo Opera City
SHINJUKU
Shinjuku Station
Yamanote Line
Seibu-Shinjuku
KABUKICHO
Koma
Shinichi-kan Restaurant
KUYAKUSHO-DORI
MEIJI-DORI
SHOKUAN-DORI
Shinjuku Ward Office
Studio Alta
EAST SHINJUKU
Kushinobo Restaurant
Shinjuku Sanchome
Nakamura-ya Honten Restaurant
Tsunahachi Restaurant
SHINJUKU-DORI
YASUKUNI-DO
Shinjuku Gyoemmae
Takashimaya Dept Store
Chuo Line
SHINJUKU-GYOEN GARDEN
Tokyo Railway Hospital
YOYOGI
Minami-Shinjuku
Yoyogi
Odakyu Line
Chuo Line
Sendagaya
Sword Museum
YAMATE-DORI
EXPRESSWAY NO.4
Meiji Treasure House
National Noh Theater
Nation Stadiu
Sangubashi
SENDAGAYA
MEIJI JIN OUTER GARDEN
Meiji Shrine
GAIEN-NISHI-DORI
Togo Shrine
YOYOGI PARK
Harajuku
TAKESHITA-DORI
Museum of Contemporary Art
Yoyogi-Hachiman
Yoyogi-Koen
Ota Memorial Museum of Art
Meiji-Jingumae
JINGUMAE
Japan Trad Crafts
YAMATE-DORI
INOKASHIRA-DORI
Olympic Stadiums
OMOTE-SANDO
Hanae Mori Building
NHK Broadcasting Station
Omotesando
MINAM AOYAM
Shibuya Ward Office
TEPCO Electric Energy Museum
Spiral Building
SHIBUYA-KU
Shibuya Tobu Hotel
KOEN-DORI
Tobacco and Salt Museum
Tokyu Hands
National Children's Castle
SHOTO
SHIBUYA
KOTTO-DORI
Les Cristalli Restaurant
Seibu Dept Store
Shibuya Tokyu Hotel
Bunkamura
CENTER GAI
BUNKAMURA-DORI
Kaitenzushi Tsukiji Honten Restaurant
MIYAMASU-ZAKA
KONNO-ZAKA
Shanpia Hotel Aoyama
ROPPONGI-DOR
DOGEN-ZAKA
EXPRESSWAY NO. 3
Shibuya
Shinsen
A
B
C

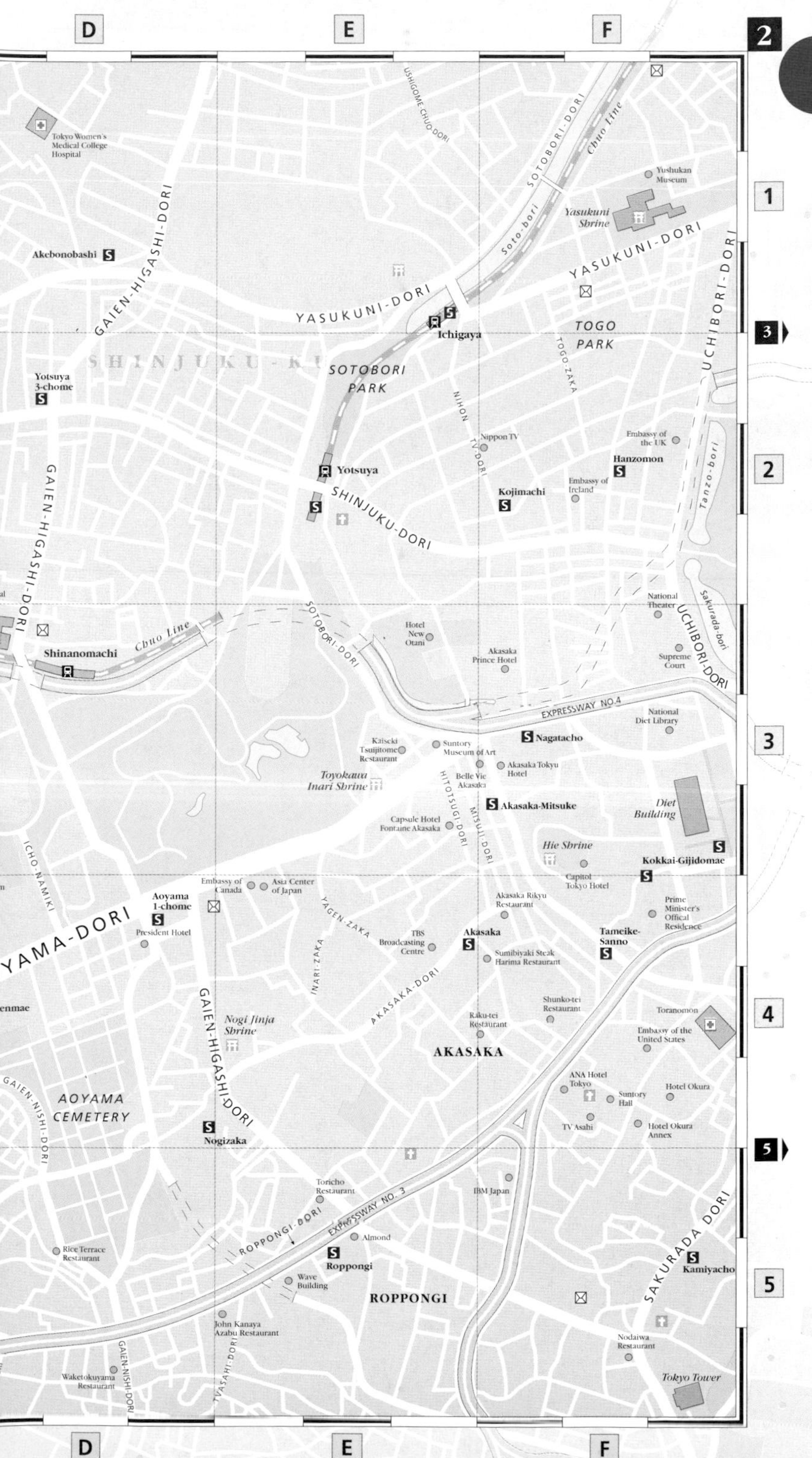

D
E
F
2
1
2
3
4
5
Tokyo Women's Medical College Hospital
GAIEN-HIGASHI-DORI
Akebonobashi
USHIGOME-CHUO-DORI
SOTOBORI-DORI
Chuo Line
Soto-bori
Yushukan Museum
Yasukuni Shrine
YASUKUNI-DORI
UCHIBORI-DORI
YASUKUNI-DORI
Ichigaya
TOGO PARK
TOGO-ZAKA
SHINJUKU-KU
SOTOBORI PARK
Yotsuya 3-chome
NIHON TV-DORI
Nippon TV
Embassy of the UK
Hanzomon
Tanzo-bori
Yotsuya
Kojimachi
Embassy of Ireland
SHINJUKU-DORI
National Theater
Sakurada-bori
UCHIBORI-DORI
Hotel New Otani
SOTOBORI-DORI
Chuo Line
Shinanomachi
Akasaka Prince Hotel
Supreme Court
EXPRESSWAY NO.4
National Diet Library
Kaiseki Tsujitome Restaurant
Suntory Museum of Art
Nagatacho
Akasaka Tokyu Hotel
Belle Vie Akasaka
Toyokawa Inari Shrine
HITOTSUGI-DORI
Akasaka-Mitsuke
Diet Building
Capsule Hotel Fontaine Akasaka
MISUJI-DORI
Hie Shrine
Kokkai-Gijidomae
ICHO-NAMIKI
Embassy of Canada
Asia Center of Japan
Capitol Tokyo Hotel
Aoyama 1-chome
Akasaka Rikyu Restaurant
Prime Minister's Offical Residence
AOYAMA-DORI
President Hotel
YAGEN-ZAKA
TBS Broadcasting Centre
Akasaka
Tameike-Sanno
Sumibiyaki Steak Harima Restaurant
INARI-ZAKA
GAIEN-HIGASHI-DORI
AKASAKA-DORI
Shunko-tei Restaurant
Toranomon
Nogi Jinja Shrine
Raku-tei Restaurant
Embassy of the United States
AKASAKA
GAIEN-NISHI-DORI
AOYAMA CEMETERY
ANA Hotel Tokyo
Suntory Hall
Hotel Okura
TV Asahi
Hotel Okura Annex
Nogizaka
Toricho Restaurant
IBM Japan
EXPRESSWAY NO. 3
ROPPONGI-DORI
Almond
Rice Terrace Restaurant
Roppongi
SAKURADA DORI
Kamiyacho
Wave Building
ROPPONGI
John Kanaya Azabu Restaurant
Nodaiwa Restaurant
Waketokuyama Restaurant
GAIEN-NISHI-DORI
TVASAHI-DORI
Tokyo Tower
D
E
F

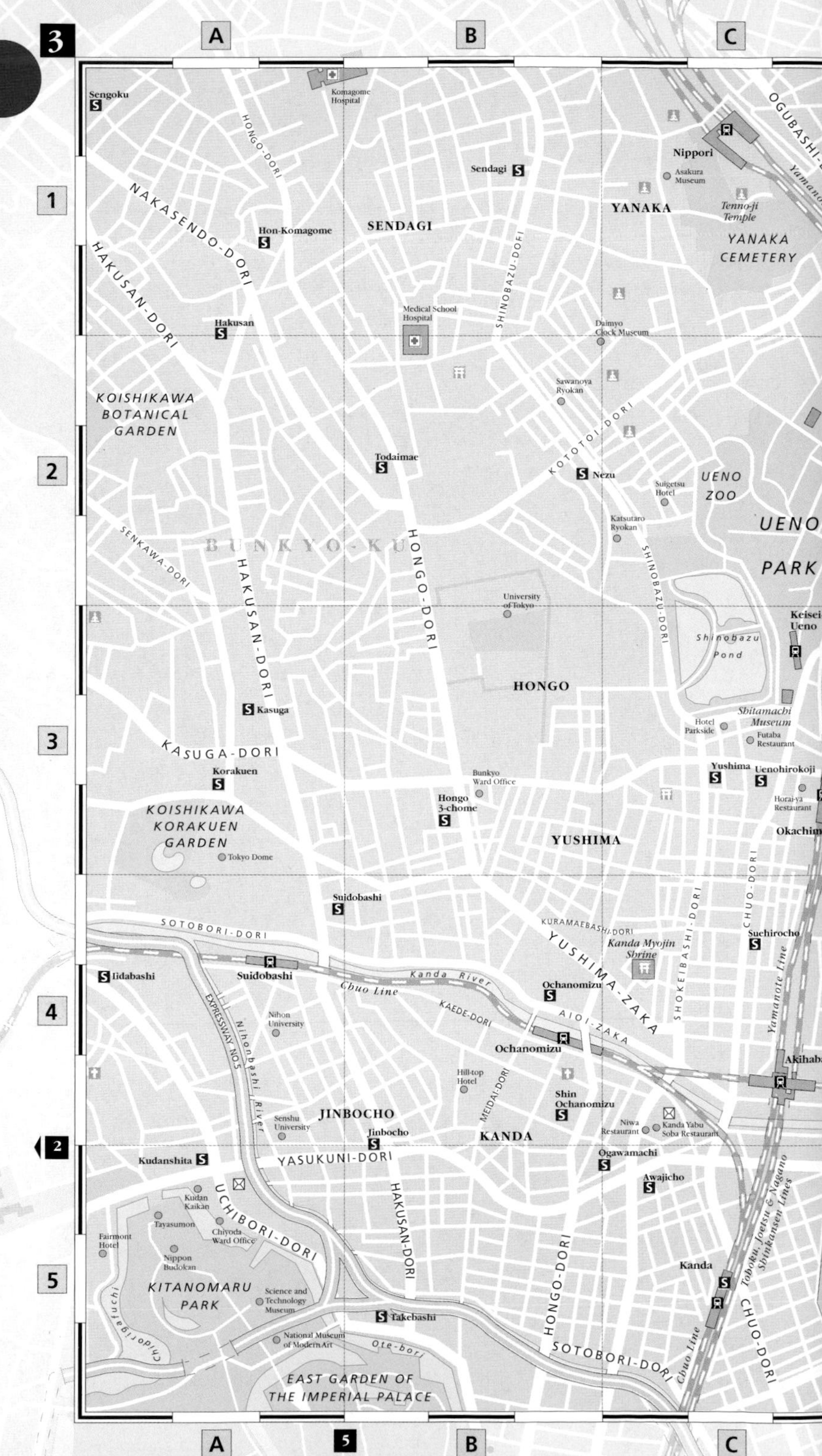

3
A
B
C
1
2
3
4
5
Sengoku
Komagome Hospital
HONGO-DORI
NAKASENDO-DORI
HAKUSAN-DORI
Hon-Komagome
SENDAGI
Sendagi
SHINOBAZU-DORI
Nippori
Asakura Museum
YANAKA
Tenno-ji Temple
YANAKA CEMETERY
OGUBASHI
Hakusan
Medical School Hospital
Daimyo Clock Museum
KOISHIKAWA BOTANICAL GARDEN
Sawanoya Ryokan
KOTOTOI-DORI
Todaimae
Nezu
Suigetsu Hotel
UENO ZOO
UENO PARK
SENKAWA-DORI
BUNKYO-KU
Katsutaro Ryokan
University of Tokyo
Keisei-Ueno
Shinobazu Pond
HONGO
Kasuga
Shitamachi Museum
Hotel Parkside
Futaba Restaurant
KASUGA-DORI
Korakuen
Yushima
Uenohirokoji
Bunkyo Ward Office
Hongo 3-chome
Horai-ya Restaurant
KOISHIKAWA KORAKUEN GARDEN
Okachimachi
Tokyo Dome
YUSHIMA
Suidobashi
CHUO-DORI
SOTOBORI-DORI
KURAMAEBASHI-DORI
Kanda Myojin Shrine
SHOKEIBASHI-DORI
Suehirocho
Iidabashi
Kanda River
Chuo Line
YUSHIMA-ZAKA
Ochanomizu
Yamanote Line
EXPRESSWAY NO.5
Nihonbashi River
Nihon University
KAEDE-DORI
AIOI-ZAKA
Akihabara
Hill-top Hotel
MEIDAI-DORI
Shin Ochanomizu
JINBOCHO
Senshu University
Jinbocho
KANDA
Niwa Restaurant
Kanda Yabu Soba Restaurant
2
Kudanshita
YASUKUNI-DORI
Ogawamachi
Awajicho
Kudan Kaikan
UCHIBORI-DORI
Tayasumon
Chiyoda Ward Office
HAKUSAN-DORI
Tohoku, Joetsu & Nagano Shinkansen Lines
Fairmont Hotel
Nippon Budokan
HONGO-DORI
Kanda
KITANOMARU PARK
Science and Technology Museum
Takebashi
CHUO-DORI
Chidorigafuchi
National Museum of Modern Art
Ote-bori
SOTOBORI-DORI
Chuo Line
EAST GARDEN OF THE IMPERIAL PALACE
5

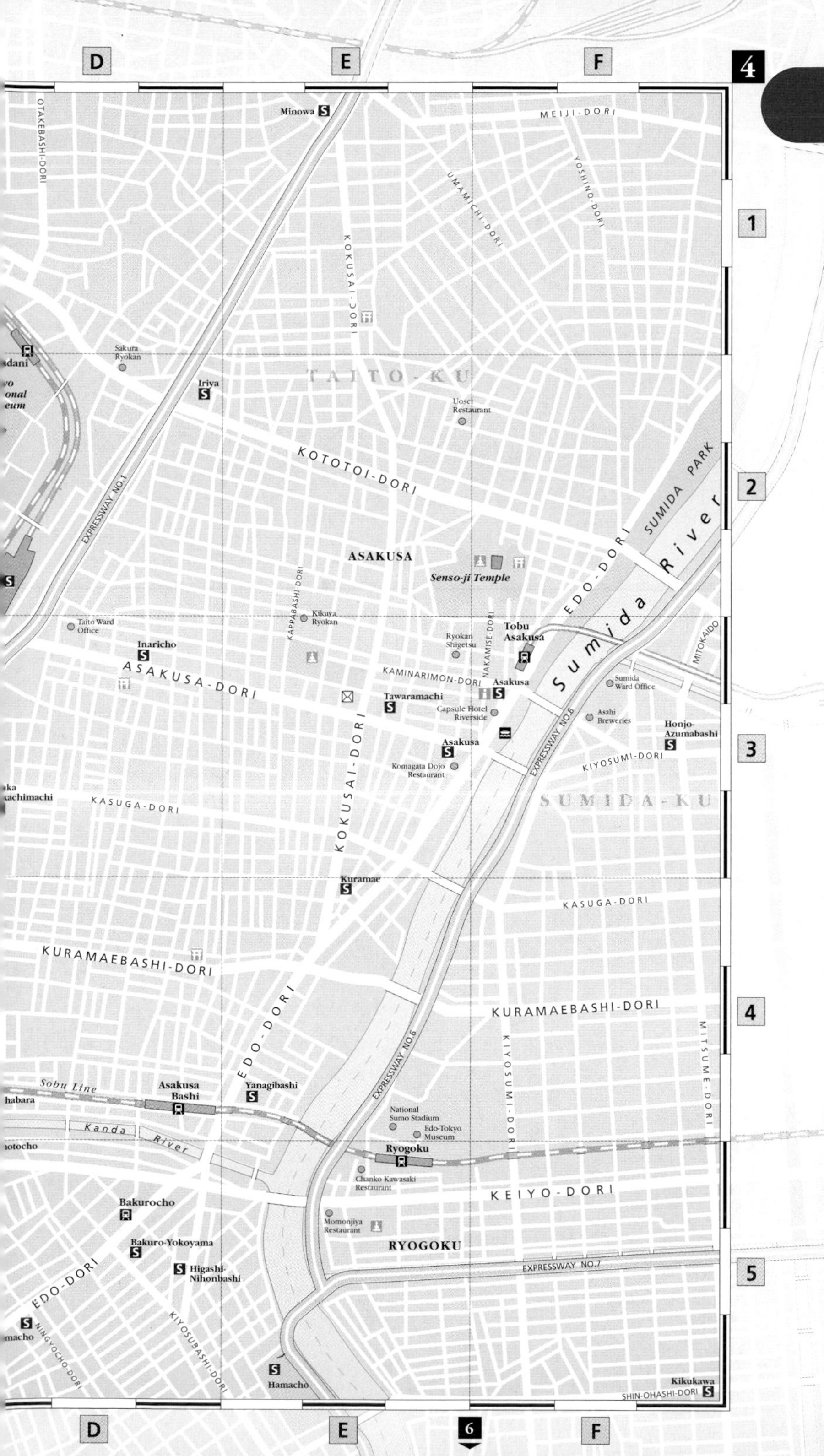

D
E
F
4
Minowa
MEIJI-DORI
OTAKEBASHI-DORI
UMAMICHI-DORI
YOSHINO-DORI
KOKUSAI-DORI
1
Sakura Ryokan
Iriya
TAITO-KU
Uosei Restaurant
KOTOTOI-DORI
SUMIDA PARK
EXPRESSWAY NO.1
2
ASAKUSA
Senso-ji Temple
EDO-DORI
Sumida River
KAPPABASHI-DORI
Kikuya Ryokan
Taito Ward Office
Inaricho
NAKAMISE-DORI
Tobu Asakusa
Ryokan Shigetsu
MITOKAIDO
ASAKUSA-DORI
KAMINARIMON-DORI
Asakusa
Sumida Ward Office
Tawaramachi
Capsule Hotel Riverside
Asahi Breweries
Honjo-Azumabashi
EXPRESSWAY NO.6
Asakusa
3
Komagata Dojo Restaurant
KIYOSUMI-DORI
SUMIDA-KU
KASUGA-DORI
KOKUSAI-DORI
Kuramae
KASUGA-DORI
KURAMAEBASHI-DORI
EDO-DORI
KURAMAEBASHI-DORI
4
KIYOSUMI-DORI
MITSUME-DORI
Sobu Line
Asakusa Bashi
Yanagibashi
EXPRESSWAY NO.6
National Sumo Stadium
Kanda River
Edo-Tokyo Museum
Ryogoku
Chanko Kawasaki Restaurant
KEIYO-DORI
Bakurocho
Momonjiya Restaurant
RYOGOKU
Bakuro-Yokoyama
Higashi-Nihonbashi
EXPRESSWAY NO.7
5
EDO-DORI
NINGYOCHO-DORI
KIYOSUBASHI-DORI
Hamacho
Kikukawa
SHIN-OHASHI-DORI
D
E
6
F

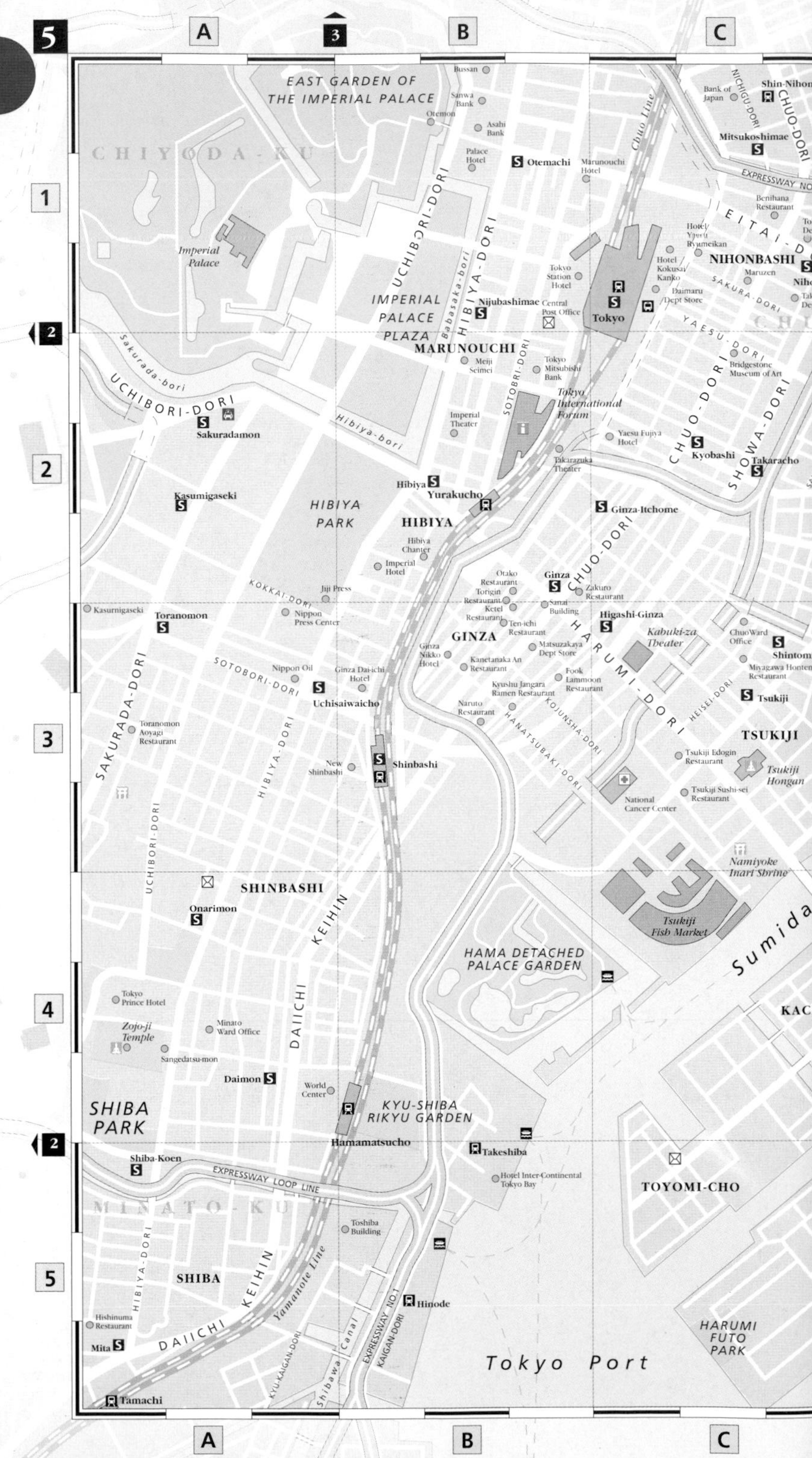
5
A
B
C
3
1
2
3
4
5
2
2
EAST GARDEN OF THE IMPERIAL PALACE
CHIYODA-KU
Imperial Palace
IMPERIAL PALACE PLAZA
MARUNOUCHI
Otemachi
Tokyo
Nijubashimae
Sakuradamon
Kasumigaseki
HIBIYA PARK
HIBIYA
Hibiya
Yurakucho
Tokyo International Forum
Kyobashi
Takaracho
Ginza-Itchome
Ginza
Higashi-Ginza
GINZA
Kabuki-za Theater
Shintomicho
Tsukiji
TSUKIJI
Tsukiji Hongan
NIHONBASHI
Mitsukoshimae
Shin-Nihonbashi
Toranomon
Uchisaiwaicho
Shinbashi
SHINBASHI
Onarimon
Daimon
Zojo-ji Temple
SHIBA PARK
Shiba-Koen
KYU-SHIBA RIKYU GARDEN
Hamamatsucho
Takeshiba
HAMA DETACHED PALACE GARDEN
Tsukiji Fish Market
Namiyoke Inari Shrine
National Cancer Center
Sumida
TOYOMI-CHO
MINATO-KU
SHIBA
Hinode
Mita
Tamachi
Tokyo Port
HARUMI FUTO PARK
UCHIBORI-DORI
HIBIYA-DORI
SOTOBORI-DORI
CHUO-DORI
HARUMI-DORI
SAKURADA-DORI
DAIICHI KEIHIN
EXPRESSWAY LOOP LINE
Chuo Line
Yamanote Line
KAIGAN-DORI
EXPRESSWAY NO.1
Shibaura Canal
EITAI-DORI
YAESU-DORI
SHOWA-DORI
SAKURA-DORI
Sakurada-bori
Hibiya-bori
Babasaka-bori
KOKKAI-DORI
HANATSUBAKI-DORI
KOJUNSHA-DORI
HEISEI-DORI
NICHIGIN-DORI
KYU-KAIGAN-DORI
Bussan
Sanwa Bank
Otemon
Asahi Bank
Palace Hotel
Marunouchi Hotel
Bank of Japan
Benihana Restaurant
Hotel Yaesu Ryumeikan
Hotel Kokusai Kanko
Maruzen
Daimaru Dept Store
Tokyo Station Hotel
Central Post Office
Meiji Seimei
Tokyo Mitsubishi Bank
Bridgestone Museum of Art
Imperial Theater
Yaesu Fujiya Hotel
Takarazuka Theater
Hibiya Chanter
Imperial Hotel
Jiji Press
Nippon Press Center
Otako Restaurant
Torigin Restaurant
Ketel Restaurant
Sanai Building
Zakuro Restaurant
Ten-ichi Restaurant
Ginza Nikko Hotel
Matsuzakaya Dept Store
Kanetanaka An Restaurant
Fook Lammoon Restaurant
Kyushu Jangara Ramen Restaurant
Naruto Restaurant
Chuo Ward Office
Miyagawa Honten Restaurant
Tsukiji Edogin Restaurant
Tsukiji Sushi-sei Restaurant
Kasumigaseki
Nippon Oil
Ginza Dai-ichi Hotel
Toranomon Aoyagi Restaurant
New Shinbashi
Tokyo Prince Hotel
Minato Ward Office
Sangedatsu-mon
World Trade Center
Hotel Inter-Continental Tokyo Bay
Toshiba Building
Hishinuma Restaurant

D
E
4
F
6
1
2
3
4
5
Ningyocho
NINGYOCHO-DORI
KIYOSUBASHI-DORI
SHIN-OHASHI-DORI
Suitengumae
Tokyo Stock Exchange
Kayabacho
Nihonbashi River
Sumida River
Morishita
Kikukawa
KIYOSUMI-DORI
Konagi River
KIYOSUBASHI-DORI
KIYO SUMI GARDENS
KOTO-KU
EXPRESSWAY NO.9
KASAIDASHI-DORI
KAJIBASHI-DORI
atchobori
EITAI-DORI
Monzen Nakacho
Hakusan
Etchujima
Tsukishima
TSUKISHIMA
Harumi Canal
KIYOSUMI-DORI
Asashio Canal
Toyosu Canal
HARUMI-DORI
Toyosu
TOYOSU PARK
TOYOSU
HARUMI
Harumi Canal
Shinonome Canal
SHINONOME
Tokyo Gas

Japan Region by Region

Japan at a Glance 120-121
Central Honshu 122-147
Kyoto City 148-179
Western Honshu 180-213
Shikoku 214-223
Kyushu 224-243
Okinawa 244-253
Northern Honshu 254-273
Hokkaido 274-285

Japan at a Glance

HONSHU, JAPAN'S LARGEST ISLAND, is characterized by its mountainous center and densely populated southern coastline. Most of Japan's ancient temples, shrines, and imperial cities are on Honshu, along with the vibrant capital, Tokyo. North of Honshu lies the island of Hokkaido, an unspoiled wilderness of national parks, snowbound for much of the year. The quiet, traditional island of Shikoku lies south of Honshu, as does Kyushu island, a varied mixture of modern cities, hot springs, and archaeological ruins. A string of subtropical islands with Okinawa at the center stretches away to the southwest.

The Inland Sea, separating Honshu and Shikoku islands

OKINAWA ARCHIPELAGO

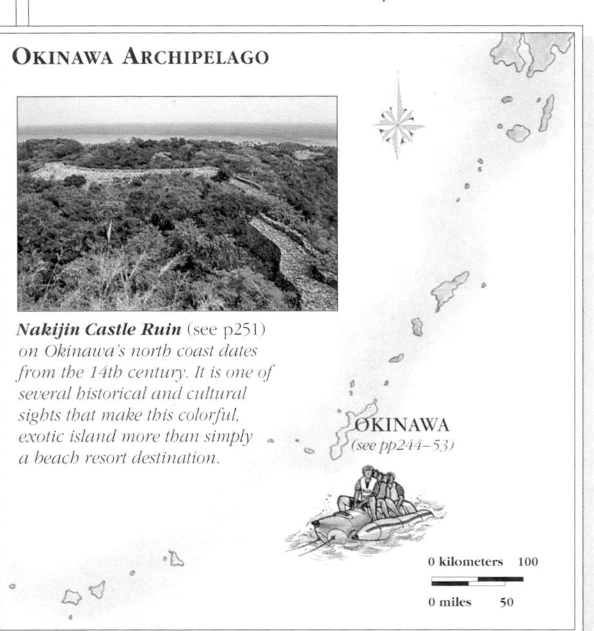

Nakijin Castle Ruin (see p251) *on Okinawa's north coast dates from the 14th century. It is one of several historical and cultural sights that make this colorful, exotic island more than simply a beach resort destination.*

Konomine-ji *is Temple 27 on Shikoku's 88-temple pilgrimage* (see pp222–3). *The thousands of pilgrims who travel the route every year are following in the footsteps of Kukai, the 9th-century founder of Shingon-sect Buddhism.*

Miyajima island's vermilion *torii* (gate) is one of Japan's most famous sights.

The Peace Park *in Nagasaki* (see pp234–7) *was the point of impact of the second atomic bomb, for which the city is now known worldwide. A cosmopolitan port for centuries, it has regenerated since the war to become a thriving urban center.*

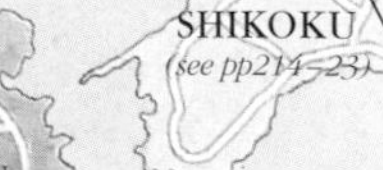

◁ **Konpon Dai-to pagoda at Mount Koya, Western Honshu**

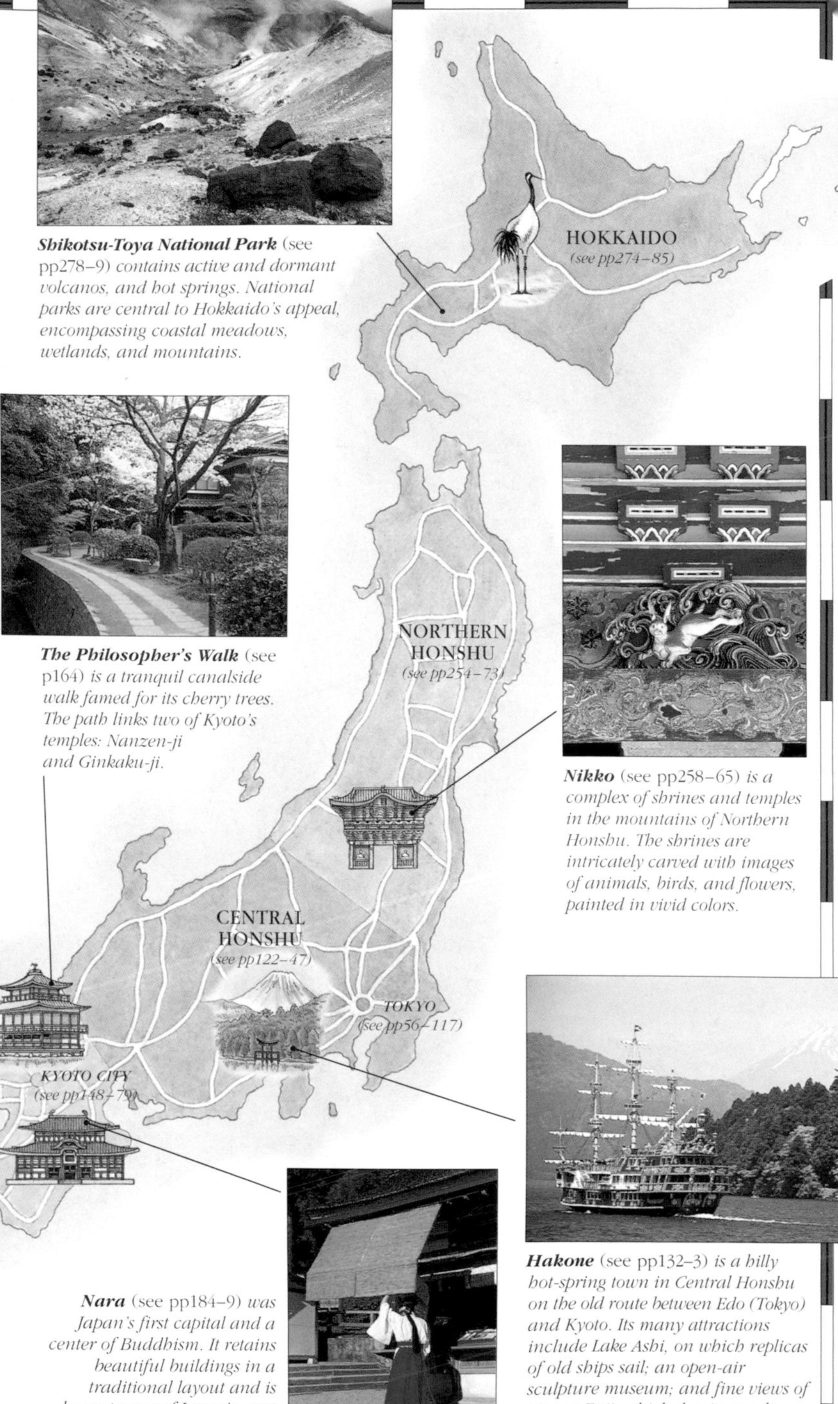

Shikotsu-Toya National Park (see pp278–9) *contains active and dormant volcanos, and hot springs. National parks are central to Hokkaido's appeal, encompassing coastal meadows, wetlands, and mountains.*

The Philosopher's Walk (see p164) *is a tranquil canalside walk famed for its cherry trees. The path links two of Kyoto's temples: Nanzen-ji and Ginkaku-ji.*

Nikko (see pp258–65) *is a complex of shrines and temples in the mountains of Northern Honshu. The shrines are intricately carved with images of animals, birds, and flowers, painted in vivid colors.*

Nara (see pp184–9) *was Japan's first capital and a center of Buddhism. It retains beautiful buildings in a traditional layout and is home to one of Japan's most spectacular festivals, Omizu-tori* (see p38), *each spring.*

Hakone (see pp132–3) *is a hilly hot-spring town in Central Honshu on the old route between Edo (Tokyo) and Kyoto. Its many attractions include Lake Ashi, on which replicas of old ships sail; an open-air sculpture museum; and fine views of Mount Fuji, which dominates the plain to the west of Tokyo.*

山妙法寺
献燈

CENTRAL HONSHU

LYING BETWEEN TOKYO AND KYOTO, *Central Honshu epitomizes the contrasts of Japan today. Its densely populated coastal belt includes the country's second- and fourth-largest cities, while the interior contains its highest, wildest mountains. Between these extremes, much of the region is relatively accessible, yet remote enough to have kept traditional rural lifestyles, architecture, and festivals.*

The mountains of Central Honshu incorporate not only Mount Fuji but also the North and South Japan Alps, with many peaks over 3,000 m (10,000 ft). They dictate the area's character, and offer hiking, skiing, and hot springs. During the Edo period (1603–1868) five post roads crossed the region, linking Edo (Tokyo) and Kyoto. Feudal lords were required to spend half their time in Edo, so long processions traveled the roads, and checkpoints and post towns grew up. Most heavily used were the Tokaido ("East Sea Way") via Yokohama, Hakone, and Shizuoka, and the Nakasendo ("Central Mountain Way") through the Kiso Valley. Remnants of both can be walked.

Postman from Tsumago in the Kiso Valley

Today there is a dramatic contrast between the modern, urban Pacific coast, including Yokohama and Nagoya, and underpopulated rural areas. Among the latter, the post towns of Kiso and thatched villages of Shokawa have found new life in tourism thanks to unspoiled architecture, while Takayama and Chichibu attract thousands to their festivals. The former regional capitals of Kamakura and Kanazawa maintain tradition in gardens, temples, culture, and crafts. Heavily forested, the region produces skilled woodwork: lacquerware in Takayama, Noto, and Kiso; carving in Kamakura; *yosegi-zaiku* in Hakone. Until the 1970s, silkworms were raised in Shokawa and Chichibu; silk was exported via Yokohama and is still dyed in Kanazawa. Central Honshu cuisine focuses on seafood coastally, while mountain fare comprises river fish, *sansai* (young ferns), tofu, and miso. Kanazawa's refined yet down-to-earth *Kaga ryori* uses fish and duck; Nagoya is known for eel, chicken, and stronger flavors.

The waterfront at Yokohama, Japan's second-largest city

◁ **The snow-capped cone of Mount Fuji dominating the landscape**

Exploring Central Honshu

THE SMOOTH CONE OF MOUNT FUJI – one of the great icons of Japan – rises from the Kanto Plain to the west of Tokyo, and is open to pilgrims and casual hikers in summer. Beyond this is the largely mountainous area known to the Japanese as Chubu. A cluster of cultural and scenic destinations, including Fuji, Hakone, Kamakura, and much of the industrialized Pacific coast, are an easy day-trip from Tokyo. Other areas, especially the more rural regions such as the Kiso and Shokawa valleys and the Noto peninsula, are harder to reach and require more time to explore.

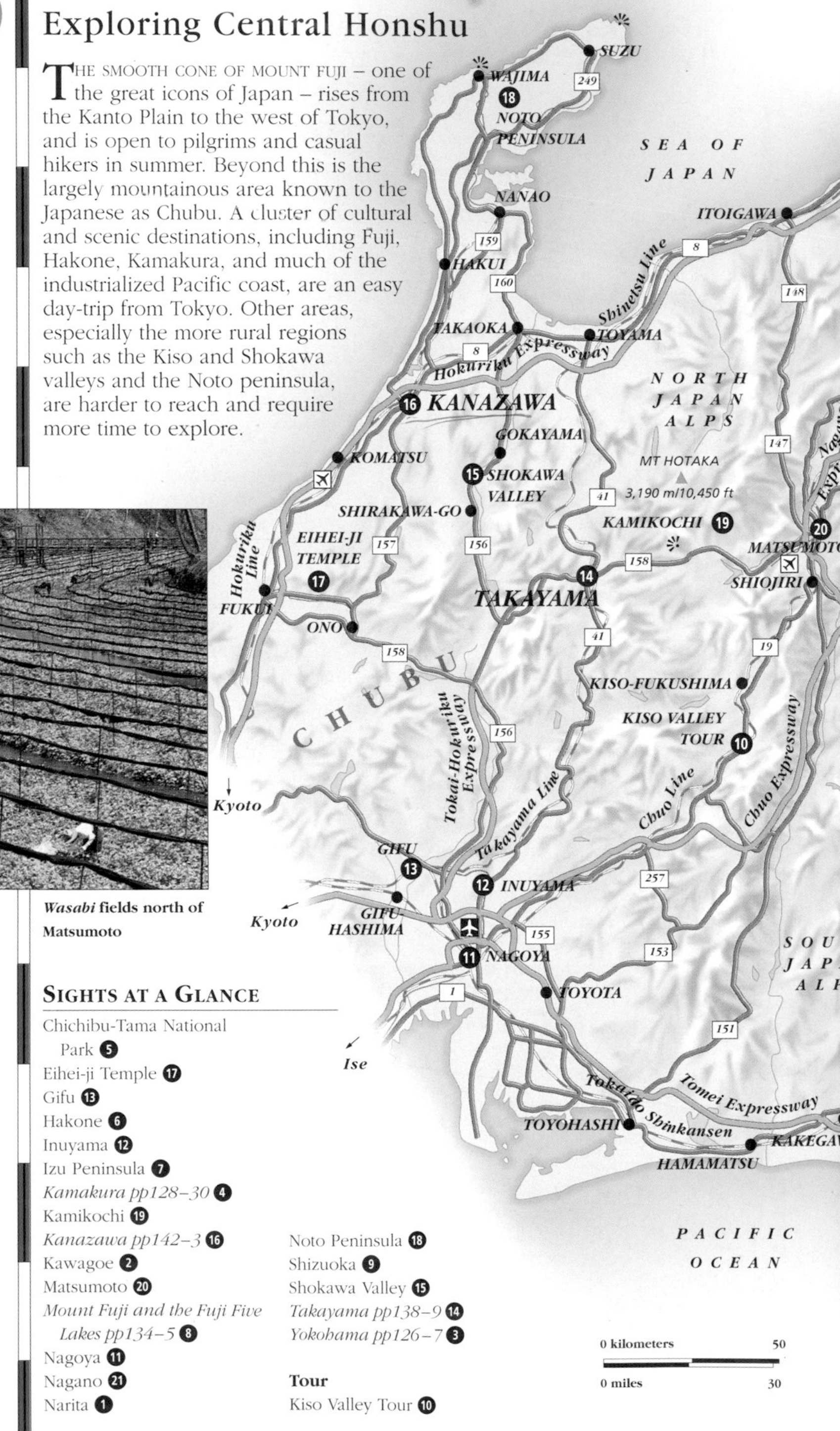

***Wasabi* fields north of Matsumoto**

Sights at a Glance

Chichibu-Tama National Park 5
Eihei-ji Temple 17
Gifu 13
Hakone 6
Inuyama 12
Izu Peninsula 7
Kamakura pp128–30 4
Kamikochi 19
Kanazawa pp142–3 16
Kawagoe 2
Matsumoto 20
Mount Fuji and the Fuji Five Lakes pp134–5 8
Nagoya 11
Nagano 21
Narita 1
Noto Peninsula 18
Shizuoka 9
Shokawa Valley 15
Takayama pp138–9 14
Yokohama pp126–7 3

Tour

Kiso Valley Tour 10

Jizo statues at Hase-dera Temple, Kamakura

Locator Map

See Also

- *Where to Stay* pp295–7
- *Where to Eat* pp327–30

Key

- International airport
- Domestic airport
- Expressway
- Major road
- JR train line
- Private train line
- Viewpoint

Getting Around

Much of Central Honshu is accessible by train. The fast Tokaido Shinkansen runs from Tokyo to Nagoya and on to Western Honshu. Another *shinkansen* line runs from Tokyo to Nagano. The main Chuo line runs to Matsumoto. Nagoya is a major transportation hub, but Kanazawa and Eihei-ji are easier to get to from Kyoto than Nagoya. Visitors will need to take a bus or rent a car for some coastal areas, including parts of the Noto and Izu peninsulas.

Narita ❶

成田

Chiba prefecture. 92,000. in front of JR stn (0476) 24-3198. www.city.narita.chiba.jp/english *Setsubun (Feb 3).*

A QUIET LITTLE town, worlds removed from nearby Narita Airport, Narita's main attraction is **Narita-san Shinsho-ji**, an Esoteric-Shingon-sect temple founded in 940 and dedicated to Fudo Myo-o, Deity of Immovable Wisdom. Several times daily, the priests burn wooden sticks to symbolize extinguishing of earthly passions. The streets are full of traditional shops for the 12 million temple visitors a year.

ENVIRONS: Near Narita are over 1,000 ancient burial mounds (*kofun*); the best are in **Boso Historical Park**. The **National Museum of Japanese History** offers a good survey of Japan.

Boso Historical Park
15 mins by taxi from Narita stn.
(0476) 95-3126. Tue–Sun.

National Museum of Japanese History
15 mins walk from Sakura stn.
(043) 486-0123. Tue–Sun.

Kawagoe ❷

川越

Saitama prefecture. 323,000. at JR stn (0492) 46-2027. www.city.kawagoe.saitama.jp *Ashi-odori (Leg-dancing, Apr 14), Kawagoe Festival (3rd weekend in Oct).*

NICKNAMED "Little Edo," Kawagoe preserves the atmosphere of 19th-century Edo (Tokyo) in its *kura*

A row of *kura* buildings in Kawagoe

Yokohama Bay Bridge

buildings. *Kura* structure, with thick clay walls, double doors, and heavy shutters, was first used for warehouses, but after a fire in 1893 left only *kura* standing, it was adopted for houses and shops. The roof finials have a cloud design, the idea being that rain protects against fire.

Of over 200 *kura*, about 30 remain; these are a 15-minute walk north of Hon-Kawagoe station. The **Kura-Zukuri Shiryokan**, formerly a *kura* tobacconist, is a museum. Nearby, **Toki-no-kane** wooden bell tower was built in 1624 to tell the time and warn of fires; it was rebuilt after the 1893 fire. Opposite, **Kashiya Yokocho** is lined with shops selling old-fashioned candies.

East of the *kura* streets is **Kita-in**, a Tendai-sect temple which includes the only extant rooms from Edo Castle, donated by the shogun Iemitsu in 1638. It also has characterful *go-hyaku* (500) *rakan*, sculptures of temple benefactors, carved in 1782–1825 to cheer people in a time of hardship.

Kura-Zukuri Shiryokan
(0492) 25-4287.
Tue–Sun.

Yokohama ❸

横浜

Kanagawa prefecture. 3,310,000. *Sanbo Center Bldg (045) 641-4759.* www.city.yokohama.jp/front/welcomeE.html *Chinese New Year (Feb), Yokohama Port Festival (May 3).*

JAPAN'S SECOND-LARGEST city, Yokohama has been a center for shipping, trade, foreign contact, and modern ideas since the mid-19th century. Formerly a small fishing village on the Tokaido road, it was made a treaty port in 1859; there followed an influx of foreign traders, especially Chinese and British, making it the biggest port in Asia by the early 1900s. The 1923 Kanto Earthquake wiped out 95 percent of the city, killing 40,000 people, then World War II bombing again destroyed half the city. After the war, Yokohama became a base for US soldiers. By the 1970s, it was once more Japan's largest port. The heart of the city is compact and walkable.

Minato Mirai 21, an area of redeveloped docks, has some creative architecture (with hi-tech earthquake-proofing) and on weekends comes alive with street performers. Its focal point is the **Landmark Tower**, built in 1993 under US architect Hugh Stubbins and, at 269 m (880 ft), Japan's tallest building. Reached by the world's fastest elevator (at 750 m (2,500 ft) per minute), the 69th-floor public lounge has a spectacular 360-degree view. To the north, Tange

Kenzo's **Yokohama Museum of Art** houses displays of modern art and photography.

In the older, more attractive part of town, the **NYK Maritime Museum** covers the history of shipping, with detailed models. Created on rubble from the 1923 Earthquake, **Yamashita Park** is a pleasant promenade overlooking ships, including the moored liner **Hikawa Maru**, which cruised between Yokohama and Seattle in 1930–60, and the 860-m (2,800-ft) long **Yokohama Bay Bridge** (1989).

Chinatown, the largest of Japan's few Chinatowns, has around 2,500 Chinese inhabitants, and a mass of restaurants, food shops, Chinese-medicine shops, and fortune-tellers. At its heart is the Chinese **Kantei-byo Temple** (1887), dedicated to ancient Chinese hero Kuan-yu, who was worshiped as a god of war but is now popular as a god of accountancy, business success, and prosperity.

Among the 4,500 tombs in the early 20th-century **Foreigners' Cemetery** is that of Edmund Morel, the English engineer who helped build Japan's first railroads, with a tombstone shaped like a railroad ticket. The lovely, landscaped **Sankei-en Garden** was the private residence of silk-trader Hara Tomitaro (1868–1939). Among the ponds and flowers are 16 architectural treasures, including a three-story pagoda from Kyoto.

Landmark Tower
(045) 222-5015. *daily.*

Yokohama Museum of Art
(045) 221-0300. *Fri–Wed.*

NYK Maritime Museum
(045) 211-1923. *Tue–Sun.*

Hikawa Maru
(045) 641-4361. *daily.*

Foreigners' Cemetery
(045) 622-1311. *Apr–Nov: Sun.*

Sankei-en Garden
30 mins by bus from Sakuragi-cho stn to Honmoku Sankei-en Mae.
(045) 621-0634. *daily.*

ENVIRONS: Outside the center are two entertaining venues: **Kirin Beer Village**, with beer-tasting tours of the automated Kirin brewery; and **Shin Yokohama Ramen Museum** *(see p329)*. On a more serious note, the **Hodogaya Commonwealth Cemetery** (a bus ride from Yokohama, Hodogaya, or Sakuragi-cho stations) contains over 2,000 Allied graves from World War II (including some POWs).

Kirin Beer Village
Namamugi stn, Keihin Kyuko line.
(045) 503-8250. *Tue–Sat.*

One of the colorful entrance gates to Yokohama's Chinatown

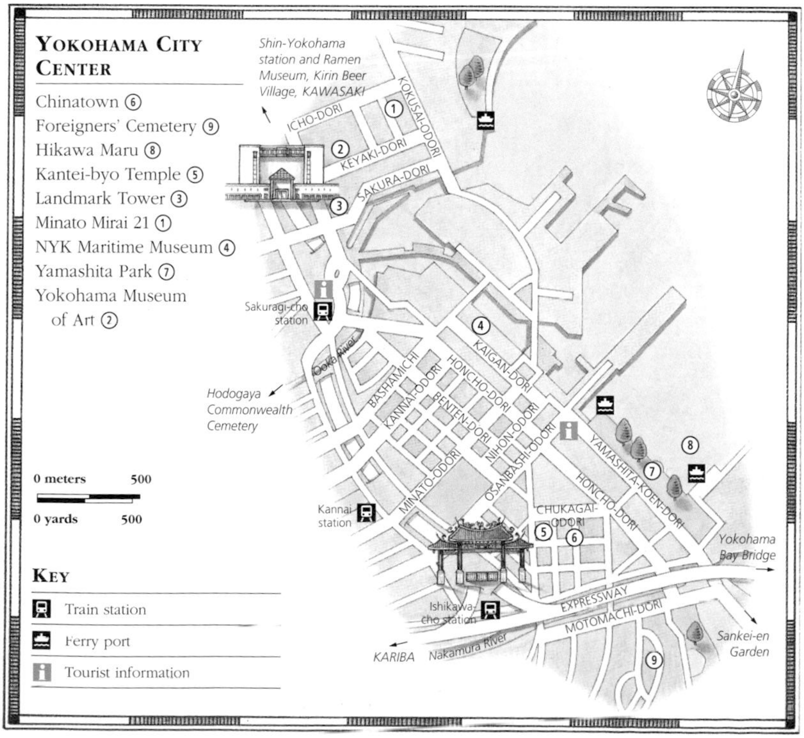

YOKOHAMA CITY CENTER

Chinatown ⑥
Foreigners' Cemetery ⑨
Hikawa Maru ⑧
Kantei-byo Temple ⑤
Landmark Tower ③
Minato Mirai 21 ①
NYK Maritime Museum ④
Yamashita Park ⑦
Yokohama Museum of Art ②

0 meters 500
0 yards 500

KEY

Train station
Ferry port
Tourist information

Kamakura 4

鎌倉

An Amida Buddha, Hase-dera temple

A SEASIDE TOWN of temples and wooded hills, Kamakura was Japan's capital from 1185 until 1333. As a legacy, today it has 19 Shinto shrines and 65 Buddhist temples, including two of Japan's oldest Zen monasteries (in Kita Kamakura, *see p130*). Many of the temples and gardens nestle against the hills ringing the town, and are linked by three hiking trails. Favored by artists and writers, Kamakura has numerous antique and crafts shops. In cherry-blossom season and on summer weekends it can be swamped by visitors. Some parts are best explored on foot, but there are one-day bus passes, and bicycles for rent at Kamakura station.

The path down the center of Wakamiya-oji, Kamakura's main street

Hase-dera Temple

Hase stn. *(0467) 22-6300.* *daily.*

Simple and elegant, Hase-dera is home to a superb 11-faced Kannon, *bosatsu* of mercy. The Treasure House displays characterful Muromachi-era carvings of the 33 incarnations of Kannon and a 1421 image of Daikokuten, god of wealth. Beside it is the sutra repository; rotating the sutras is said to earn as much merit as reading them. The 1264 bell is the town's oldest. Below it is a hall dedicated to Jizo, guardian of children, surrounded by countless statues to children who have died or been aborted.

The head of the Great Buddha, or Daibutsu

Great Buddha

Hase stn. *(0467) 22-0703.* *daily.*

The Great Buddha (Daibutsu) is Kamakura's most famous sight. Cast in 1252, the bronze statue of the Amida Buddha is 13.5 m (44 ft) tall. Having survived tidal waves, fires, earthquakes, and typhoons, it now has shock-absorbers in its base. Its proportions are distorted so that it seems balanced to those in front of it – this use of perspective may show Greek influence (via the Silk Road). The interior is open to visitors.

Sights at a Glance

Engaku-ji Temple 1
Great Buddha 12
Hachiman-gu Shrine 6
Hase-dera Temple 11
Hokoku-ji Temple 9
Kencho-ji Temple 4
Meigetsu-in Temple 3
Myohon-ji Temple 10
Sugimoto-dera Temple 8
Tokei-ji Temple 2
Zeni-arai Benten Shrine 5
Zuisen-ji Temple 7

Hachiman-gu Shrine

Kamakura stn. *(0467) 22-0315.* *daily.* **Kamakura National Treasure House Museum** *(0467) 22-0753.* *Tue–Sun.*

Hachiman shrines are dedicated to the god of war; this one is also a guardian shrine of the Minamoto (or Genji) clan. Built in 1063 by the sea, it was moved here in 1191. The approach runs between two lotus ponds: the Genji Pond has three islands (in Japanese *san* means both three and life) while the Heike Pond, named for a rival clan, has four (*shi* means both four and death). The path leads to the Mai-den stage for dances and music. The main shrine above was reconstructed in

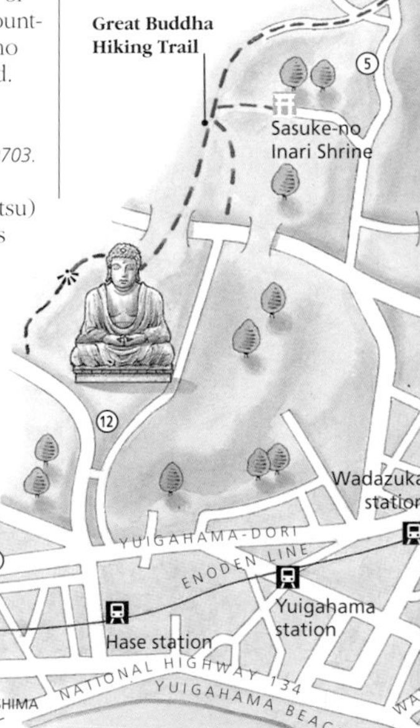

The Mai-den in front of the main shrine at Hachiman-gu shrine

1828 in Edo style. To the east, the **Kamakura National Treasure House Museum** contains a wealth of temple treasures.

Myohon-ji Temple

Kamakura stn. (0467) 22-0777. daily.

On a hillside of soaring trees, this temple, with its unusually steep, extended roof, is Kamakura's largest of the Nichiren sect. It was established in 1274, in memory of a 1203 massacre.

Hokoku-ji Temple

(0467) 22-0762. daily. (for bamboo grove).

A Rinzai Zen temple founded in 1334, Hokoku-ji's buildings are modern; its great attraction is its lovely bamboo grove. There is also a pleasant raked gravel and rock garden, and the temple's Sunday-morning *zazen* (meditation) sessions are open to all.

Visitors' Checklist

Kanagawa prefecture.
168,000. JR and Enoden lines. at Kamakura stn (0467) 22-3350. www.city.kamakura.kanagawa.jp New Year archery (Jan 5), Kamakura Festival (2nd–3rd Sun in Apr), Hachiman-gu Festival (Sep 14–16), Menkake-gyoretsu (Sep 18), Torchlight Noh (Oct 8–9).

Zuisen-ji Temple

(0467) 22-1191. daily.

This secluded temple is known for its naturalistic garden. Created in 1327 by the monk Muso Soseki, it features a waterfall-fed lake, rocks, and sand; a Zen meditation cave is cut into the cliff.

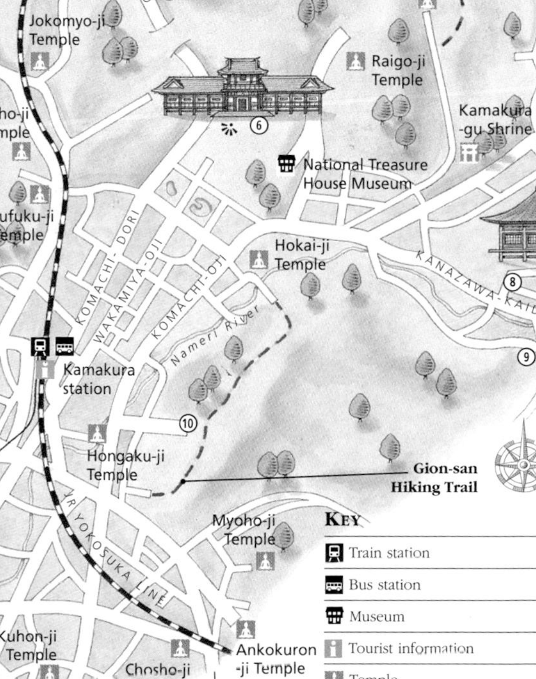

Sugimoto-dera Temple

(0467) 22-3463. daily.

Founded in 734, this is Kamakura's oldest temple and pleasantly informal. The softly thatched hall contains three wooden statues of 11-faced Kannon, protected by the ferocious guardian figures at the temple gateway.

Azalea-lined steps to the thatched hall at Sugimoto-dera temple

Exploring Kita Kamakura

Statue above Kencho-ji

ZEN BUDDHISM CAME TO JAPAN from China at the end of the 12th century. Its simplicity and accessibility appealed to the ethos of Kamakura samurai warriors as well as to ordinary people. Kita (north) Kamakura, a tranquil area of wooded gullies, includes three of Kamakura's so-called "five great" Zen temples: Kencho-ji, Engaku-ji, and Jochi-ji (the others are Jomyo-ji and Jufuku-ji). The area is served by its own train station, from which most sights can be reached on foot. Delicate vegetarian food *(see p320)*, which complies with Zen dietary rules, can be tried at several Kita Kamakura temples and restaurants.

Engaku-ji Temple

Kita Kamakura stn. (0467) 22-0478. daily.

The largest of Kamakura's "five great" Zen temples, deep in trees, Engaku-ji was founded by the Hojo regent Tokimune in 1282. An influential *zazen* (meditation) center since the Meiji era, it now runs public courses.

Although much of Engaku-ji was destroyed by the 1923 Kanto Earthquake, 17 of its more than 40 subtemples remain, and careful rebuilding has made sure that it retains its characteristic Zen layout *(see opposite)*. One of its highlights, in Shozoku-in subtemple, is the Shariden. Japan's finest example of Chinese Sung-style Zen architecture, it is open only at New Year but can be seen through a gate at other times. Farther on, the Butsunichian, mausoleum of Engaku-ji's founder, serves *matcha* tea *(see p163)*. It was the setting for Kawabata Yasunari's 1949 novel *Senbazuru* (Thousand Cranes).

***Bosatsu* statue at Kencho-ji**

Stone monuments in the peaceful cemetery at Tokei-ji temple

Tokei-ji Temple

Kita Kamakura stn. (0467) 22-1663. daily.

This quiet little temple was set up as a convent in 1285, at a time when only men were allowed to petition for divorce. However, if a woman spent three years here she could divorce her husband. Thus Tokei-ji was nicknamed the "divorce temple." In 1873 the law was changed to allow women to initiate divorce; in 1902 Tokei-ji became a monastery. It is still refuge-like, with gardens stretching back to the wooded hillside.

Meigetsu-in Temple

Kita Kamakura stn. (0467) 24-3437. daily.

Known as the "hydrangea temple," Meigetsu-in is a small Zen temple with attractive gardens. As well as hydrangeas (at their peak in June), there are irises; these bloom in late May, when the rear garden, usually only tantalizingly glimpsed through a round window, is opened to the public.

Kencho-ji Temple

Kita Kamakura stn. (0467) 22-0981. daily.

Kencho-ji is the foremost of Kamkura's "five great" Zen temples and the oldest Zen training monastery in Japan. Founded in 1253, the temple originally had seven main buildings and 49 subtemples; many were destroyed in fires, but ten subtemples remain. Beside the impressive Sanmon gate is the bell, cast in 1255, which has a Zen inscription by the temple's founder. The Buddha Hall contains a Jizo *bosatsu*, savior of souls of the dead, rather than the usual Buddha. Behind the hall is the Hatto, where public ceremonies are performed. The Karamon (Chinese gate) leads to the Hojo, used for services. Its rear garden is constructed around a pond supposedly in the shape of the kanji character for heart or mind. To the side of the temple a tree-lined lane leads to subtemples and up steps to Hanso-bo, the temple's shrine.

Zeni-Arai Benten Shrine

Kamakura stn. (0467) 25-1081. daily.

This popular shrine is dedicated to Benten, goddess of music, eloquence, and the arts, and one of the "seven lucky gods" of folk religion. Hidden in a niche in the cliffs, it is approached through a small tunnel and a row of *torii* (gates). These lead to a pocket of wafting incense, lucky charms, and a cave spring where visitors wash money in the hope of doubling its value.

Washing money at Zeni-Arai Benten shrine

The Layout of a Zen Buddhist Temple

Japanese Zen temple layout is typically based on Chinese Sung-dynasty temples. Essentially rectilinear and symmetrical (in contrast to native Japanese asymmetry), Zen temples have the main buildings in a straight line one behind another, on a roughly north–south axis. The main buildings comprise the Sanmon (main gate), Butsuden (Buddha Hall), Hatto lecture hall, sometimes a meditation or study hall, and the abbot's and monks' quarters. In practice, subtemples often crowd around the main buildings and may obscure the basic layout. The temple compound is entered by a bridge over a pond or stream, symbolically crossing from the earthly world to that of Buddha. Buildings are beautiful but natural looking, often of unpainted wood; they are intended to be conducive to emptying the mind of worldly illusions, facilitating enlightenment. The example below is based on Engaku-ji.

Bridge to Jochi-ji Temple

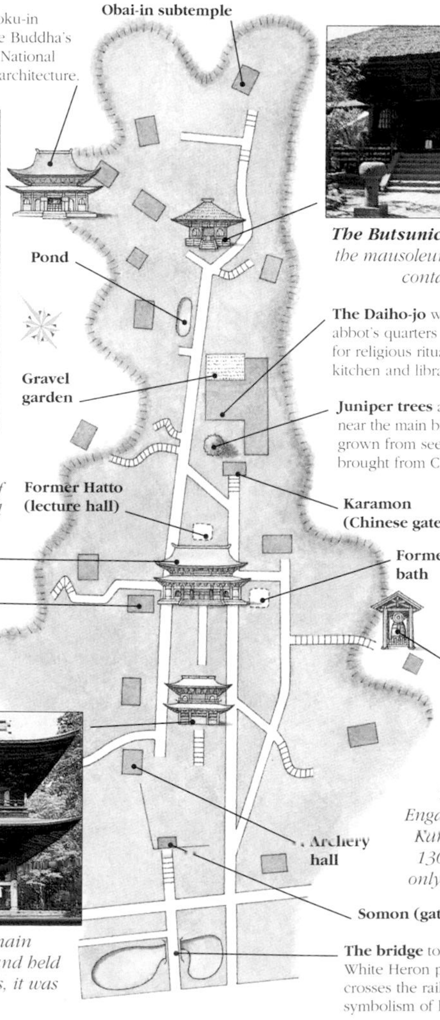

The Shariden, in Shozoku-in subtemple, enshrines the Buddha's tooth. The building is a National Treasure due to its Zen architecture.

Obai-in subtemple

The Butsunichian subtemple *is the mausoleum of Tokimune and contains a statue of him.*

Pond

The Daiho-jo was formerly the abbot's quarters and is now used for religious rituals. Next to it are a kitchen and library.

Gravel garden

Juniper trees are sometimes planted near the main buildings and are often grown from seeds supposedly brought from China by the founder.

The Butsuden *(Buddha Hall) contains an image of the Buddha. The hall at Engaku-ji was rebuilt in 1964.*

Former Hatto (lecture hall)

Karamon (Chinese gate)

Former bath

The Senbutsu-jo is a thatched building that serves as a Zen practice hall for monks.

Archery hall

The temple bell *at Engaku-ji, the largest in Kamakura, dates from 1301 and is now rung only on New Year's Eve.*

Somon (gate)

The Sanmon *is the main gate. Made of wood and held together without nails, it was built in 1783.*

The bridge to Engaku-ji crosses the White Heron pond. The path also crosses the rail track, doubling the symbolism of leaving the real world.

Chichibu-Tama National Park ❺

秩父多摩国立公園

Tokyo, Saitama, Nagano, and Yamanashi prefectures. *61,000 (Chichibu town). Seibu-Chichibu stn, Seibu-Chichibu line, Chichibu stn, Chichibu line; Okutama or Mitake stns, JR line.* *Chichibu stn (0494) 22-2211. Yo Matsuri (Dec 2–3, Chichibu town).*

Chichibu-Tama National Park is a remote region of low mountains, rich in traditions and wildlife, stretching from the narrow valleys of Okutama in the south to the basin around Chichibu town in the north. The two parts of the park are separated by mountains, crossed only by a few hiking trails, and are reached by two separate rail networks. Within the park, railroads penetrate to a few spots, but travel is mostly by bus.

Chichibu was a prime silk-producing region until the early 20th century. Today it is known for its vibrant festivals and its pilgrim route linking 33 Kannon temples. To the north, at **Nagatoro**, the Arakawa River runs past rare crystalline schist rock formations.

In the Okutama area, **Mount Mitake** has good hiking, and an attractive mountaintop shrine village, easily reached by a funicular. Stalactite caves at **Nippara** are worth visiting.

Nippara Caves

NW of Okutama. *(0428) 83-8491.* *daily.*

Yosegi-Zaiku Woodwork

Originating in the 9th century, this woodcraft looks like inlaid mosaic but in fact employs a very different technique. It has been a Hakone specialty for over 200 years, and today there are about 100 *yosegi-zaiku* practitioners in the area. Strips are cut from planks of up to 40 varieties of undyed woods and glued together to form blocks of pattern, which are in turn glued into larger blocks. These are then either shaped with a lathe into bowls and boxes, or shaved into cross-sectional sheets, used to coat items such as boxes and purses. The paper-thin sheets are flexible and can be laminated. Some of the most popular creations are "magic" boxes, opened in a sequence of moves to reveal a hidden drawer.

Craftsman making a *yosegi-zaiku* box

Environs: South of Chichibu-Tama lies **Mount Takao**, reached by the Keio line train to Takaosan-guchi. Its wooded slopes have pleasant walks with sweeping views of Tokyo and Mount Fuji.

Hakone ❻

箱根

Kanagawa prefecture. *17,000.* *698 Yumoto, Hakone (0460) 5-8911.* www2.marinet.or.jp/~kankouts/ hakone/index2_e.html *Torii-yaki (Aug 5, Lake Ashi), Daimyo Gyoretsu (Nov 3, Hakone-Yumoto).*

Hakone is a hilly hot-spring town whose scattered attractions are both cultural and natural. Popular as a resort since the 9th century, it can be very crowded. The Hakone area extends across the collapsed remains of a huge volcano, which was active until 3 to 4,000 years ago, leaving a legacy today of hot springs and steam vents.

Although Hakone can be visited as a long day trip from Tokyo, it is worth an overnight stay. Two- or three-day public-transportation passes are available on the Odakyu line from Shinjuku, Tokyo. A convenient circuit of the main sights starts from the *onsen* town of **Hakone-Yumoto**, taking the Tozan switchback train up the hillside to **Hakone Open-Air Museum**, with its modern sculptures. Continue via funicular to **Hakone Art Museum**, which has an excellent Japanese ceramic collection and garden. Farther on, via the funicular and then

Crossing the rocky scree and steaming vents of Owaku-dani valley in Hakone

A statue of *The Izu Dancer* by a waterfall near Kawazu, Izu Peninsula

a ropeway over the crest of the hill, is the fascinating **Owaku-dani** ("valley of great boiling"), an area of sulfurous steam vents, where there is a **Natural Science Museum**.

The ropeway continues to **Lake Ashi**, where replicas of historical Western-style boats run to **Hakone-machi** and **Moto-Hakone**. In clear weather there are stunning views of Mount Fuji. At Hakone-machi is an interesting reconstruction of the **Seki-sho Barrier Gate**, a checkpoint that used to control the passage of people and guns on the Edo-period Tokaido road between Edo (Tokyo) and Kyoto.

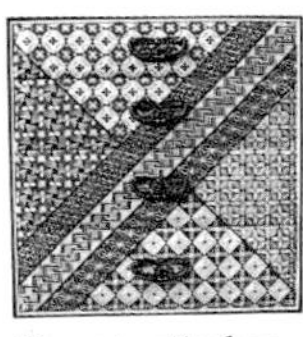
Yosegi-zaiku box, Hatajuku

From Hakone-machi it is a short walk to Moto-Hakone, along a surviving section of Tokaido road. The old road can also be followed beyond Moto-Hakone over a pass to the **Amazake-chaya** teahouse, and on to **Hatajuku** village. Hatajuku is known for *yosegi-zaiku*, a form of decorative woodwork. Infrequent buses run between Moto-Hakone and Hakone-Yumoto, via Hatajuku.

Open-Air Museum
(0460) 2-1161. daily.
Hakone Art Museum
(0460) 2-2623. Fri–Wed.
Natural Science Museum
(0460) 4-9149. daily.
Seki-sho Barrier Gate
(0460) 3-6635. daily.

Izu Peninsula ❼

伊豆半島

Shizuoka prefecture. Atami, Ito, and Shuzenji stns. Daimonji Burning (Jul 22–3, Atagawa), Anjin Festival (Aug 8–10, Ito).

A PICTURESQUE, hilly peninsula with a benign climate, Izu is popular for its numerous hot springs. It was a place of exile during the Middle Ages, and in the early 1600s was home to the shipwrecked Englishman Will Adams, whose story was the basis of the James Clavell novel *Shogun*. **Shimoda**, on the southern tip, became a coaling station for foreign ships in 1854, then opened to US traders. Today Shimoda has little of interest besides pretty gray-and-white walls, reinforced against typhoons with crisscross plasterwork.

Izu's east coast is quite developed, but the west has charming coves and fishing villages, such as **Toi** and **Heda**, offering delicious long-legged crabs and other seafood. The center is also relatively unspoiled, with wooded mountains and rustic hot springs, including **Shuzenji** *onsen* and a chain of villages from **Amagi Yugashima** to **Kawazu**. These latter were the setting for Kawabata Yasunari's short story *The Izu Dancer*, commemorated across Izu. Two-day transportation passes cover parts of the peninsula.

Mount Fuji and the Fuji Five Lakes ❽

See pp134–5.

Shizuoka ❾

静岡

Shizuoka prefecture. 476,000. in JR stn (054) 252-4247. www.pref.shizuoka.jp Shizuoka Festival (1st weekend Apr).

SETTLEMENT in this area stretches back to AD 200–300. Later a stop on the old Tokaido road, and the retirement home of Tokugawa Ieyasu *(see p52)*, Shizuoka is today a sprawling urban center, the city in Japan at greatest risk of a major earthquake. As a result it is probably the only place that is fully prepared.

The **Toro ruins** near the port have well-explained reconstructions of ancient buildings, and an excellent interactive **museum**. The view from **Nihondaira** plateau, in the east of the city, to Mount Fuji and Izu is superb. Nearby is **Kunozan Tosho-gu**, one of the three top Tosho-gu shrines.

Toro Ruins
Museum *(0542) 85-0476. Tue–Sun. last day of month.*

ENVIRONS: West of Shizuoka, **Kanaya** has one of Japan's largest tea plantations – with giant fans to protect from frost. Fields and processing plants can be visited, and the elegant **Ocha no Sato** museum portrays tea lore. Nearby, the **Oigawa steam railroad** leads into the untamed South Alps.

Ocha no Sato
(0547) 46-5588. daily. 1st & 3rd Tue of Feb–Mar, Jul, Sep–Oct, Dec.

A reconstructed dwelling at the Toro site, Shizuoka

Mount Fuji and the Fuji Five Lakes ❽

富士山と富士五湖

Decorative drain cover in Fuji-Yoshida

At 3,776 m (12,390 ft), Mount Fuji (or Fuji-san) is Japan's highest peak by far, its near-perfect cone floating lilac-gray or snow-capped above hilltops and low cloud. Dormant since 1707, the volcano first erupted 8–10,000 years ago. Its upper slopes are loose volcanic ash, devoid of greenery or streams. Until 100 years ago, Mount Fuji was considered so sacred that it was climbed only by priests and pilgrims; women were not allowed until 1872. Today pilgrims are greatly outnumbered by recreational climbers. The Fuji Five Lakes area, at the foot of the mountain, is a playground for Tokyo-ites, with sports facilities and amusement parks.

Lake Sai
This is the least spoiled of the Fuji Five Lakes and offers beautiful views of Mount Fuji.

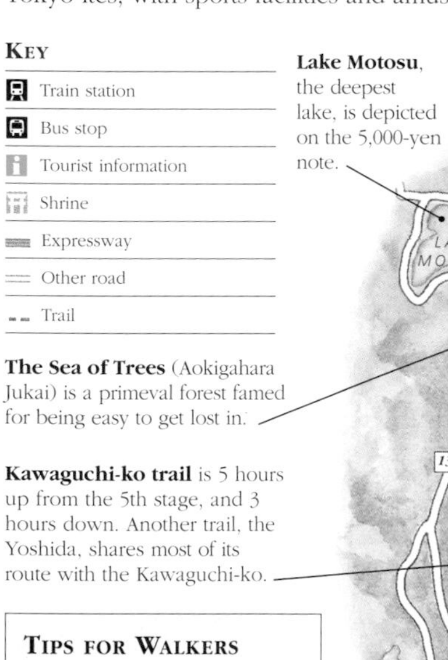

Key

- Train station
- Bus stop
- Tourist information
- Shrine
- Expressway
- Other road
- Trail

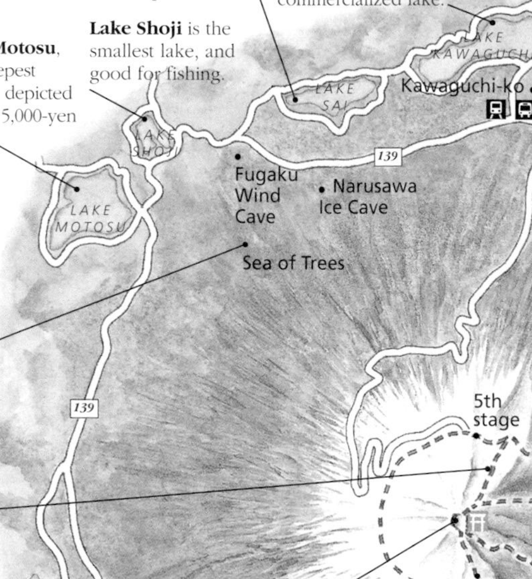

Lake Kawaguchi is the most accessible and commercialized lake.

Lake Shoji is the smallest lake, and good for fishing.

Lake Motosu, the deepest lake, is depicted on the 5,000-yen note.

The Sea of Trees (Aokigahara Jukai) is a primeval forest famed for being easy to get lost in.

Kawaguchi-ko trail is 5 hours up from the 5th stage, and 3 hours down. Another trail, the Yoshida, shares most of its route with the Kawaguchi-ko.

The top is not a single summit, but a crater rim. A circuit of the rim takes about an hour.

Fujinomiya trail is 5 hours up from the 5th stage, and 3 hours 30 minutes down.

Tips for Walkers

Planning: *The mountain is open for climbing only in July and August. Trails and huts can be very crowded on weekends.*
Stages: *The trails are divided into 10 stages. Climbers usually start at the 5th stage. To see the sunrise and avoid midday sun, it is usual to climb by night or start in the afternoon, sleep in a hut at the 7th or 8th stage, and rise around 4am to finish the climb.*
Conditions: *The climb is hard work as the steep volcanic cinder shifts underfoot like sand. Above the 8th stage, altitude sickness occasionally strikes: if you have a serious headache or nausea, descend at once. The summit is much colder than the base.*
What to take: *Sun-protection cream, hat, sweater, raincoat, hiking shoes, flashlight, and emergency drink supplies; a walking stick is useful.*

Approaching the Crater Rim
At the top, climbers and pilgrims can visit the Sengen shrine, 24-hour noodle stalls, a post office, an office for souvenir stamps, and a weather station.

Sengen Jinja
Many Sengen shrines, including this main one at Fuji-Yoshida, can be found around Fuji. The inner sanctum of Sengen shrines is on the crater rim at the summit. They are dedicated to the deity of the mountain.

Visitors' Checklist

Shizuoka prefecture. *Fuji-Yoshida, Kawaguchi-ko, Gotenba, Mishima (Tokaido Shinkansen), or Fujinomiya.* *summer only, from all stns to the nearest 5th stage, also direct from Tokyo (Shinjuku stn W side or Hamamatsu-cho) to Kawaguchi-ko, Gotenba, and Lake Yamanaka.* *Fuji-Yoshida (0555) 22-1111.* www.city.fujiyoshida.yamanashi.jp *Fuji-Yoshida Fire Festival (Aug 26 & 27).*

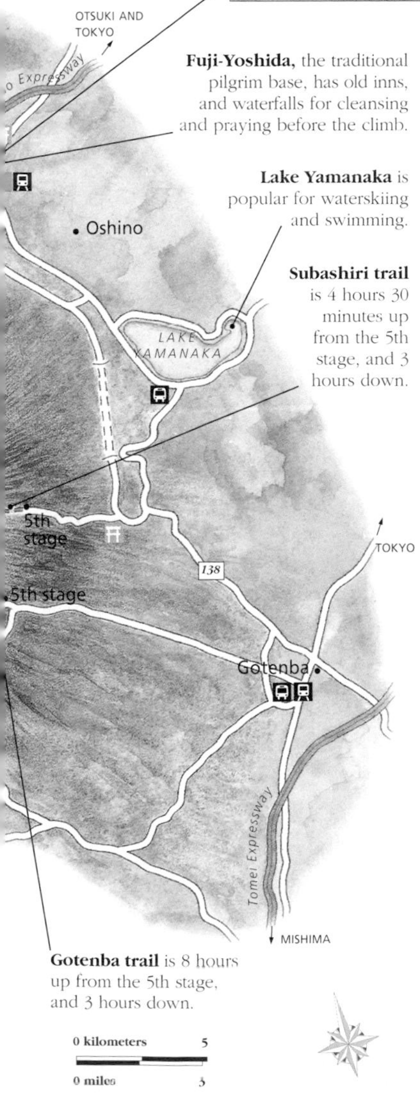

OTSUKI AND TOKYO

Expressway

Fuji-Yoshida, the traditional pilgrim base, has old inns, and waterfalls for cleansing and praying before the climb.

Lake Yamanaka is popular for waterskiing and swimming.

Oshino

Subashiri trail is 4 hours 30 minutes up from the 5th stage, and 3 hours down.

LAKE YAMANAKA

5th stage

TOKYO

138

5th stage

Gotenba

Tomei Expressway

MISHIMA

Gotenba trail is 8 hours up from the 5th stage, and 3 hours down.

0 kilometers 5

0 miles 3

Mount Fuji in Art

Mount Fuji's graceful, almost symmetrical form, its changing appearance at different seasons and times of day, and its dominance over the landscape have made it both a symbol of Japan and a popular subject for artists. The mountain features in various series of 19th-century woodblock prints: Katsushika Hokusai (1790–1849) and Ando Hiroshige (1797–1858) both published series called *Thirty-Six Views of Mount Fuji,* and Hiroshige also depicted Fuji in his *Fifty-Three Stages of the Tokaido* published in 1833–4. It often appears in the background of prints of downtown Edo (Tokyo), from where it is sometimes visible between high-rises even today. In other arts, Mount Fuji is echoed in decorative motifs, for instance on kimonos, in wood carvings, and even in the shape of window frames.

One of Hiroshige's *Thirty-Six Views of Mount Fuji*

Beneath the Wave off Kanagawa* from Hokusai's *Thirty-Six Views of Mount Fuji

Kiso Valley Tour ⑩

木曽谷

THE KISO RIVER runs through a picturesque mountain valley that was the route of the Nakasendo, one of the Edo-period post roads. Its 11 post towns, particularly Tsumago, Narai, and Magome, still retain much of that atmosphere, their narrow streets lined with wooden inns and stores. Parts of the old Nakasendo trail, especially between Tsumago and Magome, are as they were in the Edo days and can be followed past woods, farms, and milestones. More challenging hiking is found on nearby mountains such as Ontake.

Tips for Travellers

Tour length: *60 km (37 miles).*
Travel: *Car is the most flexible option. Most express trains stop only at Nakatsugawa and Kiso-Fukushima; one or two a day stop at more stations. Local trains run about every hour.* ***Information and reservations:*** *Tsumago (0264) 57-3123; Magome (0264) 59-2336; Narai (0264) 34-2001.*

Kiso-Hirasawa ①
Lacquerware is a specialty here, perfected over the years to sell to travelers passing through.

Narai ②
This well-preserved post town has streets lined with wooden buildings, plus a couple of interesting museums, giving an insight into how life was for travelers on the Nakasendo.

Torii Pass ③
This pass has one of the main remaining sections of genuine, stone-paved Nakasendo road, with no modern road nearby to spoil it. It takes about 2 hours to walk over the pass.

Kiso-Fukushima ④
This was the location of a major barrier gate on the Nakasendo road. Today it is the gateway to the sacred mountain of Ontake.

SHIOJIRI AND MATSUMOTO

Yabuhara

Miyanokoshi

Harano

MT ONTAKE

Kiso River

MT KISO-KOMAGATAKE

Agematsu

Key

- Tour route
- Other roads
- Train station
- Walk route
- Viewpoint

Nezame-no-toko ⑤
This pretty gorge, about half-an-hour's walk from Agematsu, holds turquoise waters strewn with boulders.

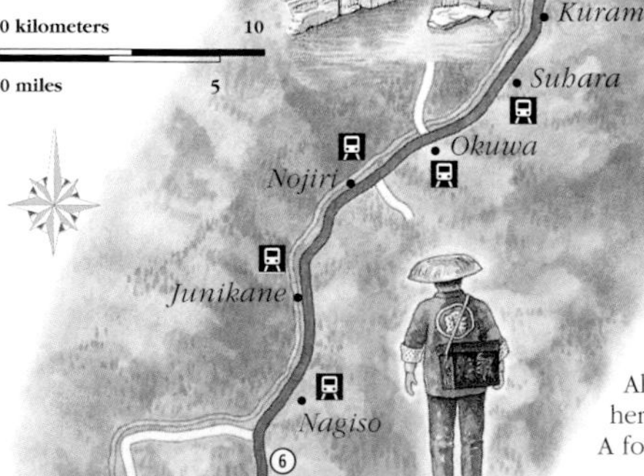

Tsumago ⑥
All signs of modernity have been hidden here – cables are buried and cars banned. A former high-class inn, the Okuya, is now an excellent museum of local and Nakasendo history.

Magome ⑦
In the hills above the Kiso Valley, Magome is a good starting point for the 8.5-km (5-mile) Nakasendo walking trail to Tsumago.

NAKATSUGAWA

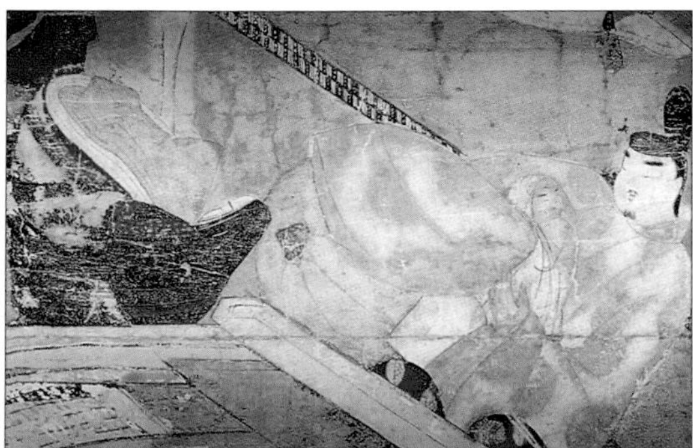

Part of the *Tale of Genji* handscroll in Tokugawa Art Museum, Nagoya

Nagoya ⓫

名古屋

Aichi prefecture. 2,160,000. at Nagoya JR stn (052) 972-2425. www.city.nagoya.jp/indexe.htm Atsuta Shrine Festival (Jun 5), Nagoya Festival (mid-Oct).

A major transportation hub for the region, Nagoya is a pleasant and convenient, if unexciting, base. It rose to prominence in the 17th century as a Tokaido castle town, birthplace of Oda Nobunaga and Toyotomi Hideyoshi *(see pp50 & 52)*. Japan's fourth-largest city and an industrial center, it was heavily bombed in World War II.

The city's one-day bus or bus-and-subway passes are good for exploring. **Nagoya Castle**, built in 1610–12 and one of the largest, most sophisticated of the Edo period, was destroyed in a bombing raid in 1945; today's concrete reconstruction has a top-floor observatory, and the modern interior contains exhibits about the castle.

A short bus ride east is the **Tokugawa Art Museum**, with superb Edo-period treasures, as well as a 12th-century illustrated handscroll of the *Tale of Genji*, part of which is exhibited each November. Photos and reproductions of the scrolls are on permanent display.

Nagoya Castle
Shiyakusho stn. Nagoya-jo Seimon-mae stop. (052) 231-1700. daily.

Tokugawa Art Museum
Shindeki stop. (052) 935-6262. Tue–Sun.

Environs: Trips from Nagoya, all on the Meitetsu rail line, include **Arimatsu**, a well-preserved Tokaido post town, known for tie-dyeing since the 17th century. The town of Toyota, home of **Toyota cars**, has interesting factory tours.

Toyota Car Factory
(0565) 29-3355. Mon–Sat.

Meiji-era post office at Meiji Mura near Inuyama

Inuyama ⓬

犬山

Aichi prefecture. 71,000. at Inuyama stn (0568) 61-1800. Tagata Honen-sai (Mar 15), Inuyama Festival (1st weekend in Apr).

Inuyama is a quiet, friendly castle town on the Kiso River. Its **castle** (1537) is the oldest in Japan. Although it places more emphasis on defense than show, it is still small, simple, and graceful, with panoramic views across the river far below. In nearby **Urakuen park** is Jo-an teahouse, a classic example of rustic simplicity, created in 1612 in Kyoto.

Inuyama Castle
(0568) 61-1711 daily.

Environs: Outside Inuyama is **Meiji Mura**, a large park containing over 60 Meiji-era (1868–1912) buildings, including the lobby of Frank Lloyd Wright's Imperial Hotel from Tokyo. A rural train ride away is **Yaotsu**, birthplace of Sugihara Chiune. Japan's consul in Lithuania in World War II, Sugihara saved around 6,000 Jews by issuing transit visas via Japan, against government orders. He is now commemorated with a monument and museum at Yaotsu's **Hill of Humanity Park**.

Meiji Mura
15 min by bus from Inuyama.
(0568) 67-0314. daily.

Gifu ⓭

岐阜

Gifu prefecture. 410,000. at Gifu JR stn (058) 262-4415. All-Japan Fireworks Contest (last Sat in Jul).

A rather garish spa town, Gifu's main attraction is *ukai* cormorant fishing *(see p40)*. This tradition involves using trained cormorants to catch fish. Nightly from mid-May to mid-October, except at full moon or when stormy, fishermen and their cormorants go out on torchlit boats; the birds dive for *ayu* (sweetfish) and trout, which they are prevented from swallowing by a ring around their necks.

The town is also known for its paper parasols and lanterns and for the largest lacquer Buddha in Japan, at **Shoho-ji temple**. Dating from 1832, it comprises a woven bamboo frame covered with sutra-inscribed paper, then coated in clay and lacquered. **Gifu Castle** is a modern reconstruction.

The small, reconstructed castle at Gifu, perched on a hilltop

Street-by-Street: Takayama ⓮

高山

TAKAYAMA IS A TOWN OF CHARACTER surrounded by mountains. Agriculturally poor but rich in timber, it produced skilled carpenters; in the 8th century, when the region was unable to produce enough rice for its taxes (usually paid in the form of rice), it sent craftsmen instead. From 1692 to 1868 the area was under direct shogunate control as a source of timber. Its isolated mountain location has meant the survival of unspoiled Edo-period streets lined with tiny shops, museums, and eating places, while the pure water is ideal for sake brewing. The town also stages one of Japan's best-known festivals.

One of the floats at the Takayama Matsuri

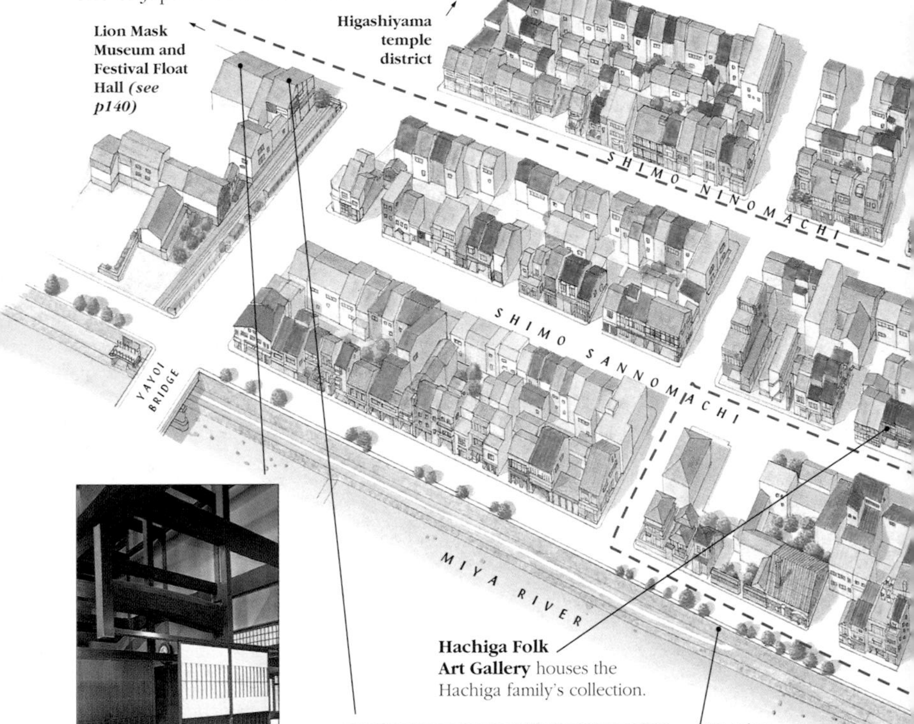

Lion Mask Museum and Festival Float Hall *(see p140)*

Higashiyama temple district

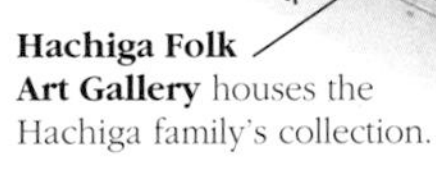

Hachiga Folk Art Gallery houses the Hachiga family's collection.

Morning market

0 meters 50

0 yards 50

Yoshijima Heritage House

This beautifully maintained sake merchant's house retains its wooden beamed interior, lit by high windows.

★ Kusakabe Heritage House

Rebuilt of Japanese cypress in 1879 after a fire, this house is a well-preserved money-lender's dwelling, and includes folk-craft items and a small garden.

STAR SIGHTS

- **★ Sannomachi Quarter**
- **★ Kusakabe Heritage House**

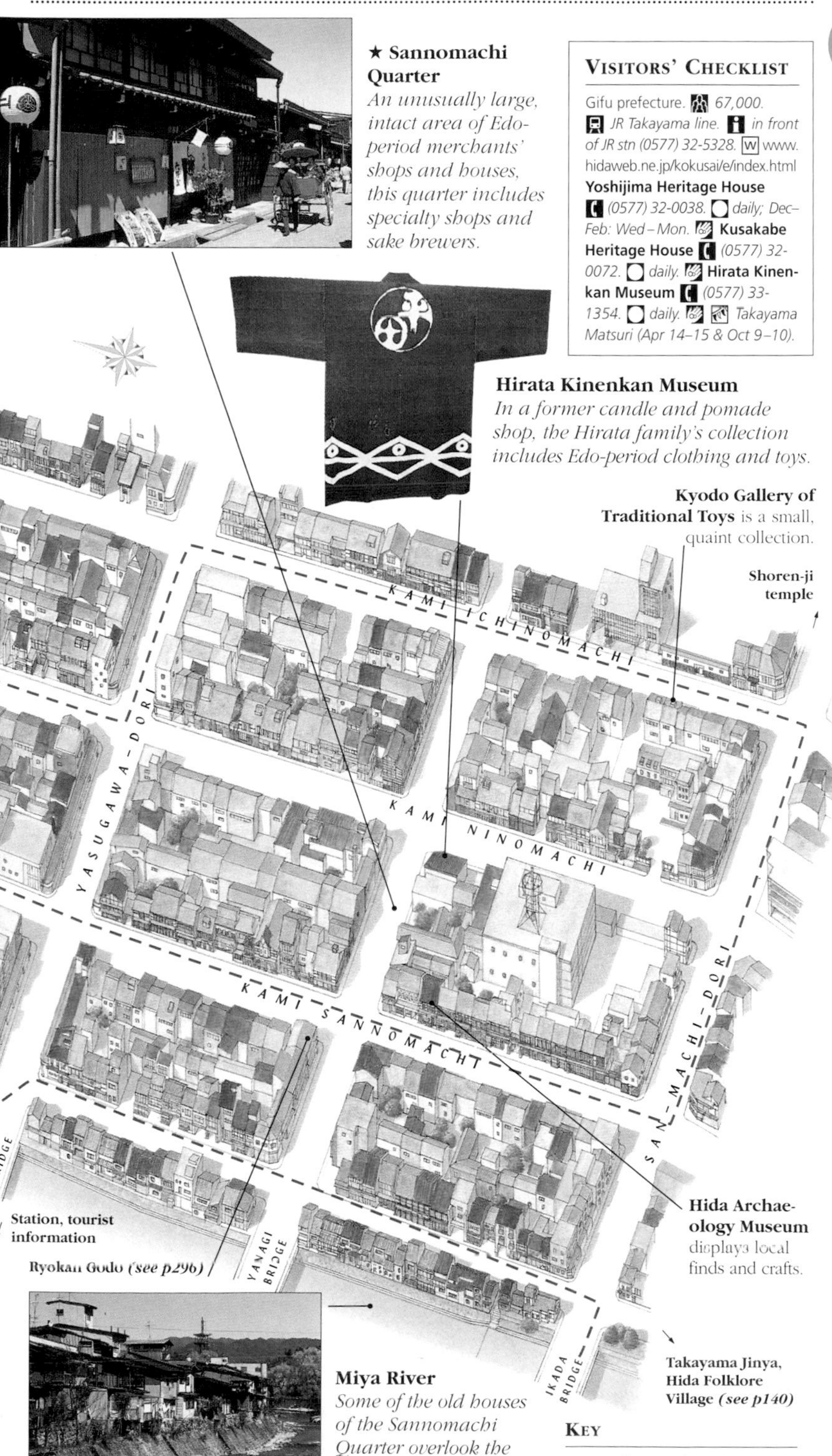

★ Sannomachi Quarter
An unusually large, intact area of Edo-period merchants' shops and houses, this quarter includes specialty shops and sake brewers.

Hirata Kinenkan Museum
In a former candle and pomade shop, the Hirata family's collection includes Edo-period clothing and toys.

Kyodo Gallery of Traditional Toys is a small, quaint collection.

Hida Archaeology Museum displays local finds and crafts.

Miya River
Some of the old houses of the Sannomachi Quarter overlook the fast-flowing Miya River.

Key

– – – Suggested route

Visitors' Checklist

Gifu prefecture. *67,000.* *JR Takayama line.* *in front of JR stn (0577) 32-5328.* www.hidaweb.ne.jp/kokusai/e/index.html **Yoshijima Heritage House** *(0577) 32-0038.* *daily; Dec–Feb: Wed – Mon.* **Kusakabe Heritage House** *(0577) 32-0072.* *daily.* **Hirata Kinenkan Museum** *(0577) 33-1354.* *daily.* *Takayama Matsuri (Apr 14–15 & Oct 9–10).*

Exploring Takayama

Takayama is best explored slowly on foot or by bicycle. Old merchant houses reveal high, skylighted ceilings, soot-painted beams, and fireproof storage rooms; the dirt-floor area at the front was the shop. The town's eight sake breweries can also be visited during the peak brewing week in January or February. To the east, the tranquil Higashiyama temple district has a 3.5-km (2-mile) walking course taking in 13 temples, five shrines, and a hilltop park.

Lion Mask Museum

(0577) 32-0881. daily.

Lion dances, to drive away wild animals and evil spirits, are integral to festivals such as Takayama's. This museum contains over 800 lively lion masks from all over Japan, plus superb armor, screens, pottery, and coins. Included in the entry fee is a performance by *karakuri* marionettes, invented in Edo (Tokyo) in 1617.

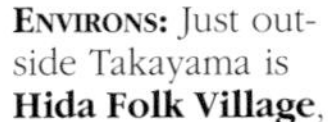

One of the masks in the Lion Mask Museum

Festival Float Hall

(0577) 32-5100. daily.

Takayama Matsuri dates from about 1690 and takes place twice a year, in spring, coinciding with planting, and in fall at harvest time. Both festivals involve processions of 11 or 12 tall, lavishly decorated floats, guided by townspeople in traditional costume. Four floats also feature *karakuri* marionettes. Between festivals, four of the magnificent floats are displayed in this museum along with photographs of the others. Admission includes access to a gallery of exquisite scale models of Nikko Toshogu Shrine *(see pp260–63).*

Takayama Jinya

(0577) 32-0643. daily.

The Jinya was built in 1615 for Takayama's lord, but in 1692 the shogunate made it their provincial government office – the only one still in existence. The front of the building comprises rooms where people of various ranks waited or met officials; behind are kitchens and living quarters of the governor's family. To one side is a prison, with a small array of torture instruments. The storehouses contain items relating to the rice-tax system.

Environs: Just outside Takayama is **Hida Folk Village**, a collection of over 30 houses from surrounding rural areas, including a *gassho-zukuri* house from the Shokawa Valley. There are also storehouses, a festival stage, and demonstrations of traditional crafts. The buildings, on a hillside with views of the Japan Alps, are interesting both architecturally and for what they reveal – such as the demands of a snowy climate or the life of a village headman.

Hida Folk Village

40 mins walk or 8 mins by bus from Takayama stn. *(0577) 33-4714. daily.*

Inside Takayama's Festival Float Hall

Gassho-zukuri houses in Shirakawa-go

Shokawa Valley ⑮

庄川渓谷

Gifu and Toyama prefectures. *from Nagoya (summer only), Takayama, Gifu & Takaoka. by main bus stop at Ogimachi (0576) 96-1013.* www.shirakawa-go.com/e_top.html *Doburoku Matsuri (Shirakawa-go, Oct 14–19).*

A remote mountain region with unique thatched houses, the Shokawa valley comprises two areas: **Shirakawa-go** (including Ogimachi) to the south and the five hamlets of **Gokayama** to the north. Under deep snow from December to March, the region was historically a refuge for the defeated and persecuted. Until the 1970s most families here produced silk, raising silkworms in *gassho-zukuri* thatched houses.

Of the original 1,800, less than 150 *gassho* houses remain. Three settlements – **Ogimachi**, **Suganuma**, and **Ainokura** – are World Heritage sites. Every April–May, a few houses are re-thatched, one roof taking 200 villagers and volunteers two days. Ogimachi is the largest village, with 59 *gassho* houses and an **Open-Air Museum**. Suganuma has nine *gassho* buildings. Ainokura is a hillside hamlet of 20 *gassho* houses (two open to visitors).

Open-Air Museum

Across the river from Ogimachi. *Fri–Tue.*

Gassho-zukuri Houses

These houses are named for their steep thatched roofs, shaped like *gassho* ("praying hands"). The climate demands strong, steep roofs able to withstand heavy snow and shed rain quickly so that the straw does not rot. *Gassho* structures meet those requirements with a series of triangular frames on a rectangular base, creating a large interior space. Generally three or four stories, they traditionally accommodated extended families of 20–30 people on the ground floor, all involved in silkworm cultivation; the upper floors housed the silkworms, permitting variations in light, heat, and air at different stages. To maximize ventilation and light, *gassho-zukuri* houses have no hipped gables, and windows at both ends are opened to allow the wind through – in Shirakawa-go, where winds always blow north–south along the valley floor, all houses are aligned on the same axis. Architectural details vary from village to village.

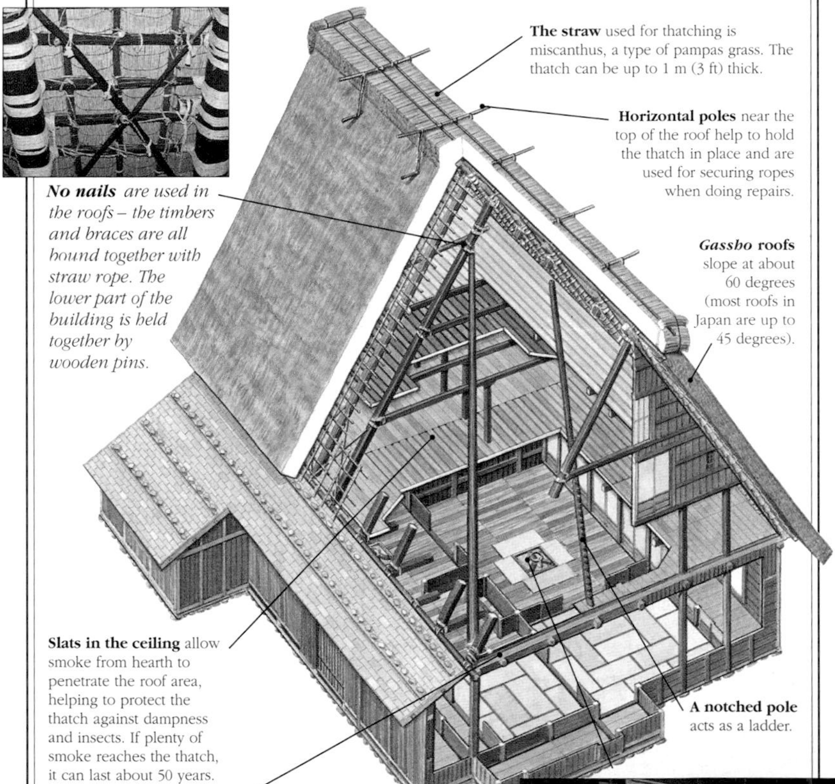

A *gassho*-style house behind a watermill

No nails *are used in the roofs – the timbers and braces are all bound together with straw rope. The lower part of the building is held together by wooden pins.*

The straw used for thatching is miscanthus, a type of pampas grass. The thatch can be up to 1 m (3 ft) thick.

Horizontal poles near the top of the roof help to hold the thatch in place and are used for securing ropes when doing repairs.

***Gassho* roofs** slope at about 60 degrees (most roofs in Japan are up to 45 degrees).

Slats in the ceiling allow smoke from hearth to penetrate the roof area, helping to protect the thatch against dampness and insects. If plenty of smoke reaches the thatch, it can last about 50 years.

A notched pole acts as a ladder.

Horizontal beams are often taken from trees that have been bent by snow; being slightly curved, they absorb stress better than straight beams.

The hearth *is a common feature of Japanese rural houses, and was used for heating, cooking, and drying. The exact style of hearth and way of hanging things over it varies between villages.*

Kanazawa ⓰

金沢

A CITY WITH A STRONG cultural identity, Kanazawa was historically shielded from outside influence by its location between alps and sea and supported by an ample rice yield. In 1583 the area, known as Kaga, passed from egalitarian government under the Ikko Buddhist sect to the firm rule of the Maeda lords; while much of Japan was still unstable, Kaga had three centuries of peace and became the richest domain in the land. Wealth encouraged cultural development, and artists from Kyoto came and developed new, more vibrant styles with less restraint. When Japan modernized, Kanazawa focused on culture; lack of industry meant the city escaped bombing in World War II and retains its heritage today.

Exploring Central Kanazawa
Most of Kanazawa's sights are located centrally. One-day bus passes are available, and bicycles can be rented at the station. **Kenroku-en Garden** is one of Japan's "great three" gardens, and is best seen uncrowded early or late in the day. Established in the mid-17th century, it was opened to the public in 1871. Kenroku-en means "garden of six qualities" (desirable in Chinese gardens): spaciousness, seclusion, air of antiquity, ingenuity, flowing water, and views. At the edge of the lake is a two-legged stone lantern *(see p27)*, known as Kotoji because it is shaped like the bridge of a *koto* (stringed instrument). Many of the garden's 12,000 trees are protected in winter by rope "tents."

The exquisite two-story **Seisonkaku Villa** adjoining Kenroku-en was built in 1863 by Maeda Nariyasu, 13th lord, for his mother. Its lower floor has formal receiving rooms: walls are coated in gold dust, and *shoji* paper doors have rare Dutch stained-glass insets. Garden design forms part of the whole, and a veranda roof is cantilevered so that no pillars spoil the view. Upstairs is more informal and colorful. The superb curved roof is made from *sawara* cypress shingles.

Kanazawa Castle, one of the largest in feudal Japan, was almost entirely destroyed by fire in 1881; only the armory and rear gate, Ishikawa-mon, survived. A section of the castle is being rebuilt and a park created; both are to be finished by 2005. The nearby **Oyama Shrine** is dedicated to Maeda Toshiie.

Spring in Kenroku-en Garden

The unusual gate to the Oyama Shrine

Walled street in the Nagamachi Samurai quarter

The **Nagamachi Samurai Quarter** retains its earthen-walled streets, even though many houses here have been rebuilt. With its quality woodwork, costly windowpanes, and serene garden, **Nomura House** gives an idea of samurai life. In the **Saihatsuan Kaga Yuzen Silk Center**, a former samurai house, an 18-step resist-dyeing process is used to produce Kaga *yuzen* silk, popular for formal kimonos.

Most of the city's museums are in the central area. **Ishikawa Prefecture Traditional Products and Crafts Museum** is an excellent starting point, with sections on more than 30 Kanazawa crafts, such as silk, ceramics, gold leaf, and folk toys. Two-day "passport" tickets give access to this and four other museums, including the **Ishikawa Prefecture Art Museum** (the Maedas' collection) and the **Honda Museum** (Honda family possessions).

Kenroku-en Garden
(076) 221-5850. daily. (free on 3rd Sun of each month).

Seisonkaku Villa
(076) 221-0580. Thu–Tue.

Kanazawa Castle
(076) 232-3113. daily.

Nomura House
(076) 221-3553. daily.

Saihatsuan Kaga Yuzen Silk Center
(076) 264-2811. Fri–Wed.

Crafts Museum
(076) 262-2020. daily. Apr–Nov: 3rd Thu in month; Dec–Mar: Thu.

Art Museum
(076) 231-7580. daily.

Honda Museum
(076) 261-0500. daily. Nov–Feb: Thu.

Exploring the Higashi (Eastern) Pleasure District
Established in 1820, this was the grandest pleasure district outside Kyoto and Edo (Tokyo). Full of atmosphere, the area has old-fashioned street lamps and wooden-lattice windows hiding elegant restaurants and crafts galleries. The evocative **Shima Geisha House** is as it was in the 19th century. On the upper floor are guest rooms with small stages where the geisha sang and danced. Downstairs are living quarters. Nearby, at **Fukushima Shamisen**, the Fukushima family have been hand-crafting musical instruments for 130 years. *Shamisen* are made from *karin* wood (a type of quince) and cat or dog skin; the three strings are silk. Visitors may play a finished instrument. The **Sakuda Gold-leaf Store** sells gold-leaf items and demonstrates production – it even has toilets tiled in gold. Kanazawa has produced gold leaf since 1593 and supplies 99 percent of Japan's needs.

Wall hanging of a geisha in the Shima Geisha House

Shima Geisha House
(076) 252-5675. *Tue–Sun.*

Fukushima Shamisen
(076) 252-3703. *Mon–Sat.*

Sakuda Gold-leaf Store
(076) 251-6777. *daily.*

Exploring Southern Kanazawa
Popularly known as the "ninja temple," **Myoryu-ji** is a Nichiren temple full of secret doors and passages. It was established in 1643 as both a place of worship for the Maedas and a watchtower on the edge of town. The architecture is highly complex, with 23 rooms linked by 29 staircases and a maze of corridors.

Nearby, **Kutani Kosen Kiln** is the only kiln in Kanazawa. Kutani porcelain originated in the village of Kutani, south of Kanazawa, in the mid-17th century. Old Kutani-ware uses deep, over-glazed blues, greens, and ochres; modern work has more delicate and varied designs. All pieces are handmade and fired two or three times.

Myoryu-ji Temple
(076) 241-0888. *daily.*
(every 30 mins, compulsory.)

Kutani Kosen Kiln
(076) 241-0902. *daily.*

Visitors' Checklist

Ishikawa prefecture. *455,000.*
Komatsu. *JR line.*
at Kanazawa JR stn (076) 220-2194. www.city.Kanazawa.ishikawa. jp/kanazawa E.html
Noh at Ono Minato Shrine (May 15), Hyakumangoku Matsuri (mid-Jun).

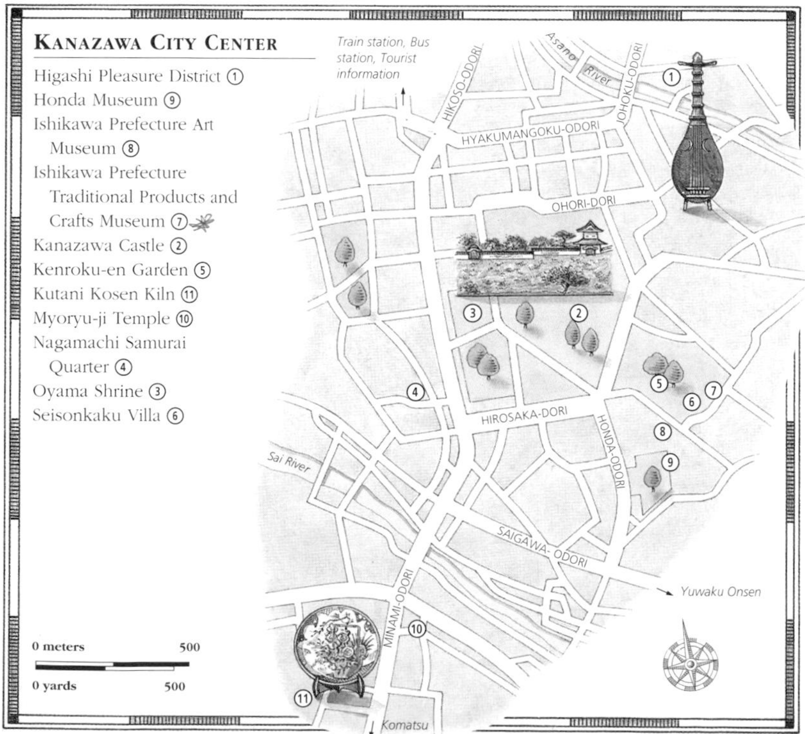

Kanazawa City Center

Higashi Pleasure District ①
Honda Museum ⑨
Ishikawa Prefecture Art Museum ⑧
Ishikawa Prefecture Traditional Products and Crafts Museum ⑦
Kanazawa Castle ②
Kenroku-en Garden ⑤
Kutani Kosen Kiln ⑪
Myoryu-ji Temple ⑩
Nagamachi Samurai Quarter ④
Oyama Shrine ③
Seisonkaku Villa ⑥

Train station, Bus station, Tourist information
Asano River
HIKOSO-ODORI
JOHOKU-ODORI
HYAKUMANGOKU-ODORI
OHORI-DORI
HIROSAKA-DORI
HONDA-ODORI
Sai River
SAIGAWA- ODORI
MINAMI-ODORI
Yuwaku Onsen
Komatsu airport

0 meters 500
0 yards 500

Chujakumon gate at the Zen temple of Eihei-ji

Eihei-ji Temple ⓱

永平寺

Fukui prefecture. *(0776) 63-3102 (bookings and Zen training). Lantern offering on the river (late Aug).*

ESTABLISHED IN 1244, Eihei-ji is one of the Soto Zen sect's two head temples and has been Japan's most active Zen meditation monastery since the late 16th century. In a classic rectilinear plan *(see p131)*, its brown-and-white halls and covered corridors climb up the wooded mountainside. Soto Zen pursues gradual enlightenment by practicing meditation away from the real world; the monastery has about 50 elders and 250 trainees.

The atmosphere is cheerful, yet life is austere, with no heating and a simple diet. In the Sodo Hall (to the left), each trainee has just one *tatami* mat for eating, sleeping, and *zazen* (meditation) – silence is observed here, as in the bath building and toilet. Laypeople wishing to experience the rigorous Zen regime must book ahead.

Noto Peninsula ⓲

能登半島

Ishikawa prefecture. *at Wajima stn (0768) 22-1503. Seihakusai (May 3–5, Nanao); Abare Festival (Jul 7–8, Ushitsu); Hoto Festival (1st Sat in Aug, Nanao); Gojinjo Daiko (Jul 31–Aug 1, Nabune).*

PROJECTING 70 km (45 miles) into the Japan Sea, Noto is a quiet region of fishing villages known for seafood and untouched traditions. The east coast and the sandy west near Kanazawa are quite developed, but the north and northwest are rocky and picturesque. Public transportation around Noto is limited; bus and train are similar in time and cost, but the bus network is wider.

Wajima, a weathered fishing town, produces top-quality, durable lacquerware with at least 70 layers of lacquer. Nearby **Hegura** island is a stopping-off point for migratory birds. Just east of Wajima, **Senmaida** is famed for its "1,000" narrow rice terraces by the sea, while **Sosogi**'s coast has unusual rock formations. Many summer festivals feature demon-masked drummers and *kiriko* lanterns up to 15 m (50 ft) tall. Between events, drums are played at Wajima and Sosogi.

To the west, **Monzen** has the major **Soji-ji** Zen temple. In **Hakui** are the important shrine of **Keta Taisha** and a 2,000-year-old **sumo ring** – Japan's oldest, still used each September. Senmaida, Sosogi, and Monzen can be reached by bus from Wajima, Hakui by bus or train from Kanazawa.

Kamikochi ⓳

上高地

Nagano prefecture. *to Shin-Shimashima, then bus. from Hirayu Onsen. 3-min walk from Onota bus stop (0263) 94-2221. Mountain-opening Festival (Apr 27).*

AN ALPINE VALLEY with a handful of hotels and campsites, Kamikochi lies in the southern part of the Chubu Sangaku (North Japan Alps) National Park, at an altitude of 1,500 m (4,900 ft), and is a good hiking and climbing base. The valley is reached by a tunnel, open from late April to early November; in July, August, Golden Week *(see p40)*, and on some weekends, private cars are banned. Although Japan's highest (after Fuji) and wildest mountains are in the South Alps, the North Alps have more snow and more impressive scenery. Plentiful mountain refuges allow hikes of several days from hut to hut, often via a hot spring. Most huts open from early May to late October (no reservations needed); the main mountaineering season is July to September. Tents and climbing gear can be rented in Kamikochi.

The most spectacular climb is a three-day route from Kamikochi taking in angular **Mount Yari** and **Mount Hotaka** – at 3,190 m (10,470 ft), the highest peak in the North Alps – while short hikes include the rocky scree of **Mount Yake**, the only active volcano in the North Alps. In bad weather, walks are constrained to the valley floor, by the rushing river and through a half-submerged landscape shaped by eruptions from Mount Yake.

DOSOJIN STONES

A man and woman, each holding a bowl of sake, on a Dosojin stone

These pairs of jaunty stone figures, a male and a female, are guardian deities of travelers. They are found at many roadsides in northern Nagano prefecture, as well as at village boundaries. Typically rounded in shape, the pair are often depicted holding hands or with the female offering sake to the male.

Matsumoto ⑳

松本城

Nagano prefecture. 205,000. at Matsumoto JR stn (0263) 32-2814. firelit Noh at castle (Aug), Taimatsu (Oct 3).

Gateway to the Japan Alps, Matsumoto's main attraction is its **castle**, a 20-minute walk northeast of the station. It has the oldest five-tiered keep in Japan (1593) and walls and moat from 1504. Functional yet beautiful, it is well preserved. Devices for defense include niches for archers, guns, and dropping stones. The sixth floor, with superb mountain views, was the headquarters when under attack, and its ceiling contains a shrine to the goddess of the 26th night who was thought to protect against fire and invasion. The other floors can also be visited.

Beside the keep, reached by a covered passage, stands the **Moon-viewing Turret**, added in the 1630s for aesthetic purposes. The castle admission includes the **Japan Folklore Museum** in the grounds, featuring local geography, wildlife, history, dolls, and tools.

Also in Matsumoto are the **Japan Ukiyo-e Museum**, an excellent collection of woodblock prints, and **Matsumoto Folkcraft Museum**, with folk art from Japan and across Asia; on the edge of the city, a 15–20-minute bus ride away from the station, **Asama** and **Utsukushigahara** have pleasant hot springs for bathing.

Matsumoto Castle
(0263) 32-2902. daily.

Japan Ukiyo-e Museum
7 mins drive W of stn. *(0263) 47-4440. Tue–Sun.*

Folkcraft Museum
15 mins by bus from stn. *(0263) 33-1569. Tue–Sun.*

Environs: Just north of Matsumoto, **Hotaka** has views over the bright-green fields of Japan's largest *wasabi* (horseradish) farm, as well as *wasabi*-tasting. The fields are a 40-minute walk from Hotaka station.

An image of the physician Binzuru, follower of Buddha, in Zenko-ji, Nagano

Nagano ㉑

長野

Nagano prefecture. 360,000. at Nagano JR stn (026) 226-5626. www.city.nagano.nagano.jp/index-e.htm *Gokaicho (showing of statue, mid-Apr–mid-May, every six years – next showings 2003, 2009).*

Surrounded by orchards and low mountains, Nagano is a skiing center and was the main venue for the 1998 Winter Olympics. In the town, the prime attraction is **Zenko-ji**, a non-sect temple that draws up to one million pilgrims a year. It has, unusually, always been open to women as well as men, and has male and female chief priests. Established in 670, it enshrines what is thought to be Japan's oldest Buddhist image, an Amida triad brought from Korea in the 6th century. This is kept hidden, and a copy shown every six years. The temple also has a pitch-dark underground passage containing a "key to paradise": touching the key, positioned on the right-hand wall just below waist height, is said to bring happiness in the afterlife.

Environs: In nearby **Obuse**, the small **Hokusai-kan** is a gallery devoted to artist Katsushika Hokusai (1760–1849), who stayed in the town as an old man. Farther into the mountains **Jigokudani Onsen**, reached by bus from Yudanaka station, is famous for the 270 or so wild macaque monkeys living in and around its hot pools.

Hokusai-kan
10-min walk from Obuse stn.
(026) 247-5206. daily.

Jigokudani Onsen
(0269) 33-4379. daily.

Bridge leading to the immaculately preserved Matsumoto castle

A row of *bosatsu* from the temple of Zenko-ji, Nagano ▷

青森県三沢市本町四丁目三ノ一〇六
宮下太郎
晃一
京都市左京区岡崎北御所町二ノ三
静岡県賀茂郡東伊豆町稲取
大宝道生
末田建設(株)
新美清式
はつえ
群馬県館林市北成島町二五三八
吉田養蜂園
株式会社
坂ノ山舗道株式会社

Kyoto City

To truly understand Japan, *the visitor must spend time in the backstreets and environs of its old imperial capital, where scores of the country's famous monuments are preserved within a lively modern city. Kyoto's citizens may grudgingly envy the economic vitality of Tokyo and nearby Osaka, but they take great pride in their refined cuisine, lilting dialect, and sensitivity to the seasons.*

Kyoto women in traditional costume, a not uncommon sight

Founded in 794 as Heian-kyo (capital of peace and tranquility), the city was modeled on the Tang Chinese city of Chang-an. Bounded on three sides by mountains and bisected by a river flowing north to south, the site was considered ideal by Emperor Kanmu's geomancers. As the population grew, however, hygiene was a problem, especially when the Kamo River flooded. A series of rituals and festivals came into being to placate the spirits responsible for plagues and other catastrophes, resulting in a tightly knit fabric of ritual and custom, mostly still observed.

Kyoto culture became an amalgam of several influences, of which the imperial court and nobility were the first and most important. Later came the samurai, patrons of Zen Buddhism and the tea ceremony. Merchants were also influential, especially the silk weavers of Nishijin. The city was reduced to ashes at various times by earthquakes, fires, and the ten-year period of civil strife known as the Onin War (1467–77). During the Edo period (1600–1868), the balance of power shifted from Kyoto to Edo (Tokyo), and Kyoto eventually lost its status of capital in 1868. At first glance, modern Kyoto may seem little different from other Japanese cities, but the pleasures of this repository of Japanese culture will soon reveal themselves. Life here is still largely tied to nature's rhythms, as can be gauged by visiting at different times of the year. *Kyo-ryori*, Kyoto's celebrated cuisine, for example, makes much of seasonality, and the city's exquisite gardens go through striking seasonal transitions.

Bridge on the northern edge of the Gion district, a remnant of old Kyoto

◁ **Avenue of *torii* gates at Fushimi Shrine, southern Kyoto**

Exploring Kyoto City

KYOTO IS BOUNDED BY MOUNTAINS to the west, north, and east. Many of the best monuments and gardens are found in the foothills, such as the Higashiyama (Eastern Mountains) district east of the Kamo River. Kyoto's treasures have to be sought out. Only by investigating side streets with their old shops and townhouses, exploring temples, and wandering through outlying districts will you begin to get a sense of the city's cultural riches.

SIGHTS AT A GLANCE

Temples and Shrines

Chion-in Temple 11
Daitoku-ji Temple 19
Ginkaku-ji: the Silver Pavilion 16
Kamo Shrines 18
Kinkaku-ji: the Golden Pavilion 21
Kitano Tenman-gu Shrine 20
Kiyomizu-dera Temple 10
Koryu-ji Temple 26
Myoshin-ji Temple 25
Nanzen-ji Temple 15
Ninna-ji Temple 24
Nishi and Higashi Hongan-ji Temples 5
Ryoan-ji Temple 23
Sanjusangen-do Temple 3
Shoren-in Temple 12
Toji Temple 1

Museums and Notable Buildings

Insho Domoto Museum 22
Kyoto National Museum 4
Kyoto Station 2
Nijo Castle pp154–5 6

Districts

Eastern Gion and the Higashiyama pp160–61 9
Gion District 8
Imperial Park 17
Okazaki Area 13
Pontocho Alley 7

Walk

The Philosopher's Walk 14

SEE ALSO

- ***Farther Afield*** pp170–73
- ***Where to Stay*** pp297–8
- ***Where to Eat*** pp330–31

KYOTO ADDRESSES

Despite its gridlike layout, Kyoto has no more logical pattern to its address system than anywhere else in Japan. Residences and shops are organized into *cho*, or neighborhoods, many formed from the boundaries of medieval guilds. Locations are often given in relation to an intersection or well-known landmark. Because the city is built on an incline rising from south to north, south is indicated in an address by the word *sagaru* (go down) and north by *agaru* (go up).

VISITORS' CHECKLIST

Kyoto prefecture. *1,450,000.* *Sanyo Shinkansen and other lines.* *(075) 343-6655.* www.spcom.co.jp/KVG *Aoi Matsuri (Hollyhock Festival, May 15); Gion Matsuri (Jul); Jidai Matsuri (Festival of the Ages, Oct 22).*

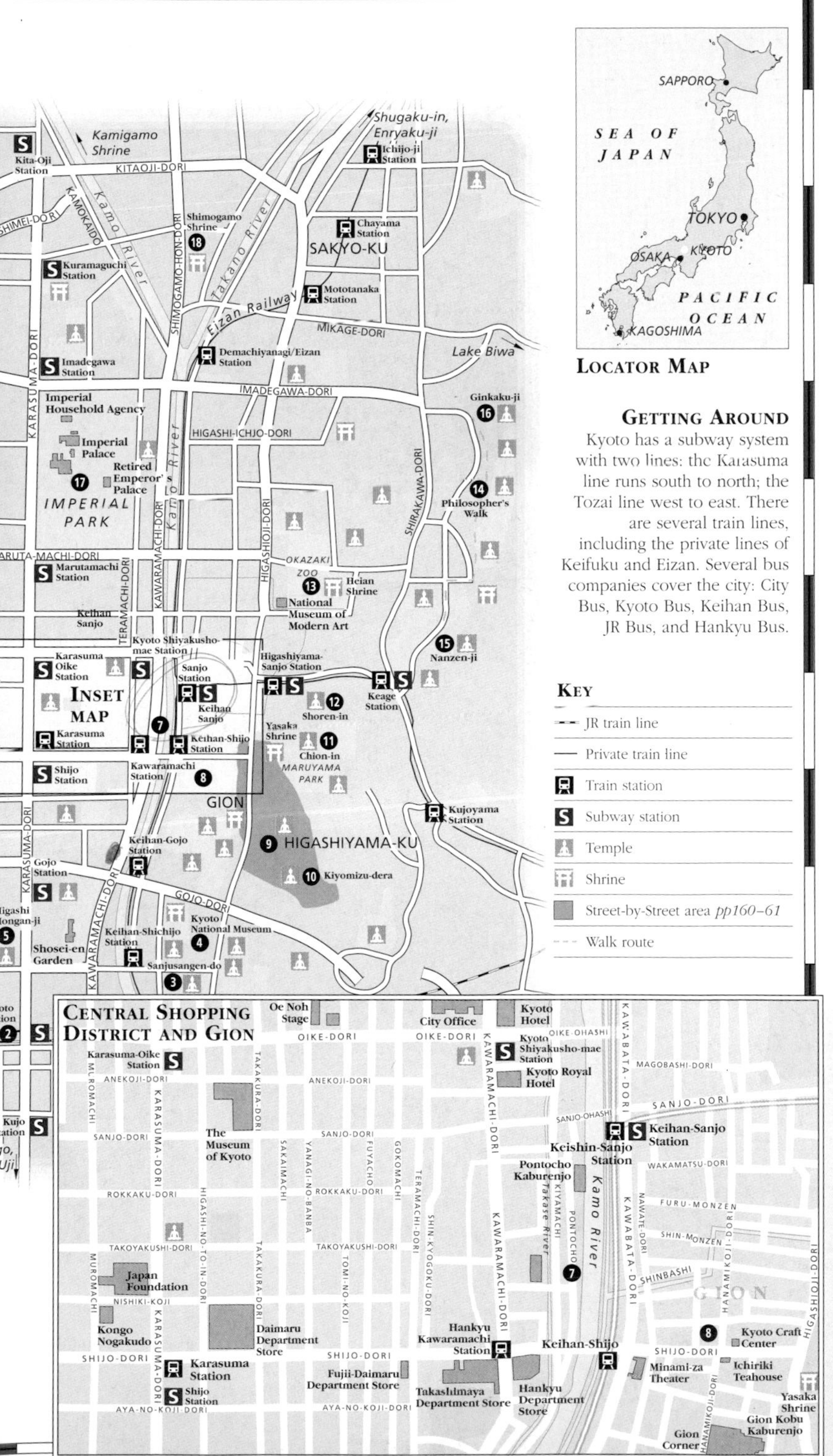

GETTING AROUND

Kyoto has a subway system with two lines: the Karasuma line runs south to north; the Tozai line west to east. There are several train lines, including the private lines of Keifuku and Eizan. Several bus companies cover the city: City Bus, Kyoto Bus, Keihan Bus, JR Bus, and Hankyu Bus.

Toji Temple ❶

東寺

Toji stn, Kintetsu line. *17 to Toji Higashimon-mae.* *9am–4:30pm daily.* **Museum** *(075) 691-3325.* *Mar 20–May 25; Sep 20–Nov 25.*

ALTHOUGH IT LACKS the mossy beauty of many Kyoto temples, dusty, hoary Toji (actual name Kyo-o-gokoku-ji) impresses by the sheer weight of its history. Its Buddhas have been watching over the city ever since Kukai *(see p223)* founded the temple in 796. The city's religious foundations were laid here, and echoes of bygone rituals seem to linger in Toji's hallowed halls.

Kukai turned Toji into the main headquarters of Shingon Buddhism. The sect's esoteric rituals relied heavily on mandalas, and in the Kodo (lecture hall), 21 statues form a three-dimensional mandala, at the center of which is Dainichi Nyorai, the cosmic Buddha who first expounded the esoteric teachings. About 1,200 years old, these and other major images were carved from single blocks of wood.

Yakushi Nyorai, the Buddha of healing, and his attendants Gakko and Nikko, are enshrined in the two-story Kondo (main hall). First built in 796, the present structure dates from 1603 and is considered a masterpiece.

Rebuilt in 1644, Toji's magnificent five-story pagoda – at 55 m (180 ft) the tallest wooden structure in Japan – has become a symbol of Kyoto. Inside are images of four Buddhas and their followers.

Toji temple's five-story pagoda, the tallest in Japan

Soaring, light-filled main hall of Kyoto Station

Northwest of the Kodo is the Miei-do or Taishi-do (great teacher's hall) where Kukai lived. It houses a Secret Buddha, a Fudo Myo-o image, shown on rare occasions, as well as an image of Kukai. A National Treasure, the graceful structure dates from 1380.

Kukai's death is commemorated on the 21st of each month, when a flea market, called *Kobo-san* by the locals, is held in the temple precincts. Many shoppers take time out for a brief pilgrimage to the Miei-do, where they offer money and incense, some rubbing the incense smoke onto whatever body part is troubling them.

Kyoto Station ❷

京都駅

Complex *2nd flr main concourse, left from escalator.* *(075) 361-4401.* *10am–7pm daily.* **Kyoto City TIC** *2nd flr main concourse, right from escalator.* *(075) 343-6655.* *8:30am–7pm daily.* **Train** *1st flr main concourse.* *(075) 352-5441.* *8am–9pm daily.*

A SLEEK COMPLEX of soaring spaces, glass surfaces, and bleacher-like staircases, Kyoto's new JR train station provides a futuristic entry to Japan's old imperial capital. Completed in 1997, the structure is the work of architect Hara Koji, a Tokyo University professor whose design triumphed in an international competition. Although it has been criticized for its refusal to incorporate traditional Japanese motifs in its design, the station is undeniably eye-catching. Thanks to its open-air spaces it also ironically resembles a traditional wooden Kyoto house: pleasant in summer, but drafty and cold in winter.

Within the station is a shopping area called **The Cube**, which includes shops specializing in Kyoto craft items and food products.

Long hall and landscaped grounds of Sanjusangen-do

Sanjusangen-do Temple ❸

三十三間堂

(075) 525-0033. *Keihan Nanajo stn.* *100, 206, 208 to Hakubutsukan Sanjusangen-do-mae.* *Apr–mid-Nov: 8am–5pm daily; mid-Nov–Mar: 9am–4pm daily.*

SANJUSANGEN-DO (popular name of Rengeo-in) induces an almost hallucinatory effect on its visitors who, once inside its elongated main hall, find themselves face to face with ranks of nearly identical Kannon (goddess of mercy) images – 1,001 of them, to be precise – all glimmering in the dark. The effect is magical, and a bit eerie.

Sanjusangen-do dates from 1164 and is the longest wooden structure in the world. Its name derives from the 33 *(sanjusan)* spaces between the building's pillars. The main, magnificent image of a 1,000-armed Kannon was carved in 1254 by Tankei at the age of 82. Upon its head are ten other heads, including a miniature image of the Amida Buddha. Stretching out on either side of the main image are 1,000 other smaller images. Kannon was believed to have 33 manifestations, so the faithful would have invoked the mercy of 33,033 Kannons.

On January 15, Coming of Age Day, the temple hosts an archery contest for young women, who shoot arrows from one end of the veranda of the main hall to the other.

Kyoto National Museum ❹

京都国立博物館

(075) 541-1151. 9am–4:30pm Tue–Sun (to 8pm Fri in Apr–Nov).

The city's National Museum was established in 1895 by the Imperial Household Agency. It is noted for its collection of pictorial works and Heian-period sculptures. Special exhibitions are held in the Meiji-era brick building to the right of the entrance.

Nishi and Higashi Hongan-ji Temples ❺

西本願寺と東本願寺

Nishi Hongan-ji
(075) 371-5181. 9, 28, 75 to Nishi Honganji-mae. May–Aug: 5:30am–6pm daily; Sep–Apr: 5:30am–5:30pm daily.
Higashi Hongan-ji *(075) 371-9181. JR Kyoto Stn. 5 to Karasuma Nanajo. Mar–Oct: 5:50am–5:30pm daily; Nov–Feb: 6:20am–4:30pm daily.*

With their massive flower-decked altars, ornately carved transoms, and shimmering expanses of *tatami* matting worn smooth by millions of stockinged feet, the cavernous Hongan-ji temples testify to the power and popularity of the Jodo-Shinshu sect.

The two temples are almost identical in their layout, reflecting their common origin. Each has a huge Goei-do (founder's hall) and a smaller Amida-do housing an Amida Buddha image. **Nishi Hongan-ji** is rich in National Treasures. Unfortunately, not all are always on view. They include the Shoin (study hall), with its lavishly decorated Shiroshoin and Kuroshoin compartments; Kokei no Niwa, a garden featuring cycad palms; two Noh stages, one of which is thought to be the oldest Noh stage in existence; Hiunkaku, a large tea pavilion; and the Karamon, or Chinese gate. The Shoin is open twice a month, but dates vary. (The Kuroshoin, however, is never shown.) Hiunkaku is open only once a year, on May 21. Entrance requires a large donation, which includes a bowl of tea and a Noh performance.

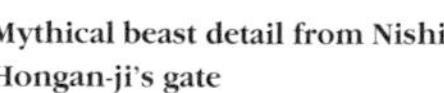

Mythical beast detail from Nishi Hongan-ji's gate

Higashi Hongan-ji's immense and lavish Goei-do gate is one of the first traditional structures visitors to Kyoto see as they head north out of Kyoto Station. The temple's Goei-do (founder's hall) dates from 1895 and claims to be the largest wooden structure in the world. The striking white plaster and gray tile walls on the temple's northern side belong to the temple *kura*, or storehouse.

Environs: Two blocks east of Higashi Hongan-ji proper is **Shosei-en** (nicknamed Kikoku-tei), a spacious stroll garden owned by the temple. Poet-scholar Ishikawa Jozan (1583–1672) and landscape architect Kobori Enshu (1579–1647) are said to have had a hand in its design. Herons, ducks, and other wildlife find refuge in this city-center oasis.

Detail of the main gate fronting the street at Nishi Hongan-ji

Nijo Castle 6

二条城

With few of the grand fortifications of other castles in Japan, Nijo is instead best known for its unusually ornate interiors and so-called nightingale floors. The latter were designed to make bird-like squeaking sounds when walked upon, a warning of possible intruders. The complex was created by Shogun Tokugawa Ieyasu (1543–1616), and symbolized the power and riches of the newly established Edo-based shogunate. Ieyasu's grandson Iemitsu commissioned the best Kano School painters for the reception halls, in preparation for an imperial visit. Ironically, in 1867 the last Tokugawa shogun resigned at Nijo Castle, in the presence of Emperor Meiji.

Cherry Trees Painting
The painting of flowering cherry trees on the sliding door panels is attributed to Kano Naonobu (1607–50).

Shiroshoin (shogun's living chambers)

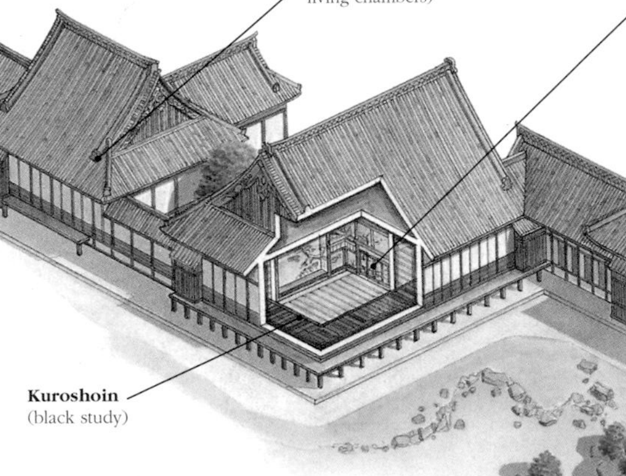

Kuroshoin (black study)

Garden
Nijo's garden is famous for the wealth and variety of its rocks.

Ninomaru Complex
The focus of Nijo Castle is the Ninomaru reception rooms, a staggered group of buildings interconnected by covered wooden walkways.

★ Ohiroma Ichi-no-ma
(first grand chamber)
Dummies representing daimyo *(feudal lords) are shown paying respects to the shogun on his dais.*

Star Features

- ★ Karamon Gate
- ★ Ohiroma Ichi-no-ma

Large Cats Painting
This dynamic animal scene was painted at a time when Japanese artists mistook leopards for female tigers.

Visitors' Checklist

Entrance on Horikawa-dori.
(075) 841-0096.
Nijojo-mae stn. *9, 12, 50, 52, 61, 67.* *8:45am–5pm daily. Last admission 4pm.*
Dec 26–Jan 4.

The nightingale floors were carefully laid so that the cramps and nails below the floorboards would rub together and squeak gently when disturbed.

Shikidai (reception chamber)

★ Karamon Gate
This Momoyama-period gate has a Chinese-style gable and gold-plated fixtures.

Entrance to Ninomaru compound

The Kano School Painters

The Kano painters, originally from a low-ranking samurai family, grew to prominence in the 15th century for their Chinese-style landscapes, figures-in-landscape, and bird and flower scenes. The paintings at Nijo Castle are the largest Kano pieces executed. Among the motifs are life-size tigers and panthers crouching among bamboo groves, wild geese and herons in a winter landscape, pine trees, flitting swallows, and frolicking peacocks.

Huge pine trees in the Shikidai, by Kano Tanyu (1602–74)

Entrance to Palace
Above the carriage porch is an unusually ornate wood carving of flying birds, peacocks, and delicately twining flowers.

Pontocho Alley 7

先斗町通り

Kawaramachi stn, Hankyu Kyoto line. 3, 4, 17, 32, 100 to Shijo-Kawaramachi.

THIS CHARMING alleyway is best appreciated after dusk, when it is reminiscent of an *ukiyo-e* print *(see p81)*. Formerly a sandbar, the stretch of land began to be developed in 1670. The area flourished as an entertainment district and was licensed as a gay quarter, a role it continues to play. Although neon and concrete are encroaching, the street largely remains the preserve of the traditional wooden *ochaya* – the type of teahouse where geisha entertain clients.

Pontocho is also home to the tiny **Tanuki (Badger) Shrine**. In 1978 a fire broke out in Pontocho, taking the life of a geisha. Where it stopped, a ceramic *tanuki (see p311)* was found shattered by the heat. Believing that Mr. Tanuki had sacrificed himself on their behalf, the residents built this little shrine to house his remains. Throw in a coin and a recorded message imparts such pearls of wisdom as "beware of fire."

From the beginning of June to mid-September, many of Pontocho's riverside restaurants erect platforms, called *yuka*, over the canal running parallel to the Kamo River.

The colorful Tanuki Shrine, dedicated to a badger in Japanese folklore

Two-story gateway to Yasaka Shrine, Gion district

Gion District 8

祇園地区

Several blocks north and south of Shijo-dori, bounded by the Kamo River to the west and the Higashiyama to the east. *Shijo stn, Keihan line. 80, 86, 100 to Gion.*

BY TURNS tawdry and sublime, the Gion is Kyoto's best-known geisha quarter and symbol to the average Japanese male of all that's good in life: wine, women, and karaoke.

The Gion's history started in feudal times, with stalls catering to the needs of pilgrims and other visitors. These evolved into teahouses fulfilling a variety of appetites. In the late 16th century, Kabuki moved from the Kamo riverbank, where it had started, into several theaters just east of the river, furthering the Gion's reputation as a playboy's paradise. One of these, **Minami-za** *(see p178)*, still exists.

The **Yasaka Shrine**, whose striking two-story vermilion gate rises above the eastern end of Shijo-dori, was established around 656 and originally called Gion Shrine. Its deities protect from illness and, in 869, were paraded through the streets to stop an epidemic – the beginning of the famous Gion Matsuri *(see p178)*. On New Year's Day, thousands flock here to pray for health and prosperity, while in early April crowds stream through its gates on their way to **Maruyama Park**, a cherry-blossom viewing site.

Gion's main shopping area is the stretch of Shijo between Yasaka Shrine and Shijo Bridge, which includes shops with expensive kimono accessories. On the southeast corner of Shijo and Hanamikoji is the Gion's most famous *ochaya*, **Ichiriki**. Easily identified by its distinctive red walls, this teahouse is the setting of a scene in the Kabuki play *Chushingura*. **Hanamikoji** itself, a historically preserved zone, shows the Gion at its classic, and classy, best. The restaurants and *ochaya* here are the haunts of politicians and company presidents, and are likely to turn a cold shoulder to people without a proper introduction. More accessible to tourists are the nearby **Gion Corner** and the **Gion Kobu Kaburenjo** venues *(see p178)*.

Running east from Hanamikoji, north of Shijo, is **Shinbashi**, a street lined with *ochaya*, and nary a neon sign to be seen. At the eastern end of this beautifully preserved area is the tiny shrine of **Tatsumi Daimyo-jin**, its red surfaces plastered with name cards of Gion geisha, hostesses, and restaurant owners who have visited to pray for prosperity.

The average Gion-goer, however, is more likely to partake of drink and karaoke than engage in geisha play at a prestigious *ochaya*. His territory is the northeastern Gion, where the cluttered streets of neon and concrete are as gaudy as Shinbashi is refined.

Geisha, Geiko, and Maiko

GEISHA are female professional entertainers whose knowledge of traditional arts, skill at verbal repartee, and ability to keep a secret win them the respect, and sometimes love, of their well-heeled and often influential male clients. The profession, dating from the 17th century, is in decline and blurred by the activities of so-called *onsen geisha* and others who offer more sexual than classical arts, or who are more glorified waitress than geisha. Kyoto's proud geisha prefer the term *geiko* (child of the arts). Less polished than their *geiko* "sisters," *maiko*, apprentice geisha, are a Kyoto-only phenomenon. The city has four geisha enclaves: Gion-kobu, Pontocho, Miyagawa-cho, and Kamishichi-ken. Public dances are staged in each district in spring and fall. At other times, the only way to see geisha perform is at private functions, often held at *ryotei*, *ochaya*, and *ryokan* (upscale restaurants, teahouses, and inns).

A Kyoto *maiko*

The white face and delicately shaped red lips are classic ideals of beauty in Japan.

Under-kimono

***Tabi* socks**

***Pontocho**, one of Kyoto's historic geisha districts, has many* ochaya, *where geisha are booked to entertain prestigious clients.*

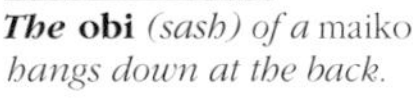

***The* obi** *(sash) of a* maiko *hangs down at the back.*

Ornamental hairpins vary with the seasons.

A *maiko's* hair is her own, not a wig.

The nape of the neck, accentuated by the unpainted part, is considered sensuous.

Embroidered collar

The Maiko Costume

Only in Kyoto do young women training to be *geiko* wear their hair in a distinctive style and sport a unique costume featuring a long, hanging *obi*, tall *koppori* clogs, and an under-kimono with an embroidered collar. When becoming full-fledged *geiko*, they exchange the embroidered collar for a white one, a transition known as *eri-kae*, or collar change.

***The geisha world** moves to the rhythm of the* shamisen, *a three-stringed instrument that originated in Okinawa. Geisha who choose not to specialize in dance will instead master the* shamisen *or another instrument. The skills of older geisha are held in high regard.*

***Poised and posture-perfect**, Umegiku, of the Kamishichi-ken district, performs classical dance with a fan as prop. For more formal occasions she will paint her face and wear a different kimono.*

Kyoto men on one of the ornate floats displayed during the city's major festival in July, the Gion Matsuri ▷

Street-by-Street: Eastern Gion and the Higashiyama ❾

Sipping the sacred, cleansing water at Kiyomizu Temple

For most of Kyoto's history, the area comprising the Higashiyama (Eastern Mountains) district lay outside the official boundaries of the capital. As a result, it was always more rustic and secluded. Furthermore, being separated from the main city by the Kamo River, it was spared the fires that often ravaged Kyoto. Consequently, Higashiyama remains one of the city's most charming and unspoiled districts. The small area shown here includes the eastern side of the Gion, leading through some delightful stone-paved roads up to Kiyomizu Temple.

Maruyama Park
Kyoto's most famous cherry-blossom viewing site is mobbed until the petals fall.

Kodai-ji was built in 1605 for the widow of Toyotomi Hideyoshi.

★ Yasaka Shrine
On the edge of Kyoto's central shopping district, the Yasaka Shrine (see p156) *oversees the religious rites of the city's main festival, the Gion Matsuri, in July.*

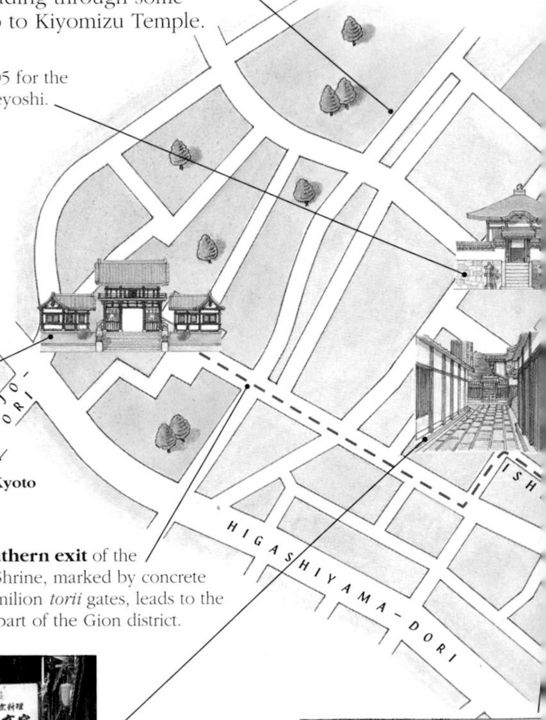

SHIJO-DORI

Central Kyoto

HIGASHIYAMA-DORI

The southern exit of the Yasaka Shrine, marked by concrete and vermilion *torii* gates, leads to the eastern part of the Gion district.

★ Ishibe-Koji Lane
This charming lane with discreet inns and teahouses is an extension of the Gion entertainment district (see p156). *The exquisite wooden buildings with tiny gardens reflect the peaceful atmosphere of old Kyoto.*

Ne-ne no Michi
Named after Hideyoshi's widow, "Ne-ne's road" is a wide flagstone-paved avenue, home to small, upscale shops and private galleries. Long, stone staircases lead up from the road to the temple of Kodai-ji and the Ryozen Kannon.

Yasaka Pagoda
Not to be confused with the Shinto shrine of the same name to its north, the elegant, five-story Yasaka Pagoda is all that remains of a Buddhist temple that once stood here.

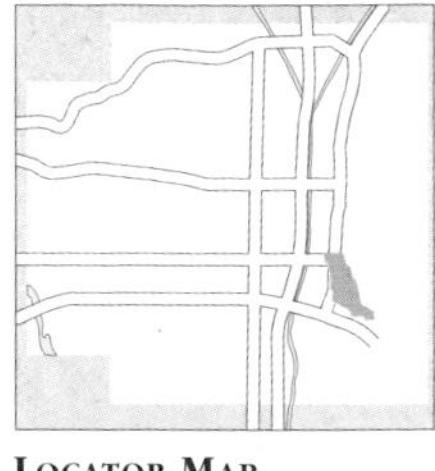

LOCATOR MAP
See Kyoto map page 151

Ryozen Kannon
The 24-m (80-ft) high concrete figure near Kodai-ji Temple is dedicated to the Japanese soldiers who died in World War II.

Kiyomizu-*yaki*, a refined, brightly colored porcelain, is sold in numerous pottery shops lining the roads leading up to Kiyomizu.

★ Kiyomizu Temple
This famous temple (see p162) *is over a thousand years old and could almost be called an institution of Kyoto life.*

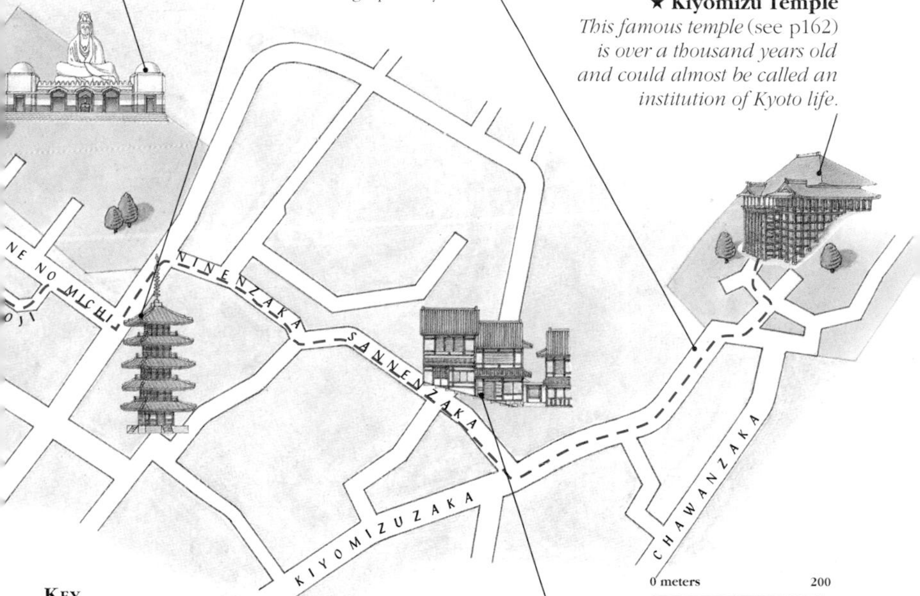

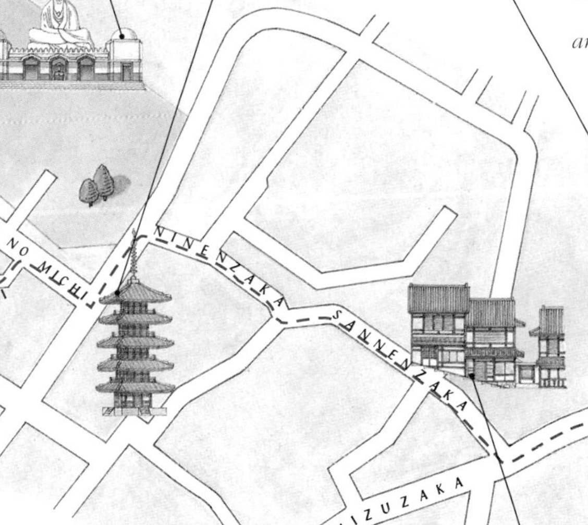

KEY

– – – Suggested route

★ Stone-Paved Roads
Two flagstone-paved streets called Sannenzaka ("three-year slope") and Ninenzaka ("two-year slope") are a preservation district. Take care on the steps – local lore maintains that a slip here will bring two or three years' bad luck.

STAR SIGHTS

- ★ Stone-Paved Roads
- ★ Ishibe-Koji Lane
- ★ Kiyomizu Temple
- ★ Yasaka Shrine

View from the veranda of the main hall at Kiyomizu-dera

Kiyomizu-dera Temple ⑩

清水寺

(075) 551-1234. 206 or 207 to Kiyomizu-michi. 6am–6pm daily.

WHILE MANY other famous temples are the preserves of certain sects, Kiyomizu-dera seems to belong to everyone. For over 1,000 years, pilgrims have climbed the slope to pray to the temple's 11-headed Kannon image and drink from its sacred spring (*kiyomizu* means pure water). The main hall's veranda, a nail-less miracle of Japanese joinery, offers wonderful views of Kyoto. To view the temple itself, walk to the pagoda across the ravine, and you'll see why the expression "to jump off Kiyomizu's stage" is the Japanese equivalent of "to take the plunge."

Statue of Kannon at Kiyomizu-dera

On the temple's north side is a small shrine where love charms can be purchased.

Chion-in Temple ⑪

知恩院

(075) 531-2111. Higashiyama stn, Tozai line. 100 or 206 to Chion-in-mae. Apr–Sep: 9am–4:30pm daily; Oct–Mar: 9am–3:40pm daily.

CHION-IN'S colossal Sanmon, the largest such gate in Japan, was built to proclaim the supremacy of Jodo-sect Buddhism, of which Chion-in is the headquarters. It was also an emphatic statement of the authority of the Tokugawa shogunate, which funded the temple's restoration in 1633.

The well-endowed complex occupies the site where Honen, the founder of the Jodo sect, started to preach in 1175. It boasts a lavish founder's hall, a smaller hall enshrining an image of Amida Buddha, and elegant reception halls decorated with Kano School *(see p155)* paintings. The Gongen-do mausoleum enshrines the spirits of Tokugawa Ieyasu, his son Hidetada, and grandson Iemitsu. The temple also possesses a huge bell that is solemnly rung 108 times (once for each sin Man is prone to commit) on New Year's Eve, an event broadcast on TV.

Shoren-in Temple ⑫

青蓮院

(075) 561-2345. Higashiyama stn, Tozai line. 5 to Jingu-michi. 9am–5pm daily.

ARISTOCRATIC Shoren-in's symbol is its ancient camphor trees whose 700-year-old gnarled limbs spread majestically on either side of the front gate. The grounds are beautifully landscaped, with a bright pond garden on one side and a mysterious, camphor tree-shaded expanse of moss on the other. The teahouse in the garden has been newly rebuilt, the original having been burned in April 1993 by left-wing radicals protesting the Emperor's visit to Okinawa.

Okazaki Area ⑬

岡崎公園一帯

5 or 100 to Kyoto Kaikan Bijutsukan-mae. Jidai Matsuri (Festival of the Ages, Oct 22, Heian Shrine).

OKAZAKI is home to museums, galleries, sports grounds, the municipal zoo, and **Heian Shrine**, one of Kyoto's largest and newest shrines. Built in 1895, the shrine was intended to help boost the city's morale and economy – both at a low ebb after Tokyo was made capital in 1868. With its vermilion pillars and green tiles, the shrine harks back to Tang Dynasty China. Its pond garden is famous for irises and a Chinese-style covered bridge.

The **National Museum of Modern Art** houses an outstanding collection of paintings by a school of Kyoto artists active in the Meiji and Taisho eras. Across the street is the venerable **Kyoto City Museum of Fine Arts**, which hosts exhibitions of European and American works. The **Kyoto Exhibition Hall** (Mikako Messe), hosts a variety of shows, while its basement museum presents scores of Kyoto crafts, including Kiyomizu-*yaki* porcelain.

Museum of Modern Art
(075) 761-4111. Tue–Sun.
Museum of Fine Arts
(075) 771-4107. Tue–Sun.
Exhibition Hall
(075) 762-2670. Tue–Sun.

Heian-jingu, the shrine built in 1895 in Okazaki

The Tea Ceremony

VALUED FOR ITS medicinal qualities, tea was imported from China in the 8th century. The nobility took to drinking it at lavish parties, and Murato Shuko (1422–1502) later developed the custom's spiritual aspects, which appealed to the samurai. The point of the ritual *(chaji)*, in which a light meal and whipped powdered tea *(matcha)* are served by a host to a few invited guests, is summed up by the samurai notion "one lifetime, one meeting" *(ichigo, ichie)*. In other words, this is a unique moment to be treasured. In Kyoto, where the tea ceremony was developed, special rituals are put on for tourists *(see p179)*, with commentary about the complex etiquette and Zen ideals. Visitors can also enjoy *matcha* and a sweet *(wagashi)* without the ritual at many temples and specialty teashops.

Seasonal flowers in the *tokonoma*

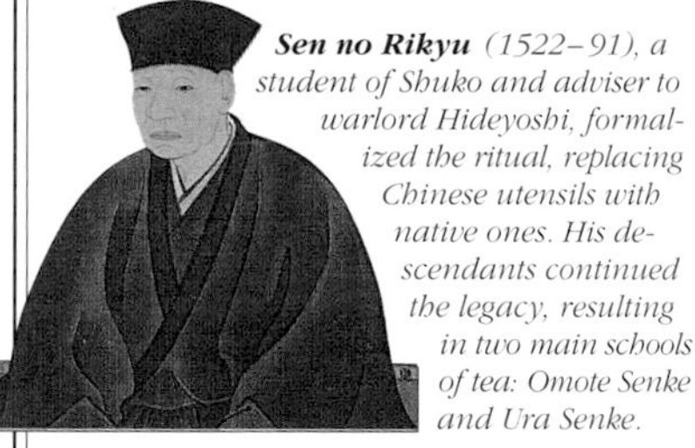

Sen no Rikyu *(1522–91), a student of Shuko and adviser to warlord Hideyoshi, formalized the ritual, replacing Chinese utensils with native ones. His descendants continued the legacy, resulting in two main schools of tea: Omote Senke and Ura Senke.*

The ceremonial teahouse *is a small, hut-like building with a garden* (see pp26–7)*, not to be confused with other types of teahouses, such as the geisha's* ochaya*, or those for wayfarers. The one shown here is at Daitoku-ji* (see pp166–7)*, the spiritual home of the tea ceremony.*

The tea utensils *reflect Zen values of simplicity, refinement, and restraint.*

To drink **matcha**, *even informally, hold the bowl with your right hand and place it in the palm of your left. Turn it clockwise about 90 degrees, raise it with both hands, then empty it in three gulps.*

The Way of Tea

The tea ceremony is a well-orchestrated series of events. The ritual involves meeting your fellow guests, walking through the grounds of the teahouse, performing ablutions, entering a cell-like room, meeting your host, admiring the features of the room and tea utensils, watching the tea being prepared, bowing, and consuming the food and tea. Each part of the ritual is symbolic; ultimately it is your appreciation of the moment that counts.

The decorative alcove *(tokonoma)* has a hanging scroll *(kakemono)* and sometimes a flower arrangement or art object to be admired.

Guests sit *seiza*, kneeling on the *tatami* matting, an uncomfortable position for the uninitiated.

Guests bow when attendants offer individual bowls of the freshly prepared tea.

The Philosopher's Walk ⓮

哲学の道

One of Kyoto's best-loved spots, the Philosopher's Walk follows a cherry-tree-lined canal meandering along the base of the scenic Higashiyama (Eastern Mountains) between Ginkaku-ji south to Nyakuoji-jinja, and connects with roads leading to the precincts of Nanzen-ji. The route is so-named because a Kyoto University philosophy professor, Nishida Kitaro (1870–1945), used it for his daily constitutional. Coffee and craft shops, restaurants, and boutiques are scattered along the route. The path becomes a veritable promenade during the cherry and maple seasons, as couples from all over the Kansai region flock to enjoy its unspoiled natural beauty.

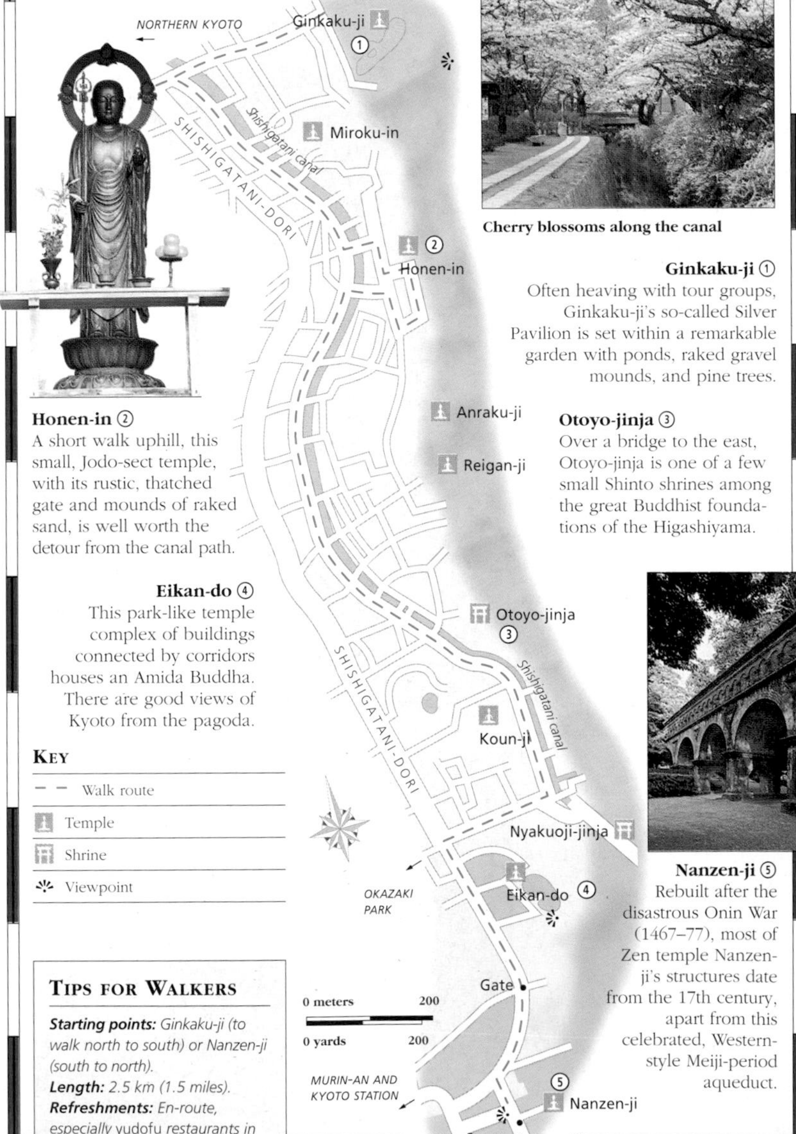

Cherry blossoms along the canal

Ginkaku-ji ①
Often heaving with tour groups, Ginkaku-ji's so-called Silver Pavilion is set within a remarkable garden with ponds, raked gravel mounds, and pine trees.

Honen-in ②
A short walk uphill, this small, Jodo-sect temple, with its rustic, thatched gate and mounds of raked sand, is well worth the detour from the canal path.

Otoyo-jinja ③
Over a bridge to the east, Otoyo-jinja is one of a few small Shinto shrines among the great Buddhist foundations of the Higashiyama.

Eikan-do ④
This park-like temple complex of buildings connected by corridors houses an Amida Buddha. There are good views of Kyoto from the pagoda.

Nanzen-ji ⑤
Rebuilt after the disastrous Onin War (1467–77), most of Zen temple Nanzen-ji's structures date from the 17th century, apart from this celebrated, Western-style Meiji-period aqueduct.

Key

- – – Walk route
- Temple
- Shrine
- Viewpoint

Tips for Walkers

Starting points: *Ginkaku-ji (to walk north to south) or Nanzen-ji (south to north).*
Length: *2.5 km (1.5 miles).*
Refreshments: *En-route, especially yudofu restaurants in precincts of Nanzen-ji.*

Colossal, free-standing Sanmon (gateway) at Nanzen-ji

Nanzen-ji Temple ⓯

南禅寺

(075) 771-0365. Keage stn, Tozai line. 5 or 100 to Nanzen-ji-Eikan-do-michi. 8:40am–5pm daily (Dec–Feb: to 4:30).

FROM ITS pine-studded outer precincts to the inner recesses of its subtemples, this quintessential Zen temple exudes an air of serenity. Nanzen ji has been at the center of Japanese Zen history since 1386, when it was placed in control of Kyoto's Gozan, or "five great Zen temples."

The **Hojo** (abbot's quarters) includes a small but exquisite dry garden attributed to Kobori Enshu (1579–1647), and Momoyama-period paintings, including the Kano Tanyu masterpiece *Tiger Drinking Water*. Nearby is a room overlooking a waterfall and garden, where a bowl of *matcha* (ceremonial tea) and a sweet can be enjoyed for a small fee.

The temple's colossal **Sanmon**, a two-story gate built in 1626 to console the souls of those killed in the Summer Siege of Osaka Castle, is said to have been the hideout of Ishikawa Goemon, a legendary outlaw hero who was later boiled alive in an iron cauldron.

SUBTEMPLES: Three of Nanzen-ji's 12 subtemples are open to the public year-round. The most impressive, **Konchi-in**, boasts one of the few authenticated works by Kobori Enshu, featuring boulders and pines arranged in a tortoise-and-crane motif. **Tenju-an** has an elegant dry garden and a small but lush stroll garden. Secluded **Nanzen-in** occupies the original site of Emperor Kameyama's villa. Restored in 1703, the temple faces a pond-centered garden backed by a thickly wooded mountainside.

The red-brick **aqueduct** in front of Nanzen-in may seem incongruous, but for Japanese tourists this "exotic" Western structure is one of Nanzen-ji's greatest attractions. Built in 1890, it formed part of an ambitious canal project to bring water and goods from neighboring Shiga prefecture into the city. It was one of Meiji Japan's first feats of engineering.

Nanzen-ji is synonymous with *yudofu*, boiled tofu, a delicacy best enjoyed during cold months. Specialty restaurants are located within the temple precincts *(see p331)*.

ENVIRONS: Gem-like **Murin-an** to the west of Nanzen-ji is the former villa of Meiji-era statesman Yamagata Aritomo. The garden's design makes good use of water from the aqueduct. Just to the north of Nanzen-ji, **Eikan-do** houses an image of Amida Buddha depicted in the act of looking back over his shoulder, a very unusual pose.

Ginkaku-ji: the Silver Pavilion ⓰

銀閣寺

(075) 771-5725. 5, 32 to Ginkaku-ji-mae. 8:30am–5pm daily (Dec to mid-Mar: 9am–4:30pm).

GINKAKU-JI – actual name, Jisho-ji; English nickname, Silver Pavilion – is considered by some to be an unequaled masterpiece of garden design; others find it overrated. Not in dispute is the importance of Ginkaku-ji to Japanese culture, for within its walls the tea ceremony, Noh, flower arrangement, and ink painting found new levels of refinement.

The temple was originally the mountain retreat of shogun Yoshimasa (1358–1408), who is remembered for an artistic renaissance now referred to as Higashiyama culture. In tribute to his grandfather, who covered Kinkaku-ji in gold leaf *(see p168)*, Yoshimasa intended to finish his pavilion in silver. However, the ruinous Onin War thwarted that ambition. Minus its final coating, the graceful Silver Pavilion now shines with the patina of age.

The Silver Pavilion, which never received its intended coating

The majestic Kenreimon gate within the Imperial Park

Imperial Park ⓱

京都御苑

Imadegawa stn, Karasuma line.
Imperial Palace *tours in English at 10am and 2pm Mon–Fri.*
Retired Emperor's Palace *tours in Japanese only at 11am and 1:30pm Sun–Fri. Under 20s not admitted.*
Both palaces *Apr, May, Oct, Nov: weekdays; Dec 25–Jan 5, public hols, and during special rituals.*
Imperial Household Agency *(075) 211-1215.* *8:45am–noon, 1–4pm Mon–Fri.*

With its stately pines and vistas of the Higashiyama, the Imperial Park (Kyoto Gyoen) is a spacious oasis in the heart of the city. On its grounds are the **Imperial Palace** (Kyoto Gosho) and **Retired Emperor's Palace** (Sento Gosho), whose impressive stroll garden was built by the Tokugawa for retired emperor Go-Mizuno'o in 1630. The **Imperial Household Agency** (Kunaicho), where tickets are issued for the imperial structures in the park, as well as to Shugaku-in and Katsura villas *(see pp170 and 172)*, is located in the park's northwest corner.

Mannequin at the Imperial Palace

At the southern end of the park is a delightful pond with an arched bridge, all that remains of one of several noble families' estates that occupied much of what is now parkland. From the bridge is an unobstructed view all the way north to the **Kenreimon**, the majestic gate in the middle of the palace's south wall, which may be used only by the emperor. The palace structures date from about 1855. The **Shishin-den** is the venue for investiture.

Kamo Shrines ⓲

上賀茂・下賀茂神社

46, 67 to Kamigamo-jinja-mae; 4, 205 to Shimogamo-jinja-mae.
Nishimura House *(075) 781-0666.* *mid-Mar to early Nov: 9:30am–4:30pm daily.* *Aoi Matsuri (Hollyhock Festival, May 15).*

At the northern reaches of the Kamo River, the **Kamigamo Shrine** has probably existed since the 7th century, while **Shimogamo**, its southern counterpart, is a century older. Both are dedicated to the thunder deity. Set in sylvan Tadasu no Mori ("the forest where lies are revealed"), Shimogamo has long played a role in ensuring the success of the rice harvest. The Aoi Festival, culminating on May 15, features a procession between the shrines, horse races, and archery. Kamigamo Shrine is noted for its Haiden hall, rebuilt in 1628, and mysterious cones of white sand. In the vicinity are several *shake*, priests' residences. One of these, the **Nishimura House**, is open to the public. Nearby **Narita** is a famous pickle shop occupying a handsome 250-year-old farm building.

***Torii* gates at Shimogamo, one of the Kamo shrines**

Daitoku-ji Temple ⓳

大徳寺

(075) 491-0019.
Kita-Oji stn, Karasuma line.
12, 204, 205, 206 to Daitoku-ji-mae. *9am–4:30pm daily.* *for most subtemples.*

An air of eloquent restraint pervades the grounds of Daitoku-ji, as befits a temple intimately connected with the world of the tea ceremony. Founded in 1325, the temple prospered in the latter half of the 16th century, when it came under the patronage of warlords (and tea ceremony aficionados) Oda Nobunaga and Hideyoshi. Today, a host of subtemples, many with famous tearooms and jewel-like gardens, continue to promote the ways of Zen and Tea.

Sen no Rikyu (1522–91), the man credited for elevating the simple act of drinking tea into a profound ritual, placed an image of himself in the upper story of the Sanmon (gate), an act of self-promotion thought to have prompted Hideyoshi to order his suicide.

Of the subtemples regularly open to the public, **Daisen-in** is famous for its Muromachi-period dry garden, a small but powerful representation in rock and sand of a Sung-style landscape painting. Ink landscape paintings by Soami and Kano Motonobu grace its interior. The south garden of **Koto-in** features a grove of slender maples rising above an expanse of moss (surreal in its beauty in the fall) and a *roji*, or tea garden, to the west. **Zuiho-in**, built in 1535 as the memorial temple of a Christian *daimyo*, has a modern garden by Shigemori Mirei featuring rocks placed in the shape of a crucifix.

Ryogen-in, founded 1502, has four gardens in different styles. Other subtemples are often included in special seasonal temple openings.

Near the east gate of the temple are **Izusen** and **Ikkyu**, two restaurants specializing in *shojin-ryori*, Zen vegetarian cuisine *(see p331)*.

Interior at Ryogen-in, a subtemple of Daitoku-ji

Kitano Tenman-gu Shrine ⑳

北野天満宮

(075) 461-0005. 10, 50, 51, 52, 203 to Kitano Tenman-gu-mae. 5:30am–5:30pm daily.

ALWAYS THRONGED with students praying for success in exams, Kitano Tenman-gu enshrines Heian statesman Sugawara Michizane, or Tenjin-san, the deity of learning. Michizane's favorite tree, the plum *(ume)*, is found throughout the grounds. On the 25th of each month, the shrine is the site of a bustling flea-market, where everything from blue-and-white Imari porcelains to nylon stockings are for sale.

Kamishichi-ken, an *ochaya* (teahouse) and bar-lined street running from Kitano Tenman-gu to Imadegawa-dori, forms the heart of Kyoto's smallest, but oldest *geiko* (geisha) district. On February 25 the *geiko* conduct a tea ceremony in the shrine's plum orchard, and they perform dances for the public every spring and fall at the local theater.

THE SYMBOLISM OF DAISEN-IN ZEN GARDEN AT DAITOKU-JI

Daisen-in's garden is a three-dimensional version of the Chinese Sung monochrome landscape paintings that inspired its creation. Mankind's fate, relationship with nature, and place in the universe are all expressed in this masterpiece of dry-landscape garden design.

A "waterfall" of white gravel *flows from a rock representing mythical Mount Horai. Other rock groupings symbolize Earth and Heaven.*

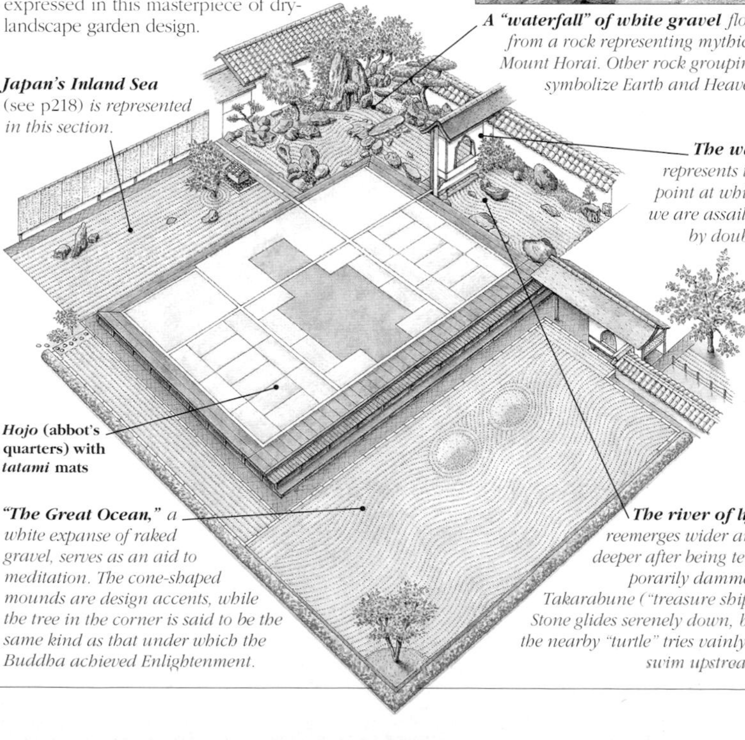

Japan's Inland Sea (see p218) *is represented in this section.*

The wall *represents the point at which we are assailed by doubts.*

Hojo **(abbot's quarters) with *tatami* mats**

"The Great Ocean," *a white expanse of raked gravel, serves as an aid to meditation. The cone-shaped mounds are design accents, while the tree in the corner is said to be the same kind as that under which the Buddha achieved Enlightenment.*

The river of life *reemerges wider and deeper after being temporarily dammed. Takarabune ("treasure ship") Stone glides serenely down, but the nearby "turtle" tries vainly to swim upstream.*

The fabulous pavilion at Kinkaku-ji, its gold-leaf outer layer shining in the sun

Kinkaku-ji: the Golden Pavilion ㉑

金閣寺

(075) 461-0013.
12 or 59 to Kinkaku-ji-mae; 101, 204, 205 to Kinkaku-ji-michi.
9am–5pm daily.

A GLIMMERING LEGACY of medieval Japan, Kinkaku-ji (formal name Rokuon-ji) is more familiar to foreign tourists as the Golden Pavilion. It was built by the third Ashikaga shogun, Yoshimitsu (1358–1408), who, relinquishing his official duties (but not his hold on power), entered the priesthood at the age of 37. The temple originally served as his retirement villa. A fervent follower of the Zen priest Soseki, Yoshimitsu directed that the finished complex become a temple after his death, with Soseki as its superior.

The visitor approaches the temple along a tree-shaded path, then emerges into a bright garden, on the other side of which stands the fabled pavilion. An exact replica of the original, destroyed by arson in 1950 (an event dramatized in Yukio Mishima's novel *The Golden Pavilion*), the graceful three-story structure is totally covered in gold leaf and topped by a bronze phoenix.

Mount Kinugasa serves as a backdrop to the garden, a stroll-type, laid out around a central pond. The harmonious interplay of its various components makes it a superb example of Muromachi-period garden design. Both pavilion and garden are especially exquisite after a snowfall.

Insho Domoto Museum ㉒

堂本印象美術館

(075) 463-0007.
12, 15, 50, 51, 59 to Ritsumeikan Univ.-mae. *9am–5pm Tue–Sun.* *(free to disabled visitors and over 65s.)*

WEST OF KINKAKU-JI, along the Kinukake-no-Michi, a stretch of road skirting the base of the Kitayama (Northern Mountains), lies the Insho Domoto Museum. It houses the impressive works of 20th-century *nihonga* master, Domoto Insho (1891–1975). Often translated as "Japanese-style painting," *nihonga* is a fresco-like painting technique that utilizes mineral pigments.

Ryoan-ji's Zen garden, the interpretation of which is up to the viewer

Ryoan-ji Temple ㉓

竜安寺

(075) 463-2216. *Ryoan-ji michi, Keifuku Kitano line (10-min walk).* *59 to Ryoan-ji-mae.*
8am–5pm daily (Dec–Feb: 8:30am–4:30pm).

FOUNDED IN 1450, Ryoan-ji's claim to fame is grounded in its rock garden, a composition of white gravel and 15 stones that many consider to be the ultimate expression of Zen Buddhism.

Although various interpretations of the rocks' symbolism have been put forth, the significance of the garden, like that of Zen itself, defies definitions. Its riddles can be unraveled only by silent contemplation, something that the hordes of high-school students, not to mention the temple's recorded explanations, do little to facilitate. To avoid both, try to arrive just as the gates open.

Though overshadowed by the famous rock garden, the temple's lower pond-garden should not be overlooked. Created at a time when Zen had not yet arrived in Japan, its soft contours serve as an interesting foil to the spiritual rigors of the rock garden.

Ninna-ji Temple 24

仁和寺

(075) 461-1155. Omuro stn, Keifuku Kitano line. 10, 26, 59 to Omuro Ninna-ji. 9am–4:30pm daily.

NINNA-JI'S colossal front gate, with formidable Nio (Deva King) guardians, serves as a reminder that this Shingon-sect temple used to be, until fires reduced it to its present size, a huge complex numbering up to 60 subtemples.

Completed by Emperor Uda in 888, Ninna-ji was formerly known as the Omuro Palace. Until the Meiji Restoration (1868), it was always headed by an imperial prince. The Kondo (main hall) and its wooden Amida image are National Treasures. Other sights include a soaring five-story pagoda and a stand of dwarf cherry trees – the last of Kyoto's many *sakura* (cherry trees) to bloom.

Situated in the southwest of the precincts is the Omuro Gosho, a compound with a lovely Edo-period garden. On the mountain behind is the Omuro 88-Temple Pilgrimage, which reproduces in miniature the temples on Shikoku's 88-Temple Pilgrimage *(see pp222–3)*. It takes about two hours to complete the full circuit.

Nio guardian figure at the gate of Ninna-ji

Ninna-ji's soaring five-story pagoda, dating from the 1630s

Myoshin-ji Temple 25

妙心寺

(075) 461-5226. Myoshin-ji stn, Keifuku Kitano line; Hanazono stn, JR Sanin line. 26 to Myoshin-ji Kitamon-mae. 9:10am–3:40pm daily.

FOUNDED at the behest of retired Emperor Hanazono in 1337, destroyed during the Onin War, and rebuilt on a grand scale, the spacious Rinzai-sect Zen temple complex of Myoshin-ji boasts some 47 subtemples rich in Kano School paintings and other art objects. The main structures, aligned in a row in typically Zen fashion *(see p131)*, include the Hatto (lecture hall), famous for a huge dragon painted by Kano Tanyu on its ceiling, and its bell, the oldest in Japan.

Subtemples normally open to the public include **Keishun-in**, noted for its four gardens and famous tea arbor, **Taizo-in**, which has both a dry garden by Kano Motonobu (1476–1559) and a modern garden by Nakane Kinsaku (1917–95). Taizo-in's prize possession is one of the most famous examples of Zen ink painting, Josetsu's *Catching a Catfish with a Gourd* (1413). A copy is on display.

Daishin-in has three gardens. Subtemples **Reiun-in**, nicknamed the Motonobu Temple because of its many Kano Motonobu works, and **Tenkyu-in**, noted for paintings by Kano Sanraku, are open on special days in spring and fall.

Ajiro, a restaurant specializing in *shojin ryori* (Zen vegetarian cuisine) is near the temple's south gate *(see p331)*.

Koryu-ji Temple 26

広隆寺

(075) 861-1461. Uzumasa stn, Keifuku Arashiyama line. 11, 61, 62, 63, 71, 72, 73 to Omuro Ninna-ji. 9am–5pm daily (Dec–Feb: to 4:30).

A MUST-SEE for lovers of Buddhist art, Koryu-ji was founded in 622, by a clan of Korean immigrants who contributed greatly to the development of Kyoto. Among the impressive images in its Reihoden (treasure hall), is a Miroku Bosatsu (Buddha of the future) believed to have been brought to Japan from Korea in the 7th century. Kyoto's oldest image, the seated figure is known throughout the nation for its beatific Mona Lisa-like smile. The temple's oldest structure, the Kodo, houses a 9th-century statue of the Amida Buddha.

Garden of subtemple Taizo-in, at the Myoshin-ji complex

Kyoto City: Farther Afield

POETS' HERMITAGES, noblemen's villas, esoteric mountain temples, and unspoiled natural scenery are among the many attractions to be found in the outskirts of the old capital. Once remote regions boasting unique characteristics and customs, they are now easily accessible, and any itinerary of Kyoto should include at least two or three of these rewarding destinations.

SIGHTS AT A GLANCE

Arashiyama District ❷
Daigo District ⓬
Enryaku-ji Temple ❾
Fushimi Shrine ⓫
Katsura Imperial Villa ❶
Kurama District ❺
Manshu-in Temple ❼
Ohara District ❿
Sagano District ❸
Shisen-do Temple ❻
Shugaku-in Villa ❽
Takao District ❹
Uji City ⓭

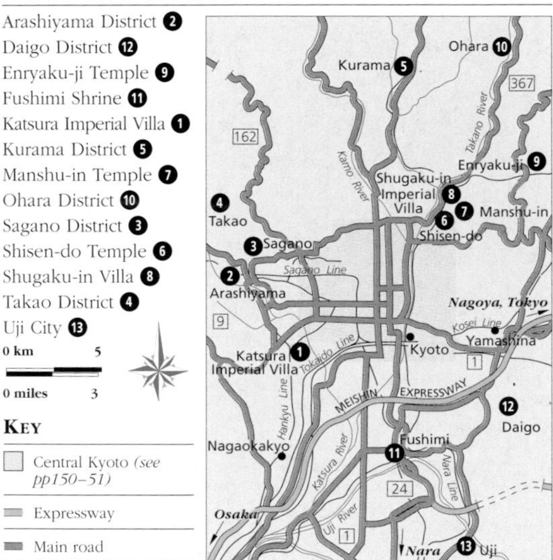

KEY

Central Kyoto *(see pp150–51)*

Expressway

Main road

Katsura Imperial Villa ❶

桂離宮

1-1 Misono, Katsura, Nishikyo-ku. *(075) 211-1215. Katsura stn, Hankyu line. 33 to Katsura Rikyu-mae. by appt only Mon–Fri: apply at Imperial Household Agency* (see p166).

WITH ITS flawless attention to detail, Katsura Imperial Villa is often cited as one of the finest examples of Japanese landscape design. Built in 1620 by Hachijo no Miya Toshihito, an imperial prince, it was later added to by his son, Toshitada. A sumptuous stroll garden *(see pp26–7)*, Katsura is famous for the manner in which its paths and stepping stones control the visitor's line of sight, resulting in a series of ingeniously planned vistas. The view from the **Shokin-tei** (pine zither) tea arbor, replicates the scenery of Amanohashidate *(see p206)*. Many of the garden's scenic allusions are to places mentioned in the Chinese and Japanese classics. The somewhat hurried tour includes the **Shoka-tei** (flower-viewing teahouse) in the highest part of the garden, then down past the **Shoi-ken** (sense-of-humor teahouse), and on to the main villa, a set of halls poetically described as resembling a flock of geese in flight.

Arashiyama District ❷

嵐山地区

Arashiyama stn, Keifuku Arashiyama line; Hankyu Arashiyama stn. 11, 28 or 93 to Arashiyama Tenryu-ji-mae.

WITH SOMETHING to please the eye in any season, Arashiyama has long held a special place in the hearts of the Japanese. Even today, despite omnipresent shops specializing in items emblazoned with the likenesses of TV and movie celebrities, the area still offers a lot of unspoiled natural beauty. At its center is timeless **Togetsu-kyo**, the graceful "moon-crossing" bridge. North of the bridge, mountainsides thickly forested with cherries and pines drop steeply to the river, which in summer becomes the stage for *ukai*, fishing done by firelight with trained cormorants. *Hozugawa-kudari*, running the Hozu River rapids from Kameoka to Arashiyama, is another popular activity. The narrow-gauge **Torokko Train** provides a different way of viewing the same scenery.

Rinzai-sect temple **Tenryu-ji** was founded by the first Ashikaga shogun, Takauji, in 1339. The serene garden has survived intact and features a pond in the shape of the Chinese character, *kokoro*, or "enlightened heart."

Another Arashiyama treasure is **Okochi Sanso**, the private villa of silent-screen star Okochi Denjiro. The meticulously laid-out grounds offer wonderful vistas of Mount Hiei and the Hozu River gorge.

Togetsu-kyo, the wooden "moon-crossing" bridge in Arashiyama

Sagano District ❸

嵯峨野地区

JR Saga stn, Sagano line. 28 or 91 to Daikaku-ji.

THE HOME of rice fields, bamboo groves, temples, and cemeteries, Sagano's varied sights are by turn pastoral and poignant. The best point from which to launch an exploration is **Torii Moto**, where a vermilion shrine gateway *(torii)* marks the beginning of an ancient trail leading up to sacred Mount Atago, abode of the fire divinity. Two thatched teahouses near the *torii* have been offering refreshment to pilgrims for centuries.

From the *torii*, head south past traditional farmhouses to **Adashino Nenbutsu-ji**. From the Heian to Edo periods, Adashino was a remote place where corpses were often disposed of. Established to offer solace for the souls of these forgotten dead, the temple gathered together their grave markers – rocks on which a likeness of the Buddha had been carved. The sight of row after row of these silent stone figures is strangely moving. On the evenings of August 23 and 24, more than 1,000 candles are offered to them.

Rickshaw in the pastoral Sagano district

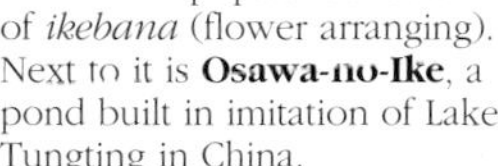

To the south is **Gio-ji**, a tiny thatched nunnery where Gio, a cast-off mistress of warlord Taira no Kiyomori (1118–81), took the tonsure. Known for the beauty of its fall foliage, the temple is bounded on one side by a magnificent stand of bamboo, while, to the front, slender maples rise from an emerald carpet of moss.

Located in central Sagano, Jodo-sect temple **Seiryo-ji** houses an image of the Sakyamuni Buddha reportedly brought to Japan in 987. **Nison-in** has standing images of Amida and Sakyamuni. The many maple trees on the temple's grounds attract large numbers of visitors in the fall. Charming **Rakushi-sha** (hut of the fallen persimmons) was the humble home of haiku poet Mukai Kyorai (1651–1704). Basho *(see p273)* composed his *Saga Diary* here in 1691.

Secluded Nichiren-sect temple **Jojakko-ji** is situated on Ogura-yama, a mountain whose beauty has been celebrated by poets since ancient times. A steep flight of stone steps leads to the temple from where there are great views of Kyoto and Mount Hiei. Halfway up the steps, a thatched gate houses two fierce-eyed Nio guards said to be the work of 13th-century sculptor Unkei. The temple's beautiful two-story pagoda is a symbol of the Lotus Sutra.

The aristocratic temple complex of **Daikaku-ji**, in the northeast of Sagano, is the headquarters of one of Japan's most popular schools of *ikebana* (flower arranging). Next to it is **Osawa-no-Ike**, a pond built in imitation of Lake Tungting in China.

Takao District ❹

高雄地区

Takao bus or 8 to Takao.

ESOTERIC mountain temples and refreshingly pristine mountain scenery are Takao's main attractions. **Jingo-ji**, founded in the 8th century, houses a wealth of National Treasures including the Yakushi Nyorai (Buddha of healing). Set in an ancient cryptomeria forest, **Kozan-ji**, founded in 774, has the look of an elegant estate. Copies of the handscroll *Choju-giga* (frolicking birds and animals) are displayed in the **Sekisui-in**, a brilliant example of Kamakura residential architecture. Japan's first tea was cultivated nearby.

Traditional restaurant in the mountainous district of Takao

Kurama District ❺

鞍馬地区

Kurama stn, Eizan line. 95 from Ohara. Kurama Matsuri (Oct 22).

FAMOUS AS the abode of gods, demons, and superheroes, Kurama was once an isolated village of foresters. Now a Kyoto suburb, it still retains an untamed feeling, a quality fully in evidence on the night of October 22, when the town celebrates its Fire Festival.

Kurama-dera was built in 770 to protect Kyoto from the evil forces that, according to Chinese geomancy, emanate from the north. A gate marks the beginning of a mountain trail to the main temple buildings; the main hall offers splendid views of the Kitayama mountains. From the Reihokan (treasure hall) a path winds beneath towering cryptomeria trees to the village of **Kibune**, a collection of inns and teahouses alongside a stream. Several Kurama shops sell pickled mountain herbs and vegetables. Watch for masks of *tengu*, a folkloric creature with a phallic-shaped nose.

Bibbed stone carvings along the wayside, Kurama

The upper garden at Shisen-do, as viewed from the veranda

Shisen-do Temple ❻

詩仙堂

27 Monguchi-cho, Ichijo-ji, Sakyo-ku. *(075) 781-2954.* *5 or 8 to Ichijo-ji Sagarimatsu-cho.* *9am–5pm daily.*

A samurai who had fallen out of favor with the shogunate, Ishikawa Jozan constructed this retirement villa in 1641. On a small plot below the Higashiyama mountains, this Confucian scholar and poet succeeded in creating a nearly perfect blend of building and garden. Although now a Soto-sect Zen temple, the hermitage retains the feel of a home.

The famous garden is divided into two levels: the upper, best viewed from the main building's veranda, features a broad expanse of packed sand bordered by clipped azalea bushes. The lower level, which also makes use of areas of sand to add light and space, offers a fine view of the villa's tile-and-thatch roof and moon-viewing chamber.

Manshu-in Temple ❼

曼殊院

42 Takenouchi-cho, Ichijo-ji, Sakyo-ku. *5 to Shugaku-in Michi.* *9am–4:30pm daily.*

Even in spring and fall when its cherries and maples draw the crowds, Manshu-in maintains an atmosphere of dignified repose. This Tendai-sect temple was restored in 1656 by the son of the prince who designed Katsura Villa *(see p170)*. Its elegant buildings, with their cleverly crafted door pulls and other carefully planned details, call to mind those of the imperial villa. The beautiful garden is composed of islands of rock and vegetation amid swaths of raked gravel, with the Higashiyama mountains forming a harmonious backdrop.

Shugaku-in Imperial Villa ❽

修学院離宮

Yabuzoe, Shugaku-in. *Shugaku-in stn, Eizan line.* *5 to Shugaku-in Michi.* *by appt only Mon–Fri: apply at Imperial Household Agency, (075) 211-1215* (see p166).

If Katsura Villa *(see p170)* could be said to be yin, then its counterpart imperial villa, Shugaku-in, could only be described as yang. While the former's garden, layered with literary and poetic allusions, is characterized by an inward-looking sensibility, spacious Shugaku-in might strike the viewer as extroverted.

Created by retired emperor Go-Mizuno'o (1596–1680), the garden was a lifetime labor of love. Divided into three levels, each with a teahouse, the complex is imbued with a spirit of understated simplicity. Yet, a surprise awaits: the approach to the uppermost teahouse is designed so that the visitor is kept unaware until the last minute of the panorama from the top of the Kitayama mountains, spread out as if an extension of the garden.

Enryaku-ji Temple ❾

延暦寺

4220 Sakamoto Honmachi, Otsu, Shiga prefecture. *(077) 578-0551.* *Yase stn, Eizan line, then cable car; or Hieizan Sakamoto stn, Kosei line, then cable car.* *Enryaku-ji bus from Kyoto or Keihan Sanjo stns.* *summer: 8:30am–4:30pm daily; winter: 9am–4pm daily.*

A once mighty monastery fortress with 3,000 subtemples and thousands of *sohei*, or warrior monks, Enryaku-ji today is but a shadow of its former self. Still, the solemnity of its isolated mountain-top setting and grandeur of its remaining buildings make the trek to Mount Hiei worthwhile. Founded by the monk Saicho in 792, Enryaku-ji became the main temple of the Tendai sect *(see p269)*. Although initially entrusted to protect the city from evil forces, the temple itself became the bane of the capital. Emperor Go-Shirakawa (1127–92) once lamented that there were only three things beyond his control: the flooding of the Kamo River, the roll of the dice, and the warrior monks of Enryaku-ji. In 1571, however, warlord Oda

Konpon Chu-do, the inner sanctum of Enryaku-ji

Nobunaga, angered by the temple's resistance to his authority, sent his army to attack the mountain. The complex was burned to the ground, and every man, woman, and child massacred.

The temple is divided into three precincts, connected by shuttle bus. The **Kokuho-den**, a museum of treasures, is in the east precinct. Here, too, is the famous **Konpon Chu-do**, the inner sanctum, which enshrines a Healing Buddha image said to have been carved by Saicho. Nearby **Jodo-in** (Pure Land Hall) is the site of Saicho's tomb.

In the **Jogyo-do** hall in the west precinct monks circumambulate the altar, chanting an invocation called the *nembutsu*; in the **Hokke-do** hall they meditate upon the Lotus Sutra, a central tenet of Tendai belief. Beyond these two buildings is the **Shaka-do**, the main hall of the west precinct.

Ohara District ❿

大原地区

17 from Kyoto stn.

KNOWN FOR thatched farmhouses, delicious pickles, and other rustic charms, Ohara is also home to two famous temples. Set in an incomparably beautiful setting, **Sanzen-in's** Amida Hall dates from 1148 and houses a meditating Amida Buddha. *Fusuma* (sliding door) paintings by Takeuchi Seiho (1864–1942) decorate the temple's Shinden. The approach to Sanzen-in is lined with shops selling such local products as *shiba-zuke*, a pickle dyed purple with the leaf of the beefsteak plant. Across the valley is tiny **Jakko-in**, a nunnery where Kenreimon-in (1155–1213) lived. The sole survivor of the Taira clan, she prayed here for the souls of her son and kin killed by the Genji.

Daigo-ji's Heian-era pagoda

Fushimi Shrine ⓫

伏見稲荷神社

68 Yabunouchi, Fukakusa, Fushimi-ku. *Fushimi Inari stn, Keihan & Nara lines.* *15 to Fushimi Inari Taisha mae.* *(075) 641-7331.* *24 hours.*

THIS MOST FAMOUS of the many thousands of shrines dedicated to Inari, the popular deity of rice and sake *(see p22)*, lies near the sake-making district of Fushimi. A much-photographed avenue formed out of hundreds of *torii* (gates) has been donated by businessmen who come here to pray for prosperity *(see p148)*.

Daigo-ji Temple ⓬

醍醐寺

22 Higashioji-cho, Daigo, Fushimi-ku. *Daigo stn, Tozai line.* **Sanpo-in** *(075) 571-0002.* *9am–4pm daily (to 5pm Mar–Oct).*

DAIGO-JI'S main draw is subtemple **Sanpo-in**. Because Toyotomi Hideyoshi took a personal interest in restoring this after a visit in 1598, it contains some of the Momoyama period's most representative works of art. The lavish garden is noted for its many magnificent rocks, which were gifts to Hideyoshi from his *daimyo* (feudal lords). The rest of Daigo-ji is more ancient. The graceful five-story pagoda, built in 951, is one of only two Heian-era pagodas in existence. Those venturing to upper Daigo are mainly pilgrims. The white-clad ones are headed for **Juntei-do**, a hall housing a Kannon image, which is number 11 of the 33 Kannon Temples pilgrimage route. Those sporting pillbox hats and baggy trousers are *yamabushi* ascetics *(see p269)*.

Uji City ⓭

宇治市

Obaku & Uji stns, Keihan-Uji line. **Temples** *9am–4:30pm daily.*

IN ADDITION to some of the best green tea grown in Japan, the small city of Uji boasts **Byodo-in**, which is featured on the 10-yen coin. Built in 1053, the temple's Phoenix Hall *(see p26)* and Amida Nyorai image housed within are marvelous remnants of one of Japan's greatest b epochs. Beneath a lavish canopy once inlaid with mother of pearl, Amida is shown meditating in the western Pure Land, while on the walls around him 52 small *bosatsu* ride on puffs of cloud.

While Byodo-in sought to imitate palaces depicted in Tang-dynasty mandalas, **Mampuku-ji** invoked the architectural traditions of Ming China. This most Chinese of Kyoto temples was established in 1661 by Ingen, a priest who fled China after the fall of the Ming dynasty. Ingen introduced the *sencha*, or leaf tea (in contrast to the *matcha*, or powdered tea) ceremony.

Mampuku-ji, a Chinese-style temple in Uji city

Shopping in Kyoto

Kyoto is famous throughout Japan for the quality of its crafts and food products, the result of many centuries of catering to the demanding tastes of its resident aristocrats, temple abbots, tea masters, and merchants. Venerable shops coexist with stores stocked with the latest fads, making shopping here a bizarre, but never boring, experience. As in other major Japanese cities, Kyoto has large branches of Japanese department store chains. Typically these offer a vast selection of goods, including foodstuffs in the basement. Specialty craft outlets are all over the city. On the west side of Teramachi, just north of Shijo, is **All Card Plaza**, where an assortment of ATM machines awaits the cash-needy tourist. A map of the central shopping district is on page 151; details of opening hours are on page 340.

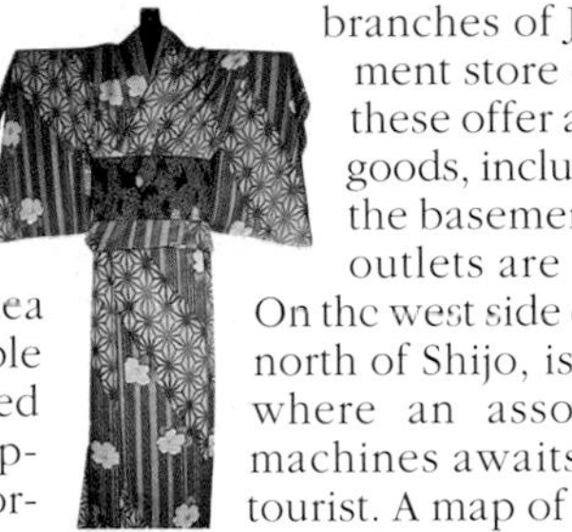

Kimono in shop window

Modern storefronts along Kawaramachi

Shopping Districts

The intersection of Shijo and Kawaramachi forms the heart of the downtown shopping district. During the day, the sidewalks of Kawaramachi, which serves as Kyoto's main street, are busy with shoppers, while at night *boso-zoku* (hot-rodders) cruise noisily along its store-lined length.

Smaller shopping districts include the area around JR Kyoto station and Kitayama-dori, where Kyoto's most upscale shops can be found.

Department Stores and Arcades

The **Hankyu** and **Takashimaya** department stores are located at the intersection of Kawaramachi and Shijo. Takashimaya is the place to head for men's and women's fashions; inside are boutiques stocking Issey Miyake and other brand-name clothing. The city's other main department store, **Daimaru**, is six blocks further west on Shijo's north side. Many of Kyoto's famous old shops, such as the Ippodo tea store, have outlets in department store basements.

On the east side of Kawaramachi are **Maruzen**, a small department store that contains an English bookstore and a contemporary crafts boutique, and the **BAL Building**, a comprehensive, multistory collection of brand-name boutiques.

Shin-Kyogoku, a street situated within the network of arcades and roads between Shijo and Sanjo, caters to Japanese youngsters on school outings. Its varied offerings run the gamut from legitimate craft items to outrageous kitsch.

On the west end of Kyoto Station is **JR Kyoto Isetan**, the newest addition to Kyoto's department store line-up. Just to the north of the station is an old standby, the **Kyoto Kintetsu** department store. **Porta**, an underground shopping arcade, is located beneath the station's north side, while to its south is **Avanti**, a building housing a variety of shops.

Within the station itself is a shopping area called **The Cube**, which contains a sizable number of souvenir shops specializing in Kyoto craft items and food products.

Nishiki Market Alley

Nicknamed "Kyoto's Kitchen," Nishiki is a fascinating market alley north of, and running parallel to, Shijo, from Teramachi west to Takakura. This is where most of Kyoto's *kaiseki* chefs buy their ingredients. Many of the items sold, such as *fu* (wheat gluten) and *yuba* (soy milk skin), are unique to Kyoto cuisine. In particular, a wide selection of pickles, another local specialty, is available. **Aritsugu**, at Nishiki's eastern end, is known for Japanese knives and other kitchen utensils.

Nishiki market, the best place to shop for food items in Kyoto

ELECTRONIC GOODS

On the north side of Shijo between Tomi-no-Koji and Yanagi-no-Banba, **Big Off** stocks discounted toiletries, watches, and Walkmans on its ground floor, and electrical appliances on its upper floors. The city's main outlet for cheap electronic goods and appliances, however, is the stretch of Teramachi running south of Shijo. This serves as Kyoto's version of Den Den Town in Osaka.

ANTIQUES

Having escaped the bombs of World War II, Kyoto's *kura* (family storehouses) continue to emit a small but steady stream of fascinating objects. The city's antiques fall into three main categories: Buddhist art, tea ceremony utensils, and everyday items. Some stores specialize in just one category, but most carry a range. Kyoto's most venerable antique shops are located between Nawate and Higashio-ji along Shinmonzen and Furumonzen streets. Especially reputable are **Kawasaki Bijutsu** (specializing in screens and chests), **Renkodo** (Imari-ware), and **Nakajima** (which sells a bit of everything).

The city's up-and-coming antique district is the section of Teramachi from Oike to Marutamachi, where a host of new shops run by young but knowledgeable owners have suddenly sprouted. The **Kyoto Antiques Center** houses many shops under one roof. **Teramachi Club**, farther up Teramachi on the same side of the street, deals mainly in Meiji and Taisho period items. Across from it is **Nagata**, which buys not at auction but directly from family *kura*, and **Tazuke**, whose minimalistic show window always features something rare and wonderful. Fans of old lacquerware should not miss **Uruwashi-ya**, on Marutamachi, one and a half blocks west of Teramachi.

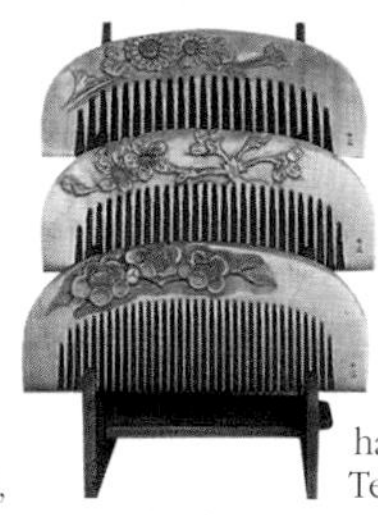

Handmade combs

Antique lovers will also want to visit **Hirooka Antique**, which is just two minutes' walk east from Exit 1 of Kitayama station. The shop is a bit out of the way but worth the trip out of the city center – Hirooka's goods are first-rate and reasonably priced.

FLEA MARKETS

Antiques, household items, plants, food, and much more are on sale at Kobo-san, the market held on the 21st of every month at Toji Temple *(see p152)*. Tenjin-san, a similar flea market, is held on the 25th at the shrine of Kitano Tenman-gu *(see p167)*.

DIRECTORY

DEPARTMENT STORES AND ARCADES

Avanti
Opp Hachijo-guchi (south) exit of JR Kyoto stn.
☎ *(075) 671-8761.*

BAL Building
E side of Kawaramachi, S of Sanjo, Nakagyo-ku.
☎ *(075) 223-0501.*

The Cube
JR Kyoto stn bldg, B2F, B1F, 1F, 11F.
☎ *(075) 371-2134.*
W www.thecube.co.jp

Daimaru
N side of Shijo, at Takakura, Shimogyo-ku.
☎ *(075) 211-8111.*
● *Wed.*

Hankyu
Corner of Kawaramachi and Shijo, Shimogyo-ku.
☎ *(075) 223-2288.*
● *Tue.*

JR Kyoto Isetan
Karasuma, S of Shiokoji, Shimogyo-ku.
☎ *(075) 352-1111.*
● *Tue.*

Kyoto Kintetsu
Kurasuma, S of Nanajo, Shimogyo-ku.
☎ *(075) 361-1111.*
● *Thu.*

Maruzen
E side of Kawaramachi, at Takoyakushi, Nakagyo-ku.
☎ *(075) 241-2161.*
● *3rd Wed of month.*

Porta
N side of JR Kyoto stn.
☎ *(075) 365-7528.*
● *3rd Tue of month, except in Aug & Dec.*

Takashimaya
Corner of Kawaramachi and Shijo, Shimogyo-ku.
☎ *(075) 221-8811*
● *Wed.*

NISHIKI MARKET

Aritsugu
On Nishiki-koji, W of Gokomachi, Nakagyo-ku.
☎ *(075) 221-1091.*

ELECTRONIC GOODS

Big Off
N side of Shijo, W of Yanagi-no-Banba, Shimogyo-ku.
☎ *(075) 221-3810.*
● *occasionally Wed.*

ANTIQUES

Hirooka Antique
34-3 Minami Shibacho, Shimogamo, Sakyo-ku.
☎ *(075) 721-4438.*
● *Mon.*

Kawasaki Bijutsu
Shinmonzen, W of Higashi-oji, Higashiyama-ku.
☎ *(075) 541-8785*

Kyoto Antiques Center
E side of Teramachi, N of Nijo, Nakagyo-ku.
☎ *(075) 222-0793.*
● *Tue.*

Nagata
On corner of Ebisu and Teramachi, Nakagyo-ku.
☎ *(075) 211-9511.*
● *Sun.*

Nakajima
Shinmonzen, E of Hanami-koji, Higashiyama-ku.
☎ *(075) 561-7771.*

Renkodo
Shinmonzen, E of Yamato-oji, Higashiyama-ku.
☎ *(075) 525-2121*
● *Tue.*

Tazuke
W side of Teramachi, S of Ebisugawa, Nakagyo-ku.
☎ *(075) 311-2188.*

Teramachi Club
E side of Teramachi, N of Nijo, Nakagyo-ku.
☎ *(075) 211-6445.*
● *Tue.*

Uruwashi-ya
Marutamachi, E of Fuyacho, Nakagyo-ku.
☎ *(075) 212-0043.*
● *Tue.*

Specialty Souvenirs

KYOTO IS ONE OF THE BEST PLACES in Japan to buy crafts and souvenirs, many of them local specialties. Some outlets are actually outside the central shopping district. Among the best places to look are the roads leading up to major temples such as Kiyomizu-dera.

Craft shop on the canalside Philosopher's Walk

GENERAL CRAFTS

THE GION, or eastern, end of Shijo has a number of interesting craft shops, including the **Kyoto Craft Center**, which carries many contemporary craft items.

CERAMICS AND TABLEWARE

KIYOMIZU-YAKI is the city's refined porcelain ware, which admirably suits its delicate cuisine. A fine selection of this and other porcelains can be found at **Tachikichi**, on the north side of Shijo at Tomi-no-Koji. **Asahi-do** offers a comprehensive range, as does **Tojiki Kaikan**. **Asobe**, on Shijo's south side at Takakura is well known for lacquerware. **Ichihara**, south of Shijo, on Sakaimachi, offers a good selection of chopsticks and bamboo utensils.

TEA

TEA IN KYOTO means Uji-cha, for neighboring Uji is, with Shizuoka, one of Japan's most famous tea-producing regions. There are many fine tea shops in town, but the renowned **Ippodo Chaho** is the granddaddy of them all.

DOLLS

KYOTO DOLLS have been famous throughout Japan for centuries. **Fujii Kei Shoten** has both new and antique dolls for sale, as well as *netsuke* and *kanzashi* (hair ornaments). One of the finest collections of antique dolls in the city is at **Nakanishi Toku Shoten**, which specializes in *Kyo-ningyo* (Kyoto dolls) of all kinds. **Gallery K1** has an impressive collection of lifelike *Ichimatsu-ningyo*, which were once considered standard trousseau items. **Tanaka-ya** is known both for its dolls and its Noh masks.

One of Kyoto's famous dolls

INCENSE

INCENSE has been a Kyoto specialty since Heian times. **Kungyoku-do**, a shop with a 400-year-old history, has an aromatic selection in stick, chip, and pellet form. **Toyoda Aisan-do**, in the Gion, has a wide selection of incense and incense burners. **Lisn** is an intriguing boutique with some novel forms of incense.

PICKLES AND SWEETS

KYOTO'S MANY vegetables are delicious; pickled *(tsukemono)*, they become sublime. In addition to Nishiki Market *(see p174)*, two stores are notable. **Narita**, east of Kamigamo Shrine, has preservative-free delicacies, including its famous *suguki-zuke* (turnip pickle). **Murakami-ju**, in the city center, has more than 20 types of pickles. Works of art, *wagashi* (sweets) come in a variety of styles. The exquisite *namagashi* are meant to be eaten the same day they are made, preferably accompanied by *matcha* (powdered tea). Those at **Tsukimochi-ya Naomasa** are traditional favorites.

FOOTWARE

ON NAWATE, **Minochu** has a stunning collection of traditional Japanese footwear, some in larger than standard sizes. The tall *koppori-geta* worn by Kyoto's apprentice geisha can be bought here.

BAMBOO PRODUCTS

AN ABUNDANCE of bamboo in neighboring Shiga prefecture and the development of the utensils used in the tea ceremony have helped make Kyoto a prime center for the production of this flexible natural material. **Kagoshin**, east of the Sanjo Bridge, makes wonderful bamboo craft items, including baskets for *ikebana* arrangements. **Tsujikura**, on Kawaramachi, north of Shijo, stocks a good selection of handsome and sturdy bamboo umbrellas, as well as various types of paper lanterns.

Umbrella with a bamboo frame, a popular shade at restaurants

Washi

Paper has been made in Japan since the 7th century. *Washi* (handmade paper) is made of tree and other plant fibers. Exquisite *washi* from all over Japan is available at **Morita Washi Wagami-no-mise**, on Higashi-no-Toin, a couple of blocks south of Shijo. **Kakimoto** also stocks an outstanding variety. **Kyukyo-do**, a shop famous for calligraphy supplies, paper, and incense, is located between Sanjo and Oike.

Other Crafts

Across from Takashimaya department store is **Terauchi**, a jewelry shop that carries a fine selection of pearls. At the corner of Rokkaku and Tomi-no-Koji is **Miyawaki Baisen-an**, an old shop that is famous for its elegant fans. **Kazurasei**, in the Gion, specializes in hair ornaments and makeup for apprentice geisha. For Japanese woodblock prints, probably the best gallery is **Nishimura** in Teramachi.

Craftswoman making *washi*, Japanese handmade paper

Directory

General Crafts

Kyoto Craft Center
Gion, N side of Shijo.
(075) 561-9660.
Wed.

Ceramics and Tableware

Asahi-do
Kiyomizu, Higashiyama-ku.
(075) 531-2181.

Asobe
S side of Shijo, at Takakura, Shimogyo-ku.
(075) 211-0803.
Wed.

Ichihara
E side of Sakaimachi, S of Shijo, Shimogyo-ku.
(075) 341-3831
Sun.

Tachikichi
N side of Shijo, at Tomi-no-Koji, Shimogyo-ku.
(075) 211-3141.
Wed.

Tojiki Kaikan
Gojo-zaka, 100 m E of Higashi-oji intersection, Higashiyama-ku.
(075) 541-1102.

Tea

Ippodo Chaho
E side of Teramachi, N of Nijo, Nakagyo-ku.
(075) 211-3421.

Dolls

Fujii Kei Shoten
Nawate, S of Shinbashi, Higasihyama-ku.
(075) 561-7863.
Tue.

Gallery K1
Muromachi-dori, S of Kita-oji.
(075) 415-1477.

Nakanishi Toku Shoten
Furumonzen, E of Yamato-oji (Nawate), Higashiyama-ku.
(075) 561-7309.

Tanaka-ya
N side of Shijo, E of Yanagi-no-Banba, Shimogyo-ku.
(075) 221-1959.
Wed.

Incense

Kungyoku-do
E side of Horikawa, across from Nishi Hongan-ji, Shimogyo-ku.
(075) 371-0162.
1st and 3rd Sun of month.

Lisn
2F Spiral Space 103 Bldg, Shimogamo-naka, N of Kitayama, Kita-ku.
(075) 721-6006.
Wed.

Toyoda Aisan-do
Gion, N side of Shijo-dori.
(075) 551-2221.
Wed.

Pickles and Sweets

Murakami-ju
Nishi-Kiyamachi, S of Shijo, behind Hankyu dept store, Shimogyo-ku.
075-351-1737.

Narita
35 Yamamoto-cho, Kamigamo, Kita-ku (E of Kamigamo Shrine).
(075) 721-1567.
Wed.

Tsukimochi-ya Naomasa
E side Kiyamachi, N of Sanjo, Kiyamachi Sanjo-agaru, Nakagyo-ku.
(075) 231-0175.
Thu.

Footware

Minochu
Yamato-oji (Nawate) at Shinmonzen, Higashiyama-ku.
(075) 561-5189.
Wed.

Bamboo Products

Kagoshin
N side Sanjo, E of Sanjo Bridge, Higashiyama-ku.
(075) 771-0209.
Mon.

Tsujikura
E side of Kawaramachi, N of Shijo, Nakagyo-ku.
(075) 221-4396.
Mon.

Washi

Kakimoto
E side of Teramachi, N of Nijo, Nakagyo-ku.
(075) 211-3481.
Sun.

Kyukyo-do
W side of Teramachi, at Anekoji, Nakagyo-ku.
(075) 231-0510.
Sun.

Morita Washi Wagami-no-mise
E side of Higashi-no-Toin, N of Bukkoji, Shimogyo-ku.
(075) 341-0123
Sun and 1st day of month.

Other Crafts

Kazurasei
Gion, N side of Shijo.
(075) 561-0672.
Wed.

Miyawaki Baisen-an
N side Rokkaku, W of Tomi-no-Koji, Nakagyo-ku.
(075) 221-0181.

Nishimura
Corner of Sanjo and Teramachi, Nakagyo-ku.
(075) 211-2849.

Terauchi
N side of Shijo, W of Kawaramachi, Shimogyo-ku.
(075) 211-3511.
Wed.

Entertainment in Kyoto

Kyoto's entertainment scene is small but varied, catering to tastes both ancient and contemporary. In addition to performances of Kabuki and *buyo* (classical Japanese dance), the city offers bars and clubs where you can hear guest musicians playing anything from blues guitar to Latin rhythms. Thanks to its more than 1,200 years of history, a traditional event takes place almost every day at one of Kyoto's hundreds of shrines and temples. While the majority of these are little more than arcane rituals, some are on a huge scale and attract visitors from all over the country. Of these, the month-long Gion Matsuri, put on by the silk merchants of the city, is probably the best-known festival. It culminates on July 14–17.

Geisha dancer

Buying Tickets

For help in obtaining tickets to events, check with the city-run tourist information counter inside **Kyoto Station** *(see p152)* or at the **Tourist Information Center**. Tickets for most major events can be purchased at any of the several branches of **PIA** ticket agency scattered throughout the city. They can also be bought in the **Shinshindo Bookstore**, or at Playguide counters inside **Takashimaya** and **Daimaru** department stores *(see p174)*.

Information Sources

For an overview of what is happening, consult the *Kyoto Visitor's Guide*, a free monthly publication available at tourist information centers and major hotels, and on the internet. *Kansai Time Out*, a guide to events in the Kansai region (Kobe, Osaka, and Kyoto), is on sale at bookstores. The website of **JNTO** (Japan National Tourist Organization) has a section on Kyoto. The *Japan Times*, and other newspapers in English also carry a listing of Kansai events at least once a week.

Festivals

Of Kyoto's many festivals, the big three are the Aoi Matsuri (Hollyhock Festival, May 15); Gion Matsuri (all of July, especially 14–17); and Jidai Matsuri (Festival of the Ages, October 22). The Aoi and Gion festivals both started as purification rites in the Heian period. The former involves a parade of costumed nobles, courtiers, horses, and ox-carts between the two Kamo shrines *(see p166)*. The latter centers around elaborately decorated floats belonging to various neighborhoods, which are pulled through the streets on the morning of July 17, then disassembled. The Jidai Matsuri was begun in 1895 to boost morale after the emperor abandoned Kyoto for Tokyo. Characters in costumes from every epoch of Kyoto's imperial past parade from the Imperial Palace to Heian Shrine.

Apprentice geisha performing at the Gion Kobu Kaburenjo theater

An old teahouse in Gion, a long-established entertainment district

Traditional Arts

For the tourist wanting a quick look at traditional arts, **Gion Corner** has a program from March to November that includes snippets of *kyomai* (classical Kyoto dance), *koto* music, Kyogen comic drama, and even *ikebana* (flower arranging). Performances take place at 7:40 and 8:40pm.

The geisha of Gion put on *Miyako Odori*, their gala dance spectacle, during April at the **Gion Kobu Kaburenjo** theater, while at Kamishichi-ken, the geisha district near Kitano Shrine, public dances, *Kitano Odori*, are staged from April 15 to 25 at the **Kamishichi-ken Kaburenjo**. Ponto-cho's geisha perform their *Kamogawa Odori* in May at the **Pontocho Kaburenjo**. Tickets for all can be bought at the theaters or at Takashimaya and Daimaru Playguide counters.

The **Minami-za** is the venue for *Kaomise Kabuki*, Kyoto's December Kabuki extravaganza. Performances of Noh and Kyogen are held at **Kyoto Kanze Kaikan** and **Kongo Nogakudo** on certain Sundays of every month. Check the *Visitor's Guide* for details.

Anyone interested in experiencing the tea ceremony can do so at **Shishigatani SABIE**. This restored Taisho-period house and garden complex offers several options including a full tea presentation with English narration.

NIGHTLIFE

KYOTO MAY NOT have as lively a nightlife as Osaka and Tokyo, but it still has plenty of bars, clubs, and live music spots, especially in the entertainment districts of Ponto-cho and Gion.

A stage event, the **Kyoto Connection**, performed by Japanese and foreign poets, musicians, dancers, comedians, and storytellers, takes place in Teatro Marron on the last Saturday of the month (except August and December).

Cafe David, a sumptuous art-filled coffee house on the south side of Sanjo, between Takakura and Higashi-no-Toin, sponsors Saturday night events showcasing local talent.

Kyoryukan, located a little north of the east gate of Shokoku-ji Temple, behind Doshisha University, also hosts a varied schedule of performances, many of *butoh* and other dance forms. The **Pig & Whistle**, a British-style pub popular with the foreign community, offers reasonably priced food and drink in a comfortable atmosphere. Occasionally bands perform. **Café Indépendants**, in the basement of the old Mainichi Newspaper Building at the corner of Sanjo Street and Gokomachi Street, is a relaxed eating and drinking spot that also occasionally features live music. **Metro** hosts monthly events, including a drag show ("Diamond Night"), and a Latin music night.

Another watering hole popular with the city's foreign residents is **Bar Isn't It**, the Kyoto branch of an Osaka establishment. It runs a Latin music night once a month, usually with a live band.

Pontocho district restaurants, with *yuka* platforms erected in summer

DIRECTORY

TICKETS

PIA
1F of the Vivre 21 Fashion Bldg on Takoyakushi, W of Kawaramachi.
(075) 223-1331.

Shinshindo Bookstore
Corner of Sanjo and Rokkaku.
(075) 730-5766.

Tourist Information Center
1F Kyoto Tower Bldg, opp JR Kyoto stn.
(075) 343-6655.

INFORMATION

Kyoto Visitor's Guide
www.city.kyoto.jp/sankan/kankoshinko/visitor/index.html

JNTO Kyoto
www.jnto.go.jp/05regional/kyoto/kyoto.html

TRADITIONAL ARTS

Gion Corner
Next to Gion Kobu Kaburenjo, E of Hanamikoji and S of Shijo, Higashiyama-ku.
(075) 561-1119.
Aug 16, Nov 30–Feb 28.

Gion Kobu Kaburenjo
1F Yasaka Kaikan, Next to Gion Corner, Higashiyama-ku.
(075) 561-1115.

Kamishichi-ken Kaburenjo
Kamishichi-ken, E of Kitano Tenman-gu Shrine, Kamigyo-ku.
(075) 461-0148.

Kyoto Kanze Kaikan
Nio-mon, W of Jingu-michi, Higashiyama-ku.
(075) 771-6114.

Kongo Nogakudo
E side of Muromachi, N of Shijo, Nakagyo-ku.
(075) 221-3049.

Minami-za Theater
Corner of Kawabata and Shijo, Higashiyama-ku.
Reservations:
(0570) 000-489.
General inquiries:
(075) 561-1155.

Pontocho Kaburenjo
On E side of Pontocho, S of Sanjo, Nakagyo-ku.
(075) 221-2025.

Shishigatani SABIE
Sakura Bridge, nr Honen-in Temple, Higashiyama-ku.
10am–5pm. *Mon.*
(075) 762-3425.

NIGHTLIFE

Bar Isn't It
B1 Forum Nishi Kiyamachi (2nd street S of Sanjo).
(075) 221-5399.

Cafe David
Sanjo, W of Takakura, Nakagyo-ku.
(075) 212-8580.
Wed.

Café Indépendants
1928 Bldg B1, corner of Sanjo and Gokomachi, Nakagyo-ku.
(075) 255-4312.

Kyoryukan
N of Shokoku-ji Temple's E gate, Kamigyo-ku.
(075) 213-0288.
Wed.

Kyoto Connection
2F Teatro Marron Ue-no-Kaido, N of Kitayama, Kita-ku.
(075) 491-5971.

Metro
Corner of Kawabata and Marutamachi (Keihan Marutamachi stn exit 2).
(075) 752-4765.
web.kyoto-inet.or.jp/org/metro

Pig & Whistle
2F Shobi Bldg, N side of Sanjo, E of Sanjo Bridge.
6pm–1am Mon, Tue, Wed; to 2am Thu, Fri, Sat; 5pm–midnight Sun.
(075) 761-6022.

Western Honshu

The cultural heartland of the country, Western Honshu is where Japan's first imperial courts held sway, in an area called Yamato. A rich fusion of literature, imagination, and religious mysticism permeates many tourist attractions, while Osaka and other teeming cities are vibrant places constantly reinventing themselves. Little wonder that this part of Japan sits high on the list of travelers.

The name Yamato refers to the Japanese mountains, where heaven and earth divide, and also to the land founded by the mythical son of the gods, emperor Jimmu. In the Japanese mind, Yamato is a holy place, a homeland "whose trees and rocks, streams and mountains," as legendary emperor Keiko expressed it in verse form almost two millennia ago, "house the gods."

Shinto priests, Miyajima Island

Legend solidified into fact in the 4th century AD when a clan called Yamato expanded its kingdom in the region. Japan's first emperors, the Yamato rulers set up court on the Yamato Plain, the site of present-day Nara prefecture.

Nature, religion, and architecture converge in the city of Nara, its antiquity evident in its aging wooden temples. Here, the rich pantheons of India and China, reinterpreted, are set against a city characterized by quiet stroll gardens, the smell of lingering incense, and the reflections of winged pagodas in green ponds.

Hiroshima, now a surprisingly pleasant city, the international port of Kobe, and Osaka are Western Honshu's great metropolitan centers. Osaka, an industrial dynamo best known for its business deals and copious appetite for good food, is being transformed by its restless inhabitants into a forum for the arts.

Elsewhere, a strong sense of regional character is apparent at such destinations as the exquisite ceramic town of Hagi, the sacred island of Miyajima, the willow-lined canals and storehouses of Kurashiki, and Ise Grand Shrine, whose inner precincts are solemnly dedicated to the Sun Goddess.

Meoto Iwa ("wedded rocks"), representing the gods Izanami and Izanagi, Ise Peninsula

◁ **Statue of Kokuzo Bosatsu, an Enlightened Being, at the temple of Todai-ji, Nara**

Exploring Western Honshu

WESTERN HONSHU INCLUDES the region called Kansai (or sometimes Kinki), centered on the major city of Osaka. Kyoto is also part of Kansai but has a separate chapter in this book *(see pp148–79).* The area west of Osaka is called Chugoku, "Middle Country," and, despite being the historic heartland of Japan, it is now less densely populated than Kansai and Tokyo to the east. A spine of mountains runs through the middle of Western Honshu, and the two coasts are quite different in character, with the San-in coast rugged and more remote.

Hikone Castle garden, Lake Biwa

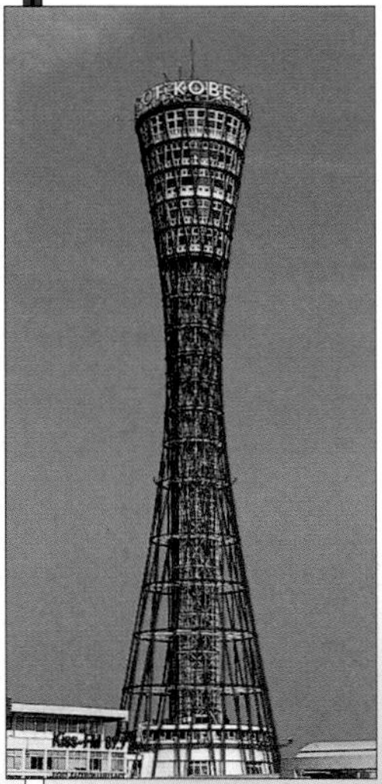

Kobe tower

SEE ALSO

- ***Where to Stay*** pp298–302
- ***Where to Eat*** pp331–4

SIGHTS AT A GLANCE

Akiyoshi-dai Tablelands 25
Amanohashidate Sand Bar 17
Asuka Plain 3
Fukiya 15
Hagi 26
Himeji Castle pp200–203 11
Hiroshima pp208–9 21
Horyu-ji Temple 2
Iga-Ueno 5
Inbe 12
Iwakuni 23
Izumo 20
Kii Peninsula 7
Kobe pp198–9 10
Kurashiki 14
Lake Biwa 16
Matsue 19
Miyajima Island pp210–11 22
Mount Koya 8
Nara pp184–9 1
Okayama 13
Osaka pp194–7 9
Tottori Sand Dunes 18
Tsuwano 27
Yamaguchi 24
Yoshino 4

Tour

Ise Peninsula Tour 6

0 kilometers 50
0 miles 30

KEY

- International airport
- Domestic airport
- Expressway
- Major road
- JR train line
- Private train line
- Viewpoint

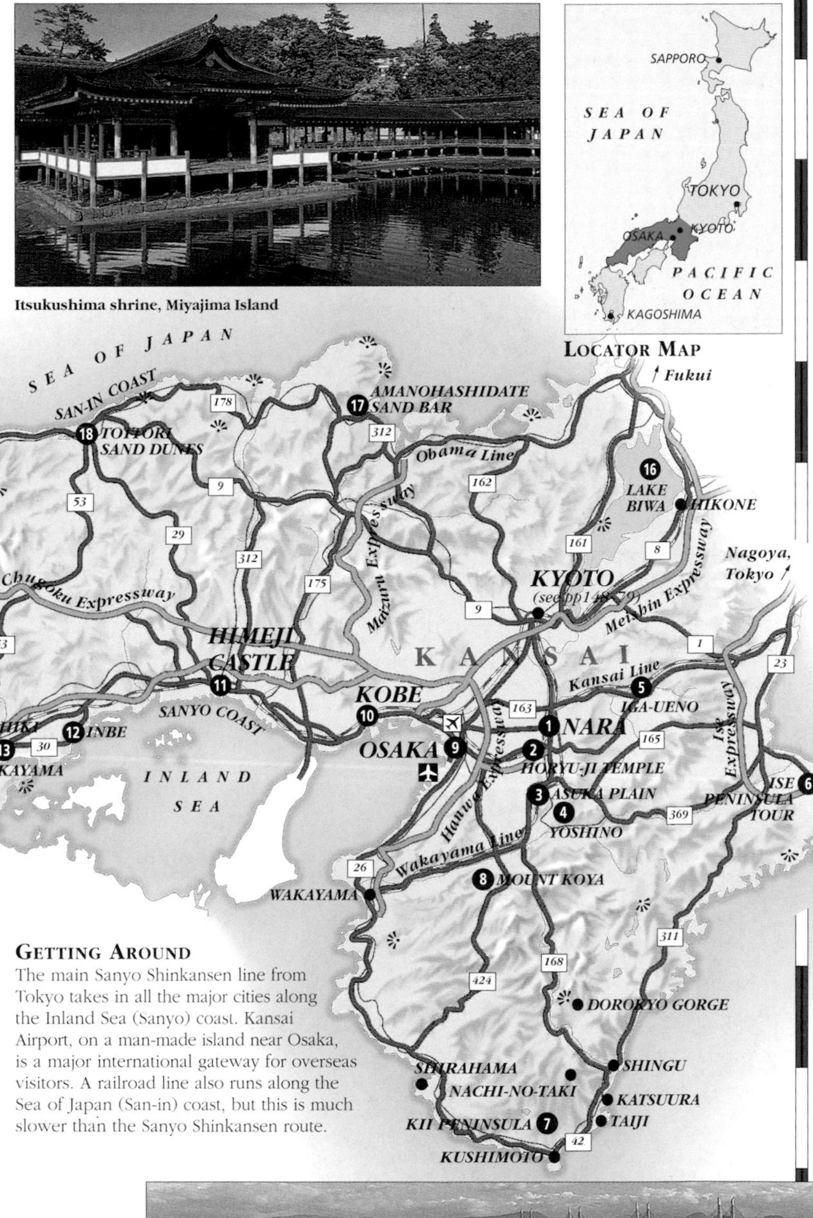

Itsukushima shrine, Miyajima Island

Getting Around

The main Sanyo Shinkansen line from Tokyo takes in all the major cities along the Inland Sea (Sanyo) coast. Kansai Airport, on a man-made island near Osaka, is a major international gateway for overseas visitors. A railroad line also runs along the Sea of Japan (San-in) coast, but this is much slower than the Sanyo Shinkansen route.

Sanyo coast near Okayama

Nara ❶

奈良

FOUNDED IN 710 on the Yamato Plain, Nara, then known as Heijo-kyo (citadel of peace), became one of Asia's most splendid cities in its 74-year spell as Japan's first capital. Avidly absorbing ideas from mainland Asia, the city became the grand diocese of Buddhism and the far eastern destination of the Silk Road. Miraculously, many buildings have survived. With its wooded hills, temple parks, and some of the world's oldest wooden buildings, this ancient city remains a symbol of tranquillity.

The tree ensconced temple of Todai-ji, as seen from hills to the east

Deer – "messengers of the gods" – in Nara Park

Nara National Museum

(0742) 22-7771. 9am–4:30pm Tue–Sun.

This important two-part museum consists of the original Beaux-arts building created in the 1870s, now housing the permanent collection, and a modern annex serving as a site for special exhibitions.

Exploring Nara

Nara's rectangular design, a checkerboard of streets based on the ancient Chinese city of Ch'ang-an, is straightforward and clearly divided into zones. The downtown area around the two stations, JR Nara and Kintetsu Nara, is within walking distance of **Nara Park**, a 1,300-acre area where most of the temples are located. Over 1,000 tame deer *(shika)*, regarded as messengers of the gods, roam the park. South of the center is **Naramachi**, the old city. Other notable areas like **Nishino-kyo** and **Horyu-ji** *(see p190)* are to the west and southwest of Nara.

Kofuku-ji Temple

(0742) 22-5370. 9am–5pm daily. for Treasure House and Eastern Golden Hall.

Kofuku-ji, approached up a wide staircase from Sarusawa Pond, was founded in 669. Of the 175 buildings in the original complex only a precious few remain. In Nara, however, even reconstructions can lay claim to antiquity. The current five-story pagoda, burned to the ground no less than five times, dates from 1426. The temple's Eastern Golden Hall, containing several priceless statues, is of similar vintage. In the Treasure House is one of Japan's foremost collections of Buddhist art, including an exquisite 8th-century statue of Ashura.

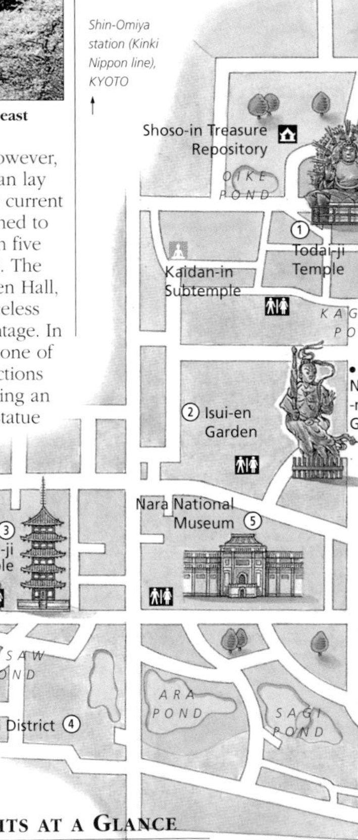

SIGHTS AT A GLANCE

Isui-en Garden ②
Kasuga Grand Shrine ⑦
Kofuku-ji Temple ③
Naramachi District ④
Nara National Museum ⑤
Shin-Yakushi-ji Temple ⑥
Todai-ji Temple ①

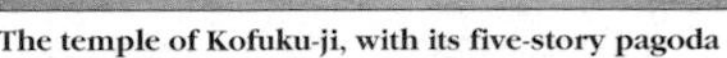

The temple of Kofuku-ji, with its five-story pagoda

Most of the exhibits, including Buddhist sculptures, paintings, objects found in sutra mounds, and calligraphy, date from the Nara and Heian periods. The museum holds an annual exhibition in October and early November of rarely seen treasures from the Shoso-in, a storehouse in the Todai-ji complex that was built to preserve Emperor Shomu's private collection. The Shoso-in itself houses over 9,000 precious objects, some of which are of Central Asian and Persian extraction, evidence of Nara's interaction with these regions through its position at the end of the Silk Road.

Some of the 3,000 lanterns at Kasuga Shrine

Isui-en Garden

(0742) 22-2173. 9:30am–4:30pm Wed–Mon.

The powerful shapes of Mount Wakakusa and Kasuga, and the megalithic roof of Todai-ji form a backdrop to this essentially Meiji-era garden, which is popular in spring for its plum, cherry, and azalea blooms, and in autumn for red maples. Stone lanterns, a meandering stream, and teahouses with thatched and cryptomeria-bark roofs complete the picture. In the teahouses, visitors can eat *mugitoro*, a potato, wheat, and rice mixture esteemed by health-food advocates.

Todai-ji Temple

See pp186–7.

Kasuga Grand Shrine

(0742) 22-7788.

9am–4pm daily. for museum.

Originally built as the tutelary shrine of the Fujiwaras, one of the families who helped to establish Nara, Kasuga is one of the best known and most photographed Shinto sites. The original building was completed in 710 but, according to the strictures of purity and renewal governing Shinto beliefs, the structure, like the Great Shrine at Ise, was demolished and rebuilt in identical fashion every 20 years. This was repeated 50 times over the centuries, but the current structure has been preserved since 1863.

Surrounded by a wood, the approach road and walkways around this vermilion-colored shrine boast an astonishing 3,000 or so stone and bronze lanterns, an impressive spectacle when they are lit in early February and mid-August.

Visitors' Checklist

Nara prefecture. *350,000.*
JR line from Kyoto, Kintetsu line from Kyoto. *at Kintetsu Nara stn (0742) 24-4858.*
www.ntt.com/japan/JNTO/Nara
Omizu-tori (Mar 1–14).

Shin-Yakushi-ji Temple

(0742) 22-3736. 9am–5pm daily.

This temple was built by Empress Komyo (701–60) as an offering to the gods whose intercession she sought in the recovery of her husband from an eye disease. Some structures were rebuilt in the 13th century, but the main hall, with 12 striking clay figures of Yakushi (Amida's incarnation as the Healing Buddha), is original.

House in the residential and crafts quarter of Naramachi

Naramachi District

The old quarter of **Naramachi** includes traditional *machiya* (merchant homes), mostly from the mid-18th–19th centuries, converted into galleries and craft shops. The buildings are distinguished by narrow frontages and surprising depth, a design that developed due to taxes that were assessed by the width of a building's frontage. The tourist office has free maps of the area.

Nigatsu do Subtemple
Sangatsu-do Subtemple
Lantern-lined walkways
⑦ Kasuga Grand Shrine
Deer enclosure
⑥ Shin-Yakushi-ji Temple
0 meters 250
0 yards 250

Key

- Train station
- Tourist information
- Temple
- Historic building
- Toilets
- Viewpoint

Exploring Nara: Todai-ji Temple

Stone lantern at Todai-ji Temple

THE TODAI-JI complex consists of a vast Buddha hall (Daibutsuden), subtemples, halls, pagodas, and gates of exceptional historical and architectural interest. The construction of Todai-ji, completed in 752, was ordered by Emperor Shomyo, ostensibly to house Nara's Great Buddha image but also to consolidate the position of the city as the capital and a powerful center of Buddhism. Natural disasters have not diminished the scale of the 16-m (53-ft) high statue. From time to time, when the figure is given a dusting, visitors may be startled to see four or five monks standing in the Buddha's upturned palm.

The 19-m (62-ft) high Nandaimon (great southern gate) of Todai-ji

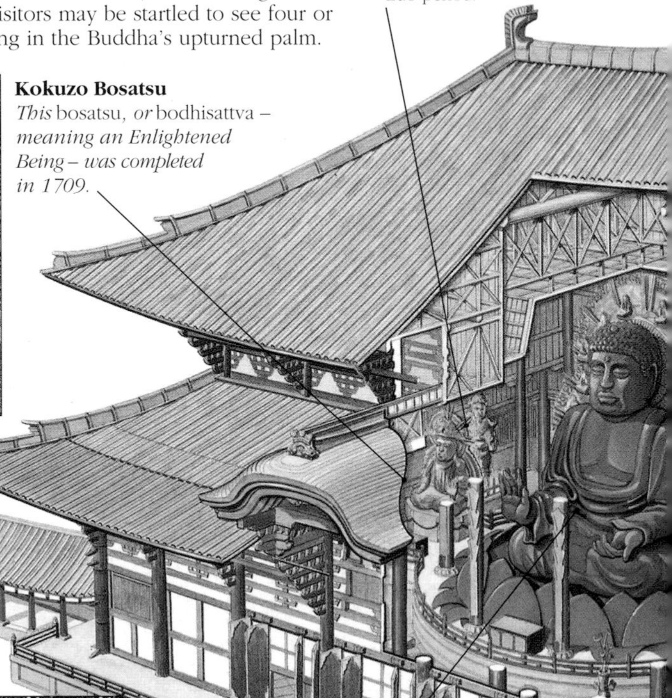

Koumokuten, a heavenly guardian, dates from the mid-Edo period.

Kokuzo Bosatsu

This bosatsu, *or* bodhisattva – *meaning an Enlightened Being – was completed in 1709.*

Entrance

★ Great Buddha Vairocana

The casting of this vast statue in 752 deployed hundreds of tons of molten bronze, mercury, and vegetable wax. Fires and earthquakes dislodged the head several times; the current head dates from 1692.

GREAT BUDDHA HALL

The main hall of Todai-ji was rebuilt several times. The current structure, completed in 1709, is only two-thirds of the original size but is still the largest wooden building in the world. The seated figure inside is the world's largest bronze image of the Buddha.

Visitors' Checklist

Nara Park. *(0742) 22-5511.* *Daibutsuden Kasuga-Taisha-mae stop.* *Apr–Sept: 7:30am–5:30pm daily; Oct: 7:30am–5pm daily; Nov–Feb: 8am–4:30pm daily; Mar: 8am–5pm daily.*

★ Wooden Hall
The unusual bracketing and beam-frame construction of this vast wooden hall, built in 1688–1709, were possibly the work of craftsmen from southern China.

Roofline
The striking roofline, with its golden "horns" and curved lintel, was an 18th-century embellishment.

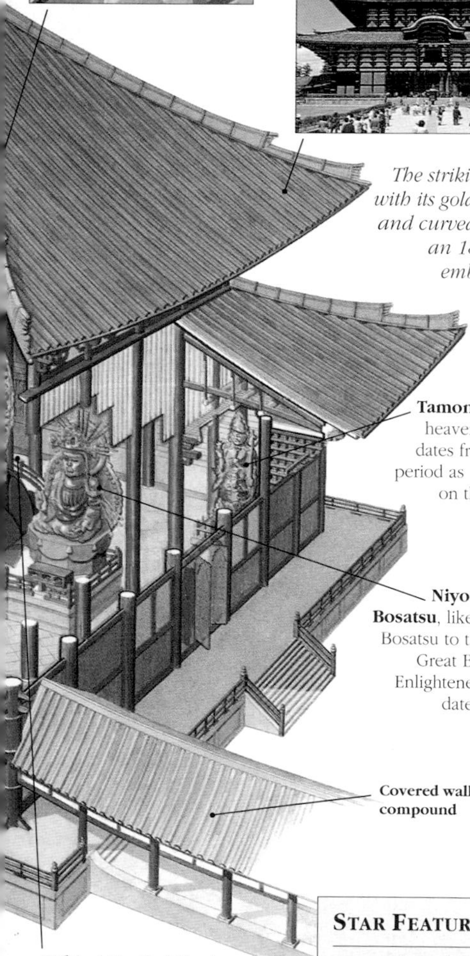

Tamonten, another heavenly guardian, dates from the same period as Koumokuten on the other side of the hall.

Niyorin Kannon Bosatsu, like the Kokuzo Bosatsu to the left of the Great Buddha, is an Enlightened Being and dates from 1709.

Covered walkway in compound

Behind the Buddha is a small hole bored into a large wooden pillar. A popular belief holds that if you can squeeze through the hole you will attain Nirvana.

Star Features

- ★ **Great Buddha Vairocana**
- ★ **Wooden Hall**

The beguiling "three-story" pagoda at Yakushi-ji

Beyond Nara Park: Nishinokyo District

Time permitting, two more temples in the Nara vicinity should not be missed.

Founded in 759 by the blind Chinese sage and priest Ganjin, **Toshodai-ji's** original main hall and lecture hall, designated National Treasures, are still standing. Be sure to visit the temple's stunning 5.5-m (18-ft) high Senju Kannon statue.

A little south of Toshodai-ji, more Buddhist statuary can be found at **Yakushi-ji**. Emperor Tenmu had the temple built in the hope of effecting a recovery for his wife, a gesture that seems to have worked as she outlived him by several years. Dedicated to the Buddha of healing, the temple's masterpiece is its famous three-story east pagoda, the only original structure remaining.

The pagoda, built in 730, appears to have six levels, but three are intermediary roofs placed between the main floors, creating an appealing optical effect. The 19th-century American scholar Ernest Fenollosa, on a visit to Yakushi-ji, compared the striking geometry of the pagoda to "frozen music."

Toshodai-ji, where its founder, Ganjin, is entombed

Classic view of the Yakushi-ji complex, with the top stories of the east pagoda visible on the right ▷

Horyu-ji Temple ❷

法隆寺

REGARDED AS THE CRADLE of Japanese Buddhism, the Horyu-ji complex is also thought to contain some of the world's oldest surviving wooden structures, dating from the early 7th century. The temple was erected by Prince Shotoku (573–621) in his effort to entrench Buddhism alongside Shinto as a pillar of the Japanese belief system. Some exceptional works of art, including ancient images of the Buddha, are housed here.

VISITORS' CHECKLIST

10 km (6 miles) SW of Nara. *JR Kansai Honsen line from Nara, then 15-min walk.* *from Kintetsu Nara stn to Horyu-ji-mae stop.* *daily: Nov–Feb 8am–4:30pm; Feb–Nov 8am–5pm.*

Gate at the Horyu-ji compound

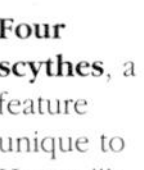

Four scythes, a feature unique to Horyu-ji's pagoda, are said to stop it from being destroyed by lightning.

The nine rings *(kurin)* of the finial are made of bronze.

Yakushi Nyorai images *dating from the 10th century are among the treasures of Horyu-ji.*

FIVE-STORY PAGODA

The pagoda is one of Horyu-ji's oldest buildings and the oldest one of its kind in Japan. The pagoda style was brought from China, which in turn had been developed from the Buddhist stupa in ancient India. The symbolism of such buildings is subject to debate. Some say that a five-story pagoda represents the elements, as shown; others disagree.

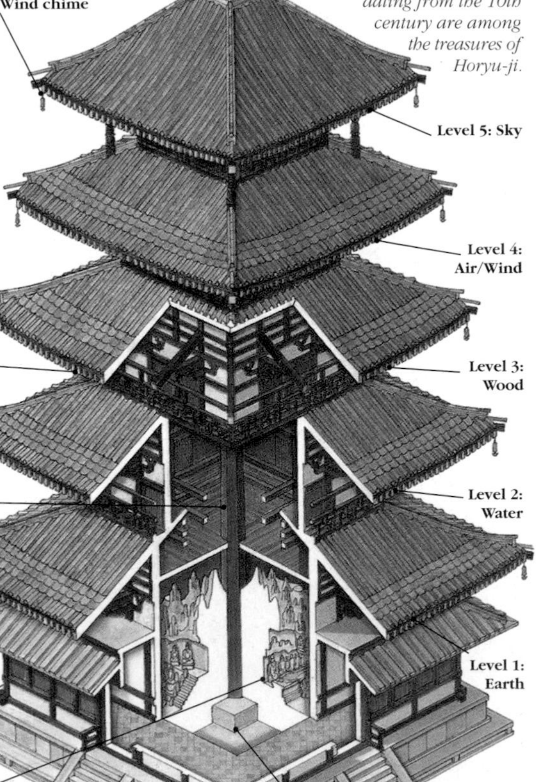

Wind chime

Level 5: Sky

Level 4: Air/Wind

Ornamental roof crays are made of bronze.

Level 3: Wood

The central column is fashioned from a single cypress tree. The bowed shape of pillars at Horyu-ji are reminiscent of classical Greek style, a legacy of the Silk Route.

Level 2: Water

Level 1: Earth

A fragment of the Buddha's bone is enshrined at the base of the central pillar.

Four sculpted scenes *from the life of the Buddha face north, south, east, and west. Here, on the north side, the Buddha passes into Nirvana.*

Asuka Plain ❸

飛鳥地方

Nara prefecture. [train] *Asuka.* [i] *(0744) 54-4577.*

THE ASUKA PLAIN is scattered with excavation sites from the proto-capital Asukakyo, which flourished in the 5th to 7th centuries. The best way to explore the burial tombs, temples, and early Buddhist statuary is by bicycle.

One of the best-known sites, **Takamatsuzuka Kofun,** is similar in design to Korean tombs of the same period and contains vivid murals of stars and mythological animals. Notable images elsewhere include **Sakabune Ishi**, a concentric stone that may have been used to make sake, **Kame and Saru Ishi**, turtle and monkey-shaped statues, and **Nimen Seki**, a stone with faces carved on each side.

Asuka-dera dates from the late 6th century. It was the country's first Buddhist temple but was overshadowed in fame by Prince Shotoku's Horyu-ji.

Takamatsuzuka Kofun, a tomb site on the Asuka Plain

Yoshino ❹

吉野

Nara prefecture. [train] [i] *at stn (0476) 3/2-3014.* [festival] *Setsubune (Feb 3); Sakura Festival (Apr 11–12).*

THE ATTRACTIVE, elevated village of Yoshino, its multistoried houses built on graduated levels on the side of a remote mountain, is one of Japan's most popular cherry blossom viewing spots. Mount Yoshino boasts

Cherry trees blossoming at altitude in Yoshino

100,000 trees planted in four groves at different altitudes. Each level blooms in succession, extending the viewing period to almost three weeks.

ENVIRONS: Uphill from the main road, **Chikurin-in** is a temple renowned for its stroll garden designed by the tea master Sen no Rikyu *(see p273)*. The two temples at the summit of **Sanjo-san**, regarded by pilgrims as the most sacred mountain here, afford superb views of the area. Another pilgrimage site, to the peak of **Omine-san**, is, unfortunately, off-limits to women climbers. **Yoshino Mikumari Shrine,** an hour's trek from the village, is a popular spot for couples who come to pray for fertility. Children's clothes and small cotton circles representing women's breasts are hung in the shrine precincts as offerings.

Iga-Ueno ❺

伊賀上野

Mie prefecture. [train] [festival] *Ueno Tenjin Matsuri (October 23–25).* [i] *at stn (0595) 24-0270.*

A PROVINCIAL castle town, Iga-Ueno was home to the ninja, the most inventive and feared spies of Japan's feudal era, and the birthplace of Japan's most revered haiku poet, Matsuo Basho *(see p163)*. Several sites in town, including Basho's house, a museum, and the odd **Haeseiden**, an octagonal building said to replicate Basho's standing figure, are dedicated to the poet.

The main attraction for most people, though, is the extraordinary **Iga Ninja Museum**, a clan farmhouse that served as the secret headquarters of the Iga sect of professional spies and assassins. The well-restored building retains hidden panels, spy holes, secret escape routes and trapdoors intended to repel night attacks from enemy warlords and rival ninja groups. Ninja methods are enthusiastically demonstrated by local guides dressed in pink day-glo ninja outfits.

Iga Ninja Museum
[tel] *(0595) 23-0311.* [open] *daily.* [fee]

THE NINJA

Ninjutsu, the "art of stealth," was developed during the bloody clan warfare of Japan's feudal era. The ninja elevated their profession of spying and assassination into a sophisticated discipline by practicing mountain ascetism and studying such subjects as astronomy, herbalism, medicine, and nutrition. They developed ingenious devices to outwit enemies, including lock picks, collapsible floats for crossing water, clothing designed to conceal swords and knives, and over 30 different kinds of *shuriken*, which are deadly throwing stars made of metal.

Ninja sword exhibit at Iga Ninja Museum

Local guide demonstrating ninja methods

Ise Peninsula Tour ❻

伊勢志摩国立公園

THE CITY OF ISE, its Grand Shrine – the most sacred in Japan – and the Ise-Shima National Park are the main tourist attractions of this peninsula. Its jagged, indented coast, the center of cultured oyster pearl production in Japan, is in striking contrast to the undulating evergreen-clad hills inland, which are the habitat of monkeys, wild boars, and flying squirrels.

Mikimoto Pearl Island ③
Just offshore from the tourist town of Toba, this island has a memorial hall to Mikimoto Kokichi who created the original cultured pearl in 1893. Women divers can be seen collecting seaweed and sea urchins.

Futamigaura Beach ②
Two rocks called the Meoto Iwa (wedded rocks), representing the parent gods of Japan, Izanami and Izanagi, are connected by a sacred rope *(see p181)*.

Ise Shrines ①
Reconstructed every 20 years in accordance with Shinto principles of purity and renewal, Ise's shrines are in two main groups: the Ge-ku (outer shrine) and Nai-ku (inner shrine, *see pp22–3*).

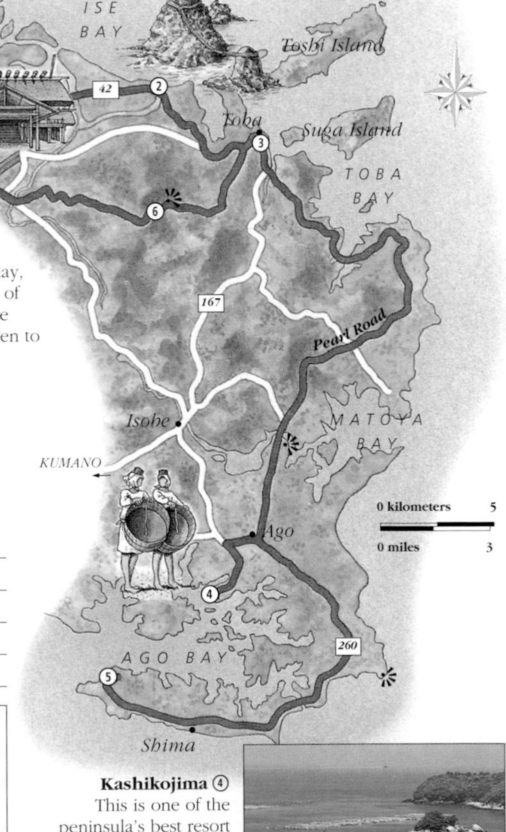

Ise-Shima Skyline ⑥
A good route back on a clear day, this road goes over the summit of Mount Asama, with views of the peninsula and, occasionally, even to Mount Fuji in Central Honshu.

Goza Beach ⑤
The most popular stretch of sand on the peninsula, Goza Beach can be reached by road or by boat from Kashikojima.

KEY

- Tour route
- Expressway
- Other road
- Viewpoint

TIPS FOR TRAVELERS

Tour length: *110 km (70 miles).*
Alternative transportation: *The area has excellent bus and train services. Trains run to Ise, Futamigaura, Toba, and Kashikojima, while buses run to many destinations from Toba, and between the Ise shrines.*

Kashikojima ④
This is one of the peninsula's best resort areas, with fine views of Ago Bay. You can take a boat trip past scenic islets, fishing boats, and hundreds of oyster rafts.

Kii Peninsula 7

紀伊半島

Wakayama, Mie, and Nara prefectures. *Shirahama.* *JR Kisei line.* *Shingu City Tourist Office (0735) 22-2840.* *Nachi no Hi-Matsuri (Jul 14).*

THE KII PENINSULA, with densely forested mountains at its center and craggy headlands, pine-covered islands, and coves along its shoreline, has largely avoided the industrial development that scars much of Japan's Pacific coastline.

A good starting point is the small port town of **Shingu**, on the east coast. From here a four-hour boat trip takes you along the emerald-green Kumano River to **Dorokyo**, one of Japan's most spectacular gorges. The river is at its best from May to early June, when rhododendrons and azaleas bloom on the banks.

A 20-minute bus ride inland from Shingu lies **Nachi-no-taki**, Japan's highest waterfall. A stone path ascending parallel to the falls leads to **Nachi Taisha** shrine, its origins reaching back over 1,400 years. The next port south of Shingu is **Katsuura**, a pleasant pine-studded bay with several picturesque islets. Visitors interested in the Japanese perspective on whaling should go to nearby **Taiji**, a whaling community since the 17th century. For insight into a complex subject, visit the **Taiji Whale Museum**.

Farther south, the resort of **Kushimoto** is known for a chain of 30 rocks, **Hashi-gui-iwa,** that seem to march out to sea, connecting the town to the island of Oshima. The peninsula's southernmost point is marked by **Shio-no-misaki**, a headland with a white lighthouse dating from 1873. One of the three best hot springs in Japan, **Shirahama Onsen**, on the west coast, also has one of the area's finest beaches.

Typically forested hillsides on the Kii Peninsula

Kano-school screens inside Kongobu-ji, Mount Koya

Taiji Whale Museum

(07355) 9-2400. *daily.*

Mount Koya 8

高野山

Wakayama prefecture. *6,000.* *Nankai line from Osaka, then cable car from Gokurakubashi stn.* *nr Senjuinbashi bus stop (0736) 56-2616.* *daily.* *some buildings.* *Aoba Matsuri (Jun 15), Rosoku Matsuri (Candle Festival, Aug 13).*

SET AMID clumps of black cedar at an altitude of 900 m (3,000 ft) in the heart of the Kii Peninsula, Mount Koya, or Koya-san, is Japan's most venerated Shingon-Buddhist site. It is host to over one million pilgrims a year. Saint Kukai (774–835), also known by his posthumous name, Kobo Daishi, established a monastic retreat here in 816. There were almost a thousand temples on the mountain by the Edo period, but typhoons and fire have since reduced the number to 123. The mountain's unique atmosphere is best experienced with an overnight stay. Traditional vegetarian cuisine is served in Koya-san's 53 temple lodgings.

The western part of Koya-san contains the grandest and most revered structures. **Kongobu-ji**, built in 1592 by Toyotomi Hideyoshi *(see p52)*, is Koya-san's chief temple. Its rhododendrons and the sliding doors of its inner chambers, painted in the 16th century by artists of the Kano school, are among its special attractions. The magnificent **Danjogaran** complex, a short walk away, includes the oldest building on the mountain, the **Fudo-do** (Fudo Hall), built in 1197, and the **Konpon Dai-to**, an impressive two-story vermilion-and-white pagoda. Rebuilt in 1937, the pagoda is regarded as the symbol of Koya-san.

The aptly named **Reihokan** (Treasure House) stands opposite the complex, a cornucopia of over 5,000 paintings, statues, and mandalas displayed in two separate buildings. The gigantic **Daimon** (great gate), the traditional main entrance to Koya-san, lies a little west of here on the edge of the plateau. It affords a matchless view of mountains, valleys and, on clear days, distant Shikoku and Awaji islands.

A burial stone at Okuno-in, Mount Koya

In the eastern half of Koya-san is a necropolis of over 200,000 tombs, and the **Okuno-in** (inner sanctum), Kukai's mausoleum. Great status is attached to burial on Koya-san. The stone-paved approach to Okuno-in is flanked with statues, monuments, and tombs housing the remains of Japan's most powerful and illustrious families. In front of Kukai's mausoleum is the **Toro-do** (Lantern Hall). Day and night 11,000 lanterns burn here, including two that are said to have remained lit since the 11th century.

Osaka ❾

大阪

Theater poster in Osaka

OSAKA'S PROMINENCE as a merchant city dates from Toyotomi Hideyoshi's building of Osaka Castle in 1586. He also encouraged traders from other parts of Japan to settle in the city. In the 1920s and '30s it became an industrial powerhouse. Nowadays, though, the nondescript skyline is being replaced with galleries, international hotels, futuristic living spaces, and exciting postmodernist architecture. The city's extravagant nightlife and culinary predilections are famous. A Japanese saying, "*Kyoto kidaore; Osaka kuidaore,*" suggests that Kyoto-ites are apt to go bankrupt from buying kimonos, Osakans from eating out too much.

Exploring Osaka

Central Osaka is split into two main districts, which meet at Chuo-odori. **Kita-ku**, the northern ward around the main Osaka and Umeda stations, is where many of the city's big hotels, restaurants, and underground shopping precincts are found. It also includes the small island of Nakanoshima, between the Dojima and Tosabori rivers. **Minami-ku**, the southern district, includes the lively downtown area called **Namba**, the core of the old merchant city where you will find Osaka's best eating and drinking options, including **Dotonbori**. This lane, running alongside the canal of the same name and crammed with pink salons, karaoke bars, and pachinko parlors, is also a mecca of cheap restaurants and bars. Namba's many pedestrian shopping zones include **America Mura** and **Europe-dori**, with their imported goods, both north of, and parallel to, Dotonbori, and **Den Den Town**, Osaka's premier electronics district which is south of Sennichimae-dori. **Chuo-ku**, the old central ward and historic center of the city is to the east; this is where Osaka Castle stands. **Osaka Port** is west of the city center.

Plenty of information and signs in English make Osaka a relatively easy place to negotiate in comparison with other major Japanese cities. The city center is served by a user-friendly loop system called the JR Kanjo Line. Its color-coded subway system is also easy to ride. Visitors who intend to cover a lot of sightseeing in a limited period will benefit from buying a one-day pass *(ichi nichi joshaken)* that offers a day's unlimited travel on subways, trams, and local train lines.

Young Osakans at leisure in the Dotonbori canal district

Sweeping view of downtown Osaka

Osaka City Museum

(06) 6949-7177. Morinomiya stn, JR Kanjo line. Tanimachi-Yonchome stn, Chuo or Tanimachi lines. Tue–Sun.

The museum has an extensive, permanent collection of historical exhibits relating to the city. Among the items on display are objects excavated from the 7th-century Naniwa Palace, photographs, and old books. It provides a good introduction to the history of Osaka. A capsule was buried outside the museum in 1970 to commemorate the inauguration of Osaka Expo; a replica of the contents can be seen in the museum.

Osaka Castle

Morinomiya stn, JR Kanjo line. Tanimachi-Yonchome stn, Chuo or Tanimachi lines. daily.

The present reconstruction of the main donjon, dating from 1931, is smaller than the castle completed by Hideyoshi in 1586 but still gives some idea of the power and majesty of the original. The largest castle in the country at the time, Osaka-jo's turbulent history began when it was besieged and destroyed by the Tokugawa shogunate in 1615. The castle was rebuilt but struck by lightning a few years later. The remains were burned down in a fire in 1868, just before the Meiji Restoration.

Some ancillary buildings, including the Tamon tower and the impressive Otemon gate have survived from the Tokugawa period. The modernized lower floors of the main keep display a collection of armor and memorabilia connected with Hideyoshi, including his

The imposing keep of Osaka Castle

letters. A modern elevator whisks visitors up to the 8th floor where there are excellent views of the city.

Panasonic Square

2nd flr, Twin 21 National Tower Bldg. (06) 6949-2122. Kyobashi stn, JR Kanjo lines. Osaka Business Park stn. daily.

From a re-creation of the past to a vision of the future, Panasonic Square, located among the skyscrapers of Osaka's Business Park just north of the castle, is the city's tribute to the achievements of high-tech. Interactive electronic equipment allows visitors to enjoy hands-on experiences at the Futuristic Electro-Fun Zone, which is divided into four sections: Experiencing, Creating, Knowing, and Learning with Electronics. Virtual Fantasia and Fantasy Studios allow you to fly over the city, create your own photo montages, and play computer games. Weekends and late afternoons, when hordes of school children descend, are best avoided.

The high-tech, neon-lit interior of Panasonic Square

Visitors' Checklist

Osaka prefecture. *2,600,000.*
Kansai 35 km (22 miles) S.
Itami 10 km (6 miles) N.
Sanyo Shinkansen, JR, Hankyu, Keihan, Nankai, Hanshin, and Kintetsu lines. in JR Osaka stn (06) 6345-2189.
www.tourism.city.osaka.jp/en
Shoryoe Matsuri (Apr 22); Tenjin Matsuri (July 24–25).

Museum of Oriental Ceramics

Nakanoshima Island. (06) 6223-0055. JR Osaka stn. Yodoyabashi stn, Midosuji line. Tue–Sun.

Housing one of the finest collections of Oriental ceramics in the world, this museum, with over 1,000 items of mostly Chinese and Korean origin, should not be missed. The display comes from the Ataka Collection, once owned by a wealthy Osaka industrialist. Computer-regulated, light-sensitive rooms highlight the surfaces of the items. A few of the Japanese pieces are National Treasures.

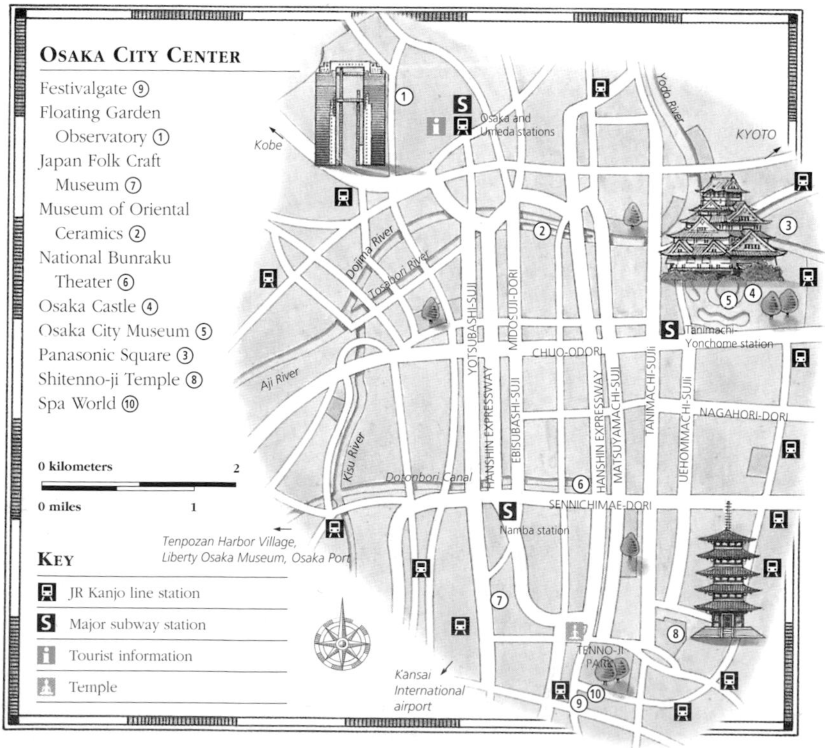

Osaka City Center

Festivalgate ⑨
Floating Garden Observatory ①
Japan Folk Craft Museum ⑦
Museum of Oriental Ceramics ②
National Bunraku Theater ⑥
Osaka Castle ④
Osaka City Museum ⑤
Panasonic Square ③
Shitenno-ji Temple ⑧
Spa World ⑩

0 kilometers 2
0 miles 1

Osaka and Umeda stations
Kobe
KYOTO
Yodo River
Dojima River
Tosabori River
Aji River
Kisu River
Dotonbori Canal
YOTSUBASHI-SUJI
MIDOSUJI-DORI
CHUO-ODORI
HANSHIN EXPRESSWAY
EBISUBASHI-SUJI
HANSHIN EXPRESSWAY
MATSUYAMACHI-SUJI
TANIMACHI-SUJI
UEHOMMACHI-SUJI
NAGAHORI-DORI
SENNICHIMAE-DORI
Tanimachi-Yonchome station
Namba station
TENNO-JI PARK
Tenpozan Harbor Village, Liberty Osaka Museum, Osaka Port
Kansai International airport

Key

JR Kanjo line station
Major subway station
Tourist information
Temple

Exploring Osaka

Today, Osaka is Japan's third largest city after Tokyo and Yokohama. It also joins Tokyo and Kyoto as the top three culinary centres of Japan, with a local cuisine known for its practicality rather than finesse – instant noodles were invented here in 1958. Working Osakans eat out about six times a week. Favorite local dishes include *oshizushi*, in which sushi is placed in stainless steel molds and sliced; *udon suki*, buckwheat noodles and meat in a rich broth served in a ceramic stew pot; and *okonimiyaki*, a batter and vegetable pancake-type dish developed in 1700 as a Buddhist ritual food. For recommended restaurants see pages 333–4.

Osaka's Umeda Sky Building, topped by the Floating Garden Observatory

Floating Garden Observatory

Umeda Sky Bldg. JR Osaka or Umeda stns. 10am–10:30pm daily.

This futuristic structure, reached by taking an exposed glass escalator to the 39th floor, is not for those who suffer from vertigo or fear of being caught in high places in earthquake-prone regions.

The observatory, 150 m (500 ft) above ground, straddles the twin towers of Hara Hiroshi's Umeda Sky Building. Views of Osaka and the port area from the top are well worth the palpitations. High-tech displays and a virtual-reality game center also occupy the observatory, but neither can really compete with the panoramas.

National Bunraku Theater

Nipponbashi stn, Kintetsu line. S Nipponbashi stn, Sennichi-mae & Sakaisuji lines. (06) 6212-2531.

Japan's main venue for Bunraku puppet dramas *(see p33)* can be spotted from the colorful banners hanging outside the theater. Bunraku performances take place every January, April, June, July, August, and November, programs running normally for about 20 days at a time with shows at 11am and 4pm. The acoustics in this specially designed theater are excellent, and headsets are available for foreign tourists, with dialogue translated into English.

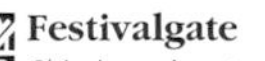

Festivalgate

Shin-imamiya stn, JR Kanjo line. S Dobutsuenmae stn, Midosuji line. (06) 6635-1000. daily. (for individual rides and activities)

Opened in the late 1990s, Festivalgate is a large outdoor and indoor amusement park with a futuristic image. Marine-themed experiences include water carousels, a submarine roller-coaster, and a dolphin ride that speeds through the complex at over 100 km (60 miles) an hour. The park itself is full of tropical decor and flora. Fast-food restaurants, virtual-reality games, and other amusements make this a perfect day out for travelers with children.

Lobster restaurant and motif in downtown Osaka

Spa World

Shin-imamiya stn, JR Kanjo line. S Dobutsuenmae stn, Midosuji line. (06) 6631-0001. 24 hours.

Built to cater to up to 5,000 people at any time, Spa World is one of the most amazing bathing experiences you are ever likely to have. Piping hot water comes from springs almost 900 m (3,000 ft) underground. The main part of the complex is divided into zones representing bathing characteristics of such parts of the world as the Middle East, Europe, India, Japan, and Asia. The Chinese section concentrates on traditional Chinese medicine, while the Turkish section has mosaic-tile flooring.

Japan Folk Craft Museum

Banpaku-Kinenkoen monorail. Nihon-teien-mae. (06) 6877-1971. Thu–Tue.

This modest building contains an outstanding collection of traditional folk arts and crafts, one of the best of its type in Japan. It offers a superb introduction to regional handicrafts centering on textiles and fabrics, ceramic ware, bamboo, furniture, toys, and more. There are examples of modern crafts by living masters.

Ceramic bowl, Folk Craft Museum

Shitenno-ji Temple

S Shitenno-ji stn, Tanimachi line. daily.

Prince Shotoku ordered the construction of the original temple here in 593. The complex is considered the birthplace of Japanese Buddhism. Destroyed many times by fire, the current concrete buildings, dating from 1965, are of no intrinsic value. As exact replicas of the originals, however, they are of interest to visitors wishing to know more about early Buddhist architecture. An excellent flea market is held on the 21st of every month.

Tempozan Harbor Village

Osaka-ko stn, Chuo line. **Suntory Museum** Tue–Sun. **Aquarium** daily.

Begun as a reclamation program in the 1830s, this waterfront project in Osaka Port is the new face of an older, Edo-period landfill. The **Suntory Museum**, a super-modern structure by world-famous architect Ando Tadao, has a formidable collection of posters by artists such as Mucha and Toulouse-Lautrec, and also rare glass art objects.

Nearby **Osaka Aquarium** is set apart by its innovative and challenging design. Built around the concept of the Pacific "Ring of Fire," the aquarium holds almost 13.5 million liters (3 million gallons) of water. Visitors descend through 14 levels representing fish and mammal habitats found within the Pacific Ocean belt. Over 35,000 creatures inhabit the aquarium, including some large specimens like manta rays and whale sharks.

The Harbor Village complex also has a theater and what is claimed to be the world's largest IMAX screen. **Tempozan Marketplace** is a large center for restaurants and shopping. There is also a huge ferris wheel, only a little smaller than the one built in 1999 in Tokyo Bay, which is the world's second largest.

Curved glass façade of the Suntory Museum, Tempozan Harbor Village

Liberty Osaka Museum

Ashiharabashi or Imamiya stns, JR loop line. Tue–Sun.

The Liberty is also known as the Osaka Human Rights Museum and provides a sobering insight into the dark side of Japan. Exhibits take a critical look at subjects rarely discussed by Japanese. Topics include the Burakumin section of society – descendants of leather-workers, who disposed of the dead and did other jobs considered polluted. Discrimination against ethnic minorities and foreigners, and environmental issues are also covered.

Environs: Situated 35 km (22 miles) south of Osaka, state-of-the-art **Kansai International Airport** (KIX) is built on a man-made island 2 km (1 mile) offshore in Osaka Bay. Connected to the mainland by a bridge, the airport is a long, thin, futuristic compression of glass and steel.

Osaka is also at the cutting edge of research into high-speed train technology in the form of magnetic-levitated trains (Maglevs). A prototype runs between Kadoma-minami and Taisho stations. Experiments with more advanced Maglevs have reached speads of 550 kph (340 mph).

Takarazuka lies northwest of Osaka, in Hyogo prefecture. The town is closely associated with the enormously popular all-female Takarazuka Troupe, which was founded in 1914. Their revues can be classified as adaptations of heroic romances. Performances at the **Takarazuka Grand Theater** are held once or twice a day except Wednesday.

Takarazuka Grand Theater

Hankyu & JR lines. (0797) 85-6770.

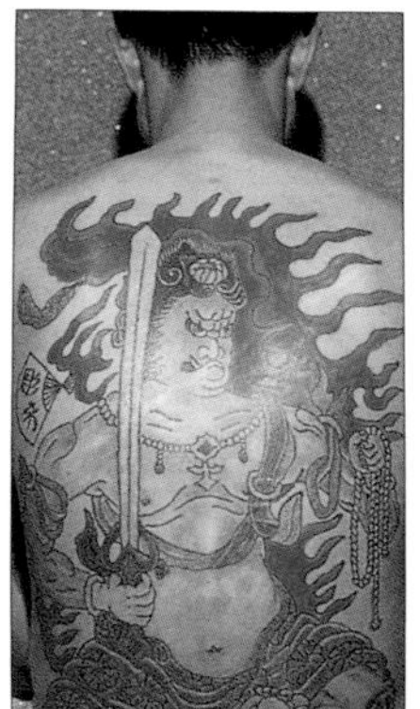

A large tattoo, often the sign of a *yakuza* member

The Yakuza

The word *yakuza* was originally used to describe the classless groups of thieves, gamblers, and outlaws who floated around large cities and ports during the Edo period. Osaka is the center of the modern *yakuza* and many of the country's largest and most influential crime syndicates. *Yakuza* are involved in a wide range of illegal activities that run from prostitution, drug- and light-arms-smuggling to loan-sharking. Gangs are also adept at corporate extortion, preventing, for a suitable fee, embarrassing questions being asked at stockholder meetings. *Irezumi* (tattoos), though traditionally an art form, are considered anti-social in Japan and are strongly associated with the *yakuza*. If you see a tattooed person with a missing finger or two – the result of a self-mutilation equated in the *yakuza* world with machismo – the chances are that the person will be a gang member.

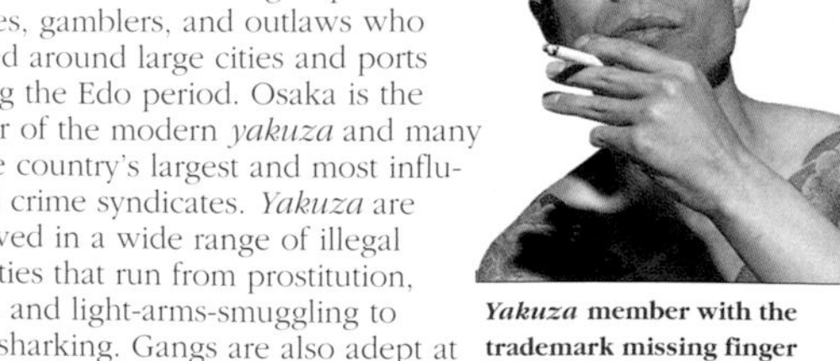

***Yakuza* member with the trademark missing finger**

Gateway detail, Chinatown

KOBE ENJOYED A BRISK TRADE with China and Korea from the 8th century on and was one of the first ports to benefit when Japan reopened to Western trade in 1868. Today, there is a large expatriate community, notably Chinese and Koreans, but also Europeans, Americans, and Indians. The city became famous overnight in 1995 when a massive earthquake struck. However, there is little evidence of the disaster now, so effectively has this lively, cosmopolitan city been rebuilt. The downtown area is famous for its nightlife. Kobe beef, meanwhile, is the world's most expensive meat.

One of the elegant European residences in Kitano-cho

Exploring Kobe

Kobe's central business, shopping, and nightlife districts, Kitano-cho, nearby Chinatown, and the narrow north-south axis of Flower Road are easily negotiated on foot. With little room left to expand beyond these urban parameters, Kobe has turned to the sea for extra space. Reclamation projects include Rokko and Port Islands.

The excellent subway system has lines running east-west. An unmanned monorail, the Port Liner, runs from Sannomiya station in a circle around Port Island. The City Loop bus offers a day pass that includes most of the city's key sights.

Kitano-cho

12-min walk from Sannomiya stn along Kitano-zaka. *some houses.*

Wealthy foreign traders and diplomats built homes in this area after Kobe was chosen to serve as one of Japan's major international ports at the start of the Meiji period. Over 20 of these beautifully preserved homes are open to the public. The stone and clapboard buildings, many in the Gothic Victorian style, are called *ijinkan*. The area, which suggests fin de siècle European elegance to many Japanese people, enjoys a reputation as one of Kobe's more fashionable districts.

Chinatown

5-min walk S of Motomachi stn.

The city's 40,000 or more Chinese residents have turned this quarter (Nankin-machi) into a lively and colorful slice of Kobe life. Approached through four large gateways, the central plaza, Nankin Park, is surrounded by Chinese restaurants, souvenir and trinket shops, and is filled with street vendors. The park has statues representing the 12 animals of the Chinese astrological calendar. Chinatown is a popular dining spot for Kobe residents.

Kobe City Museum

10-min walk S of Motomachi stn.

Tue–Sun.

This museum is an excellent introduction to the history of the city from the earliest times until its reconstruction after the 1995 earthquake. There is an intriguing display of objects retrieved from the old foreign concession in Kitano-cho and a scale model of the area. The museum also has the world's premier collection of 16th-century Nanban art. The word Nanban ("Southern Barbarian") was at first applied to all foreigners who arrived from the south, mainly the Portuguese. Later it was applied to Europeans in general.

Meriken Park

Port Liner monorail. **Museum and Port Tower** *daily.*

A little west of the monorail bridge that takes you across to Port Island lies Meriken Park. Meriken was the Meiji-

THE GREAT HANSHIN EARTHQUAKE

Shoehorned into a narrow strip of land between hills to the north and the Inland Sea to the south, Kobe paid a high price for its location on the morning of January 17, 1995. At 5:46am the Great Hanshin Earthquake struck, its epicenter 10 miles beneath the Akashi Strait near Kobe. The tremor lasted almost a minute and measured 6.9 on the moment magnitude scale. The initial quake, hundreds of aftershocks, and ensuing fires together destroyed over 100,000 buildings and killed over 5,000 inhabitants.

The center of Kobe in ruins following the January 1995 earthquake

Sake brewery in Kobe, open to visitors

era rendition of "American." From the park you will see the distinctive outline of the **Kobe Maritime Museum**, a glass structure with a roof designed like a ship. The displays inside it focus on the city's role as a port. For a good overview of the area climb the **Port Tower** on Naka Tottei Pier.

Sake Breweries

Although most of the best breweries were razed during the earthquake, reconstruction and preservation of the few that were left has been going on at a furious pace, and it is now possible once again to visit some the best-known brand-name producers. Reservations are required to visit **Kikumasamune Shuzo Kinenkan**, a brewery located within three minutes' walk of Rokko Liner Minami Uozaki station. Although its storehouses perished in the quake, the watermill cottage survived and now houses a small but interesting display of brewing utensils. At **Hamafukutsuru Ginjo Kobo**, a five-minute stroll from Hanshin Uozaki station, visitors can watch the fermenting process. Sake tasting takes place at both breweries.

Environs: On a hill behind Shin-Kobe station, the **Nunobiki Falls**, with four picturesque cascades, have been celebrated in Japanese literature since the 10th century. **Mount Rokko**, the highest peak of the chain of the same name, can be reached by cable car. The sweeping panorama of the Inland Sea and city below is sensational. On the north slope is **Arima Onsen**, a spa that has been operating since the 7th century. The waters were a favorite of the great 16th-century shogun Toyotomi Hideyoshi and his wife, who sometimes came in the company of the tea ceremony master, Sen no Rikyu.

Visitors' Checklist

Hyogo prefecture. 1,480,000. Kansai airport, 27 km (17 miles) E of Port Island, 25 mins by high-speed boat. Kobe City Air Terminal (K-CAT), Port Island. JR Shin-Kobe stn, Sanyo Shinkansen line; Sannomiya stn, JR Tokkaido, Hankyu, & Hanshin lines. in front of stn (078) 322-0220. Tsuinashiki Matsuri (Feb 3–4); Kobe Matsuri (around Jul 20).

The cable car ride up Mount Rokko

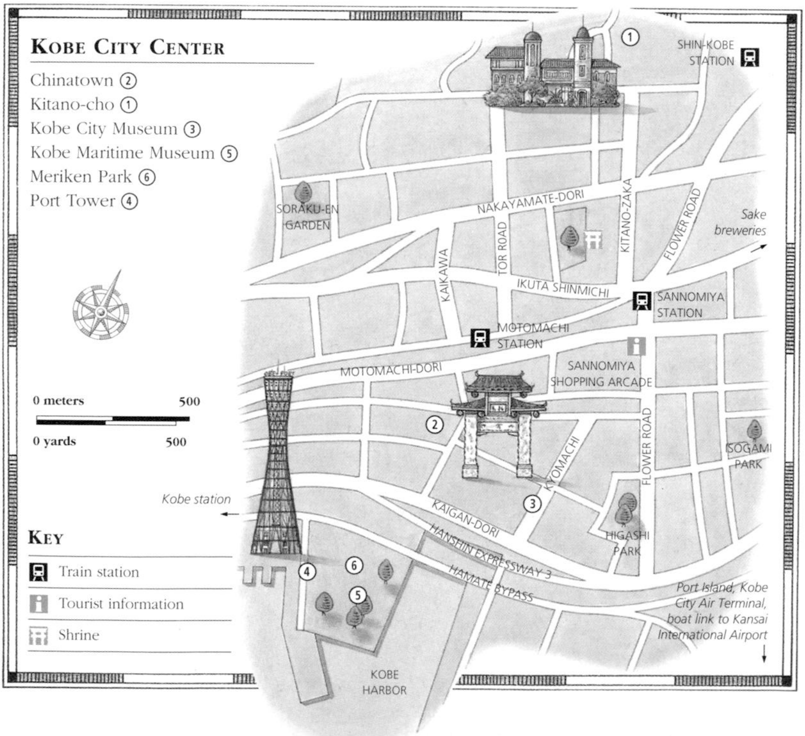

Kobe City Center

Chinatown ②
Kitano-cho ①
Kobe City Museum ③
Kobe Maritime Museum ⑤
Meriken Park ⑥
Port Tower ④

0 meters 500
0 yards 500

Key

Train station
Tourist information
Shrine

Shin-Kobe Station
Soraku-en Garden
Nakayamate-dori
Tor Road
Kitano-zaka
Flower Road
Sake breweries
Kaikawa
Ikuta Shinmichi
Sannomiya Station
Motomachi Station
Motomachi-dori
Sannomiya Shopping Arcade
Kyomachi
Isogami Park
Kobe station
Kaigan-dori
Higashi Park
Hanshin Expressway 3
Hamate Bypass
Port Island, Kobe City Air Terminal, boat link to Kansai International Airport
Kobe Harbor

Himeji Castle ⓫

姫路城

BUILT ON A HIGH BLUFF, Himeji-jo, the grandest of Japan's 12 remaining feudal castles, dominates the city of Himeji. The building is better known among the Japanese as Shirasagi-jo, the "white egret castle," because of the supposed resemblance of its plastered walls, stretched either side of the main donjon, to the image of a bird taking flight. For many people its military architecture, ameliorated by graceful aesthetic lines, qualifies Himeji-jo as the ultimate samurai castle. Its cinematic potential was exploited by Akira Kurosawa who used the castle's stunning exterior for his 1985 film *Ran*. The castle is now designated a UNESCO World Heritage Site.

View from lower floor of donjon to the modern city of Himeji

West bailey
(nishi-nomaru)

Vanity Tower
The abode of Princess Sen (1597–1667) and other women was locked each night under guard.

Gates and Passageways
Though never put to the test, the castle's labyrinth of passageways and gateways in the outer zones were designed to confuse enemies.

Entrance

Sangoku moat

TIMELINE OF HIMEJI CASTLE

1333 Norimura Akamatsu builds a fort in a strategic location on top of a hillock at Himeji

1467 Two baileys added by Akamatsu Masanori

1581 Toyotomi Hideyoshi adds a three-story donjon to the fort

1600 Battle of Sekigahara *(see pp50–51)*, after which Ikeda Terumasa, son-in-law of Tokugawa Ieyasu, is rewarded with Himeji Castle

1601 Ikeda Terumasa begins digging three moats around castle

1609 Five-story donjon completed

1618 Buildings in west bailey added by Tadamasa Honda

1749 Sakai Tadasumi and descendants live in castle until Meiji Restoration of 1867

1400 | 1500 | 1600 | 1700

17th-century crest tile from gable of castle

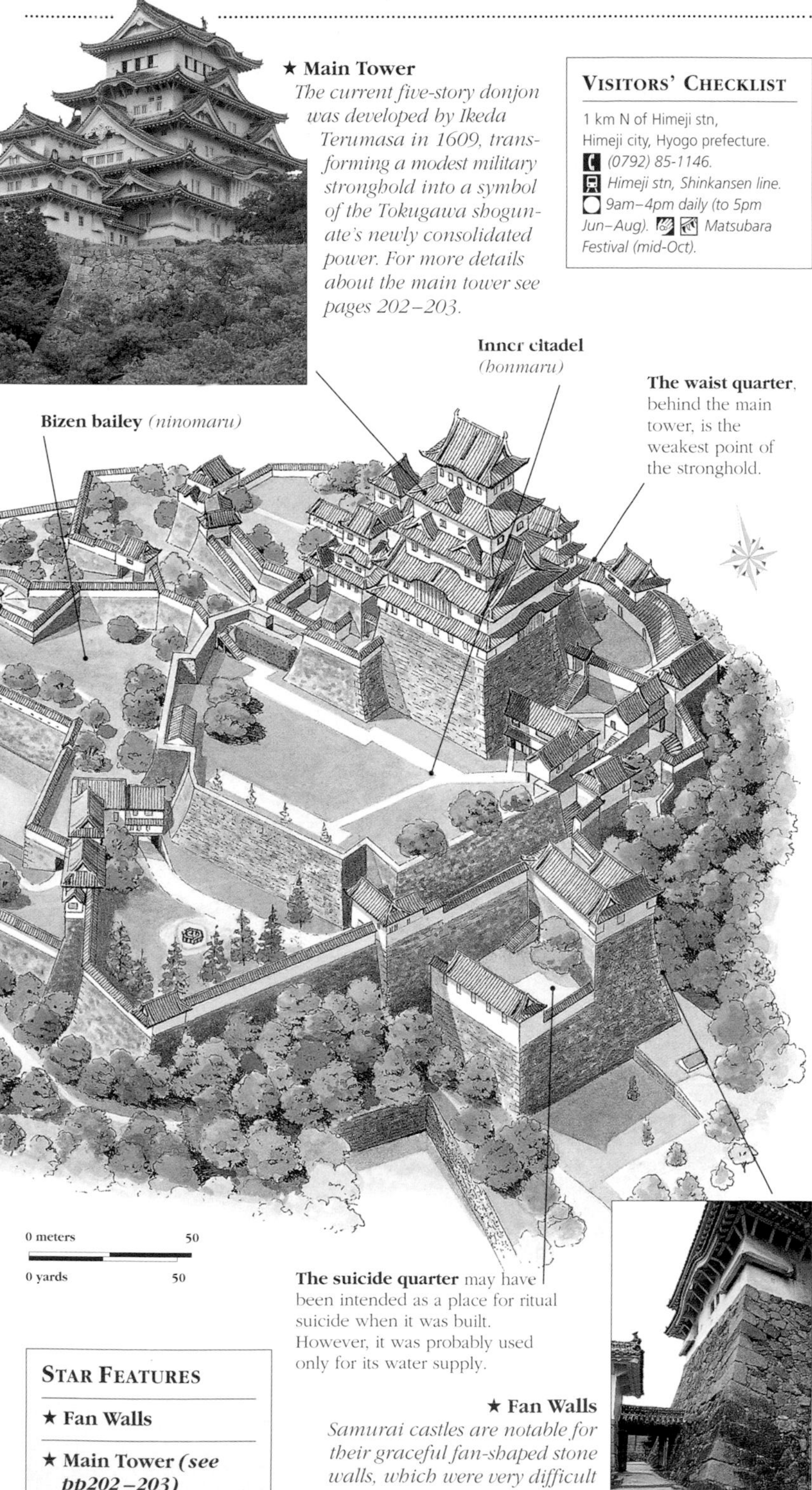

Visitors' Checklist

1 km N of Himeji stn, Himeji city, Hyogo prefecture. *(0792) 85-1146. Himeji stn, Shinkansen line. 9am–4pm daily (to 5pm Jun–Aug). Matsubara Festival (mid-Oct).*

Star Features

- ★ Fan Walls
- ★ Main Tower *(see pp202–203)*

Exploring Himeji Castle: the Main Tower

THE STRONGHOLD of Himeji Castle, the main tower was used by the feudal lords in the event of a seige or during drills. From the exterior, the tower appears to have five floors. In fact, it has six floors and a basement – the second and third floors from the top appear to be one floor from the outside. Visitors today enter the keep through its door in the basement and climb to the top.

Fish Motifs
Dolphin-like shachi-gawara *motifs on the roof are of a mythical beast believed to protect the main tower from fire.*

The uppermost chamber offers panoramas on four sides.

The division between these two floors is not obvious from the exterior.

Slippery wooden stairs ascend through rooms of diminishing size.

Interior of Keep
Originally an armaments store, the interior remains largely unadorned and houses exhibits relating to castle life.

Entrance through basement

Portholes in the shape of circles, triangles, and rectangles were for musketeers and archers.

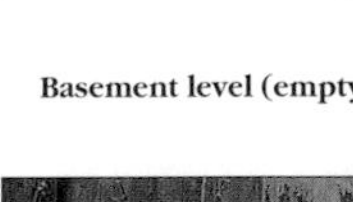

Basement level (empty)

Rock Chutes
Angled chutes set at numerous points in the walls enabled stones, boiling oil, and water to be dropped on the heads of any invaders.

Museum of Weaponry
Displays of samurai arms and armor are complemented by guns and gun powder, which were introduced to Japan by the Portuguese in the 16th century.

View of Himeji Castle in April, when the cherry trees are blossoming

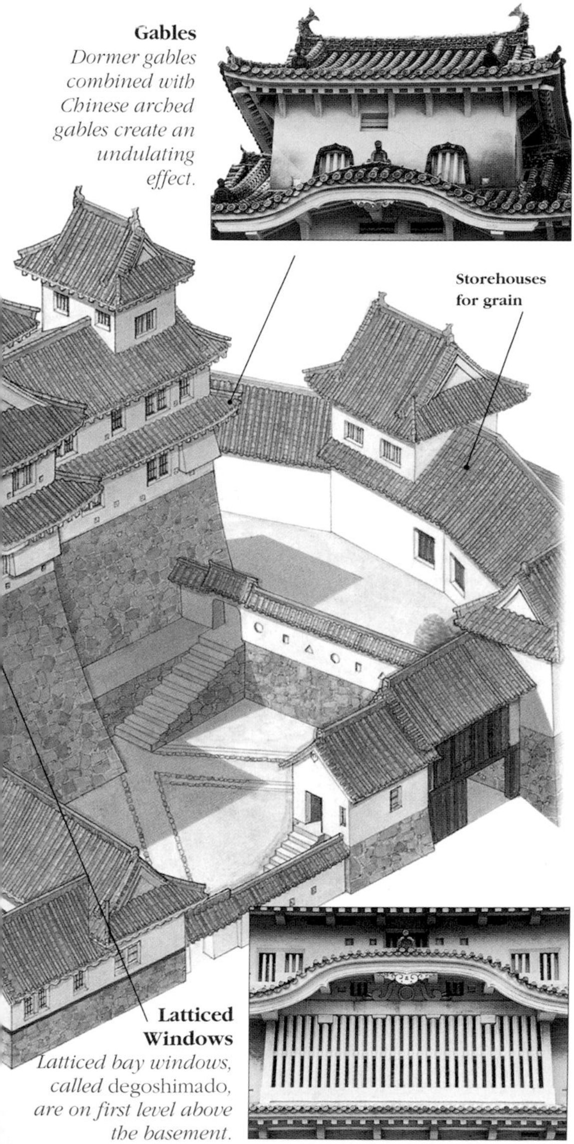

Modern facade of Hyogo Prefectural Museum of History

Gables
Dormer gables combined with Chinese arched gables create an undulating effect.

Storehouses for grain

Latticed Windows
Latticed bay windows, called degoshimado, *are on first level above the basement.*

CASTLE ENVIRONS: The grounds at Himeji are particularly attractive during April, when the cherry trees are in bloom. **Koko-en**, an elegantly arranged composite of nine separate Edo-style gardens, merits attention. It was built in 1992 on the site of former samurai homes. The **Hyogo Prefectural Museum of History** provides excellent exhibits, models, and background information on Japanese castles. It has a good section on Bunraku puppet drama, including models that can be operated by the public.

Just beyond the castle grounds, the **Himeji City Museum of Literature** pays tribute to nine influential local writers, but it is more notable for its architecture, designed by one of Japan's most respected contemporary architects, Ando Tadao *(see p21)*. **The Doll House** has a comprehensive display of Japanese and other dolls from around the world.

On the nearby hill called Shoshazan, **Shoshazan Enkyo-ji** is a well-known Buddhist training center and pilgrimage sight. Priceless sculptures include the Kongo Satta, a Buddha image carved in 1395. The Yakushido is the oldest building here, dating from the 14th-century Kamakura period.

Koko-en Garden
Castle grounds, W of main entrance.
(0792) 89-4120. *daily.*

Hyogo Prefectural Museum of History
Just behind castle.

Himeji Museum of Literature
84 Yamanoi-cho, NW of castle.
(0792) 93-8228. *Tue–Sun.*

The Doll House
68 Honmachi. E of Otemae-dori, close to Otemae Ken Park.
(0792) 98-8014. *daily.*

Koraku-en Garden in Okayama, with carefully landscaped mounds and an artificial lake

Inbe ⓬

伊部

Okayama prefecture. *30,000.* *next to Inbe JR stn (0869) 64-1100.* *Bizen-yaki Matsuri (Pottery Festival, 3rd weekend in Oct).*

THE HOME of Bizen-ware pottery, Inbe has a huge range of shops, galleries, and kilns. Originating in the Kamakura period, Bizen-ware is earthy, unglazed, and prized by tea-ceremony enthusiasts. The **Bizen Pottery Traditional and Contemporary Art Museum**, near the station, has modern pieces and superb examples from the Muromachi, Momoyama, and Edo periods.

Bizen Pottery Museum
(0869) 64-1400. *daily.* *Mon in Dec–Mar & Jun–Sep.*

Okayama ⓭

岡山

Okayama prefecture. *630,000.* *in JR stn (086) 222-2912.* *Saidai-ji Eyo (3rd Sat in Feb).*

THE FORMER center of a domain ruled by the lords of the feudal Ikeda family, Okayama today is a vibrant modern city, much visited by Japanese tourists who come to marvel at the 9-km (6-mile) long **Seto Ohashi Bridge** *(see p183)*, connecting Okayama with Shikoku. Trains now reduce the crossing time, which used to take an hour by ferry, to 15 minutes. The main sights are just over 1 km (half a mile) east of the station.

A highlight is the **Koraku-en Garden**, one of Japan's "famous three" gardens. Commissioned by Lord Ikeda, it was completed in 1700. Though a classic stroll garden, it was the first in Japan to use large expanses of lawn in the overall design. The garden is divided into three sections and features bamboo, pine, plum, and cherry trees, along with tea bushes. The nearby castle is incorporated into the composition as "borrowed scenery," a classic device in Japanese gardens. Also included are streams and a pond crossed by an elegant red bridge.

Okayama Castle is nicknamed the "Crow's Castle" due to its black walls. Destroyed in World War II, the exterior of the 16th-century castle was faithfully reconstructed in 1966. The interior has an authentic period collection of palanquins, samurai helmets, swords, and the like.

The reconstructed keep of Okayama castle, with its striking black walls

Visitor facilities include an elevator to the top of the four-story keep, and in the river below the castle, rental paddle-boats shaped like swans and teacups. More items owned by the Ikeda clan, notably armor, swords, pottery, lacquerware, and an excellent collection of Noh costumes, are on view at the **Hayashibara Museum of Art**, just south of the castle.

To the northeast is the **Orient Museum**, tracing how Near-Eastern art reached and influenced Japan via the Silk Route. The nearby **Okayama Prefectural Museum of Art** has an interesting collection of mostly 20th-century Japanese paintings and a few works by older artists including the 15th-century master Sesshu.

Koraku-en Garden
Koraku-en-mae stop. *daily.*

Okayama Castle
daily.

Hayashibara Art Museum
(862) 223-1733. *daily.*

Orient Museum
(086) 232-3636. *Tue–Sun.*

Okayama Prefectural Museum of Art
(086) 225-4800. *Tue–Sun.*

Kurashiki ⓮

倉敷

Okayama prefecture. *420,000.* *2nd flr of stn (086) 426-8681.*

CIVIC PRIDE and a strong preservation ethic have saved the Edo-period mercantile town of Kurashiki from the development that has swept away so much of

Japan's architectural heritage. Kurashiki means "storehouse village," a reference to the dozens of granaries *(kura)*, characterized by mortar and black-tiled walls, that are the main feature of the town.

In the heart of the old city, the **Bikan Historical Area** just south of the station, 200-year-old *kura* flank a tranquil canal lined with willows. Many of the *kura* have been converted into galleries, restaurants, Japanese inns, and tasteful shops and boutiques. The largest commercial conversion, a short walk from the canal, is **Kurashiki Ivy Square**, a complex of shops, restaurants, hotels, museums, and an orchid center housed in the former Kurabo Textile Mill, an attractive red-brick building covered in ivy.

In the old district the finest museum is the **Ohara Museum of Art**. The collection was commissioned by industrialist Ohara Magosaburo in 1930 on the premise that great art should be accessible – even to the people of a relative backwater such as Kurashiki. It includes some rare works by the likes of Matisse, Renoir, Picasso, Degas, and Gauguin. Some genuine masterpieces, like El Greco's *The Annunciation*, are here. The **Kogeikan** annex, converted from a traditional storehouse, houses an outstanding collection of works from Japan's *mingei* (or folk-craft) movement, among them ceramic objects crafted by Hamada Shoji, Kawai Kanjiro, and Bernard Leach, founders of the movement in the early 20th century.

Asian exhibits at the Japan Rural Toy Museum, Kurashiki

The **Kurashiki Archaeological Museum** occupies an old *kura* by the canal and includes items excavated in the region along with comparative objects from elsewhere in the world. In the **Kurashiki Folk Art Museum** are folk crafts housed in connecting *kura*. The **Japan Rural Toy Museum** has a delightful and extensive display of traditional old toys, both international and Japanese. Several of the latter are painted red, a defense, it was believed, against smallpox. A charming shop near the entrance sells traditional toys.

Woven rush shoes from Kurashiki

One of Kurashiki's storehouses, now a shop

Kurashiki Tiv... the north exit of ... an immensely pop... theme park.

Ohara Museum of A...
(086) 422-0005. Tue–Sun.
Archaeological Museum
(086) 422-1542. Tue–Sun.
Folk Art Museum
(086) 422-1637. Tue–Sun.
Japan Rural Toy Museum
(086) 422-8058. daily.
Kurashiki Tivoli Park
(086) 434-1111. variable.

Fukiya ⑮

吹屋

Okayama prefecture. 200. from Bitchu Takahashi.

A PROSPEROUS boom town at the center of a local copper and red-ochre mining industry in the 19th century, Fukiya is now a rustic hamlet tucked into some of the area's most beautiful mountain countryside. Well-to-do mine owners and merchants put much of their wealth into building grand houses. Characterized by white plaster walls and red-ochre colored latticework windows and doors, these distinctive buildings, the work of master carpenters, are the village's main cultural asset.

Several are open to the public, including the former house of the ochre-rich Katayama family, now Fukiya's **Local History Museum**, several renovated stores, and an old plaster-and-tile schoolhouse. One of the prefecture's six International Villas, an inn based on the design of a traditional soy sauce warehouse, is in Fukiya *(see p298)*.

Just outside the village is a copper and ochre mine, which can be visited. An unusual Edo-period home called the **Hirokane-tei**, about 4 km (2 miles) outside, resembles a fortified chateau.

Local History Museum
(0866) 29-2222. daily.
Hirokane-tei
(0866) 29-3182. daily. 

View of boats and hotels at Lake Biwa

Lake Biwa 16

琵琶湖

Shiga prefecture. *at Otsu stn (077) 522-3830.* *Sanno Matsuri (Apr 12–15, Otsu).*

WITH A TOTAL MASS of 674 sq km (263 sq miles), and a depth at some points of 105 m (340 ft) Biwa-ko, Japan's largest lake, covers an area greater than any Japanese city, including Tokyo. A calm expanse of water dotted with islets, the lake is named after the *biwa*, a Japanese musical instrument whose outline it is said to resemble. In the 15th century the highlights of Lake Biwa were named Omi Hakkei, "the eight views of Omi." Although development has changed some of these views radically, Lake Biwa is still one of Western Honshu's most beautiful places, its shore fringed with shrines, temples, hotels, and modest pensions.

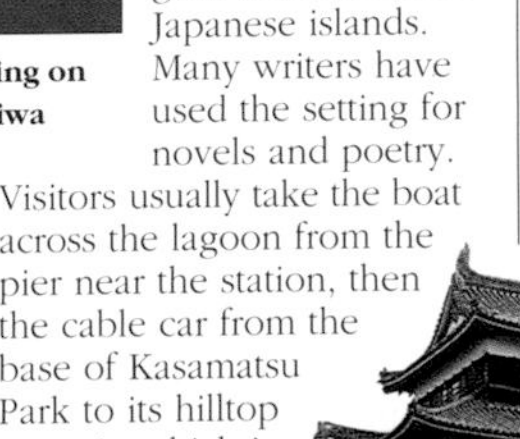

Windsurfing on Lake Biwa

Otsu, on the southwest edge, is the lake shore's largest city with a population of nearly 290,000. Visitors come here to see **Onjo-ji** temple complex of over 20 buildings, about 15 minutes' walk from the station. One of its huge gates, the Todaimon, leads to **Ishiyama-dera** temple, which has some 8th-century buildings. Murasaki Shikibu, author of the *Tale of Genji*, is believed to have used one of the chambers of the Main Hall in which to write her early 11th-century masterpiece.

Hikone, on the lake's eastern shore, has the 17th-century **Hikone Castle**, remarkable for retaining its original structure virtually intact. From the top floor of the keep is a superb view of Lake Biwa.

Hikone Castle
(0749) 22-2742. *daily.*

Amanohashidate Sand Bar 17

天橋立

Kyoto prefecture. *Amanohashidate.* *at Amanohashidate stn (0772) 22-8030.*

ONE OF THE highlights of Miyatsu Bay, along the San-in coast, is Amanohashidate, the "bridge of heaven." The 4-km (2-mile) pine-studded sand bar separates the bay from Asoumi lagoon. According to Japanese mythology, Amanohashidate is the spot where the gods conceived the Japanese islands. Many writers have used the setting for novels and poetry. Visitors usually take the boat across the lagoon from the pier near the station, then the cable car from the base of Kasamatsu Park to its hilltop summit, which is the best viewing point of the sand bar. It is said that if you look at Amanohashidate upside down through your legs it seems to be floating in mid-air.

Tottori Sand Dunes 18

鳥取砂丘

Tottori prefecture. *Tottori.* *from stn to entrance to dunes.* *at Tottori stn (0857) 22-3318.*

A HUGE EXPANSE of wavy, sahara-brown and yellow undulations, the Tottori sand dunes stretch for 16 km (10 miles) along the San-in coast. To the Japanese, the towering dunes, some rising to 90 m (300 ft), and the shifting patterns and shadows formed across the sand, are lyrical reminders of the human condition. Abe Kobo's powerful existential novel, *The Woman in the Dunes* (1962), made into a classic Japanese film, is set here. Commercialization has inevitably hit the area – head east acrosss the dunes or rent a bike for a quieter experience.

Matsue 19

松江

Shimane prefecture. *140,000.* *Yonago and Izumo.* *at Matsue JR stn (0852) 27-2598.* *Matsue Castle Festival (Apr 1–15), Doh Matsuri (Nov 3).*

SITUATED at the intersection of Lake Shinji with Miho bay and Nakaumi lagoon, Matsue is, not surprisingly, also known as the "water city." Rarely included in the itineraries

The towering keep of Matsue Castle

Lafcadio Hearn's residence with its well-tended garden, in Matsue

of foreign visitors, the area has several worthwhile cultural features. Matsue is referred to at length in *Glimpses of Unfamiliar Japan* (1894), by Lafcadio Hearn, a journalist of Irish-Greek descent who spent 15 months in the town.

Hearn described **Matsue Castle** in the colorful superlatives that mark his style as "a veritable architectural dragon, made up of magnificent monstrosities." One of the few in Japan to remain intact, the castle was built in 1611 of pine and stone, then partially reconstructed 31 years later. Its five-story keep is Japan's tallest.

Within five minutes of the castle are two more modest architectural gems. The **Buke Yashiki** is an interesting mansion built in 1730 by the Shiomi family, who were chief retainers at the castle. Furniture and household items provide an insight into their life. Above Shiome Nawate street is the **Meimei-an Teahouse** (1779), one of Japan's oldest and best preserved. Along the same street is the **Tanabe Art Museum**, with a refined collection of tea bowls and other tea-related objects.

Just north of the castle, the **Lafcadio Hearn Residence** is beautifully preserved. Its immaculate garden inspired one of Hearn's most engaging essays, *In A Japanese Garden*. Beside the house, the **Lafcadio Hearn Memorial Hall** has a good collection of his memorabilia, including such items as manuscripts, photos, and his desk and smoking pipes.

Matsue Castle
Kencho-mae stop. (0852) 21-4030. daily.

Buke Yashiki
(0852) 22-2243. Apr–Sep: daily.

Meimei-an Teahouse
(0852) 21-9863. daily.

Tanabe Art Museum
(0852) 26-2211. Tue–Sun.

Lafcadio Hearn Residence
(0852) 23-0714. daily.

Lafcadio Hearn Memorial Hall
(0852) 21-2147. daily.

Izumo ⓴

出雲

Shimane prefecture. 65,000. on main road to Izumo shrine, (0853) 53-2298. Daisairei (May 14–16), Kamiari Festival (11–17th days of 10th lunar month).

ALIVE WITH MYTHS, legends, and tales of the supernatural, Izumo, known until the 3rd century as the "eightfold-towering-thunder-head land," has an enthralling heritage. The town is well known throughout Japan for the **Izumo-Taisha**, one of the most revered and oldest Shinto shrines in the country. It is dedicated to Okuninushi-no-Mikoto, a deity who is closely associated with agriculture and medicine, as well as marriage – the latter explaining the popularity of the shrine for wedding ceremonies.

The entrance to the shrine, through 11 *torii* (gates), is impressive. Unusually tall, the **Honden** (Main Hall) is not open to the public, although the **Treasure House** can be visited. The shrine's environs are sacred and therefore ecologically pristine, with towering cryptomeria trees surrounding the main compound. Just east of the shrine are a number of old houses occupied by priests who serve here. Note the traditional clay and stone walls.

Just past Izumo-Taisha, on Route 431 to Okuni, there is a **monument** to a nun who is said to have danced on the banks of the Kamo River in Kyoto to raise money for the shrine. The dance was developed into the Kabuki theatrical form *(see pp32–3)*.

Izumo-Taisha
(0853) 53-3100. daily. (Treasure Hall).

Izumo shrine, dominated by the distinctive rafters of the Honden

Lafcadio Hearn

Lafcadio Hearn (1850–1904) arrived in Japan in 1890. He published several books, many of which are still in print and widely read, such as In *Ghostly Japan*, *Japan: An Interpretation*, and *Glimpses of Unfamiliar Japan*. The Japanese continue to be fascinated by Hearn, whose books allowed them for the first time to view their culture through the eyes of a foreigner. He was also one of the foremost interpreters of Japan for the West. A bold and unconventional thinker in his time, he was interested in the folklore and superstitions of Japan. Hearn's first Japanese home was Matsue, where he took up a teaching post, but quickly fell ill. The woman who nursed him back to health – the daughter of a local samurai family – eventually became Hearn's wife. He later acquired Japanese citizenship, changing his name to Koizumi Yakumo.

Writer and journalist Lafcadio Hearn

Hiroshima ㉑

広島

FOR THE WORST OF REASONS, Hiroshima needs no introduction. Each year millions of visitors are drawn to the city where so many people were wiped out in one instant of apocalyptic destruction. An unusual tourist attraction, the sober monuments of Hiroshima can induce an unexpected sense of listlessness and enervation in many visitors. However, there is more to the reconstructed city than its sorrowful atomic legacy.

Hiroshima's Peace Memorial Park and the A-Bomb Dome

Exploring Hiroshima

Rather than resurrect the tortuous pre-war streets, the modern city was rebuilt on a grid system, making it easy to negotiate. Trams are the most convenient form of transportation. Downtown Hiroshima lies to the east of the Peace Park. The lively nightlife area of Nagarikawa is not far away.

The A-Bomb Dome, all that remains of the old bombed city

Peace Memorial Park

Genbaku-Domu-mae. **Museum** *(082) 241-4004. daily.*

Located at the confluence of the Ota and Motoyasu rivers, just outside the park proper, the **A-Bomb Dome** is a haunting reminder of the destructive forces that were unleashed on the city. The former Industrial Promotion Hall stood close to the hypocenter, or ground zero, the point at which the bomb exploded. The occupants of the building were killed instantly. Its twisted girders, gaping holes, and piles of rubble have been preserved as a UNESCO World Heritage Site.

By the northern entrance to the park is the **Peace Bell**, which visitors can ring themselves. Nearby is the **Memorial Mound** containing the ashes of tens of thousands of people cremated on this spot. Farther into the park is the **Children's Peace Monument**, depicting a girl with outstretched hands. A crane, the Japanese symbol of longevity and happiness, passes above her. The work refers to the story of a child victim of the bomb who believed that if she could make 1,000 paper cranes she would recover from her illness. The girl did not survive, but her story is known throughout Japan, and fresh paper cranes sent by school children from all over Japan always adorn the memorial.

The Peace Memorial Museum, with exhibits on the bomb's effects

Across the road is the **Flame of Peace**, which will be extinguished only when all nuclear weapons have been eliminated from the earth. Adjacent to it is the **Cenotaph**, designed by Tange Kenzo, for the victims of the bomb. It contains the names of all those who died, together with an inscription that reads "Rest in peace. We will never repeat the error."

The centerpiece of the park is the **Peace Memorial Museum**. This graphically explains the consequences of

THE BOMBING OF HIROSHIMA

As World War II dragged on into the summer of 1945, the US decided to deploy an entirely new, untested weapon to force Japan to surrender. On August 6 a B29 bomber dropped the first atomic bomb on Hiroshima, a city that had seen little conventional bombing. It exploded at 8:15am, 580 m (1,900 ft) above the city center. Tens of thousands of people were killed instantly by the blast, and the death toll rose to 180–200,000 over the following years as after-effects took hold. Nagasaki *(see pp234–7)* suffered a similar fate three days later.

The ruins of Hiroshima in 1945, all but flattened by the atomic blast

the bomb on the city by means of photos, videos, and the personal effects of victims. Poignant exhibits inclued a half-melted bronze Buddha, a mangled tricycle, and the imprint of a dark shadow on the granite steps of the Sumitomo Bank building – the sole remains of someone who was sitting there at the time.

Outside the museum are the so-called **Phoenix trees** which were growing 1.5 km (1 mile) from the hypocenter. Transplanted here since, they still show scorch marks on one side of their crowns.

The Flame of Peace, fringed by sculpted bushes

Other Sights in Hiroshima

A look at the city's other attractions helps to dispel the gloom that descends on some visitors to the Peace Memorial Park. A relaxing spot is the **Shukkei-en** stroll garden. Its pond, islets, streams, miniature bridges, and pine-studded banks carefully replicate scenes from a legendary lake in China.

Hiroshima Castle was destroyed in the bomb, but a faithful reconstruction was completed in 1958. The **Museum of Contemporary Art** was designed by world-renowned Japanese architect Kurokawa Kisho and houses a collection of modern, post-war art. An outdoor sculpture garden is attached to the museum. The fascinating **Science and Cultural Center for Children** has lots of hands-on equipment and displays.

Visitors' Checklist

Hiroshima prefecture.
1,120,000. Hiroshima airport 40 km (25 miles) E; Hiroshima Nishi airport 4 km (2.5 miles) S. Shinkansen line. 4 km (2.5 miles) S. at JR stn (082) 263-6822. Flower Festival (May 3,4,5); Peace Park Memorial Service (Aug 6).

Shukkei-en Garden
Nr Shukkei-mae stop. *daily.*

Hiroshima Castle
Kamiya-cho. daily.

Museum of Contemporary Art
Hijiyama-shita. daily.

Science and Cultural Center for Children
10-min walk from Genbaku-dome mae. *Tue–Sun.*

Peace Memorial Park

The park was built in the 1960s, covering an area close to the hypocenter of the blast. The half-melted wreckage of the Industrial Promotion Hall (A-Bomb Dome) is the only remnant from the destruction. Scores of monuments have been erected on behalf of different groups of victims. The main memorials of interest to foreign visitors are shown here.

The Cenotaph, erected in memory of the victims of the bombing

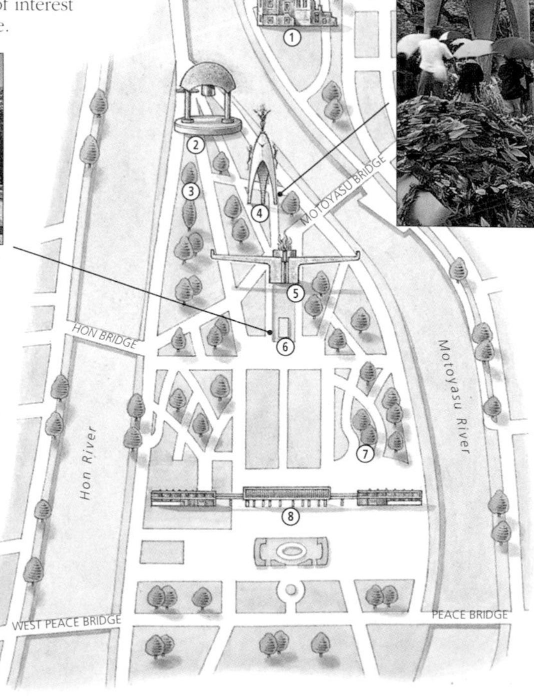

Children's Peace Monument, surrounded by paper cranes

Sights at a Glance

A-Bomb Dome ①
Cenotaph ⑥
Children's Peace Monument ④
Flame of Peace ⑤
Memorial Mound ③
Peace Bell ②
Peace Memorial Museum ⑧
Phoenix Trees ⑦

Ota River
AIOI BRIDGE
MOTOYASU BRIDGE
HON BRIDGE
Motoyasu River
Hon River
WEST PEACE BRIDGE
PEACE BRIDGE

0 meters 250
yards 250

Miyajima Island ㉒

A JEWEL OF THE SANYO COAST, Miyajima is symbolized by a looming vermilion *torii* (Shinto gate) set in the sea, which denotes that the whole island is sacred. There are no maternity wards or cemeteries because no one is permitted to give birth or die on Miyajima. Felling trees is also forbidden – the island is covered in virgin forest, which provides a habitat for scores of bird species. Tame deer are allowed to roam at will.

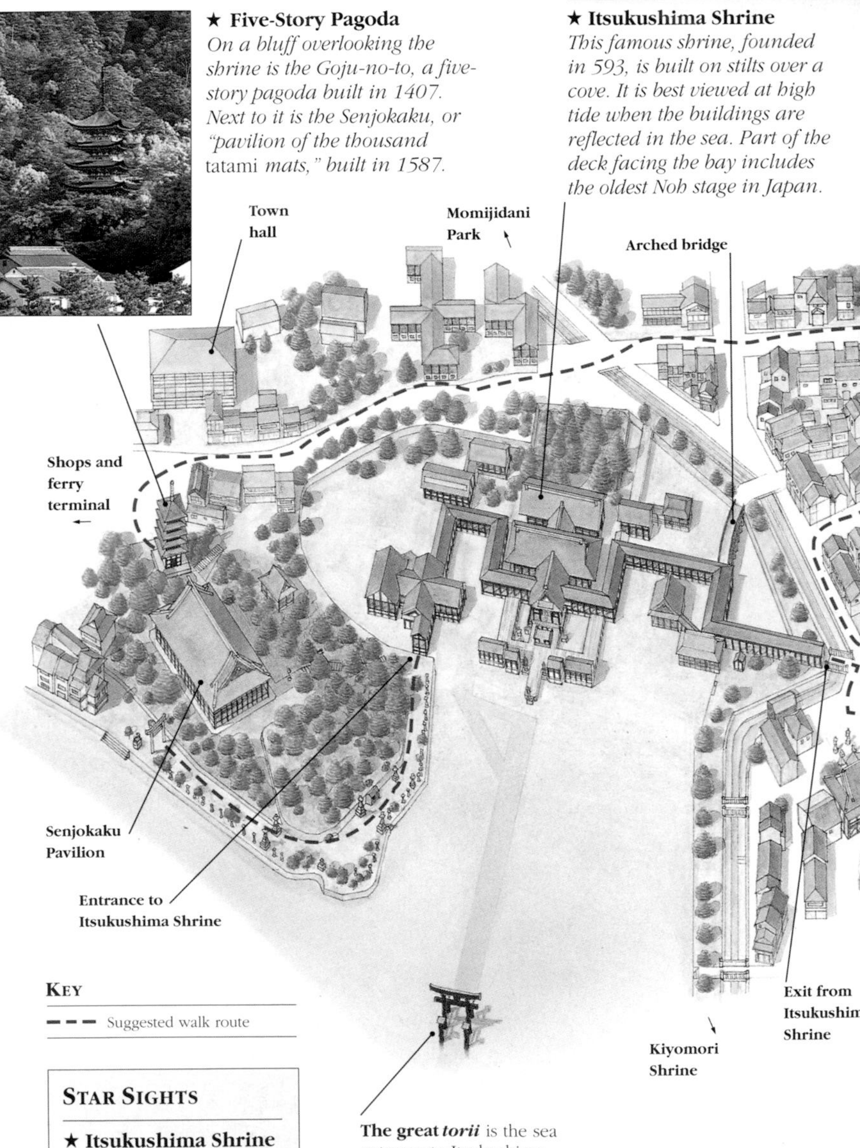

★ Five-Story Pagoda
On a bluff overlooking the shrine is the Goju-no-to, a five-story pagoda built in 1407. Next to it is the Senjokaku, or "pavilion of the thousand tatami *mats," built in 1587.*

★ Itsukushima Shrine
This famous shrine, founded in 593, is built on stilts over a cove. It is best viewed at high tide when the buildings are reflected in the sea. Part of the deck facing the bay includes the oldest Noh stage in Japan.

The great *torii* is the sea entrance to Itsukushima Shrine. At low tide it is possible to walk up to it.

KEY

– – – Suggested walk route

STAR SIGHTS

- ★ **Itsukushima Shrine**
- ★ **Five-Story Pagoda**

Mount Misen
On the slopes behind the shrine is Momijidani ("maple leaf valley") Park. A cable car station in the park goes to the summit of Mount Misen, where there is a monkey sanctuary and superb views of the Inland Sea (see p218). *There are also several nature trails on the mountainside.*

Visitors' Checklist

Hiroshima prefecture. *from Hiroshima to Miyajima-guchi, then ferry.* *high speed ferry from Hiroshima port or from Miyajima-guchi stn.*
booth at ferry terminal on island (0829) 44-2011.
Kangensai Music Festival (Jun, Jul, or Aug – varies).
All sights *daily.*

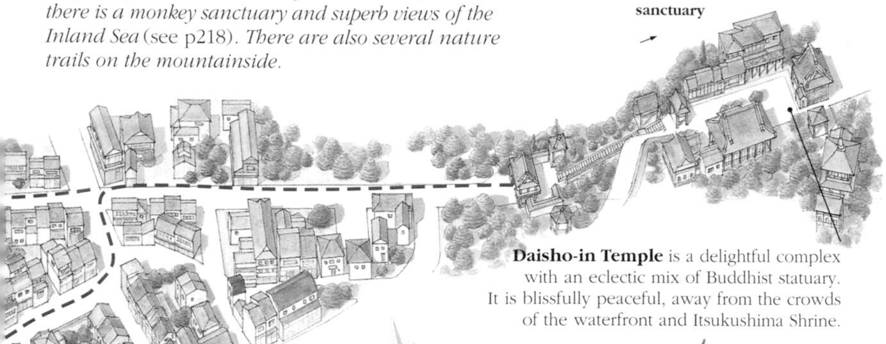

Mount Misen nature trails and monkey sanctuary

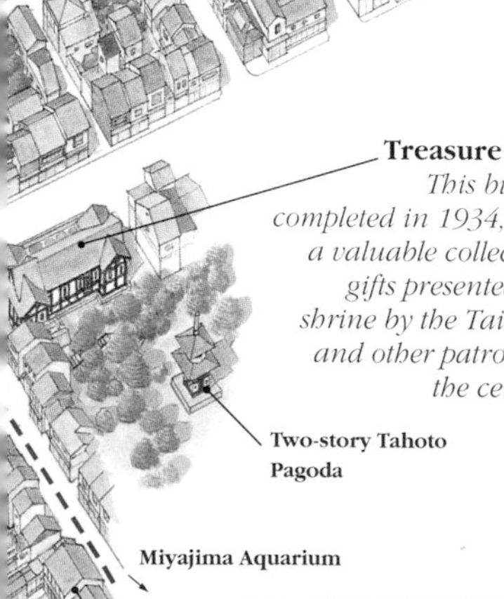

Daisho-in Temple is a delightful complex with an eclectic mix of Buddhist statuary. It is blissfully peaceful, away from the crowds of the waterfront and Itsukushima Shrine.

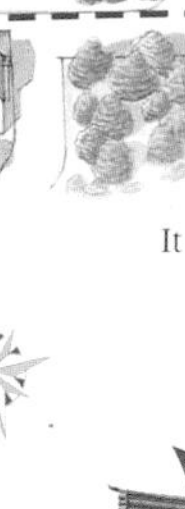

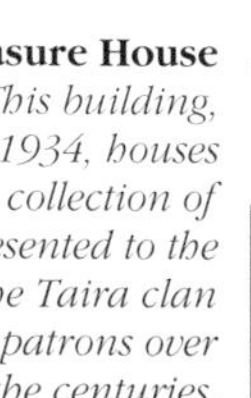

Treasure House
This building, completed in 1934, houses a valuable collection of gifts presented to the shrine by the Taira clan and other patrons over the centuries.

Two-story Tahoto Pagoda

Miyajima Aquarium

Municipal History and Folklore Museum
Housed in a beautiful mid-19th century mansion is a collection of artworks, household utensils, and furniture.

The Famous Floating Torii

Acclaimed by the Japanese as one of the country's three most scenic views (Nihon Sankei), the *torii* of Itsukushima Shrine appears to float in the water. (The sand bar Amanohashidate, *see p206*, and Matsushima Bay, *see p270*, are the two other famous sights.) The warlord Taira no Kiyomori, who provided funds for the shrine, built the first *torii* in the bay in the 12th century. The present structure dates from 1875 and is about 16 m (50 ft) high. Its four-legged *(yo-tsuashi)* style provides stability.

The *torii* at dusk

Iwakuni ㉓

岩国

Yamaguchi prefecture. 120,000. *Sanyo Shinkansen line to Shin-Iwakuni, JR Sanyo line to Iwakuni.* *at Iwakuni stn (0827) 21-6050.*

THE TOWN OF Iwakuni's main draw is the elegant **Kintai-kyo**, or "brocade sash" bridge. It earns its name from the rippling effect created by its five linked arches. The original structure, built in 1673, was destroyed by a typhoon in 1953. Rebuilt in an almost exact replica of the original, the bridge depends on first-rate joinery (no nails are used), and an invisible quantity of reinforced steel.

Beyond the bridge in **Kikko Park** are a number of samurai houses, including the beautiful **Mekata House**. A short stroll west of the park lies **Iwakuni Historical Museum**, housing an impressive display of armor and weapons. A cable car or walk uphill from here takes you to **Iwakuni Castle**, a faithful 1962 reconstruction of the original 1608 donjon. There is a good view from here of the town and surrounding countryside and, on fine days, the islands of the Inland Sea.

Mekata House
Tue–Sun.
Iwakuni Historical Museum

(0827) 41-0506. *daily.*

Yamaguchi ㉔

山口

Yamaguchi prefecture. *140,000.* *(083) 933-0090.* *Gion Matsuri (Jul 20–27).*

LAID OUT in the 14th century by the Ouchi family, Yamaguchi was modeled on Kyoto. When the Jesuit Francis Xavier visited here in 1550 he found a city of incredible wealth and sophistication. The **Xavier Memorial Chapel**, built in 1952, marks the 400th anniversary of the priest's two-month stay. The painter Sesshu (1420–1506) designed a masterly garden for the temple of **Joei-ji** on the outskirts of town. To the north of Yamaguchi, the temple of **Ruriko-ji** has a Japanese cypress-wood, five-story pagoda. Nearby is a set of tombs belonging to the Mori family, another influential local clan.

Akiyoshi-dai Tablelands ㉕

秋吉台

Yamaguchi prefecture. *from Yamaguchi.* *at bus stn (0837) 62-6304.*

AKIYOSHI-DAI IS A massive limestone plateau of grassland and rocky outcrops, which tour buses pass on their way to **Akiyoshido Cave**, one of the largest limestone grottos in Asia. The cave is 10 km (6 miles) deep, not all of it open to the public. Passageways are well lit, and a clear map is provided.

In the limestone Akiyoshido Cave in the Akiyoshi-dai Tablelands

Akiyoshido Cave
(0837) 62-0018. *daily.*

Hagi ㉖

萩

Yamaguchi prefecture. *47,000.* *nr City Hall (0838) 25-1750.* *Hagi-yaki Festival (May 1–5).*

AN INTENSELY cultural town, Hagi was a minor fishing port until Mori Terumoto fortified it in 1604. Mori samurai helped spark off the anti-Tokugawa revolt in the mid-19th century, and many of Meiji Japan's founding fathers

Five-arched "brocade sash" bridge at Iwakuni

came from Hagi. Today it is best known for its 400-year-old pottery-making tradition. Hagi's charm is in the details: its tea-houses, mossy cemeteries, and the tiny, purple bloom of bush clover *(hagi)*, the town's namesake.

Cemetery of Toko-ji temple near Hagi

The central **Teramachi** district contains old temples and shrines, each with its own special features. **Jonen-ji** is noted for its finely carved gate, **Hofuku-ji** its bibbed Jizo statues, **Kyotoku-ji** for its immaculate garden, and **Choju-ji** for an atmospheric cemetery. Camellias and *natsu mikan* (summer oranges) hanging over long, whitewashed mud walls typify the **samurai quarters** to the west of Teramachi. Several residences are located here, including the homes of the Kido and Takasugi families, and **Kikuya House**, a merchant villa with a small museum and beautiful garden attached. The **Ishii Tea Bowl Museum** has a superb ceramics collection.

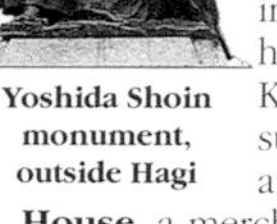

Yoshida Shoin monument, outside Hagi

Wealthy merchants appointed by the Mori clan once owned the fine collection in the **Kumaya Art Museum** to the north of here. It includes tea-ceremony utensils, literati paintings, and screens.

Little remains of the original **Hagi Castle** – about 4 km (2 miles) west of Higashi-Hagi station – except its stone walls and broad moat. The picnic grounds include **Hagijo Kiln**, a good place to watch potters at work. Beside the castle walls **Hananoe Tea House** is a lovely thatched-roof building, where green tea is served in local ware.

Kikuya House
(0838) 25-8282. daily.
Ishii Tea Bowl Museum
(0838) 22-1211. Wed–Mon.
Kumaya Art Museum
(0838) 25-5535. daily.

ENVIRONS: East over the river is the house of Yoshida Shoin, an influential late-Edo educator, philosopher, and revolutionary. **Shoin shrine** and **memorial** are dedicated to him. The nearby temple of **Toko-ji**, with its impressive three-story gate, was founded in 1691 by the third Mori lord. The Mori tombs are at the end of a path flanked by almost 500 stone lanterns.

The natural salt-water **Myojin Lagoon** is 5 km (3 miles) from town. A volcano, **Mount Kasayama**, stands beside the far end of the lake.

Tsuwano ㉗

津和野

Shimane prefecture. 6,300. next to Tsuwano stn (08567) 2-1771. Sagimai (Heron Dance Festival, Jul 20, 24, 27).

THIS TINY 700-year old former castle town, tucked into a river valley deep in the mountains, has a large number of well-preserved samurai houses. Thousands of colorful carp inhabit the town's brooks, outnumbering the residents, it is said, by ten to one.

Tsuwano's **Catholic Church** (1931) commemorates the 36 Japanese Christians who were killed here in 1868 after refusing to recant.

On the other side of town, the hillside **Taikodani Inari Shrine** is one of the most important Inari (fox) shrines in Japan. It is reached through a tunnel of vermilion *torii* (gates), 1,174 in all. A cable car goes up the other side of the slope to the scant remains of **Tsuwano Castle** with a stunning view from the top.

Nishi Amane (1829–97), a Meiji-period statesman and philosopher, was born here. **Nishi House**, now a museum, is on a quiet street in the south of town. Opposite is **Mori House**, a museum to the army surgeon, writer, and translator Mori Ogai (1862–1922), known for novels such as *The Wild Geese* and *Vita Sexualis*, and also a Tsuwano native.

Nishi House
daily.
Mori House
(08567) 2-3210. Tue–Sun.

Taikodani Inari Shrine in the town of Tsuwano

HAGI'S CERAMIC ARTS

Hagi's pink stonewear

Hagi's first kilns date from the Heian period, but the town's reputation for refined tea vessels and other wares began in the 16th century with the introduction of apprentice potters from Korea. A distinguishing mark of *hagi-yaki* (Hagi-ware) is its translucent glaze. *Hagi-yaki* improves with age, the muted pinks and pastels of the stoneware softening to beiges and umbers as tannin from the tea soaks through the porous glaze. Members of some of Hagi's oldest families, like the Sakas and Miwas, have been designated Living National Treasures.

SHIKOKU

THE INLAND SEA *formed a natural barrier for centuries, isolating Japan's fourth largest island from much of the forces of population growth and Westernization. Still relatively off the tourist track, despite the construction of three bridge systems across the Inland Sea, Shikoku offers a nostalgic glimpse of fishing and farming villages, of rice paddies set against a backdrop of forested hills, castles, and temples.*

Late Paleolithic sites and *kofun* (tumuli) dating from the 3rd century AD are evidence of early human activity on Shikoku. The Dogo Onsen (spa) in Matsuyama is referred to in the *Kojiki*, Japan's oldest chronicle, written in 712. Despite such ancient sites, however, Shikoku has mainly been on the margin of Japanese history. The island's most famous figure is Kukai, who was born into a poor aristrocratic Shikoku family in 774. This Buddhist priest, who has been called the Father of Japanese Culture, visited 88 of the island's temples in a pilgrimage that has been imitated by others for more than a thousand years.

In 1183, as chronicled in the *Tale of the Heike*, the war between the Taira and Minamoto clans for dominance of Japan spilled over into the Inland Sea and Shikoku. Some of the defeated Taira went into hiding in a gorge in central Shikoku, where many of their descendants still live.

Statue of Jizo on the 88-Temple Pilgrimage

Farmland and mountains continue to dominate Shikoku's landscape, although agriculture employs only three percent of the island's four million residents. Assembly of autos and manufacture of electronic goods, particularly in the ports along the Inland Sea, are the most important industries and are expected to be enhanced by the three new bridge links with Honshu. Other industries include fruit farming (mandarin oranges in particular), seaweed and pearl cultivation, food and chemical processing, and papermaking.

Whereas construction has altered most of Japan's coastal areas, Shikoku's coastline remains relatively unspoiled. The capes that jut into the Pacific, Muroto to the east and Ashizuri to the west, offer panoramic vistas such as are rarely seen in Japan.

Matsuyama Castle, first built in 1603 and reconstructed in 1835 after a lightning strike

◁ **Pilgrims on the steps of Konomine-ji, number 27 on the 88-Temple Pilgrimage**

Exploring Shikoku

SHIKOKU'S NORTH COAST facing the Inland Sea is much more industrialized than its south coast, but not as much so as Western Honshu's Sanyo coast. The interior of the island is mountainous and rugged and not conducive to rice cultivation. Shikoku's main cities and historical sights, including most temples on the pilgrimage circuit, are thus on or near the Inland Sea coast. Takamatsu is a popular entry point. Kochi is the main city on the Pacific coast.

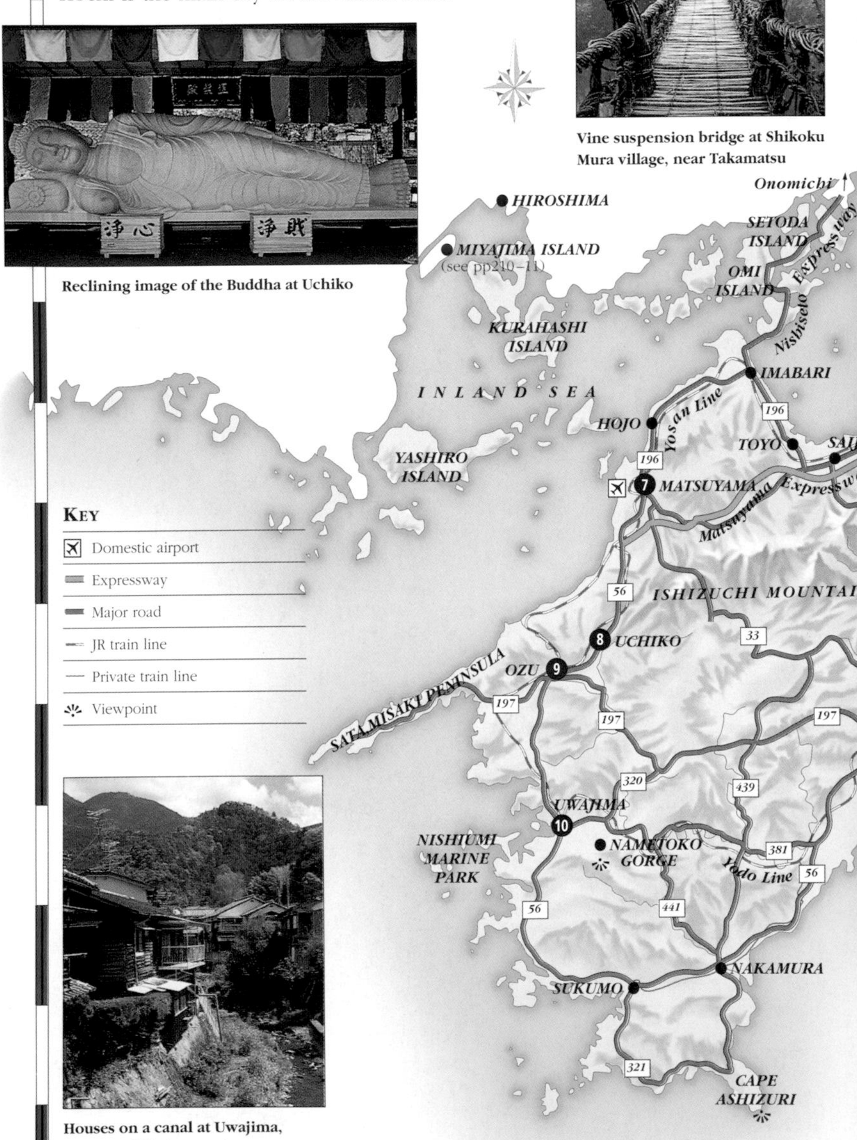

Vine suspension bridge at Shikoku Mura village, near Takamatsu

Reclining image of the Buddha at Uchiko

Houses on a canal at Uwajima, western Shikoku

Getting Around

Taking a direct train from Okayama to Takamatsu, via the Seto-Ohashi Bridge, is the most popular gateway for tourists traveling from Honshu to Shikoku. Matsuyama, the island's main city, has an airport with good links to other parts of Japan. There is no *shinkansen* line, but the other types of train lines are efficient and connect all the main towns. However, unless you plan to emulate walkers on the 88-Temple Pilgrimage, it is best to rent a car to explore the mountainous interior and visit the rugged southern capes.

See Also

- ***Where to Stay*** pp302–303
- ***Where to Eat*** pp334–5

Sights at a Glance

The Inland Sea 1
Kochi 6
Kotohira 3
Matsuyama 7
Naruto Whirlpools 4
Ozu 9
Takamatsu 2
Tokushima 5
Uchiko 8
Uwajima 10

Pilgrimage Route
The 88-Temple Pilgrimage pp222–3

Seto-Ohashi Bridge near Takamatsu, joining Shikoku to Honshu

Typical view of islands in the so-called Inland Sea, which separates Shikoku from Honshu and Kyushu

The Inland Sea ❶

瀬戸内海

(082) 263 6822 (Hiroshima). **Setonaikai-kisen (Inland Sea cruises)** *(082) 253-1212.*

THE INLAND SEA, Japan's most beautiful body of water, is not landlocked, as its name suggests, but seems almost so with its serene waters and over 3,000 pine-studded islands. Donald Richie, in his classic travelogue *The Inland Sea* (1971), sets the scene of a boat journey westward through the narrow defiles of water: "On the left are first the sharp and Chinese-looking mountains of the island of Shikoku, so different that it appears another land, and then the flat coasts of Kyushu. This shallow sea is a valley among these mountainous islands."

Bridges, local ferries, and cruise boats provide access to the 750 or so inhabited islands. The remote fishing villages on these islands, with their salt-weathered wooden houses and black ceramic-tiled roofs, seem to hail from a different era. Among the most visited are **Awaji**, the largest island, **Setoda**, **Omi**, and **Shodo**, a beautiful green island that, with its olive and orange groves, and sparkling, wine-dark seas, seems to belong more to the Mediterranean than the Orient.

Takamatsu ❷

高松

Kagawa prefecture. *330,000.* *at JR stn (087) 851-2009.* *Takamatsu Matsuri (Aug 12–14).* www.takamatsu-nct.ac.jp

THE CAPITAL of Kagawa prefecture on the Inland Sea, Takamatsu is the main hub between Shikoku and the outside world. Nonetheless, it maintains a local charm with its neighborhood shops and historic landmarks. The town expanded after Ikoma Chikamasa erected **Takamatsu Castle** in 1588, the remains of which can still be seen. When the Tokugawa shoguns assumed power in 1600, they granted the town, castle, and surrounding fiefdom to their relatives, the Matsudaira clan. The family devoted nearly a century to landscaping the six ponds and 13 artificial hillocks that make **Ritsurin Park** the city's most famous landmark.

Takamatsu's location as an entry port for Shikoku made it the setting for such historic battles as the one between the Minamoto and the Taira clans in 1185. The **Wax Museum of the Tale of the Heike** offers a surprisingly effective recreation of the story's high points, which are also the subject matter of the classic Noh play *Yashima*.

Wax Museum
(087) 823-8400. *daily.*

ENVIRONS: At Yashima volcanic plateau, **Shikoku Mura Museum** is an open-air village where immaculately preserved buildings and other artifacts of rural life display Shikoku craftsmanship.

Shikoku Mura
(087) 843-3111. *Kotoden Yashima stn.* *daily.*

Bridge within the landscaped grounds of Ritsurin Park, Takamatsu

Kotohira ❸

琴平

Kagawa prefecture. *12,000.* *booth 2 mins from stn (0877) 75-3500.* *Kotohira-gu Reitaisai (Grand Festival, Oct 9–11).*

KOTOHIRA, which can be reached by train via either the charming, old-fashioned Kotoden or the JR line from Takamatsu, is the home of famous shrine

Palanquin on the steps leading up to Kompira-san

complex **Kotohira-gu**, also affectionately known as **Kompira-san**, the spiritual guardian of seafarers. The target of pilgrimages for centuries, the shrine now attracts four million visitors per year and is believed to bestow good luck upon fishermen and sailors.

A 785-stair climb (or ride in one of the palanquins available) takes visitors up the rugged mountainside to the shrine, set in beautiful grounds. Within the complex, the Asahi shrine is built of zelkova, a rock-hard wood that forms an excellent medium for carved relief work. The nearby Omote Shoin and Oku Shoin have celebrated screen paintings by Maruyama Okyo. The first presents burly tigers bristling with Zen energy, the second includes a waterfall flowing acrosss a corner of the room.

An old wooden Kabuki theater, the **Kanamaru-za**, can also be found in the town.

Awa-Odori Dancing

Tokushima's celebrations for O-Bon, the festival of the dead on August 12–15, are the liveliest in Japan. Special dances, called Awa-Odori, are meant to welcome ancestral spirits on their yearly visit to the land of the living. Nicknamed "the fool's dance" because the refrain "you're a fool whether you dance or not, so you might as well dance" is sung, the Awa-Odori allegedly originated when rice wine was passed out to the townspeople of Tokushima to celebrate completion of a castle.

Awa-Odori dancers, Tokushima

Naruto Whirlpools ❹

鳴門の渦潮

Tokushima prefecture. Naruto stn, then bus to Naruto Park. Uzushio line ferry (088) 687-0613; Naruto sightseeing boat (088) 687-0101.

Where the tip of Awaji Island nearly touches Shikoku – a wedge between Osaka Bay, the Inland Sea, Honshu, Shikoku, and the Pacific Ocean – the tidal pull on these distinct bodies of water creates large disparities spawning powerful currents and whirlpools. Navigating the churning waters of this 1.3 km (1-mile) strait has been a part of Shikoku lore for over a millennium.

Sightseeing boats now ply the 20-kmph (13-mph) currents and whirlpools, and provide startling views of the Naruto suspension bridge, part of a bridge system linking Shikoku and Honshu via Awaji Island. When the northern end of the system was completed in 1998, it was discovered to have stretched 1 m (3 ft) as a result of ground shifts caused by the Kobe earthquake.

At the Awaji end of the bridge, the **Onarutokyo Memorial Hall** includes exhibits of *Awaji ningyo joruri*, a local variant of Bunraku puppet theater.

Votive hall at Kompira-san, near Kotohira

Memorial Hall
(079) 952-2888. daily.

Tokushima ❺

徳島

Tokushima prefecture. 260,000. at JR stn (088) 621-5232. Awa-Odori (Awa dancing festival, Aug 12–15).

Tokushima forms the gateway into Shikoku from the Kansai region of Honshu and is the traditional point of entry for those who set out to duplicate Kukai's pilgrimage *(see pp222–3)*. The old name of the province, Awa, gives its name to the town's Awa-Odori celebration in August, which is broadcast nationwide.

Environs: South of Tokushima, the scenic **Anan Coast** is known for its fishing villages, beaches, and the sea turtles that return to lay and hatch eggs between June and August.

The suspension bridge at Naruto, completed in 1985

Flooded rice fields near Kochi

Kochi 6

高地

Kochi prefecture. 310,000. at JR stn; Kochi "i" information office (088) 882-7777. *Yosakoi Matsuri (Aug 9–12).*

KOCHI CITY offers a rare blend of sandy beaches, mountain views, and well-preserved historic sites.

The Kochi region, formerly called Tosa, is known for its forging of cutlery, and shops selling knives line the street in front of **Kochi Castle**, built in 1603. A startlingly long sword, over 1.5 m (5 ft) in length, is among the weapons on display in the castle. Breathtaking views can be seen from the top floors.

At Katsurahama, a white-sand beach area in the southern part of the city, the **Sakamoto Ryoma Museum** is devoted to the Tosa patriot admired for his part in the overthrow of the shogunate and restoration of the emperor in the 1860s. He was assassinated in 1867. Most Japanese visitors make a point of viewing and paying homage at a bronze statue of the man looming over the beach. Also at Katsurahama is the **Tosa Token Center**, the venue for the Tosa Fighting Dogs. Dogfights are staged here in a caged enclosure rather like a miniature Sumo wrestling stadium. The animals are also paraded in Sumo-like garments. To create the Tosa fighting dog of today, breeders matched its local ancestors with mastiffs and other powerful Western dogs. A photo exhibition documents major events in the history of this sport, including visits by the emperor. The gambling that helped make the fights popular is now illegal, and increasing numbers of people are repulsed by the dogfights.

Statue of patriotic figure Sakamoto Ryoma, Kochi

Kochi Castle
(088) 872-2776. daily.

Sakamoto Ryoma Museum
(088) 841-0001. daily.

Tosa Token Center
(088) 842-3315. daily.

ENVIRONS: Kochi is a good starting point for day trips to **Cape Muroto** at the south-east tip of Shikoku or **Cape Ashizuri** to the southwest. Both have panoramic views of the Pacific Ocean, lush vegetation, and some unusual rock formations.

Matsuyama 7

松山

Ehime prefecture. 460,000. *at JR stn (089) 931-3914.*

THE CAPITAL of Ehime prefecture and a castle town since 1603, Matsuyama has many powerful associations for the Japanese.

The **Dogo Onsen**, a famous hot-spring spa, has been in use for over a millennium, and has a fine 19th-century bathhouse. The onsen can be reached via the city's historic streetcars.

Deeper into the mountains behind the historic bathhouse, **Oku-Dogo Onsen** is a much newer resort area.

Natsume Soseki, an author whose portrait appears on the ¥1,000 bill, moved to Matsuyama in 1895 and later wrote about the town in his popular autobiographical novel *Botchan* (1906).

The **Shiki Masaoka Museum** is devoted to Soseki's friend Shiki (1867–1902), a Matsuyama native held by many to be Japan's finest modern haiku poet. Shiki was also a fine painter, and the museum's highly visual presentation includes manuscripts, paintings, and photographs of Shiki and Soseki in the city.

Matsuyama Castle is an extensive complex on a bluff overlooking the city and Inland Sea. Plaques offer intelligent commentary on the castle's strategic features.

Dogo Onsen
from stn. (089) 921-5141. daily.

Shiki Masaoka Museum
3-min walk from Dogo Onsen.
(089) 931-5566. Tue–Sun.

Matsuyama Castle
Kencho-mae stop, then steep walk.
(089) 921-2540. daily.

Exterior of the bathhouse of Dogo Onsen, Matsuyama

Stage of the historic Kabuki Theater in Uchiko, now rarely used

Uchiko 8

内子

Ehime prefecture. 11,000. Uchiko Town Preservation Planning Dept (0893) 44-2111.

LOCATED in a small valley where the Oda River splits into three branches, the town of Uchiko is famous for its historic Kabuki theater, the **Uchiko-za**, and its sloping street of two-story wooden buildings with whitewashed walls, tiled roofs, and broad fronts. In 1982 the government moved to ensure the preservation of these structures, which date from the mid-19th century. Several are open to the public, and others function as craft shops and restaurants. The area is often used for location shooting of historical dramas for film and television. A quaint touch is the steam locomotive preserved in front of the station.

Hand-made umbrellas, Uchiko

Uchiko-za
(089) 344-2840. daily.

Ozu 9

大洲

Ehime prefecture. 40,000. at JR stn (0893) 24-7520. Kawa Matsuri Hanabi Taikai (River Festival Fireworks, Aug 3–4).

A CASTLE TOWN built where the Hiji River snakes through a valley rimmed by picturesque bluffs, Ozu has some splendid architectural surprises. Its riverfront is lined by quaint, narrow streets of tile-roofed bars and restaurants with sliding wood shutters. A riverside villa called **Garyu Sanso**, built in 1907, is one of the most spectacular buildings. On the river itself, shallow-bottomed skiffs shunt cormorant fishermen back and forth through the river breezes. Traditional culture is still alive in Ozu, where raw silk, dairy products, and vegetables form the basis for the local economy. The town's restaurants serve fish and eel caught in the river.

The panorama of seasonal change is especially vivid in the wooded hillsides of Ozu. August is marked with a festival of fireworks launched from an islet in the river.

Garyu Sanso
(089) 324-3759. Tue–Sun.

Uwajima 10

宇和島

Ehime prefecture. 65,000. 1 min from stn (0895) 24-1111.

UWAJIMA, a harbor town with a castle, old temple district, and mountain setting, is probably best known for its bullfighting, conducted on a system with ranks modeled on Sumo wrestling. The bullfights are held on six days each year, but a video presentation is available year-round at the **Shiei Togyu-jo**.

The **Taga-jinja** shrine has famously sexually explicit statues and other objects associated with fertility.

Shiei Togyu-jo
(0895) 25-3511. Mon–Fri for video; bullfights Jan 2, 1st Sun Apr, Jul 24, Aug 14, 2nd Sun Nov.

ENVIRONS: Uwajima is perhaps best appreciated as a hopping-off spot for trips by car, bus, or boat to the nearby scenic islands and beautiful coastal areas. In summer, glass-bottomed boats tour coral reefs in the **Nishiumi Marine Park** near the island of Tojima.

In the mountains northwest of Uwajima, just off Route 320, the **Nametoko Gorge** is noted for its waterfall and fine views.

Nishiumi Marine Park
Nishiumi tourism dept (0895) 82-1111. from Uwajima. daily.

Nametoko Gorge
Matsuno tourism dept (0895) 42-1111.

Grave markers in the old temple district of Uwajima

The 88-Temple Pilgrimage

四国八十八箇所巡礼

WHEN PILGRIMS retrace the route of Kukai, the founder of Shingon Buddhism *(see p269)* who made a pilgrimage of 88 of the island's minor temples in the 9th century, they are honoring a cultural icon and hoping some of the magic rubs off. Those who hope to atone for a grave error complete the pilgrimage in reverse order; it is believed they will encounter the saint as they walk or in their dreams. In Shingon, 88 represents the number of evils that can beset us. About 100,000 pilgrims complete the circuit each year; countless others follow part of it.

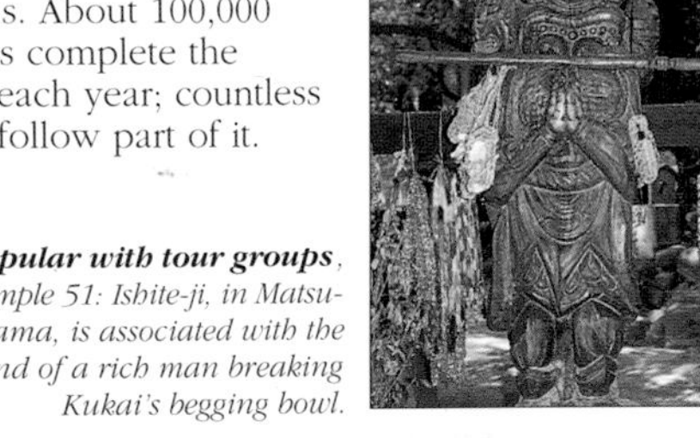

***Popular with tour groups**, Temple 51: Ishite-ji, in Matsuyama, is associated with the legend of a rich man breaking Kukai's begging bowl.*

***The birthplace of Kukai** is marked by Temple 75: Zentsu-ji, one stop from Kotohira.*

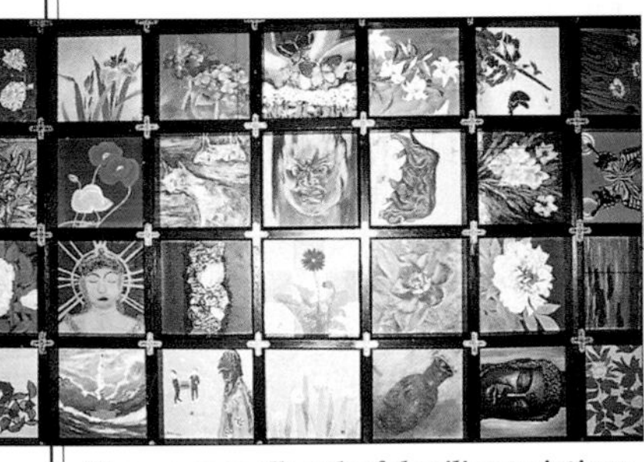

***These unusually colorful ceiling paintings** are found at Temple 37: Iwamoto-ji. The 90-km (55-mile) stretch between this temple and number 38 is the longest on the circuit.*

TIPS FOR PILGRIMS

***Length:** About 1,100 km (700 miles).*
***Walking time:** average six to eight weeks for the whole circuit.*
***Alternative transportation:** bus tours organized by numerous operators take about a week. Helicopter tours are another option.*
***Accommodations:** many temples offer lodgings and meals to pilgrims for around ¥4,000, and there are numerous inns and restaurants all along the route.*
***Official stamps:** pilgrims can collect a series of rubber stamps as they visit each temple in turn.*
***Waymarkers:** signs on rocks and posts are mostly in Japanese.*
***Information:** Tokushima (088) 621-5232.*
***Guides for foreign visitors:** Oliver Statler's book* Japanese Pilgrimage *(Tuttle, 1984) has extensive background. Personal accounts in English, French, and other languages can be found on the World Wide Web.*

***White-robed pilgrims** are called* henro, *seen here at Temple 31, Chikurin-ji.*

***Temple 1: Ryozen-ji**, near Naruto, is the start and end of the pilgrimage on Shikoku, though devout pilgrims will extend the start and end to Koya-san (see p193) on Honshu, the headquarters of the Shingon sect. Temple stalls sell the traditional garments for pilgrims: straw hats, white cotton coats, colored sashes, and staves. Visitors sign the book of completion here.*

***The Gokuraku** in the name of Temple 2: Gokuraku-ji, refers to the Pure Land, or Western Paradise, of the Amida Buddha, a fundamental concept in Shingon Buddhism.*

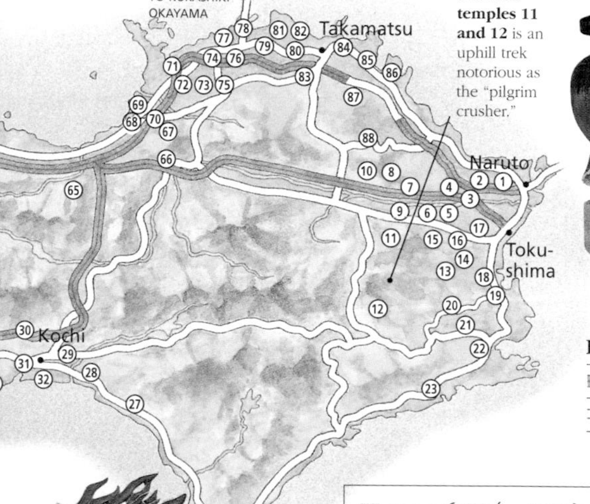

Between temples 11 and 12 is an uphill trek notorious as the "pilgrim crusher."

Incense urn at Temple 24, Hotsumisaki-ji

Key

Expressway

Other roads

0 kilometers 25

0 miles 15

***Shingon deities** come in both benign and, as this Fudo figure at Temple 27, Kounomine-ji, demonstrates, fierce guises.*

Kukai (774–835)

Kukai, who was also known as Kobo Daishi (Great Saint) after his death, helped to integrate Buddhism into Japanese life. Sailing to China as a student monk, he returned to found Japan's esoteric Shingon sect. Spending most of his time in the Kansai region of Honshu, he later returned to his native Shikoku to visit some of its temples. His accomplishments were legion: he invented the *kana* syllabary, wrote influential religious treatises, achieved lasting distinction as a poet, calligrapher, and sculptor, wrote Japan's oldest extant dictionary, and founded a school.

Statue of Kukai

KYUSHU

LONG REGARDED AS A BACKWATER *by the rest of Japan, the island of Kyushu's history of interaction with China, Southeast Asia, and Europe has, in fact, made it one of Japan's most cosmopolitan and culturally progressive regions. Such diversity creates the sensation, as you journey from prehistoric sites to urban centers like the main city of Fukuoka, of traveling through a microcosm of Japan.*

Organized communities settled in Kyushu in the Jomon period (14,500–300 BC). According to legend, it was from Kyushu that the first emperor of Japan, Jimmu, set out on his campaign to unify the country in the 6th century BC. And it was through Kyushu in the 4th century AD that Chinese and Korean culture, including Buddhism and the Chinese writing system, first infiltrated Japan. Not all foreign incursions were welcomed, however. The natives of the island repelled several Mongolian invasions, the last and most formidable in 1274 only by the intervention of a powerful storm, the *kamikaze* (divine wind), which scuttled the Mongolian fleet.

Taroemon pot from Karatsu

In the 16th century, Christianity, firearms, and medicine were introduced through the port cities of Nagasaki and Kumamoto by the merchants and emissaries of Portugal, Spain, and Holland. Later, during the two centuries of Japan's self-imposed isolation, the tiny island of Dejima off the coast of Nagasaki was the country's sole entrepôt for Western trade and learning.

The island landscape is characterized by volcanic activity. Kagoshima lies in the shadow of Sakurajima, which daily belches ash; Mount Aso is the world's largest caldera; and steaming fissures and fumeroles are found at Beppu, Unzen, and other spa towns.

Kyushu is one of the world's foremost ceramic centers. Pottery and porcelain techniques, learned from craftsmen brought from Korea, were perfected at the workshops and kilns of Arita, Imari, and Karatsu.

The island offers the visitor a rich concentration of sights, ranging from feudal castle towns and Shinto mountain shrines to hi-tech museums.

Buddhist figures carved into the cliffs at Usuki

◁ **Boatmen navigating one of the many canals in the town of Yanagawa**

Exploring Kyushu

THE NORTHERN TIP OF KYUSHU is separated from Honshu only by the narrow Kanmon Straits, less than one kilometer (half a mile) wide in parts. The island's mild climate and geothermal character has created a land of undulating green countryside, ancient volcanic cones, lava spills, hot-spring resorts, and lush, subtropical vegetation.

SEE ALSO

- ***Where to Stay*** pp303–5
- ***Where to Eat*** pp335–7

View over the rooftops of the historic port of Nagasaki

SIGHTS AT A GLANCE

Amami Island 23
Beppu 3
Chiran 22
Dazaifu 7
Fukuoka 6
Kagoshima 20
Kirishima National Park 19
Kokura 1
Kumamoto 15
Kurume 8
Mount Aso 16
Nagasaki pp234–7 13
Nichinan Coast 18
Onta 9
Sakurajima Volcano 21
Shimabara Peninsula 14
Takachiho 17
Usa 2
Usuki Stone Buddhas 5
Yanagawa 10
Yoshinogari Archaeological Site 11
Yufuin 4

Tour

Saga Pottery Towns Tour 12

Getting Around

The Sanyo Shinkansen line from Tokyo passes through a tunnel beneath the Kanmon Straits and continues to Fukuoka, where it terminates. A road bridge also links Kyushu with Honshu. The major towns of Kyushu are well served by train and bus routes, but the interior is more remote. Fukuoka is the main transportation hub, with an international airport linking to other parts of Asia, and a major ferry terminal.

Gardens surrounding Umi Jigoku, or Ocean Hell, in Beppu

Kokura ❶

小倉

Fukuoka prefecture. 400,000. *Kitakyushu International Association (093) 662-0055. Mekari Shinji (Shinto ceremony, early Feb); Tobata Gion Yamagasa (Jul 13–15).*

THE GATEWAY to northern Kyushu, Kokura is also known as Kita Kyushu. Its image as a modern city is embodied in the designs of architect Arata Isozaki, especially **Chuo Toshokan** (Central Library, 1974) and the more impressive **Kita Kyushu Municipal Art Museum**. The city and its environs – including **Dan no Ura** battlefield, where the Taira clan were defeated, and the straits of **Shimonoseki** – can be seen in one sweep from **Kokura Castle**.

Chuo Toshokan
Nr S exit of stn. *(093) 571-1481. Tue–Sun.*

Municipal Art Museum
15-min walk S of castle. *(093) 571-4466. Tue–Sun.*

Usa ❷

宇佐

Oita prefecture. 50,000. *Teiki Kanko bus tour recommended. Usa Furusato Matsuri (early Nov).*

THE CENTER of Tendai-sect sanctuaries and shrines dedicated to Hachiman, the god of war, the area including Usa and the Kunisaki Peninsula is believed to have been the nucleus of ancient Buddhist sites of Korean inspiration and origin. The most famous site, **Usa Jingu**, a shrine to the ancient Japanese deities, is also identified with the influential figure of Hachiman.

On the peninsula, to the east of Usa, are stone tombs, Heian-period statues, and, at **Kumano Magaibutsu**, the largest carved rock-face reliefs in Japan. The ancient ambience of the peninsula can be sensed near the summit of Mount Futago, where stone guardians mark the approach to **Futago-ji**. Twin avatars of the mountain are enshrined at the temple hall here, built into the side of a cliff. The oldest religious structure on Kyushu, the main hall of the **Fuki-ji**, dating from the Heian period, has faint, eerily beautiful frescoes of the Buddhist paradise.

Doorway at the vermilion hall of Usa Jingu

Beppu ❸

別府

Oita prefecture. 127,000. *Oita. from Osaka, Kobe, and Hiroshima. Beppu stn (0977) 24-2838; also Foreign Tourist Information Service at stn (0977) 21-6220.*

IF YOU CAN ACCEPT its gimmickry and brazen commercialism, Beppu, a glitzy, neon-strung hot-spring resort, situated in a wide bay and visited by over 12 million tourists a year, constitutes an amazing thermal and entertainment roller coaster. The city's porous skin is punctured by an infinite number of vents from which steam continuously rises, making it feel at times like a huge, malfunctioning boiler room.

Scalding water not only surfaces at the 3,750 hot springs and 168 public baths but is also piped into private homes to heat rooms and fuel ovens.

Beppu offers some interesting variations on the theme of a hot bath. Visitors can soak in a series of tubs of graded temperatures, plunge into thermal whirlpools, be buried in hot black sand, or sit up to the neck in steaming mud.

The most famous sights are the **Boiling Hells** (Jigoku) – pools of mineral-colored water and bubbling mud. A circuit of the Nine Hells is recommended; seven of them are within walking distance of each other in the Kannawa district in the north of Beppu.

Each has a different function, color, and mineral property. For example, the waters of Ocean Hell (Umi Jigoku) are the color of a tropical sea, while Blood Pond Hell (Chi-no-Ike Jigoku) takes its color from dissolved red clay. Visitors are shown and sold baskets of eggs that have been lowered into pools for hard-boiling.

Many of the baths are attached to hotels but also open to the public. For high kitsch and hilarity, the hugely popular **Suginoi Palace**, on the western fringes of town, is an irresistible hot-spring fantasy. Built in 1879 just inland from Beppu Bay, **Takegawara Bathhouse** is one of Beppu's oldest public baths, in which visitors are buried in black-sand baths before plunging into adjacent hot pools. Up in the hills north of Kannawa, **Myoban Hot Spring** is a quieter place to which Japanese have been coming for well over a thousand years for curative baths. For an overview of Beppu, climb the 125-m (410-ft) **Global Tower**, between the station and Suginoi Palace.

Boiling Hells
(0977) 66-1577. daily.
Suginoi Palace
(0977) 24-1160. daily.
Takegawara Bathhouse
(0977) 23-1585. daily.
Myoban Hot Spring
(0977) 66-0301. daily.

Eggs cooking at one of Beppu's Boiling Hells

Waterwheel at Yufuin Folk Art Village

Yufuin ❹

由布院

Oita prefecture. 12,000. at JR stn (0977) 84-2446. Yufuin Film and Music Festival (late Aug).

Yufuin spa town, known throughout Japan for picturesque wisps of morning mist rising from its thermally warm lake, is located at the foot of Mount Yufudake. In contrast to Beppu, it aspires to be a more refined hot spring, priding itself on elegant country inns, boutiques, summer concerts, and a host of museums and galleries.

Yufuin's more highbrow pretensions are evident from the moment you arrive at **JR Yufuin Station**, a cedarwood construction with a sooty, black exterior intended to suggest the boiler of a locomotive. The station, which was built in 1990 by Arata Isozaki, has art displays in its exhibition hall, and the floors are heated from an underground hot spring.

Serene **Lake Kinrin** is the centerpiece of Yufuin. A walking and cycling path follows the shore, passing through lakeside woods. **Shitan-yu** is an old outdoor bath with a thatched roof beside the lake. The bathing here is mixed, as baths often were before the arrival, during the Meiji period, of Americans and Europeans who shamed the Japanese into segregating their baths.

The **Sueda Art Museum** and the **Yufuin Museum** are both worth visiting for their original postmodernist architecture. A cluster of traditional samurai and thatched-roofed houses, located beside a warm stream, have been carefully converted into a collection of folk-craft galleries at the **Kyushu Yufuin Folk Art Village**. It contains a museum of crafts, and local artisans can be seen at work making ceramics, toys, and glassware, among other items. There is also an indigo dyeing house and a miso factory.

Sueda Art Museum
(0977) 85-3572. daily.
Yufuin Museum
(0977) 85-3525. daily.
Yufuin Folk Art Village
(0977) 85-2288. daily.

Usuki Stone Buddhas ❺

臼杵石仏

Oita prefecture. Usuki stn, then JR bus to Usuki-Sekibutsu. (0972) 63-1111.

Despite the wide dissemination of images of Oita's Seki Butsu (stone Buddhas) throughout Japan, the site itself is, fortunately, only a minor tourist area. Although some realignment and fissuring has been caused by centuries of earth tremors in the area, the 60 or more consummately carved Buddhas at Usuki remain remarkably intact.

One of the Usuki stone Buddhas

Though it is probable that the work was begun during the late Heian period and completed in the early Kamakura era, there appears to be no consensus regarding the origin of the site, who commissioned or executed the carvings, or why such a large, relatively remote area was dedicated for the images.

All of this adds a great deal of mystery and charm to the place. Late afternoon is very atmospheric, when sculptured sunlight draws out the earth hues from the faces and torsos of these mysterious and peaceful Buddhas.

Riverside view of the Nakasu district, Fukuoka

Fukuoka ❻

福岡

Fukuoka prefecture. 1,300,000. Hakata stn (092) 431-3003; Rainbow Plaza, IMZ Bldg, Tenjin (092) 733-2220. Hakata Dontaku Matsuri (May 3–4); Yamagasa Matsuri (Jul 1–15).

STRIKINGLY MODERN, Fukuoka bills itself as the gateway to southern Japan. Divided in two by the Naka River, the city is also known as Hakata, a name deriving from its first mercantile district. Eschewing the heavy manufacturing industries of nearby Kokura in favor of administration, wholesaling, and distribution, Japan's closest city to mainland Asia has, for at least a millennium, been the country's main port of entry for Chinese and Korean culture. This has lent it an attractive foreign Asian flavor that the local government is eager to exploit.

Tenjin, to the west of the river, is the city's commercial and shopping district, while **Nakasu**, just to the east of the river, is an entertainment district with over 3,000 nightclubs, restaurants, and bars. Most of the main sights are reached by a subway system.

A newer feature of the city is **Momochi**, a waterfront development, dominated by the **Fukuoka Tower** and the massive resort of **Hawks Town**. A little south of Fukuoka Tower lies the highly original **Saibu Gas Museum**, a combined science and art venue containing an exhibition area called the Gallery of Flame, an otherworldly collection of art objects created with natural gas. The nearby **Fukuoka City Museum** has exhibits tracing the relationship between the city and its Asian neighbors, including a gold seal sent by a Chinese emperor in the 3rd century.

Despite its modernity, Fukuoka also has religious sights of impressive antiquity.

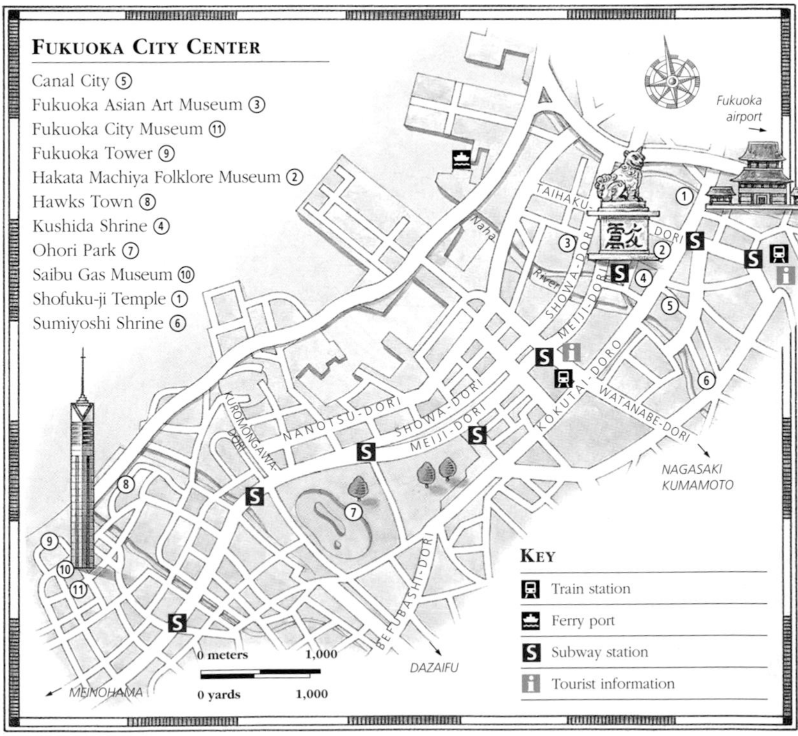

Fukuoka City Center

Canal City ⑤
Fukuoka Asian Art Museum ③
Fukuoka City Museum ⑪
Fukuoka Tower ⑨
Hakata Machiya Folklore Museum ②
Hawks Town ⑧
Kushida Shrine ④
Ohori Park ⑦
Saibu Gas Museum ⑩
Shofuku-ji Temple ①
Sumiyoshi Shrine ⑥

Fukuoka airport
Naka River
Taihaku-Dori
Showa-Dori
Meiji-Dori
Kokutai-Doro
Watanabe-Dori
Nanotsu-Dori
Kuromongawa-Dori
Befubashi-Dori
Nagasaki Kumamoto
Dazaifu
Meinohama

0 meters 1,000
0 yards 1,000

Key

Train station
Ferry port
Subway station
Tourist information

Shofuku-ji, northwest of Hakata station, is said to be the oldest Zen Buddhist temple in Japan. It was founded in the late 12th century by the priest Eisai, who introduced both Zen and tea to Japan. The **Kushida Shrine**, just to the west, dates from the 8th century and displays one of the Yamagasa festival floats. Almost opposite is the **Hakata Machiya Folklore Museum**, the exhibits and dioramas within this traditional building celebrating the heritage of the area. It is also possible to watch local artisans at work here, including demonstrations of Hakata silk weaving.

A huge and vibrant mall in the center of town, **Canal City**, features sleek shops in a setting of hanging gardens and exploding fountains, a variety theater, and a 13-screen cinema complex. The **Asian Art Museum** holds an interesting collection of contemporary Asian art.

Located on a hillside southwest of Hakata station, **Sumiyoshi Shrine**, dotted with cedar and camphor trees, hosts an annual sumo-wrestling festival in mid-October. In the southwest, **Ohori Park** is the city's most popular green space, with delightful pathways, lakes, pavilions, and islets connected by traditional bridges.

Fukuoka is regarded as one of the best places to eat in Japan and is celebrated for its *yatai*. Some of these sit-down food stalls are almost legendary, with their colorful, lamp-lit stalls serving steaming bowls of buckwheat noodles and open-pot stews.

A detail from the festival float at Kushida Shrine, Fukuoka

A Shinto priest inside the shrine of Dazaifu Tenman-gu

Saibu Gas Museum
(092) 845-1410. 305, 306 to Fukuoka Tower Minami. Tue–Sun.

Fukuoka City Museum
(092) 845-5011. Tue–Sun.

Hakata Machiya Folklore Museum
(092) 281-7761. Gion stn. daily.

Asian Art Museum
(092) 771-8600. Nakasu-Kawabata stn. Thu–Tue.

Dazaifu 7

太宰府

Fukuoka prefecture. *64,000.*
at Nishitetsu-Dazaifu stn (092) 925-1880. Usokae (Bullfinch Exchange, Jan 7); Sentomyo Festival (Jul 25 and Sep 25).

DAZAIFU was of military importance under the Yamato government *(see p181)* and an administrative center in the later Nara period. Most visitors come here today to visit the shrine of **Dazaifu Tenman-gu**. Located in a tranquil district close to the station, the shrine is dedicated to the calligrapher, scholar, and poet Sugawara Michizane. The guardian of learning, Michizane, who died in AD 903, is also known by his divine name of Tenjin. The shrine is a site of pilgrimage for students who pray for success in their exams, writing their wishes on small, votive wooden boards *(ema)*. The Treasure House can be visited, and just behind it a hall displays curious tableaux of Hakata clay dolls representing scenes in Michizane's life.

Visitors can also enjoy a stroll around the stone, sand, and moss garden of the nearby temple, **Komyo Zen-ji**. Ten minute's walk away, **Kyushu History Museum** has some good displays of Jomon-, Yayoi-, and Kofun-period items excavated at Dazaifu.

Kanzeon-ji, a temple to the southwest of the station, contains a great bell and a number of highly prized statues, including an unusual horse-headed Kannon.

Dazaifu Tenman-gu Shrine
(092) 922-8225. Wed–Mon. (for Treasure House).

Kyushu History Museum
(092) 923-0404. Tue–Sun.

Statue of a bull near the shrine of Dazaifu Tenman-gu

Kurume ❽

久留米

Fukuoka prefecture. 230,000. (0942) 30-9137. *Suiten-gu Spring Festival (May 5–7); Mizu-no-Saiten (water festival, Aug 3–5).*

THE UNATTRACTIVE, sprawling city of Kurume is the center of *kasuri* textiles. These employ a distinctive ikat weaving style, in which the threads have been tie-dyed before weaving; unlike Southeast Asian forms of ikat, both the warp and weft are patterned. The **Kurume Regional Industry Promotion Center** houses a superb display on *kasuri* weaving. *Rantai-shikki* is a local basket-weaving style whereby layers of lacquer are applied to bamboo to produce attractive, durable basketware. Examples can be bought at **Inoue Rantai-Shikki**, opposite the Honmachi-yon-chome bus stop. The **Ishibashi Bunka Center**, a five-minute bus ride from the station, has an art museum and Japanese garden. By the river is the **Suiten-gu**, the head shrine of a popular sect.

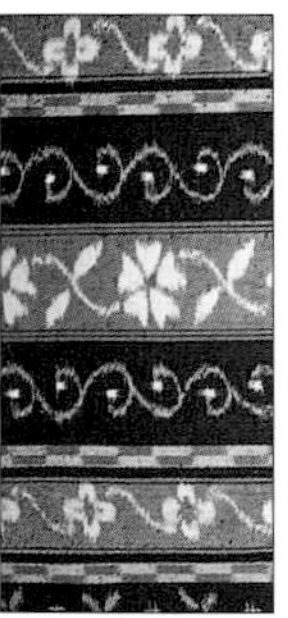

***Kasuri* cloth from Kurume**

Kurume Regional Industry Promotion Center
2nd flr, Jibasan Kurume Center.
(0942) 44-3700. daily.

Ishibashi Bunka Center
(0942) 33-2271. Tue–Sun.

ENVIRONS: Many artisans work in the secluded villages of **Hirokawa** and **Yame**, a 40-minute bus ride from Kurume station. In Hirokawa, the **Workshop of Moriyama Torao** is well worth a visit. Paper-making, using mulberry-tree fibers, dates from the 16th century. Traditional, wood-fired cauldrons can still be seen in use at **Yamaguchi Seishijo** paper workshop in Yame.

Workshop of Moriyama Torao
(0943) 32-0023. Mon–Sat.

A boatman plying one of Yanagawa's canals

Onta ❾

小鹿田

Oita prefecture. 60. *Hita, then bus.* (0973) 23-3111. *Onta Pottery Festival (2nd weekend in Oct).*

TUCKED into a wooded mountain valley, this tiny village has been producing Onta-ware since a group of Korean potters set up their kilns here in 1705. Later luminaries of the *mingei* (folk craft) movement, such as Yanagi Soetsu and Bernard Leach, praised Onta-ware for its unpretentious rustic quality. The kilns, dug into the hillside and water-powered, are still used today. Ten families producing pottery have converted their homes into open galleries. The simple, functional objects are characterized by marked, dribbled glazes in earth colors.

Potter at work in Onta

Yanagawa ❿

柳川

Fukuoka prefecture. 45,000. *Inari-machi (0944) 73-2145. Dorotsukudon Matsuri (early Oct).*

THE STONE QUAYS of Yanagawa are not as busy as they used to be, but the canals and old moats that run through this former castle town are still vital to its economy. Visitors can board gondolas to glide past old samurai villas and storehouses. The canals are at their best in spring.

Other Yanagawa sights include **Suiten-gu**, a pretty shrine used by the same sect as the shrine in Kurume; **Toshimashi-tei**, an Edo-period tea garden; and a house-museum, **Hakushu Seika**, the birthplace of Kitahara Hakushu (1885–1942), a prolific writer best known for children's poems.

Hakushu Seika
(0944) 92-6773. daily.

Yoshinogari Archaeological Site ⓫

吉野ヶ里遺跡

Saga prefecture. *Tosu, then Showa bus to Yoshinogari.* (0952) 25-7233.

PIT DWELLINGS and hundreds of burial urns excavated at Yoshinogari point to the existence of a sophisticated Yayoi-period society (300 BC–AD 300) in the region. Irrigation systems and rice cultivation were begun in this period, laying the pattern for later Japanese society. The area is believed by some to be the home of Queen Himiko, mentioned in 3rd-century Chinese annals. Watchtowers and Yayoi-period homes have been reconstructed.

Urn in the museum at Yoshinogari

Saga Pottery Towns Tour ⓬

佐賀県陶器生産地

CERAMICS ENTHUSIASTS will have a field day in Saga prefecture, where pottery towns have been producing high-quality wares for at least 500 years. Korean potters were brought to Kyushu in the 1590s and given sovereign control over the kilns they set up. The three main pottery towns – Arita, Imari, and Karatsu – are all within convenient distances of each other, and provide access to other interesting destinations nearby.

Imari ④
Imari porcelain was exported in the 17th century via the Dutch East India Company to Europe where it was highly prized. Today much Imari-ware is produced in the kilns of Okawachi-yama, a nearby village.

Yobuko ⑥
In this fishing town, the daily produce market includes stalls devoted to good-quality ceramics that are reasonably priced.

Karatsu ⑤
Karatsu-ware resembles Korean pottery and is much sought after by tea ceremony practitioners. The Nakazato Taroemon Kiln is run by descendants of the first Korean potters who lived here.

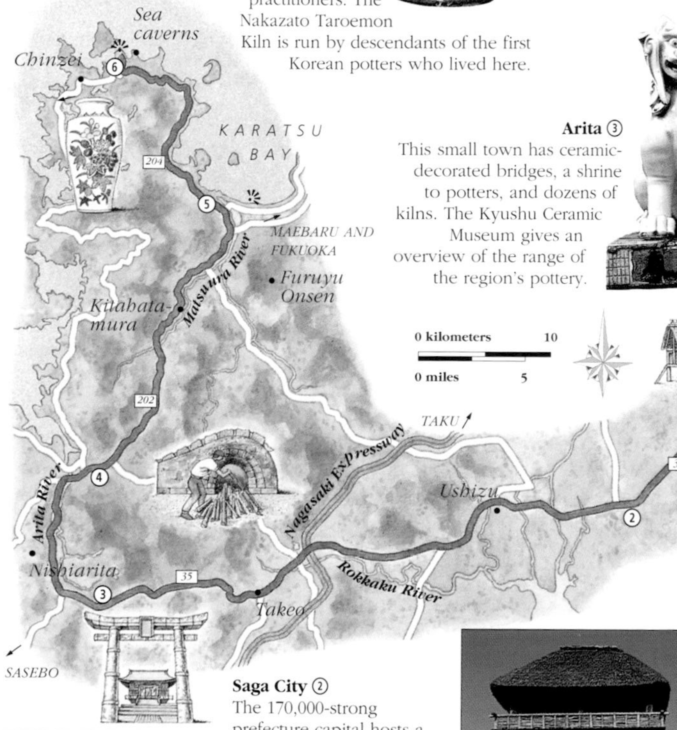

Arita ③
This small town has ceramic-decorated bridges, a shrine to potters, and dozens of kilns. The Kyushu Ceramic Museum gives an overview of the range of the region's pottery.

Sea caverns
Chinzei
KARATSU BAY
MAEBARU AND FUKUOKA
Furuyu Onsen
Kitahata-mura
Matsuura River
Arita River
Nishiarita
Takeo
Nagasaki Expressway
Rokkaku River
Ushizu
TAKU
OGORI
SASEBO
204
202
35
34

0 kilometers 10
0 miles 5

Saga City ②
The 170,000-strong prefecture capital hosts a major annual balloon competition in November.

Tips for Drivers

Length: *80 km (50 miles); allow 7–8 hours by car.*
Alternative transportation: *Some Japanese-language tour buses cover the sights. There are also some train links from Fukuoka – allow more time for these.*

Key

Tour route by car
Other roads
Viewpoint

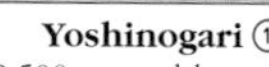

Yoshinogari ①
This site, with its 2,500-year-old ceramics and reconstructed buildings, is a good starting point for the tour.

Nagasaki ⓭

長崎

Statue in Sofuku-ji Temple

A HISTORY OF CONTACT and interaction with Europe, its tragic fate as victim of the second atomic bomb, and miraculous resurgence since the war have made Nagasaki one of the most cosmopolitan and eclectic cities in Japan. After the Portuguese were expelled from the country in 1638, the Dutch, confined to the tiny island of Dejima, were the only foreign power permitted to remain throughout Japan's long period of self-imposed isolation. When Japan opened its doors to foreigners in 1854, Nagasaki thrived once more as a center of Western trade and culture.

Ornate red gateway leading into Nagasaki's Chinatown

Getting Around Nagasaki

Despite the encroachments of modern industry, Nagasaki – with its magnificent harbor setting, meandering streets, and beautiful terraced slopes – is a city of which its inhabitants are roundly proud. Although the main sights are fairly scattered, signs in English and well-marked walking routes make Nagasaki an easily navigable city. Surprisingly inexpensive streetcars are the easiest means of transportation with four main lines running through the center of the city. Organized bus tours provide another perspective on the city. The main concentration of shops, restaurants, and nightspots is to the southeast of Nagasaki Station in the Hamanomachi arcade district, while the Peace Park, an essential place of pilgrimage for any visitor to Nagasaki, lies to the north of the station. Chinatown, once an artificial island but now attached to the mainland, is located in the district of Shinchi. Shrines, temples, and churches are scattered between.

Shrine to the 26 Martyrs

5-min walk N of stn.

Christianity was officially banned in 1587 by the shogun Toyotomi Hideyoshi who feared that conversions would lead to political intrigues and the undermining of the state by foreign powers. In that year, to emphasize the point, 26 defiant Christians (Japanese and foreigners) were rounded up and crucified on Nishizaka Hill, the first of over 600 documented martyrdoms in the Nagasaki area alone. A short walk from the station leads to the shrine built on the site of the martyrdom. A stone relief, a small chapel, and a museum honor the martyrs who, in 1862, were declared saints by the pope. Without a clergy and without a single chapel to worship in, Christianity, astonishingly, managed to survive covertly for 200 years after the martyrdoms until the end of Japan's isolationist policy.

Figures carved on the façade of the shrine to the 26 Martyrs

KEY

- Train station
- Bus station
- Ferry port
- Streetcar stop
- Tourist information
- Temple

ISAHAYA

KANKO-DORI

Nakashima River

Peace Park
Atomic Bomb Museum
SASEBO

NAGASAKI CITY CENTER

Confucian Shrine ⑧
Dejima ⑥
Glover Park ⑩
Hollander Slope ⑦
Kofuku-ji Temple ②
Oura Catholic Church ⑨
Shrine to the 26 Martyrs ⑤
Sofuku-ji Temple ③
Spectacles Bridge ④
Suwa Shrine ①

Inner gate detail at the temple of Sofuku-ji

Dejima

Dejima.

Little remains of the old Dutch enclave of Dejima as landfills have long connected it to the mainland. In its day the island was surrounded by mud walls, and the only people allowed to enter, apart from the Japanese involved in trading with the Dutch and accessing the fruits of Western medicine and science, were prostitutes and monks collecting alms. There is a scale model of the outpost on the present grounds near the Dejima streetcar stop.

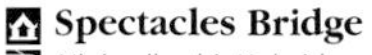

Spectacles Bridge

Nigiwaibashi, Kokaidomae.

One of the most photographed sights of Nagasaki is the modest but curious Spectacles Bridge (Megane-bashi), a Chinese bequest to the city. Built by the Chinese Zen priest Mozi in 1634, it remains the oldest stone bridge in Japan. The curve of the bridge reflected in the Nakashima River resembles a pair of glasses.

Sofuku-ji Temple

Sofuku-ji-dori. *Shianbashi.*

The Chinese provenance of this temple is proclaimed in the entrance gate. This depicts the gateway that, according to legend, is to be seen in the Chinese undersea paradise. A second, more illustrious gate farther into the temple precinct has been designated a National Treasure of the late Ming period. Also worth seeing is the Treasure Hall.

Sofuku-ji is one of the three largest Chinese places of worship in Nagasaki. The temple was founded, with the help of local Chinese residents, by a monk from Fukien province in 1629. The gigantic cooking pot that stands enigmatically in the temple grounds was used to make gruel to feed over 3,000 people each day during one of Nagasaki's worst famines in 1682. A fascinating 20-minute or so walk north from here, along narrow streets lined with a few old buildings and stores, leads to Kofuku-ji temple.

> **VISITORS' CHECKLIST**
>
> Nagasaki prefecture. *430,000.* *40 km (25 miles) NE.* *JR line.* *above bus stn (0958) 26-9407.* *Lantern Festival (2 weeks from end Jan); Kunchi Matsuri (Oct 7–9).*

Kofuku-ji Temple

Teramachi-dori. *Kokaidomae.*

Kofuku-ji, located at the heart of the Teramachi district, was Japan's first Obaku Zen Buddhist temple. Founded by a Chinese priest in 1623, the building is also known as the Nanking Temple and is often visited by residents from that city. The main buildings, including the Buddha hall, are constructed in Chinese style.

Suwa Shrine

Kaminishiyama-dori. *Suwa Jinjamae.*

Located in a wooded hilltop precinct at the top of 227 stone steps, Suwa Shrine affords fine harbor views. The original buildings were destroyed by fire in 1857 but later beautifully restored. This popular shrine was constructed with the purpose of promoting Shintoism and eradicating the last vestiges of Christianity from the area. The shrine is home to the city's pantheon of Shinto gods. The autumn festival, Kunchi Matsuri, is celebrated here, with blazing floats and dragon dances.

The Chinese-style Buddha hall in the temple of Kofuku-ji

Exploring Nagasaki

To the north and south of the city center there are many sights of interest, most of them reflecting the diverse foreign influences that have shaped Nagasaki. For a view of the city take a boat trip from Ohato Pier, or, better still, cross the harbor and take the ropeway to the lookout tower on the summit of Mount Isa.

View over Glover Park, with its 19th-century colonial-style residences

Confucian Shrine

Oura Tenshudo.

Vibrant yellow roof tiles and vermilion walls instantly announce this building as a shrine dedicated to the scholar Confucius. Built by the Chinese community in 1893, the repairs and extensions accorded the shrine after it was damaged in the atomic bombing included the addition in 1982 of a National Museum of Chinese History. The antiquities on display are on loan from the Chinese National Museum and the prestigious Palace Museum in Beijing.

Glover Park

Oura Tenshudo Shita.

daily.

With the reopening of the port to Westerners in the latter half of the 19th century, Nagasaki flowered as a prosperous and sophisticated international city. Suitable housing was required for the sudden influx of foreigners who made their homes here. Many of the comfortable stone and clapboard residencies that were built during this period survive today, preserved in Glover Park, overlooking Nagasaki harbor. The best-known European-style residence here is **Glover House**. Built in 1863, it was the setting for Puccini's opera *Madame Butterfly*.

Thomas Glover, who was responsible for bringing the first steam locomotive to Japan, was an extraordinary British entrepreneur whose ventures included coal mining, a tea import house, ship repair yards, and the founding of a beer company, the forerunner of today's Kirin Beer.

Statue of Petitjean, Oura church

Other notable buildings in the park include **Ringer House**, standing on foundation stones brought from Vladivostok, and **Walker House**, with a private garden and hall displaying the colorful floats used in the annual Kunchi festival. The **Old Hong Kong and Shanghai Bank Building** is a restored stone structure that now houses displays tracing Nagasaki's contact with Western ideas.

Oura Catholic Church

Oura Tenshudo Shita.

This white church was built in 1864 under the direction of Bernard Petitjean, a French priest who became the first Bishop of Nagasaki.

The church, which boasts some impressive stained-glass windows, was erected in order to serve the foreign community that settled in Nagasaki after the new trade treaties were signed. It was also intended to honor the city's 26 martyred saints. Shortly after its foundation, Father Petitjean was approached by members of a group of Japanese Christians who had practiced their faith in secret and at risk for over 200 years.

Classed as a National Treasure, Oura is one of the oldest churches in Japan and the country's earliest Gothic wooden structure. A wooden building beside the church contains items connected with the persecution of Nagasaki's early Christians.

Hollander Slope

Oura Tenshudo Shita.

A pleasant cobblestone street built by the Dutch, the Slope was once the center for the city's expatriate community. For a time, all Westerners, irrespective of nationality, were called "Hollanders" by the Japanese. Some of the wooden houses along the Slope are open to the public. One of the most imposing, the 1868 **Junibankan**, was once the Prussian Legation building.

Interior of the Atomic Bomb Museum

Tulips by the canal in Huis Ten Bosch

Peace Park

Matsuyama-machi.

A black stone pillar marks the spot where the US detonated its second atom bomb at 11:02 on August 9, 1945, three days after Hiroshima. The intended target was the nearby shipyards. The blast killed an estimated 75,000, while 75,000 more were injured in its wake. Small wonder that the citizens of Nagasaki have become staunch advocates of world peace, erecting several monuments in the park, including a 9-m (30-ft) tall Peace Statue. A 1959 reconstruction of the **Urakami Catholic Church**, which stood at the epicenter, stands near the park.

Atomic Bomb Museum

(095) 844-1231. *daily.*

This museum is a must for anybody visiting the city. Displays depict Nagasaki before and after the explosion and also the reconstruction. It traces with great objectivity and fairness the events leading up to the bombing, the history of nuclear weapons, and the evolution of the peace movement. Photographs, artifacts, videos, and dioramas vividly re-create the event. A clock, frozen at the moment the bomb exploded, is one of the most poignant items.

Huis ten Bosch

Near Sasebo. *Huis ten Bosch.* *(0956) 27-0001.* *daily.*

Built in 1992 at the staggering cost of US$1.75 billion, Huis ten Bosch is a reproduction of a traditional Dutch village. Replete with churches, houses, shops, windmills, a farmhouse, and canals, it is Japan's largest theme park to date. Replicas of one of Queen Beatrix's palaces and of Holland's tallest church tower are highlights. Horse-drawn carriages, old-fashioned taxis, and canal boats complete the picture.

Holland Village

from airport. *(0959) 27-0080.* *daily.*

This theme park has a replica of a famous 17th-century ship, the *Prince Willem*. A video simulates the conditions of the arduous voyage from Holland to Nagasaki.

Foreigners in Nagasaki

The Portuguese and Dutch were the first to arrive when the harbor opened to international trade in 1571, followed by Chinese merchants who established their own community. Portuguese cargos of guns and Catholicism, however, foreshadowed Kyushu's troubled history of rebellion and persecution. Only the Dutch were allowed to trade between 1638 and 1854. After the port reopened, British, American, French, German, and Prussian trade missions came to the city. The legacy of this extraordinary foreign contact survives in some of the local festivals and cuisine, like the Portuguese *castella*, an egg and flour mixture, and the Chinese *champon* noodles, invented in 1899.

Replica, in Holland Village, of the Dutch ship *Prince Willem*

The scenic Nita Pass in the Shimabara peninsula

Shimabara Peninsula ⓮

島原半島

Nagasaki prefecture. *Shimabara city.* *from Kumamoto.* *Unzen Spa (0957) 73-3434; Shimabara (0957) 63-1111.*

Ruled until 1616 by the Christian Lord Arima, Shimabara peninsula is known as the site of anti-Christian pogroms ordered by the Tokugawa shogunate. However, in the 1880s, **Unzen Spa** became a resort for Westerners. At an altitude of 700 m (2,300 ft) and surrounded by pine forests, it was an ideal retreat from the summer heat. Thousands of azaleas bloom in the peninsula in spring, and in autumn the maple leaves turn brilliant shades of red. In 1934 the **Unzen-Amakusa National Park**, Japan's first such protected area, was created.

Most hotels in Unzen Spa have their own hot-spring baths. Visitors in a more somber mood can see the notorious **Hells** (Jigoku): scalding sulfurous cauldrons in which 30 Christians were boiled alive after the outlawing of Christianity in Japan. As a demonstration of the ferocity of the waters in the Hells, elderly ladies in bonnets and smocks lower eggs placed in baskets into the pools and sell them hard-boiled to tourists.

Mount Unzen, thought to be dormant until one of its peaks erupted in 1991, can be climbed from the Nita Pass, reached by bus from Unzen.

The eaves and roofs of Kumamoto Castle, one of the great fortresses of Japan

Kumamoto ⓯

熊本

Kumamoto prefecture. *660,000.* *Prefectural Information Office (096) 325-6360.* *Hinokuni Matsuri (Fire Festival, Aug 11–13); Fujisake Hachiman-gu Shuki Reitaisai (Sep 11–15); Kumamoto Oshiro Matsuri (Kumamoto Castle Festival, mid-Oct–Nov 3).*

A CITY WITH a small-town atmosphere, a mild climate, and semitropical flora, Kumamoto was an important seat of power during the Tokugawa shogunate (1603–1868). Its star attraction, one of the largest castles in Japan, dates from this period. The city's main shopping precinct and sights are compressed into an area south of Kumamoto castle, the original location of merchants' and artisans' quarters attached to the castle.

The longevity of Kumamoto's feisty residents (the city has numerous centenarians) is ascribed to a passion for living and a healthy diet. The latter includes *karashi renkon* (deep-fried lotus root stuffed with mustard miso) and various brands of sake made from water supposedly purified by the area's rich volcanic soil.

Dominating the center of the city from an imposing hill, **Kumamoto Castle** was constructed on the orders of Kato Kiyomasa, a warrior who fought alongside Tokugawa Ieyasu at the decisive Battle of Sekigahara in 1600. He was rewarded for his loyalty with lands encompassing most of present-day Kumamoto. The castle was completed in 1607 – a hard seven-year undertaking. Unlike more decorative castles such as Himeji *(see pp200–203)*, Kumamoto's citadel is stridently martial in appearance with steep, almost impregnable walls. The original structure had 49 towers and 29 gates, but it was almost completely destroyed during the Seinan War in 1877. Although the main keep was reconstructed on a smaller scale using ferroconcrete in 1960, it is a highly effective replica, successfully evoking the fearsome magnificence of the original.

Gyobu-tei, a 300-year-old residence owned by Lord Gyobu, is located a little northwest of the castle grounds. It presents insights into the way the feudal elite lived during the Edo period.

The family possessions of the powerful Kato and Hosokawa clans can be found near the castle in the **Kumamoto Prefectural Art Museum**, a distinctive modern building with a pleasant tea room. The museum also has interesting replicas of ancient burial mounds and archaeological finds from the region.

Suizen-ji Garden, Kumamoto's other main attraction, was laid out by the Hosokawa family in 1632 as the grounds for a detached villa. With a central spring-fed lake, it is a classic stroll garden *(see pp26–7)*. Its representational designs are not labeled and not always apparent. They include scenes in miniature from the 53 stages of the old Tokaido Highway and outlines of Lake Biwa and Mount Fuji.

Kumamoto is renowned for its crafts, especially damascene inlay designs, Amakusa pearls, and Yamage lanterns. These lanterns, made from gold paper, are a feature of the city's festival in August. The **Kumamoto Traditional Crafts Center** has a good selection of these local crafts.

Kumamoto Castle
(096) 352-5900.
daily.

Gyobu-tei
(096) 352-6522.
Tue–Sun.

Kumamoto Prefectural Art Museum
(096) 352-2111.
Tue–Sun.

Suizen-ji Garden
(096) 383-0074.
daily.

Kumamoto Traditional Crafts Center
(096) 324-4930. *Tue–Sun.*
for 2nd flr.

Guard on duty outside the castle

Mount Aso ⓰

阿蘇山

Kumamoto prefecture. *Aso, then bus.* *Kyushu Kokusai Kanko sightseeing bus from Beppu or Kumamoto.* *Aso-no-hi Matsuri (Aso Fire Festival), Kuginomura (mid-Mar).*

ACTUALLY A SERIES of five volcanic cones, Mount Aso is the world's largest caldera, with a circumference of 130 km (80 miles). Of the five peaks, **Mount Daikanbo**, at about 940 m (3,100 ft), is the highest. **Mount Nakadake** is still active, emitting sulfurous fumes and hot gases, earning

Blocks of sulfuric rock on sale at the top of the Nakadake cable car

The fuming crater of Nakadake, one of the five volcanic cones in the Mount Aso caldera

Kumamoto the epithet *hi-no-kuni* ("the land of fire").

Below these peaks, the caldera is dotted with towns set among forests, grasslands, bamboo groves, and hot springs. Arriving tour buses pass a curious, grass-covered mountain resembling an inverted rice bowl, aptly named **Komezuka** (Rice Mound), and often stop at the pretty **Kusasenri Meadow**.

A cable car runs to the top of Nakadake, providing, on clear days, awesome views into the depths of the crater and its malodorous green lake. Hikers can follow a path to the summit for a closer look. A popular hiking route starts at the top of the ropeway, proceeds to **Mount Takadake** around the crater rim, and descends to **Sensuikyo Gorge**.

Mount Aso Volcanic Museum, at the base of Nakadake, offers a fascinating preview of the mountain even when the crater is closed due to a high level of dangerous, sulfuric fumes. Two cameras on the crater wall relay continuous images of the cone's volcanic activity.

Mount Aso Volcanic Museum
(0967) 34-2111. daily.

Shrine in the Mount Aso caldera

Takachiho ⓱

高千穂

Miyazaki prefecture. 16,000. (0982) 73-1212. Amano Iwato Shrine Festival (May 2–3); Yo-Kagura Kokai Festival (Nov 3).

The Takachiho mountain region, a place of homage for those with an affection for Japan's ancient pantheon of gods and goddesses, is alive with the resonances of legend.

Most of the sights on or around the 1,575-m (5,150-ft) mountain, sanctified by Shintoism, are connected with Japan's rich mythology. Kagura, a mime-dance said to have been first performed by the Sun Goddess Amaterasu Omikami, is thought to have originated here. The cave into which Amaterasu vanished, casting the world into a temporary gloom until she could be lured out, faces **Ama no Iwato Jingu**, a pavilion-style shrine noted for a sacred tree that stands in its grounds. A short walk from here, **Ama no Yasugawara** is the grotto where the gods are supposed to have convened in order to devise a way to entice the Sun Goddess from her lair. The entrance to the cavern is next to a clear, pebble-strewn river. Many visitors have placed miniature cairns there in the hope that, by association, some of the wisdom and power of the gods will rub off on them.

The area's main shrine, **Takachiho Jinja** is famous for its ancient cryptomeria trees, a common feature of Japanese shrines and temple grounds. The shrine stages nightly extracts of Kagura lasting half an hour and giving a rare opportunity to witness a performance in such atmospheric surroundings. Visitors usually try to factor into their itinerary a rowboat trip along **Takachiho Gorge**, with its scenic rock formations and waterfalls.

Waterfall in the picturesque Takachiho Gorge

Horse and sightseers dwarfed by a large eruption of smoke and ash at Mount Aso ▷

Udo Jingu, a cave shrine on the Nichinan Coast dedicated to fertility

Nichinan Coast ⓲

日南海岸

Miyazaki prefecture. *Nichinan line from Miyazaki.*

The Nichinan coastal landscape is known in Japanese as Onino Sentakuita, the "devil's washboard," an apt description for the eroded, rippled effect presented by the rock shelves.

The gateway to the coast is **Aoshima Island**, barely a mile in circumference and connected to the mainland by a walkway. An attractive vermilion shrine stands at the center of this densely forested islet, which can get crowded in summertime.

Udo Jingu, another vermilion-colored shrine about 30 km (20 miles) south of Aoshima, stands in a cave beside the ocean. The shrine is dedicated to Emperor Jimmu's father, who is believed to have been washed there at birth, and serves as a catalyst for propitious marriages and fertility. The water dripping from breast-shaped rocks is compared to mother's milk, and milk candies are sold at the shrine shop. Farther south, **Ishinami Beach** is a stretch of fine white sand.

Miyazaki city is known for its year-round flowers. The extraordinary **Miyazaki Seagaia** is a resort complex simulating a tropical paradise. Exotic flora luxuriate under a retractable roof, which allows the sun to pour in.

Miyazaki Seagaia
(0985) 21-1111. daily.

Kirishima National Park ⓳

霧島国立公園

Miyazaki and Kagoshima prefectures. *Kirishima Jingu (Nippo line from Miyazaki), then bus to Kirishima Jinja.*

This region, identified with Japanese foundation myths, centers on the volcanic plateau of **Ebino-Kogen** (Shrimp Meadow), which is surrounded by volcanoes, crater lakes, and hot springs. The Ebino-Kogen Nature Trail is the best of several hiking routes, going past three ponds, two of which are cobalt blue. The climb up to the peak of Mount Karakunidake is popular in summer. Two hot springs, **Ebino-Kogen Rotenburo** (in a beautiful location) and **Hayashida Onsen**, are the main tourist centers of the region.

Kagoshima ⓴

鹿児島

Kagoshima prefecture. *550,000. from Osaka and Nagasaki. at Nishi Kagoshima stn (099) 253-2500. Soga-don no Kasayaki (mid-Jul).*

With one of the most stunning settings of any city in Japan, Kagoshima looks out across the broad sweep of a bay to the brooding silhouette of Sakurajima, an active volcano that sometimes showers the city in a gray blanket of volcanic ash.

Historically, this semitropical city, far from the old capital of Edo, enjoyed an unusual degree of independence. Center of the feudal domain of Satsuma, Kagoshima's Shimazu clan ruled Okinawa for eight centuries, absorbing much of the culture of China and Southeast Asia transmitted through the islands. The legacy of that contact is evident today in a cuisine that relies on sweet potatoes rather than rice, and in its typically Okinawan preference for pork dishes.

Shochu, Kagoshima's favorite liquor made from sweet potatoes, is believed to have passed through Okinawa from China or Korea. There are over 120 *shochu* distilleries in Kagoshima alone. Local craft traditions, particularly Satsuma ceramics and fine silk brocades, reflect an aesthetic of Asian provenance. Kagoshima's sultry climate is apparent at **Iso Garden**, where semitropical plants grow alongside plum trees and bamboo groves. The garden's centerpiece is a pond and miniature waterfall.

Roof detail from Iso Garden, Kagoshima

On an artificial island in the harbor is the **City Aquarium**, with species from local waters and the coral reefs around the Nansei islands, southwest of Kyushu. Also worth seeing is the **Art Museum**, with its displays of Satsuma ceramics.

Japan first came into contact with Christianity at Kagoshima, in 1549, in the person of the Spanish missionary Francis Xavier. The 20th-century **St. Xavier's Church** commemorates this event. The city is also associated with Saigo Takamori (1827–77), who led

Fish in one of the tanks of Kagoshima's City Aquarium

Sakurajima volcano across the strait from Kagoshima

the ill-fated Seinan Rebellion. Japanese visitors pay their respects to him in a cave on Shiroyama Hill where he committed ritual suicide.

Iso Garden
(099) 247-1551. daily.

City Aquarium
(099) 226-2233. daily.

Art Museum
(099) 224-3400. Tue–Sun.

Sakurajima Volcano ㉑

桜島

every 15 mins from the pier near Kagoshima stn.

A DRAMATIC ERUPTION of Sakurajima in 1914 deposited three billion tons of lava in the narrow strait separating the mountain from the peninsula, thus joining the island to the mainland. The rich volcanic soil produces the world's largest white radishes, giant specimens growing to a diameter of 1.5 m (5 ft). Such is the fascination of the cone that one of Japan's foremost writers, Endo Shusaku, is said to have had himself lowered by helicopter into the smoking crater of Sakurajima, the model for his 1959 novel *Kazan (Volcano)*. One particular sight is the **Kurokami Buried Torii Gate**, the protruding lintel of a stone Shinto gate, a casualty of the 1914 eruption.

Chiran ㉒

知覧

Kagoshima prefecture. 14,500. from Kagoshima. (0993) 83-2511.

TUCKED INTO the green folds of neatly manicured tea plantations and wooded hills, exquisite Chiran was one of 102 castle-towns built to protect the feudal lords of Satsuma. Six preserved samurai houses and gardens on **Samurai Lane** can be visited with a single entrance ticket. **Sata** combines a dry-landscape garden, an expanse of white raked sand, and mountains used as "borrowed scenery." **Morishige** is a stroll garden with a pond representing the sea with islands. **Hirayama** is composed almost entirely of hedges, clipped with precision into the illusion of undulating hills blending seamlessly with a backdrop of mountains.

A hill above the village was the site of a World War II training ground for kamikaze pilots. Cherry trees are dedicated to 1,026 young men who flew their fatal missions from Chiran.

Amami Island ㉓

奄美大島

Kagoshima prefecture. 135,000. from Kagoshima to Naze. at airport (0997) 63-2295.

SUBTROPICAL Amami is home to a wealth of flora and fauna. The coral reefs and offshore islets of **Setouchi**, in the south, are part of a protected marine park offering excellent diving, snorkeling, fishing, and boat trips.

The **Amami Oshima Tsumugi Mura** is an artisan village set aside for the production of *tsumugi* (also known as Oshima pongee), a delicate handwoven silk fabric used to make kimonos. It can take up to one year to produce sufficient silk to make a single kimono.

Halfway down the east coast, two rivers form a saltwater delta, which supports the world's most northerly mangrove forest.

One of the six perfectly maintained samurai gardens in Chiran

OKINAWA

AN EXOTIC CORAL BAR *slicing through the Pacific Ocean and East China Sea, the Okinawa archipelago was a vassal of China from the 15th century; its masters named it Liu-chiu (Ryukyu in Japanese). Under the Chinese, then later suzerainty of the Satsuma domain, the islands assimilated diverse influences, creating a unique, exotic culture that still sets them apart from mainland Japan.*

Present day Okinawans, a people with a reputation for warmth and native good manners, are the heirs of a diverse racial intermingling, the result of maritime migrations from Southeast Asia, the Philippines, Mongolia, China, and the peninsula of Korea. The geography of the islands matches this rich ethnographic map. Encircled by stunning coral reefs and transparent waters, Okinawa has a richly varied topography and subtropical flora and fauna. This is one source of inspiration for the exquisite handiwork of the islanders, particularly their textiles. Created using light, natural fabrics and innovative dyeing methods, they vary from island to island.

A kimono of traditional Okinawan fabric

Okinawa, the largest and busiest island in the group, gives its name to the prefecture, which was established in 1879. In the closing stages of World War II, this was the scene of fierce fighting, in the Battle of Okinawa, and the mass suicide of thousands of civilians. Naha, the main city, was damaged in the battle but has since become a heady mix of refined civilization and neon glitz. Art galleries and teahouses stand alongside red-light bars, snake restaurants, and karaoke cabins. Ceramic *shisa* lions, topping the red-tiled roofs of traditional Okinawan houses, add to the eclectic mix of war memorials, sacred groves, flower-covered coral walls, craft shops, luxury hotels, and discos.

Those who venture to the more remote islands southwest of Okinawa itself will encounter idyllic beaches, tropical rainforests, and superb diving – the nearest thing to terra incognita it is possible to find in the Japanese archipelago.

Part of the Nakamura House on Okinawa, a fine example of traditional architecture

◁ **A sweep of coast, ending at the cape of Higashi Henna, on Miyako Island**

Exploring Okinawa

THE ARCHIPELAGO, also known as the Ryukyu islands, consists of 65 subtropical islands stretching for 685 km (425 miles) from the southwest coast of Kyushu to within television-reception distance of Taiwan. About 45 islands are inhabited. Just 135 km (80 miles) long, narrow Okinawa island is the most accessible part for tourists, with its vibrant capital Naha, beach resorts, and historical monuments. The more remote islands to the southwest are part of Okinawa prefecture; ones to the northeast are actually part of Kyushu's Kagoshima prefecture.

Battle of Okinawa war memorial at Cape Kyan

The massive remaining wall at Nakijin Castle, Okinawa

KEY

- International airport
- Domestic airport
- Expressway
- Major road
- Minor road
- Ferry route
- Viewpoint

See Also

- *Where to Stay* p305
- *Where to Eat* p337

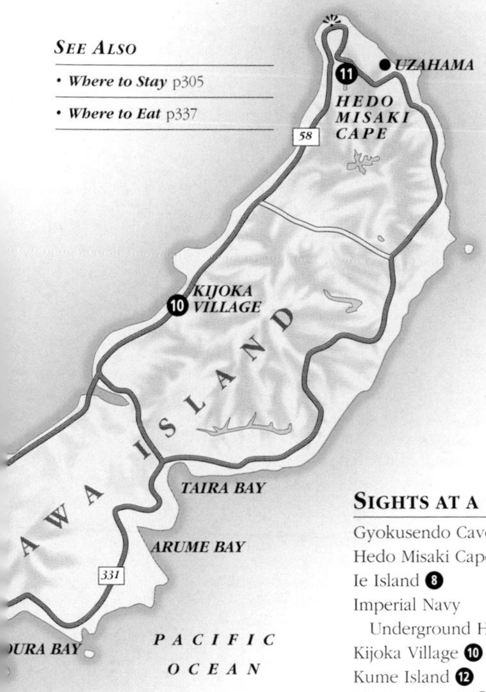

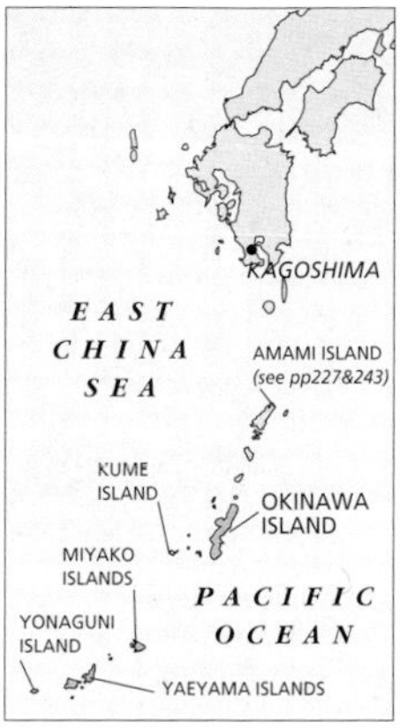

Locator Map

Sights at a Glance

Gyokusendo Cave ❹	Naha City ❶
Hedo Misaki Cape ⓫	Nakagusuku Castle Ruin ❻
Ie Island ❽	Nakamura House ❺
Imperial Navy Underground HQ ❷	Nakijin Castle Ruin ❾
Kijoka Village ❿	Okinawa Battle Sites ❸
Kume Island ⓬	Okinawa Memorial Park ❼
Miyako Islands ⓭	Yaeyama Islands ⓮

Kume Island ⓬

Miyako Islands ⓭

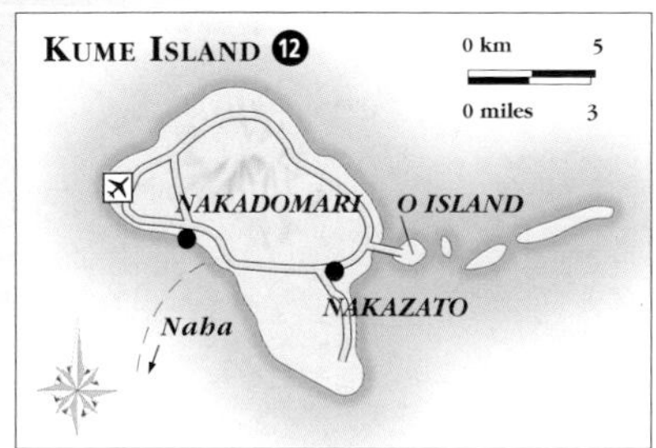

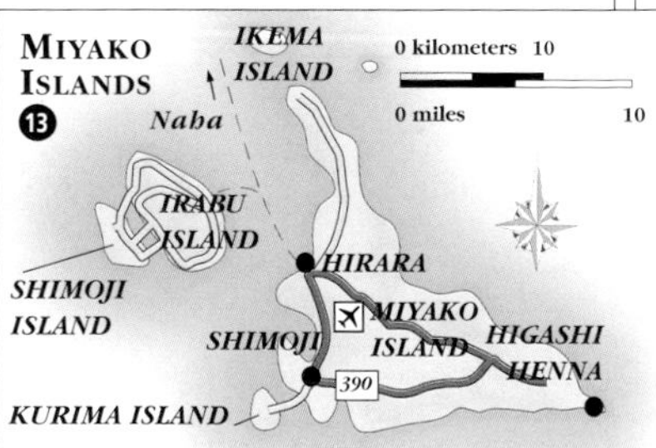

Getting Around

Flying is by far the easiest way to reach Okinawa and to travel between the islands. The flight time from Tokyo is approximately two and a half hours. Naha airport also has direct flights to other parts of Asia. Ferries serve many islands in the archipelago, but journey times are long. It is also possible to take a ferry from Taiwan. There are no train services on any of the islands. Local buses can be slow, so the best way to get around may be to rent a car, scooter, or bicycle.

Yaeyama Islands ⓮

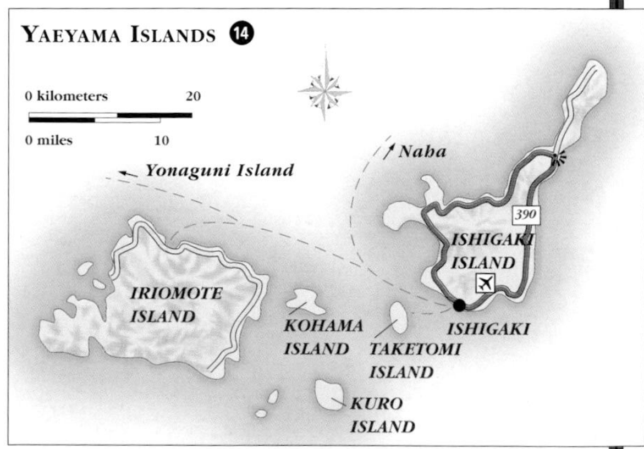

Kokusai-dori, Naha's vibrant main shopping street

Naha City ❶

那覇市

Okinawa Island. 300,000. Tomari and Naha. Airport Terminal 1 (098) 857-6884; Kumoji department store (098) 866-7515. Naha Matsuri (Oct 10).

SHURI, the most historical settlement in Okinawa, was its capital until the islands became part of Japan in 1879, after which Naha was declared the capital. The two cities have since expanded and merged. Naha prospered through its seaborne trade with other parts of Asia and, eventually, the West. The city that emerged from the ruins of World War II is a bustling center, with the archipelago's best restaurants, nightlife, and shopping.

Exploring Central Naha

A long shopping and entertainment thoroughfare in the heart of Naha, **Kokusai-dori** (International Street) typifies the new city, with its boutiques and craft shops selling Okinawan lacquerware, textiles, glassware, and local Tsuboya pottery. The atmosphere along **Heiwa-dori** market street (to the south, off Kokusai-dori) harks back to an older Naha. Started by widows who had lost their husbands in the Battle of Okinawa, the market is full of Asian aromas, crowded alleys, and market stalls selling Okinawan art, crafts, bric-a-brac, and exotic foods.

To the east, along Himeyuri-dori, the pottery quarter of **Tsuboya** dates from the late 17th century. Over 20 workshops still produce wine flasks, tea bowls, and *shisa* (statues of a legendary Okinawan lion, used all over the island as propitious roof ornaments).

Tsuboya pottery from Naha

Also of interest in central Naha are the **Sogen-ji Ishimon Gates**. Although the temple itself, originally an early 16th-century memorial to the Ryukyu kings, was destroyed in the war, three of the original arched stone gates have been restored.

The **Commodore Perry Memorial** by Tomari port marks the point where the commander of the American "black ships" landed on June 6, 1853, leading to the end of Japan's 250-year isolation.

Exploring Shuri

The 500-year-old former capital, 6 km (4 miles) east of central Naha, contains various shrines, temples, ceremonial gates, and fortifications – a reminder of the sophistication of the Ryukyu kingdom. Several fabric factories and workshops, using the specialized *ryusen* and *bingata* dyeing techniques, are open to the public. With over 4,000 exhibits, the **Okinawa Prefectural Museum** is a good introduction to the area's culture, and has the original bells from Shuri Castle and the temple Engaku-ji.

Shuri Castle was the headquarters of the Japanese High command during the war, resulting in its total destruction. **Shurei-mon**, the castle's ceremonial entrance gate, was rebuilt in 1958; as the symbol of Okinawa, it is popular with tour groups. The grand **Seiden** (hall) has also been well restored.

Natural disasters and war have led to the constant rebuilding of **Benzaiten-do** temple, north of the castle park, its foundations dating from 1502. Now it is surrounded by a lotus pond spanned by stone bridges.

The **Kinjocho Stone-Paved Road**, from the reign of King Shin in the 15th century, is an authentic vestige of old Naha, meandering past old red-roofed homes with small tropical gardens enclosed by sturdy coral walls.

Okinawa Prefectural Museum

(098) 884-2243. Tue–Sun.

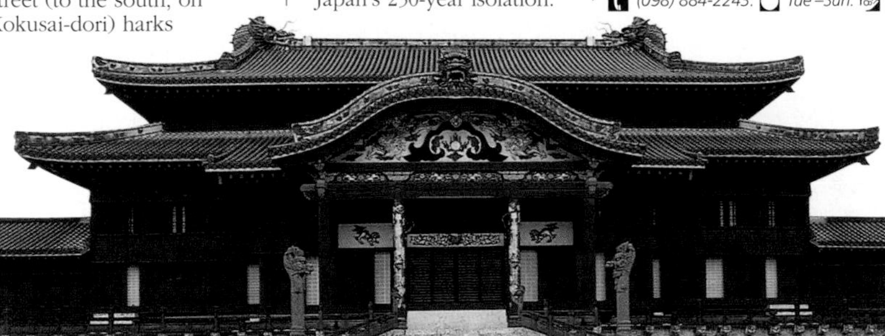

The splendid restored Seiden state hall at Shuri Castle

Cliffs at Cape Kyan, also called Cape of Tragedy

Imperial Navy Underground HQ ❷

旧海軍司令部壕

5 km (3 miles) S of Naha. from Naha bus terminal to Tomigusuku Koen-mae. (098) 850-4055. 8:30am – 6pm daily.

PARTS of the subterranean rooms and tunnels where the Japanese Navy conducted the closing stages of World War II have been restored and opened to the public. The Imperial Navy Admiral was one of over 4,000 men who committed suicide here on June 13, 1945. Many of the officers dispatched themselves by *seppuku* (ritual disembowelment); others used hand grenades – scorch marks can still be seen on tunnel walls.

Okinawa Battle Sites ❸

沖縄戦跡国定公園

15 km (9 miles) S of Naha. bus tour from Naha recommended.

AT THE SOUTHERN END of Okinawa, the scene of the heaviest fighting at the close of World War II, are various battle sites and memorials to victims and those who committed suicide rather than surrender to advancing American forces.

Cape Kyan saw some of the fiercest exchanges. Many locals jumped to their deaths here. To the northeast, **Himeyuri no To** is a much-visited memorial to a group of schoolgirls and teachers who died while working as volunteer nurses during the Battle of Okinawa. A total of 210 people died inside a cave while trying to escape. Others perished from the effects of a gas bomb fired into the cavern, or by suicide. **Konpaku no To**, 2 km (1 mile) south, is a cliffside memorial where 35,000 unknown soldiers and civilians were interred.

The single heaviest loss of life was on **Mabuni Hill**. Now a memorial park, it is dotted with monuments dedicated to both military and civilian dead. A comprehensive display, with photos, memorabilia, and personal accounts of the battle can be seen at the nearby **Peace Memorial Museum**.

Peace Memorial Museum
(098) 997-2874. Tue–Sun.

Gyokusendo Cave ❹

玉泉洞

30 km (19 miles) SW of Naha.

JAPAN'S LARGEST stalactite grottoes were discovered in 1967 by students from Ehime University. With over 460,000 stalactites, this natural fantasia is negotiated with the help of rather slippery pathways and wooden walkways. The stalactites have been likened to giant bamboo, wine glasses, organ pipes, and statues by Rodin. At the center is a pond known as Golden Cup.

The cave lies near the **Gyokusendo Okokumura**, a park and museum with a large snake collection, including the *habu*, Okinawa's most poisonous reptile.

Gyokusendo Okokumura
(098) 949-7421. daily.

Densely packed stalactites in Gyokusendo Cave

The Battle of Okinawa

Kamakazi attack on an American battle ship

Few conflicts in modern history have been fought with such ferocity on both sides as the Battle of Okinawa. The final phase in the Pacific War began when five American divisions, supported by a massive aerial and naval bombardment, landed on Easter Sunday, April 1, 1945. Although logistically outnumbered, the Japanese were well prepared for the attack with a maze of tunnels and shelters. The horrors of these engagements, utilizing flame-throwers, grenades, bayonets, and kamikaze pilots (Japanese suicide bombers), almost defies imagination. By the end of the battle, which lasted 82 days, 13,000 American soldiers and 250,000 Japanese soldiers and civilians had died.

Guest room in the Nakamura House

Nakamura House ❺

中村家

13 km (9 miles) NE of Naha City. *Ryukyu bus 21 to Futenma, then taxi. (098) 935-3500. 9am–5:30pm daily.*

A VISIT to this well-to-do 18th-century farmhouse, now a museum with exhibits about Okinawan daily life, offers rare insights into a more refined style of rural architecture. It consists of five buildings around a stone courtyard. Okinawan masons were renowned, and even the pig pens here, with their finely cut stones, are remarkably well made. A stone enclosure, with a barrier to repel evil spirits – a typical Okinawan feature – faces the entrance. Descendants of the Nakamura family continue to live in the private inner quarters of the house.

Nakagusuku Castle Ruin ❻

中城城跡

13 km (9 miles) NE of Naha City, 5-min walk E of Nakamura House. *(098) 935-5719. 8:30am–5pm daily.*

BUILT BY Lord Gosamaru in about 1450, Nakagusuku, the first stone castle to be built in Japan, is said to have strongly impressed Commodore Perry when he visited the site. The views from here along the east coast of central Okinawa are excellent.

Lord Gosamaru was betrayed by the northern noble Amawari who convinced the Shuri king, falsely, that Gosamaru was raising troops against him. The king sent forces to attack, and Gosamaru chose to commit suicide at his castle rather than oppose a ruler he loyally supported. The only structures to have survived the ravages of time, and the 1458 Amawari Rebellion, are its walls. Passages link three main compounds, each of which is enclosed by high, fortified walls.

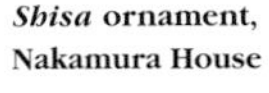

***Shisa* ornament, Nakamura House**

Okinawa Memorial Park ❼

沖縄記念公園

20 km (12 miles) NW of Nago. *Kinenkoen-mae. 9:30am–6pm Fri–Wed. for each attraction.*

THE OKINAWA International Ocean Exposition was held here in 1975; since then several new attractions have been added to this coastal park, which is also known as the Ocean EXPO Park and the Commemorative National Government Park. The **Dolphin Theater** is popular with families who come to see the regular shows. The adjacent **Aquarium** has almost 300 species of fish housed in three sections: tropical, ocean, and deep sea. The **Okinawa Cultures Pavilion** relates the development of the Okinawan people to the maritime culture of Oceania through fishing and navigation exhibits. **Okinawa-kan** specializes in antiques and Ryukyu Kingdom relics, photographic exhibitions, and a fantastic collection of sacred and festival masks.

Expo Land, a large amusement park, has a good strip of sand called Emerald Beach. **Aquapolis** aims to represent a model marine city of the future. More futuristic is the **Tropical Dream Center,** a complex of high-tech greenhouses and botanical gardens.

ENVIRONS: There are several excellent stretches of beach about 30 km (19 miles) to the south of the park, along the coast of **Nago Bay**. Between Cape Busena and Inbu Beach is one of the world's finest underwater observatories, located at the **Busena Resort**. Don't miss its excellent undersea aquarium.

Busena Resort
(0980) 52-3379. daily.

Ie Island ❽

伊江島

5,600. from Motobu port. (0980) 49-2906.

IE IS A PICTURESQUE little island ideal for bicycling. Bike rentals are plentiful, and the whole island can be explored in under eight hours. The north terminates in steep cliffs, while the interior is an expanse of sugarcane, tobacco, and pineapple fields, and old houses with kitchen gardens. **Gusukuyama**, Ie's only hill, provides a first-rate view.

Sea turtle at the Okinawa Memorial Park

View of Ie Island from the entrance to the Memorial Park

The island saw considerable action in World War II. **Nya-teiya-gama**, a cave in the southwest, was used as a shelter by locals during the fighting. The **Ernie Pyle Monument** is dedicated to the US war correspondent who died when his jeep was blown up on the island only a few weeks before the end of the conflict.

Visitors are welcome at the friendly cooperative where locals process the day's catch of fish and seaweed.

Nakijin Castle Ruin 9

今帰仁城跡

bus 66 from Nago bus terminal to Nakijin Joseki (0980) 56-4400. *8:30am–6pm daily.*

THE FOUNDATIONS, gate, and 1,100-m (3,600-ft) stretch of remaining wall give some indication of the original size of Nakijin Castle. It was built in the 14th century by King Hokuzan, founder of the North Mountain Kingdom, an esoteric and short-lived domain.

The entrance, with its flat stone ceiling, is still intact. Because the castle faced the sacred island of **Iheya**, three wooden shrines were built here to allow the local priestesses to conduct rituals, but none has survived. There are stunning views across the East China Sea toward several other offshore islands including the Amami and Yoron groups.

Okinawan Arts and Crafts

Okinawan artists and craftsmen are honored as masters or, in a few rare cases, Living National Treasures. The island's textiles are among the finest in Japan, particularly the linen-dyed *bingata* and *ryusen* fabrics, *bashofu*, and *kasuri*, a high-quality cloth made from the finest natural fibers. Equally, the glossy, black Okinawan lacquerware has been made for over 500 years, using the wood of the indigenous *deigo* tree as a base. New crafts have appeared since the war, most notably Okinawan glassware, its vibrant colors reflecting the island's sparkling coral seas.

Dyeing fabric in a *ryusen* workshop

Kijoka Village 10

喜如嘉村

25 km (16 miles) N of Nago. *300.* *from Nago.* *(0980) 44-3232.*

THE MAIN REASON for a visit to Kijoka village is to watch the making of *bashofu*, a rare textile made of plantain fiber, closely associated with Okinawa. The village is famous for the cloth, which is exported to mainland Japan and sold at prices far above those available direct from the weavers. Unlike traditional Japanese kimonos, Okinawan apparel was made from plain woven cotton, ramie, and lightweight fabrics such as *bashofu*. The stages involved in producing this increasingly scarce linen can be seen at the **Bashofu Kaikan**, a workshop with a high reputation.

Stone lion from Kijoka village

Bashofu Kaikan
(0980) 44-3033. *Mon–Sat.*

Hedo Misaki Cape 11

辺戸岬

50 km (31 miles) N of Nago. *67 from Nago to Hentona.*

THE REMOTE, northernmost point of the island is a wild and breathtaking area of great natural beauty and, mercifully, few tour buses. A grassy plateau runs to the edge of a steep, 100-m (330-ft) high cliff, beyond which are coral reefs. The views of distant Yoron, Iheya, and Izena islands are magnificent.

The road to Hedo Point passes through traditional villages. One of the most interesting is **Ogimi Mura**, renowned for pale yellow *bashofu* cloth. A short distance east of Hedo Point is the village of **Uzahama** and the remains of a prehistoric settlement.

Hedo Misaki, the northernmost cape of Okinawa

Tatami-ishi pentagonal stones on O Island, just off Kume

Kume Island ⓬

久米島

100 km (60 miles) W of Okinawa Island. ✈ from Naha. 👥 9,500. ⛴ from Naha Tomari port. ℹ (098) 985-3431.

Regarded by many as the most beautiful island in the prefecture, volcanic Kume is famous for its sugarcane and pineapple plantations, and Kumejima-*tsumugi*, an exquisite silk pongee. Buses serve many of the island's sights.

The village of **Nakadomari**, in the southwest, boasts the the oldest house in Okinawa. **Uezu-ke** was built in 1726 in the Okinawan samurai style. An extraordinary tree, the **Goeda no Matsu**, which has five separate trunks spanning out, is just a short walk from the house. Rice-planting rituals and prayers for rain are still conducted at **Chinbei-donchi**, the island's foremost shrine, north of Nakadomari. Nearby, the sacred **Yajiya-gama Cave** was used for burials 2,000 years ago.

To the north, the 200-m (650-ft) high **Hiyajo Banta** cliff affords good views toward the Aguni and Tonaki islands and the barrier reef below, one of Kume's outstanding natural sights. The Teida-ishi (sun stone), in a beautiful grove not far from the cliff, was used as a sundial.

Nakazato village, in the east of the island, is one of its most traditional settlements, with several well-preserved buildings. You can see women weaving and dyeing Kume-jima-*tsumugi* here. Nearby **Eef Beach** is Kume's largest resort.

Tiny **O Island** is well worth the 20-minute walk across a connecting bridge from Naka-zato's Tomari port. In the southwest is a mosaic of over 1,000 pentagonal stones, called Tatami-ishi, which resemble flattened tortoise shells.

Miyako Islands ⓭

宮古諸島

330 km (200 miles) SW of Okinawa Island.

Set amid coral reefs in a transparent emerald sea, Miyako consists of eight almost perfectly flat islands. Unique customs and a distinct dialect set the inhabitants of Miyako apart from Okinawan mainlanders. Spared the devastation of World War II, traditional houses are squat, one-story buildings with red-tiled roofs and surrounding coral walls that serve as shelters against typhoons.

Miyako Island

👥 35,000. ✈ from Naha and Ishigaki Island. ⛴ from Naha. ℹ 186 Nishisato, Hirara (09807) 2-0899.

Hirara, with a population of over 30,000, is the island's main business and cultural center and its principal port. North of the port is **Harimizu Utaki** shrine, dedicated to the two gods who created the island. The fascinating **mausoleum** of the 15th-century chieftain Nakasone Toimiya has graves and tombs that combine local styles with the more elaborate Okinawan style. Northeast of Hirara, the **Hirara Tropical Botanical Gardens** contain over 40,000 tree and almost 2,000 plant species from around the world.

In the backstreets of Hirara you can see women drying strips of Miyako-*jofu* indigo cloth, used as a tributary payment when the islands were under nominal Chinese rule. Just north of Hirara is the 1.4-m (55-in) stone, called the **Jintozeiseki**, used to access tax eligibility when the

Sweep of sand at Yonaha Maehama Beach, Miyako Island

islands fell under the suzerainty of the Satsuma domain in the 17th century. When someone grew to the height of the stone they were deemed old enough to start paying taxes.

At the tip of **Higashi Henna** cape on the east coast you can look out over the Pacific Ocean to the left and the East China Sea to the right.

On the southwest coast, facing Kurima island, **Yonaha Maehama Beach**, a 4-km (2-mile) stretch of pristine white sand, offers the island's best swimming, fishing, and diving.

Hirara Tropical Botanical Gardens
(09807) 2-4778. daily.

Other Islands
from Miyako Island.
Mostly set aside for sugarcane plantations, **Kurima** is of interest to ornithologists as sea hawks rest here for a few days in October on their way to the Philippines. The main sight on **Ikema**, off the far north of Miyako, is the Yaebishi reef. Also a seasonal event, it emerges in all its splendor during the low tides of spring.

Off the west coast is **Irabu**, linked by six bridges to neighboring Shimoji. On **Shimoji**, two deep green lakes called Tori-ike are connected to the sea by an underground river and tunnel. Locals believe that the lakes are haunted; for those brave enough, the area is a superb diving locale.

Yaeyama Islands ⓮

八重山諸島

430 km (270 miles) SW of Okinawa Island.

THE YAEYAMAS are Japan's most southerly islands, its last frontier of tourism. Some of the finest scuba diving in Asia is found here.

Ishigaki Island
44,000. from Naha and Miyako. from Naha and Hirara port, Miyako Island. (09808) 2-2809. Angama Festival (Jul 16, Taketomi Island).
Ishigaki's airport and harbor serve the outlying islands in the group. Glimpses of the unique Yaeyama culture can be seen at the **Shiritsu Yaeyama Museum**, near the harbor, which contains ancient ceramics, old Yaeyama-*jofu* textiles, and Polynesian-style canoes. Not far away is **Miyara Donchi,** a superb 19th-century nobleman's home. **Shiraho Reef**, off the southeastern tip of the island, is the world's largest expanse of blue coral. **Kabira Bay** on the north shore, is full of small islets and supports a cultured black pearl industry.

Shiritsu Yaeyama History Museum, Ishigaki Island

Shiritsu Yaeyama Museum
(09808) 2-4712. Tue–Sun.

Miyara Donchi
(09808) 2-2767. Wed–Mon.

Taketomi Island
280. from Ishigaki. (09808) 2-5445.
Meaning "prosperous bamboo," Taketomi is a quiet, unspoiled island. Its neatness stems from an old custom by which it was, and still is, the responsibility of all householders to sweep the street in front of their own property. The island can easily be explored on foot or by bike. Taketomi is famous as the source of *minsa*, an indigo fabric used for kimono belts, which can be seen in the main village. It also has some of Okinawa's best-preserved houses.

To the west, **Kondoi Misaki**, the island's finest beach, has star-shaped sand – the fossilized skeletons of tiny sea animals. The stunning aquamarine waters here support bountiful tropical sealife, and brilliantly colored butterflies swarm around the beach.

A dancer in traditional costume, Ishigaki Island

The orderly, sandy lanes of Taketomi Island village

Iriomote Island
1,900. from Ishigaki. (09808) 2-5445.
Possibly the wildest landmass in Japan, nine-tenths of Iriomote is forest and jungle. Visitors can take cruises along its three rivers, the **Nakama**, **Urauchi**, and **Kuira**, where black oyster beds, mangroves, and tropical trees, including the rare Yaeyama coconut palm, can be seen. The three-stage **Maryudo Falls** end the Urauchi River trip. The island is famous as the last habitat of the Iriomote wild cat.

Yonaguni Island
1,800. from Ishigaki. (09808) 7-2402.
Yonaguni is the ultimate retreat – the last island in the archipelago. Excellent swordfish and bonito fishing provide interest along with Japan's strongest sake – *awamori.*

Northern Honshu

WHEN HAIKU POET MATSUO BASHO *set out in 1689 on his five-month trek in northern Japan, he likened it to going to the back of beyond. Three centuries later,* shinkansen *lines and expressways provide easy access, and the north is as much a part of the information age as the rest of Japan. The region nevertheless retains its quiet, rural image, a place where life is lived at a more congenial pace.*

The backcountry reputation of Northern Honshu belies its rich history. Long ago it was home to indigenous people, who may have been Ainu *(see p281)*. In the 11th century, Hiraizumi was the capital of the Northern Fujiwara clan, rivaling Kyoto in splendor. During feudal times, Morioka, Tsuruoka, Hirosaki, and Aizu-Wakamatsu were thriving castle towns. Foremost, though, was Sendai, ruled by the north's most powerful clan, and now the region's largest city. These and other north-country wonders, such as the shrines and temples of Nikko and Dewa Sanzan, are now tourist attractions. Despite rapid development in recent decades, the region still has much unspoiled natural beauty: rugged mountains, virgin forests, deep lakes, *onsen* (hot-spring resorts), and dramatic coastlines. Towada-Hachimantai, Bandai-Asahi, and Nikko national parks are accessible and exciting destinations for hikers, climbers, campers, and skiers.

Kokeshi doll from Sendai

Known for its excellent rice and fine sake, northern Japan is the country's main rice-producer. Agriculture is now mechanized, but farmers still work hard for a living. Mushrooms in autumn, wild edible vegetables in spring, oysters in winter, and good seafood all year are other reasons to visit the north, while its cool summers provide relief from the heat and humidity farther south. The wealth of crafts and folk arts, such as Nanbu *testsubin* (iron kettles) in Morioka, wooden *kokeshi* dolls, Aizu and Tsugaru lacquerware, *kabazaiku* (cherry-bark craft), and Mashiko pottery, are renowned in Japan and internationally.

One of the extravagant carvings by the Yomeimon gate at Nikko's Tosho-gu Shrine

◁ **The five-story Buddhist pagoda at the start of the climb up Mount Haguro, Dewa Sanzan**

Exploring Northern Honshu

NORTHERN HONSHU is much more rural than Central and Western Honshu. Snow-covered mountains, thick forests, and rice paddies characterize most of the region, with towns and ski resorts fairly evenly scattered. North of the major city of Sendai, tiny pine-covered islands lie in calm bays facing the Pacific Ocean, forming some of the most beautiful coastal scenery in Japan. The six northeastern prefectures of Aomori, Akita, Iwate, Yamagata, Miyagi, and Fukushima make up the area known as Tohoku. This chapter also includes parts of Niigata, Tochigi, Gunma, and Ibaraki prefectures.

A *kabuto-zukuri*-style farmhouse in the grounds of Chido Museum, Tsuruoka

SIGHTS AT A GLANCE

- Aizu-Wakamatsu 4
- Aomori 20
- Bandai-Asahi National Park 6
- Dewa Sanzan 9
- Hanamaki 13
- Hiraizumi 12
- Hirosaki 19
- Kakunodate 16
- Kitakata 5
- Mashiko 3
- Matsushima 11
- Morioka 15
- *Nikko pp258–65* 1
- Nikko National Park 2
- Oga Peninsula 17
- Sado Island 7
- Sendai 10
- Shimokita Peninsula 21
- Tono 14
- Towada-Hachimantai National Park 18
- Tsuruoka 8

SEE ALSO

- ***Where to Stay*** pp305–7
- ***Where to Eat*** pp337–9

Clear waters and the rugged coastline of Sado Island

SAPPORO
SEA OF JAPAN
TOKYO
OSAKA
KYOTO
PACIFIC OCEAN
KAGOSHIMA

LOCATOR MAP

GETTING AROUND

Two main *shinkansen* lines penetrate this region: one from Tokyo to Niigata, the other from Tokyo to Morioka via Sendai. Branch *shinkansen* lines run to Yamagata and Akita. From Morioka, a main line continues north and on to Hokkaido via the Seikan Tunnel. Much slower branch lines – some private – serve towns along both coasts and in the interior. Nikko is an easy day trip from Tokyo; elsewhere allow plenty of time for travel. A rental car is a good option for getting off the beaten track.

PACIFIC OCEAN

0 kilometers 50

0 miles 30

KEY

- International airport
- Domestic airport
- Expressway
- Major road
- JR train line
- Private train line
- Tunnel
- Viewpoint

Weeping cherry trees in Hirosaki

Nikko ❶

日光

OVER 1,200 YEARS AGO, the formidable Buddhist priest Shodo Shonin, on his way to Mount Nantai, crossed the Daiya River and founded the first temple at Nikko. Centuries later, Nikko was a renowned Buddhist-Shinto religious center, and the warlord Tokugawa Ieyasu *(see p261)* chose it for the site of his mausoleum. When his grandson Iemitsu had Ieyasu's shrine-mausoleum Tosho-gu built in 1634, he wanted to impress upon any rivals the wealth and might of the Tokugawa clan. Since then, Nikko, written with characters that mean sunlight, has become a Japanese byword for splendor.

Bato Kannon, with a horse on the headdress, at Rinno-ji Temple

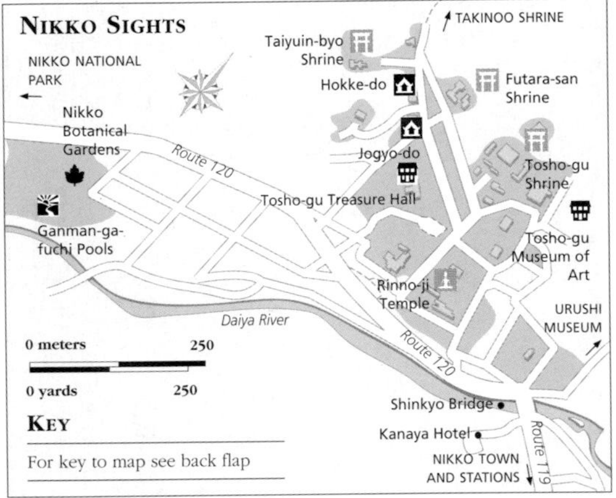

Exploring Nikko Town

Of the two stations in Nikko, the JR station, the oldest in eastern Japan, is a classic. The graceful wooden edifice, built in 1915, was designed by American architect Frank Lloyd Wright. Buses to many of Nikko's sights run from here. The 1-km (about half-a-mile) long avenue from the train stations to the Tosho-gu precincts is lined with shops, restaurants, and inns. A good shop for Nikko wood carvings and *geta* (wooden sandals) is Tezuka, on the left halfway up the street. An architectural treat is the venerable 19th-century Kanaya Hotel *(see p306)*, situated on a rise to the left, just before the Daiya River.

Shinkyo Bridge

for renovation until 2003.

This red-lacquered wooden bridge, just to the left of the road bridge, arches over the Daiya River where, legend has it, Shodo Shonin crossed the river on the backs of two huge serpents. The original, built in 1636 for the exclusive use of the shogun and imperial messengers, was destroyed by flood. The current bridge dates from 1907.

Rinno-ji Temple

daily.

The first temple founded at Nikko, by Shodo Shonin in 766, this was originally called Shihonryu-ji. When it became a Tendai-sect temple in the 17th century, it was renamed Rinno-ji. Its **Sanbutsu-do** (Three Buddha Hall) is the largest hall at Nikko. The three gilt images, of Amida Buddha, Senju (thousand-armed) Kannon, and Bato (horse-headed) Kannon, enshrined in the hall correspond to the three mountain deities enshrined at Futara-san Shrine. Beyond the hall, the nine-ringed bronze pillar, **Sorinto**, contains

The Shinkyo Bridge spanning the Daiya River

1,000 volumes of sutras (Buddhist scriptures) and is a symbol of world peace. The **Treasure Hall** (Homotsuden) has a large and fascinating array of temple treasures, mainly dating from the Edo period. Behind it is the **Shoyoen**, a lovely Edo-style 19th-century stroll garden carefully landscaped for interest in all seasons. Its path meanders around a large pond, over stone bridges, and past mossy stone lanterns.

The Sanbutsu-do hall at Rinno-ji

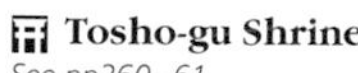

Tosho-gu Shrine

See pp260–61.

Tosho-gu Treasure Hall and Museum of Art

(0288) 54-2558 (Treasure Hall); (0288) 54-0560 (Museum of Art). *daily.*

In the Treasure Hall are shrine treasures along with armor and swords used by the Tokugawa shoguns. In the Museum of Art is an outstanding collection of early 20th-century painted doors and panels by Yokoyama Taikan and others.

Hokke-do and Jogyo-do

These two halls belong to Rinno-ji and house Buddhist relics. Linked by a corridor, they are often referred to as the twin halls.

Futara-san Shrine

daily.

Founded by Shodo Shonin in 782, this shrine is dedicated to the gods of Mounts Nantai (male), Nyotai (female), and Taro, their child. It is actually the main shrine of three; the other two are at Lake Chuzen-ji and on Mount Nantai. The bronze *torii* (gate) here is an Important Cultural Property. More interesting is the tall bronze lantern, which was said to take the shape of a monster at night. The gashes in the lantern are from the sword of a terrified samurai.

Shrine interior at Futara-san

Takinoo Shrine

(0288) 21-0765. *daily.*

A quiet 30-minute uphill walk through the woods via a stone path to the left of Futara-san Shrine, this peaceful, rustic shrine, thought to be dedicated to a female deity, draws women and those looking for love. Toss a stone through the hole in the top of the *torii* (gate) and into the shrine grounds and your wish, they say, will come true.

Painted sliding doors at the Tosho-gu Museum of Art

Visitors' Checklist

Tochigi prefecture. 19,000. JR and Tobu-Nikko lines. at Tobu Nikko stn (0288) 53-4511. Tosho-gu Grand Festival (equestrian archery and 1,000 samurai procession, May 17–18); Tosho-gu Fall Festival (Oct 17).

Taiyuin-byo Shrine

See pp264–5.

Ganman-ga-fuchi Pools

to Sogo-kaikan-mae bus stop.

Lava flows from an old eruption of Mount Nantai combine with the limpid waters of the Daiya River to make these unusual scenic pools, which are a spot sacred to Buddhism. About 70 stone statues of Jizo, the *bodhisattva* of children, line the path by the river. They are known as phantom statues because their numbers always appear to change.

Nikko Botanical Gardens

to Rengeishi bus stop. (0288) 54-0206. Tue–Sun. Dec 1–Apr 14.

Some 3,000 varieties of plants and flowers from Japan and around the world are at these gardens, a branch of the Koishikawa Botanical Gardens of the University of Tokyo. Flora from Nikko National Park are showcased. April to July, when skunk cabbages and irises bloom, is a lovely time to visit.

Urushi Museum

to Marumi bus stop. (0288) 53-6807. Mar 20–Nov 20: Tue–Sun.

This small museum, which opened in 1998 in wooded Ogurayama Park, showcases the lacquer arts of Nikko and Japan – *urushi* is Japanese for lacquer. Used in Japan for over 5,000 years, lacquer has reached the height of refinement only in the past 1,000 years. The museum collection also includes examples of lacquerware from China, India, and Egypt.

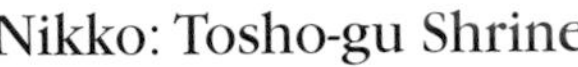

Nikko: Tosho-gu Shrine

Tokugawa Iemitsu set out to dazzle with this mausoleum-shrine for his grandfather Ieyasu. For two years some 15,000 artisans from all over Japan worked, building, carving, gilting, painting, and lacquering, to create this flowery, gorgeous Momoyama-style complex. Almost anything that can be decorated is. Although designated a shrine in the Meiji period, it retains many of its Buddhist elements, including its unusual pagoda, sutra library, and Niomon gate. The famed *sugi-namiki* (Japanese cedar avenue) leading to the shrine was planted by a 17th-century lord, in lieu of a more opulent offering.

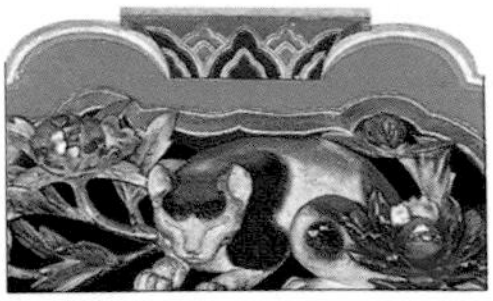

Sleeping Cat Carving
Over an entrance in the east corridor, this tiny, exquisite carving of a sleeping cat is attributed to Hidari Jingoro (Hidari the Left-handed).

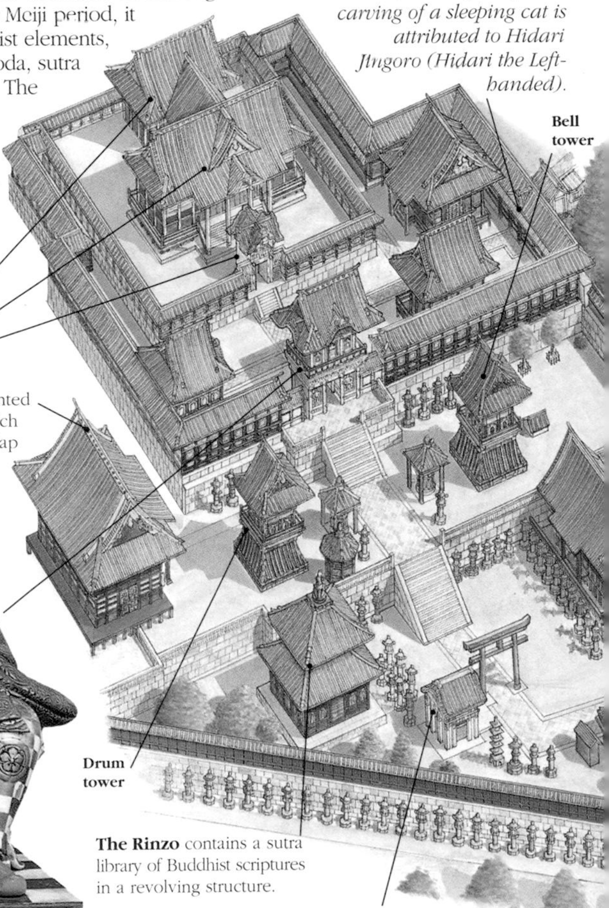

Bell tower

Honden *(inner sanctuary)*

Haiden *(sanctuary)*

The Karamon gate is the smallest at Tosho-gu.

The Honji-do's ceiling is painted with the "crying dragon," which echoes resoundingly if you clap your hands beneath it.

Drum tower

The Rinzo contains a sutra library of Buddhist scriptures in a revolving structure.

★ Yomeimon Gate
Lavishly decorated with beasts and flowers, this gate has one of its 12 columns carved upside-down, a deliberate imperfection to avoid angering jealous spirits. Statues of imperial ministers occupy the niches.

Star Sights

- ★ Yomeimon Gate
- ★ Sacred Stable
- ★ Pagoda

Sacred Fountain
The granite basin (1618), for ritual purification, is covered with an ornate Chinese-style roof.

Tokugawa Ieyasu

Ieyasu (1543–1616) was a wily strategist and master politician who founded the dynasty that would rule Japan for over 250 years. Born the son of a minor lord, he spent his life accumulating power, not becoming shogun until 1603, when he was 60. He built his capital at the swampy village of Edo (now Tokyo), and his rule saw the start of the flowering of Edo culture. He ensured that, after his death, he would be enshrined as a god and *gongen* (incarnation of the Buddha). His posthumous name was Tosho-Daigongen (the great incarnation illuminating the East).

Ieyasu's treasure tower, containing his ashes

Visitors' Checklist

(0288) 54-0560. 8am – 5pm daily (Nov–Mar: to 4pm).

To Ieyasu's tomb and treasure tower

The three sacred storehouses are built according to a traditional design.

The Niomon (or Omotemon) gate is guarded by two fearsome Nio figures, one with an open mouth to pronounce the first letter of the Sanskrit alphabet (ah), the other with a closed mouth for the last letter (un).

★ Pagoda
Donated by a daimyo *(feudal lord) in 1650, this five-story pagoda was rebuilt in 1818 after a fire. Each story represents an element – earth, water, fire, wind, and heaven – in ascending order.*

Ticket office

Granite *torii* (gate)

Entrance

★ Sacred Stable
A carving of the three wise monkeys decorates this unpainted wooden building. A horse given by the New Zealand goverment is stabled here for several hours a day.

The highly ornate Yomeimon gate at the shrine of Tosho-gu ▷

Nikko: Taiyuin-byo Shrine

Finished in 1653, Taiyuin-byo is the mausoleum of Tokugawa Iemitsu (1603–51), the grandson of Ieyasu and powerful third shogun, who closed Japan to foreign commerce and isolated it from the world for over 200 years. Tayuin is his posthumous Buddhist name. If Tosho-gu is splendid, Taiyuin-byo is sublime. Set in a grove of Japanese cedars, it has a number of ornate gates ascending to the Haiden (sanctuary) and Honden (inner sanctuary). The shogun's ashes are entombed beyond the sixth and final gate.

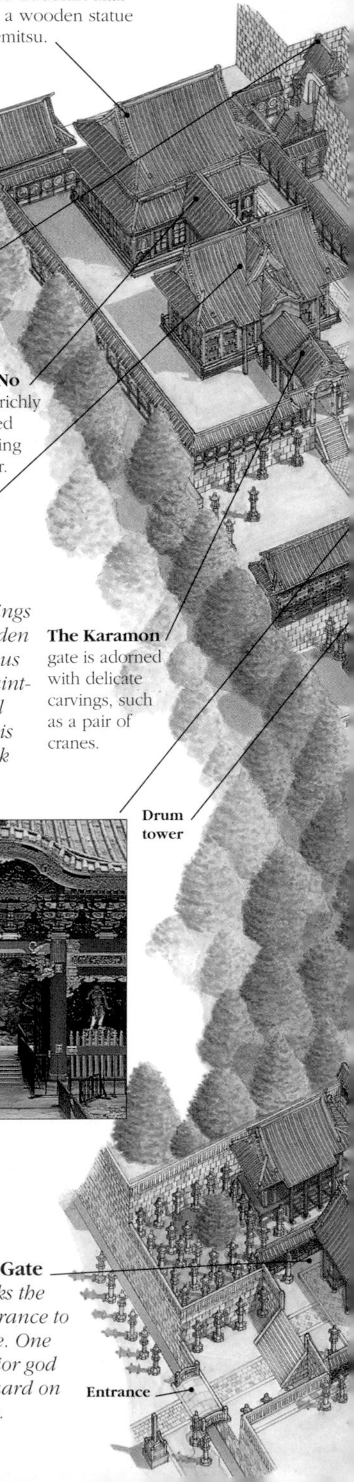

Kokamon Gate
This unusual Ming-dynasty Chinese-style gate, usually closed to the public, is beside the path to Iemitsu's tomb.

The Honden holds a gilded Buddhist altar with a wooden statue of Iemitsu.

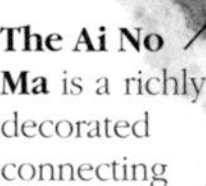

The Ai No Ma is a richly decorated connecting chamber.

★ Haiden
Decorated with carvings of dragons, the Haiden also has some famous 17th-century lion paintings by Kano School painters. Its exterior is decorated with black and gold lacquer.

The Karamon gate is adorned with delicate carvings, such as a pair of cranes.

Drum tower

Yashamon Gate
The third gate is beautifully gilded and contains four statues of Yasha, a fierce guardian spirit. It is also known as Botanmon, or peony gate, after its detailed peony carvings.

Niomon Gate
This marks the main entrance to the shrine. One Nio warrior god stands guard on each side.

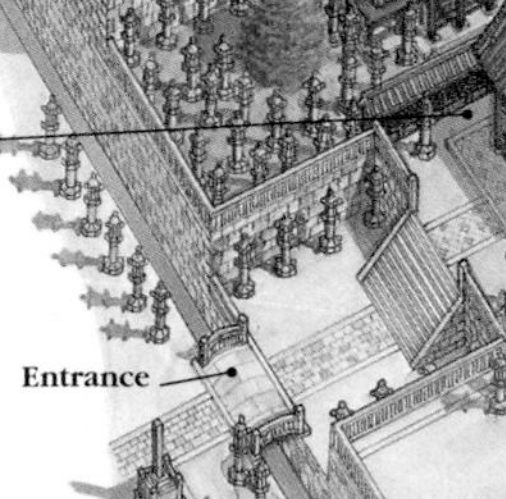

Entrance

VISITORS' CHECKLIST

(0288) 53-1567. 8am–5pm daily (Nov–Mar: to 4pm).

Bell Tower
This structure forms a pair with the drum tower. They are no longer used, but the drum signifies positive/birth, while the bell is negative/death.

★ Nitenmon Gate
Four guardian statues occupy the niches here. At the front are the gods Komoku and Jikoku, while at the back are the green god of wind and the red god of thunder.

Granite Fountain
On the ceiling above the basin is a dragon painting by Kano Yasunobu, which is sometimes reflected in the water below.

Stone lanterns were donated over the years by *daimyo* (feudal lords).

STAR SIGHTS

- **★ Nitenmon Gate**
- **★ Haiden**

A monkey by the roadside, Nikko National Park

Nikko National Park ❷

日光国立公園

Tochigi, Fukushima, and Gunma prefectures. *from Nikko stations.* *(0288) 53-4511.*

THE MAGNIFICENT national park that includes Tosho-gu and its environs is largely a mountainous volcanic plateau, studded with lakes, waterfalls, hot springs, and swamplands. For a taste of Oku-Nikko, the mountainous interior, take the bus west from Nikko to **Lake Chuzen-ji**. The hairpin curves of Irohazaka, along the old ascent to the sacred **Mount Nantai**, start at Umagaeshi (horse return), where pilgrims had to give up their horses and walk. Halfway up, at Akechidaira, there is an excellent view of Mount Nantai, which dominates the lake. At the east end of the lake, the **Kegon Falls**, named for the Buddhist principle of universal unity, cascade 96 m (315 ft) to the Daiya River below. An elevator through the cliff runs to an observation deck at the base of the falls.

At the nearby temple of **Chuzen-ji**, the main image is the Tachiki Kannon, a 1,000-armed Kannon said to have been carved from a live tree by Shodo Shoin, Nikko's founder. On July 31 hundreds of pilgrims make an overnight climb of Mount Nantai, reaching the top by sunrise. **Yumoto**, a lakeside *onsen* town, linked by bus to Nikko station and Lake Chuzen-ji, is one of several spas in the park.

Mashiko ❸

益子

Tochigi prefecture. 25,000. (local trains only). from Tobu-Utsunomiya stn. next to Mashiko stn. Mashiko Hi Matsuri (Pottery/Fire Festival, May 1–5).

KNOWN for its folk pottery, Mashiko was home to the world-famous potter Hamada Shoji (1894–1978), a founder of the *mingei* (folk art) movement. A long stretch of a town, Mashiko has hundreds of pottery shops and workshops. Bicycles are easy to rent and are the best way to explore.

The excellent **Mashiko Reference Collection Museum** contains Hamada's studio and kiln, and his eclectic collection of ceramics and other crafts, housed in beautifully restored local buildings. Moegi and Toko galleries, on the main street, showcase local potters. On the corner, by Toko, is the eighth-generation **Higeta Dyeworks** and its indigo dye vats, sunk in the floor of a thatched workshop.

Mashiko Museum
(0285) 72-5300. Mar–Jan: Tue–Sun.

Higeta Dyeworks
(0285) 72-3165. Mon–Sat.

Shimenawa **(straw rope) at the entrance to Kumano Jinja near Kitakata**

Aizu-Wakamatsu ❹

会津若松

Fukushima prefecture. 120,000. in View Plaza at JR stn. Aizu Aki Matsuri (Fall Festival, Sep 22–24).

ONCE HOME to the north's second most powerful clan, Aizu-Wakamatsu takes pride in its samurai past. With ties to the Tokugawas, the Matsudaira clan bitterly resisted the 19th-century movement to reinstate the emperor. In the 1868 Boshin War, the Byakkotai (White Tigers), a band of teenage samurai fighters against imperial forces, mistakenly thought the castle had fallen and committed mass suicide on **Iimoriyama**, the hill (east of the station) where they are now buried. On the hill is a Pompeian marble column topped by a bronze eagle, sent by Rome in 1928 as a salute from the Fascist party to the Byakkotai.

The main sights are fairly spread out: all-day bus passes are available at the station bus office. **Tsuruga Castle** has been the heart of the city for over 600 years. It was last rebuilt in 1965 as a museum. To the east, the **Samurai Residence** (Buke-yashiki), a good reproduction of a 35-room samurai manor, shows feudal life, down to a 160-year-old rice mill. Nearby, the **Oyakuen** (medicinal herb garden) of a 17th-century villa contains over 200 herbs.

For shopping, Nanuka-machi-dori, which runs east to west, is lined with old shops selling traditional crafts, including painted candles, kites, striped Aizu cotton, and the famed Aizu lacquerware.

Lacquerware bowl from Aizu-Wakamatsu

Tsuruga Castle
to Tsurugajo. (0242) 27-4005. daily. 1st Mon–Thu in July & 1st Tue–Thu in Dec.

Samurai Residence
to Higashiyama. (0242) 28-2525. daily.

Oyakuen
to Higashiyama. (0242) 27-2472. daily. 1st Mon–Thu in Jul & 1st Tue–Thu in Dec.

Kitakata ❺

喜多方

Fukushima prefecture. 37,000. next to JR stn. Suwa Jinja Matsuri (Aug 2–3).

MUD-WALLED *kura* (warehouses) were long used to keep sake, miso, rice, and other provisions from fire, theft, and vermin. Kitakata has more than 2,600, including a *kura*-style temple. Most are tucked away on back streets. South of the **Kai Honke**, a handsome sake-merchant's house with a coffee-shop inside, is a *kura*-lined walking lane. Along the way, the **Sake-Brewing**

Museum offers informative tours, with tastings of Yamatogawa sake. Kitakata is also known for its *ramen* noodles and *oki-agari* dolls, which roll upright when knocked over.

Kai Honke
(0241) 22-0001. *daily.*
Sake-Brewing Museum
(0241) 22-2233. *daily.*

Environs: Seven km (5 miles) south of the station is the remarkable open-air **Kumano Jinja**, an 11th-century shrine restored in the 1970s with natural wood columns supporting a heavy thatched roof.

Souvenir dolls from Kitakata

Bandai-Asahi National Park 6

磐梯朝日国立公園

Yamagata, Niigata, and Fukushima prefectures. *to Fukushima, Koriyama, or Inawashiro.* *at all of the stns.* *Bandai Matsuri (Jul 25–26, Inawashiro).*

On July 15, 1888, Mount Bandai erupted, killing 477 people. Dammed streams formed hundreds of lakes and marshes, creating the lush natural beauty of the Bandai-Asahi National Park. Crisscrossed by five scenic toll roads, including the Bandai-Azuma Skyline (open April 22–November 5), the park is studded with hot springs and camping grounds. The best way to explore is by car or by bus from nearby train stations.

Goshikinuma (five-colored marshes) is a popular 4-km (2-mile) trail starting at the Bandai-kogen or Goshikinuma bus stops. In Inawashiro the **Aizu Minzokukan** folk museum has over 24,000 items, and a garden of phallic rocks associated with fertility.

Aizu Minzokukan
from JR Inawashiro stn. *(0242) 65-2600.* *Apr 1–Nov 15: daily; Nov 16–Mar 31: Fri–Wed.*

Lake on the Bandai-Asahi plateau

Sado Island 7

佐渡島

Niigata prefecture. *80,000.* *ferry or hydrofoil from Niigata (city) to Ryotsu.* *Niigata port (025) 245-1234.* *frequently, spring to fall.*

Though it receives more than a million visitors a year, Sado Island still feels remote. This mellow little island, 60 km (37 miles) off Honshu's northwest coast, offers a chance to enjoy fresh seafood and meet friendly people. For centuries, Sado was home to political exiles, including the emperor Juntoku in 1221, the priest Nichiren in 1271, and Zeami, the Noh actor and playwright, in 1433. Of the 88 Noh theaters once here, about 35 are left. In 1601 the discovery of gold in Aikawa brought an influx of convicts to work as slaves in the mines.

Buses connect the island's small towns, and tour buses stop at major attractions. In the main port of **Ryotsu** in the east, outdoor Noh performances are held at the **Honma Noh Stage**. In **Aikawa**, on the west coast, the touristy **Gold Mine** has mechanical dolls recreating the harsh mining conditions. **Aikawa Museum** has exhibits on gold mining, ragweaving, and the local red-clay pottery.

Recently, the **Kodo** drummers have put Sado on the international map. The group, based in **Ogi**, in the southwest, should be contacted directly for further information. Nearby **Shukunegi**, with outlying rice paddies, is one of the island's loveliest villages.

Gold Mine
to Aikawa Eigyosho. *(0259) 74-2389.* *daily.*
Aikawa Museum
to Aikawa Eigyosho. *(0259) 74-4312.* *daily.* *Dec–Feb: Sat, Sun & nat hols.*
Kodo
148-1 Kaneta Shinden, Ogi-machi, Sado-gun, Niigata 952-0611. *(0259) 86-3630.* www.kodo.or.jp

Clear seas and jagged rocks off the coast of Sado Island

The Kodo Drumming Group

A Kodo drummer beating a huge *o-daiko* drum

Kodo, one of the most famous and dynamic *taiko* drumming groups, formed in 1981, is known for performances of drum, flute, song, and dance. Kodo means both "children of the drum" and "heartbeat". The throbbing heart of Kodo is the *o-daiko*, a convex wooden drum used in Japanese folk festivals. Kodo spends much of the year performing in Japan and worldwide, and hosts an annual three-day Earth Celebration, when international musicians come to Sado to perform.

Tsuruoka ❽

鶴岡

Yamagata prefecture. *100,000.* *outside JR stn (0235) 25-2111.* *Tenjin Matsuri (May 25), Oyama Inu Matsuri (Jun 5).*

GATEWAY TO Dewa Sanzan, Tsuruoka was the Sakai clan's castle seat. Best of this friendly town's attractions is the **Chido Museum**, west of the former castle grounds. It includes a *kabuto-zukuri* (helmet-style) farmhouse, and marvelous folk objects such as lacquered sake caskets, bamboo fishing poles, and decorative straw *bandori* (backpacks). Southeast of the castle is the 1806 **Chidokan**, a school for young samurai. For the famous local painted candles, visit the 300-year-old Togashi Candle Shop.

***Bandori* backpack, Chido Museum**

Chido Museum
(0235) 22-1199. *daily.*

Chidokan
(0235) 23-4672. *Tue–Sun.*

Dewa Sanzan ❾

出羽三山

Yamagata prefecture. *from Shoko Mall near JR Tsuruoka stn.* *Haguro-machi (0235) 62-2111.* **Mt Haguro** *daily.* *Hassaku Matsuri (Aug 31), Shoreisai Matsuri (Dec 31).* **Mt Gassan** *Jul 1–Oct 10.* **Mt Yudono** *late Apr–Nov 3.*

DEWA IS THE OLD NAME for this region and Sanzan are its three mountains – Haguro-san (Mount Black Wing), Gassan (Mount Moon), and Yudono-san (Mount Bath) – opened for religious purposes 1,400 years ago by Hachiko, an imperial prince turned wandering priest. The three are sacred to *yamabushi*, followers of the Shugendo sect.

Millions of pilgrims and sightseers visit Dewa Sanzan on foot or by toll road. The route to the peak of **Mount Haguro** is a climb up the 2,446 stone steps of the Japanese cedar-lined path. Take the bus to Haguro Center to start the climb. At the second stage is a teahouse with a grand view of the Mogami River valley. A side path goes to the ruins of a temple where Basho stayed. At the top is the **Dewa Sanzan Shrine**, an impressive lacquered building with the largest thatched roof in Japan, and Prince Hachiko's tomb. After the 1868 Meiji Restoration, all Shugendo temples were turned into Shinto shrines. The only true Buddhist structure left is the graceful five-story **pagoda** *(see p254)* at the foot of the stone steps.

Mount Gassan, also topped by a shrine, offers alpine flowers and summer skiing. It is a two-hour hike to the top from the Hachigome bus stop. The shrine on **Mount Yudono**, a 2.5-km (2-mile) hike from the Yudonosan Hotel bus stop, has a sacred hot-water spring in which pilgrims bathe their feet. Mummified priests, examples of *sokushin jobutsu* (living Buddhas), can be seen at the temples of **Dainichi-bo** and **Churen-ji**, on the way to Mount Yudono.

Cedar-lined stone steps up to Mount Haguro

Statue of Masamune, Sendai

Sendai ❿

仙台

Miyagi prefecture. *1,000,000.* *at Tohoku Shinkansen stn.* *Sendai Aoba Matsuri (3rd weekend in May), Sendai Tanabata (Weavers' Festival, Aug 6–8).*

LAID OUT in a grid pattern in the 1600s by the dynamic lord Date Masamune, Sendai is the north's largest city. The few historic sights to survive World War II bombing lie outside the town center. **Osaki Hachiman Shrine** is a black lacquer architectural beauty in the northwest of the city. Overlooking the ruins of **Aoba Castle** from 1602 is a statue of the warrior Masamune, nicknamed the "one-eyed dragon." The ruins are set in a park a bus ride to the west of the station at the end of Aoba-dori. Nearby, the ornately carved Date mausoleums at **Zuihoden**, rebuilt after the war, are remarkable replicas of Momoyama-period architecture.

With tree-lined avenues and a dense, lively downtown, modern Sendai is fun. Intriguing shops and restaurants line the shopping arcades Ichibancho and Chuo-dori. Shimanuki, in Ichibancho, on the left as you come from the station, has *kokeshi* dolls and other crafts from all over Miyagi. Gourmets will want to try *hoya* (sea squirt), a regional specialty, at the city's many good seafood eateries.

Buddhist Sects

In the course of 1,500 years or so, since the time that priests from mainland Asia first brought Buddhism *(see pp24–5)* to the archipelago, hundreds of separate Buddhist movements, sects, and subsects developed in Japan. Contrasting beliefs appealed to different groups of nobility, samurai, and commoners, who each adapted practices to their own ends. In the eyes of many foreigners today, Zen, one-time favorite of the samurai, is the quintessential religion of Japan, but it is just one of several major movements originating in China, and is itself subdivided into various sects. Of other movements flowering in Japan, the Tendai and Shingon sects of esoteric Buddhism still have millions of devotees.

Priest, Nara

Zen Buddhism

The Taoist-inspired Chan school from China first gained popularity in Japan during the Kamakura period (1185–1333). There are three main Zen sects: Soto, Rinzai, and Obaku. All place emphasis on *zazen* (sitting meditation) and self-help. As developed in the great Zen temples of Kyoto during the feudal era, the rigorous mindset and uncluttered aesthetics of Zen have had a profound influence on Japanese culture at large.

Zen gardens *express a sublime harmony between humanity and nature.*

At Zuiho-in, *a subtemple of the great Zen temple Daitoku-ji* (see p167) *in Kyoto, priests use percussion instruments while chanting the sutras as part of their daily training.*

Shingon

This branch of esoteric Mahayana Buddhism was founded in Japan in the 9th century by Kukai *(see p223)*. It incorporates such Hindu elements as mandalas and multi-armed deities, and places emphasis on hand gestures *(mudra)* and the chanting of mantras. The headquarters are at Mount Koya *(see p193)*, and there are 50 or so subsects today.

Shingon sect follower

Shingon deity from Mount Koya *displaying the* yogan semui-in *mudra with the hands.*

Tendai

Brought to Japan in the 9th century by Saicho, Tendai is another branch of esoteric Buddhism and places emphasis on selfless devotion. From its base at Mount Hiei, Tendai helped spawn the Jodo (Pure Land), Jodo Shin, and Nichiren sects.

The Amida Buddha *(Amida Nyorai) of the Tendai sect leads the way to the Pure Land.*

Shugendo

Dewa Sanzan in Northern Honshu is the most sacred site for the Shugendo sect. This offshoot of Shingon combines Buddhism and Shinto, and promotes ascetic practices on mountain retreats.

Yamabushi **(ascetic) Shugendo-sect Dewa Sanzan**

Irregularly shaped pine-covered islands in Matsushima bay

Matsushima ⓫

松島

Miyagi prefecture. *17,000.* *to Shiogama and Matsushima-Kaigan.* *from Shiogama.* *outside JR Matsushima-Kaigan stn (022) 354-2618.* *Toronagashi Hanabi Taikai (floating lanterns, Aug 15), Osegakie (Consolation Festival, Aug 16, Zuigan-ji).*

TAKE A HINT from Matsuo Basho's 1689 visit to the bay of Matsushima and make Shiogama your starting point. The fishing grounds off Miyagi are among the world's richest, and the busy **Shiogama Wholesale Fish Market**, active from early morning until about 1pm, is known for its huge tuna auctions. Dedicated to both mariners and mothers-to-be is the beautiful hilltop **Shiogama Shrine**. Make time to lunch at one of Shiogama's superb sushi restaurants before taking the ferry to Matsushima.

Dotted with hundreds of islets, Matsushima bay has been known for centuries as one of Japan's "three famous views." Now, however, it is clogged with sediment and marred by forgettable tourist venues. In Matsushima itself is **Zuigan-ji**, a handsome Zen training temple; its carved kitchen and corridors are National Treasures. One side of its wooded grounds is lined with meditation caves.

Hiraizumi ⓬

平泉

Iwate prefecture. *10,000.* *next to JR stn (0191) 46-2110.* *Fujiwara Matsuri (May 1–5 & Nov 1–3).*

NINE HUNDRED years ago, the Northern Fujiwara clan, under Fujiwara Kiyohira, made this small town into a cultural and economic capital, second only to Kyoto. Three generations later, Hiraizumi was in ruins. Yoshitsune, Japan's archetypal tragic hero, sought refuge here from Yoritomo, his jealous brother and Japan's first shogun, but was betrayed by Yasuhira, the last Fujiwara leader, and killed. Yoritomo then turned against Yasuhira and had the clan wiped out.

At its peak, Hiraizumi had a population of 100,000. Wishing to create a Buddhist paradise on earth, Kiyohira enriched the 9th-century temples Chuson-ji and Motsu-ji. **Chuson-ji** is 10 minutes by bus from the station, followed by a long climb lined with towering Japanese cedars. Only two of its many original buildings remain: the small **Golden Hall**, splendid with gold leaf, lacquer, and mother of pearl, where the first three Fujiwara leaders are buried; and the **Sutra Hall**. In the **Treasure Hall** are remarkable treasures from the Fujiwara coffins and the temple.

All that remains of the original **Motsu-ji** (a 5-minute bus ride from the station) are its foundations and beautiful Heian-period paradise garden, the best in Japan.

Steps up to Hiraizumi's Golden Hall at Chuson-ji, Hiraizumi

Hanamaki ⓭

花巻

Iwate prefecture. *72,000.* *at JR Shin-Hanamaki and JR Hanamaki stns.* *Hanamaki Matsuri (Fri–Sun, weekend of the 2nd Sat in Sep); Kenji Sai (Kenji Festival, Sep 21).*

MIYAZAWA KENJI (1896–1933), one of Japan's best-loved writers, was born in Hanamaki, a thriving *onsen* town. He wrote more than 1,200 poems and 90 children's stories, and worked selflessly to improve conditions for poor farmers in Iwate. Each year some 250,000 people visit the **Miyazawa Memorial Museum**. Exhibits reflect Kenji's lifelong interests in minerals, astronomy, wildlife, agriculture, Esperanto, and Buddhism. There is also a quirky little garden and the Ihatov, a free arts and research center. Ihatov was Kenji's Esperanto name for Iwate.

Miyazawa Memorial Museum
(0198) 31-2319. daily.

A wooden *torii* (gate) to Mount Hayachine

Tono 14

遠野

Iwate prefecture. 28,000
by JR stn (0198) 62-1333.
Tono Matsuri (Sep 14–15).

IN TONO PEOPLE STILL LIVE in rhythm with nature, and observe old ways and traditions. Much has changed, though, since folklorist Yanagita Kunio compiled the *Legends of Tono* in 1910. Few of the *magariya* (L-shaped houses, shared by people and horses) are left, but the mountains ringing the Tono basin are still beautiful. Storytellers tell the age-old story of *oshirasama*, about a young woman falling in love with a horse.

Tono is divided into the town center and seven outlying districts. Attractions are best reached by car or bicycle, both of which can be rented at the station. At the private **Nakayama House**, in Kamigo district, you can see wonderful 350-year-old *oshirasama* dolls. The **Municipal Museum** in the town center introduces local folkways. At **Denshoen**, a mellow tourist venue in Tsuchibuchi district, local experts teach traditional crafts. A short walk away are **Kappabuchi** stream and the temple of **Joken-ji**, both traditionally the home of *kappa* (water imps). **Hayachine Shrine**, a 30-minute drive from the station in Tsukimoushi district, is known for its Kagura (sacred dances), and **Mount Hayachine** is popular with climbers. Most evocative is the **Ravine of the 500 Rakan** (Buddha's disciples), a 10-minute drive west of town, with natural boulders carved centuries ago to appease the souls of famine victims.

Japanese Dolls

More than a thousand years ago, simple cloth dolls called *sarukko* were attached to babies' clothing as charms against harm. The thousands of clay dolls unearthed at Jomon-period sites are also believed to have had symbolic functions. These dolls remind some scholars of *oshirasama* dolls – stick figures, usually of a horse and a girl, made of mulberry or bamboo and draped in layers of cloth – still found, and venerated, in parts of northern Japan. Other favorites include: the limbless painted *kokeshi* dolls, made by woodturners at *onsen* towns around northern Japan; *ohinasama*, the elaborate tiered arrays of silk court dolls displayed each Girls' Day (March 3); and *anesan ningyo* (big sister dolls), ingenious figures folded from paper.

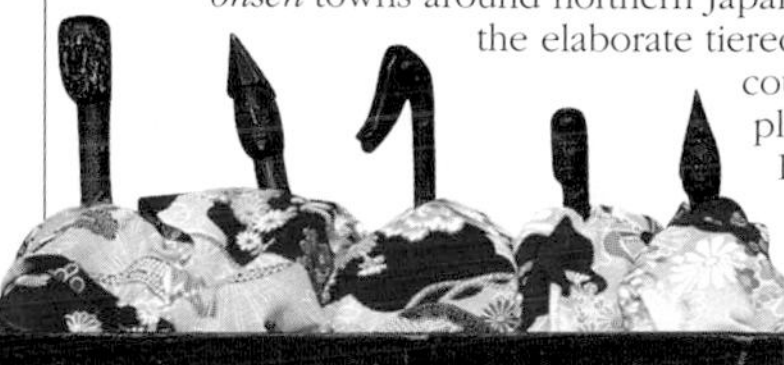

***Oshirasama* dolls in Tono's Nakayama House**

Morioka's "stone-splitting" tree

Nakayama House
(0198) 65-2609. phone for appointment.

Municipal Museum
(0198) 62-2340. Tue–Sun. Nov–Mar: last day of month; New Year, 2nd Mon in Jan, Feb 11, Mar 1–4, Nov 24–30, Dec 23.

Morioka 15

盛岡

Iwate prefecture. 290,000.
2nd flr, JR stn (019) 651-3111.
Chagu-chagu Umakko (Horse Festival, Jun 15).

AN OLD CASTLE TOWN, once the center of the Nanbu domain, Morioka is now Iwate's capital and a transportation hub for the north, known for its Nanbu *tetsubin* (iron kettles) and Mount Iwate, the majestic volcano overlooking it. In October salmon run up the Nakatsu River, one of three bisecting the city.

Nanbu iron kettle

All that remains of **Morioka Castle**, in Iwate Park, are its stone walls and moats. Nearby is the "stone-splitting" cherry tree. Over Nakatsu River is the **Morihisa Iron Studio**, with superb iron pieces. For folk crafts, head for **Konya-cho** (dyers' street), to the north, and **Zaimoku-cho** (lumber street), to the left across Asahi bridge. A 30-minute bus ride northeast is **Morioka Hashimoto Art Museum**, with a wide range of Western and Japanese art.

Morihisa Iron Studio
(019) 622-3809. daily.

Morioka Hashimoto Art Museum
(019) 652-5002. daily.

Kakunodate ⑯

角館

Akita prefecture. 15,000.
outside JR stn (0187) 54-2700.
Aki Matsuri (Fall Festival, Sep 7–9).

FAMED FOR ITS SAMURAI quarter and weeping cherry trees, Kakunodate has only a sprinkling of its original samurai houses remaining on Uchimachi, to the northwest of the station. However, the broad avenue, faced with the gated houses, wonderfully evokes the past. More than 150 of the weeping cherries on Uchimachi, brought from Kyoto almost 300 years ago, have been designated National Natural Treasures.

Among the samurai houses that are open to the public, the large **Aoyagi-ke** has three small museums in its grounds. Look for the ceilings painted with waves as protection from fire. At the classic **Ishiguro-ke**, known for its beautiful garden, note the transoms between rooms, carved to project shadows by candle-light. Also on Uchimachi, the red-brick **Denshokan Museum** has exhibits of historical and craft items and demonstrations of outstanding local crafts, including *kabazaiku* (objects of polished cherry bark) and *itayazaiku* (baskets and folk objects woven of split maple).

Aoyagi-ke
(0187) 54-3257. daily.

Ishiguro-ke
(0187) 55-1496. daily.

Denshokan Museum
(0187) 54-1700. daily.

Looking into the garden from Ishiguro-ke samurai house, Kakunodate

Oga Peninsula ⑰

男鹿半島

Akita prefecture. JR Oga stn.
next to JR Oga stn (0185) 23-2111. Namahage Sedo Matsuri (Feb 13–15); Namahage (Dec 31).

KICKING 20 KM (12 miles) into the Sea of Japan, this foot-shaped peninsula has a scenic rocky coastline, pleasant little fishing villages, good seafood, and hills covered with Akita cedar. The lookout on **Mount Kanpu**, at the neck of the peninsula, offers a panoramic view of mountains, sea, and spreading rice fields. The peninsula is best known for its Namahage Festival, held on New Year's Eve, when men dressed in horned demon masks and bulky straw coats go from house to house, scaring children into being good and idlers into working. A tourist version of the festival, the Namahage Sedo Matsuri, is held at **Shinzan Shrine**, in the city of Oga.

Towada-Hachimantai National Park ⑱

十和田八幡平国立公園

Akita, Aomori, and Iwate prefectures.
JR Morioka & JR Aomori stns.
from stns to Lake Towada. 2nd flr, JR Morioka stn (019) 625-2090.

TOUCHING THREE prefectures, the Towada-Hachimantai National Park is in two sections with the mountainous Hachimantai section 60 km (37 miles) south of the Towada section. Car is the best way to get around: trains are limited and buses not available in winter. **Hachimantai** offers hiking and ski trails, frozen lava flows, alpine flora, and mountain views. A favorite with Japanese tourists, it has scenic toll roads, hot-spring and ski resorts, and a variety of tourist facilities. Good stopping places include **Goshogake** *onsen*, **Higashi-Hachimantai** ski complex, and the tourist village of **Putaro**.

In the **Towada** section highlights include **Lake Towada**, a lovely caldera lake. Its symbol, a statue of two maidens (1953) by Takamura Kotaro, is on the southern shore. More dramatic is the 9 km (6-mile) **Oirase Gorge** to the east of the lake. While it is possible to travel the gorge by bus, car, or bike, it is best to get off the busy highway and walk. Also impressive are Towada's virgin beech forests, rightly dubbed an ocean of trees. North of the lake are some atmospheric spa inns, such as the excellent Tsuta Onsen *(see p306)*.

Beech forest in the Towada section of Towada-Hachimantai National Park

Hirosaki ⓳

弘前

Aomori prefecture. *180,000.* *Kankokan, Otemon Square (0172) 37-5501.* *Neputa Matsuri (Aug 1–7).*

LONG THE CULTURAL and educational center of Aomori, Hirosaki is a delight to explore, its main attraction being its castle, a pocket of feudal history in a thriving modern city. Most streets lead, more or less, to **Hirosaki Park**, the old castle grounds of the Tsugaru lords, to the northwest of the station. The castle was destroyed by lightning but its picturesque 1810 keep, some smaller towers, several gates, and three moats remain. **Kamenokomon**, the imposing main gate, is on the north, where historic samurai houses still stand. Nearby is the **Tsugaruhan Neputa Mura**, displaying the Neputa floats used in Hirosaki's more refined version of Aomori's Nebuta festival. The wooded castle park is famous for its cherry blossoms, at their best in late April. The **Municipal Museum**, inside the park, has exhibitions of local history, including old photographs of the Neputa Festival.

One of the temples en route to Chosho-ji, Hirosaki

Twenty-two temples line the approach to **Chosho-ji**, the family temple of the Tsugaru, about a 15-minute walk southwest of the park, built on a bluff overlooking the Hirosaki plain and Mount Iwaki. Its handsome two-story gate has extra-deep eaves because of the heavy snows common in the area. A side hall contains interesting polychrome statues of the Buddha's 500 disciples. The naturally mummified body of the 12th Tsugaru lord is displayed in the main hall.

Like most feudal towns, the streets around the castle were designed to twist and turn to confuse enemy forces. The large **Kankokan** (municipal information center) just south of the park is a good place to get oriented. It also has displays of local crafts. Other good craft outlets include Tanakaya, on the corner of Ichiban-cho, which has a fine selection of traditional and contemporary Tsugaru lacquerware. Miyamoto Kogei, on Minami Sakura-cho, handles baskets of *akebi*, a vine that grows wild in the mountains. Not to be missed is the bar-restaurant Yamauta *(see p338)*.

Tsugaruhan Neputa Mura
NE corner outside castle park.
(0172) 39-1511. *daily.*

Municipal Museum
(0172) 35-0700. *Tue–Sun.*

Chosho-ji
(0172) 32-0813. **Main hall** *Apr–mid-Dec: daily (at other times by appointment).*

Reconstructed dwellings at Sannai-Maruyama

Aomori ⓴

青森

Aomori prefecture. *295,000.* *in JR stn (0177) 34-1111.* *Nebuta Matsuri (Aug 2–7).*

REBUILT AFTER World War II, Aomori is a nondescript city with two outstanding attractions. One is the Nebuta Matsuri *(see p42)*; the other **Sannai-Maruyama**, a Jomon-period (10,000–300 BC) archaeological site. Since its discovery in 1993, the site has yielded invaluable relics and ruins from 4,000–5,500 years ago, including a woven pouch, red lacquerware, and clay figures. Most impressive are the reconstructed pit dwellings and a standing-pillar building.

Sannai-Maruyama
from JR stn to Unten Menkyo Center. *(0177) 22-1111.* *daily.*

Shimokita Peninsula ㉑

下北半島

Aomori prefecture. *JR Tanabu stn at Mutsu.* *at JR Tanabu stn.*

THIS AX-SHAPED peninsula offers unspoiled beauty. In the interior is the desolate **Osorezan** (Mount Dread), one of three Japanese mountains sacred to spirits of the dead, with a crater lake and sulfur hot springs. It is open from May to October. Blind mediums communicate with the spirits from July 20–24. Take the ferry from Sai along the west coast to **Hotoke-ga-ura** (Buddha Coast) with sea-worn cliffs and rock formations. In the southwest the port of **Wakinosawa** is home to sassy snow monkeys. A ferry runs from here to Aomori.

MATSUO BASHO AND HAIKU

Matsuo Basho (1644–94), a master of style and a thinker to whom life and art were one, perfected the haiku form. Originating in Japan, haiku is now practiced internationally. A classical haiku is 17 syllables (written 5-7-5), includes a seasonal word, and refers to an objective image in the present. Basho spent most of his life traveling and writing haiku. His most famous travel journal, a superb guide to northern Japan, is *The Narrow Road to the Deep North*, about his five-month pilgrimage in 1689; the northernmost point of his journey was Akita prefecture.

Statue of Basho

HOKKAIDO

*J*APAN'S NORTHERNMOST ISLAND *is on the Pacific "ring of fire" at the southern edge of the Okhotsk Sea. Russia lies to the north, west, and east, while the deep Tsugaru Strait to the south separates Hokkaido from Honshu. With both sea-ice and active volcanoes, it is truly a land of fire and ice. Dramatic peaks, gorges, and lakes all contribute to making Hokkaido the part of Japan where nature is at its most vivid.*

First settled 20,000 years ago, this remote northern island became the only homeland of the indigenous Ainu people after the 12th century. The Japanese made early forays to Yezo, as the island was called, from 659, but it was perceived as remote, inhospitable, and cold. For centuries only the persecuted Ainu, refugee warriors, and banished criminals lived here. In the late 1860s, however, the new Meiji government decided officially to settle the island. Thereafter it became known as Hokkaido, or "north sea road."

Skiing in central Hokkiado

Since then, the population has risen to just under 6 million. The few Ainu left number somewhere between 24,000 and 60,000. Fishing, farming, forestry, and mining are the main industries, but tourism draws several million people north each year.

Sapporo, the capital, is a lively, fast-growing city, home to spectacular festivals. Outside Sapporo, the lifestyle of the Ainu is about the only point of cultural and historical interest for the visitor. By contrast, numerous national parks offer boundless opportunities for outdoor enthusiasts, including camping, hiking, and hotspring bathing. Extensive forests, broad mountain ranges, numerous lakes and wetlands, and a long coastline support a wealth of plant, animal, and birdlife.

The prevailing winter winds blow in from Siberia, resulting in a sub-arctic winter climate, with temperatures sometimes dropping to -30°C (-22°F). This means a guaranteed snow season with perfect powder snow for skiers. Between May and September temperatures rise into the 20s (70s Fahrenheit).

Nighttime scene in Suskino, the entertainment district of Hokkaido's modern capital, Sapporo

◁ **Dramatic view of Sounkyo gorge, in Daisetsu-zan, Japan's largest national park**

Exploring Hokkaido

Just five percent of the Japanese population has settled on Japan's second-largest island, mainly in the capital, Sapporo, and the port of Hakodate. Volcanic mountains, caldera lakes, and rocks stained by yellow sulfur characterize the wild interior, while forests and wetlands provide breeding grounds for wildlife. Wildflowers are bountiful on coasts and mountains in spring and summer. Information in English is scarce outside Sapporo and Hakodate, and distances between sights are great, so planning ahead is essential if time is limited. Allow at least a week to explore the island.

Hakodate harbor and city from Mount Hakodate

Getting Around

Sapporo international airport is the main gateway to Hokkaido and also offers internal flights to many parts of the island. Hokkaido is connected by rail to Honshu via a 25-km (16-mile) tunnel; it is possible to take an overnight train all the way from Tokyo to Sapporo. Several JR rail lines cover the island, offering relatively fast links. Buses run to many destinations, although a car or bicycle provides more flexibility. Numerous hiking routes crisscross the national parks.

Key

- International airport
- Domestic airport
- Expressway
- Major road
- Minor road
- JR line
- Tunnel
- Viewpoint

Sights at a Glance

Akan National Park 8
Akkeshi Bay 10
Daisetsu-zan National Park 7
Hakodate 1
Kushiro Wetlands National Park 9
Lake Furen 11
Nemuro Peninsula 12
Niseko Ski Resort 3
Onuma Quasi-National Park 2
Rishiri Rebun-Sarobetsu National Park 6
Sapporo 5
Shikotsu-Toya National Park 4
Shiretoko National Park 13

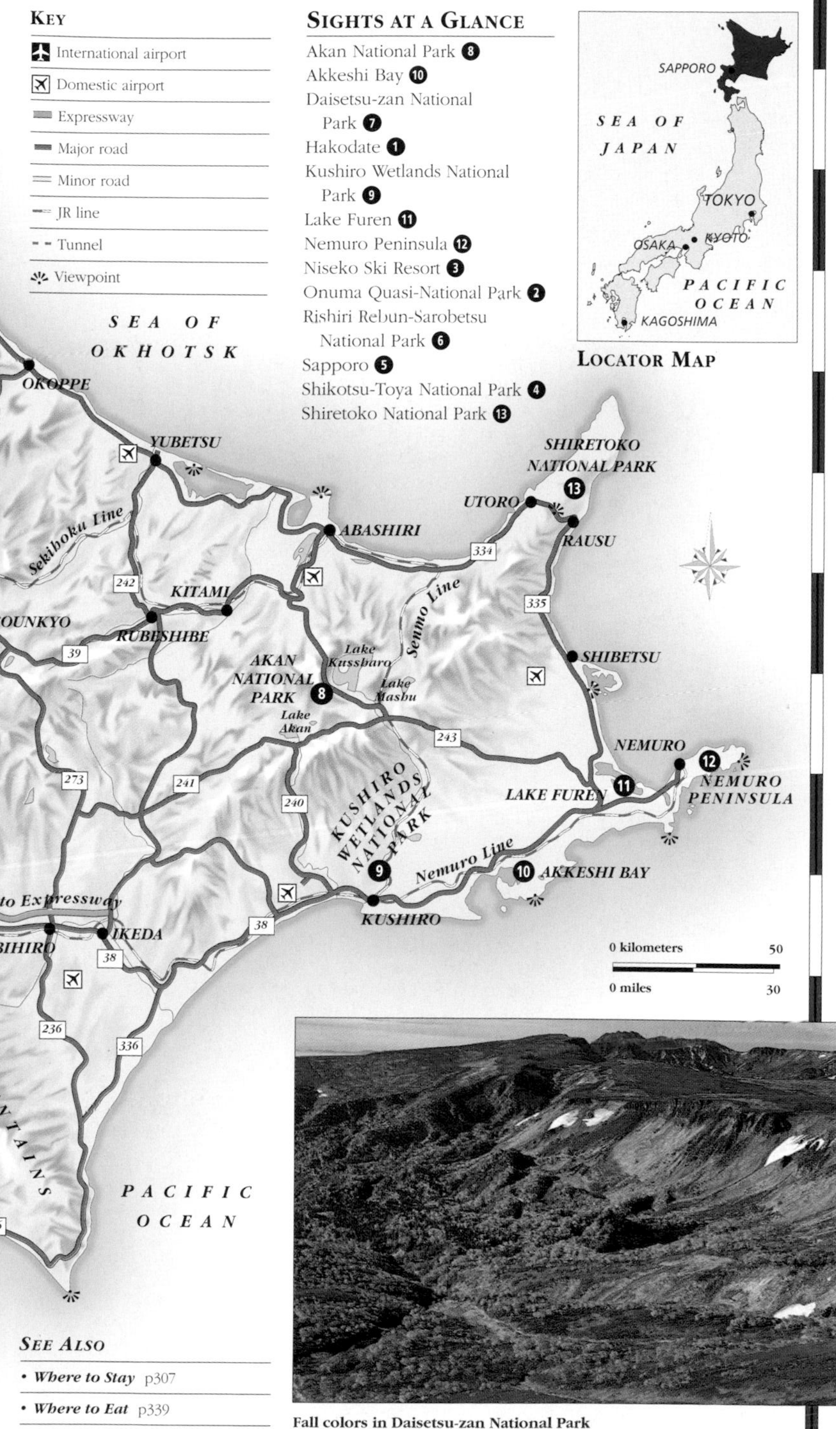

Fall colors in Daisetsu-zan National Park

See Also

- *Where to Stay* p307
- *Where to Eat* p339

Blossom-viewing in Hakodate's Goryokaku Park

Hakodate ❶

函館

290,000. Hakodate. from Sapporo. from Aomori. next to stn (0138) 23-5440. www.hakodate.or.jp/city/index.htm Hakodate Port Festival (Aug 1–5).

ONCE AN ISLAND, the fan-shaped city of Hakodate now straddles a low sandbar that links it to the mainland. In 1854, Hakodate was designated one of the first treaty ports in Japan. Fifteen years later the city was the scene of one of the last battles heralding the Meiji Restoration.

Within easy reach of the center is **Mount Hakodate**, the peak of which can be reached by cable car, road, or on foot. There are pleasant country walks and spectacular panoramas – at night the shimmering city lights can be seen fanning out between two dark arms of the sea.

The quiet **Motomachi** district, nestling beneath Mount Hakodate in the south of the city, is the most attractive area. Western-style buildings are a feature here, a legacy of the treaty-port status. They include the **Old Public Hall**, with its stately blue-and-yellow clapboarding; the **Russian Orthodox Church** with its spire and onion domes; and, nearby, the **Old British Consulate**.

In the north, **Goryokaku Park** provides a peaceful haven for strolling, and its more than 1,500 cherry trees create a popular springtime spectacle. The pentagon-shaped **Goryokaku Fort** was built in 1865 to defend against the Russians, but it fell to imperial forces in 1869.

ENVIRONS: Hot-spring enthusiasts will want to stay at the *onsen* resort of **Yunokawa** 15 minutes from the center. An hour's drive to the east of the city is the still-active **Mount Esan** volcano, with nearby azalea gardens, and densely forested slopes.

Onuma Quasi-National Park ❷

大沼国定公園

Onuma-Koen stn. from Hakodate. next to stn (0138) 67-2170.

THREE LARGE, islet-studded lakes – Onuma, Konuma, and Junsainuma – are surrounded by forest and form the Onuma Quasi-National Park. Deer and foxes inhabit the forests, and the lakes support several kinds of waterfowl, particularly during the spring and fall migrations. Wildflowers are abundant in summer, while overhead Latham's snipe perform the bizarre zigzag display flights that earn them the local name of "lightning bird." The graceful form of **Mount Komagatake** provides a stunning backdrop to the north.

An easily followed hiking trail from the north side of Lake Onuma to the upper mountain provides a fabulous view of southwestern Hokkaido.

Niseko Ski Resort ❸

ニセコスキーリゾート

Niseko stn. from Sapporo.

SOME OF JAPAN'S BEST skiing can be found in the Niseko Mountains. Snowboarders and skiers alike favor this area for its long, cold winter season, numerous slopes, and quality off-piste powder. In summer it offers adventure-sports vacations. At **Hirafu**, the main ski runs are linked physically but run by competing companies – you need to buy a separate pass for each. The beauty of the slopes is not matched by the resort – its cluster of hotels and pensions lacks style, and few facilities are available outside the package accommodations.

Shikotsu-Toya National Park ❹

支笏洞爺国立公園

Toya stn. from Sapporo. at Toya stn (0142) 75-2446.

THE DISJOINTED Shikotsu-Toya National Park is like an open-air museum to vulcanology. It contains the 1,900-m (6,230-ft) high **Mount Yotei** (also known as Ezo-Fuji, due to its conical shape), two large crater lakes, and the

Mount Komagatake across Lake Onuma

spa towns of **Jozankei** in the north and **Noboribetsu** in the south. Summer weekends and fall tend to be busy with visitors from nearby Sapporo.

By **Lake Shikotsu** is the popular hot-spring resort of **Shikotsu Kohan**, as well as the remarkable moss-covered **Kokenodamon** gorge. The lake is dominated to the north by the rugged peak of **Mount Eniwa**, and to the south by the recumbent forms of **Mount Fuppushi** and **Mount Tarumae**, with its cinder cone.

Lake Toya, 40 km (25 miles) farther southwest, contains the picturesque central island of Oshima and three smaller satellite islands. Nearby stands Japan's youngest volcano, the bare-sloped **Showa Shinzan** (formed 1943–5), beside the extremely active **Mount Usu**.

The mountains in the park make for rewarding day hiking; trails are well defined, and the views from the tops of Eniwa and Tarumae are superb.

Sapporo ❺

札幌

1,600,000. Shin-Chitose. Okadama. Sapporo International Communication Plaza (011) 211-3678; booth in stn (011) 213-5062. www.city.sapporo.jp/english/indexe.html Snow Festival (1 week, early–mid-Feb); Hokkaido Shrine Festival (Jun 14–16); Summer Festival (Jul 21–Aug 20); Bon Odori (mid-Aug).

CAPITAL OF HOKKAIDO, the modern city of Sapporo lies on the Ishikari plain, straddling the Toyohira River. Four subway lines, street cars, and a well laid-out grid structure make getting around fairly straightforward. At Sapporo's heart lies the long **Odori Park**, dominated at the east end by the metal television tower and at the west by a view to the mountains. One block north, opposite the historic wooden **Tokei-dai** clocktower, is the **Sapporo International Communication Plaza**, an essential stop for information on travel all over Hokkaido, with friendly staff to help with planning and booking.

Neon lights in Sapporo's busy Susukino district

The city gives its name to the famous local beer; its brewing is shown at the **Sapporo Beer Garden and Museum** south of the station *(see p339)*. Nightlife is focused in the **Susukino** area, two stops south of the station on the Nanboku subway line, with thousands of restaurants and bars. Local specialties include "Genghis Khan" – mutton and vegetables barbecue-grilled in a cast-iron pan.

A huge collection of Ainu artifacts is displayed at the **Ainu Museum** in the **Botanical Gardens**. The gardens themselves are a refreshingly quiet spot, with a representative collection of Hokkaido's flora. The large-scale outdoor sculptures at the **Sapporo Art Park**, set amid wooded hills, make for an interesting hands-on excursion.

Sapporo Beer Museum
(011) 731-4368. daily.

Botanical Gardens and Ainu Museum
10-min walk SW of stn. *(011) 221-0066. Apr 29–Nov 3: Tue–Sun.*

Sapporo Art Park
(011) 592-4123. daily. Nov 4–Apr 28: Mon.

ENVIRONS: Lying 14 km (9 miles) east of the city, the excellent **Historical Village of Hokkaido** commemorates the official settlement of the island in the 1860s. This cluster of over 60 evocatively restored late 19th-century buildings has been gathered from around Hokkaido. Some contain interesting displays about traditional life.

Historical Village of Hokkaido
(011) 898-2692. Tue–Sun.

SAPPORO SNOW FESTIVAL

The annual Snow Festival (Yuki Matsuri) transforms Sapporo's Odori Park and the nearby Susukino area and Makomanai Park into a fairytale land of snow sculptures and ice carvings, drawing up to two million visitors. Watching the making of these imaginative and complex forms (from about a week before the start of the festival) can be even more interesting than seeing the finished objects. The festival overlaps with the Sapporo White Illumination: from mid-November to mid-February, strings of white lights adorn Odori Park and Ekimae-dori. A nighttime visit to the area is magical.

One of the elaborate snow carvings at Sapporo's Snow Festival

Rishiri-Rebun-Sarobetsu National Park ❻

利尻礼文サロベツ国立公園

Wakkanai. Wakkanai stn. from Wakkanai to both islands.

Consisting of the Sarobetsu coast of north Hokkaido and the two islands of Rishiri and Rebun, this park is within sight of the Russian island of Sakhalin. Although remote – at least a 6-hour drive north of Sapporo – the park is easily accessible by plane or train. The coastal meadows in the **Sarobetsu** area and the shores of the shallow lagoons in the coastal plain, are carpeted with flowers in summer, including yellow-orange lilies, white cotton grass, white rhododendrons, and purple irises.

About 20 km (12 miles) offshore, the startling 1,720-m (5,650-ft) high conical peak of **Mount Rishiri** (Rishiri-Fuji) appears to rise straight from the sea. A road runs around its coastline, making for scenic cycling and linking the various settlements including **Oshidomari**, the main port, and **Kutsugata**, the second port on the west side. Trails to the top of Mount Rishiri thread through a host of alpine summer flowers. Those less inclined to hike may choose to fish or simply relax and enjoy the excellent fresh fish at local restaurants.

Rebun, Rishiri's partner and Japan's northernmost island, is lowly in comparison but is renowned as the "isle of flowers." **Kabuka** is its main port; the fishing village of **Funadomari** is at the opposite, north end of the island. There's great hiking (sometimes hard-going), especially on the west coast; the island's youth hostel organizes guided walking groups.

Women cutting dried kelp at Kutsugata on Rishiri Island

Daisetsu-zan National Park ❼

大雪山国立公園

Okadama.and Asahikawa. Asahikawa and Obihiro stns.

At 2,310 sq km (890 sq miles), Daisetsu-zan is Japan's largest national park. A huge raised plateau ringed with peaks, right in the center of Hokkaido, the park was established in 1934. **Asahikawa** to the northwest or **Obihiro** to the south make the best starting points for visiting the park, with easy car access by routes 39 and 273. Buses connect the major *onsen* resorts of **Sounkyo**, **Asahi-dake**, and **Tenninkyo**. The plunging **Sounkyo gorge**, with the cascading Ryusei and Ginga waterfalls, is best explored by bicycle or on foot. The ropeway at Sounkyo and the cable car at Asahi-dake tend to be packed but offer quick access; away from the top stations people become scarcer and the views more spectacular.

In Ainu legend the peaks of the Daisetsu mountains are the dwelling places of benevolent but powerful god-spirits who, in human form, helped in times of need. To hike among these mountains is certainly to feel among the gods. A network of trails provides everything from day hikes to week-long tramps, and it is worth taking the time to hike or take the cable car up from the low access roads to the higher levels for the breathtaking views. The dramatic, conical, steam-venting peak of **Mount Asahi** (or Asahi-dake), Hokkaido's highest at 2,290 m (7,500 ft), offers an uplifting panorama across the high plateau. June and July bring alpine flowers, while fall colors are at their best in late August and September. En route, you may see bears and pika, rubythroats and nutcrackers among other species.

An excellent route for the fit day-hiker starts from Sounkyo *onsen*. From there take the ropeway and cable car, then hike southwest over Mount Kurodake, continuing along well-marked trails to Mount Asahi. From the top, descend via the cablecar to Asahi-dake *onsen*. It should take around 7 hours in total.

Snow-capped peaks in Daisetsu-zan National Park

Lake Mashu, one of Hokkaido's most beautiful sights, in Akan National Park

lake has no inlets or outlets. The panoramic view from the crater rim takes in Mount Shari to the north, the Shiretoko Peninsula to the northeast, and Lake Kussharo and beyond to the Akan volcanoes in the west.

The park's forests are home to many woodpeckers, including the black woodpecker, other forest birds, red foxes, sika deer, red squirrels, and Siberian chipmunks.

For those interested in geothermal activity, in addition to active Me-Akan, there are simple outdoor hot-spring pools at **Akan Kohan** and **Wakoto**, both on Lake Kussharo's south shore, steaming sulfuroles on **Mount Iwo** (between Kussharo and Mashu lakes), and "bokke" (small areas of bubbling mud) beside Lake Akan. The larger and more tourist-oriented spa resorts of **Kawayu** and **Akan** are crowded with souvenir shops selling Ainu carvings.

Akan National Park 8

阿寒国立公園

Memanbetsu (Abashiri), Nakashibetsu, and Kushiro. Teshikaga and Kawayu stns. from Kushiro stn. near Akan Kohan bus terminal (0154) 67-3200. Marimo Festival (Oct 8–10).

This enormous National Park of 905 sq km (350 sq miles) in east-central Hokkaido is possibly the most beautiful in Japan. Travel around the park is limited; there are tour buses, but cycling, hitching, or rental-car are all better options.

The western portion, around **Lake Akan** (famed for its bizarre green spherical algae known as *marimo*) is dominated by a pair of volcanic peaks: in the southeast is the 1,370-m (4,500-ft) **Mount O-Akan** while in the southwest is the still-active **Mount Me-Akan**, at 1,500 m (4,920 ft). The day hike up Me-Akan from **Akan Kohan** *onsen* and down the other side on a well-trodden trail to attractive **Lake Onetto** affords marvelous views in any season, but especially in fall. O-Akan is a more serious hike but also possible in a day.

East of Akan, over the pass toward **Teshikaga** (a spectacular drive in itself), are splendid views back to the two volcanoes. Farther east lies **Lake Kussharo**, in a huge caldera with a 57-km (35-mile) perimeter. Beautiful all year, this enormous lake freezes over almost entirely in winter when the harmonics created by pressure in the ice make the lake sound as if it is singing. Thermal vents keep tiny portions ice-free; here flocks of whooper swans remain throughout the winter.

Farther east again lies **Lake Mashu**, prized as one of the greatest scenic spots in all Hokkaido, especially when the weather is kind. The crater's steep internal cliffs rise 200 m (650 ft), the water of the lake is astonishingly clear, and the

Ainu Culture

Ainu culture in Japan is believed to have developed its distinctive characteristics between the 8th and 14th centuries. Physically large, typically bearded, and often with wavy hair, the Ainu more closely resemble Caucasians than do Japanese. Their relationship with nature was a powerful one, linked to their dependence on it for food, clothing, and building materials. Animals they hunted or encountered were often revered as *kamui* (gods), and killing for food was a necessity that invoked rituals to thank the god-spirits. The lives of many animal and bird species were intimately known. Ainu dances, including a crane dance, mimic nature, and their crafts include implements and clothing made from locally available materials such as salmon skin and deer antlers.

After the Japanese settled Hokkaido in the 1860s, Ainu land was confiscated and hunting and fishing rights suppressed. Much of the traditional orally transferred wisdom disappeared as the Ainu were encouraged to "assimilate." Only recently have many of the old oral epics or *yukars* been transcribed. Few people now use the language, even though there has been something of a revival since 1990.

A traditionally dressed Ainu man and woman

Whooper swans on Lake Kussharo in Akan National Park ▷

Kushiro Wetlands National Park ❾

釧路湿原

Kushiro. Kushiro stn. from Kushiro. Kushiro City Office (0154) 31-4549.

If any creature represents Japan, it is the beautiful *tancho*, or red-crowned crane, regarded as a symbol of happiness and long life (myth has it that it lives a thousand years). To the Ainu, the crane is a god of the marshes – *sarurun kamui*. The Kushiro Wetlands National Park is typical of its natural environment. This enormous peat swamp, an expanse of undulating reed beds bisected by streams, north of the coastal port city of Kushiro is one of the main homes of these enormous, graceful birds that stand 1.4 m (4 ft 6 in) high. The cranes are also found in other wetlands of southeast Hokkaido, albeit in smaller numbers.

In the early 20th century, the cranes were pushed to the verge of extinction in Japan by a combination of hunting and loss of habitat, but now protection and provision of food for them during the winter months has helped the young cranes survive, boosting the population to around 700 birds.

During the winter nights (December to March) the cranes roost in the safety of flowing rivers. By day, they forage along streams and marsh edges, or fly to one of three major feeding sites north of Kushiro: two in **Tsurui** village and one in **Akan** village. These sites offer the best opportunities for viewing the cranes year round. On late winter days, the birds display, calling and dancing to one another in the snow as they prepare for the breeding season ahead.

A red-crowned crane

In summer (May to September), the cranes are territorial, occupying large, traditional nesting grounds where they usually raise just one chick, or occasionally two. In the lush green summer reed beds, even these tall birds are well hidden, but may be spotted at the marsh fringes.

Akkeshi Bay ❿

厚岸湾

Kushiro. Akkeshi stn.

Akkeshi's sheltered tidal lagoon is renowned for the quality of its oysters. The bay is extensively farmed, and there is a shrine to the oysters on a rocky islet. Throughout the winter, and especially during spring and fall migration, hundreds of whooper swans gather in the inner bay, while in summer red-crowned cranes breed upriver and at the nearby **Kiritappu wetland**. The coastal road from Akkeshi around to Kiritappu is well worth driving – both for the scenery and for an insight into the fishing and seaweed-harvesting lifestyles of some of the people in this region. Walking at the cape beyond Kiritappu is exhilarating, but early summer mornings are best avoided because this is when a sea mist is most likely to conceal the view.

Whooper swans congregating at Akkeshi Bay

Lake Furen ⓫

風蓮湖

Kushiro. Nemuro stn.

A far cry from Japan's crowded cityscapes, the huge 52 sq-km (20 sq-mile) lagoon of Lake Furen is surrounded by expansive, eye-relaxing landscape. Situated on Hokkaido's east coast, this lake is the seasonal haunt of hordes of birds: migrating waterfowl in spring and fall, sea eagles in winter, and breeding red-crowned cranes during summer.

Nearly 20 km (12 miles) long and up to 4 km (2 miles) wide, the lagoon is only 2 m (6 ft) deep or less in places. It is fringed by forests of fir and spruce, with alder and birch scrub in wetter areas. Some easy forest walks start from the south end of the lake, at **Hakkuchodai** and **Shunkunitai**, offering a wealth of birdwatching opportunities and plenty of wildflowers en route. In winter, the frozen lagoon and adjacent areas are good for cross-country skiing.

Kushiro Wetlands, Japan's largest peat swamp

Nemuro Peninsula ⓬

根室半島

✈ *Kushiro.* 🚉 *Nemuro stn.*

In contrast to the rugged, mountainous Shiretoko Peninsula of northeast Hokkaido, the Nemuro Peninsula in the southeast is low-lying, essentially a coastal plateau carved by streams into steep-sided gullies, and well loved by naturalists. The best way to explore the area is by car.

The red fox is common here and, in forests around the base of the peninsula, particularly in the Onetto area, there are also many sika deer. In summer, lilies, fritillaries, and other wildflowers are abundant, while in winter, although the cape appears bleak and inhospitable, both white-tailed and Steller's sea eagles can be seen. Offshore and in the many sheltered harbors and bays, there are flocks of sea duck, particularly scoter and harlequin, and many other seabirds can be spotted in the coastal waters.

At the base of the peninsula, the quiet town of **Nemuro**, with its declining population, has little to offer the visitor apart from a practical base. At **Cape Nosappu** the viewing tower overlooks the Russian-occupied islands across the narrow Nemuro Channel.

Shiretoko National Park ⓭

知床半島

✈ *Memanbetsu (Abashiri) or Nakashibetsu.* 🚉 *Shiretoko-Shari stn.* ℹ *Shiretoko Shizen center (01522) 4-2114.*

This rugged finger of land, jutting 65 km (40 miles) northeast into the Okhotsk Sea, was named Shiretoko ("the end of the earth") by the Ainu. Japan's wildest national park, its 386 sq km (150 sq miles) consist of a well-forested mountainous ridge of volcanic peaks dominated by the 1,660-m (5,450-ft) **Mount Rausu**. The peninsula supports one of the healthiest remaining populations of brown bears left in Hokkaido. Sightings are few and far between, although the boat ride from **Utoro** (on the northwest coast) north to the cape during the summer is one possible way of seeing them as they forage along the coastal strip.

A red fox, often seen on the Nemuro Peninsula

Minke whales, dolphins, and porpoises may be seen in summer, too, along with seabirds such as spectacled guillemots, Japanese cormorants, and migratory short-tailed shearwaters. Several pairs of white-tailed sea eagles nest along the peninsula. In winter their numbers are swollen by hundreds more arriving from Russia, but then they are overshadowed by the world's largest and most magnificent eagle: Steller's sea eagle. Both types of eagles are best seen in winter north of **Rausu** on the southeast coast.

Steller's sea eagle

North of Utoro lie the pretty **Shiretoko Five Lakes,** reflecting Mount Rausu. There is an easy 2-km (1-mile) trail starting beyond the Visitor Center, and *onsen*-enthusiasts will not want to miss the hot waterfall known as **Kamuiwakka**, northeast of here. From June to October the high pass from Utoro to Rausu (Route 334) is open, and the view east from here to Kunashiri island is dramatic. This road passes through the subalpine zone, which is dominated by dwarf stone pine trees. From near the pass, a hiking trail strikes off south for Lake Rausu and Mount Onnebetsu, while another heads north for Mounts Rausu, Io, and Shiretoko and the cape beyond. For most levels of fitness, Mount Rausu is a manageable day hike along a good trail. The journey to the cape, however, requires several days and careful planning. The long, cold winters and short summers here make hiking possible only from June to September.

Utoro lighthouse on the northwest coast of Shiretoko National Park

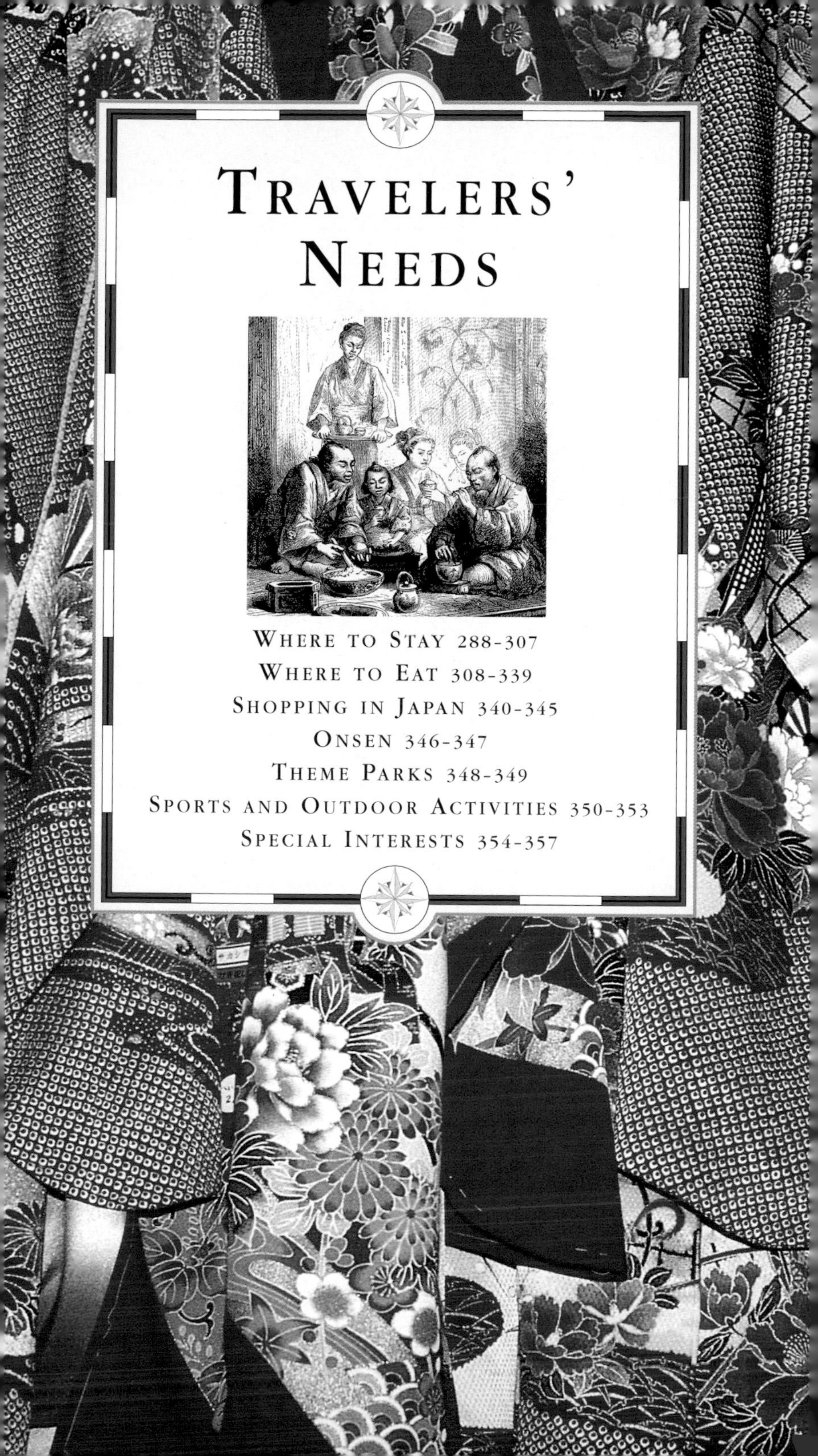

Travelers' Needs

Where to Stay 288-307
Where to Eat 308-339
Shopping in Japan 340-345
Onsen 346-347
Theme Parks 348-349
Sports and Outdoor Activities 350-353
Special Interests 354-357

WHERE TO STAY

THE TRADITION of hosting travelers is so deep-rooted in Japan that every town is well endowed with welcoming places to stay. There are two basic classifications of accommodations: Western-style and traditional. No visit to Japan is complete without staying at least one night in a traditional Japanese inn, called a *ryokan (see pp290–91)*. These tend to be multi-generational enterprises, offering a glimpse into a more traditional way of life. The range of hospitality is diverse in every sense – style, price, the size and quality of rooms, and facilities provided. There is also a certain amount of cultural crossover. Only the quality of service is a non-variable: friendly and eager to please. Sadly, there are rare instances of foreigners being turned away. This is usually due to anxiety to give of their best on the part of staff who are lacking communication skills in any language other than their own.

Sign for the Palace Hotel, Central Tokyo *(see p292)*

HELPFUL ORGANIZATIONS

DESIGNED for overseas visitors, the **Welcome Inn Reservation Center** (WIRC) arranges bookings for an approved range of traditional inns *(ryokan)*, government-run lodges, business hotels, and pensions. The service is free of charge. JNTO offices *(see p363)* stock the *Directory of Welcome Inns*, which includes maps, a full listing, and a reservation form.

Many of the traditional inns approved by the WIRC also belong to the **Japanese Inn Group**, which covers about 80 moderately rated *ryokan* that are geared to receiving mainly foreign visitors. JNTO offices have listings.

The **Japan Hotel Association**, composed of leading hotels, has overseas representatives and online information about member hotels and advance bookings.

Sleek curves of the Portopia Hotel in the port area of Kobe

Western-style façade of the Japanese airline-owned ANA hotel, Nagasaki

The **Japan Economy Hotel** (JEH) **Group** is a newer organization offering clean, modern rooms at reasonable rates in locations that are convenient for sightseeing.

BOOKING AND PAYING

BOOKING accommodations in advance is advisable, especially at times of major public holidays *(see p43)*. If you make a reservation from abroad without going through one of the organizations just mentioned, it is best to confirm by letter, fax, or e-mail. Note that the rates quoted are often per person, not per room.

Most hotels accept the best-known international credit cards. The bill is usually payable on departure, but business hotels and some others request advance payment.

A 10 to 20 percent service charge (on top of the 5 percent consumption tax) is generally added, depending on the style and quality of the hotel.

DELUXE HOTELS

TOP AMERICAN chains such as the Hilton, Sheraton, Hyatt, Westin, and Four Seasons are well established in Japan.

Among Japanese-owned hotels, there is a vast range: staid conservatism; over-the-top opulence; discreet exclusivity; chic minimalism; quaint eccentricity. Increasingly common are "intelligent" hotels, that monitor internal temperature and advise on the weather outside; also electronic cards in place of room keys, computerized toilets, and a voice-mail message system.

MID-RANGE HOTELS

MANY HOTELS in Japan offer an appealing combination of Western-style rooms with their own bathrooms, and Japanese-style flourishes such as an optional communal bath. Often there is a choice of Western-style or *tatami*-matted, Japanese-style rooms.

◁ **Okinawan fabrics for sale at an indoor market in Naha**

Pensions

Western-style pensions have become popular in recent years. Located mostly in resort areas, they are rustic and relaxed in style and offer good hearty meals. Generally managed by married couples, they fall somewhere between a *minshuku* *(see p291)* and the more service-oriented pamperings of a small hotel.

Business Hotels

As the name suggests, business hotels *(bijinesu hoteru)* cater to budget-concious business travelers. Anyone can stay, and being generally located in city centers around train stations, they are very convenient. Do not expect English to be spoken.

Rooms are Western-style, small, and clean. Slippers and a cotton robe are generally supplied. There is no room service, but vending machines offer the ubiquitous "health drinks," beer, and sake. There is usually at least one restaurant with a choice of Japanese or Western-style breakfasts.

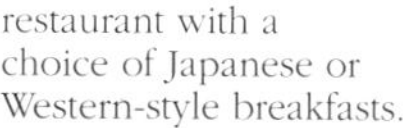

Sign showing rates for a Tokyo love hotel

Capsule Hotels

Unique to Japan, these custom-built hotels feature encapsulated beds in and out of which guests must slide, since there is no room to sit up, let alone stand up. Rattan blinds or curtains can be pulled across for a degree of privacy. Usually constructed in two tiers, they cater mainly to "*salarymen*" who are too tired or inebriated to make the last train home. Most are clustered around major train stations or nightlife areas.

Facilities include a personal TV (with porno channel), radio, alarm call system, and air-conditioning. Smoking is not allowed. Vending machines may be nearby. Baths and sometimes saunas are included in the price.

The size of such hotels varies widely, ranging from 50 capsules to over 600. Most cater only to men; sometimes there is a floor for women.

Love Hotels

Love hotels are designed especially for dating couples and married partners living in extended families, who may feel that they need some privacy. They are mainly found in entertainment areas and along expressways and highways, much like motels. Prices are twofold: "rest" (for a quickie) and "stay" (up to an overnight stay). The most entertaining offer thematic decor as an additional turn-on.

Youth Hostels

Some 360 youth hostels are scattered across Japan, mostly in out-of-the-way places or on the edges of built-up areas. The quality is variable, and house-parents range from the welcoming to dictatorial. A membership card is required for the cheapest rates, but anyone can stay for an additional charge, and there is no upper age limit.

Lobby of a youth hostel in Sendai, a mix of traditional and modern

Typical capsule hotel, with two tiers of encapsulated beds

Camping

There are about 2,800 official campsites, where tents, lodges, and bungalows can be rented. A minimum charge applies for setting up independently. Facilities include running water, toilets, baths and showers, stoves for cooking, restaurants, and vending machines. The JNTO leaflet *Camping in Japan* gives details. Overcrowding is common in holiday seasons.

Directory

Japan Economy Hotel Group
Tel *(075) 533-0490.*
FAX *(075) 533-0790.*
W www.jnto.go.jp/jeh-group.html

Japan Hotel Association
Tel *(03) 3279-2706.*
FAX *(03) 3274-5375.*
W www.j-hotel.or.jp

Japanese Inn Group
Tel *(03) 3843-2345.*
FAX *(03) 3843-2348.*
W www.roy.hi-ho.ne.jp/shigetsu

Welcome Inn Reservation Center
Tel *(03) 3211-4201.*
FAX *(03) 3211-9009.*
For JNTO offices and website see page 363.

Traditional Accommodations

A RYOKAN is a unique fusion of private and communal styles of living. Such Japanese traditions as removing shoes at the right point are important, no matter what the cost of the room, and the most expensive of these traditional inns may demand a high level of etiquette. A family-run *minshuku* – a type of guesthouse – is an even more intimate way to experience the Japanese lifestyle. There are also options that are *ryokan* at heart, but with Western-style touches such as private bathrooms.

Bamboo fencing at a guesthouse on Miyajima Island

What is a Ryokan?

A RYOKAN is a traditional inn, as likely to be found in a city area as a mountain hamlet. Some are set in Edo-period buildings – confections of wood, glass, bamboo, paper screens, and *tatami* matting. Others have a more contemporary setting. Of the 80,000 *ryokan* scattered nationwide, most cater only to Japanese tourists, but they will usually welcome foreigners. About 1,500 *ryokan* are registered as well-suited to providing for foreign visitors.

Certain important Japanese customs apply: the biggest difference and surprise for many foreigners is that bathing facilities are traditionally communal, not private. The bathing facilities may be quite elaborate, and when part of a hot spring resort the establishment is called an *onsen* *(see pp346–7)*.

Most *ryokan* place emphasis on the quality of their meals, and the room price often includes breakfast and dinner (as specified in the listings). This can be ideal in quiet towns where few restaurants are open in the evening, but a constraint elsewhere. Another possible problem, mainly for elderly foreigners, is the Japanese tradition of living at floor level, using legless chairs and beds.

Note that many *ryokan* impose a curfew around 11pm, so make special arrangements about keys in advance if you plan to stay out late.

Arriving at a Ryokan

GUESTS GENERALLY check into a *ryokan* in the mid- to late afternoon, to allow plenty of time for bathing and dinner. At larger *ryokan*, there may be a doorman to smooth the way, but in smaller establishments, guests should slide open the front door and politely call *"gomen kudasai"* to announce arrival.

Do not step up into the lobby proper until the *okamisan* (female owner or manager) appears. This is the signal to remove outdoor shoes and step up into a pair of waiting house slippers *(see p365)*. Then, before entering the guestroom, remove the house slippers and leave them outside the door.

Typical Rooms

GUESTROOMS are floored in *tatami* mats *(see p29)*. In one corner of the room is an alcove, called *tokonoma*, which may contain a hanging scroll, flowers, or other artifacts. The *tokonoma* is to be respected: no suitcases, ashtrays, or drinks. There will also be a low table surrounded by cushions *(zabuton)*, or folding chairs. On the table top will be a tray, bearing a tea set and possibly traditional sweets *(wagashi)*.

Your futon mattress and bedding will be stowed in cupboards when you first enter the room. These will usually be laid out discreetly for you in the evening while you are out of the room.

Ordinarily a room will be further supplied with a TV and air conditioner and/or heater. There is usually a telephone, although it may not have an international connection. You should also find a small towel in a box or basket, which you can take to the communal bathroom to use as a washcloth. A personal outdoor bath *(rotenburo)* counts as luxury. A screened-off veranda, with Western-style table and armchairs, is more commonplace. There may be other Western-style touches.

Handle everything in the room with care, and walk only in bare feet or socks on the fragile *tatami*.

Room with *tatami* mats, low table, and *zabuton*, and additional Western-style daybed

Small communal bath and separate low shower for actual cleansing

Wearing Yukata

SOMEWHERE in the room will be traditional robes for you to wear, called *yukata*. Most people change into *yukata* for the duration of their stay, since the loose cotton kimonos symbolize relaxation and leisure time. In resort towns and hot springs, they are even worn outside on the streets, together with the high wooden sandals called *geta*. A loose jacket may also be provided. It is best to follow the example of others as to exactly where and when to wear the robes.

Fold *yukata* left-side over right. Right-side over left symbolizes death in Buddhism and can cause upset. Use the *obi* sash provided to secure the gown.

Bathing Arrangements

WITHIN THE *ryokan* will be at least one communal bath and a toilet block with either Western-style cubicles or Japanese squat toilets or a choice of the two styles.

In smaller *ryokan* with only one bath, bathing times may differ for men and women. In larger establishments bathing is segregated, with one entrance for men, another for women *(for symbols see page 371)*. Mixed-sex bathing used to be the norm but is very rare these days. The size of the bath and bathroom naturally dictate how many people can bathe at any one time. Check with the *okamisan* if you are unsure about the house rules, which vary between establishments.

In the bathroom there will be an area for undressing; a low shower or tap area; and the large bath itself. The golden rule to observe is that you must perform ablutions with the shower first and not enter the hot bath until you are clean. The bath itself is intended only for therapeutic relaxation. The same bathwater is used by other guests, thus it is considered extremely bad manners to contaminate the water either with an unwashed body or soap and shampoo.

People wearing *yukata*, the design of which is specific to each *ryokan*

Eating Arrangements

MEALS ARE sometimes served in a dining room, but more often in the room by a maid or the *okamisan*. The more exclusive the establishment, the more likely meals will be served in private.

Meal times are usually set quite early in the evening. Depending on the situation, the *okamisan* may stay for a while, explaining the dishes, demonstrating how they should be eaten, and to chat. Or she may leave discreetly, returning only to clear the table.

Staying in a Minshuku

THESE FAMILY-RUN enterprises open the family home to travelers as and when demand requires. With rates from ¥4,000–¥10,000, this is an economical option as well as a good opportunity to see how regular working people live. The atmosphere is more homey than professional; guests are treated as part of the family at mealtimes and bathtime, and should fold up and stow away their own bedding.

Staying in a Temple

SOME TEMPLES, for example Mount Koya *(see p300)*, are geared to accepting overnight visitors. Food is vegetarian in the Buddhist tradition *(see p320)*. Gates to the compound may close early in the evening. You should follow rituals, including morning prayers, with due reverence even if you are not Buddhist. Fees start from around ¥3,000.

Staying in Lodges

PEOPLE'S LODGES, or **Kokumin-Shukusha**, are moderate-rated accommodations within the national parks. Rooms, baths, and toilets are Japanese style. Meals based on local produce are often very good. Mountain lodges, Yamagoya, are aimed at hikers and range from the relatively comfortable to spartan.

Directory

Japan Ryokan Association
Tel *(03) 3231-5310.*
FAX *(03) 3201-5797.*

Japan Minshuku Center
Tel *(03) 3216-6556.*
FAX *(03) 3216-6557.*
W www.minshuku.co.jp

Kokumin-Shukusha Association
Tel *(03) 3581-5310.*
FAX *(03) 3581-5315.*

Choosing a Hotel

The hotels in this guide have been selected across a wide price range for their locations, character, and good value. The chart lists the hotels by region corresponding to the color-coded thumb tabs. Readers are strongly advised to request a map showing any hotel's location when booking, as Japanese addresses can be difficult to find *(see pp376–7)*.

	Credit Cards	Number of Rooms	Ryokan or Minshuku	Business or Western Style	Japanese/Western Rooms
Tokyo					
Central Tokyo (Chidorigafuchi): *Fairmont Hotel* ¥¥¥ **Map** 3 A5. *(03) 3262-1151.* FAX *(03) 3264-2476.* W www.fairmont.co.jp Friendly hotel that is a bit old but holding up well with its light rooms, and pleasant and quiet location overlooking the palace moat. There is a French café and restaurant. all rooms.	AE DC MC V	197		●	
Central Tokyo (Ginza): *Ginza Nikko Hotel* ¥¥¥ **Map** 5 B3. *(03) 3571-4911.* FAX *(03) 3571-8379.* Reliable, mid-range hotel affiliated with JAL (Japan Air Lines), in a convenient location near Ginza's main department stores. all rooms.	AE DC MC V	112		●	
Central Tokyo (Ginza): *Ginza Dai-ichi Hotel* ¥¥¥¥ **Map** 5 B3. *(03) 3542-5311.* FAX *(03) 3542-3030.* Part of a famous Japanese hotel chain with lots of Western-style facilities and services, including a good selection of eateries. all rooms.	AE DC MC V	801		●	
Central Tokyo (Hibiya): *Imperial Hotel* ¥¥¥¥¥ **Map** 5 B2. *(03) 3504-1111.* FAX *(03) 33581-9146.* W www.imperialhotel.co.jp Deluxe hotel right by Hibiya station, with all the services and spacious rooms, but not a very warm, friendly feeling. all rooms.	AE DC MC V	1059		●	
Central Tokyo (Kanda): *Hill-top Hotel* ¥¥¥ **Map** 3 B4. *(03) 3293-2311.* FAX *(03) 3233-4567.* A small establishment with lots of 1930s character and class, near Meiji University. Oxygen and negative ions are pumped into the rooms, supposedly to promote an atmosphere of well-being. all rooms.	AE DC MC V	75		●	
Central Tokyo (Nr Kitanomaru Park): *Kudan Kaikan* ¥¥¥ **Map** 3 A5. *(03) 3261-5521.* FAX *(03) 3221-7238.* A cozy, mid-range hotel right by the palace moat and just a one-minute walk from Kudanshita station on the Tozai subway line. all rooms.	AE DC MC V	193	■		■
Central Tokyo (Marunouchi): *Marunouchi Hotel* ¥¥¥ **Map** 5 B1. *(03) 3215-2151.* FAX *(03) 3215-8036.* The decor may be rather old and dark, and the rooms may be small, but the Marunouchi's location is very handy, near Tokyo Station. all rooms.	AE DC MC V	192		●	■
Central Tokyo (Marunouchi): *Palace Hotel* ¥¥¥¥¥ **Map** 5 B1. *(03) 3211-5211.* FAX *(03) 3211-6987.* Many of the big rooms here overlook the palace moat and Ote-mon gate. Good value all around for a deluxe hotel. all rooms.	AE DC MC V	389		●	
Central Tokyo (Tokyo Station): *Hotel Kokusai Kanko* ¥¥¥ **Map** 5 C1. *(03) 3215-3281.* FAX *(03) 3215-1140.* The rooms are small, but the location is the prime point of this mid-range hotel, just beside the north exit, Yaesu side, of Tokyo station. all rooms.	AE DC MC V	94		●	
Central Tokyo (Tokyo Station): *Yaesu Fujiya Hotel* ¥¥¥ **Map** 5 C2. *(03) 3273-2111.* FAX *(03) 3273-2180.* Business hotel with good service and larger than typical rooms, in an excellent location near Yurakucho and Tokyo stations. all rooms.	AE DC MC V	376		●	■
Central Tokyo (Tokyo Station): *Hotel Yaesu-Ryumeikan* ¥¥¥ **Map** 5 C1. *(03) 3271-0971.* FAX *(03) 3271-0977.* @ ryumeikan@ma2.justnet.no.jp Great location about three minutes from the Yaesu exit of Tokyo station, but the rooms are not particularly bright, cheery, or new. 23 rooms.	AE DC MC V	30	■		■
Northern Tokyo (Asakusa): *Capsule Hotel Riverside* ¥ **Map** 4 F3. *(03) 3844-1155.* FAX *(03) 3841-6566.* Cheap capsule hotel by the station, one of the few to accept women, with about 16 units available for them. It almost always has vacancies.	AE DC MC V	160			

Price categories per night for two people sharing a room, including tax and service charges.

¥ under ¥8,000
¥¥ ¥8,000–15,000
¥¥¥ ¥15,000–25,000
¥¥¥¥ ¥25,000–35,000
¥¥¥¥¥ over ¥35,000

CREDIT CARDS
AE American Express; DC Diners Club; MC MasterCard; V VISA.

RYOKAN OR MINSHUKU
Traditional Japanese accommodations, usually with *tatami*-mat rooms and shared bathing facilities *(see pp290–91)*.

BUSINESS OR WESTERN STYLE
Business hotel *(see p289)* or hotel with mainly Western-style rooms and facilities.

JAPANESE/WESTERN ROOMS
Both Japanese-style and Western-style rooms are available.

NORTHERN TOKYO (NR ASAKUSA): *Kikuya Ryokan* ¥¥
Map 4 E3. *(03) 3841-4051.* **FAX** *(03) 3841-6404.*
Modern, concrete building, but in a district with lots of Shitamachi ("low city") atmosphere. Western breakfasts available. 6 rooms.

NORTHERN TOKYO (ASAKUSA): *Ryokan Shigetsu* ¥¥
Map 4 E3. *(03) 3843-2345.* **FAX** *(03) 3843-2348.* **W** www.shigetsu.com
Within the delightful network of streets leading up to Senso-ji Temple, this peaceful inn has small, viewless, but comfortable rooms, and a 6th-floor communal bath overlooking the pagoda. all rooms.

NORTHERN TOKYO (UENO): *Katsutaro Ryokan* ¥¥
Map 3 C2. *(03) 3821-9808.* **FAX** *(03) 3821-4789.*
W www.pacificmall.com/ryokan/ryokan/htm
A small inn in a pleasant residential location, near Ueno Park. 4 rooms.

NORTHERN TOKYO (UENO): *Sakura Ryokan* ¥¥
Map 4 D2. *(03) 3876-8118.* **FAX** *(03) 3873-9456.*
Built in 1989 in an interesting old neighborhood, this inn is very welcoming to foreigners, but don't expect any views. 9 rooms.

NORTHERN TOKYO (UENO): *Suigetsu Hotel/Ongaiso* ¥¥
Map 3 C2. *(03) 3822-4611.* **FAX** *(03) 3823-4340.*
What sets this hotel apart is its baths using water from a private hot-spring well. There are two buildings, one of them a *ryokan*. 122 rooms.

NORTHERN TOKYO: (UENO): *Hotel Parkside* ¥¥¥
Map 3 C3. *(03) 3836-5711.* **FAX** *(03) 3831-6641.* **W** www.parkside.co.jp
Good-value hotel beside Shinobazu Pond. Rooms are large and bright, though the hotel is generally starting to show its age. all rooms.

NORTHERN TOKYO (YANAKA): *Sawanoya Ryokan* ¥¥
Map 3 B2. *(03) 3822-2251.* **FAX** *(03) 3822-2252.* **W** www.tctv.ne.jp/members/sawanoya
Located in a pleasant residential area, this small, modern Japanese inn is run by a family who are very used to foreigners. 2 rooms.

WESTERN TOKYO (AKASAKA): *Capsule Hotel Fontaine Akasaka* ¥¥
Map 2 E3. *(03) 3583-6554.* **FAX** *(03) 3584-3163.*
More upscale than other capsule hotels, this one accepts female visitors, but only on weekends and national holidays.

WESTERN TOKYO (AKASAKA): *Akasaka Prince Hotel* ¥¥¥¥¥
Map 2 F3. *(03) 3234-1111.* **FAX** *(03) 3262-5163.* **W** www.princehotels.co.jp
One of the premier hotels of a famous Japanese chain, in a building designed by Tange Kenzo. Some find the gleaming white and glass sterile and off-putting, while others enjoy its simplicity. all rooms.

WESTERN TOKYO (AKASAKA): *ANA Hotel Tokyo* ¥¥¥¥¥
Map 2 F4. *(03) 3505-1111.* **FAX** *(03) 3505-1155.* **W** www.ananet.or.jp/anahotels
The flagship of the ANA airlines chain, which has a good reputation, this establishment lies within the huge Art Hill complex in Roppongi, which includes restaurants and shops. All rooms have a view of either Mount Fuji or the palace. all rooms.

WESTERN TOKYO (AKASAKA): *New Otani* ¥¥¥¥¥
Map 2 E3. *(03) 3265-1111.* **FAX** *(03) 3237-3408.* **W** newotani.co.jp/tokyo/en
Tokyo's biggest deluxe hotel, and practically a city unto itself with many hundreds of rooms and dozens of restaurants and shops. all rooms.

WESTERN TOKYO (MINAMI-AOYAMA): *The President Hotel* ¥¥¥
Map 2 D4. *(03) 3497-011.* **FAX** *(03) 3401-4816.* **@** reservations@president-hotel.co.jp
It would be hard to top this mid-priced hotel, with its good-sized rooms, large windows, and friendly staff. all rooms.

Hotel	Credit Cards	Number of Rooms	Ryokan or Minshuku	Business or Western Style	Japanese/Western Rooms
Kikuya Ryokan	AE MC V	10	■		
Ryokan Shigetsu	AE MC V	24	■		■
Katsutaro Ryokan	AE MC V	7	■		
Sakura Ryokan	AE MC V	20	■		■
Suigetsu Hotel/Ongaiso	AE DC MC V	124	■		■
Hotel Parkside	AE DC MC V	128		●	■
Sawanoya Ryokan	AE MC V	12	■		
Capsule Hotel Fontaine Akasaka	AE DC MC V	294			
Akasaka Prince Hotel	AE DC MC V	761		●	■
ANA Hotel Tokyo	AE DC MC V	901		●	
New Otani	AE DC MC V	1,600		●	■
The President Hotel	AE DC MC V	210		●	

Price categories per night for two people sharing a room, including tax and service charges.
¥ under ¥8,000
¥¥ ¥8,000–15,000
¥¥¥ ¥15,000–25,000
¥¥¥¥ ¥25,000–35,000
¥¥¥¥¥ over ¥35,000

Credit Cards
AE American Express; DC Diners Club; MC MasterCard; V VISA.

Ryokan or Minshuku
Traditional Japanese accommodations, usually with *tatami*-mat rooms and shared bathing facilities *(see pp290–91)*.

Business or Western Style
Business hotel *(see p289)* or hotel with mainly Western-style rooms and facilities.

Japanese/Western Rooms
Both Japanese-style and Western-style rooms are available.

	Credit Cards	Number of Rooms	Ryokan or Minshuku	Business or Western Style	Japanese/Western Rooms
Western Tokyo (Roppongi): *Asia Center of Japan* ¥¥ Map 2 E4. *(03) 3402-6111.* FAX *(03) 3402-0738.* W jcha.yado.jozu.ne.jp/english/index.htm A good-value, basic hotel in a convenient location. It is especially popular with foreign visitors for long stays. 141 rooms.	MC V	166		●	
Western Tokyo (Nr Roppongi): *Hotel Okura* ¥¥¥¥¥ Map 2 F4. *(03) 3582-0111.* FAX *(03) 3582-3707.* W www.travelweb.com/okura/tokyo Timeless Japanese-style decor, including a Japanese tearoom, and excellent service in this top-rated hotel near Kamiyacho station. all rooms.	AE DC MC V	857		●	■
Western Tokyo (Shibuya): *Shanpia Hotel Aoyama* ¥¥¥ Map 1 B5. *(03) 3407-2111.* FAX *(03) 3407-2879.* Mid-range hotel with pleasant rooms, close to the young and hip shopping areas of Shibuya. all rooms.	AE DC MC V	135		●	
Western Tokyo (Shibuya): *Shibuya Tobu Hotel* ¥¥¥ Map 1 B5. *(03) 3476-0111.* FAX *(03) 3476-0903.* Probably the best out of Shibuya's limited selection of hotels. Rooms are small but bright, in white and pastel colors. There is a coffee shop, bar, and several restaurants with different cuisines. all rooms.	AE DC MC V	197		●	
Western Tokyo (Shibuya): *Shibuya Tokyu Hotel* ¥¥¥ Map 1 B5. *(030 3403-1541.* FAX *(03) 3498-0189.* Part of a well-known chain, though far from the chain's grandest or most roomy hotel. Tremendous location just across the street from Shibuya station, with a lively, youthful atmosphere to match the area. all rooms.	AE DC MC V	223		●	
Western Tokyo (Shinjuku): *Shinjuku Washington Hotel* ¥¥¥ Map 1 A2. *(03) 3343-3111.* FAX *(03) 3342-2575.* A white tower famous for its round windows. Rooms are small but well kept. Part of a well-known chain, it has a restaurant, coffee shop, bar, and excellent views from the upper floors. all rooms.	AE DC MC V	1,301		●	
Western Tokyo (Shinjuku): *Hilton Tokyo* ¥¥¥¥¥ Map 1 A1. *(03) 3344-5111.* FAX *(03) 3342-6094.* W www.hilton.com Always gets a top rating, with its excellent service and facilities. The average-sized rooms are well furnished with *shoji*-screen windows. all rooms.	AE DC MC V	803		●	■
Western Tokyo (Shinjuku): *Park Hyatt Tokyo* ¥¥¥¥¥ Map 1 A2. *(03) 5322-1234.* FAX *(03) 5322-1288.* W www.parkhyattokyo.com Starting 39 floors above Shinjuku, this hotel is extremely popular. It has a more youthful feel than other luxury hotels in Tokyo. all rooms.	AE DC MC V	178		●	
Farther Afield (Ebisu): *The Westin Tokyo* ¥¥¥¥¥ 1-4-1 Mita, Meguro-ku. *(03) 5423-7000.* FAX *(03) 5423-7600.* W www.westin.co.jp Grand, "European-style" hotel, part of the pleasant Ebisu Garden Place complex. The lobby is all black marble floors and columns, and the very large rooms have pseudo-antique furniture. all rooms.	AE DC MC V	444		●	
Farther Afield (Gotanda): *Sansuiso Ryokan* ¥¥ 2-9-5 Higashi-Gotanda, Shinagawa-ku. *(03) 3441-7475.* FAX *(03) 3449-1944.* A basic but friendly *ryokan* near Gotanda station. It is part of the Japanese Inn Group, and is used almost exclusively by foreigners. 2 rooms.	AE V	9	■		
Farther Afield (Ikebukuro): *Kimi Ryokan* ¥ 2-36-8 Ikebukuro, Toshima-ku. *(03) 3971-3766.* FAX *(03) 3987-1326.* Very basic *ryokan*, but good value and with an extremely relaxed atmosphere. An established favorite with long-stay foreigners. none.		50	■		
Farther Afield (Odaiba): *Le Meridien Grand Pacific* ¥¥¥¥¥ 2-6-1 Daiba, Minato-ku. *(03) 5500-6711.* FAX *(03) 5500-4507.* W www.htl-pacific.co.jp Tokyo's newest big luxury hotel, with all the latest services and amenities; a little out of the way, but some visitors will consider that a plus. all rooms.	AE DC MC V	884		●	

Central Honshu

Hotel	Price	Cards	Rooms			
Chichibu-Tama National Park: *Komadori Sanso Shukubo* 155 Mitake-san, Ome-shi. + FAX *(0428) 78-8472.* W www.komadori.com An old pilgrims' lodge on Mount Mitake, dating from 1776 but with the comforts of a modern *ryokan*. Close to Mitake Shrine, it has great views and a cypress bathtub. none.	¥¥	AE DC MC V	10	■		
Fuji Five Lakes: *Daikokuya Minshuku* 5-10-25 Kami-Yoshida (7 mins from Fuji-Yoshida stn). + FAX *(0555) 22-3778.* Housed in a 400-year-old building with a large *onsen*, this inn is welcoming to foreign guests and has good access to Mount Fuji and the Five Lakes. Rates incl meals. none.	¥¥		10	■		
Fuji Five Lakes: *Masu-no-ie Minshuku* 195 Shibokusa, Oshino-mura. + FAX *(0555) 84-2013.* Beside Oshino's eight small lakes, with classic views of Mount Fuji, this 200-year-old thatched *minshuku* also has a traditional Japanese garden. Rates incl meals. none.	¥¥¥		5	■		
Hakone: *Nobohon Yumeya* 817-211 Sengokubara. *(0460) 4-9000.* FAX *(0460) 4-5892.* Friendly, flexible *ryokan* with outdoor *onsen*. All the rooms have cozy *horigotatsu*, which are hearth-like quilt-covered heating areas in the floor. Rates incl meals. none.	¥¥¥	AE DC MC V	10	■		
Hakone: *Fujiya Hotel* Nr Miyanoshita stn on Hakone Tozan railway. *(0460) 2-2211.* FAX *(0460) 2-2210.* W www.fujiyahotel.co.jp @ info@fujiyahotel.co.jp Opened in 1878, this classic hotel has a unique combination of Japanese and Western architecture and decor, and is well attuned to foreigners. It also has extensive gardens and its own golf course. all rooms.	¥¥¥¥	AE DC MC V	146		●	
Inuyama: *Hasshokaku Mizuno-o* 6-264 Unuma-Minami-machi. *(0583) 85-4611.* FAX *(0583) 85-4621.* Overlooking the river and castle, this is a stylish modern hotel with *tatami* flooring throughout and an outdoor *onsen*. Cormorant-fishing trips *(see p137)* can be arranged. Rates incl meals. all rooms.	¥¥¥	AE DC MC V	24	■		■
Izu: *Asaba* 3450-1 Shuzenji-machi (in Shuzenji Onsen). *(0558) 72-7000.* FAX *(0558) 72-7077.* This stunning *onsen* hotel, in updated traditional style, is a member of the prestigious French Relais & Chateaux. Noh theater is performed on an open-air stage floating on a pond. Rates incl meals. all rooms.	¥¥¥	AE DC MC V	19	■		
Izu: *Minshuku Teppo* 175 Nashimoto, Kawazu-machi. *(0558) 35-7501.* FAX *(0558) 36-8276.* Once the home of a gunmaker, this 200-year-old house with attractive crisscross plaster walls is known for meals cooked over an open hearth, such as local wild boar stew. Rates incl meals. none.	¥¥¥		8	■		
Izu: *Osawa Onsen Hotel* Osawa Onsen, Matsuzaki-cho, Oku-izu. *(0558) 43-0121.* FAX *(0558) 43-0123.* An Edo-period headman's mansion in a sleepy *onsen* village, with beautiful old rooms, gardens, and cedar *onsen* baths. Beds are Western-style despite the Japanese ambience. Rates incl meals. all rooms.	¥¥¥	AE DC MC V	25	■		
Kamikochi: *Kamikochi Imperial Hotel* Nr Kamikochi bus terminal and car park. *(0263) 95-2001/2006.* FAX *(0263) 95-2412.* W www.imperialhotel.co.jp Quality hotel on a Swiss Alpine theme, lying in the heart of the valley and open from late April to mid-November. It is sister to Tokyo's Imperial Hotel *(see p292)*. all rooms.	¥¥¥¥	AE DC MC V	75		●	
Kamikochi: *Nishi Itoya Sanso* By Kappa Bridge. *(0263) 95-2206.* FAX *(0263) 95-2208.* Modern lodge with excellent views. The annex is less expensive and more basic than the main building. The hotel is open only from late April to mid-November. Rates incl meals. 2 rooms.	¥¥ – ¥¥¥¥	DC MC V	40	■		■
Kanazawa: *Yogetsu Minshuku* 1-13-22 Higashiyama. *(0762) 52-0497.* A former geisha house in the attractive Higashi Pleasure District, over 100 years old and full of atmosphere. Rates incl meals. none.	¥¥		5	■		

Price categories per night for two people sharing a room, including tax and service charges.

- ¥ under ¥8,000
- ¥¥ ¥8,000–15,000
- ¥¥¥ ¥15,000–25,000
- ¥¥¥¥ ¥25,000–35,000
- ¥¥¥¥¥ over ¥35,000

Credit Cards
AE American Express; DC Diners Club; MC MasterCard; V VISA.

Ryokan or Minshuku
Traditional Japanese accommodations, usually with *tatami*-mat rooms and shared bathing facilities *(see pp290–91)*.

Business or Western Style
Business hotel *(see p289)* or hotel with mainly Western-style rooms and facilities.

Japanese/Western Rooms
Both Japanese-style and Western-style rooms are available.

Hotel	Credit Cards	Number of Rooms	Ryokan or Minshuku	Business or Western Style	Japanese/Western Rooms
Kiso Valley: *Onyado Daikichi* ¥¥¥ Koino, Tsumago (toward Nagiso end of village). *(0264) 57-2595.* FAX *(0264) 57-2203.* A small, quiet, family-run *minshuku* with excellent food and a fragrant cypress bath. A video of the local festival is often shown after dinner. Advisable to book through the tourist office. Rates incl meals. none.		5	■		
Kiso Valley: *Echigoya Ryokan* ¥¥¥¥ Narai, Narakawa-mura. *(0264) 34-3011.* Over 200 years old, this posting inn *(see p136)* on the old Nakasendo road is still as it was in the Edo period. Little English is spoken, but service is courteous. Book through the tourist office. Rates incl meals. none.		5	■		
Matsumoto: *Marumo Ryokan* ¥¥ 3-3-10 Chuo (10-min walk from stn toward the castle, by river). *(0263) 32-0115.* FAX *(0263) 35-2251.* W www.avis.ne.jp/~marumo A *ryokan* since the Edo period, located in an attractive converted *kura* storehouse. Rates incl breakfast. none.		8	■		
Nagano: *Fujiya Ryokan* ¥¥¥ Just in front of main gate to Zenko-ji. *(0262) 32-1241.* FAX *(0262) 32-1243.* @ fuziya@avis.ne.jp Behind a fading 1920s façade is a graceful *ryokan* dating from the Edo period, with courteous, welcoming service. All rooms face a tranquil garden. Rates incl meals. 3 rooms.	AE DC MC V	23	■		
Nagoya: *Taikan-so* ¥¥¥ 15 Hiyoshi-cho. *(052) 471-2151.* FAX *(052) 471-2153.* An old-fashioned *ryokan* with traditional garden in a quiet area, convenient for central Nagoya. Rates incl meals. 5 rooms.		29	■		
Narita: *Wakamatsu Honten* ¥¥¥¥ By Narita-san temple gate. *(0476) 22-1136.* FAX *(0476) 24-1347.* A *ryokan* built to look old but comfortably new and convenient. The owners are accustomed to foreign guests. Rates incl meals. 8 rooms.	AE DC V	19	■		
Noto Peninsula: *Chiaya-so Minshuku* ¥¥ 18–51, Hakui-shi (nr Shibagaki-naka bus stop.) *(0767) 27-1304.* FAX *(0767) 27-1260.* *Minshuku* in a quiet fishing village with a beach. A specialty, seasonal oyster meal is available on request (extra charge) from July to August. The owners are used to foreigners. Rates incl meals. none.		12	■		
Seki (Gifu): *U-no-ie* ¥¥¥ 78 Oze, Seki-shi (train from Gifu). *(0575) 22-0799.* FAX *(0575) 24-4878.* A 250-year-old fisherman's home with a modern annex. Cormorants trained for catching fish are kept in the garden, and their catch of the day is served at meal times. Rates incl meals and fishing trip. none.		15	■		
Shirakawa (Shokawa Valley): *Minshuku Koemon* ¥¥¥ 456 Ogimachi (nr Shirakawa Jinja-mae bus stop). *(05769) 6-1446.* FAX *(05769) 6-1748.* Traditional *gassho-zukuri* house with added modern amenities, whose friendly proprietors show a video about the village and happily answer questions. Several similar *minshuku* are nearby. Advisable to book through a tourist office (locally or in Takayama). Rates incl meals. none.		5	■		
Shizuoka: *Business Hotel Tomita* ¥¥ 3-6-8 Mabuchi (10 mins from stn). *(054) 283-6800.* FAX *(054) 283-6042.* Despite its appearance as a business hotel, this is a relaxed, family-run establishment, to which vacationers often return. all rooms.	AE DC MC V	18		●	■
Takayama: *Goudo Ryokan* ¥¥¥ 46 Kami-Sanno-machi, in front of Fujii Museum. *(0577) 33-0870.* Small, family-run inn at the heart of the old merchant district. The rooms are decorated with local folk-art items. Rates incl breakfast. none.		4	■		

Hotel	Cards	Rooms			
TAKAYAMA: *Nagase Ryokan* ¥¥¥¥ 10 Kami-Nino-machi (10-min walk from stn). (0577) 32-0068. FAX (0577) 32-1068. A beautiful 250-year-old *ryokan* in the old merchant district. Each room has its own garden with a stream. Rates incl meals. all rooms.	V	10	■		
YOKOHAMA: *Yamashiroya Ryokan* ¥¥ 2-159 Hinode-cho (nr Hinode-cho stn). (045) 231-1146. FAX (045) 231-1147. A reasonably priced, family-run *ryokan* conveniently located near Yokohama's Yamashita Park. none.		13	■		■
YOKOHAMA: *Hotel New Grand* ¥¥¥¥ 10 Yamashita-cho (by Yokohama Bay and Yamashita Park). (045) 681-1841. This is the hotel where General MacArthur stayed at the beginning of the US Occupation in 1945. It was renovated in the early 1990s and has views across the port and Bay Bridge. all rooms.	AE DC MC V	264		●	

KYOTO

Hotel	Cards	Rooms			
JR KYOTO STATION VICINITY: *Ryokan Hiraiwa/Annex Hiraiwa* ¥ 314 Hayao-cho. (075) 351-6748. FAX (075) 351-6969. A wooden two-story inn located near the Takase River, Ryokan Hiraiwa welcomes foreigners. The ferroconcrete annex is also pleasant, if somewhat less atmospheric than the main building. none.	AE MC V	21	■		
JR KYOTO STATION VICINITY: *Ryokan Murakamiya* ¥¥ 270 Sasaya-cho. (075) 371-1260. FAX (075) 371-7161. Basic but comfortable traditional accommodations in a convenient downtown location. The bath and shower room can be used either communally or privately. none.	AE MC V	8	■		
JR KYOTO STATION VICINITY: *Hotel Granvia Kyoto* ¥¥¥ Shiokoji. (075) 344-8888. FAX (075) 344-4400. www.hotels.westjr.co.jp Kyoto's newest deluxe hotel, the Granvia is very conveniently located inside the sleek, new JR station building. all rooms.	AE DC V	539		●	
CITY CENTER: *Hearton Hotel Kyoto* ¥¥ Higashi-no-Toin/Oike agaru. (075) 222-1300. FAX (075) 222-1313. hearton@mail.hearton.co.jp A reasonably priced hotel that offers excellent service and facilities, the Hearton is within walking distance of the downtown shopping areas and the Imperial Palace. all rooms.	AE DC MC V	294		●	
CITY CENTER: *Ishihara* ¥¥ Yanagi-no-Banba/Anekoji agaru. + FAX (075) 221-5612. A charming inn run by a very friendly couple, Ishihara was where movie director Akira Kurosawa chose to spend his Kyoto visits. 2 rooms.		5	■		
CITY CENTER: *Hotel Marmol* ¥¥ 346 Iseya-cho, Gokomachi-dori/Rokkaku sagaru. (075) 213-2456. FAX (075) 213-3518. A small, friendly hotel in the heart of downtown Kyoto, the Marmol offers great value. There are no frills, but rooms are not too small. all rooms.	AE DC MC V	16		●	
CITY CENTER: *Kyoto Royal Hotel* ¥¥¥ Kawaramachi/Sanjo agaru. (075) 223-1234. FAX (075) 223-1702. www.kyoto-royal.co.jp A fine, high-class, efficient hotel typical of its type, offering quality service and dedicated to pleasing its customers. all rooms.	AE DC MC V	332		●	
CITY CENTER: *Kinmata* ¥¥¥¥ Gokomachi/Shijo agaru. (075) 221-1039. FAX (075) 231-7632. Located just south of the Nishiki market street, this charming traditional inn boasts fine food. Rates incl meals. none.	AE DC MC V	7	■		
CITY CENTER: *Kyoto Hotel* ¥¥¥¥ Kawaramachi/Oike. (075) 211-5111. FAX (075) 221-7770. www.kyotohotel.co.jp This recently rebuilt deluxe hotel is conveniently located in the city center and is known for fine service and food. all rooms.	AE DC MC V	322		●	
CITY CENTER: *Hiiragiya Ryokan/Hiiragiya Annex* ¥¥¥¥¥ Fuyacho-dori/Anekoji agaru. (075) 221-1136. FAX (075) 221-1139. hiiragiya.co.jp Considered by many to be the quintessential Kyoto *ryokan* (and thus the best in the whole of Japan), Hiiragiya has a history of excellence dating back to 1818. Rates incl meals. 28 rooms.	AE DC MC V	33	■		

For key to symbols see back flap

Price categories per night for two people sharing a room, including tax and service charges.
¥ under ¥8,000
¥¥ ¥8,000–15,000
¥¥¥ ¥15,000–25,000
¥¥¥¥ ¥25,000–35,000
¥¥¥¥¥ over ¥35,000

Credit Cards
AE American Express; DC Diners Club; MC MasterCard; V VISA.

Ryokan or Minshuku
Traditional Japanese accommodations, usually with *tatami*-mat rooms and shared bathing facilities *(see pp290–91)*.

Business or Western Style
Business hotel *(see p289)* or hotel with mainly Western-style rooms and facilities.

Japanese/Western Rooms
Both Japanese-style and Western-style rooms are available.

	Credit Cards	Number of Rooms	Ryokan or Minshuku	Business or Western Style	Japanese/Western Rooms
City Center: *Tawaraya* ¥¥¥¥¥ Fuyacho/Anekoji agaru. ☎ *(075) 211-5566.* FAX *(075) 211-2204.* One of Kyoto's best-known inns, Tawaraya has hosted the likes of Charlie Chaplin. Old Kyoto at its best. Rates incl meals. TV all rooms.	AE DC V	18	■		
Imperial Palace Vicinity: *Hotel Harvest Kyoto* ¥¥ Karasuma-dori/Marutamachi sagaru. ☎ *(075) 251-1092.* FAX *(075) 251-1239.* Located very near the Imperial Palace, the Harvest is a fine medium-sized hotel with a comfortable lounge bar off the lobby. TV all rooms.	AE DC MC V	81		●	
Imperial Palace Vicinity: *Kyoto Palace-Side Hotel* ¥¥ Karasuma-dori, Shimo-dachiuri agaru. ☎ *(075) 431-8171.* FAX *(075) 414-2018.* Small-scale, friendly, and pleasant hotel conveniently located just a three-minute walk from the Marutamachi subway stop. TV all rooms.	AE DC MC V	119		●	
Imperial Palace Vicinity: *Kyoto Brighton Hotel* ¥¥¥¥¥ Shinmachi/Naka-dachiuri. ☎ *(075) 441-4411.* FAX *(075) 431-2360.* Located just west of the Imperial Palace, the Brighton offers impeccable service and top-class facilities in a quiet neighborhood. TV all rooms.	AE DC MC V	183		●	
Eastern Kyoto: *Miyako Hotel* ¥¥¥ Sanjo/Keage. ☎ *(075) 771-7111.* FAX *(075) 751-2490.* @ yoyaku@miyakohotel.co.jp Beautifully situated on a wooded hillside close to Nanzen-ji Temple, the Miyako is one of the grande dames of Kyoto hotelery. TV all rooms.	AE DC MC V	528		●	■
Eastern Kyoto: *Ryokan Murasaki* ¥¥¥ 570-7 Gion-machi Minamigawa. ☎ + FAX *(075) 541-7004.* A small inn with helpful owners, located in the heart of the historic Gion district. Book in advance. Rates incl breakfast. TV none.		5	■		
Eastern Kyoto: *Hotel Sunflower Kyoto* ¥¥¥ 5/1 Higashi Tenno-cho. ☎ *(075) 761-9111.* FAX *(075) 761-1333.* Medium-sized hotel close to the Heian Shrine and Kurodani Temple. It has more atmosphere than a business hotel. TV 123 rooms.	AE DC MC V	156	■	●	■
Northern Kyoto: *Green Peace Kyoto* ¥ 14-1 Matsugasaki/Shibamoto-cho. ☎ + FAX *(075) 791-9890.* A low-budget traveler favorite, this guest house is especially good for long stays. Dormitory and private rooms are available, with shared showers, toilets, kitchen, and living room. Min stay 3 nights. TV none.		15	■		
Northern Kyoto: *Tani House* ¥ 8 Daitokuji-cho, Murasakino. ☎ *(075) 492-5489.* FAX *(075) 493-6419.* A favorite with budget travelers, Tani House lies near the Zen monastery complex Daitoku-ji. Advance reservations required. TV none.	AE DC MC V	8	■		
Northern Kyoto: *Ryokan Rakucho* ¥¥ 67 Hangi-cho, Shimogamo-higashi. ☎ *(075) 721-2174.* FAX *(075) 791-7202.* Clean, quiet, comfortable, and welcoming to foreigners, Ryokan Rakucho is located in a residential area. TV none.	AE MC V	8	■		
WESTERN HONSHU					
Amanohashidate: *Genmyoan* ¥¥¥¥¥ 32 Monju, Miyazu. ☎ *(0772) 22-2171.* FAX *(0772) 25-1641.* @ genmyoan@mxa.nkansai.ne.jp A small deluxe hotel with good views of the bay. Rooms are quite spacious and comfortable. Rates incl meals. TV all rooms.	AE MC V	28	■		
Fukiya: *Fukiya International Villa* ¥ 836 Fukiya, Nariwa-cho. ☎ *(086) 256-2535.* FAX *(086) 256-2576.* W www.harenet.ne.jp/villa Modeled after a traditional Okayama soy sauce warehouse, this villa is part of a local organization offering high-quality accommodations at discount prices only to foreigners and their Japanese guests. TV none.		5			■

Hotel	Price	Credit cards	Rooms			
HIMEJI: *Himeji Castle Hotel* 210 Nishinomachi. *(0792) 84-3311.* FAX *(0792) 84-3729.* With staff who are accustomed to dealing with foreign visitors, this is one of the most stress-free hotels in town. Cheap-end twins with separate bathrooms are a good value. all rooms.	¥¥	AE V	257		●	
HIROSHIMA: *Mikawa Ryokan* 9-6 Kyobashi-cho (nr stn). *(082) 261-2719.* FAX *(082) 263-2706.* Another great bargain, the Mikawa, not surprisingly, is very popular, so it is best to book well in advance. none.	¥	AE V	13	■		
HIROSHIMA: *World Friendship Center* 8-10 Higashi-Kannon. *(082) 503-3191.* FAX *(082) 503-3179.* @ wfc@ma7.seikyou.ne.jp Cozy bed-and-breakfast place run by a welcoming American couple working for the non-profit WFC, which is an organization promoting international friendship and peace across borders. Rates incl breakfast. none.	¥	AE DC MC V	4			
HIROSHIMA: *Hotel Sunroute* 3-3-1 Otemachi, Naka-ku. *(082) 249-3600.* FAX *(082) 249-3677.* W http://sunroute.aska. or.jp A well-run business hotel facing the river and Peace Park, and with good extra facilities such as no-smoking rooms. all rooms.	¥¥¥	AE DC MC V	284		●	
HIROSHIMA: *Mitakiso* 1-7 Mitaki-cho, Nishi-ku. *(082) 237-1402.* FAX *(082) 237-1403.* Graceful rooms, some with sliding doors opening onto an elegant landscaped garden, and cuisine with a good reputation. Rates incl meals. 3 rooms.	¥¥¥¥¥	AE DC MC V	10	■		
ISE: *Hoshidekan* 2-15-2 Kawasake. *(0596) 28-2377.* FAX *(0596) 27-2830.* @ mblu@e-net.or.jp Very good value in an old-fashioned *ryokan* that is conveniently close to Ise-shi station. A small extra charge is made for meals. none.	¥	AE MC V	12	■		
IWAKUNI: *Iwakuni Youth Hostel* 1-10-46 Yokoyama. *(0827) 43-1092.* FAX *(0827) 43-0123.* Friendly staff, shared *tatami* rooms with TVs, and a tranquil setting make up for the slightly rundown state of the building. Rates incl meals. none.	¥		12			
IZUMO: *Takenoya* 857 Kizuki-Minami, Taisha-machi. *(0853) 53-3131.* FAX *(0853) 53-3134.* A wooden inn right opposite Izumo Shrine. The wooden corridors and *tatami* rooms have a nicely weathered feel. Rates incl meals. 28 rooms.	¥¥¥	AE DC MC V	44	■		
KOBE: *Kobe Sauna and Spa* 2-chome, Shimoyamate-dori, Chuo-ku. *(078) 322-1126.* FAX *(078) 393-4126.* Capsule hotel for both men and women between JR Sannomiya station and the Washington Hotel. Sauna and showers are available. The check in/out times are 5pm–10am.	¥					
KOBE: *Hana Hotel* 4-2-7 Nunobiki-cho (nr Sannomiya stn). *(078) 221-1087.* FAX *(078) 221-1785.* Classic, good-value business hotel with all the usual amenities. The staff are helpful, and the layout of the hotel spacious. all rooms.	¥¥	AE DC MC V	47		●	
KOBE: *Hotel Grand Vista* Nr Shin-Kobe stn. *(078) 271-2111.* FAX *(078) 271-1171.* @ info@grandvista.co.jp Most rooms have good views in this well-appointed hotel with English-speaking staff. Good-value Italian food in the restaurant. all rooms.	¥¥¥		108		●	
KOBE: *Hotel Okura Kobe* 2-1 Hatoba-cho, Chuo-ku. *(078) 333-0111.* FAX *(078) 333-6673.* Part of the prestigious Okura flagship, this hotel is well situated next to Kobe's Meriken Park and the Port Tower. A business center, travel agent, tea ceremony room, and health club are among facilities. all rooms.	¥¥¥¥	AE DC MC V	489		●	■
KURASHIKI: *Minshuku Kamoi* 1-24 Honmachi. *(086) 422-4898.* FAX *(086) 427-7615.* Clean, simple *tatami* rooms in an exceptionally cheap *minshuku*. The food is excellent, because the owner runs the Kamoi Restaurant *(see p332)*. Rates incl meals. none.	¥¥		17	■		
KURASHIKI: *Kurashiki Kokusai Hotel* 1-1-44 Chuo. *(086) 422-5141.* FAX *(086) 422-5192.* A modern hotel designed to blend in with the local architecture. There are just four Japanese-style rooms. all rooms.	¥¥	AE DC MC V	106		●	■

Price categories per night for two people sharing a room, including tax and service charges.
¥ under ¥8,000
¥¥ ¥8,000–15,000
¥¥¥ ¥15,000–25,000
¥¥¥¥ ¥25,000–35,000
¥¥¥¥¥ over ¥35,000

Credit Cards
AE American Express; DC Diners Club; MC MasterCard; V VISA.

Ryokan or Minshuku
Traditional Japanese accommodations, usually with *tatami*-mat rooms and shared bathing facilities *(see pp290–91)*.

Business or Western Style
Business hotel *(see p289)* or hotel with mainly Western-style rooms and facilities.

Japanese/Western Rooms
Both Japanese-style and Western-style rooms are available.

	Credit Cards	Number of Rooms	Ryokan or Minshuku	Business or Western Style	Japanese/Western Rooms
Kurashiki: *Ryokan Kurashiki* ¥¥¥ 4-1 Honmachi. *(086) 422-0730.* FAX *(086) 422-0990.* Classic Japanese hospitality in Kurashiki's oldest, most elegant inn, which has an inner garden where you can sip tea, and a restaurant famous for regional dishes. 8 rooms.	AE DC MC V	17	■		
Lake Biwa: *Biwako Hotel* ¥¥¥ 2-40 Hamamachi, Otsu. *(0775) 24-1511.* W www.biwakohotel.co.jp A comfortable international hotel near the lake shore, which has a relaxing and quiet atmosphere. all rooms.	AE DC MC V	171		●	
Matsue: *Ryokan Terazuya* ¥ 60-3 Tenjin-machi. *(0852) 21-3480.* FAX *(0852) 21-3422.* This small intimate inn has been run by the same kindly family since 1893, who have no inhibitions about taking in foreigners. none.		10	■		
Matsue: *Hotel Ichibata* ¥¥¥ 30 Chidori-cho. *(0852) 22-0188.* FAX *(0852) 22-0230.* Located in the hot-spring section of town, this hotel has indoor and outdoor baths. The Japanese rooms have fine views of the lake. none.	AE DC V	148		●	■
Miyajima Island: *Guesthouse Kikugawa* ¥ 796 Miyajima. *(0829) 44-0039.* FAX *(0829) 44-2773.* Ask for one of the beautiful *tatami*-mat rooms with high-tech toilets at this small, friendly place with a tiny garden. all rooms.	AE DC MC V	8		●	■
Miyajima Island: *Iwaso* ¥¥¥¥ Miyajima, Saeki-gun. *(0829) 44-2233.* FAX *(0829) 44-2230.* The island's oldest and most gracious accommodation. Be sure to stay in the older wing, not the new addition. Rates incl meals. 31 rooms.	AE V	42	■		
Mount Koya: *Mount Koya Monastery* ¥¥¥ Cable car from Gokurakubashi stn. *(0736) 56-2616.* Basic lodgings at a spectacular mountain temple *(see p193)*. Be sure to take warm clothes if staying in wintertime. Rates incl meals. none.					
Nara: *Ryokan Seikan-so* ¥ 29 Higashi Kitsuji-cho (nr Kofukuji). + FAX *(0742) 22-2670.* One of Nara's best budget accommodations, where the rooms look onto a spacious garden. none.	AE MC V	11	■		
Nara: *Edo-san* ¥¥¥ 1167 Takabatake-cho. *(0742) 26-2662.* FAX *(0742) 26-2663.* This lovely old *ryokan* began life as a restaurant in 1907 before converting to an inn, composed of cottages positioned around a beautiful garden. It still has a high reputation for its cooking. none.	AE MC V	11	■		
Nara: *Nara Hotel* ¥¥¥ 1096 Takabatake-cho. *(0742) 26-3300.* FAX *(0742) 23-5252.* W www.hotels.westjr.co.jp One of Japan's few hotels designed in the style of the grand old hotels of the Orient, like the Strand in Rangoon and the E&O in Penang. Try to stay in the old wing with its high ceilings, period fixtures and fittings, and cypress paneling and eaves. all rooms.	AE DC MC V	132		●	■
Nara: *Kikusuiro* ¥¥¥¥ 1130 Takabataka-cho. *(0742) 23-2001.* FAX *(0742) 26-0025.* Rooms in this first-class, 140-year-old *ryokan* are decorated with genuine antiques and artworks. Rates incl meals. none.		14	■		
Okayama: *Ark Hotel* ¥¥ 2-6-1 Shimoishii (nr stn). *(086) 233-2200.* FAX *(086 225-1663.* Clean and efficient business hotel that is used to foreigners. all rooms.	AE DC MC V	178		●	■

Hotel	Price	Cards	Rooms			
OKAYAMA: *Chisan Hotel Okayama* 1-1-13 Marunouchi. (086) 225-1212. FAX (086) 225-1322. Close to the Koraku-en garden, this ten-story business hotel with reasonably priced singles and twin rooms is part of a chain. all rooms.	¥¥	AE DC MC V	212		●	
OKAYAMA: *Okayama Plaza Hotel* 2-3-12 Hama. (086) 272-1201. FAX (086) 273-1557. The rooms here are of a generous size considering the price, and facilities include two restaurants and a local products and craft shop. all rooms.	¥¥	AE DC MC V	85		●	■
OSAKA: *Capsule Inn Namba* Namba-Naka, 1-7-16. (06) 6633-2666. Well-located capsule hotel near Namba station, with a good choice of single and double units, for both men and women. Operates 3pm–10am.	¥					
OSAKA: *Yu-ing-Yu* Sakuragawa, 2-1-1 (nr Sakuragawa subway stn). (06) 6562-9551. One of the city's oldest capsule hotels, this is also one of its least expensive, and women are admitted as well as men. Operates 4pm–10am.	¥					
OSAKA: *Ebisu-so Ryokan* 1-7-33 Nihonbashi-Nisi, Naniwa-ku. (06) 643-4861. This 50-year-old inn has seen better days, but its friendly owner, intimate atmosphere, and decent rates make it an option. none.	¥¥	AE MC V	11	■		
OSAKA: *Hotel Hokke Club* 12-19 Togano-cho (nr Osaka stn). (06) 6313-3171. FAX (06) 6313-4637. A good bargain for semi-budget travelers, this is one of the city's inexpensive, and older, business hotels. Standard rooms with public baths. none.	¥¥	AE DC MC V	247		●	■
OSAKA: *D-Hotel* 2-5-15 Dotonbori, Chuo-ku. (06) 6212-2995. FAX (06) 6212-7462. Trendy, post-modernist-style hotel with lovely simple, minimalist lines to rooms. A good location for Dotonbori's lively nightlife scene. all rooms.	¥¥¥	AE MC V	12		●	
OSAKA: *Rihga Grand Hotel* 2-3-18 Nakanoshima (next to Osaka Festival Hall). (06) 6202-1212. FAX (06) 6227-5054. The 40-year-old Grand combines a faded European appeal and modern facilities such as cable TVs in each room. all rooms.	¥¥¥	AE DC MC V	310		●	
OSAKA: *Rihga Royal Hotel* 5-3-68 Nakanoshima Kita-ku. (06) 6448-1121. FAX (06) 6448-4414. One of Osaka's older hotels, the Royal has over 20 restaurants catering to every taste, and a lovely swimming pool and Jacuzzi. all rooms.	¥¥¥	AE DC MC V	993		●	■
OSAKA: *Hotel Nikko Kansai Kuko* By Kansai airport. (0724) 55-1111. FAX (0724) 55-1155. Good facilities and reasonably sized rooms; excellent for airline passengers with early departures or late arrivals. all rooms.	¥¥¥¥	AE DC MC V	576		●	
OSAKA: *Hotel Hankyu International* 19-19 Chayamachi, Kita-ku. (06) 6377-2100. FAX (06) 6377-3622. W www.hhi.co.jp One of the most cosmopolitan hotels in Osaka, offering spacious guest rooms, marble bathrooms, and top-notch service. all rooms.	¥¥¥¥¥	AE DC MC V	168		●	■
SHIRAHAMA: *Hotel Kawakyu* 3745 Shirahama-cho, Nishimuro-gun. (0739) 42-2661. FAX (0739) 42-2666. A very comfortable, medium-size deluxe hotel. Ask for one of the rooms overlooking the Pacific. all rooms.	¥¥¥¥	AE DC MC V	88		●	
TSUWANO: *Ryokan Meigetsu* Tsuwano-cho, Kanoashi-gun. (08567) 2-0685. FAX (08567) 2-0637. An old-fashioned *ryokan* with wonderful cypress bathtubs. Rates incl meals. 8 rooms.	¥¥	AE MC V	13	■		
TSUWANO: *Minshuku Wakasagi no Yado* Tsuwano-cho, Kanoashi-gun. + FAX (08567) 2-1146. The friendly staff from this small *minshuku* will come by car to meet you at the station if asked. Rates incl meals. none.	¥¥		8	■		
YAMAGUCHI: *Matsudaya Hotel* 3-6-7 Yuda Onsen. (083) 922-0125. FAX (083)925-6111. A Meiji-era bath and elegant teahouse are attached to this historically important inn, which is celebrated for its local cuisine. none.	¥¥¥	AE DC MC V	34	■		

For key to symbols see back flap

Price categories per night for two people sharing a room, including tax and service charges.
¥ under ¥8,000
¥¥ ¥8,000–15,000
¥¥¥ ¥15,000–25,000
¥¥¥¥ ¥25,000–35,000
¥¥¥¥¥ over ¥35,000

Credit Cards
AE American Express; DC Diners Club; MC MasterCard; V VISA.

Ryokan or Minshuku
Traditional Japanese accommodations, usually with *tatami*-mat rooms and shared bathing facilities *(see pp290–91)*.

Business or Western Style
Business hotel *(see p289)* or hotel with mainly Western-style rooms and facilities.

Japanese/Western Rooms
Both Japanese-style and Western-style rooms are available.

Hotel	Price	Credit Cards	Number of Rooms	Ryokan or Minshuku	Business or Western Style	Japanese/Western Rooms
Yoshino: *Keisho-no-yado Ho-un Kan* Yoshino-yama. (07463) 2-3001. FAX (07463) 2-8633. Traditional *ryokan* with cherry and Yoshino cedar wood interiors. Rates incl meals. all rooms.	¥¥¥	AE DC MC V	32	■		
SHIKOKU						
Anan Coastal Area: *Hotel Riviera Shishikui* Matsubara, on Hwy 55 nr Shishikui stn. (0884) 76-3300. FAX (0884) 76-3910. All rooms face the sea at this hotel with a great "Riviera" façade, rooftop garden pool, and floating restaurant. Rates incl meals. all rooms.	¥¥¥¥	AE MC V	28		●	■
Cape Ashizuri Area: *Bellreef Otsuki* Otsuki-cho, Hata-gun. (0880) 74-0222. FAX (0880) 74-0080. The bright, airy maisonettes with lofts here are situated next to an ecology camp and surrounded by coastal scenery. all rooms.	¥¥	V	20		●	■
Kochi: *Sansuien* Takashomachi-cho. (088) 22-0131. FAX (088) 22-0145. @ sansuien@i-kochi.or.jp Centrally located on the river, with enormous gardens, this famous estate has over 180 years of history. all rooms.	¥¥¥¥	AE DC MC V	131	■		■
Kochi: *Joseikan* 2-chome, Kamimachi. (088) 75-0111. FAX (088) 24-0557. @ joseikan@mb.inforyoma.or.jp Luxury hotel where the emperor stays. Famous for its bath with a view of Kochi Castle, and its attached tearoom. Rates incl meals. all rooms.	¥¥¥¥¥	AE DC MC V	72	■		■
Kotohira: *Kotohira Riverside Hotel* 246-1 Kotohira-cho (on river). (0877) 75-1800. FAX (0877) 75-2890. Modern-style *ryokan* with nice views and friendly service. Unusually, one third of the rooms are singles. There is an *onsen* at the affiliated Kotohira Grand, one block away. all rooms.	¥¥	AE DC V	30		●	
Kotohira: *Kotohira Kadan* Kotohira. (0877) 75-3232. FAX (087) 75-3235. Classic *ryokan* on a large scale, with a historic garden praised by the late 19th-century novelist Mori Ogai. Rates incl meals. all rooms.	¥¥¥¥	AE DC MC V	57	■		■
Matsuyama: *Dogokan* 7-26 Dogo-tako-cho. (089) 41-7777. FAX (089) 41-7707. With this contemporary interpretation of Edo luxury, you get a view of the castle from the communal bath, tearooms, sauna, and daily concerts on a historic *orgel* music box. Rates incl meals. all rooms.	¥¥¥¥	AE DC MC V	90	■		■
Naruto: *Naruto Hotel Hama* 65 Aza-maehama. (088) 685-2600. FAX (088) 686-4800. Business hotel with all the usual amenities and extremely well located, two-minutes' walk from JR Kotohira station. all rooms.	¥¥	AE DC V	71		●	■
Naruto: *Sanukiya* 39 Aza-Mitsuicho. (088) 686-3301. FAX (088) 686-3347. Low-key *ryokan* in a useful location, just three-minutes' walk from JR Kotohira station. Meals are available for an additional cost. 3 rooms.	¥¥	AE MC V	15	■		■
Ozu: *Ninomiya Ryokan* 2 Naka-machi (20-min walk from JR Iyo-Ozu stn). (089) 324-2747. Modest *ryokan* with low prices; slightly more if you decide to take the reasonable quality meals. none.	¥		7	■		
Takamatsu: *Rihga Hotel Zest Takamatsu* 9-1 Furujin-machi. (087) 822-3555. FAX (087) 822-7516. Bright, elegant, and modern business hotel in a central location. There are French, Japanese, and Chinese restaurants, and a coffee shop. all rooms.	¥¥¥	AE DC MC V	133		●	■

Hotel	Credit cards	Rooms			
TAKAMATSU: *Hotel Jingoro* ¥¥¥¥ 1831-5 Higashimachi, Yashima. Tel *(087) 841-3335.* FAX *(087) 843-2170.* The most spacious *ryokan* on Yashima, located on a summit with splendid views. Can be reached by road or cable car. Rates incl meals. 35 rooms.	AE DC MC V	49	■		■
UWAJIMA AREA: *Mori no Kuni Hotel* ¥¥¥ Meguro. Tel *(0895) 43-0331.* FAX *(0895) 43-0333.* @ nametoko@morinokuni.or.jp Classic resort hotel famed for its setting on the Nametoko Gorge as well as its high ceiling, Art Deco touches, and fireplace. You can reach it by bus on winding mountain roads. Its lodge has Western-style showers. 7 rooms.	DC MC V	15		●	■
KYUSHU					
AMAMI ISLAND: *Resort Hotel Marine Station Amami* ¥¥ Yadorihama, Setouchi-cho, Oshima-gun. Tel *(09977) 2-1001.* FAX *(09977) 2-3932.* Beautifully located on a quiet white beach at the southern tip of Amami Island, this hotel has first-rate boating and diving services as well as outdoor and indoor pools. all rooms.	AE MC V	53		●	■
BEPPU: *Sakaeya* ¥¥ Ida, Kannawa. Tel *(0977) 66-6234.* FAX *(0977) 66-6235.* Beppu's oldest *minshuku* and one of its most charming, with Meiji-period fixtures and fittings in some rooms. A stone oven in the courtyard is powered by steam from a hot spring. 7 rooms.		12	■		
BEPPU: *Tenjuso* ¥¥¥¥ Minami-soencho 6 Kumi. Tel *(0977) 23-0131.* FAX *(0977) 25-8455.* A 70-year-old *ryokan* with some rooms overlooking the sea, and lovely indoor and outdoor hot springs. Rates incl meals. 9 rooms.		13	■		■
FUKUOKA: *Toyoko Inn* ¥¥ 1-38 Gion-cho, Hakata-ku. Tel *(092) 281-1045.* FAX *(092) 281-1046.* A new, inexpensive inn that attracts young people, with its light and spacious rooms in a clean, efficient setup. Preferably book in advance. all rooms.	AE DC MC V	176		●	
FUKUOKA: *Hakata Miyako Hotel* ¥¥¥ By main stn. Tel *(092) 441-3111.* FAX *(092) 481-1306.* @ info@hakatamiyako.co.jp Part of a well-known and respected chain, and used to foreign clients. Facilities include a beauty salon, souvenir shop, and medical clinic. all rooms.	AE DC MC V	266		●	■
FUKUOKA: *Lakeside Hotel Hisayama* ¥¥¥ Kubara, Hisayama-machi (20 km NW of Hakata stn). Tel *(092) 976-1800.* FAX *(092) 976-1840.* Large, airy rooms in a modern spa hotel, which has an unusual red-wine bath for women and crushed pearl baths for both sexes. Excellent French-Japanese fusion cuisine and acupuncture also available. Rates incl meals. 24 rooms.	MC V	46		●	■
FUKUOKA: *Il Palazzo* ¥¥¥ 3-13-1 Haruyoshi, Chuo-ku. Tel *(092) 716-3333.* FAX *(092) 724-3330.* The creation of Italian architect Aldo Rossi and top-notch Japanese interior designers, this hotel has spacious rooms with marble baths and excellent Italian food. all rooms.	AE DC MC V	62		●	■
KAGOSHIMA: *Nakazono Ryukan* ¥ 1-18 Yasui-cho. Tel *(099) 226-5125.* FAX *(099) 226-5126.* @ shindon@satsuma.ne.jp This Japan Inn Group *ryokan* doesn't offer meals or its own bath, but it is well located, and you can use the 24-hour public baths nearby. none.	AE V	10	■		
KAGOSHIMA: *Kagoshima Tokyu Hotel* ¥¥¥ 22-1 Kamoike Shinmachi. Tel *(099) 257-2411.* FAX *(099) 257-6083.* Located on the waterfront, this hotel's balcony rooms have a good view of Kagoshima's volcano, especially at sunset. Natural hot-spring Jacuzzis and two outdoor swimming pools add to the hotel's assets. all rooms.	AE DC MC V	206		●	
KAGOSHIMA: *Shigetomiso* ¥¥¥¥¥ 31-7 Shimizu-cho. Tel *(099) 247-3155.* FAX *(099) 247-0960.* An aristocratic *ryokan* for an expensive, first-rate splurge. The setting is perfect, within a hillside garden overlooking the sea. The older rooms date from the early 19th century and reek of history. A scene from one of the James Bond films was shot here. Rates incl meals. all rooms.	AE DC MC V	8	■		■
KUMAMOTO: *Ark Hotel* ¥¥ 5-16 Joto-machi. Tel *(096) 351-2222.* FAX *(096) 326-0909.* @ ark-kumamoto@mb.infobears.ne.jp Close to the castle, the Ark has a flower theme including a bamboo garden in the lobby and pleasant flower-patterned rooms. all rooms.	AE MC V	222		●	

For key to symbols see back flap

Price categories per night for two people sharing a room, including tax and service charges.

¥ under ¥8,000
¥¥ ¥8,000–15,000
¥¥¥ ¥15,000–25,000
¥¥¥¥ ¥25,000–35,000
¥¥¥¥¥ over ¥35,000

CREDIT CARDS
AE American Express; DC Diners Club; MC MasterCard; V VISA.

RYOKAN OR MINSHUKU
Traditional Japanese accommodations, usually with *tatami*-mat rooms and shared bathing facilities *(see pp290–91)*.

BUSINESS OR WESTERN STYLE
Business hotel *(see p289)* or hotel with mainly Western-style rooms and facilities.

JAPANESE/WESTERN ROOMS
Both Japanese-style and Western-style rooms are available.

	Credit Cards	Number of Rooms	Ryokan or Minshuku	Business or Western Style	Japanese/Western Rooms
KUMAMOTO: *Maruko Hotel* ¥¥¥ 11-10 Kamitori-cho (just E of castle). *(096) 353-1241.* FAX *(096) 353-1217.* The majority of the Maruko's rooms are Japanese style. Meals, if you choose to have them here, are served in the room, a practice normally associated with more expensive inns. Rates incl meals. 6 rooms.	AE DC MC V	46		●	■
MIYAZAKI: *Pension Hyugaji* ¥ 2-4-32 Aoshima. + FAX *(0985) 65-1290.* A *minshuku*-style pension conveniently located opposite JR Aoshima Station. Simple, but clean and serviceable. 5 rooms.		16	■		■
MIYAZAKI: *Aoshima Palm Beach Hotel* ¥¥¥ 1-16-1 Aoshima. *(0985) 65-2929.* FAX *(0985) 65-2655.* Set in beautiful grounds, the hotel has rooms with large windows looking out over the sea. Guests can use the hot-spring baths, sauna, gym, and swimming pool. It is ideal for families. Rates incl breakfast. all rooms.	AE DC MC V	214		●	■
MOUNT ASO: *Seifu-So* ¥¥ Kawayo, Choyo-son, Aso-gun. *(09676) 7-0005.* FAX *(09676) 7-1678.* A modest but pleasant inn located in Jigoku Onsen. Meals are cooked by guests themselves sitting around an open hearth in traditional style. Hot springs are available. Rates incl meals. all rooms.		39	■		
MOUNT ASO: *Aso Prince Hotel* ¥¥¥ Komezuka Onsen, Akamizu, Aso-machi. *(0967) 35-2111.* FAX *(0967) 35-1124.* A top-notch international hotel located right next to Mount Nakadake, with luxurious mineral baths, tennis courts, and two golf courses designed by American champion Arnold Palmer. all rooms.	AE DC MC V	180		●	
NAGASAKI: *Nagasaki Youth Hostel* ¥ 1-1-16 Tateyama. *(095) 823-5032.* FAX *(095) 823-4321.* A conveniently located youth hostel open to non-members. A laundry service is available. There are 122 beds in dormitories. Rates incl breakfast. none.					■
NAGASAKI: *Tredia Hotel Dejima* ¥¥ 1-25 Dejima-machi. *(0958) 26-4176.* FAX *(0958) 25-0081.* One of the best business hotels in the city offering simple, clean accommodations at modest rates. A good location near the shopping center with access to several sights. all rooms.	AE DC V	129		●	
NAGASAKI: *Hotel Majestic* ¥¥¥ 2-28 Minami Yamate-machi. *(095) 827-7777.* FAX *(095) 827-6112.* True to its name, this small hotel's rooms, each with a different design theme, offer majestic views, especially the bayside terrace rooms. There is a small European restaurant and bar. all rooms.	AE DC MC V	23		●	
NAGASAKI: *Sakamoto-ya* ¥¥¥¥ 2-13 Kanaya-machi. *(095) 826-8211.* FAX *(095) 825-5944.* Small, early Meiji-era Japanese inn at the center of the city. Most rooms have private, Japanese-style wooden tubs for bathing. One even has a private garden attached. Rates incl meals. all rooms.	AE DC V	17	■		
UNZEN SPA: *Seiunso Kokumin Shukusha* ¥ 500-1 Unzen, Obamacho, Minami Takaki-gun. *(0957) 73-3273.* FAX *(0957) 73-2698.* The least expensive accommodations in the area, with superb views, a small restaurant, public bath, and laundry facilities. none.		52	■		
UNZEN SPA: *Unzen Kanko Hotel* ¥¥ 320 Unzen, Obamacho, Minami-Takaki-gun. *(0957) 73-3263.* FAX *(0957) 73-3419.* The wood and stone construction is covered in ivy, while the rooms, with their high ceilings, wooden ceiling beams, and stately balconies speak of a bygone age. all rooms.	AE DC MC V	59		●	■

Hotel	Price	Credit cards	Rooms			
YUFUIN: *Pension Momotaro* 839-1, Kawakami, Yufuin, Oita-gun. ☎ *(0977) 85-2187.* FAX *(0977) 85-4002.* Located in a quiet wood with two inside baths and one open-air spa. The friendly owners serve regional specialties such as sweet river fish and wild chicken. Some A-frame chalets available. Rates incl meals. 💧 🖥 all rooms.	¥¥¥		14	■		■

OKINAWA

Hotel	Price	Credit cards	Rooms			
IRIOMOTE ISLAND: *Pension Iriomote* 750 Tsuchigahama-Iriguchi, Taketomi-cho, Yaeyama-gun. ☎ *(09808) 5-6555.* Set in a pretty bay, this pension has an attached beachside club-restaurant serving good food. You can arrange to rent diving and windsurfing gear here. 🖥 2 rooms.	¥¥¥		5		●	
ISHIGAKI ISLAND: *Hotel Miyahira* 4-9 Misaki, Ishigaki-shi. ☎ *(09808) 2-6111.* FAX *(09808) 3-3236.* @ hotel@miyahira.co.jp A resort hotel with a good pool. Some of the accommodations are in bungalows. Rates incl breakfast. 🖥 all rooms.	¥¥	AE MC V	158		●	
KUME ISLAND: *Eef Beach Hotel* 548 Janado, Nakazato-son, Shimajiri-gun. ☎ *(098) 985-7111.* FAX *(098) 985-7117.* Owned by ANA (All Nippon Airways), this smallish hotel has a marvelous beach and offers the best services and facilities for watersports. 🖥 all rooms.	¥¥¥	AE MC V	80		●	■
MIYAKO ISLAND: *Hotel New Irabu* 57-2 Kuninaka, Irabu-cho. ☎ *(09807) 8-3421.* FAX *(09807) 8-3066.* A nicely located *minshuku* beside the Kuninaka Straits; an inexpensive and friendly option. 🖥 none.	¥¥		8	■		
NAHA: *Ryokan Narumi* 2-17-46 Makishi. ☎ *(098) 67-2138.* FAX *(098) 867-2517.* Small but conveniently located inn near Kokusai-dori. The reasonable price includes two meals. 🖥 none.	¥		16	■		■
NAHA: *Naha Tokyu Hotel* 1002, Ameku, Naha. ☎ *(098) 868-2151.* FAX *(098) 868-7895.* There are good harbor views from many of the rooms in this luxury, international standard hotel. 🖥 all rooms.	¥¥¥	AE DC MC V	208		●	
NAHA: *Okinawa Harbor View Hotel* 2-46 Izumizaki, Naha-shi, Okinawa. ☎ *(098) 853-2111.* FAX *(098) 834-6103.* This swanky international resort standard hotel owned by ANA is considered the number-one accommodation in Naha. 🖥 all rooms.	¥¥¥	AE MC V	368		●	
TAKETOMI ISLAND: *Minshuku Izumiya* 377 Taketomi, Taketomi-cho, Yaeyama-gun. ☎ *(09808) 5-2250.* A friendly little place that can organize diving trips and rent gear for guests. Rates incl meals. 🖥 none.	¥¥		7	■		

NORTHERN HONSHU

Hotel	Price	Credit cards	Rooms			
AIZU-WAKAMATSU: *Shibukawa Donya* 3-28 Nanoka-machi. ☎ *(0242) 28-4000.* FAX *(0242) 26-6464.* This intriguing inn was once home to a wholesaler of dried fish, and cod and herring are still featured on its eclectic menu. Writer Mishima Yukio (1925–70) once stayed here. Rates incl meals. 🖥 none.	¥¥¥		16	■		
AIZU-WAKAMATSU: *Mukaitaki* Higashiyama-cho. ☎ *(0242) 27-7501.* FAX *(0242) 28-0939.* W www.mukaitaki.com An old wooden spa inn with a classic elegance not often found. Its 11 *sukiya*-style (tea ceremony) rooms face an intimate garden, which is illuminated at night. A geisha service is available. Rates incl meals. 💧 🖥 3 rooms.	¥¥¥¥¥	AE DC V	28	■		
HANAMAKI: *Kikusuikan* 123 Hikageza ka, Yuguchi. ☎ *(0198) 25-2233.* FAX *(0198) 25-2233.* Charming old-fashioned spa inn, a favorite of writer Miyazawa Kenji (1896–1933) when he was a boy. It has a variety of baths including an open-air one for mixed bathing. Rates incl meals. 💧 🖥 none.	¥¥	V	15	■		
HIRAIZUMI: *Hotel Musashibo* 15 Osawa. ☎ *(0191) 46-2241.* FAX *(0191) 46-2250.* This newly renovated inn, located next to Motsu-ji, has large communal baths with panoramic garden views. Maesawa beef, a local product much prized by gourmets, is on the menu. Rates incl meals. 💧 🖥 42 rooms.	¥¥¥	AE DC MC V	48	■		■

For key to symbols see back flap

Price categories per night for two people sharing a room, including tax and service charges.
¥ under ¥8,000
¥¥ ¥8,000–15,000
¥¥¥ ¥15,000–25,000
¥¥¥¥ ¥25,000–35,000
¥¥¥¥¥ over ¥35,000

Credit Cards
AE American Express; DC Diners Club; MC MasterCard; V VISA.

Ryokan or Minshuku
Traditional Japanese accommodations, usually with *tatami*-mat rooms and shared bathing facilities *(see pp290–91)*.

Business or Western Style
Business hotel *(see p289)* or hotel with mainly Western-style rooms and facilities.

Japanese/Western Rooms
Both Japanese-style and Western-style rooms are available.

Hotel	Price	Credit Cards	Number of Rooms	Ryokan or Minshuku	Business or Western Style	Japanese/Western Rooms
Hirosaki: *Hotel Hokke Club* 126 Dotemachi. *(0172) 34-3811.* FAX *(0172) 32-0589.* Efficient business hotel whose location, on a busy shopping street, is hard to beat. The entrance is up an escalator next to Kinokuniya bookstore, which caters to Hirosaki's foreign population. all rooms.	¥¥	AE DC MC V	122		●	
Kakunodate: *Folkloro Kakunodate* 14 Nakasudazawa, Iwase (next to stn). *(0187) 53-2070.* FAX *(0187) 53-2118.* Like the others in JR East's popular new chain of small town hotels, this offers excellent value and convenience. Credit card reservations can be made at any JR East View Plaza. all rooms.	¥¥		26		●	
Kakunodate: *Ishikawa Ryokan* 32 Iwase-cho, Kakunodate-machi, Senboku-gun. *(0187) 54-2030.* FAX *(0187) 54-2031.* This cozy inn, run by the same family for ten generations, has a reputation for hospitality and good food. 2 rooms.	¥¥¥		12	■		
Kamikita: *Tsuta Onsen Ryokan* Okuse, Towadako-machi. *(0176) 74-2311.* FAX *(0176) 74-2244.* Vines twine around the trees in the local beech forests and also decorate the banisters, posts, transoms, and bathrooms of this old-fashioned inn. There is a recent hotel-style annex too. 4 rooms.	¥¥¥	DC	50	■	●	
Kitakata: *Sasaya Ryokan* 4844 3-chome. *(0241) 22-0008.* FAX *(0241) 22-0238.* In business for over 100 years, this *kura* (storehouse) inn has several artworks by Yumeji Takehisa (1884–1934), who stayed here twice. none.	¥¥¥		15	■		
Morioka: *Hotel Metropolitan* 1-44 Morioka Eki-mae dori. *(019) 625-1211.* FAX *(019) 625-1210.* @ metro@nnet.ne.jp This modern, comfortable hotel, right next to JR Morioka station, has staff positively brimming with helpfulness and goodwill. all rooms.	¥¥¥	DC MC V	234		●	■
Nikko: *Nikko Kanaya Hotel* 1300 Kamihatsuishi-cho. *(0288) 54-0001.* FAX *(0288) 53-2487.* Opened in 1873, this classic hotel combines effortless, old-fashioned elegance with excellent service. all rooms.	¥¥	AE DC MC V	70		●	
Nikko: *Yumoto Itaya* Yumoto Onsen. *(0288) 62-2131.* FAX *(0288) 62-2575.* Recently renovated, this handsome 150-year-old spa inn in Oku-Nikko has indoor and outdoor baths. all rooms.	¥¥¥¥	AE DC V	24	■		■
Sado Island: *Akanashiya* 355 Onyado, Ogi, Ogi-machi. *(0259) 86-2058.* FAX *(0259) 86-3751.* This inn started out 50 years ago as a restaurant. Both food and service are outstanding, and the cypress-paneled bathrooms are lovely. none.	¥¥¥		5	■		
Sendai: *Hotel Central Sendai* 2-6 4-chome, Chuo, Aoba-ku (nr stn). *(022) 711-4111.* FAX *(022) 711-4110.* Women and solo travelers are welcome at this new business hotel which is eager to please. all rooms.	¥¥	DC MC V	97		●	
Tono: *Minshuku Magariya* 30-58-3 Niisato, Ayori-cho. *(0198) 62-4564.* Set in a hillside apple orchard, this family-run inn is housed in a beautifully restored *magariya* (L-shaped house shared by horses and people). The owner is a good source of local lore. none.	¥¥¥		10	■		
Tsuruoka: *Tokyo Dai-ichi Hotel Tsuruoka* 2-10 Nishiki-machi (nr stn and bus terminal). *(0235) 24-7611.* FAX *(0235) 24-7621.* Part of a reliable chain, this convenient business hotel has *onsen* baths on the top floor. all rooms.	¥¥	AE DC MC V	124		●	■

Hotel	Price	Credit cards	Rooms			
YAMAGATA: *Saikan* Toge, Haguro-machi. (0235) 62-2357. FAX (0235) 62-2352. These spacious shrine lodgings at the top of Mount Haguro offer meals featuring local mushrooms and edible wild vegetables. Guests have a unique chance to observe the morning service. Hundreds can stay. none.	¥¥	MC V				
HOKKAIDO						
AKAN NATIONAL PARK: *Hotel Yamaura* Akan-ko Onsen. (0154) 67-2311. FAX (0154) 67-2330. Well-appointed lakeside hotel, which has its own hot-spring baths. Rates incl meals. all rooms.	¥¥	AE DC MC V	92		●	■
DAISETSU-ZAN NATIONAL PARK: *Pension Milky House* Sounkyo. (01658) 5-3737. FAX (01658) 5-3404. Excellent value pension, built in the late 1990s, with Japanese-style rooms and food. There is a public hot bath. Rates incl meals. none.	¥¥		60	■		
HAKODATE: *B&B Pension Hakodatemura* 16-12 Suehiro-cho. (0138) 22-8105. FAX (0138) 22-8925. Clean, affordable, and centrally located, the rooms at this inn are mostly Western style. It is a member of the Japanese Inn Group and the Welcome Inn Reservation Center. 1 room.	¥	AE	18		●	
HAKODATE: *Niceday Inn* 9-11 Otemachi. (0138) 22-5919. A small and surprisingly inexpensive inn run by an amiable couple who speak English. There is no restaurant at the inn but plenty nearby. none.	¥		6	■		■
HAKODATE: *Wakamatsu Ryokan* 1-2-27 Yunokawa-cho. (0138) 59-2171. FAX (0138) 59-3316. @ wakamatsu@hakodate.ne.jp Patronized by the Imperial family, this traditional inn, over a century old, should be reserved for a special treat. It has indoor and outdoor baths and is well known for its cuisine. Rates incl meals. 26 rooms.	¥¥¥¥¥	AE DC MC V	29	■		■
KUSHIRO: *Castle Hotel* 2-5 Okawa-cho. (0154) 43-2111. FAX (0154) 42-0318. Less like a castle, more like a ship with peaked turrets and a nautical feel, this moderately sized hotel was designed by architect Mozuna Kiko in 1991. It is comfortable and full of light. all rooms.	¥¥¥¥	AE MC V	48		●	■
RISHIRI-REBUN-SAROBETSU NATIONAL PARK: *Hera-san no Ie* Rishiri-Fuji cho, Oshidomari. (01638) 2-2361. FAX (01638) 2-2366. A relaxed and homely little place that attracts travelers from all over the world – despite its size. Meals are excellent, usually with healthy fresh fish and vegetable dishes. Bicycles can be rented from the house. Rates incl meals. none.	¥¥¥		8			■
SAPPORO: *Fujiya Santus Hotel* Kita 3-jo (nr Botanical Gdns). (011) 271-3344. FAX (011) 241-4182. A small, good-value hotel with a friendly atmosphere. One restaurant serves European and Japanese dishes. all rooms.	¥¥	DC MC V	40		●	■
SAPPORO: *Nakamura-ya Ryokan* Kita 3-jo, Nishi 7 (opp Botanical Gdns). (011) 241-2111. FAX (011) 241-2118. All rooms are six-*tatami* mats in size and have built-in cupboards and alcoves to create a feeling of extra space. The hot-spring communal tub is luxurious. all rooms.	¥¥	AE MC V	29	■		
SAPPORO: *Hotel Arthur* Minami 10-jo, Nishi 6, Chuo-ku. (011) 561-1000. FAX (011) 521-5522. Completed in 1989 in a quasi Art Deco style, the Arthur enjoys a quiet location and good reputation for service. all rooms.	¥¥¥	AE DC MC V	229		●	■
SAPPORO: *Sapporo Grand Hotel* Kita 1-jo (nr stn). (011) 261-3311. FAX (011) 231-0388. W www.mitsuikanko.co.jp/sgh European-style hotel with old and new wings, both with modern facilities. Great food and drink options include a highly regarded French eatery and a superb bakery. all rooms.	¥¥¥	AE DC MC V	565		●	■
SAPPORO: *Hotel New Otani Sapporo* 1-1 Nishi, Kita-2, Chuo-ku. (011) 222-1111. FAX (011) 222-5521. Part of the excellent New Otani Chain, this hotel has up-to-date facilities. The lower-priced singles can be rather small. all rooms.	¥¥¥¥	AE DC MC V	340		●	■

For key to symbols see back flap

WHERE TO EAT

CONSIDERING the country's present profusion of restaurants (about 80,000 in Tokyo alone) and its wealth of regional and foreign cuisines, it is hard to believe that for centuries the average Japanese diet consisted of little more than rice, miso soup, and pickles. In a land of limited resources austerity was the rule, but it taught the Japanese to make the most of seasonal foods, and to serve them artfully so that a little looked appetizing.

Typical *bento* box

Tokyo, Osaka, and Kyoto are the celebrated culinary centers, but each town takes pride in its specialties. Budget and mid-range restaurants can often be found clustered around train stations, in malls, and taking up whole floors of department stores. Many eateries can be identified by the half-curtains *(noren)* above the door, with the name of the restaurant written on them in Japanese. Some may have small mounds of salt near the entrance.

Multistory building entirely full of restaurants, Ginza, Tokyo

MEALS AND MEAL TIMES

MOST *ryokan (see pp290–91)* and some hotels serve traditional breakfasts *(see p316)* from 7–9am. When Japanese eat breakfast out, they usually do so in coffee shops that serve sets called *moningu* (morning), consisting of coffee, toast, a hard-boiled egg, and a small salad.

Lunch runs from about 11:30am to 1:30 or 2pm. Many restaurants then re-open for dinner around 6. Upscale restaurants generally stop serving around 9 or 10, while establishments catering to the after-hours office crowd stay open to around 11 or midnight.

Soba (noodle) shops generally open around 11:30am and continue to serve until early evening. In major cities, street stalls selling *ramen* (Chinese noodles) and other snacks might open for business late in the evening and serve beyond midnight. In smaller towns and rural areas, few restaurants may be open after 7pm in the evening, because most visitors will be dining at their *ryokan*.

RESERVATIONS AND DRESS CODE

RESERVATIONS are essential at many *kaiseki* restaurants *(see p321)* – occasionally months in advance – but it is quite normal to turn up at others, even good places, without a reservation. Hotel concierges are usually willing to help with bookings, and to draw a map of a restaurant's location *(see p376–7)* for you.

Jeans and casual shirts are acceptable in most places, provided they are not torn or dirty. Women may find long, loose clothing advantageous when dining at a place with *zashiki* seating *(see p312)*. Also be sure to wear clean socks or stockings without holes if traditional seating on *tatami* mats is involved, as you will have to take off your shoes. Avoid wearing strong perfumes or colognes if dining at a *kaiseki* restaurant or participating in a tea ceremony.

SET DISHES AND TEISHOKU

BUDGET RESTAURANTS often have wonderfully realistic-looking plastic "dishes" in their windows, or photographs on the menu or wall. Simply point to the item you want if you don't know its name. At some canteens, you may need to use a ticket machine with buttons corresponding to certain dishes, before you eat.

Many restaurants offer *teishoku* (set menus), especially at lunch, allowing you to choose *teishoku* A or B. You may be met with bewilderment if you request any variations within a set menu. In upscale restaurants *(see p310)*, you will probably need to choose among various elaborate set menus ("courses") for each diner. For advice about ordering à la carte, including communal dishes, see page 312.

PRICES AND PAYING

THE PRICE RANGE between restaurants in Japan is vast. While you can eat a satisfying bowl of noodles for

Realistic-looking plastic "food" display in restaurant window

just ¥500, a single dish with the famous Kobe steak – with beer-fed, hand-massaged beef – may cost up to ¥20,000.

Many upscale restaurants, whose dinner courses may start at ¥10,000 or ¥20,000, might offer excellent value at lunchtime in the ¥3,000–5,000 range.

The consumption tax of 5% is added to restaurant bills at the end. (Prices on the menu do not usually include it.) At coffee shops and lunch places, the bill is usually automatically placed on your table, and you should take it to the cashier to pay. Even if you have exact change, do not leave it on the table and walk out.

At bars and certain restaurants you have to ask for the bill. The amount, written on a slip of paper, will generally be presented to you on a small tray. You place the money on this tray, and your change will be returned on the same tray.

Tipping is not expected, even when the tray is used, and may even be refused. Rounding the bill up rather than taking the change ("*Otsuri wa ii dess*" means "I don't need change") is sometimes welcomed, but many places will still insist that you take the change.

The Japanese usually divide the bill equally among diners, or one person pays for all. Asking for an itemized breakdown for groups of three or more is rarely done and is most unpopular.

Vegetarian Food

Japanese cuisine is rich in vegetables and non-animal high-protein foods such as tofu, *natto* (fermented soybeans), and other soy products. Unfortunately, it is not quite a vegetarian's paradise, because almost every dish relies to some degree for its flavoring on the *bonito*-based fish stock called *dashi*. The exception to this rule is *shojin ryori (see p320)*, which uses kelp- and mushroom-based stocks.

Lunchbox counter in shopping mall

Fast Food and Convenience Stores

Western chains such as McDonald's are everywhere. Japan has its own fast-food chains, too, including one called Mosburger, which has come up with some innovative twists on the hamburger theme.

Convenience stores offer a good selection of *bento* boxes *(see p317)* and snack foods such as *onigiri (see p314)*.

Food Halls and Market Stalls

Cavernous food halls are found in the basements of many department stores. The colorful delicatessen-type stalls might include uncut sushi rolls, *bento* boxes, and imported foodstuffs. About an hour before closing time, stores lower the prices of many food items by ¥100–300. You may also be offered free samples, with no obligation to buy.

Food markets have artful displays and stalls offering snacks and presentation boxes of sweets, tea, rice crackers, and fruit.

Bakeries

Bakeries abound but much of what is sold tends to be of the sweet-bun variety; bread for the Japanese is still more snack than staple. Do not be surprised if that innocent-looking French croissant turns out to be filled with red-bean paste.

In large cities almost every kind of bread, including most recently bagels, can be found. In rural areas the plain white loaf bread called *shokupan* (meal bread) is still predominant.

Vending Machines

You won't travel far in Japan without passing a public vending machine, one of the bonuses of Japan's almost vandal-free society. These dispense all kinds of snacks, soft drinks, chilled or hot coffee, green tea, and even cans of beer. The machines are easy to use, prices (written in Arabic numerals) are reasonable, and change is automatically dispensed with the item.

Types of Restaurants and Bars

JAPAN HAS A RESTAURANT to suit every taste and budget, from hole-in-the-wall noodle stands to havens of haute cuisine called *ryotei*. If you have difficulty distinguishing between different types, stick to restaurants with a menu and prices posted outside near the door. Lanterns mark out restaurants by name or description, though in some places they may bear the name of a district or event.

Restaurant with white lantern and *noren* (half curtains) in Takayama

RYOTEI AND KAISEKI RESTAURANTS

SANCTUMS of manicured courtyard gardens and spare but elegant private rooms, *ryotei* are the ultimate in Japanese dining. These are where the politicians and business elite entertain their customers with *kaiseki* *(see p321)*, the haute end of Japanese cuisine, and also maybe *geisha* *(see p157)* hired for the evening Used to catering to an established clientele, many *ryotei* will not accept new customers without introductions.

More accessible to tourists are what are termed *kaiseki* restaurants, which serve the same food as *ryotei*, but in a less exclusive setting.

KYO-RYORIYA

A KYO-RYORIYA (Kyoto-style restaurant) is usually another name for a *kaiseki* restaurant, Kyoto being the place where *kaiseki* achieved its apotheosis. Outside Kyoto, the name will emphasize that flavors conform to Kyoto standards, being delicate and light, and that typical Kyoto ingredients (*fu*, wheat gluten, and *yuba*, soy-milk skin, for example) will be featured.

SHOJIN RYORIYA

SHOJIN RYORI *(see p320)* also developed in Kyoto, in the kitchens of the city's Zen monasteries. The vegetarian cuisine is served on lacquered utensils in private rooms. Most *shojin ryoriya* are located near large monastery complexes.

KAPPO, IPPIN-RYORIYA, KORYORIYA, AND IZAKAYA

AKIN TO French bistros or Spanish tapas restaurants, these are places where one goes to drink and eat, rather than eat and drink. Most dishes are à la carte. *Kappo* tend to be pricey; the quality and seasonality of food is closer to that of *kaiseki* restaurants. *Ippin-ryoriya* and *izakaya* (the two are almost synonymous) feature fancier versions of Japanese home-cooking. Many will have large platters of pre-cooked items on their counter tops. *Koryoriya* means a "small dish" restaurant. Without reading Japanese, visitors may find such places hard to distinguish from one another.

NOMIYA AND AKA-CHOCHIN

TAVERN-LIKE *nomiya* (literally "drink shop") and *aka-chochin* are proletariat versions of the restaurants described above. The *aka-chochin*, or "red-lantern restaurant," is named after the gaudy lantern often hanging over the door (but note that not all red lanterns denote a "red-lantern restaurant"). They rarely have menus, the shop's offerings being written on strips of paper pasted on the wall or handwritten on a blackboard. They tend to be frequented almost entirely by locals.

SUSHI RESTAURANTS

RESTAURANTS specializing in sushi *(see pp318–19)* vary in style from low-priced *kaiten-zushi* shops, where the sushi comes to you on a conveyor belt, to astronomically expensive places where

Restaurants in Kyoto decorated with lanterns naming a local festival

everything, from the fish to the ginger, is of optimum freshness and quality. As a general rule, if there are no prices listed anywhere, you are in for an expensive dinner.

If you sit at the counter, it is customary to order *nigiri-zushi* (hand-pressed sushi) a serving at a time. A serving consists of two "fingers," which are placed on the counter in front of you. If you sit at a table or on a *zashiki* *(see p312)* then it is customary to order a combo of *nigiri-zushi*. It will be brought all at once on a platter or slab of polished wood.

Noodle Bars

Noodles in Japan come in two main forms: the domestic variety and the Chinese version known as *ramen* *(see p317)*. The former is found at *sobaya*, which in spite of the name, sell not only *soba* (brown buckwheat) but also white wheat *udon* noodles. *Sobaya* usually also offer a selection of *donburi* *(see p316)*. *Ramen* are served in cheap Chinese restaurants called *chuka-ryoriya*, in specialty shops called *ramenya*, and at night street stalls called *yatai*.

Specialty Restaurants

Many restaurants in Japan specialize in one dish, such as tempura, *tonkatsu*, or *shabu-shabu* *(see pp316–17)*. Restaurants featuring *kani-nabe* (crab hot pot) are popular during the cold months. *Oden-ya* serve *oden*, a simmered dish. *Unagiya* specialize in eel, grilled to perfection over charcoal. *Yakitori-ya* accomplish the same thing with chicken. *Fugu* restaurants serve up that delight of the adventurous gourmet, the poisonous globefish, raw and cooked.

The Tanuki

In Japanese folklore badgers are celebrated as lovable buffoons or drunken rascals. This is one of the reasons why the ceramic likeness of the *tanuki* is often found at the entrance of *nomiya* and other drinking places.

Foreign Asian Restaurants

Yakinikuya are Korean-style barbecue restaurants with plenty of red meat, as well as the more esoteric parts of the cow, plus the standard spicy *kimchi* pickles. *Chuka-ryori-ya* are cheap Chinese restaurants. So-called *esunikku* (ethnic) restaurants, found only in urban centers, serve a mixed bag of Southeast Asian-inspired dishes.

French-style restaurant and bar in the Akasaka district, Tokyo

Western Restaurants

Yoshoku (Western meal) restaurants are modest places that serve such things as *ebi-furai* (fried shrimp) and *korokke* (croquettes). These items became immensely popular among Japanese during the Meiji and Taisho periods. The Japanese still think of these dishes as Western although outside of Japan they would hardly be recognized as such. Rice is served on a plate, not in a bowl, and eaten with a fork.

Famiri resutoranto (family restaurants) are American-style chains (Royal Host is a typical example), whose extensive picture menus, late hours, and parking lots have won them a devoted following in Japan.

Specialty *dengaku* restaurant *(see p337)*

In the major cities, French and Italian restaurants are abundant. Servings, especially of wine, however, tend to be skimpy, and bread comes by the piece, not the basket.

Kissaten, Coffee Shops, and Bars

For decades the Japanese have taken their breaks at tea rooms called *kissaten*, where, over an unrefillable cup of painstakingly brewed *kohi* (coffee), served either *hotto* (hot) or *aisu* (iced), they can spend hours leafing through magazines and chain smoking. *Kissaten* also offer such standbys as *kare raisu* *(see p316)*, *pirafu* (rice pilaf), and *sando* (sandwiches, of the pale English variety).

The neighborhood *kissaten* still exists but is increasingly being challenged by international coffee shop chains such as Douter and Starbucks, which offer the novel items espresso and cappuccino.

Any fair-sized Japanese town will have a bar quarter, a warren of hole-in-the-wall places each presided over by a *"mastaa"* (master) or *"mama."* In large cities, entire buildings will be filled with such places, each its own little universe. Customers come as much for the atmosphere as the drinks.

Karaoke is the main form of entertainment in "hostess bars." Note that some are little more than rip-off joints.

Food Customs and Etiquette

EATING FOOD IN JAPAN is markedly different from eating in Western countries. Seating arrangements, tableware, and much of the etiquette surrounding the social eating of food differ even from those in nearby countries such as Korea and China. The main point of etiquette is to remove your shoes for traditional seating. The Japanese assume that you will not be able to use chopsticks properly and will be impressed if you show any finesse at all.

Sitting *seiza*-style on *zabuton* cushions

Seating Arrangements

MANY JAPANESE restaurants have a few Western-style tables and chairs, and/or a counter, as well as traditional *zashiki* seating.

The *zashiki* is a low wooden platform covered with *tatami* mats and low tables. Diners sit here on cushions *(zabuton)*, feet tucked behind. Remove your shoes before you step up onto the *zashiki*.

Women wearing skirts sit *seiza* (on their knees with their buttocks on their heels) or mermaid-style. Men usually sit cross-legged, although if there is a formal toast they will adopt the more uncomfortable *seiza* pose until it is over.

Some *zashiki* actually have sunken areas for the diners' legs, a definite plus for long-legged customers and foreigners who find sitting on the floor uncomfortable. Alternatively, chairs may be used that have backs but not legs.

In restaurants with a choice of seating, the counter is by no means regarded as a second-rate option. In sushi places, particularly, it is the preferred seat of the gastronome who wants to watch the food being skillfully prepared by chefs with years of training.

How to Order

IF A SET MENU *(see p308)* is not available, then follow these guidelines for ordering à la carte.

Specify drinks *(see pp322–3)* first, usually from a choice of sake, beer, *shochu* liquor, perhaps wine, and whiskey.

If you are in an area frequented by foreigners, the menu may have some English translations. Menus are often divided into the main categories of Japanese cuisine: grilled, simmered, and so on *(see p315)*. Sashimi is ordered first. If you can't decide on one fish, ask for a *moriawase*, or combination.

The custom is to have about three or four dishes to start and more later as you deem fit. Calling *"sumimasen!"* (excuse me!) is the standard method of attracting attention.

Alternatively, tell the chef behind the counter how much you want to spend (between ¥3,000 and ¥5,000 per person is reasonable), and let him make the decisions for you.

Polite Phrases and Toasts

JAPANESE people say *"Itadakimass"* ("I humbly receive") before eating, and *"gochisosama desh'ta"* ("I have been treated") at the end.

Japanese drinking etiquette requires that you pour for the other person and vice versa. When on the receiving end, you should pick up your glass, supporting the bottom with the fingers of the other hand. When a toast *(kanpai)* is made, beer and whisky glasses should be clinked, while sake cups are generally raised in a salute.

What to Do with the Oshibori

MOST RESTAURANTS offer customers an *oshibori* at the beginning of a meal. This small damp cotton or paper towel is used first to wipe your hands (in strict etiquette, not the face and neck). You then leave it on the table top and use it discreetly to dab fingers and spills, rather than placing it on your lap. It is fine to use your own handkerchief as a napkin on your lap. However, remember never to blow your nose into the *oshibori* or any handkerchief in public *(see p364)*.

Using Chopsticks

CHOPSTICKS *(hashi)* are shorter and more delicate than Chinese chopsticks, with a pointed lower end. The use of disposable wooden

Sitting on stools at the counter of a *yatai* noodle stall in Fukuoka

chopsticks in restaurants is widespread. Knives and forks are rarely seen except in staunchly Western restaurants and for certain dishes still regarded as foreign such as *kare raisu (see p316).*

Spearing food with your chopsticks is considered bad form, as is pushing food straight from the bowl into the mouth (entirely acceptable in China). Passing food from your chopsticks to those of another and sticking them upright in a bowl of rice are both associated with funerary customs and are therefore strictly taboo at the dinner table. Gesturing and pointing with your chopsticks are also definite no-nos, as is using them as levers to pull or push things around the table.

If some morsel proves difficult to cut on the plate, you can take a chopstick in each hand and make a sawing motion to cut it. This may not be the most elegant of moves but is unavoidable in some situations.

Ceramic teapot

When they are not in use, lay the chopsticks on your chopstick rest *(hashi-oki),* or if a rest is not provided then across the lowest dish. Lay them neatly and uncrossed, and parallel with your side of the table.

Using Tableware

Japanese tableware is wonderfully eclectic and can run to over a dozen vessels per person, of wildly differing shapes and materials such as porcelain, lacquer, wood, and even leaves. When several dishes are served at once, feel free to take morsels from them in whatever order you please, including from lidded pots containing soups.

Many small bowls and plates are designed to be picked up and brought to about chest level, easing the path of each morsel to the mouth. Do this rather than bending your head down to get to the food. It is perfectly good manners to sip directly from small bowls of soup.

How to Hold Chopsticks (Hashi)

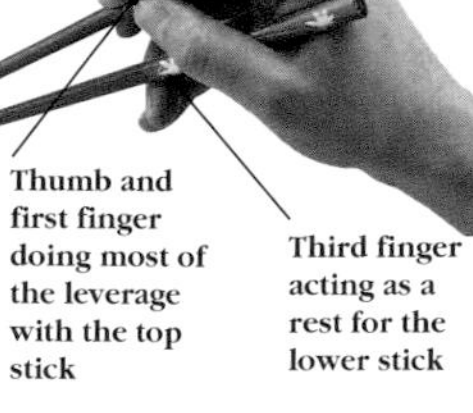

A common mistake by foreigners is to hold chopsticks too close to the ends instead of a third of the way down, thus losing leverage. They also often hold them too tightly, leading to hand cramps and dropped food. The lower stick should rest in the crook of the thumb and on the third finger, while the thumb, first, and second fingers control the movement of the top stick. Note that the *hashi* and technique are slightly different from those used in China.

However, do not eat directly from any communal serving platters and bowls. Instead, put one or two bite-sized portions first onto the *kozara,* which is a small saucer-like plate provided for each diner.

Use the separate chopsticks and spoons, if provided, for communal dishes.

Note that it is fine to bite off part of a piece of food and return the uneaten part to your *kozara* until ready for the next bite.

Eating Rice

Japanese rice has a slightly glutinous, heavy texture. Japanese people treat it with respect, and do not feel they have truly eaten until they have consumed rice in some form.

In a meal with several dishes, rice is always served in a separate bowl. If alcohol is drunk, then the bowl of rice is saved till the end of the meal, when it is eaten with miso and pickles *(see p321).* Since sake is a rice derivative, the two are often considered too similar to consume together.

***Kamameshi*, a one-pot rice dish**

No matter how tempted, do not take rice from the bowl and put it on your plate to soak up any juices or sauces or pour juices (even soy sauce) onto it. As acceptable as this is elsewhere, it will be an unappetizing sight in Japan. The exception to this rule is one-pot rice dishes, in which vegetables and meat are placed on the rice in a deep bowl, almost hiding the rice.

Seasonal Eating Patterns

The seasons have a major influence on Japanese eating habits. The temperature of food is seen as an important way of regulating body temperature. Hence, tea and sake are drunk hot in winter and cold in summer. Similarly, *nabemono* (hot pot) dishes are consumed during cold months, while cold noodles are welcomed in warm ones. Tempura is normally a cold weather dish, and the desire of tourists to eat it on a hot summer day is baffling to some Japanese. Some restaurants famous for seasonal fish such as *fugu (see p319)* may serve an entirely different menu at other times.

Slurping

The Japanese slurp with gusto when eating noodles or soupy rice dishes. Indeed, an audible intake of air is necessary to eat piping hot noodles without scorching the mouth. Many foreigners are loathe to make this noise, with the result that it takes them three times as long to eat *soba.*

Reading the Menu

General vocabulary likely to be useful when eating out is given in the *Phrase Book* on pages 407–8. Individual ingredients are also listed there. A selection of some of the most popular dishes and styles of cooking are listed in this glossary, including Japanese script to help you read menus in Japanese. Further details about some of the dishes follow on pages 316–21.

Donburi: Rice-Bowl Dishes

Katsudon
カツどん
Rice bowl topped with a breaded, deep-fried pork cutlet and semi-cooked egg.

Nikudon
肉どん
Rice bowl with beef, tofu, and gelatinous noodles.

Oyakodon
親子どん
Rice bowl with chicken, onions, and runny, semi-cooked egg *(see p316).*

Tamagodon
卵どん
Rice bowl topped with a semi-cooked egg.

Tendon
天どん
Rice bowl that has one or two shrimp tempura and sauce.

Unadon
鰻どん
Rice bowl with grilled eel.

Other Rice Dishes

Kamameshi
釜飯／かまめし
Rice and tidbits steamed in a clay or metal pot with a wooden lid. Served in the container it was steamed in *(see p313).*

Kare raisu
カレーライス
"Curry rice" *(see p316).* Can be *ebi-kare* (shrimp curry), *katsu-kare* (with deep-fried pork cutlet), etc.

Makunouchi bento
幕の内弁当
Classic *bento (see p317).*

Ocha-zuke
お茶漬け
Rice in a bowl with a piece of grilled salmon, pickled plum, etc., over which tea is poured.

Omu-raisu
オムライス
Thin omelet wrapped around rice mixed with tomato sauce and chicken or pork bits.

Onigiri
おにぎり
Two or three triangular chunks of rice wrapped with strips of dried seaweed *(nori).*

Onigiri* and *yaki-onigiri

Unaju
鰻重
Grilled eel served over rice in a lacquered, lidded box.

Yaki-onigiri
焼おにぎり
Variation of *onigiri*, without seaweed, grilled over a flame.

Zosui
雑炊
Rice soup made with the leftover stock of a one-pot *(nabemono)* meal.

Noodle Dishes

Kitsune soba/udon
きつねそば／うどん
Soba or *udon* noodles in flavored *dashi* broth with pieces of fried tofu.

Nabe yaki udon
鍋焼うどん
Udon noodles simmered in a lidded ceramic pot *(donabe)* with a flavored *dashi* broth, perhaps with shrimp tempura, shiitake mushroom, and egg *(see p317).* Popular in winter.

Ramen
ラーメン
Chinese noodles in pork broth *(see p317).* Usually there are some thin slices of roast pork on top, along with sliced leeks, spinach, and a slice of fish-paste roll.

Reimen (Hiyashi chuka)
冷麺（冷やし中華）
Chinese noodles topped with strips of ham or roast pork, cucumbers, and cabbage. Dressed with a vinegar and sesame oil sauce. A popular summer dish.

Somen
そうめん
Very thin white noodles, usually served in ice water. A summer dish.

Tamago-toji soba/udon
卵とじそば／うどん
Soba or *udon* in a flavored *dashi* broth into which an egg has been dropped and stirred to cook gently.

Tempura soba/udon
天ぷらそば／うどん
Soba or *udon* in a flavored *dashi* broth with one or two pieces of shrimp tempura.

Yakisoba
焼そば
Soft Chinese noodles sautéed on a griddle with vegetables and some form of meat or fish.

Zarusoba
ざるそば
Soba noodles served cold on a bamboo rack *(see p317).* Variation: *ten-zarusoba* has shrimp and vegetable tempura next to noodles.

Rice Crackers and Nibbles

Crackers *(senbei* or *osenbe)* are sold in supermarkets all over Japan. Beautifully made and presented, they are also sold at station gift counters and stalls at the popular tourist attractions.

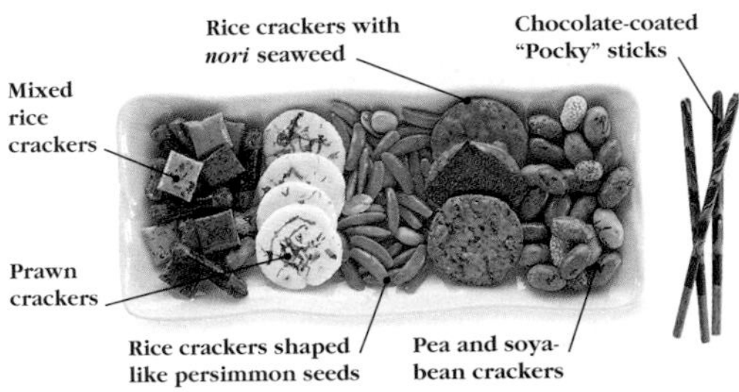

Dishes Prepared at the Table

Mizutaki/Chirinabe
水焚き／ちり鍋
Nabemono (one-pot meal) of vegetables, tofu, and chicken *(mizutaki)* or fish *(chirinabe)*.

Okonomiyaki
お好み焼
Thick pancake-shaped mix of cabbage, egg, shrimp, squid, or pork cooked on a griddle.

Shabu-shabu
しゃぶしゃぶ
Nabemono (hot pot) with thinly sliced beef and vegetables *(see p316)*, cooked in a brass pan.

Table condiments: seven-spice *shichimi* powder, jar of soy sauce, and *ichimi* ground chili pepper

Sukiyaki
すき焼き
High-quality pan-cooked beef and vegetables.

Teppanyaki
鉄板焼
Meat and/or shrimp or squid and vegetables grilled on a griddle in front of the diner.

Udon-suki
うどんすき
Udon noodles, chicken, and sometimes clams or shrimp simmered in a soup.

Sushi

Chirashi-zushi
ちらし寿司／鮨
"Scattered" sushi *(see p318)*.

Nigiri-zushi
握り寿司／鮨
"Fingers" of sushi *(see p318)*.

Maki-zushi
巻寿司／鮨
"Rolled" sushi *(see p319)*.

Set Meal

Teishoku
定食
A set meal *(see p308)*, with rice, soup, some vegetables, salad, a main meat dish, pickles.

Menu Categories

Aemono
和え物
Dressed salad dishes.

Agemono
揚げ物
Deep-fried foods.

Nimono
煮物
Simmered foods.

Sashimi (Otsukuri)
刺身（お造り）
Raw fish *(see p319)*.

Sunomono
酢の物
Vinegared dishes.

Yakimono
焼き物
Grilled foods.

À la Carte

Agedashi-dofu
揚げだし豆腐
Deep-fried tofu (bean curd) in a stock.

Chikuzen-ni
筑前煮
Vegetables and bits of chicken simmered together.

Eda mame
枝豆
Soybean steamed in the pod. Popular summer snack.

Hiya-yakko/Yudofu
冷やっこ／湯豆腐
Cold/simmered tofu *(see p317)*.

Kinpira
きんぴら
Sautéed burdock and carrot strips seasoned with sauces.

Natto
納豆
Fermented soybeans.

Niku-jaga
肉じゃが
Beef or pork simmered with potatoes and other ingredients.

Oden
おでん
Hot pot with fried fish cakes and various vegetables.

Ohitashi
おひたし
Boiled spinach or other green leafy vegetable with sauce.

Shio-yaki
塩焼
Fish sprinked with salt and grilled over a flame or charcoal.

Tamago-yaki
卵焼
Rolled omelet.

Tonkatsu
豚カツ／トンカツ
Breaded, fried pork cutlet *(see p317)* with shredded cabbage.

Grilled eel *(unagi)* basted in a sweet sauce, a *yakimono* dish

Tori no kara-age
鶏の空揚げ
Fried chicken pieces.

Tsukemono no moriawase
漬物の盛り合わせ
Combination of pickles.

Yakitori
焼鶏／やきとり
Chicken grilled on skewers.

Yakiniku
焼肉
Korean-style beef barbecue.

Chinese-Style Dishes

Gyoza
餃子／ギョウザ
Fried dumplings *(see p316)*.

Harumaki
春巻
Spring roll.

Shumai
焼売／シュウマイ
Small, pork dumplings crimped at the top and steamed.

Yakimeishi
焼めし／チャーハン
Fried rice.

Izakaya Snacks

Cucumber and seaweed

Dried squid

Onion and bonito

At *izakaya* and *ippin-ryoriya* establishments *(see p310)*, which are tavern-like places serving food rather than restaurants, dishes such as dried strips of squid and pickles complement the beer, *shochu* and other drinks *(see pp322–3)*.

Classic Dishes

***Shimeji* mushrooms**

JAPANESE FOOD is never more than lightly cooked, the ideal being to do only what is necessary to bring out the natural flavor of ingredients. Cooked fish is moist and flaky, while chicken is slightly pink near the bone. Vegetables remain crisp and retain their colors. Even when deep fried, food is not allowed to become greasy: oil is heated enough to seal the meat and vegetables. Two liquid ingredients are central to most dishes: a light stock called *dashi* made from giant kelp *(konbu)* and dried bonito shavings *(katsuo-bushi)*; and Japanese soy sauce, called *shoyu*.

Kare raisu *("curry rice") is a sweet, mild, Japanese-style curry served throughout the land. It is accompanied by pickled ginger and pickled scallions* (rakkyo).

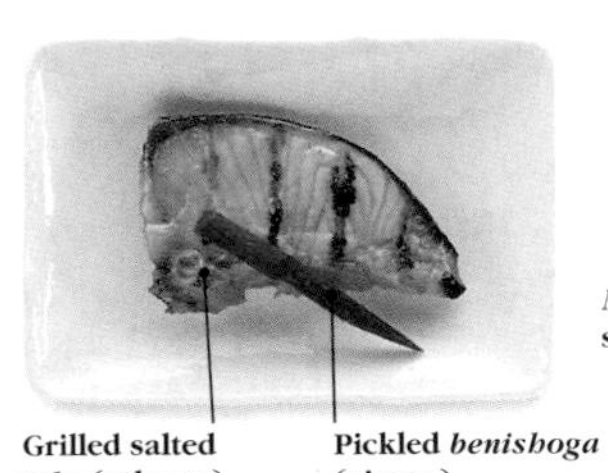

Chopped scallions

***Karashi* (mustard)**

***Natto* (fermented soybeans)**

***Umeboshi* (dried plums)**

***Nori* (seaweed)**

Marinated *tara* (cod roe)

Grated *daikon*

Slice of *tamago-yaki* (egg omelet)

Simmered *hakusai* (Chinese cabbage)

Simmered *kabocha* (squash)

Simmered *sato-imo* (taro)

***Gohan* (rice)**

Miso soup

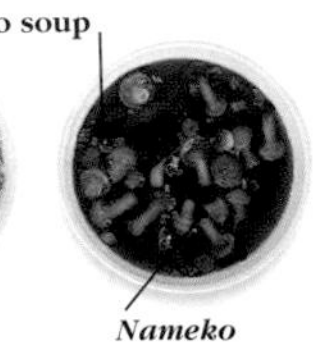

Pickled *kyuri* (cucumber)

***Hashi* parallel with near edge of table**

***Takuan* (pickled *daikon*)**

***Hashi-oki* (chopstick rest)**

THE TRADITIONAL JAPANESE BREAKFAST

Breakfast is a filling and salty meal, with fish, rice, pickles, *natto* (fermented soybeans, disliked by some), miso, omelet, grilled and salted fish, maybe a simmered dish, and strips of seaweed.

Dashi

Sesame sauce for *shabu-shabu*

Shabu-shabu *is a winter dish cooked in a* nabe *(hot pot) by diners themselves at the table. From two plates of raw beef and vegetables, cook each item as you please, swirling the beef with chopsticks.*

Donburi *is a deep-filled all-in-one rice-bowl dish.* Oyako donburi, *meaning "mother and child," contains chicken and egg.*

Gyoza *are Chinese-style dumplings filled with minced pork, cabbage, and onions, either steamed or deep fried.*

Soba *noodles are made of brown buckwheat. For the classic* zarusoba *dish, cold soba covered with shreds of* nori *(seaweed) are placed on a bamboo rack.*

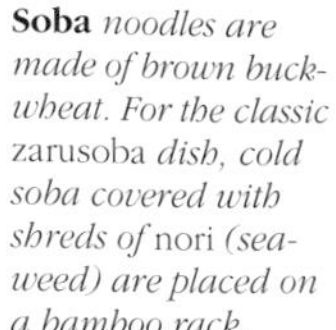

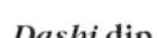

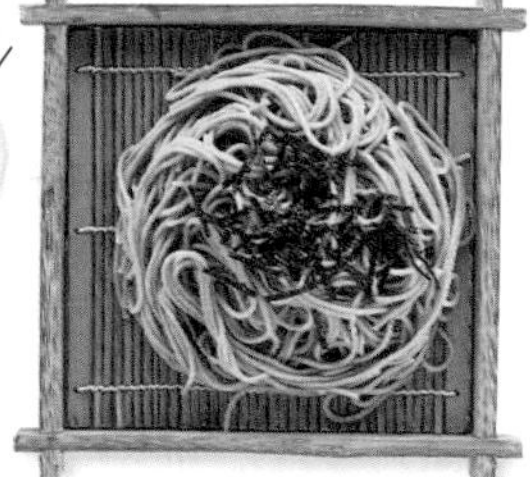

Ramen *are Chinese-style noodles in a pork or chicken broth and maybe* naruto *fish-paste roll, pickled bamboo, and beansprouts.*

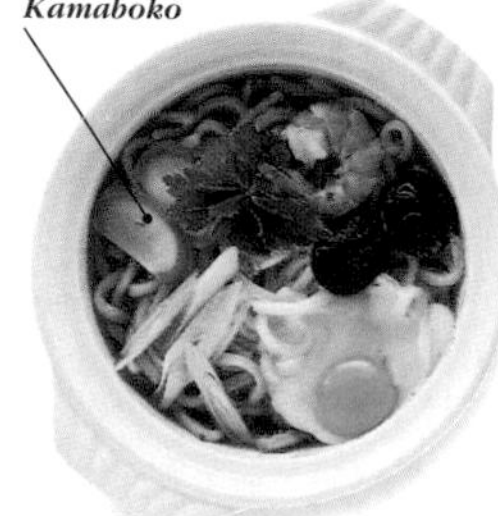

Udon *noodles are thick, white wheat noodles, here simmered in a broth with a softly poached egg and* kamaboko *fish-paste roll.*

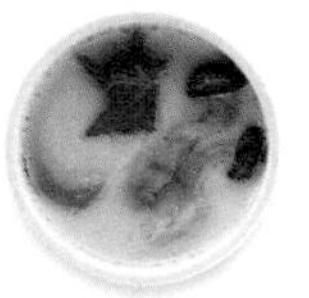

Chawan mushi *is a thick egg custard steamed in a small lidded pot with vegetables, shrimp, and other seafood.*

Yakitori *is skewered, grilled chicken coated with a sweet sauce.* Shichimi *and* sansho *pepper accompany it.*

Tempura *was originally a Portuguese dish of battered, deep-fried vegetables and* kuruma ebi *(large shrimp).*

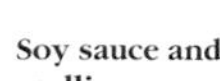

Yudofu *is a tofu (beancurd) dish, in which large cubes of tofu are simmered in a mild broth with kelp.* Shojin ryori *restaurants* (see p320) *often serve it.*

Tonkatsu *is a fried, breaded pork cutlet, with cabbage and a version of English Worcestershire* ("usuta") *sauce.*

THE BENTO BOX

Bento is an all-in-one lunch box with separate compartments for different morsels. The classic *makunouchi bento* shown here originated as a refreshment during the intervals between Kabuki plays. In restaurants, red and black lacquered boxes tend to be used; cardboard and plastic boxes are a take-away version.

Sushi and Sashimi

Shiso leaf garnish for sashimi

Newcomers to Japan are often both fascinated and intimidated by these native dishes. The term "sushi" applies to a variety of dishes (usually written with the suffix "*-zushi*") in which cold, lightly sweetened and vinegared sushi rice is topped or wrapped up with raw fish or other items such as pickles, cooked fish, and meat. Sliced fillets of raw fish served without rice are called sashimi. Even those visitors used to Japanese restaurants abroad may be surprised at how ubiquitous such foods are in Japan. There is no need to worry unduly about hygiene: Japan's highly trained chefs always use fresh fish, and the vinegar in sushi rice is a preservative.

Sushi bar counter and sushi chefs with years of training

Nigiri-Zushi

Here, thin slices of raw fish are laid over molded fingers of sushi rice with a thin layer of *wasabi* (green horseradish) in between. Using chopsticks or fingers, pick up a piece, dip the fish lightly in soy sauce, and consume in one mouthful.

Shredded *daikon*

***Hirame* (turbot)**

***Ebi* (shrimp)**

***Hotategai* (scallop)**

***Wasabi* (Japanese horseradish)**

***Gari* (ginger), eaten separately**

***Hokkigai* (type of clam)**

***Suzuki* (Japanese sea bass)**

***Kazunoko* (salted herring roe)**

***Toro* (belly flesh of a tuna)**

***Aji* (scad)**

***Maguro* (tuna)**

***Shimesaba* (salted, vinegared mackerel)**

***Ika* (squid)**

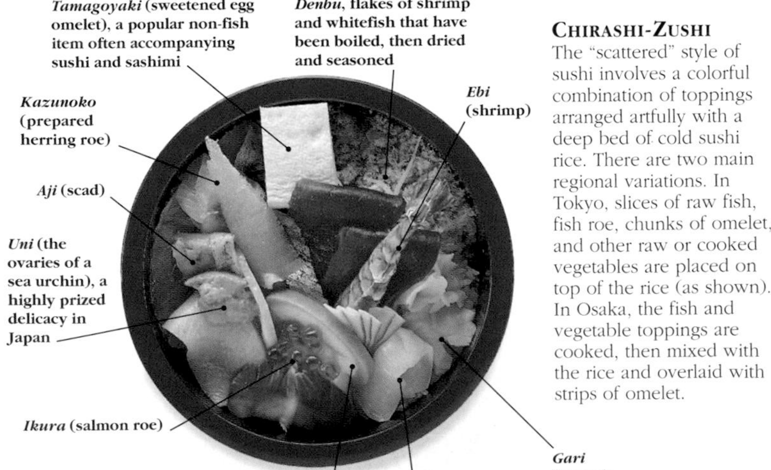

Chirashi-Zushi

The "scattered" style of sushi involves a colorful combination of toppings arranged artfully with a deep bed of cold sushi rice. There are two main regional variations. In Tokyo, slices of raw fish, fish roe, chunks of omelet, and other raw or cooked vegetables are placed on top of the rice (as shown). In Osaka, the fish and vegetable toppings are cooked, then mixed with the rice and overlaid with strips of omelet.

MAKI-ZUSHI

"Rolled" sushi is becoming increasingly familiar outside Japan – the California roll, for instance, is a version using avocado and other non-Japanese ingredients. For *maki-zushi* the sushi rice is combined with slivers of fish, pickles, or other morsels, and rolled up in a sheet of toasted seaweed *(nori)*.

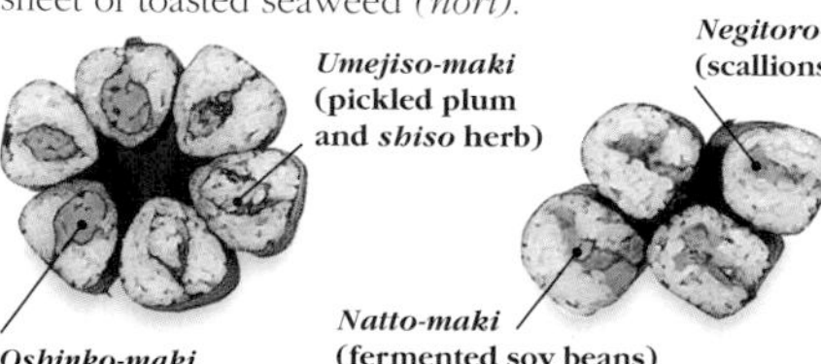

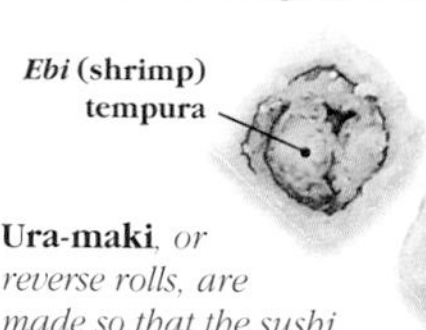

Hoso-maki, *or thin-rolled sushi, has one central ingredient at its core. It is rolled into a cylindrical shape with the help of a bamboo mat.*

Ebi **(shrimp) tempura**

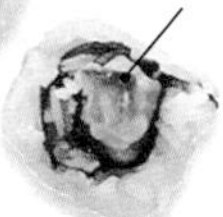

Tail end of *ebi*

Ura-maki, *or reverse rolls, are made so that the sushi rice, rather than the* nori, *forms the outside of the cylinder.*

Hotategai **(scallop) arranged in the shell**

Thick slices of raw *maguro* (tuna)

Tarako, **cod roe rolled up in squid and strips of seaweed**

Red seaweed garnish

Hotate **(scallop) arranged with thin strips of *nori* (seaweed)**

Hokkigai**, out of its shell**

Tako **(octopus)**

Aji **(scad), topped with finely sliced scallions**

Wasabi **(green horseradish) molded into the shape of a *shiso* leaf**

SASHIMI

Sliced fillets of the freshest uncooked fish may be served as a single course. Sashimi is delicate and creamy, and the only accompaniments should be soy sauce, *wasabi*, *daikon*, and maybe a *shiso* leaf.

Fish display at Kochi street market

POPULAR FISH IN JAPAN

Of the 3,000 or so varieties of fish eaten in Japan, the most common, available year-round, are *maguro* (tuna), *tai* (sea bream), *haze* (gobies), *buri* (yellowtail), *saba* (mackerel), crustaceans such as *ebi* (shrimp) and *kani* (crab), and fish that are usually salted such as *sake* (salmon) and *tara* (cod). Spring is the start of the season for the river fish *ayu* (sweetfish), traditionally caught by trained cormorants *(see p41)*. *Bonito* is available in spring and summer, *unagi* (eel) in midsummer, *sanma* (saury) in the fall. Winter is the time for *dojo* (loach), *ankou* (monkfish), and the famous *fugu* (globefish), prized for its delicate flavor but also feared for deadly toxins in its liver and ovaries.

Haute Cuisine

A TYPICAL BANQUET, such as might be served at a *ryotei* *(see p310)*, may have up to 20 small courses. Much is made of seasonal ingredients, and decorative flourishes, such as leaves, are also carefully chosen to match the season. A specialty vegetarian cuisine, called *shojin ryori*, uses such protein-rich foods as tofu rather than meat or fish. This was developed by Zen Buddhists and is now found in restaurants located in or near the precincts of many Zen temples; some are as exclusive as *kaiseki* restaurants. The Japanese have also elevated tea snacks to an art form: *wagashi* are beautifully packaged and popularly given as gifts.

***Enoki* mushrooms**

***Shojin ryori* restuarant at Daitoku-ji Zen temple, Kyoto**

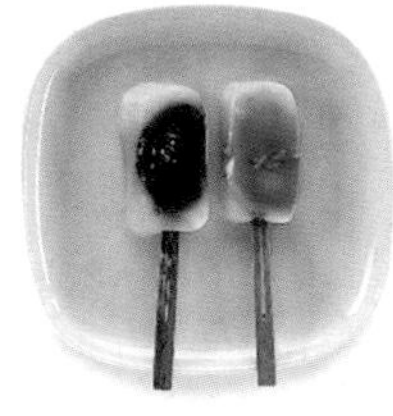

Miso dengaku *is* konnyaku *(devil's tongue), tofu, or taro, skewered and grilled with white or black miso paste on top.*

Tofu shinjo *is pounded tofu with* hijiki *(seaweed), wrapped in* abura-age, *which are thin strips of deep-fried tofu.*

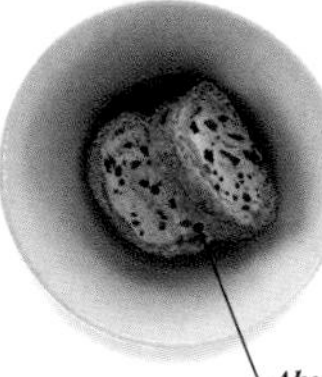

Abura-age

Shira-ae *is ground tofu and sesame seeds tossed with* horenso *(spinach). It is eaten cold.*

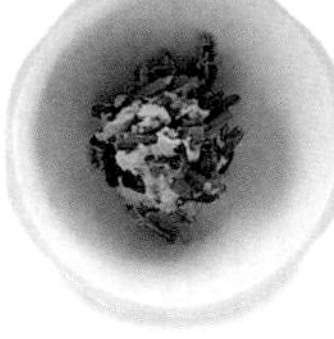

SHOJIN RYORI

The Buddhist principle of vegetarianism was introduced to Japan in the 6th century and developed into a proper cuisine by Zen Buddhists in the 13th century. Tofu, soybean curd, was found to be particularly versatile, and it fulfills the Japanese love of delicately flavored foods. Mountain vegetables are also used creatively.

WAGASHI

Wagashi is variously translated as Japanese sweets, confections, cakes, or candy, but in Japan is a more serious style of food than suggested by such translations. The delicate-looking confections, often made of sweet bean-paste, are traditionally associated with the tea ceremony *(see p163)*, being served immediately before the tea. They are also sold as gifts. There are numerous regional variations and specialties for each season; a selection of brands is shown here.

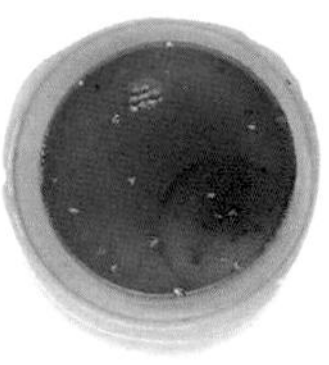

Kohakukan-ume, *dusted with flakes of real gold, is a jelly with a whole plum inside.*

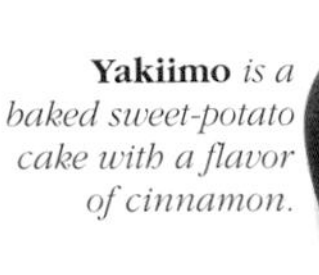

Yakiimo *is a baked sweet-potato cake with a flavor of cinnamon.*

Chofu *is a sweet rice cake wrapped in a light cake. The word* "chofu" *is written on it.*

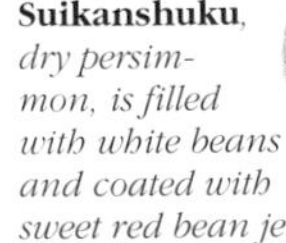

Suikanshuku, *dry persimmon, is filled with white beans and coated with sweet red bean jelly.*

Oribenishiki *is made of a bean jam and chestnut rice cake coated with raw cane sugar, and with a flower pattern on the outside.*

Jonainagashi, *shown here in six variations, is made from mashed white beans. Being raw, it should be eaten on the day it is made.*

KAISEKI

Kaiseki is a traditional style of cuisine with a dozen or more small, carefully presented dishes for each person, which on the menu are categorized according to cooking methods *(see p315)*, not ingredients. The dishes are served in an order that contrasts well on the palate; together they are called a course. Like *wagashi*, *kaiseki* originated in the tea ceremony. Sake *(see p323)* is the usual accompaniment.

***Appetizers* (zensai)** *are usually arranged in odd numbers.*

***Clear soup* (suimono)** *usually follows the appetizer. Here, a knotted fillet of* sawara *fish floats in the mild broth with a sprig of* kinome.

Sashimi *often follows the clear soup, the mild flavors of extremely fresh raw fish working well with warm dishes eaten before and after it.*

***Simmered food* (nimono)** *comes here in the form of a pork-stuffed* kabu *(turnip) in a light broth. The colorful vegetables are cooked separately.*

***Deep-fried food* (agemono)** *is one of the middle courses. A selection of tempura is shown here.*

***Grilled food* (yakimono)** *is demonstrated by this* ishikyaki *dish, which is cooked on a hot stone at the table by the diners themselves.*

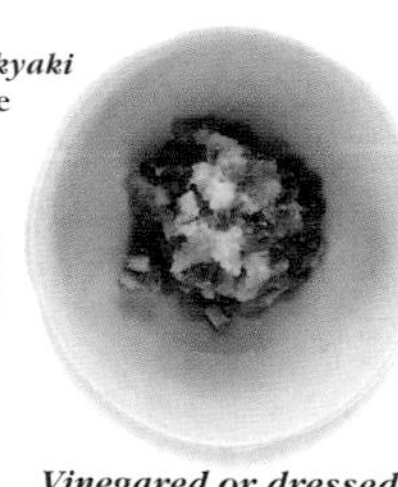

***Vinegared or dressed salad* (sunomono *or* aemono)** *follows the hot dishes. Shown here is salmon roe with grated* daikon *and diced cucumber.*

Boiled rice, miso soup, and pickles *are not side dishes, but are brought together after the main dishes.*

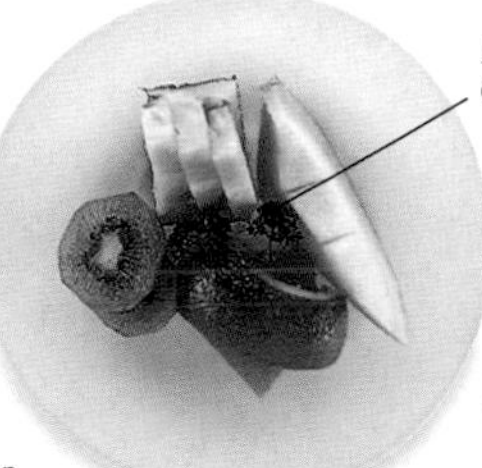

Fresh fruit and green tea *mark the end of the full* kaiseki *course.*

What to Drink in Japan

Tea ceremony

GREEN TEA AND SAKE are the traditional drinks of Japan. Both have ancient histories, and the appreciation of each has been elevated to connoisseurship. The tea ceremony *(see p163)* is the ultimate expression of tea appreciation, a social ritual imbued with Buddhist ideals. Sake (rice wine) has long associations with Shinto – the fox god Inari presides over sake *(see p22)* – and some Shinto festivals still involve the drink as a central theme. Other Japanese drinks include *shochu* spirit and "health" drinks.

Picking green tea in May, when leaves are at their most tender

TYPES OF TEA

Green tea leaves are divided into three main grades – *gyokuro*, which are the most tender, protected leaves that come out in May; *sencha*, which are tender leaves picked in May or June; and *bancha*, which are large leaves left until August. Leaves are sterilized with steam and then dried. *Bancha* is often roasted or mixed with other ingredients such as brown rice to form robust teas. Other teas are available; of foreign ones the Japanese especially enjoy imported fine English teas.

Basic green tea *is sold loose or in tea bags.*

Mugicha *is a tea brewed from roasted barley.*

Hojicha *is roasted* bancha, *a coarse tea.*

Genmaicha *is brown rice* (genmai) *and* bancha.

Sencha *is a popular medium-to-high grade of tea.*

Gyokuro *is a delicate, high grade of tea.*

Powdered **matcha** *is used at the tea ceremony.*

SOFT DRINKS

With names that conjure up disturbing images for English-speaking foreigners, Calpis and Pocari Sweat are among the most popular Japanese brands of canned soft drinks. Some are marketed as quick energy and vitamin boosters. Vending machines *(see p309)* stock them alongside canned green tea and coffee, and a wide range of fruit juices in cartons.

Tea leaves, *usually loose, are placed in a teapot.* Bancha *is brewed with boiling water, but* sencha *and* gyokuro *should be brewed with boiled water that has been allowed to cool slightly first. The brewing tea should then stand for about a minute.*

Sake (Rice Wine)

Sake is made from rice and water, which are fermented together then pasteurized to create a superb alcoholic "wine." Many connoisseurs judge sake on the five qualities of sweetness, sourness, pungency, bitterness, and astringency. Sake can be drunk warm, but the finer types should be lightly chilled to retain the subtle flavors. Unlike grape wine, sake is rarely expected to improve in the bottle. Store it in a cool, dry place for no more than a few months.

Everyday *bon-jozo* type by Gekkeikan

Fine *ginjo* type by Nihonsakari

Finer *dai-ginjo* by Tsukasa Botan

Taruzake ***(cask sake)*** *is matured in wooden casks made of cypress. Casks are often presented to Shinto shrines as offerings. The brewer's logo is displayed prominently.*

***The finest grade of sake**, dai-ginjo, is made from the hardest core of the rice – more than 50 percent of each grain is shaved away. For the* ginjo *type about 40 percent is shaved; for* hon-jozo, *the average sake, about 30 percent. Some are brewed with added alcohol; those without are called* junmai, *"pure rice."*

***A classic serving set** consists of a ceramic bottle* (tokkuri) *and matching cups* (sakazuki). *The bottle can be placed in hot water to warm the sake to about 50°C (122°F).*

***Sake breweries** traditionally hang a ball of cedar leaves* (sakabayashi) *and sometimes a sacred rope* (shimenawa) *over their entrance.*

Other Alcoholic Drinks

Japan has several beers that have become well known around the world. Suntory whisky is also sold abroad, popular with those who prefer a milder whisky. Less well known abroad, *shochu* is a name for a group of Japanese spirits made from barley or other grains, or potatoes.

The alcohol content of *shochu* varies from 40 to 90 proof. The distilled spirit is often mixed with hot water or used as a base for cocktails, but it is also drunk neat, either heated or on the rocks. It is also used to make bottled fruit liqueurs such as *umeshu*, which uses whole Japanese apricots.

Suntory whisky

Sapporo beer

Asahi beer

Barley *shochu*

Rice *shochu*

Choosing a Restaurant

The restaurants in this guide have been selected across a wide price range for their exceptional food and good value. This chart highlights some of the factors that may influence your choice; color-coded thumb tabs show the regions covered on each page. As with hotels, it is best to check the location before trying to find any restaurant.

Tokyo

Restaurant	Kaiseki Cuisine	Sushi or Seafood Specialties	Noodles	Vegetarian Specialties	Non-Japanese Cuisine
Central Tokyo (Ginza): *Kyushu Jangara Ramen* ¥ **Map** 5 B3. 1F New Ginza Bldg (2 blocks E of Yamaha Hall). *(03) 3289-2307.* Kyushu *ramen* in pork-bone soup is the most popular of numerous regional variations. *Jangara* is a lighter soup; *ponshan* the richest. *11am–11:30pm (to midnight Fri, to 10:30pm Sun & public hols).*			■		
Central Tokyo (Ginza): *Yakitori Bars* ¥ **Map** 5 B2. Under railroad bridge around Yurakucho stn. On both sides of Harumi-dori under and along the railroad are numerous cheap drinking places, mostly *yakitori* bars, where office workers mix with laborers to enjoy a carefree drinking binge. *variable.*					
Central Tokyo (Ginza): *Otako* ¥¥ **Map** 5 B2. In alleyway S of Sony Bldg at Sukiyabashi crossing. *(03) 3571-0057.* At this 100-year-old *oden* (fish-cake hot pot) restaurant, choose from mainly fish-based ingredients in the large pot simmering on the counter. A winter favorite with *salarymen*. *4:30–11pm (to 10:30pm Sun & public hols).*		●			
Central Tokyo (Ginza): *Torigin* ¥¥ **Map** 5 B2. B1 Five Bldg (in alleyway behind Sony Bldg). *(03) 3571-3333.* All-time favorite *yakitori* restaurant with a wide range of superb *kamameshi* (mixed rice in pot) as well as traditional varieties. *11:30am–10pm.*					
Central Tokyo (Ginza): *Ketel* ¥¥¥¥ **Map** 5 B3. B1/1F Hideyoshi Bldg (1 block W of Ginza stn). *(03) 3571-5056.* Enjoy German beers and excellent steak tartar, Viennese schnitzel, and other hearty meat dishes. *5–11pm (noon–10pm Sat, Sun & public hols).* *Mon.*					■
Central Tokyo (Ginza): *Naruto* ¥¥¥¥ **Map** 5 B3. 8-10-16 Ginza (nr Yamaha Hall). *(03) 3571-5338.* From late September to March, the best wild *tora-fugu* from Shimonoseki is served as sashimi and *chiri* (hot pot). There is fish *kaiseki* at other times. *11:30am–1:30pm, 5–10pm.*	■	●			
Central Tokyo (Ginza): *Zakuro* ¥¥¥¥ **Map** 5 B2. Sanwa Bldg (next to Matsuya dept store). *(03) 3535-4421.* Branch in a chain of *sukiyaki*, *shabu-shabu*, and steak restaurants. Fresh, seasonal produce and organic sugar, vinegar, and soy sauce are used. There are three other branches nearby and two in Akasaka. *11am–10:30pm.*		●			
Central Tokyo (Ginza): *Fook Lammoon* ¥¥¥¥¥ **Map** 5 B3. 1–2F Ginza Wall Bldg (1 block N of Ginza Tobu Hotel). *(03) 3543-1989.* This famous Cantonese restaurant offers Chinese delicacies such as steamed shark's fin and dried abalone slices cooked in oyster sauce. *Yamcha* (dim sum) served at lunchtime. *11:30am–3pm, 5–10pm (to 9pm Sun).*					■
Central Tokyo (Ginza): *Kanetanaka An* ¥¥¥¥¥ **Map** 5 B3. 2F Kanetanaka Bldg (corner of Namiki & Hanatsubaki). *(03) 3289-8822.* This branch of famous *ryotei* Kanetanaka serves authentic *kaiseki* at a more affordable price than the others. *5:30pm–1am.* *Sat, Sun, public hols.*	■				
Central Tokyo (Ginza): *Ten-ichi* ¥¥¥¥¥ **Map** 5 B3. 6-6-5 Ginza (2 blocks W of Ginza stn). *(03) 3571-1949.* Atmospheric tempura restaurant frequented by distinguished foreigners. Seasonal fish and vegetables are fried in pure sesame oil. *11:30am–9:30pm.*					
Central Tokyo (Nr Hibiya Park): *Toranomon Aoyagi* ¥¥¥¥¥ **Map** 5 A3. 1F Tokushima-ken Toranomon Bldg, 1-22-10 Toranomon. *(03) 3580-3456.* Upscale *kaiseki* restaurant using the freshest produce such as *tai* (sea bream) from Tokushima, Shikoku. *11:30am–2pm, 6–10pm.* *Sun, public hols.*	■	●			

Price categories for an average-size dinner for one. Lunchtime special menus are often cheaper.

- ¥ under ¥1,500
- ¥¥ ¥1,500–3,000
- ¥¥¥ ¥3,000–6,000
- ¥¥¥¥ ¥6,000–10,000
- ¥¥¥¥¥ over ¥10,000

KAISEKI CUISINE
Japanese haute cuisine *(see p321)*.

SUSHI OR SEAFOOD SPECIALTIES
Specializing in sushi, sashimi, or a seafood ingredient such as *fugu* or *unagi (see pp318–19)*.

NOODLES
Soba, ramen, or other type of noodle restaurant *(see p317)*.

VEGETARIAN SPECIALTIES
Specializing in tofu and/or other vegetarian dishes *(see p320)*.

NON-JAPANESE CUISINE
Including Chinese and other Asian restaurants.

Restaurant	Price	Kaiseki Cuisine	Sushi or Seafood Specialties	Noodles	Vegetarian Specialties	Non-Japanese Cuisine
CENTRAL TOKYO (KANDA): *Kanda Yabu Soba* **Map** 3 C4. 2-10 Kanda Awaji-cho (nr Awaji-cho subway stn). *(03) 3251-0287.* Established in 1880, this famous *soba* restaurant's *seiro* (*soba* served in a steamer) may be too delicate for some, but *kamo-nanban* (*soba* with duck) and tempura *soba* are also excellent. *11:30am–7:30pm (last order).*	¥			■		
CENTRAL TOKYO (KANDA): *Niwa* **Map** 3 C4. 2-6 Kanda Awaji-cho (1F Tokyo Green Hotel). *(03) 3255-4161.* Stylishly decorated tempura restaurant that also serves inexpensive *kaiseki*. *11:30am–2pm, 5–9:30pm.*	¥¥¥	■				
CENTRAL TOKYO (NIHONBASHI): *Benihana* **Map** 5 C1. Off Chuo-dori, nr Chuo-dori & Eitai-dori crossing. *(03) 3271-0600.* Original branch of the world-famous *teppanyaki* restaurant chain. Don't pass up the fresh abalone, *ise-ebi* (Japanese lobster), and Kobe beef. *11am–10pm (to 9pm Sat, Sun & public hols).*	¥¥¥¥					
CENTRAL TOKYO (NR TOKYO TOWER): *Nodaiwa* **Map** 2 F5. 1-5-4 Higashi Azabu. *(03) 3583-7852.* Tokyo's best *unagi* restaurant, using wild eel most of the time, grilled over charcoal and coated with their special *taré* sauce. Try *shirayaki* with *wasabi* if you don't like a sweet taste. *11am–1:30pm, 5–8pm.* *Sun.*	¥¥¥		●			
CENTRAL TOKYO (TSUKIJI): *Miyagawa Honten* **Map** 5 C3. 1-4-6 Tsukiji (2nd block W of Shintomicho subway stn). *(03) 3541-1292.* Very popular, small *unagi kabayaki* (grilled eel) restaurant, established in 1893. Try *unadon* or *unaju* (both with rice) or *shiroyaki* (white grill, without sauce). *11:30am–2pm, 5–8:30pm (to 8pm Sun, public hols).* *Sat.*	¥¥¥		●			
CENTRAL TOKYO (TSUKIJI): *Tsukiji Edogin* **Map** 5 C3. 4-5-1 Tsukiji. *(03) 3543-4401.* Established Edo-style sushi restaurant, where a thick slice of fish covers the rice completely. It is so popular that there are now three branches nearby, employing over 100 chefs. *11am–9:30pm (11:30am–9pm Sun, public hols).*	¥¥¥		●			
CENTRAL TOKYO (TSUKIJI): *Tsukiji Sushi-sei* **Map** 5 C3. 4-13-9 Tsukiji (in market next to Tsukiji Fish Market). *(03) 3541-7720.* A restaurant that has been serving an enormous choice of sushi to fish dealers for over 110 years. Sushi-sei now has about 30 branches including one in New York. *8am–1pm, 5–8pm.* *Sun, public hols.*	¥¥¥		●			
NORTHERN TOKYO (ASAKUSA): *Komagata Dojo* **Map** 4 E3. 1-7-12 Komagata (very nr Asakusa stn). *(03) 3842-4001.* *Dojo* (loach) is another Edo delicacy, and this restaurant is one of the few still to do it. Sake-steamed *dojo* is cooked over charcoal at the table with added scallions, and eaten with boiled rice. *11am–9pm.*	¥¥¥		●			
NORTHERN TOKYO (ASAKUSA): *Uosei* **Map** 4 E2. 4-35-2 Asakusa (nr Asakusa 4-chome crossing). *(03) 3874-2390.* *Fugu*, the winter delicacy of blowfish, is on the menu all year here (using farmed fish), bought fresh from Tsukiji. *5–10pm.* *Jan–Sep: Wed.*	¥¥¥¥¥		●			
NORTHERN TOKYO (UENO): *Futaba* **Map** 3 C3. 2-8-11 Ueno (nr Ueno Park). *(03) 3831-6483.* One of the best of Ueno's good *tonkatsu* restaurants. The dish is merely a deep-fried pork cutlet, but the art is to make it crisp and golden yet soft and juicy, like they do here. *11:30am–7pm.* *Mon, Thu; 2–5pm Tue, Wed, Fri.*	¥¥					
NORTHERN TOKYO (UENO): *Horai-ya* **Map** 3 C3. 3-28-5 Ueno (back of Matsuzakaya dept store). *(03) 3831-5783.* Horai-ya is said to have been the first to sell *hirekatsu* (fillet *tonkatsu*) in the 1920s, and the tiny, popular restaurant takes pride in keeping old traditions. *11:30am–1:30pm, 4:30–7pm (from 4pm Sun & public hols; Apr–Oct: 5–7:30pm).* *Wed.*	¥¥					

For key to symbols see back flap

Price categories for an average-size dinner for one. Lunchtime special menus are often cheaper.

- ¥ under ¥1,500
- ¥¥ ¥1,500–3,000
- ¥¥¥ ¥3,000–6,000
- ¥¥¥¥ ¥6,000–10,000
- ¥¥¥¥¥ over ¥10,000

Kaiseki Cuisine
Japanese haute cuisine *(see p321).*

Sushi or Seafood Specialties
Specializing in sushi, sashimi, or a seafood ingredient such as *fugu* or *unagi (see pp318–19).*

Noodles
Soba, ramen, or other type of noodle restaurant *(see p317).*

Vegetarian Specialties
Specializing in tofu and/or other vegetarian dishes *(see p320).*

Non-Japanese Cuisine
Including Chinese and other Asian restaurants.

Restaurant	Kaiseki Cuisine	Sushi or Seafood Specialties	Noodles	Vegetarian Specialties	Non-Japanese Cuisine
Western Tokyo (Akasaka): *Akasaka Rikyu* ¥¥¥¥ **Map** 2 F4. B1 Plaza Mikado Bldg, 2-14-5 Akasaka. *(03) 5570-9323.* A famous TV chef cooks Cantonese dishes at this grand, modern Chinese restaurant. A popular dish is roast goose and fried rice with baby clams. *Yamcha* (dim sum) at lunchtime. *11:30am–3pm, 5:30–10pm (last order).*					■
Western Tokyo (Akasaka): *Shunko-tei* ¥¥¥¥ **Map** 2 F4. 1F Muto Kopo, 2-17-69 Akasaka. *(03) 3585-8671.* Unique, imaginative cooking combining East and West, where 13 or 14 small dishes such as chorizo with potato in aioli and curry-flavored *matsutake* mushroom pilaf are served *kaiseki* style. *noon–1pm, 6–9pm.* *Sun L, Mon L.*	■				
Western Tokyo (Akasaka): *Sumibiyaki Steak Harima* ¥¥¥¥ **Map** 2 F4. 2F Mitoko Bldg, 6-2-4 Akasaka (nr Akasaka stn). *(03) 3583-4150.* Small counter restaurant offering the world-famous Matsuzaka beef grilled on charcoal. The low-fat dish is enhanced by the special light sauce with grated *daikon.* *11:30am–2pm, 5:30–10pm.* *Sat, Sun, public hols.*					
Western Tokyo (Akasaka): *Kaiseki Tsujitome* ¥¥¥¥¥ **Map** 2 E3. B1 Toraya No. 2 Bldg, 1-5-8 Moto Akasaka. *(03) 3403-3984.* Sophisticated Kyoto-style *kaiseki* courses are served here in such a serene, old Japanese atmosphere that you will forget you are in a modern office building. *noon–9pm.* *Sun.*	■				
Western Tokyo (Akasaka): *Raku-tei* ¥¥¥¥¥ **Map** 2 F4. 1F Music In, 6-8-1 Akasaka (3 blocks S of Akasaka stn). *(03) 3585-3743.* Counter-only tempura restaurant where the chef-patron fries for all diners. His meticulous attention to detail, such as using cottonseed oil with white sesame oil, is legendary. *noon (to arrive for L), 5–8:30pm (last order).* *Mon.*					
Western Tokyo (Nr Keio University): *Hishinuma* ¥¥¥¥ **Map** 5 A5. 1F Aurora Mita (nr Keio University main gate). *(03) 3453-0772.* Modern Japanese *kaiseki* with wine is the theme of this little restaurant. Based mainly on seasonal vegetables and fish, the seven- or eight-course menu changes daily. *6–11pm.* *Sun, public hols.*	■				
Western Tokyo (Minami-Aoyama): *Rice Terrace* ¥¥¥ **Map** 2 D5. 2-7-9 Nishi Azabu (opp Aoyama Cemetery). *(03) 3498-6271.* Thai royal banquet cooking with dishes such as spicy salad with *aji* (scad). *noon–2pm, 6–11pm.* *Sun, public hols.*					■
Western Tokyo (Minami-Aoyama): *Les Cristallines* ¥¥¥¥¥ **Map** 1 C5. 1F Casa Serena (5 mins from Omotesando stn B1/B3 exit). *(03) 5467-3322.* Imaginative French haute cuisine, with hors d'oeuvres and desserts subtly illuminated from below table level. *11:30am–2pm, 6–9:30pm.*					■
Western Tokyo (Roppongi): *Toricho* ¥¥¥ **Map** 2 E5. 1F Hosho Bldg, 7-14-1 Roppongi. *(03) 3401-1827.* Modern *yakitori* in a sophisticated Japanese atmosphere. The *omakase* course, in which 13 or 14 meat and vegetable *yakitori* are grilled over charcoal one by one, is highly recommended. *5–11pm (to 10pm Sun, public hols).*					
Western Tokyo (Roppongi): *John Kanaya Azabu* ¥¥¥¥¥ **Map** 2 E5. 2F Kanaya Hotel Mansion, 3-1-25 Nishi Azabu. *(03) 3402-4744.* One of the world's most expensive French restaurants, but the skillfully executed 7- to 15-course degustation menu is truly worth it. Reservations essential. *11:30am–2pm, 5:30–11pm.* *Sun, public hols.*					■
Western Tokyo (Shibuya): *Kaitenzushi Tsukiji Honten* ¥ **Map** 1 B5. 24-8 Udagawa-cho (off Shibuya Center-gai). *(03) 3464-1178.* Probably Japan's cheapest conveyor-belt sushi restaurant. Any plate with two pieces is merely ¥100, but you have to finish within 30 minutes, or 10 minutes if taking only five or six plates. *11am–6am (11am–11pm Sun).*		●			

WESTERN TOKYO (SHINJUKU): *Kushinobo* ¥¥¥
Map 1 B1. 6F Isetan Kaikan (back of Isetan dept store). *(03) 3356-3865.*
Over 30 items, such as shiitake mushroom, asparagus with *shiso* herb, shellfish, and meat, are skewered and fried in front of you at this *kushikatsu* bar.
11:30am–2pm, 5–9:30pm weekdays; 11:30am–9:30pm Sat, Sun. *Wed.*

WESTERN TOKYO (SHINJUKU): *Shinichi-kan* ¥¥¥
Map 1 B1. 2-28-13 Kabukicho (in the center of Kabukicho). *(03) 3209-8426.*
Popular Korean restaurant where you grill your own meat over charcoal at the table. Japanese beef such as *karubi* (rib loin) and *rosu* (sirloin) is exceptionally tender. *4pm–6:30am (to 11pm Sun).*

WESTERN TOKYO (SHINJUKU): *Tsunahachi* ¥¥¥
Map 1 B1. 3-31-8 Shinjuku (nr Shinjuku 3 chome subway stn). *(03) 3352-1012.*
Established over 70 years ago, Tsunahachi is the largest tempura chain in Japan and this is their main branch. "Freshly fried tempura for a reasonable price" is their motto, and you won't be disappointed. *11:15am–10pm.*

WESTERN TOKYO (SHINJUKU): *Nakamura-ya Honten* ¥¥¥¥
Map 1 B1. 2F Shinjuku Nakamura-ya Honten, 3-26-13 Shinjuku. *(03) 3352-6161.*
All-time favorite *yoshokuya* (Western restaurant), actually most popular for its Indian curry, introduced in the 1920s and developed meticulously ever since, using only free-range chickens from the owners' farm. *11am–10pm.*

FARTHER AFIELD (EBISU): *Tsukushi-ro* ¥¥¥¥
1-10-2 Ebisu Minami (nr JR Ebisu stn S exit). *(03) 3760-0016.*
Try shark's fin, the most delicate food from China, here as sashimi or simmered in casserole with noodles. *11:30am–2:30pm, 5–10:30pm.*

FARTHER AFIELD (HIROO): *Danoi* ¥¥¥¥
B1 Azabu Shikendo Bldg, 4-6-7 Nishi Azabu (nr Hiroo subway stn). *(03) 3797-4444.*
Da noi means "our place" in Italian, and the owners welcome customers to this little Italian restaurant as to their own home. Popular items include spaghetti with cabbage and anchovy. *6–10pm (last order).* *Mon.*

FARTHER AFIELD (MEGURO): *Tonki* ¥¥
1-1-2 Shimo Meguro (nr Meguro stn). *(03) 3491-9928.*
Tokyo's most famous *tonkatsu* restaurant, using pork only from black pigs. Long lines likely. *4–10:45pm (last order).* *Tue, 3rd Mon of month.*

FARTHER AFIELD (NISHI AZABU): *Waketokuyama* ¥¥¥¥¥
3F Yahata Bldg, 4-2-13 Nishi Azabu (nr Nishi Azabu crossing). *(03) 3400-2968.*
Chef-patron Nozaki's exclusive *kaiseki* restaurant offers imaginative, seasonal cuisine and a specialty sake list. *5–11pm.* *Sat, Sun & public hols.*

FARTHER AFIELD (OGIKUBO): *Marufuku/Harukiya* ¥
Marufuku: 1F Fukazawa Bldg (nr stn); Harukiya: one street E. *(03) 3391-6523/4868.*
Unremarkable suburb Ogikubo has become the center of Tokyo *ramen*, thanks to these two bars. Both Marufuku's rich soup and Harukiya's light one have avid followers. Try both to compare. *11:30am–9:30pm.* *Mon.*

FARTHER AFIELD (RYOGOKU): *Chanko Kawasaki* ¥¥¥
Map 4 E5. 2-13-1 Ryogoku (nr W exit of Ryogoku stn). *(03) 3631-2529.*
Chanko-nabe is a chicken-based hot pot known as the sumo wrestlers' main diet. This old *chanko* house offers a refined version that won't make you quite as fat. *5–10pm.* *Sun, public hols.*

FARTHER AFIELD (RYOGOKU): *Momonjiya* ¥¥¥
Map 4 E5. 1-10-2 Ryogoku (nr Ryogoku bridge). *(03) 3631-5596.*
This restaurant specializes in wild mountain animals. Wild boar is the most popular, eaten as *sukiyaki*. The menu includes venison sashimi, bear steak, and raccoon hot pot. *5–9pm, also noon–2pm in winter.* *Sun.*

CENTRAL HONSHU

FUJI FIVE LAKES: *Mama-no-mori Tamura-tei* ¥¥¥
On N side of Lake Yamanaka nr Mount Fuji. *(0555) 62-0346.*
Kaiseki meals in a thatched-roof restaurant with good views of Mount Fuji. *11:30am–2:30pm, 5–8pm.* *Feb; May–Nov: Thu; Dec–Apr: Wed & Thu.*

GIFU: *Kawara-ya* ¥¥¥¥¥
Nr Jozai-ji. *(0582) 62-1530.*
Ayu (sweetfish or river smelt) straight from the river, including sashimi and grilled fish, served in private *tatami* rooms. *11am–2pm, 5–9pm.* *Tue.*

Price categories for an average-size dinner for one. Lunchtime special menus are often cheaper.
¥ under ¥1,500
¥¥ ¥1,500–3,000
¥¥¥ ¥3,000–6,000
¥¥¥¥ ¥6,000–10,000
¥¥¥¥¥ over ¥10,000

Kaiseki Cuisine
Japanese haute cuisine *(see p321)*.
Sushi or Seafood Specialties
Specializing in sushi, sashimi, or a seafood ingredient such as *fugu* or *unagi* *(see pp318–19)*.
Noodles
Soba, ramen, or other type of noodle restaurant *(see p317)*.
Vegetarian Specialties
Specializing in tofu and/or other vegetarian dishes *(see p320)*.
Non-Japanese Cuisine
Including Chinese and other Asian restaurants.

Restaurant	Price	Kaiseki Cuisine	Sushi or Seafood Specialties	Noodles	Vegetarian Specialties	Non-Japanese Cuisine
Hakone: *Shikajaya*	¥¥				●	
Inuyama: *Oi Gyuniku-ten*	¥¥¥					
Izu: *Iso Ryori Maruto*	¥¥		●			
Izu: *Sasano*	¥¥					
Kamakura: *Hachinoki*	¥¥¥	■			●	
Kamakura: *Kita Kamakura Monzen*	¥¥¥¥	■			●	
Kanazawa: *Yuiga*	¥¥					■
Kanazawa: *Hana Anzu*	¥¥¥					
Kanazawa: *Kotobukiya*	¥¥¥¥	■			●	
Kawagoe: *Apron-tei*	¥¥				●	
Kawagoe: *Ichinoya*	¥¥¥¥	■	●			

Hakone: *Shikajaya* ¥¥
Hakone Yumoto (1F of Ebisu Ryokan, 5 mins from stn). *(0460) 5-5751.*
A variety of dishes based on tofu, served at tables around an open hearth. *11am–2:30pm, evening times vary.* *Thu.*

Inuyama: *Oi Gyuniku-ten* ¥¥¥
Just inside main gate of Meiji Mura. *(0568) 67-0318.*
This 1887 Meiji-period restaurant, moved from Kobe, serves Kobe beef *sukiyaki* and *nabe* hot pot, with beer. *11am–3:30pm.*

Izu: *Iso Ryori Maruto* ¥¥
Toi, Izu W coast (1-min walk from Toi-Banba bus stop). *(0558) 98-1155.*
Fresh seafood from the neighboring fishmonger is served in a restaurant blending Japanese and Western styles, situated in a scenic fishing village. *11am–8pm.* *Wed.*

Izu: *Sasano* ¥¥
Tsukigase, on Route 414 in Yugashima. *(0558) 87-0736.*
A small, unpretentious eatery in central Izu offering regional specialties such as *inoshishi* or *botan nabe* (wild boar hot pot), pheasant sashimi, and grilled *ayu* (sweetfish or river smelt). *11am–8pm.*

Kamakura: *Hachinoki* ¥¥¥
By entrance to Kencho-ji. *(0120) 22-228719 (toll free) or (0467) 22-8719.*
Elegant *shojin ryori* (Buddhist vegetarian *kaiseki*), served in airy private rooms or larger dining rooms in an old thatched building. The staff are used to foreigners. *11am–4pm (last order); to 6pm (last order) Sat, Sun.* *Mon.*

Kamakura: *Kita Kamakura Monzen* ¥¥¥¥
2 mins from Kita Kamakura stn. *(0467) 25-1121.* W www.i-breeze.com/monzen
A traditional restaurant famous for *shojin ryori*, the specialty of Kamakura's Zen temples. Nobel-prizewinning novelist Kawabata Yasunari ate here. *11am–7:30pm (last order).*

Kanazawa: *Yuiga* ¥¥
Just E along Saigawa Odori from Kata-machi crossing. *(076) 261-6122.*
A tiny gem of a bistro, serving delicious, creative variations on Japanese, French, and Italian fare. Relaxed atmosphere, with a chef-owner who speaks some English and French. *11:30am–1:30pm, 5pm–midnight.*

Kanazawa: *Hana Anzu* ¥¥¥
In local crafts center. *(076) 222-5188.*
A good place to try Kanazawa cuisine without breaking the bank. Tofu dishes and classics like *jibuni* (duck or chicken hot pot with *wasabi* horse-radish), tiny squid, and local fish. *11am–7pm.* *1st & 3rd Tue of month.*

Kanazawa: *Kotobukiya* ¥¥¥¥
Just N of Oyama shrine, nr Owari-cho bus stop. *(076) 231-6245.*
This lovely 120-year-old mansion with an Edo-period atmosphere offers classy *shojin ryori* on beautiful Wajima lacquer trays. *11:30am–2pm, 5–9pm (enter by 7pm).*

Kawagoe: *Apron-tei* ¥¥
Moto-machi, nr Toki-no-kane bell tower. *(0492) 26-3370.*
This restaurant, in a 100-year-old *kura* house in the old district, focuses on the local specialty, sweet potatoes, with some unusual and delectable dishes. *11:30am–2:30pm.* *Mon, 1st Sun of month.*

Kawagoe: *Ichinoya* ¥¥¥¥
1-18-10 Matsue-cho (W of Kita-in N entrance). *(0492) 22-0354.*
Established in 1832, this elegant restaurant with its stone lanterns combines traditional and modern style. It is known for *kaiseki* and eel dishes, served in private rooms or a general area. *11:30am–9pm.*

MATSUMOTO: *Kiso-ya* ¥

4-6-26 Ote, 10 mins E of castle. *(0263) 32-0528.*
A small restaurant in the old *kura* storehouse area, specializing in *dengaku* (food coated in miso). *11:30am–2:30pm, 5–9pm (last order at 7:30). Tue.*

NAGANO: *Chikufu-do* ¥

By post office, 10 mins from Obuse stn. *(0262) 47-2569.*
Light meals and snacks featuring locally grown chestnuts, in savory dishes with rice, and in desserts and cakes. *10am–6pm (to 7pm summer). Wed.*

NAGANO: *Suki-tei* ¥¥

112-1 Tsumashina (behind prefectural govt office). *(0262) 34-1123.*
Local apple-fed beef, served at a wooden counter in the form of *sukiyaki*, *shabu-shabu*, and steak. *11am–2pm, 4–8:30pm (last order). Sun.*

NAGOYA: *Sennari Honten* ¥

1-16-13 Izumi (nr Hisaya Odori stn). *(052) 951 6389.*
Kishimen, fettuccine-like ribbon noodles, are a well-known Nagoya specialty, and the chef-patron of Sennari makes his own every day.

NAGOYA: *Ibasho* ¥¥

5 mins from Sakae subway stn. *(052) 951-1166.*
A little restaurant specializing in Nagoya-style *unagi* (eel): grilled without being steamed first, and eaten with scallions and soup or tea. *11am–2:30pm, 4–8pm. Sun, 2nd & 3rd Mon of month.*

NAGOYA: *Toriei* ¥¥¥

8 mins from Sakae subway stn. *(052) 241-5552.*
Nagoya has been known for its chicken since the mid-19th century. This elegant, traditional restaurant, with a choice of private *tatami* rooms or general tables, has tasty chicken dishes of every guise – raw, fried, and *nabe* hot pots. *11am–2:30pm, 4:30–9:30pm. Wed.*

NARITA: *Kikuya* ¥¥¥

385 Naka-machi (10 mins from stn, toward Narita temple). *(0476) 22-4246/0236.*
This traditional restaurant on the lane to Narita-san Temple offers standards such as sashimi, tempura, eel, and *yakitori*. Very accommodating to foreigners. *10am–9pm. Tue.*

NOTO: *Shoya no Yakata* ¥¥¥

Suzu-shi, nr Sosogi, N of Wajima (N of beach on Rte 249). *(0768) 32-0372.*
A little thatched-roof restaurant with local specialty seafood *kamameshi* (rice bowl). *11am–9pm. once a month, varies.*

SHIZUOKA: *Toro Mochi-no-ie* ¥

Tono-iseki-suiden Nishi-dori (by museum at Toro ruins). *(054) 283-1663.*
Delicious homemade *mochi* riceballs and *soba* noodles, served in a farmhouse-type building. *9am–4:30pm.*

TAKAO: *Ukai Toriyama* ¥¥¥¥

3426 Minami Asakawa-cho (10-min bus ride from Takao-san-guchi stn).
(0426) 61-0739. W www.tokyo.to/dining/ukai-toriyama.html
At the foot of Mount Takao, *ryotei* thatched cottages in a tranquil, lantern-lit garden offer traditional fare (fish, chicken, beef). It's worth going just for the restaurant, but the food tastes even better after hiking up the mountain. *11am–9:30pm (to 8:30pm Sun & public hols).*

TAKAYAMA: *Suzuya* ¥¥¥

24 Hanakawa-cho (off Kokubunji-dori). *(0577) 32-2484.*
Regional specialties including Hida beef, *sansai* ferns, and tasty *hoba miso* (tofu, miso, and vegetables on a magnolia leaf), as well as local sake, in a rustic old house decorated with folk art. *11am–3pm, 5–9pm. Tue.*

TAKAYAMA: *Susaki* ¥¥¥¥¥

4-14 Shinmei-cho (by Nakabashi bridge). *(0577) 32-0023.*
A 250-year-old house and garden redolent of the tea ceremony is the venue for exquisite *honzen* cuisine, a type of *kaiseki*, served on local amber-colored lacquerware. *11:30am–2pm, 5–7pm. Tue or Wed.*

YOKOHAMA: *Shin Yokohama Ramen Museum* ¥

2-14-21 Shin Yokohama, Kohoku-ku (nr Shin Yokohama stn). *(045) 471-0503.*
Japan's *ramen* craze has resulted in this museum. In the basement eight *ramen* shops represent regional variations in the form of a reconstructed street from 1958. *11am–11pm (from 10:30am Sun & public hols).*

For key to symbols see back flap

Price categories for an average-size dinner for one. Lunchtime special menus are often cheaper.

¥ under ¥1,500
¥¥ ¥1,500–3,000
¥¥¥ ¥3,000–6,000
¥¥¥¥ ¥6,000–10,000
¥¥¥¥¥ over ¥10,000

Kaiseki Cuisine
Japanese haute cuisine *(see p321)*.
Sushi or Seafood Specialties
Specializing in sushi, sashimi, or a seafood ingredient such as *fugu* or *unagi (see pp318–19)*.
Noodles
Soba, *ramen*, or other type of noodle restaurant *(see p317)*.
Vegetarian Specialties
Specializing in tofu and/or other vegetarian dishes *(see p320)*.
Non-Japanese Cuisine
Including Chinese and other Asian restaurants.

Yokohama: *Chinatown (Chuka-gai)* ¥¥¥
Central Yokohama (10 mins from Ishikawa-cho stn).
In a few lively blocks, over 160 restaurants serve cuisines from all parts of China (some toned down to Japanese tastes). Many have *gyoza* dumplings and *yamcha* (dim sum). Prices vary widely. ○ *daily.* ▣

Kyoto

City Center: *Daikoku-ya* ¥
Takoyakushi Nishi-iru, Kiyamachi. ☎ *(075) 221-2818.*
Mid-city *soba* restaurant with a classy feeling. Quality artwork on walls and an old-fashioned waterwheel used for grinding *soba* contribute to the atmosphere. ○ *11:30am–9:45pm.* ● *Tue.* ▣

City Center: *Honke Owariya* ¥
Kurumaya-cho/Nijo sagaru (nr Karasuma-Oike subway). ☎ *(075) 231-3446.*
Kyoto's oldest *soba* shop set within a cozy old house. *Horai-soba*, the house specialty, is especially good. ○ *11am–6pm.* ● *Wed.* ▣

City Center: *Bio-tei* ¥¥
2F M & I Bldg, Higashi-no-Toin/Sanjo (nr post office). ☎ *(075) 255-0086.*
Generous portions of healthy, natural food at low prices. Try the plum-liquor soda-water cocktail *(umeshu no sodawari)*, and black-bean tofu if available. ○ *11:30am–2pm, 5–8:30pm.* ● *Mon, Thu L, Sat D, Sun, public hols.*

City Center: *Gontaro* ¥¥
Main branch: Fuyacho/Shijo agaru. ☎ *(075) 221-5810.*
Excellent *soba* and *udon* served in quietly elegant surroundings by waitresses attired in kimono. ○ *11:30am–10pm.* ● *Wed.*

City Center: *Obanzai* ¥¥
1F Ichii Bldg, Koromo-no-Tana-dori/Oike agaru. ☎ *(075) 223-6623.*
All-you-can-eat buffet of home-style Japanese cooking in a spacious room paneled with Kitayama cedar. Both *haigamai* (half-polished) and *genmai* (unpolished) rice available. ○ *11am–2pm, 5–9pm.* ● *Wed D.*

City Center: *Eitaro-ya* ¥¥¥
Muromachi/Oike (nr Oike subway). ☎ *(075) 221-4604.*
Intimate *izakaya (see p310)* featuring *obanzai*, Kyoto home-style dishes. Friendly service, some English spoken. ○ *5:30–11pm.* ● *Sun.*

City Center: *Gekkeikan Katsura* ¥¥¥
B1 Wako Shoken Bldg, Shijo/Fuya-cho nishi-iru. ☎ *(075) 241-1666.*
Owned by sake-maker Gekkeikan, this *kaiseki* restaurant naturally features Gekkeikan sake. Lunch sets and *bento* are especially good value. ○ *11:30am–1:30pm, 5:30–9:30pm.* ▣

City Center: *La Masa* ¥¥¥
1F Wakabayashi Bldg, Teramachi/Nijo sagaru. ☎ *(075) 255-6093.*
An intimate Spanish restaurant overseen by a cheerful young Kyoto native who has worked in kitchens in Spain and Guatemala. Good seafood and wine selections. ○ *noon–3pm, 5–11pm.* ● *Wed.*

City Center: *Misoka-an Kawamichi-ya* ¥¥¥
Fuyacho/Sanjo agaru. ☎ *(075) 221-2525.*
An old-fashioned *soba* shop with an Old Kyoto atmosphere. *Hokoro*, the house specialty noodle hot pot, serves two. ○ *11am–8pm.* ● *Thu.* ▣

City Center: *Tosai* ¥¥¥
Takoyakushi/Sakaimachi. ☎ *(075) 213-2900.*
Tofu, *yuba* (beancurd skin), and other delicacies in a refurbished Kyoto townhouse. Gracious husband and wife team contribute to the comfortable at-home atmosphere. Reservations essential. ○ *5–10pm.* ● *Sun, Mon.*

Restaurant	Kaiseki Cuisine	Sushi or Seafood Specialties	Noodles	Vegetarian Specialties	Non-Japanese Cuisine
Yokohama: Chinatown (Chuka-gai)					■
City Center: Daikoku-ya			■		
City Center: Honke Owariya			■		
City Center: Bio-tei				●	
City Center: Gontaro			■		
City Center: Obanzai					
City Center: Eitaro-ya					
City Center: Gekkeikan Katsura	■				
City Center: La Masa					■
City Center: Misoka-an Kawamichi-ya			■		
City Center: Tosai				●	

IMPERIAL PALACE AREA: *Mankamero* ¥¥¥¥¥
Inokuma/Demizu agaru. (075) 441-5020.
Classic Kyoto cuisine in a beautiful old building with small gardens. *Takekago* (bamboo-basket) *bento* is a lunch favorite.
noon–7:30pm (last order), bento until 2:30pm.

EASTERN KYOTO: *Nanzen-ji Okutan* ¥¥¥
86-30 Fukuchi, Nanzen-ji (part of temple precincts). (075) 771-8709.
Sub-temple-like restaurant that has been serving delicious *yudofu* (a classic boiled-tofu dish) for generations. 11am–5:30pm (last order). Thu.

EASTERN KYOTO: *Omen* ¥¥¥
Ginkaku-ji branch: 74 Ishibashi-cho, Jodo-ji. (075) 771-8994.
Gokomachi branch: 310 Daimon-ji, Gokomachi/Shijo agaru. (075) 255-2125.
House specialty is *Omen*, *udon* noodles with a dipping sauce and vegetables. *Taruzake*, barrel-sake, available in cool months. 11am–10pm. Thu.

EASTERN KYOTO: *Taam Sabaai* ¥¥¥
2F Kiyosumi Bldg, 51-6 Minamishiba-cho, Shimogamo. (075) 781-7758.
Authentic Thai cuisine prepared by a friendly couple from Chiang Mai.
11:30am–1:40pm, 5:30–9:30pm. Thu twice a month (varies).

EASTERN KYOTO: *Nanzen-ji Hyotei* ¥¥¥¥¥
35 Kusakawa-cho, Nanzen-ji. (075) 771-4116.
Considered by many to offer the consummate *kaiseki* experience, Hyotei is famous for the beauty of its gardens, dishes, decor, and, needless to say, the quality of its food. 11am–9:30pm (for D enter by 7:30pm).

NORTHERN KYOTO: *Kushibachi* ¥¥¥
Hakubai-cho branch: 33-1 Kami Hakubai, Kitano. (075) 461-8888.
Ginkaku-ji branch: 83 Nishida, Jodo-ji. (075) 751-6789.
Part of a popular chain offering good food at reasonable prices in a fun atmosphere. The *kushi* items – grilled or deep-fried tidbits served on spits – go well with beer and sake. 5–11:30pm. Hakubai-cho branch: 3rd Mon of month.

NORTHERN KYOTO: *Yamaga* ¥¥¥
7-3 Nishimoto-cho, Shimogamo (nr Furitsu Daigaku bus stop). (075) 722-0776.
Intimate *izakaya* with good seasonal specials, free-range chicken dishes, and selection of sake and *shochu* (a vodka-like spirit).
11:30am–2:30pm, 6pm–midnight. Sun L, Thu D.

NORTHERN KYOTO: *Daitoku-ji Ikkyu* ¥¥¥¥
20 Daitoku-ji-monzen, Murasakino (nr SE cnr of Daitoku-ji). (075) 493-0019.
Ikkyu has been serving *shojin ryori* (Zen vegetarian cooking) at its best for over 500 years. Reservations essential. noon–6pm.

WESTERN KYOTO: *Ajiro* ¥¥¥¥
28-3 Tera-no-mae, Hanazono (nr south gate of Myoshin-ji). (075) 463-0221.
Excellent *shojin ryori* (Zen vegetarian cooking). The shop's *bento* and *yuba* (a tofu by-product) are not to be missed. 11am–6:30pm (last order). Wed.

WESTERN HONSHU

HIMEJI: *Fukutei* ¥¥
75 Kamei-machi. (0792) 23-0981.
Moderately priced, moderately sized *kaiseki* lunches, with background Japanese instrumental music. 11am–3pm, 4pm–9pm (last order). Thu.

HIROSHIMA: *Okonomimura* ¥
5-13 Shin Tenchi. (082) 241-8758.
A rather decrepit building crammed with over 20 stalls selling *okonomiyaki*, a Hiroshima specialty resembling a pancake layered with seafood, meat, vegetables, and savory sauces. 11:30am–midnight.

HIROSHIMA: *Suishin Restaurant* ¥¥¥
6-7 Tate-machi. (082) 247-4411.
Small but well-known sushi and sashimi restaurant. Oysters and blowfish are also available. 11:30am–10pm. Wed.

HIROSHIMA: *Kanawa* ¥¥¥¥
A boat moored E of the Peace Park on the Motoyasu River. (082) 241-7416.
Hiroshima is famous for its oysters, which are cultivated on rafts in the bay. Oysters are served here in various ways from baked, fried, and steamed to marinated, and in soup dishes. 11am–2pm, 5–10pm. Sun.

Price categories for an average-size dinner for one. Lunchtime special menus are often cheaper.

¥ under ¥1,500
¥¥ ¥1,500–3,000
¥¥¥ ¥3,000–6,000
¥¥¥¥ ¥6,000–10,000
¥¥¥¥¥ over ¥10,000

Kaiseki Cuisine
Japanese haute cuisine *(see p321).*
Sushi or Seafood Specialties
Specializing in sushi, sashimi, or a seafood ingredient such as *fugu* or *unagi (see pp318–19).*
Noodles
Soba, ramen, or other type of noodle restaurant *(see p317).*
Vegetarian Specialties
Specializing in tofu and/or other vegetarian dishes *(see p320).*
Non-Japanese Cuisine
Including Chinese and other Asian restaurants.

Restaurant	Kaiseki Cuisine	Sushi or Seafood Specialties	Noodles	Vegetarian Specialties	Non-Japanese Cuisine
Kobe: *Sanda-ya* ¥¥ Kitano-zaka. *(078) 222-0567.* A good place to try the famous Kobe beef at affordable prices. Their set lunch menu is under ¥1,500 and includes slices of the celebrated beef, rice, vegetable side dishes, and soup. *11:30am–8:30pm.* *3–5pm Mon–Fri.*		●			
Kobe: *Gandhara* ¥¥¥ 4F Nikaku Bldg, 1-2-3 Kitanagasa-dori. *(078) 391-4975.* Authentic, moderately priced Indian food in a pleasant setting. Lunch menus are exceptionally good value. *11:30am–3pm, 5–10pm.*					■
Kobe: *Marrakech* ¥¥¥ 1-20-15 Nakayamate, in basement of Maison de Yamate. *(078) 241-3440.* Excellent Moroccan restaurant with an interior evoking the Maghreb. Classic couscous dishes, plus fish and brochette set dinners with mouth-watering Moroccan bread and mint tea. *noon–2pm (Sat, Sun only), 5–11pm.* *Mon.*					■
Kobe: *Kitano Club* ¥¥¥¥ 1-5-7 Kitano-cho. *(078) 222-5123.* French/Continental restaurant popular for its lunch specials and views. The dinner menu has several delicious fish dishes and an excellent lamb and filet mignon. It may be wise to reserve. *11:30am–2:30pm (last order), 5:30–11pm.*					■
Kobe: *Okagawa* ¥¥¥¥ 1-5-0 Kitano-cho (next to Kitano Club). *(078) 222-3511.* Modern tempura restaurant which also serves *kaiseki, shabu-shabu,* and *sukiyaki* in a room with sliding doors and paper screen windows. *11am–2pm, 5–9pm (last order).* *1st & 3rd Tue of month.*	■				
Kurashiki: *Kamoi* ¥¥ 1-3-17 Chuo (just across from Ohara Museum). *(086) 422-0606.* Set in an old rice storehouse along a willow-lined canal, Kamoi offers sushi set meals, eel dishes, and local specialties like *daikon-zushi*, a rice, seafood, and vegetable dish traditionally served during festivals. *9am–5:30pm.* *Mon.*		●			
Kurashiki: *Kiyutei* ¥¥¥ 1-2-20 Chuo (opp Ohara Museum). *(086) 422-5140.* Run by the Kurashiki Kokusai Hotel, Kiyutei has a good Western menu including salmon, stew, and steak dishes. *11am–8:30pm.* *Mon.*					■
Kurashiki: *Tsuta* ¥¥¥¥ Ivy Square, 7-2 Hon-machi. *(086) 422-0011.* Local cuisine, including *kaiseki* dishes. The cheaper set meals are good value, especially *obento rikyu*, a dish of fried tofu and vegetables, red beans, sashimi, and rice. *7:30–9:30am, 11:30am–2:30pm, 5–9:30pm.*	■				
Matsue: *Yakumo-an* ¥ 308 Kitabori-cho. *(0852) 25-0587.* An excellent lunch spot located in an old samurai house with a lovely garden. The novelty here is *wariko soba*, handmade noodles served in a number of round dishes placed on top of each other. *9am–4:30pm.*			■		
Matsue: *Daikichi* ¥¥ Asahi-machi, Matsue, 690. *(0852) 31-8308.* A *yakitori* joint easily identified by two large red lanterns hanging outside. A friendly place with an owner who speaks very good English. *5pm–1am*					
Miyajima Island: *Tachibana* ¥ On the path connecting Itsukushima Shrine & ferry terminal. *(0829) 44-0240.* The specialty of this small restaurant is *anago donburi*, a flavorsome dish with eels fresh from the Inland Sea. *10am–6:30pm.* *Fri.*		●			

MIYAJIMA ISLAND: *Tonookajaya* ¥
Omachi, nr five-storied pagoda. (0829) 44-2455.
This popular and inexpensive noodle shop serves different types of *udon* and rice cakes. 10am–5pm.

NARA: *Momoya* ¥
1286 Takabatake Fukui-cho. (0742) 22-8797.
Momoya specializes in *chagayu*, a rice porridge cooked in green tea, traditionally a breakfast staple in Nara. 11am–5pm. Mon, Thu.

NARA: *Harishin* ¥¥¥
15 Nakashinya-machi, nr Gango-ji on road S of Sarusawa-ike pond. (0742) 22-2669.
Lovely 200-year-old restaurant offering only one set lunch and dinner *obento*, the contents of which vary and are meant to be a surprise. Expect liberal amounts of soup, rice, meat, fish, and fresh vegetables.
11:30am–2:30pm, 6–9pm (evenings by reservation only). Mon.

NARA: *Yanagi Chaya* ¥¥¥
4-48 Noborio-ji-cho, next to Kofuku-ji main hall. (0742) 22-7560.
Made by chefs who are monks from Kofuku-ji and Todai-ji, the vegetarian dishes include *chameshi*, a rice porridge with tofu cooked in green tea. Nonvegetarian set lunches also served. Reserve for dinner.
11:30am–5pm. Mon.

NARA: *Yoshikawa Tei* ¥¥¥
1F San-Fukumura Bldg, 17 Hanashiba-cho. (0742) 23-7675.
Inexpensive French restaurant with good bistro-style food. The three-course set lunches are a real bargain. 11:30am–2pm, 5:30–8pm. Mon.

OKAYAMA: *Azumazushi* ¥¥¥
3-11-48 Omote-machi. (086) 231-0158.
Try the *azuma teishoku* set dish of fresh fish with various side dishes at this regional seafood restaurant. 11am–9pm. Wed; 2:30–4:30pm Sun & public hols.

OKAYAMA: *Maganedo* ¥¥¥
1-8-2 Uchisange. (086) 222-6116.
Opened in the 1920s and still run by the same family, this small restaurant usually recommends the delicious *inaka soba* (country soba) to visitors; *soba kaiseki* is served in the evenings. 11am–9pm. Sun.

OKAYAMA: *Matsunoke-tei* ¥¥¥
20-1 Ekimoto-machi. (086) 253-5410.
Well-known and graceful restaurant with a reasonably priced *kaiseki* menu and good *shabu-shabu* options. 11am–10pm. Sun.

OSAKA: *Daikoku* ¥
2-2-7 Dotonbori. (06) 6211-1101.
Well-known tofu and fish restaurant dating from the early Taisho period. Sea bream and yellowtail are always good, and the *kayaku gohan*, a mixture of rice, tofu, and vegetables, is inexpensive and nutritious.
11:30am–3pm, 5pm–8pm. Sun, Mon & public hols.

OSAKA: *Itoya* ¥
4F Itoya Bldg, 1-6-21 Sone-zaki Shinchi. (06) 6341-2891.
Geisha used to frequent this well-known Osaka *okonomiya* restaurant built in 1937. Several types of pancakes include octopus, shrimp, and vegetarian versions. 5pm–1am. Sat, Sun & public hols.

OSAKA: *La Bamba* ¥¥
2-3-23 Dotonbori (nr Dotonbori Hotel). (06) 6213-9612.
Economical place to try such Mexican dishes as burritos, tacos, avocado salads, and Spanish enchiladas. 5–11pm (from 2pm Sat, Sun). Mon.

OSAKA: *Namaste* ¥¥
1F Rose Bldg, 3-7-28 Minami Semba, off Shinsaibashi-Suji. (06) 6241-6515.
Authentic Indian curries and tandooris prepared and served by Indian staff. Tell the waiter how hot and spicy you would like the dish to be.
11:30am–3pm, 5:30–11pm.

OSAKA: *Shin Miura Jidoritei Yakitori* ¥¥
Takimikoji Village, in basement of Umeda Sky Bldg. (06) 6440-5957.
A re-created 1920s village with about 10 restaurants serving traditional Japanese food like noodles, *okonomiyaki*, *teppanyaki*, and chicken, beef, and pork *yakitori*. 11:30am–2pm, 5pm–10pm (from 4pm Sun & public hols).

For key to symbols see back flap

Price categories for an average-size dinner for one. Lunchtime special menus are often cheaper.

- ¥ under ¥1,500
- ¥¥ ¥1,500–3,000
- ¥¥¥ ¥3,000–6,000
- ¥¥¥¥ ¥6,000–10,000
- ¥¥¥¥¥ over ¥10,000

KAISEKI CUISINE
Japanese haute cuisine *(see p321)*.

SUSHI OR SEAFOOD SPECIALTIES
Specializing in sushi, sashimi, or a seafood ingredient such as *fugu* or *unagi* *(see pp318–19)*.

NOODLES
Soba, *ramen*, or other type of noodle restaurant *(see p317)*.

VEGETARIAN SPECIALTIES
Specializing in tofu and/or other vegetarian dishes *(see p320)*.

NON-JAPANESE CUISINE
Including Chinese and other Asian restaurants.

OSAKA: *Takoume* ¥¥
1-1-8 Dotonbori. ☎ *(06) 6211-0321.*
Another one of Osaka's classic *oden* (hot pot with fish cakes) restaurants, this one is special because of its Edo-period decor. Seating is at a counter where you choose your dish and ingredients. ○ *5–10pm.* ● *Sun.*

OSAKA: *Victoria Station* ¥¥
B2F Hilton Plaza, 1-8-16 Umeda. ☎ *(06) 6347-7470.*
A steak chain with an excellent, as-much-as-you-like salad bar and other Western-style dishes. ○ *11am–11pm.* 💳

OSAKA: *Kani Doraku* ¥¥¥
1-6-18 Dotonbori. ☎ *(06) 6211-8975.*
All the dishes are a variation on crab *(kani)*, from steamed and salt-roasted to broiled. A giant crab mobile hangs above the door. ○ *11am–11pm.* 💳

OSAKA: *Mimiu Honten* ¥¥¥
4-6-18 Hirano-cho. ☎ *(06) 6231-5770.*
A well-known Osaka dish called *udon suki* was first made at this high-class *udon* restaurant. The dish, including chicken, shrimp, clams, and various seasonal vegetables, is made at your table. ○ *11:30am–8:30pm (last order).* ● *Sun.* 💳

OSAKA: *Yotaro Honten* ¥¥¥
2-3-14 Koraibashi. ☎ *(06) 6231-5561.*
The specialty here is *tai gohan*, sea bream cooked at your table and served on top of a pile of rice steamed in a clay pot. ○ *11am–2pm, 4:30–8pm.* ● *Sun & public hols.*

TSUWANO: *Furusato* ¥
Gion-machi, nr the post office. ☎ *(08567) 2-0403.*
A small local restaurant whose specialty is *uzumemeshi*, a tofu, mushroom, and vegetable mixture served under rice. ○ *11am–3pm.*

TSUWANO: *Yuki* ¥¥
Hon-machi, Tsuwano-cho. ☎ *(08567) 2-0162.*
Carp sashimi and carp *miso* soup are specialties at Yuki, which has a stream passing through the middle of its dining room. ○ *11am–6pm.* ● *Thu.*

YAMAGUCHI: *Yamabuki* ¥
2-13-9 Eki-dori. ☎ *(0839) 22-1462.*
One of Yamaguchi's oldest noodle shops with such options as *soba-zushi* and Choshu *soba*, made from rolled buckwheat. ○ *11:30am–6pm.* ● *1st and 15th of month, and Obon Festival.*

SHIKOKU

KOCHI: *Amigo Nijudai-ten* ¥¥
15-21 Nijudai. ☎ *(088) 875-0618.*
Italian restaurant using local ingredients and Japanese names on the menu. The *umi-no-sachi* (seafood salad) is terrific. ○ *11:30am–9pm.* ● *Mon.*

KOCHI: *Tokugetsuro* ¥¥¥¥¥
Opposite Dentetsu-Taminarubiru-mae streetcar stop. ☎ *(088) 882-0101.*
The type of swanky *kaiseki* restaurant that would once have required a personal introduction to patronize, Tokugetsuro offers exquisite service, such as a plum bonsai on your table in the winter. ○ *9am–11pm.* 💳

KOTOHIRA: *Soba Restaurants* ¥
Street at foot of stairs leading to Kotohira-gu shrine
This street's historic *soba* restaurants (Tora-ya, Tanuki-ya, Hayashi-ya) have served pilgrims for centuries. The area includes a sake brewery, and a green tea and snack restaurant (Henkotsu-ya).

	Kaiseki Cuisine	Sushi or Seafood Specialties	Noodles	Vegetarian Specialties	Non-Japanese Cuisine
Osaka: Takoume			■		
Osaka: Victoria Station					■
Osaka: Kani Doraku		●			
Osaka: Mimiu Honten			■		
Osaka: Yotaro Honten		●			
Tsuwano: Furusato				●	
Tsuwano: Yuki		●			
Yamaguchi: Yamabuki			■		
Kochi: Amigo Nijudai-ten					■
Kochi: Tokugetsuro	■				
Kotohira: Soba Restaurants			■		

MATSUYAMA: *Goshiki* ¥¥
3-5-4 Sanban-cho. (089) 933-3838.
The place to enjoy the regional specialty *goshiki somen* (five-color thin noodles), Goshiki uses no dyes but colors its noodles using green tea, plums, and other natural items. 11am–8:30pm.

MATSUYAMA: *Sushimaru* ¥¥
2-3-2 Niban-cho. (089) 941-0447.
A superb sushi restaurant with exceptional river fare, especially *unagi* (eel) so fresh that it melts in your mouth. *Somen* (light noodles) and other non-sushi items are also memorable. 11am–9pm.

OZU: *Arcade Seafood Restaurants and Bars* ¥
Arcade leading from JR stn to Hijikawa bridge.
This old-fashioned arcade street is the perfect place to engage in *bashigo-zake* ("ladder liquor," meaning bar-hopping). Specialty dishes include *ayu* (sweetfish) and tiny bullhead fish from the Hiji River. daily.

TAKAMATSU: *Wara-no-Ie* ¥
91 Naka-machi, Yashima (5 mins N of Kotoden Yashima stn). (087) 843-3115.
Fresh *udon* noodles, tempura, and *inari* sushi in relocated historic thatched-roof inn connected to a folk museum. 10am–7pm.

TAKAMATSU: *Nicho* ¥¥¥¥¥
7-7 Hyakuma-cho (2 mins S of Kotoden Katawaramachi stn). (087) 851-7166.
A landmark *kaiseki* restaurant on a street of dignified traditional homes, Nicho features 13 individual rooms, a table area, and a sushi counter.
11:30am–2pm, 5–9pm. Aug 13–15, table area Sun & hols.

TOKUSHIMA: *Takashima Kohiten* ¥
2-20-1 Happyakuya-machi. (088) 652-1071.
A throwback to Japan's golden age of jazz coffeehouses, this bar and coffee-house plays recorded jazz and offers over 50 kinds of sandwiches.
6am–8pm.

UWAJIMA: *Kadoya* ¥¥
8-1 Nishiki-machi (across first street to right of JR stn). (089) 522-1543.
Along with local beef dishes, the house specialty is *taimeshi*, which is rice steamed with minced sea bream. 11am–8:45pm (last order). Thu L.

KYUSHU

BEPPU: *Amamijaya* ¥
1-4 Jisoji. (0977) 67-6024.
Dangojiru, flat noodles in a vegetable broth, set a good standard. There is also a sweet version made with soybeans and sugar called *yaseuma*.
10am–10pm.

BEPPU: *Shinanoya* ¥
6-32 Nishinoguchi (behind the stn). (0977) 21-1395.
A good quick lunch stop in an old villa built in the early Showa era. Their own creation, *Shinanoya teishoku* consists of a thick soup replete with beef slices, dumplings, rice, and pickles. 10am–10pm.

BEPPU: *Fugumatsu* ¥¥¥¥
3-6-14 Kita-hama. (0977) 21-1717.
A good opportunity to sample the potentially deadly *fugu*, or blowfish, fresh from the nearby Bungo Straits. Also flatfish from Beppu Bay in the summertime. 11am–10pm.

CHIRAN: *Takian* ¥
In samurai district. (0993) 83-3186.
A charming, inexpensive restaurant offering local dishes within a samurai house with a lovely garden. 10:30am–4:30pm.

FUKUOKA: *Hakuryu* ¥
Stall just in front of the Mitsubishi Bank in Tenjin. no phone.
Like many *yatai* in Fukuoka, this one is a family-run affair, renowned in this instance for its *gyoza* (dumplings) and Hakata-style noodles. evenings.

FUKUOKA: *Gyosai* ¥¥¥
3-30-26 Hakata-ekimae. (092) 471-9327.
Locally caught seafood, especially sashimi. This and other branches have a good fish, soup, and rice set. 11:30am–1:30pm, 5–11pm. Sun.

For key to symbols see back flap

Price categories for an average-size dinner for one. Lunchtime special menus are often cheaper.
¥ under ¥1,500
¥¥ ¥1,500–3,000
¥¥¥ ¥3,000–6,000
¥¥¥¥ ¥6,000–10,000
¥¥¥¥¥ over ¥10,000

Kaiseki Cuisine
Japanese haute cuisine *(see p321)*.
Sushi or Seafood Specialties
Specializing in sushi, sashimi, or a seafood ingredient such as *fugu* or *unagi (see pp318–19)*.
Noodles
Soba, ramen, or other type of noodle restaurant *(see p317)*.
Vegetarian Specialties
Specializing in tofu and/or other vegetarian dishes *(see p320)*.
Non-Japanese Cuisine
Including Chinese and other Asian restaurants.

Restaurant	Price	Kaiseki Cuisine	Sushi or Seafood Specialties	Noodles	Vegetarian Specialties	Non-Japanese Cuisine
Fukuoka: *Ristorante Il Palazzo* 3-13-1, Haruyoshi, Chuo-ku. (092) 716-3330. The chef at this opulent Italian affair trained in Europe for eight years, and it shows. The "Three Pastas" course is recommended. *7:30am–10pm.*	¥¥¥					■
Fukuoka: *Shin Miura* 21-12 Sekijo-machi. (092) 291-0821. Friendly and well-known restaurant serving *mizutaki*, a course that includes raw and lightly braised chicken, a rich vegetable and chicken broth, and a chicken and scallion hot pot dish. *11:30am–8pm (last order).*	¥¥¥¥					
Kagoshima: *Satsuma* 27-30 Chuo-machi. (099) 252-2661. A tiny restaurant specializing in local delicacies like *tonkatsu, Satsuma-jiru* soup, and *kibinago*. *5–11pm.* *Mon.*	¥					
Kagoshima: *Shochu Tengoku* 1F Edo Yoshi Bldg, 9-33 Yamanokuchi-cho. (099) 224-9750. The name of this snack and drinking bar means "*shochu* heaven," and it has over 150 different kinds of the *shochu* spirit to be sampled alongside extremely tasty side dishes. *5pm–midnight.* *Sun & public hols.*	¥					
Kagoshima: *Yudofu Gonbe-e* 8-12 Higashi Sengoku-machi. (099) 222-3867. Homemade tofu dishes with a lemon dipping sauce are the specialty of this cozy, friendly restaurant. *5–11pm.* *Sun.*	¥¥				●	
Kumamoto: *Aoyagi* 1-2-10 Shimotori. (096) 353-0311. One of Kumamoto's best-known restaurants, Aoyagi is a good, all-round introduction to local dishes such as rice casserole. *11:30am–10pm.*	¥¥					
Kumamoto: *Gozan* Basement of Taigeki Kaikan Bldg, 4-1 Tedorihoncho. (096) 351-2869. Mud walls, a plastic bamboo grove, and volcano with optic lights create one of Kyushu's most surreal dining encounters. Dishes include steaks, tofu, and *basashi* (raw horse meat in vinegar sauce). *5pm–midnight.*	¥¥¥					
Kumamoto: *Okumura* 1-8-8 Shin-machi. (096) 352-8101. Reservations are necessary for this elegant *kaiseki* restaurant. Their lunchtime set courses are good value. *11:30am–3pm, 5–10pm.*	¥¥¥¥	■				
Mount Aso: *Ofukuro Kan* 2827 Oaza Hisaishi, Kuginomura. (09676) 7-0848. A down-to-earth restaurant whose name translates as "mother's kitchen." Sample the *Ofukuro teishoku*, a set meal consisting of fresh mountain vegetables, vinegared rice, tofu, and salad. *10am–5pm.*	¥				●	
Nagasaki: *Yosso* 8-9 Hama-cho. (0958) 21-0001. Specializing in *chawan mushi*, a popular egg-custard dish of shrimps and various vegetables *(see p317)*. *11am–8pm.* *2nd & 4th Tue of month.*	¥¥					
Nagasaki: *Hamakatsu* 6-50 Kajiya-machi. (095) 826-8321. Another good place to try the Nagasaki specialty of *shippoku* and various other local dishes. *11:30am–10pm.*	¥¥¥					
Nagasaki: *Harbin* 2-27 Kozen-machi. (095) 822-7443. Blend of Russian/French cuisine, such as Georgian spicy lamb, Russian "salon pie," and duck in redcurrant sauce. *11:30am–2:30pm, 6–10:30pm.* *Sun.*	¥¥¥					■

NAGASAKI: *Ichiriki* ¥¥¥¥¥
8-20 Suwa-machi, on Teramachi Street. (0958) 24-0226.
Well known for *shippoku*, a traditional Nagasaki meal that combines Chinese, Japanese, and Western dishes using sashimi, soup, and tender stewed pork among other ingredients. Served on low red lacquer tables. noon–2pm, 5–7:30pm (last order).

YANAGAWA: *Fukuryu* ¥¥
29-1 Okinohata-machi. (0944) 72-2404.
Yanagawa is famous for its tasty canal eel dishes such as *unagi no seiro mushi*, which is eel on omelet over a bed of rice, and Yanagawa *nabe*, which is an eel-and-vegetable hot pot. These and more are available at Fukuryu. 11am–7pm.

OKINAWA

ISHIGAKI ISLAND: *Iso* ¥¥
Opposite the harbor. (09808) 2-7721.
A good place to sample typical Yaeyama cuisine. Try the shredded pork ear with cucumber and a vinegar dressing if you dare. 11am–10:30pm.

NAHA: *Naha Soba* ¥
Hwy 331, Onoyama. No telephone.
A good initiation into Okinawan-style buckwheat noodles. Liberal slices of pork, onion, ginger, and maybe a twist of lemon or lime. 10am–9:30pm.

NAHA: *States Size* ¥
In the Tsuji area, one street behind Wakasa-dori. (098) 868-4318.
Popular with foreigners for succulent tenderloin and other steaks. Very reasonably priced considering the quantities. 11am–3:30am.

NAHA: *Taiwan Hanten* ¥¥
1-3-14 Wakasa-dori, on the NE edge of the Tsuji area. (098) 868-2010.
Good-quality Chinese food at affordable prices. 11:30am–11pm.
Obon Festival.

NAHA: *Yunangi* ¥¥
3-3-3 Kumochi. (098) 867-3765.
A friendly, rustic, drinking venue that also serves as a small restaurant for local dishes. Expect pork and also *chanpura* (sponge gourds), and bitter melons. A good place to try *awamori*, the fiery Okinawan version of sake. noon–3pm, 5:30–10:30pm (last order).

NAHA: *Ayajo* ¥¥¥
3-25-13 Kumochi. (098) 861-7741.
This pretty restaurant has a varied selection of Ryukyu cuisine served on local ceramic ware to the accompaniment of Okinawan folk music. 5–10pm.

TAKETOMI ISLAND: *Yarabo* ¥
Taketomi-cho. (09808) 5-2268.
A good selection of local cuisine. Try the *awamori* sake served with slices of sautéed bitter melon. 11am–4pm

NORTHERN HONSHU

AIZU-WAKAMATSU: *Mitsutaya* ¥
1-25 1-chome Omachi (just off Nanokamachi shopping st). (0242) 27-1345.
Dengaku, skewers of vegetables, tofu, taro, and fish dipped in a miso sauce and grilled over charcoal, is the specialty of this popular old restaurant *(see p311)*. Try to get a seat at the counter where the grilling is done. 10am–5pm. Jan–Mar: Wed; Apr–Jul: 1st & 3rd Wed of month.

AIZU-WAKAMATSU: *Takino* ¥¥¥
5-31 Sakae-machi. (0242) 25-0808.
The specialty here is *wappameshi*, steamed rice topped variously with salmon, sweetfish, and wild vegetables, and served in wooden containers. Like Mitsutaya, the shop is an Aizu institution. 11am–9pm.

HIROSAKI: *Kajimachi District* ¥ – ¥¥¥¥
Eating district S of Chuo-dori and Dote-machi.
All kinds of restaurants, bars, coffeeshops, and pubs fill the narrow streets of this friendly eating district. Local delights include *takenoko dengaku* (skewered grilled bamboo shoot with miso), *kaiyaki* miso (eggs and miso grilled in a scallop shell), and *jappa-jiru* (simmered cod and vegetables). variable.

Price categories for an average-size dinner for one. Lunchtime special menus are often cheaper.

¥ under ¥1,500
¥¥ ¥1,500–3,000
¥¥¥ ¥3,000–6,000
¥¥¥¥ ¥6,000–10,000
¥¥¥¥¥ over ¥10,000

Kaiseki Cuisine
Japanese haute cuisine *(see p321)*.

Sushi or Seafood Specialties
Specializing in sushi, sashimi, or a seafood ingredient such as *fugu* or *unagi* *(see pp318–19)*.

Noodles
Soba, ramen, or other type of noodle restaurant *(see p317)*.

Vegetarian Specialties
Specializing in tofu and/or other vegetarian dishes *(see p320)*.

Non-Japanese Cuisine
Including Chinese and other Asian restaurants.

Columns: Kaiseki Cuisine | Sushi or Seafood Specialties | Noodles | Vegetarian Specialties | Non-Japanese Cuisine

Hirosaki: *Yamauta* ¥¥¥
2-7 1-chome Oh-machi (nr JR Hirosaki stn). *(0172) 36-1835.*
This great restaurant-bar, opened in 1964 by master musician Yamda Chisato, showcases live performances of *Tsugaru-jamisen*, a gutsy, bluesy kind of music. The food, too, is good. *5pm–11pm.* *once a month (varies).*

Kakunodate: *Shokudo Inaho* ¥
Tamachi Kami-cho. *(0187) 55-1717.*
This local favorite has *kiritanpo* (pounded rice on a skewer), *inatei udon* (light noodles), and other regional dishes. *11:30am–4pm (to 7pm Sat).* *Thu.*

Kakunodate: *Ryotei Inaho* ¥¥¥
Tamachi Kami-cho. *(0187) 54-3311.*
This 50-year-old *ryotei*, next to Shokudo Inaho, offers superb regional cuisine. Specialties include duck and wild vegetables. *11:30am–2pm, 5–8pm.*

Mashiko: *Guine Handcrafted* ¥¥¥
3479-4 Ichihana, Ichikai-machi, Haga-gun. *(0285) 68-2729.* FAX *(0285) 68-2729.*
Caribbean-style chicken, fish, and smoked ribs in a remarkable mountaintop farm-gallery-restaurant run by George and Yoko Guine. Dinner entertainment includes jazz and blues, and Japanese classical dance. Minimum of eight required for reservations. *call for reservations.*

Morioka: *Azumaya* ¥¥
1-8-3 Nakanohashi-dori. *(019) 622-2252.* FAX *(019) 654-8166.*
This old shop, decorated with folk art, is one of the best of Morioka's many good *soba* shops. *Wanko soba* courses, saucer-sized servings of chilled noodles, start at ¥2,500. *Soba kaiseki* is also served. *11am–8pm.*

Nikko: *Nikko Kanaya Hotel* ¥¥¥¥¥
1300 Kamihatsuishi-cho. *(0288) 54-0001.*
Try the trout at the main dining room of this hotel, which also has a coffeeshop, bar, and steakhouse. *noon–3pm, 6–8pm (last order).*

Sado Island (Ogi): *Shichiuemon* ¥
Saiwai-cho, Ogimachi. *(0259) 86-2046.*
Everyone in Ogi knows this handsome old *soba* shop, famous for its noodles of buckwheat-flour stone-ground on the day the noodles are made. *11am–2pm; other hours by reservation.* *Sep–Mar: 1st & 15th of month.*

Sendai: *Sendai Kakitoku* ¥¥¥
4-9-1 Ichiban-cho. *(022) 222-0785.*
Miyagi oysters are world-famous and this restaurant's specialty. The atmosphere is rustic but the presentation is sophisticated. The oyster tofu delicacy is a tasty combination of ingredients. *11am–2pm, 5–9pm.* *Mon.*

Shiogama: *Shirahata* ¥¥¥
3-min walk from JR Shiogama stn. *(022) 364-2221.*
One of Shiogama's many good sushi restaurants. Order the special course, some of the excellent miso or fish soup, some beer or sake, and enjoy. *11am–10pm.* *Tue; 3–4:30pm Mon–Fri.*

Tono: *Ichiriki* ¥¥
5-27 Chuo-dori (5-min walk from JR Tono stn). *(0198) 62-2008.*
Good unpretentious food made with a light touch and using local freshwater fish and wild vegetables. The *kamameshi*, rice in a pot with scallops, chestnuts, or other items, is delicious. *11am–8pm.* *four times a month (varies).*

Tsuruoka: *Kanazawaya* ¥
Daihoji-machi (about 10-min walk from JR Tsuruoka stn). *(0235) 24-7208.*
Northern Japan is known for its *soba* restaurants, and this is one of the best. The *tenzaru* chilled *soba* with tempura is great. *11:30am–2:30pm, 5:30–10pm.* *Wed.*

YAMAGATA: *Saikan* ¥¥
Toge, Haguro-machi. *(0235) 62-2357.* FAX *(0235) 62-2352.*
If you do not stay at Saikan, atop Mount Haguro, then try to have lunch here. The *shojin ryori*, temple (in this case, shrine) cooking, features local mushrooms and wild vegetables, and is a bargain. *by reservation.*

HOKKAIDO

AKAN NATIONAL PARK: *Mingei Kissa Poronno* ¥
Akankohan. *(0154) 67-2159.*
Sample rustic Ainu cuisine at an Ainu village, perhaps the *poteimo*, a fried-potato cake, along with bark tea, called *shikurebe.* *May–Oct: 9am–10:30pm.*

DAISETSU-ZAN NATIONAL PARK: *Yama-no-Shokubo* ¥
Sounkyo. *(01658) 5-3521.*
Popular with locals, this budget eatery offers noodles, curry, and the inevitable spaghetti dishes. *11am–9pm.*

HAKODATE: *Bay Hakodate* ¥¥
11-5 Toyokawa-cho (on promenade). *(0138) 22-1300.*
Housed inside a typical Hakodate-style red-brick warehouse, this waterfront restaurant has a sumptuous buffet lunch and expanded dinner spread. There is also a bar with sashimi and raw shellfish choices. *summer: 11am–3:30pm, 5–10pm; winter: 11:30am–3pm, 5:30–9:30pm.*

HAKODATE: *Hakodate Beer* ¥¥
5-22 Ote-machi. *(0138) 23-8000.*
A beer hall with a great choice of seafood. Hokkaido smoked salmon and scallops are recommended. Also Northern-style meat dishes like roasted duck and copious amounts of stewed beef. *11am–10pm.*

HAKODATE: *Tarozushi* ¥¥
32-8 Moto-machi. *(0138) 22-0310.*
With superb views of Hakodate Bay, Tarozuchi serves some of the freshest and best-cut sushi in town. *11:30am–11pm Tue–Sun.*

KUSHIRO: *Kushiro Pacific Hotel* ¥
2-6 Sakae-cho. *(0154) 24-8811.*
This hotel has a good all-round menu that includes Japanese, Western, and Chinese cuisine served by attentive staff who speak some English. Weekend buffet lunches are good value. *11am–2pm.*

RISHIRI-REBUN-SAROBETSU NATIONAL PARK: *Sakatsubo* ¥
Kafuka, Rebun-cho. *(01638) 6-1894.*
Specializing in sea urchins, Sakatsubo has varieties such as the purple *murasaki uni*, on steaming rice. Snacks, like rice balls stuffed with sea urchin, are tasty with beer or sake. *May–Sep: 11am–3pm; Oct–Apr: 10:30am–4pm.*

SAPPORO: *Taj Mahal* ¥¥
5-min walk S of Odori stn nr Mitsukoshi dept store. *(011) 231-1168.*
One of Sapporo's best Indian restaurants. A good choice of curries, kebabs, and tandooris, mostly lamb and chicken. *11am–11:30pm (last order).*

SAPPORO: *Yagumo* ¥¥
B2 Plaza Bldg, Odori 4-chome. *(011) 231-0789.*
Traditional noodle shop in an interesting setting with folk-art objects. Specialties include sesame *soba.* *10:30am–8:30pm.* *2nd & 3rd Mon of month.*

SAPPORO: *Sapporo Beer Garden* ¥¥¥
Kita 7, Higashi 9. *(011) 742-1531.*
An inexpensive blowout, the brewery's specialty is an all-you-can-eat lamb barbecue and all-you-can-drink within 100 minutes. The beer hall seats up to 3,500 people. *11:30am–9pm daily.*

SAPPORO: *Suginome* ¥¥¥¥
Minami 5, Nishi 5. *(011) 521-0888.*
A well-known Sapporo institution, this rather expensive restaurant specializes in local Hokkaido dishes, particularly fish ones grilled at an open hearth. It is advisable to reserve. *5–11pm.* *Sun & public hols.*

SAPPORO: *21 Club* ¥¥¥¥¥
25F Hotel Arthur, Minami 10-jo, Nishi 6. *(011) 561-1000.*
One of the most chic restaurants in town, with great views. The specialty is *teppanyaki.* *11:30am–3pm, 5–9:30pm (last order).*

For key to symbols see back flap

Shopping in Japan

Shopping in Japan is an amazing experience. With as many traditional arts and crafts products as contemporary and imported items, there is the most fascinating choice imaginable. Equally interesting is the range of shops – from glitzy department stores and huge shoppings malls to roadside stalls and tiny craft workshops. Within 24 hours, the constant greetings of *irasshaimase* (Welcome!) on entering a shop are either driving visitors crazy or have become part of the general background noise. Japan is no longer the most expensive country in the world, but still the price of certain commodities may shock. Some goods made in Japan, such as cameras and other electronic items, are actually cheaper to buy abroad. On the other hand, it is possible to buy original and unusual souvenirs surprisingly inexpensively. For details on shopping in Tokyo, see pages 100–103; for Kyoto, see pages 174–7.

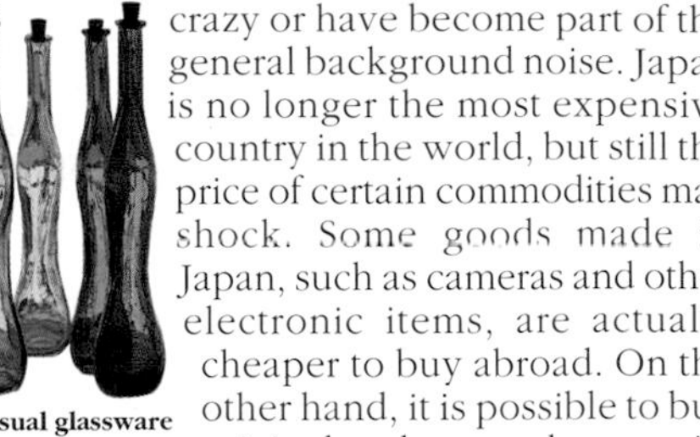

Unusual glassware for sale in Nagasaki

Canal City shopping complex in Fukuoka, Kyushu

Shopping Hours

Supermarkets and department stores are usually closed one day a week between Monday and Friday, depending on the custom of the particular locality. A number of specialty shops – boutiques included – may not open on Sundays and national holidays. Family-run businesses are generally open daily, including Saturdays, Sundays, and national holidays.

Opening hours of most shops are 10am to 8pm. Department stores usually close one hour earlier. Convenience stores – chains such as **Seven-Eleven** and **Lawson's** – are open seven days a week, 24 hours a day. Vending machines *(see p309)* are widespread in hotels and at roadsides, offering drinks, some food, plus batteries, CDs, and other practical items 24 hours a day.

Prices and Sales Tax

In department stores and boutiques, and in inner-city areas, prices are nearly always marked in Arabic numerals. In local shops and supermarkets, and in areas where non-Japanese are few and far between, prices may be written only in kanji characters. When shopkeepers are unable to make themselves understood verbally to visitors, they may type the numbers on a calculator, write them down, or sign with their fingers. If you are traveling off the beaten track, it is useful to learn the characters for the numbers one to ten, one hundred, and one thousand, and for the word *yen (see pp404–8).*

All purchasable items and services are subject to a government-imposed consumption tax of five percent. The price displayed does not necessarily include the tax, which will be added automatically when you pay.

In the booming 1980s, all prices were fixed, but in more recessive times, the emphasis is on discount shopping, with stores lowering prices to match strong competion. Flea markets and antique fairs are the only places where haggling is accepted as an integral part of the proceedings.

How to Pay

The Japanese yen continues to be regarded as a stable currency, despite various ups and downs since the late 1980s. Cash is by far the easiest method to pay for goods. There need be no anxieties about being given the right change; Japanese are scrupulously honest – especially in handling guests from abroad.

Prices displayed in Arabic numerals in a sweet shop

Inside Mikimoto Pearl shop in Ginza, Tokyo's premier shopping district

It is customary, when paying, for a small tray to be offered; you should place money on it, and your change will be returned without hand-to-hand contact. International credit cards are still surprisingly unpopular in smaller shops. In general, the larger the emporium, the wider the range of international cards taken. VISA, American Express, Diners Club, and MasterCard are the most widely accepted.

Rights and Refunds

Refunds are not encouraged but are legal if the sales slip can be produced, and the item in question has not been tampered with. Some stores give redeemable coupons rather than money, so that they do not lose out. Without a receipt, return is impossible.

Tax-Free Shopping

Japan tax-free shops offer a good range of domestically made and imported brand items all free of the five percent sales tax added elsewhere. You will need to show your passport. Authorized outlets are mainly located in shopping districts and urban areas frequented by tourists, as well as the international airports. The best-known in the capital are the **Tokyo International Arcade** (near the Imperial Hotel) and **Laox** *(see p103)* for electronic goods; and in Kansai, the **Kyoto Craft Center** *(see pp176–7)*. It is a good idea, however, to compare the prices of goods in these shops with those in specialty and discount stores, as the latter may work out the same or even cheaper.

In some shops, particularly department stores, you may have to pay the full price for an item, then obtain a refund and customs document from a tax-exemption counter. This document is retained by customs as you leave Japan.

Exporting Large Items

Most specialty duty-free outlets will arrange packaging of bulky goods for export if required. The same applies to antiques such as *tansu* (chests) and screens. There are also a large number of moving companies that specialize in handling large-size items; shop around in English-language newspapers and listings publications.

Compatibilty of Electrical Goods

Great care should be taken when buying electrical or electronic products. Make absolutely sure that circuits are either compatible with, or can be easily adjusted to, a home country's power system *(see p363)*. Also, the FM radio band is different (from 76 to 90) from that used elsewhere in the world.

Japan uses the NTSC system for video, which is compatible with Canada, the US, and much of South and Central America. PAL video systems, used in other parts of Asia, Australia, and Europe, among other places, are available at electronic specialists such as those in the Akihabara district of Tokyo *(see p69)*.

Clothing Sizes

Buying clothing in Japan can be a problem. Young people are growing to Western sizes now, but a lot of clothing is still cut for older-style Japanese physiques. That means smaller overall and with shorter sleeves in particular. The range of sizes available tends toward small to medium with a few large (not as large as Western large). Remember to take your shoes off when entering a fitting room.

Men's Suits and Coats

Japanese	S	M	L	XL
US	34	38	42	46
British	34	38	42	46
Continental	44	48	52	56

Women's Clothes

Japanese	4	5	7	9	11	13
US	5	6	8	10	12	14
British	6	8	10	12	14	16
Continental	34	36	38	40	42	44

Shoes

Japanese	23	24.5	25	26	27	28	29
US men's	5	6	7	8	9	10	11
US women's	6	7	8	9	10	11	12
British	4	5	6	7	8	9	10
Continental	37	38	39	40.5	42	43	44.5

An elegant display of watches in the window of Tokyo's Wako store

Department Stores

JAPAN'S MAINSTREAM department stores often fulfill a remarkable number of functions, housing ticket agencies, art galleries, and currency exchanges, alongside a huge range of consumer goods. Some stores are built over or enclose major train stations, resembling a city in microcosm. The early *depato* developed out of Edo-period kimono suppliers, with stores such as **Takashimaya** and **Mitsukoshi** leading the way. Others were rooted in the fortunes of industrialists seeking in patriarchal fashion to meet the needs of the masses.

Most major stores are laid out in a similar fashion. Food – together with rich pickings of free samples – is usually located in the basement; the first floor is often given over to candies, cosmetics, or accessories; restaurants serving a range of different cuisines tend to be on the top floor; playgrounds for small children are often on the roof. In between are fashion, furniture and furnishings, electrical goods, kitchenware, kimonos and traditional crafts, even pets. Customers tend to ride to the top by elevator and then descend by escalator, browsing and buying en route; Japan calls this the "shower effect." Sales are held in spring, summer, fall, and winter, and there are additional special discount events.

The really top-notch department stores are more specialized. **Matsuya** is associated with upscale fashion brands. **Wako**, regarded by many as the most elite department store in Japan, sells expensive jewelry, lingerie, and accessories. At the other end of the scale, Seibu's **Parco** caters to the affluent youth market, housing new-wave fashion and the full range of contemporary arts all under one roof.

Restrooms are often luxuriously appointed with areas for feeding and changing babies.

Shopping Malls and Arcades

A JAPANESE CITY is not a city without its fair share of malls and arcades. Many date from the postwar period and, being generally located in downtown areas, are old-fashioned in style and appearance. Nevertheless they are where most people eat and play *pachinko* *(see p93)* in between routine shopping and bargain hunting.

Imaemon pottery from Arita in Kyushu

Adjoining Senso-ji Temple in Tokyo *(see pp82–3)* is an old-fashioned arcade of shops selling a mixture of tourist souvenirs and quality traditional crafts. In Osaka, Umeda Underground Arcade is famed.

Discount Stores and Supermarkets

IN MANY RESPECTS, supermarkets are the same in Japan as elsewhere. A few sections and products may seem strange and exotic, such as the extensive displays of noodles, tofu, *kamaboko* (fish-paste products), tempura, sashimi, and *bento* (prepared lunch boxes). Under the same roof as the supermarket may be a florist, bakery, dry cleaners, and drugstore *(kusuri)*.

Kinokuniya and **Meiji-ya** supermarkets specialize in high-quality imports. At the other end of the scale, **Jusco** offers economically priced store-brand goods with an emphasis on recycling and environmental concern. The name **Daiei** is connected with high-volume chain and discount stores operating nationwide. **Ito-Yokado**, **Seiyu**, and **Daikuma** cater to families; newcomers like **Aoki** and **Konaka** specialize in men's suits. Being cheap, cheerful, in strong competition, and often near train stations, they are always packed.

Arts and Crafts Centers

ARTS AND CRAFTS are held in equally high esteem in Japan. A finely lacquered comb is therefore regarded with as much respect as *nihonga* (traditional Japanese painting). Nowhere else in the world can such a wealth of techniques and genuine appreciation of this labor-intensive work be found. There are 2,000 potters in Tokyo alone, and all make a living. Bamboo has 2,000 traditional uses, many of which are still employed for brushes, baskets, tableware, and furniture.

A basketware shop in Yufuin, Kyushu

The best place to see a full range of what is available nationwide is at a handicraft center. Both Tokyo and Kyoto have excellent craft centers *(see pp102–3 and pp176–7)*, with regular demonstrations of traditional arts and crafts as well as items on sale, often at tax-free prices.

Regional arts and crafts centers abound, displaying the work of local artists and artisans. Ask at the nearest TIC for details of local centers. Certain areas specialize in ceramics, *washi* (handmade paper), marquetry, ironware, or textiles, for example. Boutiques mixing indigo-dyed or specialty woven fabrics with other crafts, such as woodturning, glassware, and ceramics, are popular.

A colorful range of food stalls in Nishiki market alley, Kyoto

Markets

Food markets provide an insight into the Japanese enthusiasm for food and cooking. The basement food floor of a major department store is a good place to start.

Small local markets, where farmers sell fresh produce, are usually operated by the agricultural cooperatives *(nokyo)*. These markets can be found all over the country and even in inner city areas, since vegetable plots nestle between homes, factories, and *pachinko* parlors.

Markets for manufactured goods flourish in urban wholesale districts, where industries are concentrated, selling everything from kitchenware to TVs.

Stalls en route to the shrine of Tenman-gu in Dazaifu, Kyushu

Temple and Shrine Stalls

In these sacred precincts, there are usually a number of stalls selling religious charms and votive plaques. These are reasonably priced and make good souvenirs. Other types of shopping here fall into two categories: flea markets, and traditional goods associated with seasonal festivals and changes of climate. Regular flea markets, which are listed in English-language publications in Japan, provide rich pickings of everything from junk to rare treasures. Items are not as inexpensive as they used to be, but these markets are still cheaper than antique and secondhand shops for kimono, books, and so on.

Many fairs are staged toward the end of the year. Two examples in the capital are Torii-no-ichi at Otori Shrine in mid-November *(see p42)*, and Hagoita-Ichi (Toshi-no-ichi), held December 17–19 at Senso-ji Temple *(see p43)*. New Year decorations to hang above doorways and on gateposts also draw a lot of business. In summer there are often stalls selling potted *asagao* (morning glory) plants, and metal and glass wind chimes *(furin)*, which catch the breeze.

The Japanese Art of Wrapping

Japanese culture is quintessentially wrapping based: the body is wrapped and tied into kimono; tasty tidbits are encased in rice, the staple of everyday life, and further cloaked in seaweed to make *onigiri* (rice balls); hand luggage is innovatively wrapped and tied for ease of carrying in a decorative cloth *(furoshiki)*. Shops will almost invariably wrap goods exquisitely in handmade paper *(washi)*, often in several layers. While the beauty, intrigue, and ultimate revelation of such a tradition has obvious appeal – and is ideal when the purchase is a present – the level of waste is high: now even Japanese consumers are beginning to question the custom.

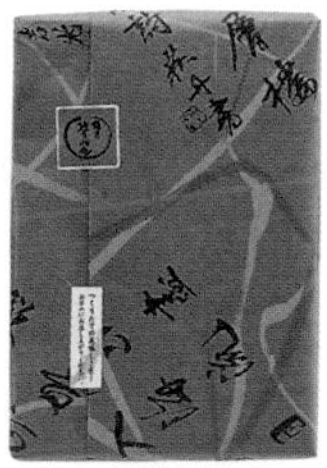

Decorative paper wrapping

Ribbon adorning a packet of spice

A set of chopsticks, boxed

What to Buy in Japan

Wooden doll from Miyajima

Origami paper

The abundance of specialty shops and craft outlets in Japan makes shopping a pleasure. Items available range from beautiful handmade crafts to useful everyday objects and kitsch toys. As a result, there should be something for every budget, and many of the most interesting souvenirs are also compact and light to carry home. Tokyo and Kyoto have the widest choice of shops that are used to dealing with foreign visitors, and many towns around the country have specialty craft centers or workshops. If time is limited, visit a large department store or a crafts emporium.

Ceramics

Ordinary pottery shops sell a wide selection of attractive bowls, dishes, cups, and sake bottles for everyday use. For a more unique – and expensive – souvenir, visit regions that specialize in pottery *(see p34)*, or a large craft shop, which should stock a good selection of the main regional styles.

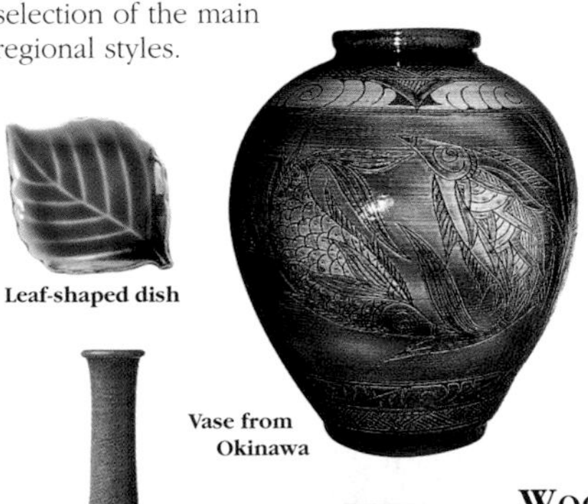
Leaf-shaped dish

Vase from Okinawa

Paper and Calligraphy

Traditional Japanese paper *(washi)* is handmade and often dyed in bright colors or embedded with petals or colored flecks. It is available as stationery, or made into boxes and various origami shapes.

Mobile made of paper

Calligraphy Set
An inkstone, water pot, brush, and ink make up a calligraphy set. The components can be bought separately or boxed.

Wood and Bamboo

A huge range of wood and bamboo souvenirs is available. Lacquerware trays, bowls, and boxes can be expensive but make original souvenirs. They need to be kept in humid conditions to last. Wooden combs, boxes, and dolls are also good buys. Large wooden chests, new and antique, are well designed but costly to ship.

Bizen-ware Vase
A form of unglazed earthenware pottery, Bizen-ware has been produced in Inbe (see p204) *for almost 1,000 years. Firing at a high temperature produces different surface finishes. Sake bottles, vases, and other storage vessels are popular.*

Echizen-ware vase

Umbrella
Made of bamboo and paper, this umbrella is typical of those seen at onsen *resorts. These traditional umbrellas are also available from craft shops.*

Lacquer bowl

Woven basket

Woodblock Prints

Known as *ukiyo-e* *(see p81)*, woodblock prints are uniquely Japanese mementoes. Antique and original prints are sold in specialty shops and can be very expensive; modern reproductions are widely available and often of good quality.

Print of a scene in a women's bath house by Yoshiiku

Woodblock print of Mount Fuji by Takamizawa

Ironware

The center for iron tea kettles *(tetsubin)* in Japan is Morioka in Northern Honshu *(see 271)*. These items were orignally manufactured for use in the tea ceremony. Many are now mass-produced. Nonetheless, they make useful, durable purchases but are heavy to carry home.

Iron tea kettle

Toys and Lucky Charms

Decorative figures and toys are enormously popular in Japan, and there are plenty to choose from. Wooden dolls may be expensive as many are handmade and have become collectors' items.

Charms
Charms, such as this classic lucky cat, are often sold at temple and shrine stalls.

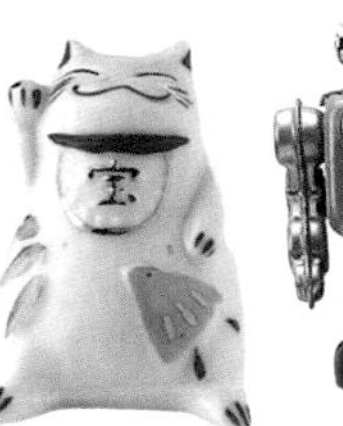

Tin robot

Clothing and Textiles

Kimonos run into thousands of yen to buy new but will last for years; second-hand ones are more affordable. Light cotton kimonos, known as *yukata*, are also less expensive to buy. Lengths of silk or hand-dyed fabrics are readily available in department stores.

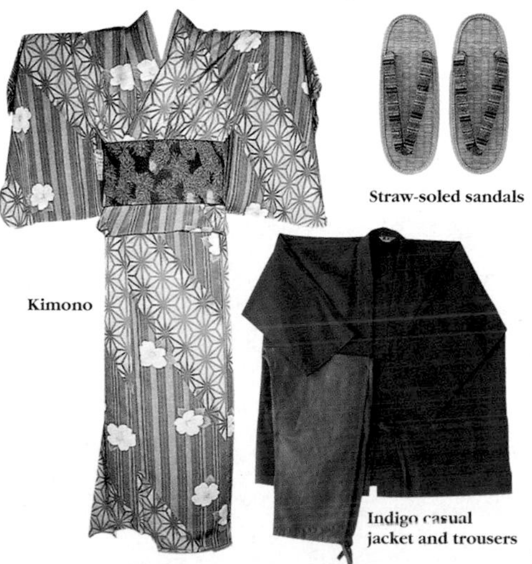

Kimono

Straw-soled sandals

Indigo casual jacket and trousers

Sweets

All manner of sweets, cookies, and rice crackers can be found in specialty shops and in department stores. You can usually choose from a selection and have your choice decoratively wrapped. Some tourist sites sell their own distinctively shaped sweets.

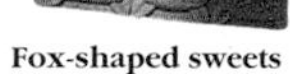

Fox-shaped sweets from Tsuruoka

Biscuit shaped like a leaf

Boxed Sweets
The Japanese themselves often give boxes of sweets as gifts. These are decorated as characters in a Kabuki play (see p32).

Onsen

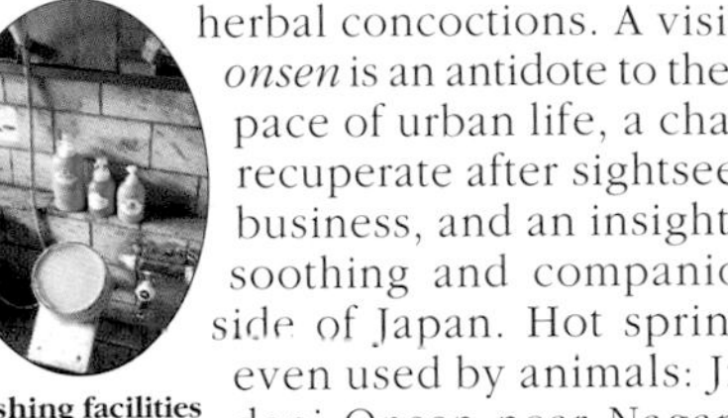

Washing facilities

Japan is peppered with volcanic hot springs, known as *onsen*. Communal bathing in these has been a custom for centuries, as a religious ritual (from the Shinto emphasis on purification), health cure, or just for pleasure. Many spa baths tap into natural volcanic activity, taming the thermal waters; some are artificially heated and enhanced with therapeutic herbal concoctions. A visit to an *onsen* is an antidote to the hectic pace of urban life, a chance to recuperate after sightseeing or business, and an insight into a soothing and companionable side of Japan. Hot springs are even used by animals: Jigokudani Onsen near Nagano, for example, is popular with wild monkeys, who sit in the pools to keep warm.

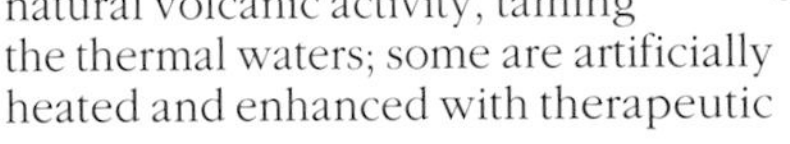

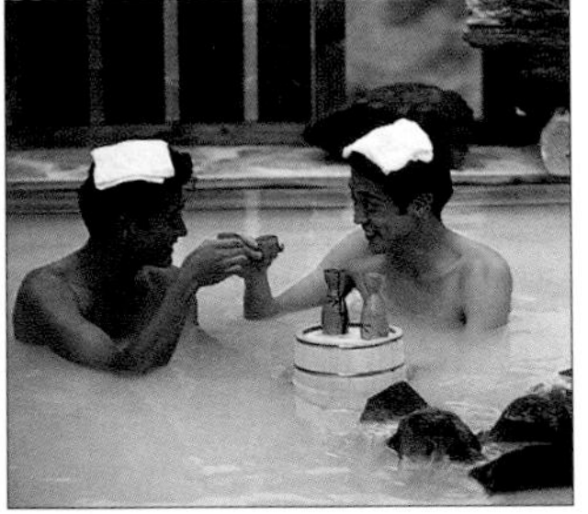

Enjoying a cup of sake in a traditional *onsen*

Types of Onsen

The variety of *onsen* is phenomenal. They come in every format: natural and man-made; indoors and outdoors; as small as a bath and as large as a swimming pool; lobster-hot and lukewarm; milky and clear; sulfurously foul-smelling and sweetly earthy. Certain chemical compositions in the waters are said to help different ailments, such as arthritis, hypertension, and skin problems.

Outdoor baths are generally rustic, made of wood or stone, and often by a river or the sea. Some are in caves, under jungle canopies, or behind waterfalls, or take the form of thermal mud or sand baths. Many *onsen* are in the mountains: after hiking, a dip in an outdoor pool in deep snow with a mountain view is perhaps the ultimate *onsen* experience. Exotic indoor *onsen* include baths in cable cars.

Many *onsen* operate as hotels, with meals and *onsen* facilities all included in the room price per person. Staying overnight allows you to sample the pleasures of night-time bathing. Entire *onsen* resorts have been developed so that between baths guests may wander around the town in their *yukata* (lightweight kimonos) or dine on local fare, often excellent. Other *onsen* hotels are in isolated hamlets in spectacular settings. At some *onsen* hotels and public bathhouses it is possible to stay for just a few hours rather than overnight. Fees can be very reasonable for these short visits – from ¥300 to ¥2,000. For details of individual *onsen*, consult a TIC or local tourist office, or *A Guide to Japanese Hot Springs* *(see p401)*. English may not be spoken at *onsen* hotels and local tourist offices; try to have a Japanese-speaker help you book accommodations.

Onsen Etiquette

Etiquette at *onsen* is similar to that for communal baths in *ryokan (see p291)*. Pools are usually single-sex; women rarely use mixed pools, except perhaps at night, when mixed bathing is more acceptable. Occasionally people in outdoor pools *(rotenburo)* wear swimsuits, but mostly everyone is naked. Nonetheless, the atmosphere is not sleazy, and visitors need have no qualms.

If you're staying overnight, change into the *yukata* provided in your room; either way, when you reach the baths, leave all clothes and possessions in the changing room. As with any Japanese bath, wash and rinse yourself thoroughly at the showers and taps provided outside the bath and take great care not to get any soap or shampoo in the bath itself.

The small towel provided can be used as a washcloth, draped across strategic parts of your body, placed on your head while in the pool (said to prevent fainting), or used to dry yourself when you emerge.

Keep all jewelry well away from steam, as the minerals can tarnish metal. Pregnant women, babies and young children, and anyone with high blood pressure should not enter the hottest baths without consulting a doctor first.

A steaming sand bath in Ibusuki, southern Kyushu

Selected Onsen Areas in Japan

There are over 2,000 hot spring areas across the country, concentrated particularly in Kyushu, the Izu Peninsula west of Tokyo, and the mountainous backbone of Northern and Central Honshu.

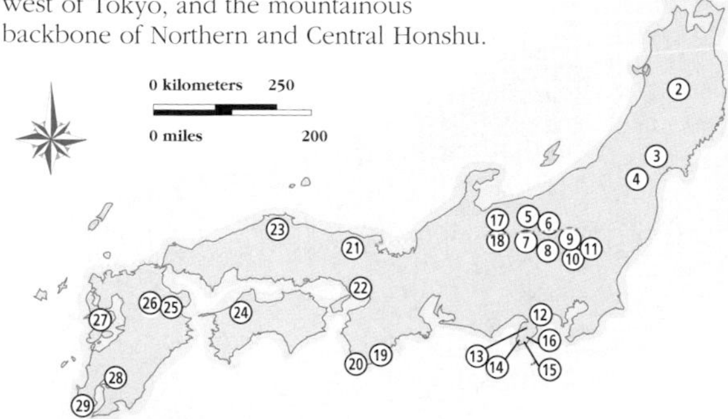

Outdoor hot spring at Yufuin, Kyushu

Key to Onsen Areas Map

(1) **Noboribetsu**
Hokkaido prefecture. Numerous hotels and huge choice of baths, playfully themed or medicinal. *(01438) 4-3311.*

(2) **Kuroyu**
Akita prefecture. Remote and unspoiled, with a single thatched inn; inaccessible in winter. *(018) 831-7067.*

(3) **Narugo**
Miyagi prefecture. Medium-size *onsen* town known for fall foliage. *(0229) 83-3441.*

(4) **Zao**
Yamagata prefecture. Popular ski resort and summer hiking base, but not over-commercialized. *(0236) 694-9328.*

(5) **Jigokudani**
Nagano prefecture. Famed for *onsen*-loving monkeys; a single, simple inn, plus hotels in nearby villages. *(0269) 33-3111.*

(6) **Echigo Yuzawa**
Niigata prefecture. Traditional resort (on *shinkansen* line); atmospheric setting for Kawabata's novel *Snow Country*. *(0257) 85-5505.*

(7) **Kusatsu**
Gunma prefecture. Three-minute "time baths" in the scalding water here. Numerous public baths and inns. *(0279) 88-0800.*

(8) **Hoshi**
Gunma prefecture. One lovely traditional *ryokan* with large wooden bathhouse, situated in woodland. *(0278) 66-0005 (ryokan).*

(9) **Takaragawa**
Gunma prefecture. Perhaps the best riverside pools in Japan, plus a pool for bears; one thatched *ryokan*. *(0278) 75-2121 (ryokan).*

(10) **Nikko Yumoto**
Tochigi prefecture. Small *onsen* village in Nikko National Park; good hiking. *(0288) 54-2496.*

(11) **Yunishigawa**
Tochigi prefecture. Atmospheric old *onsen* village in remote valley. *(0288) 97-1126.*

(12) **Hakone**
Kanagawa prefecture. Famous old *onsen* town, sprawling up hillside; wide range of inns and baths. *(0460) 5-7751.*

(13) **Shuzenji**
Shizuoka prefecture. Traditional *onsen* town, commercialized but charming; many good inns. *(0558) 72-2501.*

(14) **Osawa**
Shizuoka prefecture. A handful of picturesque *onsen* hotels in rural serenity. *(0558) 42-2799.*

(15) **Odaru**
Shizuoka prefecture. Numerous pools, waterfalls, and caves; several inns. *(0558) 32-0290.*

(16) **Hottawa**
Shizuoka prefecture. Coastal *onsen* with inns and pools overlooking the sea. *(0557) 37-3291.*

(17) **Renge**
Niigata prefecture. High in the alps, Renge has a choice of pools around a single inn (closed in winter). Ideal for hikers. *(0255) 52-1063* (inn).

(18) **Shirahone**
Nagano prefecture. Relaxed mountain town near skiing and hiking areas. *(0263) 94-2301.*

(19) **Katsuura**
Wakayama prefecture. An established resort, with jungle-theme and seaside pools, including a cave-bath. *(0735) 52-0048.*

(20) **Shirahama**
Wakayama prefecture. Popular, coastal resort town with sandy beaches. *(0739) 43-5511.*

(21) **Kinosaki**
Hyogo prefecture. Picturesque old-style town with traditional inns. Tasty crabs. *(0796) 32-3663.*

(22) **Arima**
Hyogo prefecture. Commercial resort with many hotels; pleasantly secluded. *(078) 904-0708.*

(23) **Takamatsukuri**
Shimane prefecture. Japan's oldest recorded hot spring and largest outdoor pool. *(0852) 62-9109.*

(24) **Dogo**
Ehime prefecture. Old-established spa town with classic bathhouse; many inns. *(089) 921-5141.*

(25) **Beppu**
Oita prefecture. One of the world's most thermally active places. Vintage complex of hot-spring towns *(see pp228–9)*. *(0977) 21-1111.*

(26) **Yufuin**
Oita prefecture. Small craftsy spa town with horse-drawn carriages and very little nightlife. *(0977) 84-3111.*

(27) **Unzen**
Nagasaki prefecture. Bubbling pools in Unzen-Amakusa National Park. *(0957) 73-3434.*

(28) **Ebino Kogen**
Miyazaki prefecture. Beautiful scenery and good hiking by Mount Karakuni. Rocky outdoor pools. *(0984) 35-1111.*

(29) **Ibusuki**
Kagoshima prefecture. Modern resort with tropical atmosphere and hot-sand baths. *(0993) 22-2111.*

Theme Parks

Japan has an astonishing number of theme parks, and Japanese tourists are especially drawn when the theme is new. This has created a lot of competition among managements to come up with fresh and innovative attractions. While many overseas visitors have little interest in this aspect of tourism in Japan, others – especially families and visitors from other Asian countries – travel thousands of miles to these vast playgrounds. Indeed, some foreigners find the Japanese fascination with theme parks fascinating in itself. Enthusiasts go back again and again, seeking to gain a sense of the outside world in complete security, or in search of an escape from the responsibilities of adulthood in an artificially created, idealized notion of childhood.

Interactive scientific exhibit

History Theme Parks

Even those overseas visitors who do not usually visit theme parks may be interested in those devoted to Japanese history and culture. North of Tokyo, the **Nikko Edo Village** has re-created 18th-century buildings and has guides dressed in period costume. Under the same management, **Noboribetsu Date Jidai Mura** in Hokkaido's Shikotsu-Toya National Park has assembled over 90 reconstructed 16th–19th-century buildings from all over the country.

Ise Sengoku Jidai Mura is a 16th-century theme park with a reproduction of Azuchi Castle, which used to stand on the shores of Lake Biwa. Near Inuyama, **Meiji Mura** *(see p137)* is an open-air museum that preserves and exhibits fine examples of Meiji-period architecture. On a smaller scale, **Nihon Minka-en**, between Kawasaki and Yokohama, has local traditional buildings, including farmhouses, a Shinto shrine, and a Kabuki theater, all in a garden setting.

Foreign Culture Theme Parks

These hugely popular theme parks give overseas visitors an insight into the way their own cultures are perceived by the Japanese. For example, Hokkaido's **Glucks Okoku** reproduces a medieval German town. **Niigata Russian Village** is on the same lines. **Tazawako Swiss Village** in Akita includes a reproduction of Heidi's cottage and a movie theater introducing Swiss culture. **Tivoli Park** *(see p205)* in Kurashiki is based on Copenhagen's pride and joy.

Tobu World Square near Tokyo reproduces more than 100 famous buildings from all over the world in miniature. **Nijinosato** in Shizuoka prefecture is an international mishmash with Canadian, British, and Japanese villages and a "fairy garden." **Reoma World** in Kagawa, northeast Shikoku, includes reproduction temples and pagodas from Thailand, Nepal, and Bhutan. Best of all is **Huis ten Bosch** in Nagasaki *(see p237)*. The whole development is ecologically designed, with faithful reproductions of Dutch architecture. On-site hotels are connected to the sea by inland waterways.

The Dutch-themed Huis ten Bosch park in Nagasaki

Amusement Parks

Since opening in 1983, **Tokyo Disneyland** has welcomed up to 17 million visitors each year. Situated on the outskirts of the capital, east of Daiba, in Chiba prefecture, it attracts visitors from all over Asia. In 2001, **Tokyo Disney Sea** is due to open on an adjacent site, with a monorail system to link the two parks.

In Tokyo itself, **Amazing Square** offers hi-tech interactive space battle games; **Dr. Jeekans** has a futuristic casino; **Sanrio Puroland** made history as Japan's first

Frontage of Frank Lloyd Wright's Imperial Hotel in Meiji Mura, Inuyama

completely indoor theme park. North of the capital, **Unesco Village** is (confusingly) a dinosaur amusement park with 250 life-size creatures moving, roaring, and fighting. Attractions include Japan's largest merry-go-round. **Kinugawa Western Mura** is an American Western theme park town with live shows, country-and-western music, and hi-tech robots of famous American movie stars.

South of Tokyo, **Yomiuri Land** features the White Cyclone, which is the only all-wood roller coaster in the country. **Joypolis** *(see p99)*, designed by Sega, has many interactive attractions, including the world's first virtual-reality motion ride.

Yokohama's dockside **Minato Mirai 21** complex *(see p237)* boasts a huge Ferris wheel, capable of carrying up to 480 people at a time.

Science Parks

Despite being on the cutting edge of invention, Japan is not well endowed with science parks. Tokyo Bay is now home to **Palette Town** *(see p99)*, which houses several technically based attractions, including Toyota City Showcase, the History Garage, Future World, driving courses, and the E-Com ride. **Space World** is a huge complex in Fukuoka prefecture, with many hi-tech rides. It incorporates a Space Camp where children can experience astronaut training imported from NASA.

Marine Theme Parks

Hokkaido's **Noboribetsu Marine Park Castle Nixe** offers marine and European themes in whimsical combination. In the Kanto region are **Kamogama Sea World** and

Viewing turtles in one of Japan's many spectacular aquariums

Yokohama's **Hakkeijima Sea Paradise** – a man-made island with Japan's largest aquarium. The highlight of Osaka's Tempozan Harbor Village *(see p197)* is the huge **Osaka Aquarium**, housing 580 marine species. **Paradiso**, also in Osaka, combines an aquarium with a swimming pool complex. Kyushu's **Seagaia** is an artificial water park; its Ocean Dome includes the world's largest indoor beach and bay facility, with 2.5-m (8-ft) high waves.

Directory

History Theme Parks

Ise Sengoku Jidai Mura
1201-1 Oaza Mitsu, Futami-cho, Watarai-gun, Mie-ken.
(0596) 43-2300.

Nihon Minka-en
7-1-1 Masukata, Tama-ku, Kawasaki-shi, Kanagawa-ken.
(044) 922-2181.

Nikko Edo Village
470-2 Karakura, Fujiwara-machi, Shioya-gun, Tochigi-ken.
(0288) 77-1777.

Noboribetsu Date Jidai Mura
53-1 Noboribetsu-cho, Noboribetsu-shi, Hokkaido.
(0143) 83-3311.

Foreign Culture Theme Parks

Glucks Okoku
Kofuku-cho, Obihiro-shi, Hokkaido.
(0155) 64-5300.

Niigata Russian Village
1956-82 Aza Hayama, Oaza Sasaoka, Sasakami-mura, Kita Kanbara-gun, Niigata-ken.
(0250) 63-1111.

Nijinosato
4279-3 Shuzenji, Tagata-gun, Shizuoka-ken.
(0558) 72-7111.

Reoma World
40-1 Kurikuma Nishi, Ayauta-cho, Ayauta-gun, Kagawa-ken.
(0877) 86-5533.

Tazawako Swiss Village
77-6 Kata-aza Arasawa, Tazawako-machi, Senboku-gun, Akita-ken.
(0187) 43-2939.

Tobu World Square
209-1 Oaza Ohara, Fujiwara-machi, Shioya-gun, Tochigi-ken.
(0288) 77-1000.

Amusement Parks

Amazing Square
19-1 Senju-Sekiya, Adachi-ku, Tokyo.
(03) 3882-8011.

Dr. Jeekans
2-4 Maruyama-cho, Shibuya-ku, Tokyo.
(03) 3476-7811.

Kinugawa Western Mura
315-1 Kurihara, Imaichi-shi, Tochigi-ken.
(0288) 218731.

Sanrio Puroland
1-31 Ochiai, Tama-shi, Tokyo.
(0423) 39-1111.

Tokyo Disneyland
1-1 Maihama, Urayasu-shi, Chiba-ken.
(047) 354-0001.

Unesco Village
2227 Kamiyamaguchi, Tokorozawa-shi, Saitama-ken.
(0429) 22-1370.

Yomiuri Land
3294 Yanokuchi, Inagi-shi, Tokyo.
(044) 966-1111.

Science Parks

Space World
8-1 Edamitsu Hon-machi, Hachiman Higashi-ku, Kita-Kyushu.
(093) 672-3600.

Marine Theme Parks

Hakkeijima Sea Paradise
Hakkeijima, Kanazawa-ku, Yokohama, Kanagawa-ken.
(045) 788-8888.

Kamogawa Sea World
1464-18 Higashi-cho, Kamogawa-shi, Chiba-ken.
(0470) 92-2121.

Noboribetsu Marine Park Castle Nixe
1-22 Noboribetsu Higashi-machi, Noboribetsu-shi, Hokkaido.
(0143) 83-3800.

Paradiso
1-2-3 Benten, Minato-ku, Osaka.
(06) 6576-1526.

Seagaia
Hamayama, Yamazaki-cho, Miyazaki-shi, Miyazaki-ken, Kyushu.
(0985) 21-1111.

SPORTS AND OUTDOOR ACTIVITIES

JAPAN enjoys many traditional sports activities as well as imports from abroad. Some sports that are closely identified with Japan – judo, for instance, which is a matter of extreme national pride at international competition level – have been adopted worldwide. Others, like sumo wrestling, are more exclusively Japanese. It is relatively easy to see most sports in action; participation, especially in some of the martial arts, takes more planning. As competitive and spectator sports, sumo and baseball rank uppermost, with soccer not far behind. Golf and fishing are immensely popular pastimes. With its long coastline, mountainous interior, and range in climate, Japan is also ideal for outdoor pursuits, from water sports to mountain climbing, a perfect complement to the pleasures of urban Japan.

Boating through Takachiho, Kyushu

Sumo wrestlers preparing for a bout, Tokyo

SUMO

A UNIQUE MIX of sport and ritual, sumo *(see pp30–31)* has had new life breathed into it in recent years by the successes and scandals surrounding the brothers and *yokozuna* (grand champions) Takanohana and Wakanohana.

There are numerous opportunities to watch sumo live, with six major tournaments *(sumo basho)* a year, held bimonthly in four different locations: Tokyo (January, May, and September); Osaka (March); Nagoya (July); and Fukuoka (November).

Tokyo *basho (see p106)* are held in the **National Sumo Stadium** (Kokugikan) in Ryogoku *(see p98)*. The venue in Kyushu is the **Fukuoka Kokusai Center**; in the Kansai region of Western Honshu, the **Osaka Prefectural Gymnasium** (Osaka Furitsu Taikukaikan); and in Nagoya, **Aichi Prefectural Gymnasium** (Aichi-ken Taikukan).

It is best to buy tickets in advance, via **Playguide** service centers and other outlets. The most expensive tickets buy a boxed off-area *(masu)* for four near the ring, with *zabuton* (cushions) for seating. While ringside vantage points have the added luster of 100 kg (220 lb) plus of naked muscle and flab landing in the lap, most people settle for bench-style seating, rising in tiers.

Each *basho* lasts 15 days. The wrestling starts early morning, a good time to see newcomers in action. Champions compete last, between 5 and 6pm. The Japanese crowds tend to side with winners rather than the underdogs. If you can't make it to see the action live, NHK provides expert TV commentary by native English speakers.

The stables *(beya)* most likely to accept non-Japanese who wish to train in sumo are usually run by foreign stable-masters under the auspices of the **Japan Sumo Association** (Nihon Sumo Kyokai).

OTHER MARTIAL ARTS

THESE FALL INTO two categories, traditional *(budo)*, and the others. They can be further classified as those involving weapons, and those that are open-handed *(see p31)*. While it is relatively easy to view most sports in action, to be accepted for training in one of the traditional martial arts usually requires personal introductions.

Kendo, under the official eye of the **All-Japan Kendo Association,** is the only form of traditional weaponry practiced widely in schools and clubs. Championships are usually held in the **Nippon Budokan**, which has a school.

Judo is the most popular of the open-handed sports. It is also big internationally; many students come to Japan for intensive practice. For all English-speaking services, contact the Department of International Affairs at the **Kodokan Judo Institute** (Zen Nippon Judo Renmei) in downtown Tokyo.

Karate expert breaking roof tiles with one blow of the elbow

Landscaped golf course at the Horin Country Club, Ichihara, southeast of Tokyo

The **International Aikido Federation** promotes the sport according to the ideals of founder Ueshiba Morihei. It welcomes visitors, and classes are often held in the early mornings and late afternoons.

The **Japan Karate-Do Federation** is the official karate organization, but there are many offshoots. The **International Karate Organization**, for example, is eager to promote *kyokushin* karate. The **Japanese Karate Association** has weekday classes open to observers (phone first). At Kyoto's **Budo Center** (Butokuden), ex-Canadian champion Mark Dodds teaches Okinawan karate *(goju ryu)*, which is used exclusively for self-defense, never in competition.

There have been moves in recent years to combine various martial arts, often to extremely violent effect. **World Pancrase Create**, which established its first amateur pancrase *dojo* (practice hall) in 1997, invites interest in this new form of "total fight."

The increasingly popular **K-1** is an amalgamated form of those martial arts not categorized under *budo*. The international tournament K-1 Grand Prix is now an annual event.

Golf

Of the 50 million people who play golf worldwide, 17 million are swinging clubs in Japan. Vistors staying in major hotels should have little problem in finding a game; most have ties to a reputable golf club. The same applies to visiting executives; Japanese corporations consider a game basic to establishing relationships and will effect all the necessary introductions.

Courses are either private or public. An introduction by a member is essential to gain entry to a private club. If invited, expect to be treated; if reciprocating, expect the day to be very expensive. Public courses are less expensive but often less challenging. The attitude of staff may also be daunting; some welcome non-Japanese players, others may be cautious. JNTO *(see p362)* should be able to recommend public courses. A fun alternative might be to practice at one of the netted driving ranges in urban areas.

For the ultimate treat, book a golf-hotel weekend package, such as offered in Hakone by the **Sengoku Golf Course** in collaboration with the Fujiya Hotel *(see p295)*.

Baseball

Japanese baseball is America's national game transplanted. It is believed to have taken root in the 1870s from American expatriates in Yokohama. Pro baseball is organized into two leagues of six teams each: the **Central League** and the **Pacific League**. The season is between April and October. NHK broadcasts games live on TV, and the seven national sports dailies become increasingly hysterical as the season progresses, especially when the Japan Series gets underway. The spring and summer Koshien high-school baseball tournaments at **Koshien Stadium** in Hyogo Prefecture, hold the nation's attention.

Soccer and the 2002 World Cup

Though played for as long as baseball, soccer has not yet captured the same level of public interest and acceptance in Japan. The professional **J-League** kicked off in 1993 with 10 teams. By 2000, there were two divisions: J1 with 16 teams, and J2 with ten.

The decision for Japan and Korea to share the 2002 FIFA World Cup was rooted in the historically fraught relationship between the two countries. It was made to avoid diplomatic tangles should one nation be chosen ahead of the other.

The **Japan Organizing Committee for the 2002 FIFA World Cup Korea/Japan (JAWOC)** has selected stadiums in Yokohama, Shizuoka, Osaka, Kobe, Oita, Saitama, Sapporo, Miyagi, Niigata, and Kashima. Some of these cities are quite industrial, not known for tourist attractions, but all have good transportation connections, mostly on the *shinkansen* (bullet train) tracks. The final will be played at Yokohama.

Team members playing Japan's most popular sport

Hiker resting by a marker post on Mount Fugen, Kyushu

Hiking

Japan is a hiker's heaven. Mountainous and hilly regions, including the many national parks, are crisscrossed with a comprehensive network of trails. Signboards often give precise distances and the average time to be allowed between each stage, but usually just in Japanese.

Much of north and west Japan is covered in deep snow for up to five months a year. Winter and spring hiking should be avoided unless you have an experienced guide and adequate clothing.

Summer and early autumn offer different challenges: extremes of heat and humidity, and thick vegetation that may be difficult to penetrate. But the comfort and clean green of lower slopes, and the wild beauty of many remote places make hiking Japan's most rapidly growing pastime.

Mountaineering

Chains of peaks run through all four of Japan's main islands. Among the Japan Alps of Central Honshu, for example, many mountains rise steeply to 3,000 m (10,000 ft) and can be as challenging as anywhere in the world. Others are gentler and ideal for less experienced climbers.

Japan's mountains claim fatalities every season. While there is no law forbidding climbing at any particular time, many mountainous areas and peaks have designated climbing seasons – check for dates in advance. Volcanoes also occasionally take lives; even if an active volcano is not actually in the process of erupting, dangerous gases can be emitted without warning. Check up-to-date safety announcements with local tourist information centers.

There are usually facilities for overnight stays on the foothills and peaks of mountains, though these can be heavily overcrowded. Expect the standard and quality of hospitality in such mountain huts to be variable. Many close outside the climbing season.

Skiing

The great skiing that Japan has to offer is spoiled only by the numbers of people in the most popular resorts. Long lines for lifts are common, and accommodations are often sold out. Snow is generally of an excellent quality, though, and in most resorts there are courses marked for beginners and intermediates.

Weekend trips, daily excursions, and skiing tours linked to domestic air, road, and rail routes are widely available inside Japan and to many agents abroad. Sometimes these include equipment rental. Large-size ski-boots are hard to find, so check on availability or bring your own.

The most popular areas are in Hokkaido, Northern Honshu (Tohoku), and Central and Western Honshu. JNTO *(see p362)* publishes a Top 20 ski resorts list, with full details and contact numbers.

Skiers setting off for the piste at Niseko Ski Resort in Hokkaido

Watersports

In a country with over 4,000 islands and innumerable inland rivers and lakes, water is naturally a favorite playground for the Japanese. Since the sea is often polluted around major conurbations, indoor and outdoor complexes of pools, wave machines, and water slides are popular. Unfortunately many outdoor pools are open for a limited time in midsummer only, coinciding with the time the sea is officially open for swimming from mid-July to the end of August.

Jet skiing, wind surfing, and yachting are all popular. Renting equipment is no problem on good beaches close to major cities; piloted yachts can be chartered from marinas. **Hayama Marina** near Kamakura is as classy and expensive as might be expected. To sail a cruiser in Japan, a specially issued license is necessary. Apply to Kanto's **Ministry of Transport**: a foreigner's registration card is required.

Many parts of the coastline lend themselves to scuba exploration. Around any developed area, diving can be murky to say the least; by contrast, waters around the islands of Okinawa *(see pp244–53)* are a tropical paradise.

Lively day at the Korakuen swimming pool in Tokyo

Eco-Tourism

Though Japan lags behind many nations in ecological conservation, concern about the environment has been building since the 1970s, when pollution reached record levels.

The **Nature Conservation Society of Japan** has a list of accommodations in unspoiled areas, run by people who are concerned with putting guests in touch with nature.

Birdwatching is a very popular activity. The **Wild Bird Society of Japan**, founded in 1935, has 80 chapters nationwide, each organizing local events. In areas where whaling was once a way of life, whale- and dolphin-watching now provide an alternative source of income. The best season in the remote Ogasawara Islands (a 25-hour ferry trip south of Tokyo) is March–April; in Ogata, Kochi prefecture, the chance of seeing whales between April and October is 80–90 percent.

In the Kanto area, **Wanderlust Adventures** mixes hiking, kayaking, and rock climbing with *taiko* drumming. The **Earth Steward Institute** in Nagano prefecture, founded by an American eco-engineer, has courses in sustainable development. The organizer gives tours of his homes; one in a tree, the other underground.

Directory

Sumo

Aichi Prefectural Gymnasium
1-1 Ninomaru, Naka-ku, Nagoya.
(052) 971-2516.

Fukuoka Kokusai Center
Sogo Hall, 2-2 Chikuko-Honmachi, Hakata-ku, Fukuoka.
(092) 272-1111.

Japan Sumo Association
1-3-28 Yokoami, Sumida-ku, Tokyo.
(03) 3623-5111.
www.sumo.or.jp/index_e.html

Osaka Prefectural Gymnasium
3-4-36 Namba Naka, Naniwa-ku, Osaka.
(06) 6631-0121.

Other Martial Arts

All-Japan Kendo Association
2F Yaskuni Kudan-minami Bldg, 2-3-14 Kudan-minami, Chiyoda-ku, Tokyo.
(03) 3234-6271.

Budo Center
46-2 Shogoin, Sakyo-ku, Kyoto.
(075) 751-1255.

International Aikido Federation
17-18 Wakamatsu-cho, Shinjuku-ku, Tokyo.
(03) 3203-9236.

International Karate Organization
2-38-1 Nishi-Ikebukuro, Toshima-ku, Tokyo.
(03) 5992-9200.
www.kyokushin.co.jp/english/profiles/ren.htm

Japan Karate-Do Federation
1-11-2 Toranomon, Minato-ku, Tokyo.
(03) 3503-6637.
www.karatedo.co.jp/jkf/e_index.htm

Japanese Karate Association
29-33-408 Sakuragaoka-cho, Shibuya-ku, Tokyo.
(03) 3462-1415.

K-1 Corporation
3-31-4 Jingumae, Shibuya-ku, Tokyo.
(03) 3796-2995.

Kodokan Judo Institute
1-16-30 Kasuga, Bunkyo-ku, Tokyo.
(03) 3818-4172.
www.kodokan.org/index.html

Nippon Budokan
2–3 Kitanomaru Koen, Chiyoda-ku, Tokyo.
(03) 3216-5100.

World Pancrase Create
4-2-25 Minami-Azabu, Minato-ku, Tokyo.
(03) 5792-7080.

Golf

Sengoku Golf Course
1237 Sengokubara, Hakone-machi, Ashigara-Shimo-gun, Kanagawa-ken.
(0460) 4-8511.

Baseball

Central & Pacific Leagues
Asahi Bldg, 6-6-7 Ginza, Chuo-ku, Tokyo.
(03) 3572-1673 (Central); (03) 3573-1551 (Pacific).

Koshien Stadium
1-82 Koshien-cho, Nishinomiya-shi, Hyogo-ken.
(0798) 47-1041.

Soccer and the 2002 World Cup

J-League
(03) 3568-3320.
www.j-league.or.jp/index-j.html

JAWOC
(03) 3589-2002.
www.jawoc.or.jp/index_e.htm

Watersports

Hayama Marina
50-2 Horiuchi, Hayama-cho, Miura-gun, Kanagawa-ken.
(0468)-75-2670.

Ministry of Transport
Crew Dept, Shipping Staff Affairs, Yokoyama No.2 Godo-Chosha, 5-57 Kita-Nakadori, Naka-ku, Yokohama-shi, Kanagawa-ken.
(045)-211-7234.

Eco-Tourism

Earth Steward Institute
3846 Higashi Ina Komagane, Nagano-ken.
(0265) 82-6770.

Nature Conservation Society of Japan
Yamaji Sanbancho Bldg, 5-24 Sanbancho, Chiyoda-ku, Tokyo.
(03) 3265-0521.

Wanderlust Adventures
(0422) 46-0734.
cbernatt@gol.com

Wild Bird Society of Japan
1F Odakyu Nishi-Shinjuku Bldg, 1-47-1 Hatsudai, Shibuya-ku, Tokyo.
(03) 5358-3510.

Special Interests

Besides the more obvious tourist sights, Japan has many attractions for visitors who wish to learn more about diverse aspects of Japanese culture. Traditional medicine and Buddhist lore, for example, are of great interest to many Western tourists, and various organizations exist in Japan to promote foreigners' understanding of these subjects. Other visitors are more interested in modern Japan and will want to take the opportunity to visit factories or design showcases. Various systems have been developed to facilitate more contact and exchange of ideas between Japanese and overseas visitors. Goodwill Guides are locals, often housewives and retired people, who want to practice and maintain their foreign language skills, and who are willing to show foreigners around the local sights free of charge. Invariably, such individuals are enthusiastic about their own and other people's cultures. Using conversation lounges is an excellent way to establish intercultural friendships, while the Homestay and Home Visit systems offer unique insights into Japanese culture.

A woman practicing moxibustion to improve her health

Participating in a tea ceremony, often possible via a Goodwill Guide

Goodwill Guides, Home Stays, and Home Visits

Established in 30 prefectures on Honshu, Kyushu, and Shikoku, the **Goodwill Guide** system is made up of Japanese volunteers, registered with JNTO *(see p362)*, all eager to assist vistors from overseas. Totalling some 46,000, the Goodwill Guides each wear a badge for identification. JNTO and local TICs have a list of contact numbers, and visitors may phone a local Guide to ask for information or to be guided on a tour free of charge.

EIL Japan (the Japanese Association of Experiment in International Living) runs the Japanese Homestay Program, which enables people from abroad to stay with a Japanese family for one to four weeks in various locations on Honshu, Hokkaido, Kyushu, and Shikoku. Visitors, who must bear all their own costs, are treated as one of the family and involved in regular daily activities. Contact EIL Japan at least eight weeks before your intended visit, requesting an application form.

The **Home Visit System** offers the opportunity to visit a Japanese family at home, usually in the evening after dinner. Four or five guests are invited at a time. English is spoken by most host familes, but some family members may speak other languages. About 1,000 familes are involved, in 14 cities and towns on Honshu and Kyushu. TICs have a list of contact numbers.

Conversation Lounges

The basic premise of conversation lounges is to bring together Japanese who want to practice their English and other foreign languages, and visitors from abroad who want to meet Japanese people in relaxed surroundings. Sometimes also described as coffee lounges, these conversation venues can vary in both intent and tone.

Micky House in Shinjuku is free for native English speakers; others can pay each visit, or purchase a set of ten coupons valid for two months. Other venues in Tokyo, such as **Com'sInn** and **K's Place** have different systems of charging. Conversation lounges come and go fairly regularly, or may change direction to become more like language schools; listings magazines are the best source of information for finding up-to-date spots. Be aware that

Japanese woman showing a Western visitor how to play a video game

some lounges operate as commercial matchmaking enterprises – for Western men and Japanese women, rarely the other way around.

Specialty Tours

Visitors interested in thematic tours rather than the usual kind of sightseeing can try **Sunrise Tours** in Tokyo, operated by the Japan Travel Bureau. A tour might focus on a visit to a calligraphy studio, participation in a tea ceremony, or exploring a downtown area. Sunrise also runs tours specializing in sumo or Tokyo nightlife, including trips to see traditional Japanese theater.

The **Hato Bus Tour Company** has a similar range of half-day, full-day, and nighttime tours for non-Japanese tourists, including a visit to a tea ceremony and a garden tour. **Greyline** runs trips around Tokyo as well as to places such as Mount Fuji and Hakone, and will also arrange private tours tailored to a customer's wishes; the more individual a tour is, the more the cost will be.

State-of-the-art electronics in Tokyo

Traditional Japanese ingredients

In Tokyo, **Mr. Oka's Sunday Walks**, which cover historical areas of the city, are regularly advertised in the English-language press. In Kyoto, details about Hirooka Hajime's personally guided tours, **Walk in Kyoto, Talk in English**, are available from hotels and information centers; the tours take place on selected weekdays.

For an Oriental tour of the taste buds, try **Konishi's Japanese Cooking Class**. At these classes, run by Konishi Kiyoko in her own home on weekdays and evenings, you will learn how to create healthy, economical, and seasonal dishes from traditional Japanese ingredients.

Factory Visits

Three automobile manufacturers – **Toyota** (in Aichi prefecture), **Nissan** (in Kanagawa), and **Mazda** (in Hiroshima) – welcome visitors to their various plants. Tours in English can be arranged. The electronics-oriented **Toshiba Science Insitute** in Kanagawa prefecture offers an hour-long tour.

Most tours are on weekdays only, exclusive of national holidays, and it is best to contact the relevant organization in advance.

Directory

Home Stays

EIL Japan
3F Hirakawacho Fushimi Bldg, 1-4-3 Hirakawa-cho, Chiyoda-ku, Tokyo.
(03) 3261-3451.

Conversation Lounges

Com'sInn
5F Arai Bldg, 1-3-9 Ebisu-Minami, Shibuya-ku, Tokyo.
(03) 3710-7063.

K's Place
K's Place, 4F Hoshino Bldg, 1-56-5 Higashi-Nakano, Nakano-ku, Tokyo.
(03) 3364-6065.

Micky House
4F Yashiro Bldg, 2-14-4 Takadanobaba, Shinjuku-ku, Tokyo.
(03) 3209-9686.

Specialty Tours

Greyline
3-3-3 Nishi-shinbashi, Shinbashi, Minato-ku, Tokyo.
(03) 3433-5745.

Hato Bus Tour Company
2-4-1 Hamamatsucho, Minato-ku, Tokyo.
(03) 3435-6081.

Konishi's Japanese Cooking Class
Nissei Meguro Mansion 1405, 3-1-7 Meguro, Meguro-ku, Tokyo.
(03) 3714-8859.

Mr. Oka's Walks
(0422) 51-7673.

Sunrise Tours
Tokyo branch
(03) 5620-9500.
Kyoto branch
(075) 341-1413.

Walk in Kyoto, Talk in English
(075) 622-6803.
h-s-love@mbox.kyoto-inet.or.jp

Factory Visits

Mazda
General Affairs Dept, 3-1 Shinchi, Fuchu-cho, Aki-gun, Hiroshima-ken.
(082) 286-5700.

Nissan
6-17-1 Ginza, Chuo-ku, Tokyo.
(03) 5565-2143.

Toshiba Science Institute
1 Komukai-Toshiba-cho, Saiwai-ku, Kawasaki-shi, Kanagawa-ken.
(044) 549-2200.

Toyota
Toyota Kaikan, 1 Toyota-cho, Toyota-shi, Aichi-ken.
(0565) 23-3922.

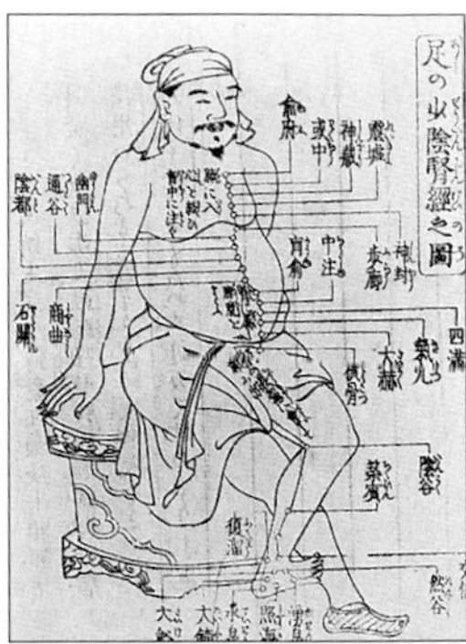

Illustration of traditional acupuncture points on the body

Traditional Medicine

In the Meiji period, with its emphasis on all things foreign, it became fashionable in Japan to reject traditional healing methods and instead to embrace Western science and medicine. Today, as alternative medicine, including Eastern methods, is burgeoning in popularity in the West, the trend in Japan is also toward a blend of ancient and modern practices.

Natural ingredients prescribed in accordance with traditional Chinese medical custom are known as *kampo*. Ready-mixed and prepared *kampo* products are available from pharmacies, often alongside manufactured prescription drugs. Some restaurants specialize in *kampo* cuisine, designed to balance the metabolism. *Kampo* can also be made up to suit individual needs in specialty stores. In Yokohama or Kobe, Chinatown is the place to go. Beware of some traditional products that may incorporate ingredients obtained from endangered species.

Acupuncture and moxibustion, a form of heat therapy, are often used in combination. **Zen Nihon Shinkyu Massage Shikai** in Tokyo and **Meiji University of Oriental Medicine** in Kyoto have information. **Akahige-do** in Yoyogi, Tokyo, teaches shiatsu body massage as well as acupuncture. **Imoto Seitai** practices and teaches what it describes as traditional manual therapy.

There are numerous other forms of alternative healing derived from Oriental wisdom. The **Japan Academy of Colorpuncture** uses colored light to restore well-being. **World Kai-igaku Network** helps people to cure themselves. **Lifeforces** practices and teaches reiki, a form of energy healing originally developed in Japan, and *sekhem*, a form of energy healing which originated in Egypt, backed by many complementary forms of holistic healing. The same organizers run **Circle of Light**, which holds twice-monthly meetings in Tokyo, aiming to bring the full range of traditional therapies to a wider audience.

Pilgrimage Routes

For many centuries pilgrimages provided Japanese farmers and townspeople with a reason to leave behind work and responsibilities and take to the open road. Nowadays pilgrimages are regarded as a form of spiritual meditation, concerned with making amends and preparing for death. Some non-purists drive or ride the pilgrim routes.

Many of the oldest pilgrimages were connected with a mystical Shugendo cult of mountain worship, which combined elements of Shinto and Buddhism. Its most devout followers, laymen known as *yamabushi* (mountain priests), still practice in the **Dewa Sanzan** mountains in Northern Honshu *(see p268)*. During the Edo period, **Mount Fuji** *(see pp134–5)* became a similar object of worship. Even today, among the thousands of tourists who climb every summer, aged white-clad pilgrims (*henro*) wearing conical straw hats can be seen.

Sticks carried by traditional pilgrims

The most famous and demanding route is the **88-Temple Pilgrimage** on Shikoku *(see pp222–3)*. The **Western Japan 33 Kannon Temple Circuit** involves visiting temples to Kannon, the goddess of mercy *(see p25)*, in Western Honshu. It includes temples in Kyoto, Nara, Ise, and Mount Koya. There is a shorter route for pilgrims in Kamakura *(see pp128–31)*, starting a brief bus ride away from the main station and finishing at the temple of Engaku-ji in Kita Kamakura.

Religious Studies

Based in downtown Tokyo, the **International Shinto Foundation** was formed in 1994 to disseminate understanding of Japan's native religion. The **Association of Shinto Shrines** publishes a range of free English-language pamphlets and booklets. There are displays on Shinto history and rituals at **Kokugakuin University Shinto Museum**.

Resting pilgrims on the 88-Temple pilgrimage in Shikoku

The **Zen Buddhist Center for International Exchange** provides non-Japanese visitors with access to Zen practices. Their temple, located near Mount Fuji, is remote, with no electricity or telephone. Other Buddhist foundations offering English-language instruction include the **International Buddhist Association**, which conducts a meeting in English toward the end of each month, **Rissho Kosei-Kai**, which offers dharma seminars four times a year, and the **Tokyo University Young Buddhists Association**, which holds twice-monthly *zazen* (Zen meditation) sessions. The main purpose of the **Hosen-ji Zen Center** is to teach *zazen*; an introduction to Buddhist sutra calligraphy and Buddhist painting is also available. A number of temples around the country offer religious instruction; contact TICs for more information.

Visitors interested in the fascinating history of Christianity in Japan are also catered to. The **Tokyo Martyrs Tour**, conducted several times a year by the Reverend Higashiki Tadahiko, visits sites linked to the persecution during the Edo period of Japanese Christians and foreign priests and missionaries. **Eastern Cross Tours** organizes trips by bus to sights linked with Christian history in Japan. These tours can be organized in Tokyo, Kyushu, Kyoto, Sendai, Aomori, and other parts of the country. The Tokyo tour ends with a video presentation and a tour of the Eastern Cross Museum. The same organization also provides useful information on Christian-related sights and history, so that visitors can plan their own itinerary.

The 19th-century Oura church, Nagasaki

DIRECTORY

TRADITIONAL MEDICINE

Akahige-do
2F Nasu Building,
1-38-8 Yoyogi,
Shibuya-ku,
Tokyo.
Tel *(03) 3370-5015.*

Circle of Light and Lifeforces
202 & 202 Mizushima House,
Shinomachi 18,
Shinjuku-ku,
Tokyo.
Tel *(03) 5368-8827.*
@ hari@japan.co.jp

Imoto Seitai
1F Casita Kyushuya,
3-22-11 Jingumae,
Shibuya-ku,
Tokyo.
Tel *(03) 3403-0185.*

Japan Academy of Colorpuncture
2-12-5 Okusawa,
Setagaya-ku,
Tokyo.
Tel *(03) 3718-7613.*

Meiji University of Oriental Medicine
Hiyoshi-cho, Funai-gun,
Kyoto.
Tel *(0771) 72-1181.*
W www.meiji-u.ac.jp/meiji-e.html

World Kai-igaku Network
7F Kapala Bldg, 5-16-14
Okikubo, Suginami-ku,
Tokyo.
Tel *(03) 3398-0023.*

Zen Nihon Shinkyu Massage Shikai
3-12-17 Yotsuya,
Shinjuku-ku, Tokyo.
Tel *(03) 3359-6049.*

RELIGIOUS STUDIES

Association of Shinto Shrines
1-2-2 Yoyogi,
Shibuya-ku,
Tokyo.
Tel *(03) 3379-8011.*

Eastern Cross Tours
2-2-3-833 Marunouchi,
Chiyoda-ku, Tokyo.
W www.keikyo.com/easterncross
@ tour@keikyo.com

Hosen-ji Zen Center
1-503 Minaminokuchi-cho,
Ushigase, Nishiky-ku,
Kyoto.
Tel *(095) 382-2250.*
W www.zen.or.jp/

International Buddhist Association
Tsukiji Hongan-ji Temple, 3-15-1 Tsukiji,
Chuo-ku,
Tokyo.
Tel *(03) 3541-1131.*

International Shinto Foundation
3F Tanaka Bldg,
5-22-9 Hirai, Edogawa-ku,
Tokyo.
Tel *(03) 3610-3975.*
W www.shinto.org
@ umeday@msn.com

Kokugakuin University Shinto Museum
1F Tokiwamatsu No 3 Bldg,
4-10-28 Higashi,
Shibuya-ku, Tokyo.
Tel *(03) 5466-0210.*

Rissho Kosei-Kai
2-11-1 Wada,
Suginami-ku,
Tokyo.
Tel *(03) 3383-1111.*
W www.kosei-kai.or.jp/english/index.html

Tokyo Martyrs Tour
c/o Fr. Higashiki,
Shimoigusa Catholic Church,
2-31-25 Igusa,
Suginami-ku,
Tokyo.
Tel *(0424) 82-3997.*

Tokyo University Young Buddhists Association
2F 3-30-5 Hongo,
Bunkyo-ku,
Tokyo.
Tel *(03) 3929-4680 (telephone information available to Japanese speakers only).*

Zen Buddhist Center for International Exchange
Hatsukari-cho,
Otsuki-shi,
Yamanashi-ken.
FAX *(0554) 25-6282.*

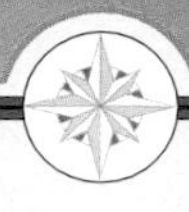

SURVIVAL GUIDE

PRACTICAL INFORMATION 360-377
TRAVEL INFORMATION 378-385

Practical Information

From a practical point of view, Japan is much easier for foreign tourists to negotiate than is generally believed. Being unable to speak or read Japanese is rarely a serious problem. Many everyday signs in major cities and at tourist attractions are displayed in Roman script along with Japanese characters. English-speaking locals are generally quick to offer assistance. The infrastructure for tourism (public transportation, accommodations, sightseeing, and so on) is highly developed, because the Japanese are well used to traveling around their own country. Where problems can arise for foreigners, however, is in the surprising contrasts in Japan's unique East-West culture – for instance, the contrast between the ease with which even foreigners can get around on the rail network compared with the difficulty everyone, including the Japanese, has with finding an address *(see p376–7)*.

北山通り
Kitayama dori

Street sign in Japanese and Roman script

Picnics in Tokyo's Ueno Park at cherry-blossom time

When to Visit

The best times to visit Japan are spring (April and May) and fall (October and November). Temperatures within the country vary widely according to latitude *(see pp44–5)*, but July and August are mostly very humid and better avoided.

Japan has numerous festivals throughout the year *(see pp40–43)*. Cherry-blossom time brings out large blossom-viewing groups who fill the parks day and night, while late summer is a time for local festivals. Peak vacation periods for the Japanese are New Year (December 29 to January 4), "Golden Week" (April 29 to May 5), and the period around Bon, the Buddhist Festival of the Dead (in mid-August). At these times flights and some accommodations are sold out, and some hotels, offices, and tourist attractions may close for up to a week.

What to Bring

It is a good idea to take a variety of clothing, as modern buildings tend to be overheated in winter and overcooled in summer, while traditional buildings are relatively vulnerable to the elements. The weather can be changeable: an umbrella is more useful than a raincoat, especially in midsummer heat. Clothes, even if casual, should be neat, clean, and not too revealing; a short, tight skirt makes it awkward to sit on the floor. Comfortable footwear is a good idea; shoes will be removed frequently, so wear some that are easily slipped on and off, and make sure there are no holes in your socks or tights. Keep luggage to a minimum, and choose items that are easy to carry: stations have many steps and few porters.

A colorful display of practical and souvenir fans for sale

Almost anything you need can be bought in Japan, although it may be expensive, and clothes or shoes may be available only in small sizes. Film can be pricey but is reasonable in general discount stores or electrical shops (note that slide film is not usually process-paid); developing is quite cheap, and of good quality, although standard print size is small.

As with any destination, good travel insurance is advisable. If you plan to travel around within Japan, consider obtaining a Japan Rail Pass before you go *(see p381)*.

Visas and Passports

Citizens of most Western countries may enter Japan for short visits as a Temporary Visitor simply with a valid passport. There is no need to obtain a visa. The usual period of stay for a Temporary Visitor is 90 days. Visitors are allowed to enter on this basis for tourism, sports, visiting

◁ **Participant in the Jidai Matsuri (Festival of the Ages), Kyoto**

Film and cameras in a discount camera shop

friends or relatives, study, or business, but may not undertake paid employment in Japan or stay longer than the specified period. (Journalists with US passports are an exception and must obtain a visa before traveling to Japan on business, even for a short stay.)

Citizens of some countries, including the UK and Germany, may extend this 90-day stay by up to another 90 days at immigration offices in Japan (at least 10 days before the original expiration date), but the length of extension is at the discretion of immigration officers.

On the plane you will be given a landing card: you need fill in only the first part, relating to arrival – the second part will be attached to your passport to be completed when you depart. There are no immunization requirements for entering Japan.

Anyone planning on undertaking paid work, long-term study, or voluntary work in Japan should obtain a visa from a Japanese embassy before going to Japan. It is generally not possible to obtain a visa, or change status, once in the country *(see pp368–9)*. Foreigners who stay in Japan for more than 90 days must also apply for a Certificate of Alien Registration from the Ward Office of the area in which they are living, within 90 days of arrival in the country. This certificate, or your passport, must be carried at all times – not doing so can occasionally lead to arrest. Visa-holders who want to leave the country and return within the duration of their visa need to obtain a re-entry permit from an immigration office. Contact the **Ministry of Foreign Affairs** for more visa information.

Customs

There is no need to fill in a written declaration of your belongings unless you are arriving in Japan by ship, have unaccompanied baggage, or if you are exceeding the duty-free allowances.

Duty-free allowances on entering the country are 400 cigarettes or 500 grams of tobacco or 100 cigars; three 0.76 liter (27 oz) bottles of alcohol; 57 g (2 oz) of perfume; and gifts and souvenirs of a total value up to ¥200,000 (not counting items less than ¥10,000).

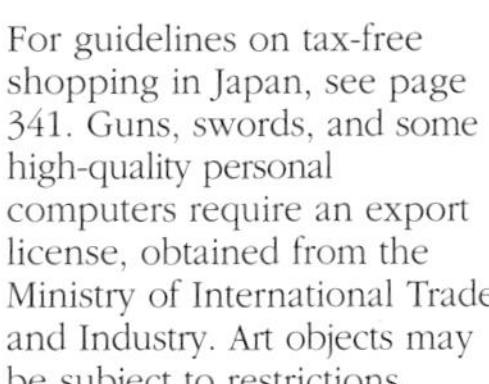

Shop selling perfume and cosmetics

Certain articles are prohibited: narcotic drugs or stimulants; counterfeit money; pornography; articles that infringe on patents or copyrights; and firearms and ammunition. Animals and plants are subject to quarantine inspection. There is no limit on the amount of currency that may be taken into or out of the country, but sums over ¥1 million must be declared at immigration.

For guidelines on tax-free shopping in Japan, see page 341. Guns, swords, and some high-quality personal computers require an export license, obtained from the Ministry of International Trade and Industry. Art objects may be subject to restrictions.

Facilities for Disabled Visitors

Facilities for the disabled are of mixed quality. Blind people are well provided for, but the elderly and those in wheelchairs face problems with stations and pedestrian overpasses, as there are endless steps and often no escalator or elevator; the situation is improving, but slowly. Most modern offices and hotels have excellent toilet facilities for the disabled.

Facilities for Children

Children are welcomed, and parents can forget their usual worries about safety. Taking children to a restaurant poses no problems, discreet breast-feeding in public is accepted, and baby food, milk, disposable diapers, and boiled water are easily obtainable. Hotels tend to be geared toward adults, but top ones usually offer baby-sitting and nurseries, while at traditional inns a maid may be willing to baby-sit. Many theme parks and museums are great fun for kids, but some very cultured temples and galleries do not allow children. Rush hour travel and very hot *onsen* pools should also be avoided.

Children playing on the sidewalk

Logo of the Japan National Tourist Organization (JNTO)

Information Centers

Outside Japan, tourist information can be obtained from branches of the **Japan National Tourist Organization (JNTO)**. The JNTO has a large range of useful material: general background information, practical leaflets, and brochures on particular locations and specialist interests. The JNTO does not, however, make recommendations or reservations or sell Rail Pass vouchers, but can provide a list of travel agents that do.

Within Japan, there are four **TICs** or Tourist Information Centers: in Tokyo, Kyoto, and Narita and Kansai Airports; these cover the whole country. Staff in Tokyo and Kyoto are especially knowledgable and helpful. TICs offer information, travel literature, and suggestions on tour itineraries, but do not make hotel reservations *(see p288)*.

Information on a local level can be obtained in Japan from the Tourist Information Offices found in almost every town, usually in or near the station; they can often also make hotel reservations. Nearly 100 of these offices are designated **"i"** Tourist Information Offices, meaning they have multilingual staff and carry pamphlets in English.

Telephone Information

There are several telephone information services in English. The **Teletourist Service** offers recorded information 24 hours a day on travel topics, entertainment, and major events. **Japan Travel-Phone** provides travel information and assistance *(see p379)*. Information on local events is available from **Japan Hotline** and from **Information Corner** in Yokohama, Osaka, and Nagoya.

Events Information and Tickets

In major cities, details of attractions and events can be gleaned from local publications such as *Tokyo Journal* and *Tokyo Classified (see p104)*, *Kansai Time Out*, and free brochures – all available at hotels, bookstores, and TICs.

Hotels will usually help reserve tickets for entertainment venues. Ticket-agency booths located in most of the larger cities, inside major department stores, and near train stations also book seats in advance and sell tickets up to the last minute. **PIA**, **Ticket Saison**, and **CN Playguide** are the main agencies *(see p107)*.

Welcome Cards

Several cities have begun to issue a Welcome Card to foreign visitors. Intended to reduce the cost of a visit, the card can be used to obtain discounts on accommodations, shopping, food and drink, and various other tourist facilities and services. Obtain the card with a booklet of participating services on arrival from a TIC or an **"i"** information center.

Opening Hours and Admission Fees

Temple buildings are typically open from 8 or 9am to 4pm in winter, and until 5pm in summer, though exact times and the number of buildings closed vary widely. Shrines are often open 24 hours. Admission to many temples and shrines is free; others charge a small admission fee, usually between ¥200 and ¥500.

Museums, art galleries, and many other tourist attractions such as technology centers and aquariums are usually open from 10am until 4 or 5pm. Many of these sights are open every day except Monday; when Monday is a

Todai-ji Temple at Nara – like many temples, open longer in summer than in winter

Canal City mall in Fukuoka, containing many shops offering discounts with a Welcome Card

public holiday, they often close on Tuesday instead. Most of these attractions may close for a week or more over the New Year period. Entrance fees to tourist attractions are occasionally under ¥1,000, but are usually more. Certain Kyoto sights – Katsura and Shugaku-in Imperial Villas, for example – require reservations well in advance of visiting.

For shopping hours, see page 340; for banking hours see page 372; and for post offices see page 376.

Time and the Calendar

Japan is 9 hours ahead of Greenwich Mean Time and 14 hours ahead of US Eastern Standard Time. There is no daylight-saving time; when countries that use daylight-saving time switch to summer time, the time difference is one hour less.

Stamps to mark the 10th year of the Heisei era

The Japanese calendar combines the Western system with the Chinese system: years are designated Year of the Tiger, Rabbit, and so on, but they begin on January 1 and not, as in China, in mid-February. Years are numbered both by the Western system and according to the reigning Japanese emperor. The present era, Heisei (meaning "achieving peace"), began when Emperor Akihito came to the throne in 1989, so that year was known as "Heisei 1"; Akihito's father's era was called "Showa." The Japanese system is generally used within the country, especially on official documents, while Western years are used in international contexts.

Misunderstandings about timings and dates are common, and it is advisable to confirm arrangements clearly and, when booking accommodations, to state the number of nights as well as the dates of your stay.

Electricity

Japan runs on 100 volts, AC – a system similar to that of the US – but the country has two different cycles: 50 cycles in eastern Japan (including Tokyo) and 60 cycles in western Japan. Plugs with two flat pins are standard; this means that appliances that can be used in America can also be used in Japan, but sometimes at a reduced efficiency.

Most British and other European appliances can be used only with transformers suitable for US voltage (which are large and expensive). If in doubt, consult the appliance's instructions.

Some international hotels have two outlets, of 110 and 220 volts, although these accept only two-pin plugs – adapters are available from electrical stores. In older buildings, ceiling lights are often operated by both a switch on the wall and a pull cord on the light itself; each pull of the cord gives a different degree of brightness.

Directory

JNTO Offices Outside Japan

US
One Rockefeller Plaza, Suite 1250, New York, NY 10020.
☎ *(212) 757-5640.*

401 N Michigan Ave, Suite 770, Chicago, IL 60611.
☎ *(312) 222-0874.*

360 Post St, Suite 601, San Francisco, CA 94108.
☎ *(415) 989-7140.*

515 South Figueroa St, Suite 1470, Los Angeles, CA 90071.
☎ *(213) 623-1952.*

UK
Heathcoat House, 20 Savile Row, London W1X 1AE.
☎ *(020) 7734-9638.*

Australia
Level 33, Chifley Tower, Chifley Sq, Sydney, NSW 2000.
☎ *(02) 9232-4522.*

Canada
165 University Ave, Toronto, Ontario M5H 3B8.
☎ *(416) 366-7140.*

Other Information Sources

Information Corner
Nagoya ☎ *(052) 581-0100.*
Osaka ☎ *(06) 6772-5931.*
Yokohama ☎ *(045) 671-7209.*

JNTO
W www.jnto.go.jp

Japan Hotline
☎ *(03) 3586-0110.*

Ministry of Foreign Affairs
W www.mofa.go.jp

Teletourist Service
☎ *(03) 3201-2911.*

Conversion Chart

Metric to US/UK Standard
1 millimeter = 0.04 inch
1 centimeter = 0.4 inch
1 meter = 3 feet 3 inches
1 kilometer = 0.6 mile
1 gram = 0.04 ounce
1 kilogram = 2.2 pounds
1 liter = 2.1 US/1.8 UK pints

Attitudes and Etiquette

ETIQUETTE IS IMPORTANT in Japan – the social lubricant for a crowded community. In recent decades attitudes have relaxed, yet even the most apparently rebellious Japanese won't break certain rules. What constitutes correct behavior often varies according to the situation and status of individuals. Foreigners will be forgiven most gaffes, but good manners will earn you respect. The best approach is to be as sensitive as possible to situations, avoid loud or dogmatic behavior, and follow the lead of those around you.

Paying respects to ancestors at a Tokyo cemetery

Gauze mask, worn to stop the spread of colds

Taboos

FEW ALLOWANCES are made even for foreigners on certain points, mainly relating to Japanese standards of hygiene. Surprisingly for many foreigners, it is considered unforgivable to get soap or shampoo in a bathtub; washing belongs in the shower area *(see p291)*. It is also a serious mistake to wear shoes indoors, or wear the wrong slippers into or out of a toilet area.

When it comes to table manners, serious errors include touching food in a communal dish with your chopsticks but then not taking it, shoveling food direct from bowl to mouth, and standing chopsticks upright in rice – explanations as to why this latter is a no-no vary, but all relate to rituals for the dead. For more about eating etiquette, see pages 312–13.

On a lesser level, eating on the move (even chocolate) is frowned on, at least by the older generation, though eating on longer train trips is fine. Smoking, in contrast, is accepted almost anywhere. Emissions from the body are considered very rude, while anything drawn inward is acceptable. Thus, sniffing is fine, but blowing your nose in public is reviled. Gauze face masks are worn in public both to stop infecting others with, and catching, colds.

The Hierachy

RESPECT FOR seniors is fundamental to Japanese society even today. The emphasis on seniority has its roots in both the native Shinto religion (which is based on ancestor worship) and Confucianism (a set of social rules imported from China that reinforced the establishment).

All older people are treated with respect: not only parents, grandparents, company bosses, and teachers but even those a year or two senior in school or employment. The term *sensei* ("teacher") is used for all elders and experts. In the Japanese language, different vocabulary is used to speak to those above and those below, so it is vital for a Japanese to know the relative status of other people; this is one reason why business cards *(meishi)* are so widely used *(see p368)*.

The ultimate parent in such a social system is the royal family: until the end of World War II, emperors were worshiped as the ancestors of the nation. Today, some liberals reject the emperor system and national anthem even as symbols of the country, while right-wing groups fiercely protect the royal family and go so far as physically attacking those who speak out against it. Most people, however, show a lot of respect for the emperor, but stop short of veneration.

Bowing

THE TRADITIONAL greeting in Japan is a bow, its depth reflecting the relative status of participants. Foreigners, however, rarely need to bow – a handshake is fine. In many situations, bows are part of the service, for instance, in elevators, department stores, restaurants, and hotels. They can be ignored or met with a

Bow between business colleagues close in status to each other

brief smile. If you feel the need to bow, hold your arms and back straight, bend from the waist, and pause for a moment at the low point.

BODY LANGUAGE

This is not as sensitive an issue as in many other Asian countries, although it is considered rude to point your feet at people, and it is preferable to avoid wild gesticulation or talking loudly. The Japanese appreciate that sitting on the floor can be a strain for those not used to it, but try not to stretch out your legs. Men may sit cross-legged, while women should tuck their feet to one side.

Personal space is smaller than in the West, and on crowded trains it is worth following the Japanese example and creating a psychological bubble around you by closing your eyes or even taking a nap.

The Japanese practice good posture from childhood: a straight back is respected.

ATTITUDES TO PHYSICAL CONTACT AND SEX

Members of the same sex are physically easy with each other. Don't be surprised if a near-stranger touches you on the arm or massages your shoulders. The atmosphere in single-sex public baths is relaxed. Between the sexes, however (outside immediate family, who often bath together), a public display of contact is very limited. Despite a fashion among some young couples for public passion, most people would not even hold hands in public. Kissing is viewed as purely sexual. A "hello" kiss on the cheek would cause embarrassment, and hugging barely exists.

Fertility statue at Uwajima's Taga Shrine museum

Skimpy clothing is worn by some girls and will not cause offense, but a shapely or hirsute Westerner in revealing clothes, or topless on a beach, can expect stares and giggles.

In general, sex is seen as free from shame, but something to be indulged discreetly. Shinto emphasizes fertility, and some objects in shrines can be quite explicit *(see p23)*. Homosexual activity, though widely practiced by samurai in the feudal era, on the whole is less openly accepted today than in many Western nations.

Sadly, the sleazier side of the sex trade includes schoolgirl prostitution, and cartoon pornography is widely sold in convenience stores. Nonetheless, everyday life is relatively sanitized, and it is important to remember that geisha *(see p157)* and most bar hostesses are not prostitutes.

Traditional footwear neatly lined up on racks outside a temple

SHOES

Shoes are an important element of etiquette. When you go indoors, take off your outdoor shoes and put on slippers, if provided, before you step on to the raised floor. If there are no slippers, or if they are too small for Western feet, go in socks or stockings. The principle is not to contaminate clean interiors with dirt from the outside, so be careful not to rest a shoe on the indoor floor or put a stockinged foot on the dirty part.

The same protocol applies in private homes, temples, and Japanese-style inns *(ryokan)*. In a Western-style hotel, however, "indoors" starts when you enter your own room. If you are unsure where "indoors" begins or, for instance, whether to take your shoes off to enter a restaurant (it depends on the type of restaurant), take your cue from other shoes or slippers in the entrance. (Also place umbrellas in a rack or plastic sleeve if provided at the entrance to the restaurant.)

Leave shoes neatly, by the step or in a pigeonhole – at an inn, staff may do this for you. To walk on *tatami* matting, remove slippers and go in stockinged feet.

Most restrooms, public and private, have special toilet slippers waiting outside: be sure to change into them as you go in (this is one way people know the restroom is occupied!) and to change back again when you emerge.

ETIQUETTE AT TEMPLES AND SHRINES

The atmosphere in temples and shrines is casual. Visitors should show respect, and not be noisy, but there are few of the taboos found in some other Buddhist nations. Japan is a superstitious society rather than a religious one, its religions mingling unexclusively and priests leading down-to-earth lives.

If you enter buildings in a shrine or temple, except those with stone floors, leave your shoes at the entrance or carry them with you. Plastic bags are often provided for this, especially if you can use a different exit. Some temples allow photography, some only without flash, others not at all. For advice about paying respects in Shinto and Buddhism see pages 22–5.

Group Mentality

One key to understanding Japanese society is its emphasis on the group, which may, for instance, be a family, village, school, company, or the Japanese nation as a whole. Foreigners are likely to gain insight to Japanese group mentality at major tourist sights.

Within a group, peer pressure leads everyone to conform to accepted ways of doing things. A popular saying is "the nail that stands out will be hammered down." Even artists and those on the fringes of society only occasionally show genuine individualism. Foreigners, however, are expected to be more individualistic. The group mentality permeates everything: attitudes and behavior in any situation largely depend on whether the people concerned are inside or outside the group.

How the Japanese React to Foreigners

Thanks to a fundamentally courteous culture, visitors meet with warm hospitality. But you will also encounter curiosity and occasional rudeness. Do not be surprised by apparently naive and insular attitudes – Western culture may flood the country but it is filtered and Japanized. Foreigners are still a curiosity in many parts of Japan (especially blondes and black people) and expected to be different. This can often lead to comments that are unintentionally racist. Young Japanese and those who travel abroad are changing the nation's perception of foreigners, but only slowly.

Because of the "them-and-us" group mentality, foreigners *(gaijin)* inevitably remain outsiders however much they are welcomed with warmth and open arms. Anyone who shows sensitivity to Japanese culture, speaks the language well, or is of Oriental racial origin may be accepted to some extent (and will be expected to conform to Japanese ways), but even they can never fully belong.

Group posing for a photograph while on a religious pilgrimage

Meeting Japanese People

Japanese have a reputation for reserve and politeness, but in fact their social behavior is more complex, dictated by the situation, the place, the people involved, and the social expectation. The contrast between, say, the formal etiquette required at a tea ceremony *(see p163)* and the casual abandon expected in a bar, is extreme.

You will find classic manners in hotels, restaurants, and shops, where courteous, efficient service is seen as simply the correct way of doing a job, and not demeaning. The response to waitresses and sales assistants is up to you: some Japanese treat them as invisible, but a token inclination of the head or quiet *"domo"* ("thanks") does no harm.

Sometimes officials such as tour guides seem autocratic, but this is largely due to imperfect English intonation and the expectation of Japanese travelers. If you somehow clash with authority, such as a traffic policeman, use a quiet conciliatory demeanor, not the loud assertiveness that might get results in your own country. This same applies to poor service: complain, but do so quietly and politely. In conversations generally, avoid confrontation and causing loss of face (although this is not as vital as in some parts of Asia). The purpose of conversation for Japanese is not discussion of ideas but building a relationship. Therefore, small talk is important.

Wherever you go, expect to be asked to pose for photographs or to practice English with strangers.

Language Difficulties

Despite the profusion of brand names written in Roman script and often using Western-sounding words, Western visitors may face some language problems outside the main tourist areas. Signs for transportation systems are transliterated in many areas, though inconsistently *(see pp380–83)*.

Helpful sign written in both Japanese and transliteration for English-speaking visitors

Linguistically as culturally, the scope for misunderstanding is vast. The American English taught in schools is heavily weighted to grammar rather than conversation, so few Japanese are comfortable with everyday spoken English. When English is spoken, it is generally pronounced as if it were Japanese, and understood only in this way.

In Japanese all syllables are evenly stressed; no consonant except *n* occurs without being followed by a vowel; *r* and *l* merge into something between, and many words are abbreviated. Thus, for instance, taxi becomes *takushi*, hotel is *hoteru*, Coca-Cola becomes *kora*, and personal computer becomes *pasokon*; London is *Rondon*, New York is *Nyu Youku*, Sydney is *Shidoni*, and Los Angeles often simply *Ros*. For guidelines about pronunciation, see the Phrase Book on pages 404–408.

Further confusion comes from words imported from English that have been changed in meaning, for example *manshon*, not a palatial house but an apartment house; or *roman*, a romance novel. Resulting product names, such as the isotonic drinks Pocari Sweat and Calpis *(see p323)*, and "Japlish" text on t-shirts can be entertaining for visitors.

Even with fluent English speakers, subtleties are often lost in translation. If a Japanese says "yes," it usually means "I understand," not "I agree"; if they say "it's difficult," this means "no." For clarity, avoid negative and either/or questions.

Japanese Names

The order of Japanese names is traditionally family name followed by given name, as in this book. However, many Japanese automatically reverse this order when giving names to Westerners, so you may need to check which is the "first" name and "surname." Japanese generally call each other by the family name, even if they are quite close friends, but will happily call you by your first name if you prefer.

When speaking to or about an adult other than yourself, add "-san" to their name, which stands for Mr., Mrs., Ms., etc – for instance, Smith-san or John-san. For babies and young girls add "-chan," for young boys "-kun."

Gift-Giving

Gift-giving is big business in Japan, one of the most important aspects of etiquette. Any trip means bringing home souvenirs for colleagues and friends, usually something

Box of cookies gift-wrapped first in paper, then cloth

edible. Small gifts may be exchanged at a first business meeting, and if you visit someone's home, never go empty-handed: buy a luxury food item or take a small gift from your home country, especially local specialties and fine teas.

Keep gifts small, to avoid placing obligation on the recipient. Do not expect them to be opened in front of you. Likewise, if someone offers you a gift, it may be best not to open it in front of the giver.

Appearance matters: the Japanese wrap gifts beautifully *(see p343)*. A shop will usually do the wrapping for you, and a carrier bag from an elegant store is also good. Wine, chocolates, or flowers are acceptable gifts, although not the norm, but avoid chrysanthemums, which are used at funerals; do not give four of anything, because in Japanese the words for "four" and "death" sound similar; nor knives, lest they cut the friendship. Be aware that white is the color of mourning (though also worn by brides), and red is for celebration.

Tipping

Tipping is not necessary anywhere unless stated, and may even cause offense to a proud Japanese. If a receipt or change is placed on a tray, this is through a sense of decorum when handling money rather than the expectation of a tip. When handing over larger sums of money on a more intimate level, for instance, to a guide or babysitter, the custom is to wrap it in an envelope or sheet of paper.

Lining Up and Jaywalking

As with so much in Japan, social behavior is full of contradictions. When waiting for a train, people line up neatly *(see pp380–81)* but may resort to pushing and shoving in order to get on. To get off a crowded train, simply push your way out, wordlessly. If you are completely stuck and cannot reach the door, call out *"orimass"* ("I'm getting off").

In situations where you want to break into a line – for instance, driving – the key is to catch someone's eye: as long as you are anonymous you can be ignored, but once you are acknowledged you must be treated politely.

As a pedestrian, be careful about jaywalking. It is heavily discouraged and rarely done by the Japanese. If you do it, others may assume you are crossing correctly and follow you unthinkingly, or you may be reprimanded by the police.

Commuters waiting patiently in line on a train station platform

Doing Business and Working in Japan

IN BUSINESS, AS IN OTHER AREAS, Japan is a complex blend of hi-tech and old-fashioned. Practicalities are fairly easy in a land that is courteous and technologically up to date. In other respects, doing business in Japan can be a challenge. The structure and culture of business are so different from the West that misunderstandings often arise. With a little luck and planning, it is possible to find work in Japan, although living expenses, especially for accommodations, can be high.

Employees doing communal exercises before starting work

Business Attitudes and Structures

JAPANESE BUSINESS attitudes are dominated by the long term. This shows in corporate planning and the slow pace of decision-making, as well as individual attitudes. Lifetime employment at a single firm may no longer be the norm, but the company is still a community around which *salarymen* build their lives – if you ask someone what they do, the answer will be not their trade but the company for which they work.

The system is hard for foreigners to break into. Companies tend to be bound together, officially or unofficially, in huge industrial groups *(keiretsu)*, comprising networks of subsidiaries and subcontractors. Japan also has a reputation for protectionism over imports, and, although the situation has eased, there are high import taxes on items relating to industries that the government wishes to protect, such as furniture and medicines. Exporting is not so difficult, but dealing with the bureaucracy and paperwork for import and export can be time-consuming. Nonetheless, effort invested in groundwork and building contacts and relationships can pay dividends.

Business Facilities

MOST MAJOR hotels have excellent business facilities and can provide e-mail and Internet access – often direct from your hotel room – arrange rooms for meetings and conferences, and recommend interpreters. Business services also advertise in Yellow Pages and English-language magazines and newspapers. Outgoing telephone calls from hotels, including e-mail from your laptop, are charged at near-normal rates, without exorbitant surcharges. For details on mobile phones, and fax, e-mail, and Internet facilities, see page 375. Convenience stores offer inexpensive photocopying and faxing.

***Salaryman* relaxing at lunchtime in the park**

Business Cards

KNOWN AS *meishi*, business cards are an essential part of business and social transactions in Japan. They are vital for learning a person's status as well as their name; bear in mind that job titles may not correspond to Western equivalents, and people may have varied experience within a company. Have a large stock of business cards printed, preferably in English on one side and Japanese on the other. Major hotels and department stores in Japan often provide this service overnight, and Japan Airlines has an inflight service.

The card's design is not important, but avoid rounded corners, as these were traditionally used by geisha and other women in the entertainment world, and the implication of frivolity lives on.

Business cards should be treated with respect: when meeting someone for the first time, proffer your card with both hands, and say your name clearly; then hand over the card with your right hand, taking the other person's card with your left. Keep their card in front of you during the meeting. Forgetting their card or putting it in a pocket where it may be crumpled are seen as signs of disrespect to the other person.

Negotiating

PATIENCE and good manners are the keys to successful negotiation in Japan. Japanese who are used to dealing with foreigners will make allowances for Western ways, but to stand the best chance of success it is worth being open to Japanese expectations. Familiarize yourself with the basics of etiquette outlined on pages 364–7. Even in hot weather, avoid dressing too informally; arrive for meetings on time or early; speak respectfully; and initially decline the seat of honor (farthest from the door).

Improving personal connections through small gifts or business entertaining is very much part of the system, but overt bribery is not. Japanese companies reach decisions by consensus, so elements of face-saving vagueness or flexibility can be useful. On the other hand, to miminize linguistic confusion it is essential to speak simply and unambiguously. In some situations, an interpreter may help. Be aware, however, that you will not be given a clear "no," even if that is what is meant. Discussion of money is usually left until last and should not be approached too bluntly.

Business Entertaining

Socializing with business contacts is essential: there is little chance of establishing a good working relationship if you have not built a rapport over a few drinks or a game of golf *(see p351)*. Expect the Japanese to extend the first invitation, and allow them to pay – usually the person who does the inviting picks up the tab. If you would like to return the compliment but are not sure where to take people, ask their advice, or choose a hotel bar (where prices are clearly marked).

Socializing in a bar after work

Conversation can include business matters, but should not be intense. Drunken words or behavior on either side are normal and rarely taken seriously. Although the world of business entertaining is fundamentally male, foreign women are mostly treated as honorary men and, despite the underlying sexist attitudes, should have few problems. For eating and drinking etiquette, see pages 312–13.

Computerized bidding at the Tokyo Stock Exchange

Finding Work

Finding work in Japan is not as easy as it was during the economic boom of the 1980s. Most common are English-teaching jobs, which usually require a university degree, and sometimes a TEFL (Teaching English as a Foreign Language) qualification.

The **JET (Japan Exchange and Teaching) Programme** sends college graduates under age 35 to work in Japan, initially for a year, sometimes extendable to two or three. It has over 5,000 participants annually, from 34 countries. For details, contact the Japanese embassy in your country.

There are also limited opportunities in Japan for editorial work, particularly polishing translations of corporate publicity material or technical documents. The best place to look for such jobs is in Japan's English-language newspapers.

Visas

Staying in Japan long term generally means qualifying for either a working visa (with a commitment for two or three years working for one firm) or a student visa (which permits you to work part-time). New Zealand, Australian, French, and Canadian citizens between 18 and 30 can also obtain a working-holiday visa, allowing part-time work, for up to a year. Though officially discouraged, it is sometimes possible to enter Japan as a Temporary Visitor and then arrange a job or study course.

Long-Term Accommodations

Some apartments can be found at rental rates similar to those in Western cities, but with a lot less space for the money, and the initial start-up costs are extremely high. Cheaper options include "*gaijin* houses," accommodations for foreigners ranging from pleasant shared apartments for three or four to scruffy hostels with 20 sharing a kitchen. The next step up is a weekly or monthly apartment, at the cost of a budget hotel or less, which is like a regular apartment but requires little or no deposit. In descriptions, room size is measured by the number of *tatami* mats, and apartments may be said to have, for instance, "2DK" – two bedrooms, a dining room, and kitchen.

Long-term visitors outside a "*gaijin* house" in Kyoto

Personal Security and Health

HYGIENE STANDARDS are as high as in Western countries, and crime rates are extremely low. Pickpockets occasionally operate in crowds, but bags can generally be put down freely in a store or at a station, and there is little risk in carrying large amounts of cash. *Koban* (manned police boxes) are found in every neighborhood; their presence helps to keep crime down.

A uniformed Tokyo policeman

In an Emergency

EMERGENCY CALLS are free. Your hotel, embassy, or consulate may also be able to help, while Tokyo Police have an assistance phone line for foreign visitors. For personal problems, contact the **Tokyo English Lifeline** (TELL), a crisis hot line organization whose trained volunteers (mostly foreigners who are resident in Japan) provide telephone counseling. Lost possessions are very likely to be returned to you; contact the appropriate local police or transport authorities.

Earthquakes, Typhoons, and Volcanoes

EACH YEAR, Japan experiences more than 1,000 earthquakes large enough to be felt by humans, although most are no more disruptive than the vibrations of a passing truck and are nothing to worry about. Earthquakes are more noticeable in tall buildings, which sway markedly but usually have mechanisms to absorb the motion. In a larger earthquake, especially in an old building, open doors (to prevent them from buckling and jamming) and turn off any gas. Do not go outside, where debris may fall on you, but shelter under something protective – the ideal is a reinforced doorway, but a sturdy table will do. Avoid placing fragile items near the edge of a shelf, and back up computer data in case of power cuts.

Typhoons generally pose no great hazard, although the worst bring winds so strong that it is wise to stay indoors.

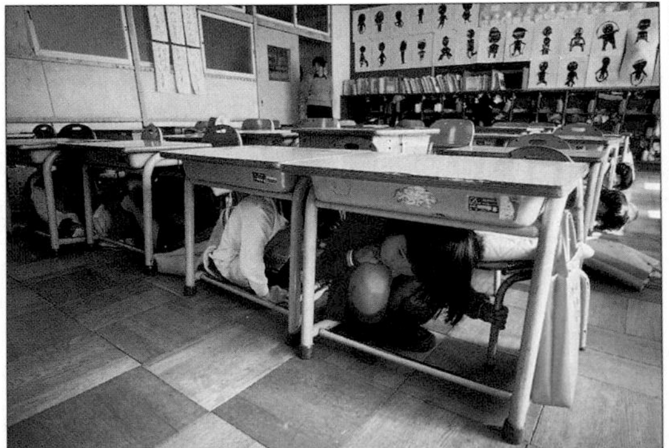

Schoolchildren practicing earthquake drill

The main typhoon season is in September. Active volcanoes usually have fences around them to ensure that no one goes dangerously close. Poisonous fumes occasionally seep from the ground nearby, but this is unpredictable; look out for warning notices.

Things to Avoid

DON'T WALK IN wet rice-paddy fields, as there is a risk of schistosomiasis, a disease caused by parasites. There are few "off-limits" areas in Japan, but it is advisable to avoid the *yakuza* (mafia, *see p197*), extremist political groups, and some religious sects.

Women Travelers

WOMEN ARE SAFE to go almost anywhere, alone and late at night. Unwanted propositions from men can usually be shaken off with a simple no. Groping hands on crowded trains, however, can be a nuisance, though the perpetrator will be embarrassed if reprimanded publicly.

In the countryside anyone of either sex choosing to travel alone is cause for surprise, and there are tales of innkeepers sitting up half the night with a lone female guest, on the assumption that the only possible reason for traveling alone was in order to commit suicide.

On a more practical level, tampons are widely available, but the Pill is difficult to obtain.

Food Safety

FOOD POISONING is rare thanks to good hygiene standards, and an upset stomach is likely to be simply due to a change in diet. The problem, if anything, is over-reliance on science – organic foods are uncommon. Tap water is drinkable throughout Japan, although in cities it may taste chlorinated. Avoid drinking from mountain streams.

Raw fish in sushi and sashimi is not a risk, nor are oysters. *Fugu* (blowfish) is safe provided it is correctly prepared. Raw pork can be eaten, but avoid raw bear

Food stall at in indoor market in Naha, Okinawa

(kuma) and raw wild boar *(botan)* because of risk of trichinosis, borne by parasites. Fruit and vegetables are clean, although insecticides and chemicals are widely applied so it may be wise to do as the locals do and peel the fruit.

Medical Facilites

Facilities are generally as good as in the US or Europe but can be expensive. If you are sick, go to a hospital; for minor problems, consulting a pharmacist is another option.

To find a hospital, doctor, or dentist, contact the International Affairs Division of the prefectural office, the **AMDA (Asian Medical Doctors Association) International Medical Information Center**, or a TIC. The hospitals listed in the directory have some English-speaking doctors. Look, too, for advertisments in foreign-language magazines; international hotels have doctors on call.

Dental care varies in quality and may not meet Western aesthetic standards. Medicines are dispensed at hospitals and pharmacies; a prescription from abroad is more likely to be understood at a hospital. Western brands are available, if expensive, at international pharmacies such as Tokyo's **American Pharmacy**. Contact lenses can be obtained with relative ease, and Western-brand lens solutions are very reasonably priced. Japan is big on pick-me-ups containing ginseng, caffeine, and the like, which can work wonders with a hangover. Local mosquito repellents and bite medicines are also good, as are pocket handwarmers *(kairo)*, sold in pharmacies and convenience stores. Chinese herbal medicine is widely available *(see p356)*.

Public Conveniences

Japanese toilets range from highly sophisticated to very basic. The latter are simple troughs to squat over, facing the end with the hood, making sure nothing falls out of trouser pockets. If squatting is difficult, seek out Western-style toilets; many public facilities, including trains, have both. The usual way of finding out if a cubicle is occupied is to knock on the door and see if anyone knocks back. Toilet paper and hand towels are often not provided, so carry tissues with you.

Traditional sign for a men's toilet

Traditional sign for a women's toilet

Older Western-style toilets often have the option of small or large flush. They may also have a panel that, if pressed, plays a tune or makes a flushing sound to discreetly mask natural noises. Newer hi-tech toilets may have heated seats, automatic seat covers, and bidet and hot-air-drying facilities. For protocol on toilet slippers, see page 365.

Directory

Emergency Numbers

Fire/Ambulance
☎ *119.*

Police
☎ *110 (emergencies only).*
Tokyo ☎ *(03) 3503-8484 (assistance service for foreigners).*

Tokyo English Lifeline
☎ *(03) 3968-4099.*
W www.tell.gol.com

Medical Facilities and Hospitals

AMDA International Medical Information Center
☎ *(03) 5285-8088.*

American Pharmacy
Hibiya Park Bldg, 1-8-1 Yurakucho, Chiyoda-ku, Tokyo.
☎ *(03) 3271-4034.*

Hospital Information
Tokyo ☎ *(03) 3212-2323.*
Hiroshima ☎ *(0120) 16-9912.*

International Catholic Hospital
2-5-1 Naka-Ochiai, Shinjuku-ku, Tokyo.
☎ *(03) 3951-1111.*

International Clinic
1-8-3 Irifune, Minato-ku, Nagoya.
☎ *(052) 651-6496.*

Japan Baptist Hospital
47 Yamanomotocho, Kitashirakawa, Sakyo-ku, Kyoto.
☎ *(075) 781-5191.*

Japanese Red Cross Medical Center
4-1-22 Hiro, Shibuya-ku, Tokyo.
☎ *(03) 3400-1311.*

St. Luke's International Hospital
9-1 Akashicho, Chuo-ku, Tokyo.
☎ *(03) 3541-5151.*

Tokyo Medical and Surgical Clinic
32 Mori Bldg, 3-4-30 Shiba-koen, Minato ku, Tokyo.
☎ *(03) 3436-3028.*

Banking and Local Currency

For visitors used to easy and instant access to cash 24 hours a day in their home country, Japan's banking system can prove frustrating. Japan is largely a cash economy – personal checks are unknown – and cash is still the most popular way to pay for almost everything. Since the economic "bubble" burst in late 1989, the economy has been in a state of flux. Various scandals have resulted in the closure of several banks and financial institutions; a comprehensive restructuring is underway.

ATM with signs indicating that it accepts some foreign cards

Banks and Banking Hours

The nation's central bank, the Bank of Japan (Nippon Ginko), issues newly minted yen currency; it is also the bank of banks, and the government bank. However, this and the prefectural and local city banks are not geared to tourists. Buying yen, exchanging travelers' checks, and any other regular banking transactions may be more easily conducted via major Japanese banks that are authorized money exchangers, such as **Daiichi-Kangyo**, **Sumitomo**, **Sakura, Tokyo-Mitsubishi**, and **Fuji**. Some foreign banks also offer useful services. Local banks in rural areas may charge large fees.

Sign for an ATM at Fuji Bank

Banks open 9am–3pm on weekdays, and close on weekends and national holidays. The exchange rate is posted at about 10am for US dollars, and after that for other currencies. Banks usually exhange currency between 10am and 3pm; some city banks offer exchange facilities from 9am.

Travelers' Checks

Although travelers' checks provide a convenient way to carry money around Japan, they are usually accepted only in major city banks and large hotels. Thomas Cook, American Express, and VISA checks are the most widely recognized. It is advisable to bring cash as well as checks, especially if you are traveling away from main tourist centers.

Credit and Debit Cards

International credit cards such as American Express, MasterCard, VISA, and Diners Club are generally accepted by leading banks, hotels, and stores in major cities. There may sometimes be a charge to use a credit card. Obtaining cash with credit cards is rare but possible at some city ATMs. The more rural the location, the less likely that outlets will accept any cards at all, or they will accept only Japanese-issued cards such as JCB.

Changing Money

It is possible to change cash and travelers' checks at banks, major hotels (which offer the same exchange rates as banks), *ryokan*, main post offices, and some department stores in cities. Banks and post offices may also offer money transfer facilities. Even leading city banks may be unfamiliar with foreign currency apart from dollars, so be prepared for bank tellers to check with their superiors if they have not experienced such notes before. In city centers, staff may speak English, and forms are often supplied in English – if not, staff will indicate to a customer where to write. Transactions are relatively simple, but usually time-consuming. Always carry your passport as your identity will be checked.

At airports handling international flights, currency exchange counters may be

Directory

Japanese Banks

Daiichi Kangyo Bank
1-1-5 Uchi-saiwai-cho, Chiyoda-ku, Tokyo.
(03) 3596-1111.

Fuji Bank
1-5-5 Otemachi, Chiyoda-ku, Tokyo.
(03) 3216-2211.

Sakura Bank
1-3-1 Kudan-Minami, Chiyoda-ku, Tokyo.
(03-3230 3111)

Sumitomo Bank
4-6-5 Kitahama, Chuo-ku, Osaka.
(06) 6227-2111.

Tokyo-Mitsubishi
2-7-1 Marunouchi, Chiyoda-ku, Tokyo.
(03) 3240-1111.

Foreign Banks

Barclays PLC
Urbannet Otemachi Bldg, 2-2-2 Otemachi, Chiyoda-ku, Tokyo.
(03) 3276-5100.

Citibank
2-3-14 Higashi-Shinagawa, Shinagawa-ku, Tokyo.
(03)-5462-5000.

Credit Card Loss Numbers

American Express
(0120) 020120.

Diners Club
(03) 3499-1181.

VISA
(0120) 13331363.

open for longer than regular banking hours; at Tokyo International Airport at Narita, for example, the counter is open from 6am to 11pm. Since it is illegal for public transportation, stores, and restaurants to accept payment in foreign currencies, a small amount of Japanese yen will be required on arrival to cover immediate needs. It is always wise to obtain cash before traveling in the countryside.

ATM Services

The large majority of automatic teller machines are located inside banks. Outside bank opening hours, they are separated from the main banking area and remain open to the public, though not usually for 24 hours. Times of closure vary, but many ATMs close at 8pm and all day Sundays. Some ATMs have an English-language facility, but the opportunities for obtaining cash from an ATM using an international credit card are extremely limited.

Currency

The Japanese currency is the yen, indicated by the symbol ¥. Coins are minted in denominations of ¥1, ¥5, ¥10, ¥50, ¥100, and ¥500. Bank notes are printed in denominations of ¥1,000, ¥2,000 (introduced in mid-2000), ¥5,000, and ¥10,000. Unused Japanese bank notes (but not coins) can be reconverted to foreign currency at the point of departure; the amount is limited only by the funds carried by the airport exchange center.

JTB Coupons

Japan Travel Bureau, a specialty travel agency with branches in North America, Europe, Asia, and Australia, sells hundreds of different kinds of coupons that can be exchanged by visitors for services (such as travel, car rental, and accommodations) inside Japan. These can be a convenient means of paying, but work best when combined with a JTB-planned itinerary. Contact a nearby JTB office for further details.

Bank Notes
Each of the banknote denominations carries a portrait of an historical figure, such as the scholar and novelist Natsume Soseki, on the ¥1,000 note.

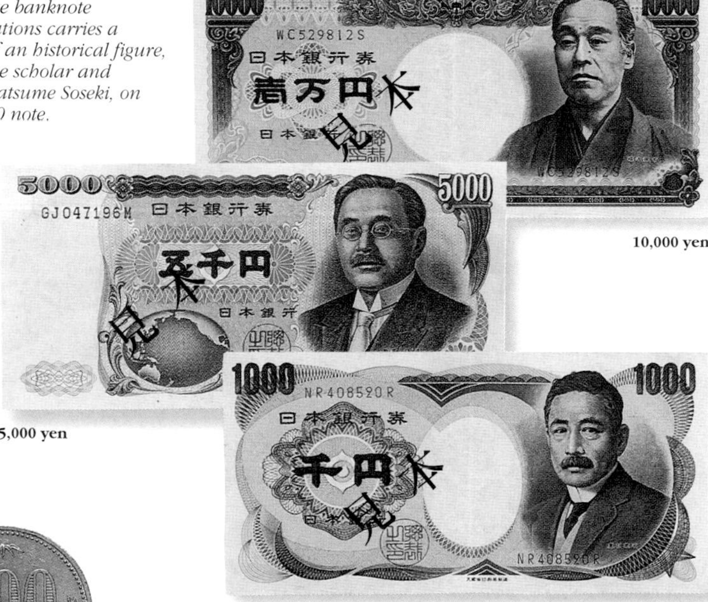

10,000 yen

5,000 yen

1,000 yen

500 yen

Coins
The denominations of Japan's coins are all marked in Arabic numerals, except for the ¥5. On the reverse side of most of the coins is a flower or plant design; on the ¥10 is a temple.

100 yen

50 yen

10 yen

5 yen

1 yen

Communications

Phonecard dispenser

As befits a country on the cutting edge of technology, the range of communication tools is extensive and state-of-the-art. But with such tools often used all at the same time, noise pollution is quite a problem, especially in busy shopping districts and at major train stations. Public phones are easy to find, though not all are suitable for making international calls. Newspapers and magazines are printed in abundance, and English-language versions are readily available in major cities. The postal system is fast and efficient.

MAINICHI
Daily News
Female condoms get
The Japan Times
Blackmail arrests latest Kanagawa police scandal
U.N. punishes Afghanistan with sanctions

The English-language *Mainichi Daily News* and *The Japan Times*

Newspapers and Magazines

The range of newspapers in Japanese is extensive. The most demanding of the reader is *Asahi Shimbun*; the least, *Gendai*, a tabloid containing a fair amount of pornographic material. Somewhere in between, selling around ten million copies daily, is the *Yomiuri Shimbun*. Japanese magazines come and go, seeking to follow news, business, and leisure trends. As for *manga* comic books *(see p21)*, they cover every subject imaginable; the regular bestseller is *Shonen Jump*, aimed at young men.

Four English-language newspapers are printed in Japan. The most widely available is *The Japan Times*; the other three are the *Daily Yomiuri*, the *Asahi Evening News*, and the *Mainichi Daily News*. *The Japan Times* includes a large classified section every Monday. All are sold at kiosks in train stations, major hotels, and foreign-language bookstores *(see p107)*.

A few English-language magazines are published, often with extensive listings and classified advertisements. These include *Tokyo Classified, Tokyo Journal,* and *Kansai Time Out*. Foreign-language bookstores often stock imported magazines, though these tend to be expensive. Newsletters in various languages are produced by community groups all over the country and are widely available.

Television and Radio

NHK is the state broadcaster, running two broadcast channels, plus two satellite channels, which are available at an extra cost. The nightly 7pm news on NHK has an English-language translation, available on bilingual TVs, which are often found in hotels. Other nationwide networks include Nihon TV, TBS, Fuji TV, and TV Asahi.

Cable and satellite TV are also widely available. In addition to the usual MTV and CNN, there are numerous Japanese channels, each specializing in news, sports, soaps, movies, and so on.

The state radio station NHKFM broadcasts news and mainly classical music. There are also several commercial radio stations; some, such as J-WAVE and Inter FM in Tokyo, and CO-CO-LO in Central Honshu, offer a choice of programs in English and other languages. Check up-to-date listings pages for frequencies and for times of programs.

***Tokyo Journal* and *Shukan ST* student paper**

A red call box with a gray phone, suitable for international calls

Types of Telephones and Telephone Cards

Several kinds of public phones are found in Japan. The most common are green in color and situated everywhere from stations to inside trains, outside convenience stores, and on street corners. Older versions of the green phones accept ¥10 and ¥100 coins only; newer models take a wider range of coins plus telephone cards. These phones are for domestic calls only.

Japan Telecom's gray public phones have an LCD display, a button for converting information into English, volume control (handy in noisy public places), and an emergency button for dialing police, fire, and ambulance *(see pp370–71)*. These phones are the most likely to offer international direct-dialing; if so, they will be labeled as such.

The most eccentric model is the old-fashioned pink phone, which is still found in many *kissaten (see p311)*. These are for local calls and accept ¥10 coins only.

Telephone cards worth ¥500 and over may be purchased from a wide variety of outlets,

Green public phone, the most widespread type

including station kiosks, vending machines, and convenience stores. Three international telephone companies, **Japan Telecom**, **IDC**, and **KDD**, each offer their own phone cards; use the appropriate company's access code when dialing. IDC also offers the 0061 Love Homecard; on the card is a number which can be dialed to call abroad from any type of phone (except pink public phones), even mobiles. Decorated phone cards are sometimes given away, or are for sale at tourist spots.

Beautiful designs on Japanese telephone cards

Making International Calls

If making an international call direct, first dial one of the international access codes for the three international operators Japan Telecom, IDC, and KDD. Then dial the country code, followed by the area code (minus any initial zero), then the number. The three companies are in competition, so charges and service details are constantly changing; each has a toll-free number for up-to-date information.

To make an international call from a public phone, use a telephone card or credit card. All major hotels and many others offer international direct-dialing, sometimes from pay phones, sometimes from your room. Calls from your room are not usually subject to a high surcharge. If you are calling from a private phone and wish to know the cost of the call, dial the operator, who will place the call and phone you afterward to tell you the total charge. **KDD** and **NTT** offer international collect calls; dial the appropriate access code and ask the operator to place a collect call.

The cheapest rates for international calls are from 11pm to 8am daily; the second-cheapest are between 7pm and 11pm.

Local Calls

The charge for a local call is ¥10 per minute. Use small coins or phone cards in a public phone; unused coins will be returned to you. In this guide area codes are given in brackets; omit the code if calling from inside the area.

Mobile Phones

It is not usually possible to use a mobile phone from abroad in Japan as neither of the two systems used are compatible with other countries – check with your mobile network before arriving in Japan. If you are staying for a while, mobiles are cheap to buy and there is a huge choice. For shorter stays, it is possible to rent mobiles from NTT, though this is expensive. Some public areas, including bullet trains, have areas set aside for mobile phone use.

Fax, E-mail, and Internet Facilities

Fax machines for public use are located at many convenience stores and at main post offices. Hotels will often have machines available for guests to use, too; they often charge to send faxes but not to receive them.

Internet cafés are rare but can be found in major cities; access is also available in some city halls and public libraries.

Directory

International Access Codes

IDC
0061.

Japan Telecom
0041.

KDD
001.

International Call Information

IDC
0120-03-0061 (toll-free).

International Directory Enquiries
0051.

Japan Telecom
0088-41 (toll-free).

KDD
0057 (toll-free).

NTT
0033 (toll-free).

Other Useful Numbers

Domestic Directory Enquiries
104.

Domestic Operator
100.

International Dialing Codes

Use these codes after the international access codes to dial the following countries:
Australia **61**, Brazil **55**, Canada **1**, China, **86**, France, **33**, Germany **49**, Hong Kong **852**, India **91**, Indonesia **62**, Ireland **353**, Israel **972**, Republic of Korea **82**, Malaysia **60**, Netherlands **31**, New Zealand **64**, Peru **51**, Philippines **63**, Russia **7**, Singpore **65**, Spain **34**, Sweden **46**, Switzerland **41**, Taiwan **886**, Thailand **66**, United Kingdom **44**, and US **1**.

Mail

Post offices *(yubin-kyoku)* and mailboxes in Japan can easily be identified by the character looking like the letter "T" with an extra horizontal bar across the top. Main post offices are usually open 9am–7pm on weekdays, 9am–5pm on Saturdays, and 9am–12:30pm on Sundays. Smaller post offices may open 9am–5pm on weekdays and 9am–12:30pm on Saturdays. Stamps are also sold at some convenience stores and larger hotels. Make sure any mail is addressed correctly and legibly; the postal code is especially important.

International mail is best sent from a main post office. There may be a counter where English is spoken, indicated by a sign. The clerk will weigh the letter to be mailed and sell you the correct stamp. An express mail service is available for more urgent mail inside Japan and abroad; either write "Sokutatsu" on the express item or, at a post office, say "express," and staff will stamp it accordingly. Should an item be especially urgent, send it from **Tokyo Central Post Office**, or **Tokyo International Post Office** (which has an all-night counter).

Items mailed from a mailbox may take slightly longer to reach their destination. Some boxes have two slots; the one on the left is for domestic letters, and the one on the right is for other mail. Use the right-hand slot for international and express mail. Parcels must be mailed from a post office: fill in the green coupon supplied, but do not attach it to the package; this will be done by staff over the counter. Boxes and bags are available for sending larger items.

Japanese mailbox

Couriers and Other Mail Services

Japan is well served with prompt and efficient door-to-door delivery services *(takkyubin)*. The best known of these domestic companies is **Yamato**; **Sagawa-Kyubin**, which is based in Kyoto, also serves all of Japan. Small packages can be sent via these courier services from convenience stores; larger items will be picked up at the source. There are also a number of courier services for sending printed materials and packages abroad. **FedEx** and **DHL** are among the best known. **Nippon Courier Services** is also prompt and reliable.

Colorful examples of Japanese postage stamps

Logo identifying post offices and also found on mailboxes

Finding an Address

There are few street names in Japan, and no consistent numbering system for buildings. Indeed, the numbering of buildings in a block is often dictated by the order in which they were built, so finding an address can be a puzzle, even for the Japanese. It is slightly easier in cities such as Nara, Kyoto, and Sapporo, which were built on a grid pattern, as at least the blocks are numbered in sequence. Tokyo, however, was designed in a spiral around the castle and then allowed to develop higgledy-piggledy, in order to confound enemies of the shogunate. Even taxi drivers have a tough time locating addresses in the capital. (All Tokyo sights, hotels, and restaurants listed in this guide are marked on the Street Finder.)

Most Japanese carry name cards with maps. Hotels should provide guests with a map, preferably in Japanese and English, of their location and nearby landmarks.

Addresses in Japanese start with the name of the prefecture, and work backward through various districts to the number of the building. When Japanese addresses are

Directory

Mail

Tokyo Central Post Office
2-7-2 Marunouchi, Chiyoda-ku, Tokyo.
(03) 3284-9539 (for domestic mail).
(03) 3284-9540 (for international mail).

Tokyo International Post Office
2-3-3 Otemachi, Chiyoda-ku, Tokyo.
(03) 3241-4877 (international mail service).

Courier Companies

DHL
(03) 5479-2580.
www.dhl.co.jp

FedEx
(03) 3201-4320.
0120-003200 (toll-free).
www.fedex.com

Nippon Courier Services
(03) 5461-3550.

Sagawa-Kyubin
(075) 691-6500.

Yamato
(03) 3541-3411.

Information on Addresses

Japan Yellow Pages
(03) 3239-3501.
www. yellowpage-jp.com

NTT Town Pages
(03) 3356-8511.
www.english.itp.ne.jp/jtd/

written in Roman letters, the order is reversed, so that the block number comes first, following Western convention.

In an address, the first number of, for example, 2-3-4 Otemachi refers to the *chome*, or main block. The second number points to a smaller block of buildings within the original *chome*. The last is the number of the building itself. On city streets, the numbers of the *chome* are given on telephone poles and lampposts, reading in this instance 2-3; it is then a matter of finding building number 4.

Local police boxes are used in large part to help people reach their destinations. Officers on duty have maps, and may even call an address to pinpoint the location. Telephone operators will not supply an address, even if a number is known. Consult NTT's **Town Pages**, and **Japan Yellow Pages** (which publishes English-language editions).

Japan's Prefectures

The four main islands of Honshu, Hokkaido, Shikoku, and Kyushu are divided into 47 areas called *ken* or prefectures. Each prefecture is governed independently under the overall control of central government. The prefectural office is usually located in the largest conurbation, which also has its own city or town office. Honshu's prefectures are grouped into the larger, historical regions of Tohoku, Chubu, Kanto, Kinki, and Chugoku. Tokyo has its own metropolitan government; each of the capital's wards has its own office.

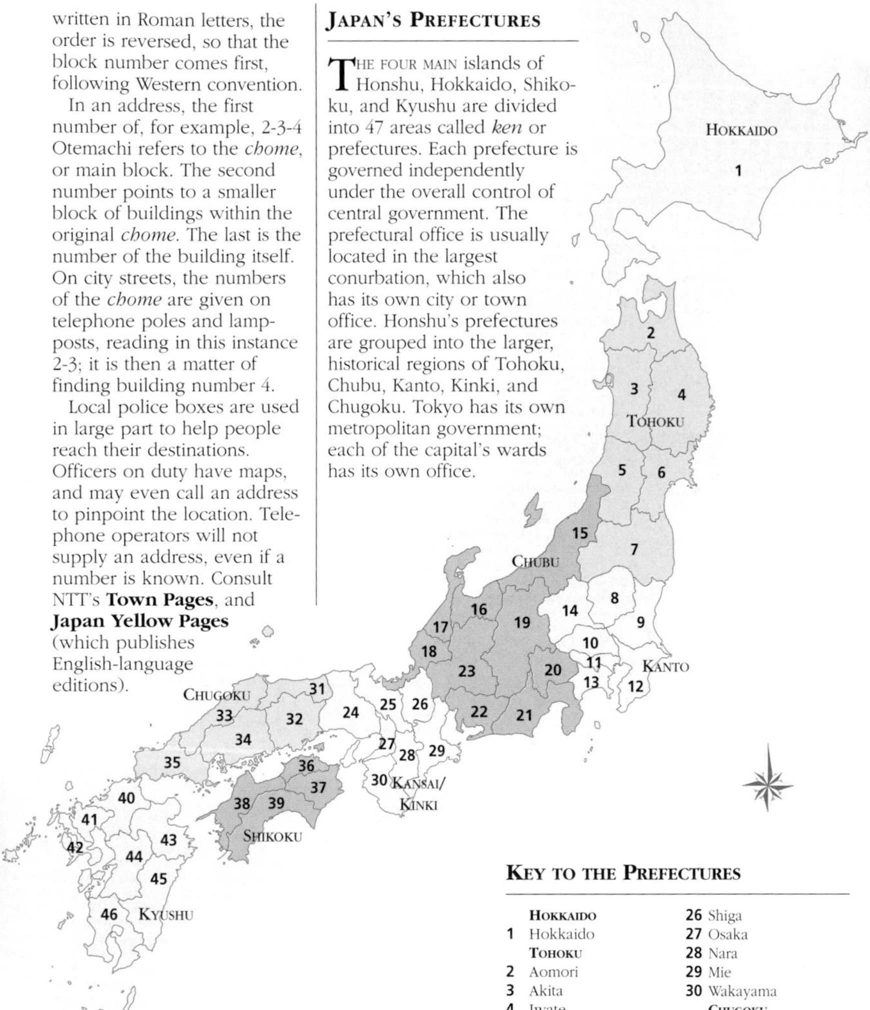

Key to the Prefectures

Hokkaido
1 Hokkaido
Tohoku
2 Aomori
3 Akita
4 Iwate
5 Yamagata
6 Miyagi
7 Fukushima
Kanto
8 Tochigi
9 Ibaraki
10 Saitama
11 Tokyo
12 Chiba
13 Kanagawa
14 Gunma
Chubu
15 Niigata
16 Toyama
17 Ishikawa
18 Fukui
19 Nagano
20 Yamanashi
21 Shizuoka
22 Aichi
23 Gifu
Kansai/Kinki
24 Hyogo
25 Kyoto
26 Shiga
27 Osaka
28 Nara
29 Mie
30 Wakayama
Chugoku
31 Tottori
32 Okayama
33 Shimane
34 Hiroshima
35 Yamaguchi
Shikoku
36 Kagawa
37 Tokushima
38 Ehime
39 Kochi
Kyushu
40 Fukuoka
41 Saga
42 Nagasaki
43 Oita
44 Kumamoto
45 Miyazaki
46 Kagoshima
Okinawa
47 Okinawa

Travel Information

Most foreigners fly to Japan and then use the country's excellent railroad system. Many of the famous sightseeing areas lie on or near the fast train lines between Tokyo, Osaka, and Fukuoka – visiting such places as Kyoto, Himeji Castle, and Hiroshima is easy, despite the distances involved. Slower trains connect to popular sights such as Nara and Nikko. Local public transportation systems are efficient, but you may need to rent a car to explore remote regions. An English-language information service about various forms of transportation, called **Japan Travel-Phone**, is provided by JNTO (the Japan National Tourist Organization). Their booklet contains useful maps, gives details of access between major airports and cities, and lists every "i" information office *(see p362)* in the country. It also describes the various services provided by the organization.

JAL

Logo of Japan Airlines

Japan Airlines (JAL) airplane

International Airports

The usual gateways for foreigners entering Japan are Narita Airport, near Tokyo, which is also called Tokyo New International Airport, and Osaka's Kansai International Airport. Other major airports handling international flights, mainly from Asia, include Naha, in Okinawa; Fukuoka and Nagasaki, in Kyushu; Hiroshima, Nagoya, Niigata, and Sendai, in Honshu; and Sapporo, in Hokkaido.

Japan Airlines (JAL) and **All Nippon Airways (ANA)** are the main airlines of Japan. JAL is particularly popular with foreign tourists.

Arriving via Narita Airport

Tokyo's Narita Airport has two terminals connected by a free shuttle bus, which takes about 10 minutes. The Narita Tourist Information Center (TIC) is located in the arrival lobby of Terminal 2, and has a multi-lingual staff.

Visitors who have bought a Japan Rail Pass Exchange Order *(see p381)* before arriving in Japan should visit the Japan Railways (JR) ticket counter. If validated from the day of arrival in Japan, the Pass can be used to make the trip from the airport into central Tokyo by JR train.

Narita Airport is located 60 km (35 miles) northeast of the center of Tokyo, thus the journey by taxi will cost at least ¥22,000. For travelers with heavy or excessive luggage, airport limousine buses are convenient but often slow, depending on traffic conditions. Buses run non-stop to Tokyo, Yokohama, and other nearby airports.

The **Narita Express (N'EX)** train, located beneath the terminal building, travels non-stop and in some luxury to Tokyo station in less than one hour, and then on to Shinjuku and Ikebukuro in the capital, or to Yokohama and Ofuna, near Kamakura. The Japan Rail Pass can be used on this train, but you will need to reserve a seat (free of charge) at the ticket booth. All signs and announcements for the N'EX are in Japanese and English, and English-language information is available via an onboard telephone service. Remember to reserve a seat when returning to the airport on the N'EX.

Travelers without a JR Pass will find Keisei trains cheaper than the N'EX and almost as fast. The Keisei line connnects with JR at Nippori, with an easy transfer. Board the Keisei Skyliner at Keisei Narita airport station (also below the terminal building); it terminates at Keisei Ueno station, within walking distance of JR Ueno train station and Ueno subway station.

The JR Sobu railway line, which changes name to the JR Yokosuka line at Tokyo station, is the cheapest but slowest form of travel from the airport.

Terminal 2 of Tokyo New International Airport, at Narita

Interior of check-in lobby at Kansai International Airport

Arriving via Kansai Airport

JAPAN'S second-largest international airport, Kansai, has direct connections with Europe, North America, and other countries, and is located on a manmade island 5 km (3 miles) off the coast in Osaka Bay. Taxis, limousine buses, and trains are all efficient ways to get into Osaka. There is also a high-speed boat service to Kobe. For Kyoto, Kansai Airport is most convenient. Kansai Tourist Information Center (TIC) is in the arrivals lobby. Rail Pass Exchange Orders may be exchanged at the JR Information Counter, Tis-Travel Service Center, or *Midori-no-madoguchi* (Green Windows, *see p382*).

Luggage Delivery

LUGGAGE can be delivered from airports to either a hotel or a private address the following day, and it can be picked up for the return trip. A number of companies offering this service operate counters at Narita and Kansai airports. The basic cost is for one item of luggage weighing no more than 30 kg (66 lb).

Domestic Flights

THE AIRLINES JAL and ANA maintain an extensive network of flights covering the four main islands and many of the smaller ones, too. **Japan Air System (JAS)** also operates domestic flights to many cities. For trips up to 600 km (350 miles), bullet trains *(see p380)* are often faster and more convenient than planes.

On domestic flights JAL and ANA offer economy seats and, at an extra cost, a "Super Seat" service, which is a combination of first and business class. Make reservations through a travel agent or directly through the airline's reservation office. For short distances, propeller aircraft are sometimes used.

The domestic "no-frills," low-cost airline **Skymark** was launched in 1998. It has two planes to date, operating between Haneda Airport (Yokohama) and Osaka, Fukuoka, and Sapporo.

The runway of Nagasaki Airport, built on the sea

Airport Tax

PASSENGERS TRAVELING from Kansai, Narita, or Fukuoka airports are subject to a Passenger Service Facilities Charge (PSFC). At Kansai this is about ¥2,650 per person, payable at a machine located near the departure gate. At Narita and Fukuoka the charge – around ¥2,040 and ¥945 respectively – is conveniently included in the cost of your airline ticket. Other airports do not make this charge.

Directory

Japan Travel-Phone

When calling from within the Tokyo (03) phone-code area:
3201-3331 9am–5pm Mon–Fri, and Sat morning.

When calling from within the Kyoto (075) phone-code area:
371-5649 9am–5pm daily.

When calling from outside Tokyo and Kyoto:
0088-22-4800 (toll-free) 9am–5pm daily.

Airlines

Japan Airlines (JAL)
In Japan:
0120-25-5931 (toll-free) for international reservations.
0120-25-5971 (toll-free) for domestic reservations.
www.jal.co.jp

In USA and Canada:
1-800 525 3663.
www.japanair.com

In Europe:
(020) 7408-0744 from UK.
(+44 20) 7408-0744 from outside UK.
www.jal-europe.com

All Nippon Airways (ANA)
0120-029-222 (toll-free).
www.ana.co.jp

Japan Air System (JAS)
0120-51-1283 (toll-free).

Skymark
(03) 3433-7670 (Tokyo).

Arriving by Boat

IT IS POSSIBLE to travel to Japan by boat from some parts of mainland Asia, including Pusan in South Korea, and Shanghai in China, from where boats run to Kobe and Osaka. The Far Eastern Shipping Line connects Niigata/Takaoka on the west coast of Japan's Honshu island with the port of Vladivostock in Russia, which is where the Trans-Siberian Railway begins and ends its journey to and from Europe.

Traveling by Train

Tourist train, Nagasaki

JAPAN'S RAIL SYSTEM leads the world in terms of safety, efficiency, and comfort. Trains linking major cities tend to have announcements and digital displays running tickertape style in both Japanese and English. In rural areas, the names of train stations may not be given in translation, but railway staff and members of the public generally try to be helpful to foreigners. The Japan Rail Pass is highly recommended. Advice about buying individual tickets and reserving seats is on page 382.

Ticket office and advance reservation center at JR train station

The Railway Network

THE JAPAN RAILWAYS GROUP, known as **JR**, is the main operator. It includes all the *shinkansen* super expresses (bullet trains) and a nationwide network of over 21,000 km (13,000 miles) of tracks. There are also many private railroads linking smaller communities in more remote regions. Often travelers have a choice of lines to the same destination.

The Shinkansen: Bullet Trains

THE FIRST "BULLET TRAIN," as it was quickly nicknamed by a marveling media worldwide, drew out of Tokyo Station in 1964, the year of the Tokyo Olympics. Symbolic of Japan's economic recovery and future drive, it became, and remains, a source of national pride.

They are no longer the world's fastest trains, and there are still only a few *shinkansen* lines linking the major cities, but their efficiency, as proved by long-distance journeys timed to the minute, is legendary. There are three types of *shinkansen* in current use: **Kodama**, which stops at many stations en route; **Hikari**, serving only major stations; and **Nozomi**, the fastest and most expensive.

English-language announcements and clear signs make the *shinkansen* an appealing form of transportation for foreigners, often more convenient than flying, though there is surprisingly little space for large suitcases. It is best to reserve a seat *(see p382)*, as the non-reserved carriages can be very crowded. Be sure to reserve a seat well in advance if you are traveling over a holiday period.

Aerodynamic nose of the fabled *shinkansen*, or "bullet train"

Other Trains and Lines

OTHER major train types include **Tokkyu** ("limited express," the fastest), **Kyuko** ("express"), **Kaisoku** (misleadingly called "rapid"), and **Futsu** local trains.

The main train stations in the Tokyo metropolitan area are all on the JR **Yamanote line**. This loop line is easy for foreigners to use.

Every year there are new train models, including "specials" for tourists; trains with *tatami* flooring; trains with swing seats and panoramic windows; even party trains with karaoke systems.

Station Signs and Facilities

TOKYO'S Shinjuku station *(see p89)* is the world's busiest, and several others in Tokyo and major cities are on a vast scale. Finding a particular line or exit during rush hour can be intimidating and exhausting for newcomers with heavy baggage. It is a good idea to find out which named or numbered exit is best for you before arriving at one of the major stations.

The level of signs in English varies greatly. Tokyo's Shibuya station, for example, is a major hub but notoriously bad for navigation. By contrast, Kyoto's new station is geared to tourists, Japanese and foreign, and most of the major tourist destinations are trying to make navigation easier.

Even at large stations, *shinkansen* lines are clearly marked, and other lines are color coded. The yellow bobbles on the floor are intended to help blind people navigate but can be a problem for suitcases with wheels, as is the lack of consistently placed escalators.

Note that trains, especially the *shinkansen*, stop only briefly in order to maintain their timetables. Thus, travelers are encouraged to line up

Modern train in the Kansai region of Western Honshu

on some platforms: look out for floor markings relating to each set of doors. There may also be numbers correlating to carriage numbers for trains with reserved seats. Despite these measures, central Tokyo's trains, especially on the Yamanote loop line, often get overcrowded, and white-gloved staff are even employed to help push people in.

Train stations in major tourist areas have baggage lockers and information booths; staff here may speak English and occasionally other languages.

On-Board Facilities

Services on shinkansen and other long-distance routes usually include trolleys for snacks and beverages, and the sale of *bento* lunchboxes and edible *omiyage* (souvenirs). There is often a choice of Western- (sit-down) and Japanese-style (squat) toilets. Toilets and washrooms may be electronically operated, requiring a hand to be passed in front of a panel for flushing, or under a tap to start water flowing.

The Japan Rail Pass

In a country with some of the world's highest train fares, the Japan Rail Pass is a wonderful deal specially devised for people visiting Japan on tourist visas. However, the Pass must be purchased from an agent abroad, before the visit. It is not for sale inside Japan itself.

The Pass gives unlimited travel on all JR lines and affiliated buses and ferries, including the N'EX train *(see p378)* from Narita into Tokyo, city-center JR trains including Tokyo's Yamanote loop line, and *shinkansen*, except Nozomi. (If you board a Nozomi, you will be asked to pay for the entire fare.) Subways and private railroads are not included. You may still have to reserve a seat on long-distance trains, but the reservation will be free.

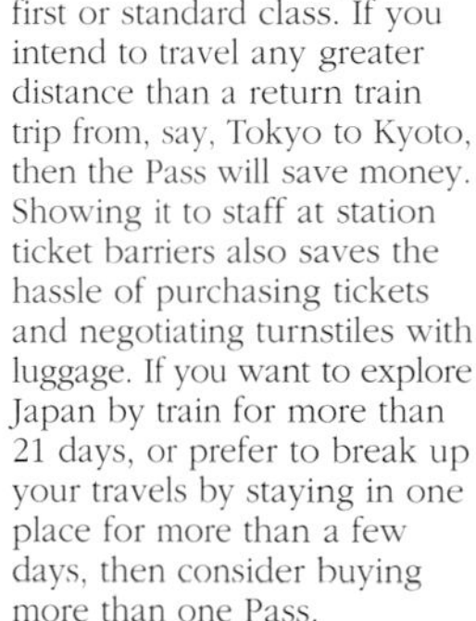

The Japan Rail Pass

You can choose a 7-day, 14-day, or 21-day Pass, first or standard class. If you intend to travel any greater distance than a return train trip from, say, Tokyo to Kyoto, then the Pass will save money. Showing it to staff at station ticket barriers also saves the hassle of purchasing tickets and negotiating turnstiles with luggage. If you want to explore Japan by train for more than 21 days, or prefer to break up your travels by staying in one place for more than a few days, then consider buying more than one Pass.

JNTO offices *(see p362)* will have a full list of Rail Pass agents in your country (they do not sell Passes themselves).

Staffed exit lane for holders of the Japan Rail Pass

The agent will issue a **Japan Rail Pass Exchange Order**, usually at a price based on the day's rate of exchange with the yen. This voucher must be exchanged for the Japan Rail Pass proper at designated JR Travel Service Centers in Japan, including Narita and Kansai airports and major train stations. You need to show your passport. When you exchange your voucher for a Pass, you must specify the date on which you wish to start using it; this can be any date within three months of issue of the Exchange Order.

Bear in mind that after the start date of the Pass, its cost cannot be refunded, and neither the Exchange Order nor the Pass can be replaced if lost or stolen.

Other Passes

There are also other less expensive regional rail passes. The **JR East Rail Pass** covers Honshu northeast of Tokyo, and can only be purchased outside Japan. There are two types of **JR West Rail Pass**: the **Sanyo Area Pass** covers the Nozomi *shinkansen*, as well as regular bullet trains from Osaka to Okayama, Hiroshima, and Hakata; the **Kansai Area Pass** includes Osaka, Kobe, Kyoto, and Nara. Both can be purchased within or outside Japan.

Most cities have their own special tickets: ask at local TICs or "i" centers. The **Tokyo Free Kippu** covers most of the JR and subway lines in the central Tokyo area.

Directory

JR Network Information

JR Infoline
English-language service:
(03) 3423-0111, 10am–6pm Mon–Fri, exc public hols.

JR Travel Service Center (View Plaza Tokyo)
Tokyo stn, Yaesu side.
(03) 3212-7059, 10am–6:30pm Mon–Fri; 10am–5pm, Sat, Sun, and public hols.

Using Train Ticket Machines

Basic fare tickets for short distances are usually available from vending machines. Some machines accept ¥1,000, ¥5,000, and ¥10,000 notes, and all should supply change. At some stations, maps are provided in English translation, showing in which fare zone your destination lies.

If you are in doubt about the cost of a trip, simply buy a cheap ticket and pay any excess at the destination by using the Fare Adjustment machine near the exit barrier. Some have an English translation facility in the style of an ATM. The machine will supply you with another ticket.

If there is no such machine, or you cannot understand it, the staff will work out the excess for payment. You will not be penalized for having the wrong value ticket.

Vending machines for basic fare train tickets

Using Green Windows

Tickets and seat reservations for longer trips can be purchased at *Midori-no-madoguchi* (Green Windows) at JR train stations. You can also buy tickets at Travel Service Centers in the larger stations, and from authorized travel agents. Note that credit cards are not always accepted.

Seat reservations are recommended for most long-distance trips, for a small extra charge or free if you have a Pass. The reservation ticket will bear the date and time of the train and also the coach and seat number. Ask the vendor to point out which numbers refer to each element if you are in doubt. On the platform, find the number that corresponds with the coach number, and line up.

Other Forms of Public Transportation

Kagoshima sightseeing bus

There are numerous systems of local transportation in the major cities, all of which are efficient, safe, and clean. The only complication for foreigners is in the purchase of tickets: systems vary from city to city, vending machines tend to be only in Japanese, and few staff speak English.

Subway Systems

The Tokyo subway system *(see Back Endpaper)* is extensive and color-coded on maps to match the color of the cars. The second largest subway system is in Osaka. Yokohama, Fukuoka, Kyoto, Sapporo, and some other cities also have systems. Modes of operation differ slightly.

The JR Rail Pass is not honored on the Tokyo Subway or any other subway tracks. Purchase a ticket from either a vending machine or a ticket window.

Subway ticket vending machines, even in Tokyo, are usually only in Japanese. This may seem daunting at first, but with a color-coded transliterated map, such as the one of the Tokyo Subway System at the back of this book, you should find that matching the Japanese characters of your destination with those on the fare chart by the machine is not too difficult. The chart will show in Arabic numerals how much to pay. Press the corresponding fare key on the machine and insert the money. Change will be dispensed with the ticket.

As with overland train tickets, if you are in any doubt about how much to pay, then simply buy the cheapest ticket and pay the excess at the end. The ticket may be punched when passing through the gate, but increasingly more likely has to be put through an automatic machine.

Station names are often displayed on platform signboards in romanized *(romaji)* form as well as Japanese.

All mass-transit systems close at around midnight until about 5am.

Entrance to subway tracks at Hakata station, Fukuoka

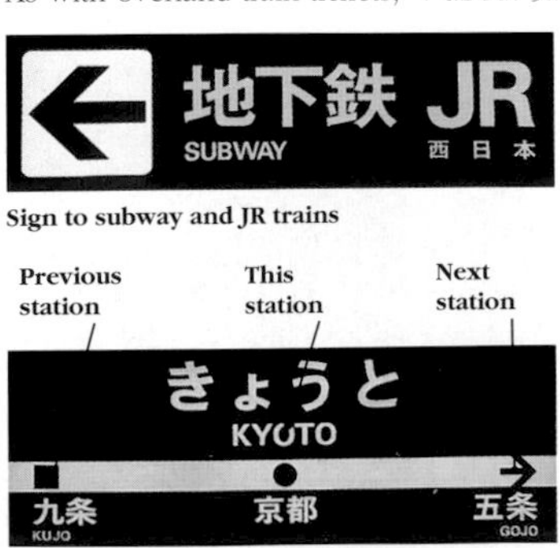

Sign to subway and JR trains

Previous station **This station** **Next station**

Destination sign on wall of subway platform

Tokyo Subway ticket machine

Interior of public tram in Nagasaki

Trams

Hiroshima and Nagasaki still have street cars, or trams; Sapporo retains this mode of transportation, too. Only one tram line remains in Tokyo, the Arakawa *(see p97)*. There are also a few oddities, like the Enoden Railway, at Kamakura, which is part-train, part-tram, sometimes running down the center of the street.

Fares and systems for paying on trams differ from city to city; some charge a flat fare, whatever the distance traveled. The fare machine is sometimes manned separately. Follow the example of other passengers as to when to pay, and whether to pay the fare collector or put money into the box.

Kochi bus dog logo

Monorail Systems

Many cities now operate monorail systems. They are all easy to negotiate and ride. Hiroshima enjoys one such line, which was installed for the Asian Games of 1994. In Tokyo, the monorail from Hamatsucho links with Haneda Airport; the new Yurikamome line links Shinbashi with Tokyo Teleport Town and the far side of the Rainbow Bridge *(see pp98–9)*.

City Buses

Bus depots *(basu noriba)* are often located close to train stations in cities, usually on the same side as where taxis line up. The method of paying fares varies. Some buses are boarded at the front, and the fare – usually a flat rate – deposited into a slot beside the driver. If in doubt, state your destination and offer the driver a selection of small coins to pick out. Disembark from the door in the middle of the bus.

A second system invites passengers to step aboard toward the center or back of the bus; a small machine distributes numbered tickets. The number on this ticket should be matched to a lighted panel at the front of the bus, which shows fares to be paid. If the ticket reads "2," look along the line at the top of the panel and check the sum in yen below the corresponding figure. Drop this amount into the box by the driver when you get off.

Do not step down from either exit until the bus comes to a complete halt, or the doors will not open automatically. When in doubt, observe how local people ride the bus and follow suit.

Long-Distance Buses

The efficiency and extent of the rail network in Japan is such that very few foreign tourists attempt to use long-distance buses. However, the bus network is comprehensive, and for those without a JR Rail Pass, a bus is a much cheaper option. While styles of seating and services may vary, such buses are uniformly comfortable, often with guides, toilets, and even onboard food and beverage services. Local information centers have timetable details.

Ferries and Tourist Boats

Tickets for most ferries can be bought at the ferry terminal on the day of departure. Usually there is a form to fill in, which enables the ferry company to compile a list of passengers. JNTO's travel manual details the main services. There are many long-distance ferry routes, including to mainland Asia *(see p379)*, but tourists will probably find flying more convenient.

Many boats these days are for tourism purposes only. Flat-bottomed punts are quite popular, with boatmen in traditional clothing.

Gaily painted tourist boat at Matsushima, Northern Honshu

Private Transportation

JAPAN IS AN ENJOYABLE and relatively safe country in which to take to the road. In the countryside, renting a car is by far the best and most flexible way to get around. It is also easy and surprisingly inexpensive to rent a vehicle, though the cost of road tolls and parking charges can quickly mount up. Road surfaces and rental cars are generally well maintained. Driving is on the left. The main problem for foreigners on the road is in trying to decipher road signs in already unfamilar territory. Other problems include such hazards as roads blocked by snow in winter, flooding during the rainy season, and occasional landslides.

Taxi with smartly dressed driver, typical in Japan

TAXIS

ALL LICENSED TAXIS in Japan have green license plates; avoid unlicensed vehicles. A red light on top of the vehicle indicates that it is free. You can flag a taxi or look for a stand – a number of taxi companies operate in each city. Costs are quite high: on a par with, say, yellow cabs in New York. Space for luggage is limited.

The doors of Japanese taxis are operated electrically by the driver from inside; it is not advisable to close or open the taxi door yourself.

Few taxi drivers speak much English. As with finding the location of anything in Japan *(see p376)*, it is best to carry a map marked with instructions in Japanese and the phone number of your destination.

RENTING A CAR

VEHICLES ARE available for rental at ports of entry, from major train stations, and local dealers. Visitors must produce an international driver's license (International Driving Permit) at the car-rental agency. Unfortunately, some countries, like Germany and Switzerland, have no reciprocal arrangement with Japan for honoring international driver's licenses.

The two largest car-rental companies with English facility are **Nippon Rent-A-Car** and **Nissan Rent-A-Car**. Costs are on a par with the US and Western Europe, in some cases cheaper.

Drivers with rental cars are protected financially from breakdown with insurance. It is a good idea to take out membership of the **Japan Automobile Federation**, which issues a booklet with emergency numbers for foreigners in case of breakdown, and is linked with similar organizations abroad.

Quiet road in the Mount Aso caldera

ROAD TOLLS

MOST NATIONAL HIGHWAYS are free, but many private roads charge tolls. There is no consistent system of charging: a short distance may cost anything from ¥100 to ¥10,000.

Road sign at a crossing in Kyoto, with some *romaji* transliteration

SERVICING

FUEL IS readily available in Japan. The cost of it compares favorably with Europe, but is double the price of Canadian fuel and nearly three times the cost of gas in the US. The international chain ESSO is familiar to drivers in Japan. JOMO is a popular Japanese chain, the name derived from the phrase "Joy of Motoring."

PARKING

PUBLIC PARKING is available – at a price. The general rule is that the closer to any city center, the more expensive parking fees become. To overcome the problem of lack of sufficient space, the Japanese have developed various innovative parking solutions. Lifts and roll-over systems are common; two-car families with only a single parking space often resolve the problem with a two-tier stacking system.

"Beware of bears" road sign in forested mountain region

Rules of the Road

Japanese drive on the left-hand side of the road. On local roads, the maximum speed allowed is 40 kph (25 mph); on bigger roads, 50 kph (31 mph); on highways (expressways) maximum speeds vary from 80–100 kph (50–62 mph). One important difference with roads in Japan is that drivers may not turn left on a red light, as allowed in some other countries.

While in general the Japanese drive carefully and safely, they have a habit of driving over intersections after a light has turned red. It is not a good idea to follow suit, and vehicles to the front and rear should be observed carefully when approaching traffic lights.

Signs are easier to decipher in cities, but the pressure of traffic and the network of roads, which may include several one on top of another, can be daunting for even the most experienced driver from abroad. A wide berth should be given to dump trucks, whose drivers are paid by the load and are therefore under pressure to drive fast; also watch out for large gangs of notorious *boso-zoku* ("crazy drivers") who gather on weekends in convoys of customized cars and motorcycles, with the sole intention of waking up neighborhoods and causing trouble.

Road Maps

Most foreign drivers rely on *Japan: A Bilingual Atlas*, published by Kodansha International, which gives route maps but does not indicate toll roads or charges. For longer-term visitors who are seriously interested in driving around Japan, Shobunsha's thick *Road Atlas Japan* is the best investment. The atlas can be purchased at specialist travel book stores abroad or any book store in Japan that has a good foreign book section.

Renting a Motorbike

In the capital, **SCS** (Sato Credit Service) is a motorbike sports shop that specializes in offering rentals. For renting a motorbike outside of Tokyo, check for local motorbike dealers through the nearest TICs and "i" centers. A 50cc scooter can be ridden on an international driver's license; anything above this capacity will require an international motorcycle license.

Rickshaw, an old-fashioned mode of transportation

Bicycles and Rickshaws

The great number of bikes, even in cities such as Tokyo, can be a surprising sight to foreigners with a perception of Japan as a land full of high-tech cars. Rickshaws *(jin-riki-sha)* are also back in fashion in predominantly tourist areas such as Kyoto and even Ginza in Central Tokyo. In rural areas, horse-drawn open carriages are common and are popular for weddings.

Cyclists leisurely cruising down Yufuin's main street

There are often bicycle rental companies in tourist areas. The main thing to note is that sidewalks are not off-limits to cyclists. Indeed, some towns prefer cyclists to use sidewalks rather than roads, ringing their bells to alert pedestrians. Japanese roads do not have designated cycle lanes, as in China, but there is a good network of cycling paths throughout the country. Bicycles are among the few items that are often stolen in Japan, so be sure to use a bicycle lock if one has been provided.

Directory

Japan Automobile Federation
3-5-8 Shiba-Koen, Minato-ku, Tokyo 105-0011.
(03) 3436-2811.
www.jaf.or.jp

Nippon Rent-A-Car
(03) 3485-7196 or (03)-3469 0919.

Nissan Rent-A-Car
(03) 5424-4123 for reservations.

SCS
2-1-16 Haksan, Bunkyo-ku, Tokyo 112-0001.
(03) 3815-6221.

General Index

Page numbers in **bold** type refer to main entries.

A

Abe Kobo
The Woman in the Dunes 206
Accommodations
long-term 369
see also Hotels
Adams, William 53, 133
Adashino Nenbutsu-ji Temple (Kyoto City) 171
Addresses 376–7
in Kyoto 150
Aichi Prefectural Gymnasium (Nagoya) 350, 353
Aikawa (Sado Island) 267
Aikawa Museum (Sado Island) 267
Aikido *see* Martial arts
Ainokura 140
Ainu
culture **281**
population 275
Ainu Museum (Sapporo) 279
Air Travel 378–9
airports 378–9
domestic flights 379
Kansai International (Osaka) 197, 379
Narita (Tokyo) 378
Aizu Minzokukan Folk Museum (Inawashiro) 267
Aizu-Wakamatsu **266**
hotels 305
restaurants 337
Akan 281
Akan Kohan 281
Akan National Park **281**
hotel 307
restaurant 339
Akasaka Blitz (Tokyo) 105, 107
Akasaka District (Tokyo) **95**
Sanno Matsuri 41
Akasaka Prince Hotel (Tokyo) 95
Akihabara Electronics Distirict (Tokyo) **69**
Akihito, Emperor 55
Akiyoshi-dai Tablelands **212**
Akiyoshido Cave 212
Akkeshi Bay **284**
All-Japan Kendo Association (Tokyo) 350, 353
All-Nippon Airways 378, 379
Almond (Tokyo) 94–5
Amagi Yugashima 133
Amami Island 243
hotel 303
Amami Oshima Tsumugi Mura 243
Amanohashidate Sand Bar **206**
hotel 298
Amaterasu 22, 47, 239
Ameyoko Market (Tokyo) **80**
Amida Buddha 25
Amlux Toyota (Tokyo) 97
Anan Coast 219
hotel 302
Ando Hiroshige *see* Hiroshige
Ando Tadao 21
Himeji City Museum of Literature 203
Suntory Museum (Osaka) 197
Annunciation, The (El Greco) 205
Antiques
shops in Kyoto City 175
Aoba Castle (Sendai) 268
Aoi Matsuri (Kyoto City) 38, 40, 166, 178
Aomori **273**
Nebuta Matsuri 39
Aoshima Island 242
Aoyagi-ke (Kakunodate) 272
Arakawa Nature Park (Tokyo) 97
Arakawa Tram Line (Tokyo) **97**
Arakawa Yuen Park (Tokyo) 97
Arashiyama District (Kyoto City) **170**
Arata Isozaki
Cho Toshokan (Kokura) 228
JR Yufuin Station 229
Kita Kyushu Municipal Art Museum (Kokura) 228
Archery
equestrian 39
see also Kyudo
Architecture
Buddhist 24–5
modern 20–21
traditional houses **28–9**
Shinto 22–3
Zen Buddhist temple layout **131**
see also Houses
Arima Onsen 199, 347
Arimatsu 137
Arita 233
Aritsugu (Kyoto City) 174, 175
Armor, samurai **51**
Art Museum (Kagoshima) 242
Arts and Crafts **34–5**
books 401
in Okinawa **251**
shopping 342–3
shops in Kyoto 176–7
shops in Tokyo 102, 103
see also Museums and Galleries, and under individual crafts
Asahikawa 280
Asahi-dake 280
Asahi-do (Kyoto City) 176, 177
Asakura Fumio 80
Asakura Museum (Tokyo) 80
Asakusa Jinja (Tokyo) 83
Asakusa Kannon (Tokyo) *see* Senso-ji Temple
Asama 145
Ashikaga family 49
Ashikaga Yoshiaki 52
Ashikaga Yoshimasa 49
Ashikaga Yoshimitsu 168
Aso, Mount *see* Mountains
Asobe (Kyoto City) 176, 177
Asuka Plain **191**
Atomic Bomb Museum (Nagasaki) 237
ATM services 375
Automobiles
Amlux Toyota (Tokyo) 97
factory visits 355
industry 20
renting 384
Avanti Building (Kyoto City) 174, 175
Awa-Odori Festival (Tokushima) 42, **219**

B

BAL Building (Kyoto City) 174, 175
Bamboo
buying 344
crafts 35
groves 18
shops in Kyoto 176, 177
Bandai-Asahi National Park **267**
Bank of Japan (Tokyo) **66**
Banks and banking 372–3
banknotes 373
Bar Isn't It (Kyoto City) 179
Baseball 351, 353
in Tokyo 106, 107
Basho, Matsuo **273**
birthplace 191
Narrow Road to the Deep North, The 273
Saga Diary 171
Bashofu fabric 251
Bashofu Kaikan 251
Basketware
akebi 273
Basketware (cont.)
itayazaiku 272
Bathing 346
at *ryokan* 291
Battle of Okinawa 245, **249**
Battle of the Sea of Japan 91
Battle of Ueno 74–5
Battledore Fair 43
Beaches
Eef (Kume Island) 252
Futamigaura 192
Goza 192
Ishinami 242
Kondoi Misaki (Taketomi Island) 253
Yonaha Maehama (Miyako Island) 253
Bean-Throwing Festival 43
Beer Museum Ebisu (Tokyo) 99
Beishu (Tokyo) 102, 103
Bengara (Tokyo) 101, 102, 103
Bento box *see* Food and Drink
Beppu **228–9**, 347
hotels 303
restaurants 335
Bicycles
renting 385
Big Off (Kyoto City) 175
Bingata dyeing 248, 251
Birdland (Tokyo) 105, 107
Birds *see* Wildlife
Birthrate 15
Biwa *see* Lake Biwa
Bizen Pottery Traditional and Contemporary Art Museum (Inbe) 204
Blue Note Tokyo 105, 107
Blues Alley Japan (Tokyo) 105, 107
Bon 39, 41, 42
Bon Odori dancing 39, 42
Bonsai 35
Books
further reading **401**
Bookstores
Jena (Tokyo) 63, 104, 107
Kinokuniya (Tokyo) 86, 104, 107
Jinbocho Booksellers' District (Tokyo) **68**
Maruzen (Kyoto City) 174, 175
Maruzen (Tokyo) 104, 107
Shinsendo (Kyoto City) 178, 179
Bosatsu 25
Boshin War 266
Boso Historical Park 126
Botanical Gardens (Sapporo) 279
Botchan (Natsume Soseki) 220
Bowing 364–5
Brancusi, Constantin 66
Bridgestone Museum of Art (Tokyo) 66
Buddha 25
Amida Nyorai (Byodo-in, Uji City) 173
Dainichi Nyorai (Toji, Kyoto City) 152
Great Buddha (Kamakura) 15, 128
Great Buddha Vairocana (Nara) 186–7
Kokuzo Bosatsu (Nara) 180, 186
Miroku Bosatsu (Koryu-ji, Kyoto City) 169
Nadi Botokesan Buddha (Tokyo) 82
Ryozen Kannon (Kyoto City) 161
Tachiki Kannon (Chuzen-ji, Nikko) 265
Usuki Stone Buddhas **229**
Yakushi Nyorai (Horyu-ji) 190
Yakushi Nyorai (Toji, Kyoto City) 152
Buddhism 15, **24–5**
festivals 24, 38–43
Hana Matsuri (Buddha's birthday) 40

Buddhism (cont.)
introduction to Japan 47
Jizo statues **24**
meditation 25
organizations 257
Paradise gardens 26
pilgrimages 25
Pure Land 25
religious studies 257
sects **269**
traditional arts and crafts 34–5
see also Pagodas, Temples, and under individual sects
Budo Center (Kyoto) 351, 353
Buke Yashiki (Matsue) 207
Bullfighting 221
Bullfinch Exchange (Dazaifu) 43
Bunkamura (Tokyo) 92
cinema 105, 107
Bunraku **33**
see also Theaters
Bunsendo (Tokyo) 101
Busena Resort (Okinawa) 250
Buses 383
Business 368–9
attitudes and structures 368
cards 368
entertaining 369
facilities 368
negotiating 368–9
Buto 105
Butsudan 25, 29
Byakkotai (White Tigers) 266
Byodo-in Temple (Uji City) 26, 173

C

Cafe David (Kyoto City) 179
Café Indépendants (Kyoto City) 179
Calendar 363
Chinese lunar 40
Gregorian 40
Japan through the year **40–43**
Calligraphy 34
buying calligraphy sets 344
Camera Doi (Tokyo) 101, 103
Camera equipment
shops in Tokyo 101, 103
Camping 289
Cape Ashizuri 220
hotel 302
Cape Kyan 249
Cape Muroto 220
Cape Nosappu 285
Castles
Aoba (Sendai) 268
Gifu 137
Hagi 213
Hikone 206
Himeji **200–3**
Hirosaki 273
Hiroshima 209
Inuyama 137
Iwakuni 212
Kanazawa 142
Kochi 220
Kumamoto 238
Matsue 207
Matsumoto 145
Matsuyama 220
Morioka 271
Nagoya 137
Nijo (Kyoto City) **154–5**
Okayama 204
Osaka 194
Shuri 248
Takamatsu 218
Tsuruga (Aizu-Wakamatsu) 266
Tsuwano 213
Catching a Goldfish with a Gourd (Josetsu) 169
Cemeteries
Foreigners' Cemetery (Yokohama) 127
Cemeteries (cont.)
Hodogaya Commonwealth Cemetery (Yokohama) 127
Center Gai (Tokyo) 92
Central Honshu **122–47**
climate 45
hotels **295–7**
map **124–5**
regional cuisine 123
restaurants **327–30**
transportation 125
Central Tokyo **60–71**
hotels **292**
maps 58–9, **61**
restaurants **324–5**
transportation 61
Ceramics 34
Bizen-ware 204, 344
buying 344
Hagi-ware **213**
Imari-ware 233
Karatsu-ware 233
Kutani-ware 143
Kyomizu-yaki 161, 176
Onta-ware 232
Saga Pottery Towns Tour **233**
shops in Kyoto 176, 177
shops in Tokyo 102, 103
Tsuboya pottery 248
Chagu-chagu Umakko (Morioka) 41
Charms 23
Cherry blossom 13, 17
Chichibu-Tama National Park **132**
hotel 295
Chido Museum (Tsuruoka) 268
Children, facilities for 361
Chinatowns
Kobe 198
Yokohama 127
Chion-in Temple (Kyoto City) **162**
Chiran **243**
restaurant 335
Christianity
introduction to Japan 49
persecution of Christians 53, 234, 237
tours 357
see also Churches
Chubu region 124, 256, 377
Chugoku region 182, 377
Churches
Oura Catholic Church (Nagasaki) 236
Russian Orthodox Church (Hakodate) 278
Shrine to the 26 Martyrs (Nagasaki) 234
St. Xavier's Church (Kagoshima) 242
Tsuwano Catholic Church 213
Urakami Catholic Church (Nagasaki) 237
Chushingura 51, 99, 157
Cinema *see* Film
Clavell, James 53, 133
Climate **44–5**
seasons 40
when to visit 360
Clothes
buying 345
clothing sizes 341
etiquette 365
maiko costume 157
traditional **36–7**
shops in Tokyo 101, 104
what to bring 360
see also Kimonos
Club Quattro (Tokyo) 105, 107
Communications 374–7
Conversion chart 363
CN Playguide 104, 107
Comme des Garçons (Tokyo) 101, 103
Commuter culture 89
Confucianism 15
Confucian Shrine (Nagasaki) 236
Conversation lounges 354–5
Cormorant fishing
Arashiyama 170
Gifu 40, 41, 137
Courier companies 376
Crafts *see* Arts and Crafts
Credit cards 372, 373
in hotels 288
Cube, The (Kyoto City) 174, 175
Currency 373
Customs information 361

D

Daiba (Tokyo) **98–9**
Daigo-ji Temple (Kyoto City) **173**
Daikaku-ji Temple (Kyoto City) 171
Daily Yomiuri 104, 374
Daimaru Department Store (Kyoto City) 174, 175
Daimonji Bonfire (Kyoto City) 42
daimyo 50
Daimyo Clock Museum (Tokyo) 80
Daimyo Gyoretsu (Hakone) 42
Daisan Daiba Historic Park (Tokyo) 99
Daisen-in Subtemple (Kyoto City) 26, **166–7**
Daisetsu-zan National Park **280**
hotel 307
restaurant 339
Daishin-in Subtemple (Kyoto City) 169
Daisho-in Temple (Miyajima Island) 211
Daitoku-ji Temple (Kyoto City) 163, **166–7**
Dance
Awa Odori **219**
Bon Odori 39, 42
venues in Tokyo 105, 107
see also Buto, Geisha, Kagura
Date Masamune 268
Dazaifu **231**
Usokae 43
Degas, Edgar 205
Dejima (Nagasaki) 235
Denshokan Museum (Kakunodate) 272
Department stores 342
in Kyoto 174, 175
in Tokyo 100, 103
see also names of individual stores
Dewa Sanzan **268**
Dewa Sanzan Shrine 268
Dewanoumi Beya (Tokyo) 106, 107
Dezomeshiki (Tokyo) 43
Diet Building (Tokyo) **67**
Disabled visitors 361
Doburoku Matsuri (Shirakawa-go) 42
Dogen-zaka (Tokyo) 92
Dogfighting 220
Dogo Onsen (Matsuyama) 220, 347
Doll Festival 40
Doll House (Himeji) 203
Dolls **271**
anesan ningyo 271
buying 345
kokeshi 268, 271
ohinasama 271
oki-agari 267
oshirasama 271
sarukko 271
shops in Kyoto 176, 177
Domoto Insho 83, 168
Doors
fusuma 29
shoji 29
Dorokyo gorge 193
Dosojin stones **144**

Dress *see* Clothes
Driving 384–5
parking 384–5
renting a car 384
road maps 385
road tolls 384
rules of the road 385
Dry-landscape gardens 26
Duty-free allowances 361

E

Earthquakes 18
Great Hanshin (Kobe) **198**
Great Kanto 58
safety guidelines 370
East Shinjuku (Tokyo) 16, 58
Street-by-Street map **86–7**
Ebisu District (Tokyo) **99**
Ebisu Garden Place (Tokyo) 99
cinemas 105
Economy 16–17
growth since World War II 55
recession in 1990s 16–17
Edo (Tokyo)
history 58
Edo period
culture 53
floating world of *ukiyo-e* **81**
post roads 123, 133, 136
Edo-Tokyo Museum (Tokyo) 98
Eef Beach (Kume Island) 252
Eihei-ji Temple **144**
Eikan-do Temple (Kyoto City) 164, 165
Eisai *see* Zen Buddhism
Electrical and electronic goods
Ameyoko Market **80**
shops in Kyoto 175
shops in Tokyo 101, 103
Electricity 341, 363
E-mail facilities 375
Emergencies 370, 371
Endo Shusaku
Kazan (Volcano) 243
Enryaku-ji Temple (Kyoto City) **172–3**
Entertainment
information and tickets 362
in Kyoto **178–9**
in Tokyo **104–7**
Ernie Pyle Memorial (Ie Island) 251
Etiquette **364–7**
bowing 364–5
food and drink 312–13, 364
onsen 346
tea ceremony 163

F

Factory visits 355
Fan Zhongyan 69
Fans 37
Fax facilities 375
Fenollosa, Ernest 187
Ferries 379, 383
Festival of the Ages (Kyoto City) 39, 42
Festival of the Dead *see* Bon
Festival Float Hall (Takayama) 140
Festivalgate (Osaka) 196
Festivals (Matsuri) **38–43**
Fifty-Three Stations of the Tokaido (Hiroshige) 81, 135
Film
Tokyo International Film Festival 105, 107
venues in Tokyo 105, 107
Floating Garden Observatory (Osaka) 196
Food and drink **312–33**
Bento Box 317
Central Honshu's cuisine 123
Food and drink (cont.)
Classic Dishes **316–17**
etiquette **312–13**
Haute Cuisine 320
Kyoto's cuisine 149
Osaka's cuisine 196
popular fish in Japan 319
Reading the Menu **314–5**
rice 313
rice crackers **314**
safety 370–71
seasonal patterns 313
Sushi and Sashimi **318–19**
tuna fish supplies **64**
vegetarian 309, 320
wagashi (sweets) 320, 345
What to Drink in Japan **322–3**
Zen cuisine 130, 320
see also Restaurants
Fugetsudo sweet shop (Tokyo) 62
Fuji Five Lakes **134–5**
hotels 295
restaurants 327
Fuji, Mount *see* Mountains
Fuji TV headquarters (Tokyo) 99
Fujii Kei Shoten (Kyoto City) 176, 177
Fujiwara family 48, 270
Fujiwara Kiyohira 270
Fujiwara Takayoshi 96
Fuji-Yoshida 135
Fukiya **205**
hotel 298
Fukuoka **230–31**
Hakata Dontaku Matsuri 40
hotels 303
map 230
restaurants 335–6
Yamagasa Matsuri 41
Fukuoka Asian Art Museum 231
Fukuoka City Museum 230
Fukuoka Kokusai Center 350, 353
Fukushima Shamisen (Kanazawa) 143
Funadomari (Rebun Island) 280
Furoshiki 343
shops in Tokyo 101, 103
Fushimi 14
Fushimi Shrine **173**
Futamigaura Beach 192
Futara-san Shrine (Nikko) 259

G

Galleria Grafica (Tokyo) 102, 103
Gallery Center Building (Tokyo) 62
Gallery K1 (Kyoto City) 176, 177
GameBoy 20
Ganjin 187
Ganman-ga-fuchi Pools (Nikko) 259
Gardens (general) **26–7**
"borrowed landscape" 26
seasons 27
types 26–7
Gardens (individual)
Botanical Gardens (Sapporo) 279
Byodo-in Temple (Uji City) 26, 173
Daisen-in Subtemple (Kyoto City) 26, **166–7**
Daishin-in Subtemple (Kyoto City) 169
Dembo-in (Tokyo) 82
East Garden of the Imperial Palace (Tokyo) 67
Ginkaku-ji Temple (Kyoto City) 26, 164
Hama Detached Palace (Tokyo) **64–5**
Hirara Tropical Botanical Gardens (Miyako Island) 252
Hirayama (Chiran) 243
Ishibashi Bunka Center (Kurume) 232
Iso Tei-en (Kagoshima) 26, 242
Isui-en (Nara) 185
Gardens (cont.)
Joei-ji Temple (Yamaguchi) 212
Katsura Imperial Villa (Kyoto City) **170**
Keishun-in Subtemple (Kyoto City) 169
Kenroku en (Kanazawa) 27, 142
Kinkaku-ji Temple (Kyoto City) **168**
Koishikawa Korakuen (Tokyo) **69**
Koko-en (Himeji) 203
Koraku-en (Okayama) 204
Koto-in Subtemple (Kyoto City) 167
Meigetsu-in Temple (Kamakura) 130
Minami-ike Shobuda (Tokyo) 90
Morishige (Chiran) 243
Motsu-ji Temple (Hiraizumi) 26
Murin-an (Kyoto City) 27, 165
Nai-en (Tokyo) 90
Nanzen-ji Temple (Kyoto City) **165**
Nanzen-in Subtemple (Kyoto City) 165
Nikko Botanical Gardens 259
Ninna-ji Temple (Kyoto City) **169**
Oyakuen Herb Garden (Aizu-Wakamatsu) 266
Reiun-in Subtemple (Kyoto City) 169
Retired Emperor's Palace (Kyoto City) 166
Rikugi-en (Tokyo) **97**
Ryoan-ji Temple (Kyoto City) 26, **168**
Ryogen-in Subtemple (Kyoto City) 167
Sankei-en (Yokohama) 127
Sata (Chiran) 243
Shin Edogawa (Tokyo) 97
Shisen-do Temple (Kyoto City) **172**
Shosei-en (Kyoto City) 153
Shoyoen (Nikko) 259
Shugaku-in Imperial Villa (Kyoto City) **172**
Shukkei-en Garden (Hiroshima) 209
Suizen-ji (Kumamoto) 238
Taizo-in Subtemple (Kyoto City) 169
Tenju-an Subtemple (Kyoto City) 165
Tenryu-ji Temple (Kyoto City) 170
Toshi-mashi-tei (Yanagawa) 232
Zuiho-in Subtemple (Kyoto City) 167
Zuisen-ji (Kamakura) 129
see also Parks
Gassho-zukuri houses **141**
Gateway Country (Tokyo) 101, 103
Gauguin, Paul 205
Geiko see Geisha
Geisha 17, **157**, 167
dance performances in Kyoto 178, 179
geiko 157
in Kanazawa 143
maiko 157
Ghostly Japan (Hearn) 207
Gift-giving 367
Gifu **137**
cormorant fishing 40, 41, 137
hotel 296
restaurant 327
Gifu Castle 137
Ginkado (Tokyo) 101
Ginkaku-ji Temple (Kyoto City) 26, 164, **165**
Ginza (Tokyo) 59
Street-by-Street map **62–3**
Ginza Art Space (Tokyo) 102, 103
Ginza Graphic Gallery (Tokyo) 102, 103

Gio-ji Temple (Kyoto City) 171
Gion, Eastern and the Higashiyama (Kyoto City) 160–61
Gion Corner (Kyoto City) 156, 178, 179
Gion District (Kyoto City) **156**
Gion Kobu Kaburenjo (Kyoto City) 156, 178, 179
Gion Matsuri (Kyoto City) 41, 178
Glimpses of Unfamiliar Japan (Hearn) 207
Glover, Thomas 236
Glover Park (Nagasaki) 236
Go-Mizuno'o 172
Gokayama 140
Golden Gai (Tokyo) 87
Golden Pavilion (Mishima) 167
Golden Pavilion *see* Kinkaku-ji Temple
Golden Week 40, 360
Golf 351, 353
Goodwill Guides 354
Goryokaku Fort (Hakodate) 278
Goryokaku Park (Hakodate) 278
Gosamaru, Lord 250
Goshikinuma trail (Bandai-Asahi National Park) 267
Goshogake *onsen* 272
Goto Art Museum (Tokyo) **96**
Goto Keita 96
Goza Beach 192
Grass Fire Festival (Nara) 43
El Greco 205
Gyokusendo Cave **249**
Gyokusendo Okokumura 249

H

Hachijo no Miya Toshihito 170
Hachiko, Prince 268
Hachiko statue (Tokyo) 93
Hachiman-gu Festival (Kamakura) 39, 42
Hachimantai 272
Hagi **212–13**
Hagi Castle 213
Hagoita Ichi (Tokyo) 43
Haiden 23
Haiku **273**
  see also Basho and Shiki
Hair
  combs 37, 101
  geisha styles 157
  hairpins *(kanzashi)* 37, 100, 101
  traditional styles 37
Hakata *see* Fukuoka
Hakata Dontaku Matsuri (Fukuoka) 40
Hakata Machiya Folklore Museum (Fukuoka) 231
Hakkeijima Sea Paradise (Yokohama) 349
Hakkuchodai 284
Hakodate **278**
  hotels 307
  restaurants 339
Hakone 121, **132–3**
  Daimyo Gyoretsu 42
  hotels 295
  restaurant 328
Hakone Art Museum 132
Hakone-machi 133
Hakone Open-Air Museum 132
Hakone-Yumoto 132, 347
Hakui 144
Hama Detached Palace Garden (Tokyo) **64–5**
Hamada Shoji 205, 266
Hamamatsu Matsuri 40
Hana Matsuri 40
Hanae Mori 91
  shop 101, 103
Hanabi Taikai (Tokyo) 41
Hanamaki **270–71**
  hotel 305
Hanami see Cherry blossom
Hanami-koji (Kyoto City) 156
Hanazono Shrine (Tokyo) 87
Haniwa sculptures 79
Hankyu Department Store (Kyoto City) 174, 175
Hara Hiroshi
  Umeda Sky Building (Osaka) 21, 196
Hara Koji 152
Hara Shobu (Tokyo) 102, 103
Hara Tomitaro 127
Harajuku District **91**
Harunobu, Suzuki 81
Hatajuku 133
Hayashi Kimono (Tokyo) 101, 103
Hayashibara Museum of Art (Okayama) 204
Health **370–71**
  hospitals 371
  medical facilities 371
  traditional medicine **356**, **357**
Hearn, Lafcadio **207**
  Ghostly Japan 207
  Glimpses of Unfamiliar Japan 207
  Japan: An Interpretation 207
  In a Japanese Garden 207
Heda 133
Hedo Misaki Cape **251**
Hegura island 144
Heian period 48
Heian Shrine (Kyoto City) 162
Hibiya Chanter 105, 107
Hibiya District (Tokyo) **67**
Hida Folk Village (Takayama) 140
Hidari Jingoro 260
Hie Jinja (Tokyo) 95
Higashi Henna Cape (Miyako Island) 253
Higashi Hongan-ji Temple (Kyoto City) **153**
Higashi Pleasure District (Kanazawa) 143
Higashi-Hachimantai 272
Higashiyama (Kyoto City) **160–61**
Higeta Dyeworks (Mashiko) 266
High-tech Japan **20–21**
  factory visits 355
  science parks 349
  toys and games 20
Hikawa Maru (Yokohama) 127
Hiking 352
  books 401
Hikone 206
Hikone Castle 206
Himeji Castle **200–3**
  hotel 299
  restaurant 331
Himeji City Museum of Literature 203
Himiko, queen of Yamatai 47, 232
Hina Matsuri 40
Hinode Pier (Tokyo) 65
Hirafu 278
Hiraizumi **270**
  hotel 305
Hirara (Miyako Island) 252
Hirara Tropical Botanical Gardens (Miyako Island) 252
Hirata Kinenkan Museum (Takayama) 139
Hirohito, Emperor 55
Hirokane-tei (Fukiya) 205
Hirooka Antique (Kyoto City) 175
Hirosaki **273**
  hotel 306
  restaurants 337–8
Hirosaki Castle 273
Hiroshige 91
  birthplace 66
  Fifty-Three Stations of the Tokaido 81, 135
Hiroshige (cont.)
  Thirty-Six Views of Mount Fuji 135
Hiroshima **208–9**
  hotels 299
  restaurants 331
Hiroshima Castle 209
Historical parks 348
  Boso Historical Park 126
  Hida Folk Village (Takayama) 140
  Historical Village of Hokkaido 279
  Ise Sengoku Jidai Mura 348, 349
  Kyushu Yufuin Folk Art Village 229
  Meiji Mura 137, 348
  Nihon Minka-en 348, 349
  Nikko Edo Village 348, 349
  Noboribetsu Date Jidai Mura 348, 349
  Shikoku Mura Museum 218
History **46–55**
  books 401
  historical periods 47
Hojo Tokimune 130
  mausoleum 131
Hokkaido **274–85**
  climate 45, 275
  hotels **307**
  map **276–7**
  prefecture 377
  restaurants **339**
  transportation 276
Hokusai, Katsushika 81
  Thirty-Six Views of Mount Fuji 135
Hokusai-kan (Obuse) 145
Holland Village (Nagasaki) 237
Hollyhock Festival (Kyoto City) 38, 40
Home Visit System 354
Homestay Program 354, 355
Honda Museum (Kanazawa) 142
Honden 23
Hondo 25
Honen *see* Jodo Sect Buddhism
Honen-in Temple (Kyoto City) 164
Honshu *see* Central, Western, and Northern Honshu
Horse Festival (Morioka) 41
Horyu-ji Temple **190**
Hot springs *see Onsen*
Hotaka 145
Hotels **288–307**
  booking 288
  business 289
  capsule 289
  Central Honshu 295–7
  deluxe 288
  Hokkaido 307
  Homestay Program 354, 355
  Kyoto City 297–8
  Kyushu 303–5
  love hotels 289
  mid-range 288
  Northern Honshu 305–7
  Okinawa 305
  pensions 289
  Shikoku 302–3
  Tokyo 292–4
  traditional 290–91
  Western Honshu 298–302
Hotoke-ga-ura 273
Houses (general)
  gassho-zukuri **141**
  kabuto-zukuri 28
  kura 126, 266
  living in small spaces **97**
  magariya 271
  roof types **28**
  town houses *(machiya)* 28
  traditional Japanese **28–9**
Houses (individual)
  Aoyagi-ke (Kakunodate) 272
  Buke Yashiki (Matsue) 207
  Garyu Sanso (Ozu) 221
  Glover House (Nagasaki) 236

Houses (cont.)
Gyobu-tei (Kumamoto) 238
Hakushu Seika (Yanagawa) 232
Hirayama (Chiran) 243
Hirokane-tei (Fukiya) 205
Ishiguro-ke (Kakunodate) 272
Kai Honke (Kitakata) 266
Kikuya House (Hagi) 213
Kusakabe Heritage House (Takayama) 138
Mekata House (Iwakuni) 212
Miyara Donchi (Ishigaki Island) 253
Mori House (Tsuwano) 213
Morishige (Chiran) 243
Nakamura House **250**
Nakayama House (Tono) 271
Nishi House (Tsuwano) 213
Nomura House (Kanazawa) 142
Ringer House (Nagasaki) 236
Samurai Residence (Aizu-Wakamatsu) 266
Sata (Chiran) 243
Seisonkaku Villa (Kanazawa) 142
Shima Geisha House (Kanazawa) 143
Uezu-ke (Kume Island) 252
Walker House (Nagasaki) 236
Yoshijima Heritage House (Takayama) 138
see also Historical Parks
Hospitals 371
Huis Ten Bosch (Nagasaki) 237, 348
Hyogo Prefectural Museum of History (Himeji) 203

I

Ichihara (Kyoto City) 176, 177
Ichiriki (Kyoto City) 156
Ie Island **250–51**
Iga Ninja Museum 191
Iga-Ueno **191**
Iheya Island 251
Ikebana 35
Ikebukuro District (Tokyo) **97**
Ikema Island 253
Imari 233
Immigration regulations *see* Visas
Imperial family 14
descent from goddess Amaterasu 47
renounces divine status 55
social attitudes 364
Imperial Household Agency (Kyoto City) 166
Imperial Navy Underground HQ **249**
Imperial Palace (Kyoto City) 166
Imperial Palace (Tokyo) **67**
Imperial Park (Kyoto City) **166**
Imperial Theater (Tokyo) 66
In a Japanese Garden (Hearn) 207
Inari shrines *see* Shrines
Inaricho District (Tokyo) **80**
Inbe **204**
Indigo 35
Information Corner 362, 363
Inland Sea **218**
Inland Sea, The (Richie) 218
Insho Domoto Museum (Kyoto City) **168**
Insurance
car 384
travel 360
International Aikido Federation (Tokyo) 351, 353
International Karate Organization (Tokyo) 351, 353
Internet facilities 375
Inuyama **137**
hotel 295
restaurant 328
Inuyama Castle 137
Ippodo (Kyoto City) 176, 177
Irabu Island 253
Irezumi see Tattoos
Iriomote Island 253
hotel 305
Ise
Grand Shrine 14, 192
hotel 299
Inner Grand Shrine 22–3, 192
Ise Peninsula Tour **192**
Ise Sengoku Jidai Mura 348, 349
Ise-Shima National Park 192
Isetan Department Stores
Kyoto 174, 175
Tokyo 87
Isetatsu (Tokyo) 102, 103
Ishibashi Bunka Center (Kurume) 232
Ishibe-Koji Lane (Kyoto City) 160
Ishigaki Island 253
hotel 305
restaurant 337
Ishiguro-ke (Kakunodate) 272
Ishii Tea Bowl Museum (Hagi) 213
Ishikawa Goemon 165
Ishikawa Jozan 153, 172
Ishikawa Prefecture Art Museum (Kanazawa) 142
Ishikawa Prefecture Traditional Products and Crafts Museum (Kanazawa) 142
Ishimaru (Tokyo) 101, 103
Ishinami beach 242
Iso Garden (Kagoshima) 242
Issey Miyake 35
shops 101, 103
Isui-en Garden (Nara) 185
Itoya (Tokyo) 102, 103
Itsukushima Shrine (Miyajima Island) 210
Iwakuni **212**
hotel 299
Iwakuni Castle 212
Iwakuni Historical Museum 212
Iwasaki Yataro 97
Iztsu Beya (Tokyo) 106, 107
Izu Dancer, The (Kawabata Yasunari) 133
Izu Peninsula **133**
hotels 295
restaurants 328
Izumo **207**
hotel 299
Izumo no Okuni *see* Okuni
Izumo-Taisha Shrine 207

J

Jakko-in Temple (Kyoto City) 173
Japan Air System 379
Japan Airlines 378, 379
Japan Alps
Kamikochi 144
Japan: An Interpretation (Hearn) 207
Japan Economy Hotel Group 288
Japan Folk Craft Museum
Osaka 196
Tokyo **96**, 102
Japan Folklore Museum (Matsumoto) 145
Japan Hotel Association 288
Japan Hotline 362, 363
Japan Karate-do Federation (Tokyo) 351, 353
Japan National Tourist Organization (JNTO) 362, 363
Japan Rail (JR)
network information 381
pass 381
Japan Rural Toy Museum (Kurashiki) 205
Japan Sumo Association 350, 353
Japan Times 104, 374
Japan Traditional Craft Center (Tokyo) 94, 102, 103
Japan Travel-Phone 362, 378, 379
Japan Ukiyo-e Museum (Matsumoto) 145
Japanese Inn Group 288
Japanese Karate Association (Tokyo) 351, 353
Jena (Tokyo) 63, 104, 107
Jewelry
shops in Kyoto 177
shops in Tokyo 101, 103
Jidai Matsuri (Kyoto City) 39, 42, 178
Jigokudani Onsen 19, 145, 347
Jinbocho Booksellers' District (Tokyo) **68**
Jingo-ji Temple (Kyoto City) 171
Jingu Stadium (Tokyo) 106, 107
Jinja see Shrines
Jintozeiseki stone (Miyako Island) 252–3
Jisho-ji *see* Ginkaku-ji
Jizo statues **24**
JNTO *see* Japan National Tourist Organization
Jodo Sect (Pure Land) Buddhism
at Chion-in Temple (Kyoto City) 162
in gardens 26
Honen 162
Jojakko-ji Temple (Kyoto City) 171
Jomon period 47, 273
dolls 271
pottery 79
Josetsu
Catching a Goldfish with a Gourd 169
Joypolis (Tokyo) 99, 349
Jozankei 279
JTB coupons 373
Judo *see* Martial arts
Jusanya (Tokyo) 101, 103

K

Kabuka (Rebun Island) 280
Kabuki **33**
Chushingura 51, 99, 156
theaters in Kyoto 178, 179
theaters in Tokyo 104, 107
see also Theaters
Kabukicho (Tokyo) 86
Kabuki-za Theater (Tokyo) **64**, 104
Kagoshima **242–3**
hotels 303
restaurants 336
Kagoshin (Kyoto City) 176, 177
Kagura 239, 271
Kakimoto (Kyoto City) 177
Kakunodate **272**
hotels 306
restaurants 338
Kamakura **128–131**
Great Buddha 15
Hachiman-gu Festival 39, 42
Kita Kamakura 130
restaurants 328
Kamakura National Treasure House Museum 129
Kami 22
role in festivals 38
Kamigamo Shrine (Kyoto City) 166
Kamikaze 225
Kamikochi **144**
hotels 295
Kamishichi-ken Kaburenjo (Kyoto City) 178, 179
Kamo Shrines (Kyoto City) **166**
Kan'ami Kiyotsugo 32
Kanaya 133
Kanaya Hotel (Nikko) 258
Kanazawa **142–3**
hotel 295
restaurant 328
Kanazawa Castle 142

Kanchan-in Temple (Tokyo) 80
Kanda Myojin Shrine (Tokyo) **69**
festival 38–39, 40
Kangensai Music Festival (Miyajima) 41
Kannon (goddess of mercy) 25
at Sanjusangen-do Temple (Kyoto City) 152–3
at Senso-ji Temple (Tokyo) 82–3
Kano School Painters **155**, 193, 264
Kano Motonobu 169
Kano Naonobu 154
Kano Sanraku 169
Kano Tanyu 165, 169
Kano Yasunobu 265
Kansai International Airport (Osaka) 197
Kansai region 182
Kansai Time Out 178
Kanto Matsuri (Akita) 42
Kanto region 125, 256–7, 377
Kanze Noh-gakudo (Tokyo) 104, 107
Kappabashi-dori (Tokyo) **80**
Karate *see* Martial arts
Karatsu 233
Karatsu Kunshu 42
Karesansui 25
Kashikojima 192
Kasuga Grand Shrine (Nara) 185
Kasuga Shrine Festival (Nara) 40
Kasugano Beya (Tokyo) 106, 107
Kasurasei (Kyoto City) 177
Kasuri dyeing 35, 232, 251
Kato Kiyomasa 238
Katsura Imperial Villa (Kyoto City) **170**
Katsushika Hokusai *see* Hokusai
Katsuura 193, 347
Kawabata Yasunari 17
The Izu Dancer 133
Senbazuru (Thousand Cranes) 130
Kawagoe **126**
restaurant 328
Kawai Kanjiro 205
Kawasaki Bijutsu (Kyoto City) 175
Kawayu 281
Kawazu 133
Kazan (Endo Shusaku) 243
Kegon Falls (Nikko National Park) 265
Keishun-in Subtemple (Kyoto City) 169
Kendo *see* Martial arts
Kenka Matsuri (Himeji) 42
Kenroku-en Garden (Kanazawa) 27, 142
Kibune 171
Kii Peninsula **193**
Kijoka Village **251**
Kikko Park (Iwakuni) 212
Kimonos
buying 345
maiko costume 157
man's 37
shops in Tokyo 101, 103
woman's 36
yukata 36, 345
Kinkaku-ji Temple (Kyoto City) **168**
Kinki region 183, 377
Kinokuniya bookstore (Tokyo) 86, 104, 107
Kintai-kyo Bridge (Iwakuni) 212
Kirin Beer Village (Yokohama) 127
Kirishima National Park **242**
Kiritappu Wetland 284
Kiso Valley Tour **136**
hotels 296
Kiso-Fukushima 136
Kiso-Hirasawa 136
Kita Kyushu *see* Kokura
Kita Kyushu Municipal Art Museum (Kokura) 228
Kitagawa Utamaro *see* Utamaro
Kitahara Hakushu 232
Kitakata **266**
hotel 306
Kitano Tenman-gu Shrine (Kyoto City) **167**
Kitanomaru Park (Tokyo) **68**
Kitchenware Town (Tokyo) *see* Kappabashi-dori
Kite-Flying Festival 40
Kiyomizu-dera Temple (Kyoto City) 161, **162**
Kobayashi Kiyochika 81
Kobe **198–9**
hotels 299
map 199
restaurants 332
Kobe City Museum 198
Kobe Maritime Museum 199
Kobori Enshu 153, 165
Kochi **220**
hotel 302
restaurants 334
Kochi Castle 220
Kodaimaru (Tokyo) 101, 103
Kodo Drumming Group **267**
Kodokan Judo Institute (Tokyo) 350, 353
Kofuku-ji Temple (Nara) 184
Koishikawa Korakuen Garden (Tokyo) **69**
Koizumi Yakumo *see* Hearn, Lafcadio
Kokenodamon Gorge 279
Koko-en Garden (Himeji) 203
Kokumin-Shukusha (lodges) 291
Kokura **228**
Koma Theater (Tokyo) 86, 105, 107
Konchi-in Subtemple (Kyoto City) 165
Kondoi Misaki Beach (Taketomi Island) 253
Kongo Nogakudo (Kyoto City) 178, 179
Koraku-en Garden (Okayama) 204
Koransha (Tokyo) 102, 103
Koryu-ji Temple (Kyoto City) **169**
Kotatsu 29
Kotohira **218–9**
hotels 302
restaurant 334
Koto-in Subtemple (Kyoto City) 167
Koya, Mount *see Mountains*
Kukai *see* Shingon Sect Buddhism
Kumamoto **238**
hotels 303–4
restaurants 336
Kumamoto Castle 238
Kumamoto Prefectural Art Museum 238
Kumamoto Traditional Crafts Center 238
Kumano Magaibutsu (Usa) 228
Kumaya Art Museum (Hagi) 213
Kume Island **252**
hotel 305
map 247
Kunchi Matsuri (Nagasaki) 42
Kungyoku-do (Kyoto City) 176
Kurama District (Kyoto City) **171**
Kurama Matsuri (Kyoto City) 42
Kurama-dera Temple (Kyoto City) 171
Kurashiki **204–5**
hotels 299–300
restaurants 332
Kurashiki Archaeological Museum 205
Kurashiki Folk Art Museum 205
Kurashiki Tivoli Park 205, 348
Kura-Zukuri Shiryokan (Takayama) 126
Kurima Island 253
Kurodaya (Tokyo) 102
Kurokawa Kisho
Museum of Contemporary Art (Hiroshima) 209
Kurosawa Akira
Ran 200
Kurume **232**
Kurume Regional Industry Promotion Center 232
Kusakabe Heritage House (Takayama) 138
Kushimoto 193
Kushiro Wetlands National Park **284**
hotel 307
restaurant 339
Kutani Kosen Kiln (Kanazawa) 143
Kutsugata (Rishiri Island) 280
Kyogen 32
Kyoryukan (Kyoto City) 179
Kyoto City **148–79**
addresses 150
Aoi Matsuri 38, 40, 166, 178
court life 48
cuisine 149
Daimonji Bonfire 42
Eastern Gion and the Higashiyama Street-by-Street map **160–61**
entertainment **178–9**
Farther Afield **170–73**
Gion Matsuri 41, 178
hotels **297–8**
Jidai Matsuri 39, 42, 178
Kurama Matsuri 42
maps **150–51**
Mifune Matsuri 41
Okera Mairi Ceremony 43
restaurants **330–31**
shopping **174–7**
transportation 151
Kyoto Antiques Center 175
Kyoto City Museum of Fine Arts 162
Kyoto Connection 179
Kyoto Craft Center 176, 177
Kyoto Exhibition Hall 162
Kyoto Gosho *see* Imperial Palace
Kyoto Gyoen *see* Imperial Park
Kyoto Kanze Kaikan 178, 179
Kyoto Kintetsu Department Store 174, 175
Kyoto National Museum **153**
Kyoto Station **152**
Kyoto Visitor's Guide 178, 179
Kyudo *see* Martial arts
Kyukyo-do (Kyoto City) 177
Kyushu **224–43**
climate 44
hotels **303–5**
map **226–7**
region 377
restaurants **335–7**
transportation 227
Kyushu Ceramic Museum (Arita) 233
Kyushu History Museum (Dazaifu) 231
Kyushu Yufuin Folk Art Village 229

L

Lacquerware 35
buying 344
in Okinawa 251
see also Museums and Galleries
Lafcadio Hearn Memorial Hall (Matsue) 207
Lafcadio Hearn Residence (Matsue) 207
LaForet (Tokyo) 91
Lakes
Akan 281
Ashi 121, 133
Biwa **206**
Chuzen-ji 265
Fuji Five **134–5**
Furen **284**
Junsainuma 278
Kinrin 229
Konuma 278

Lakes (cont.)
Kussharo 280
Mashu 280
Myojin 213
Onetto 281
Onuma 278
Shikotsu 279
Shiretoko Five 285
Towada 272
Toya 279
Yamanaka 135
Landmark Tower (Yokohama) 126
Landscape of Japan **18–19**
bamboo groves 18
plate movements 18
volcanoes 19
see also Onsen
Language 366–7
Phrase Book **404–8**
Lantern Festival (Nara) 43
Laox (Tokyo) 101, 103
Leach, Bernard 205
Legends of Tono (Miyazawa Kenji) 271
Liberal Democratic Party 55
Liberty Osaka Museum 197
Lion Mask Museum (Takayama) 140
Liquid Room (Tokyo) 105, 107
Lisn (Kyoto City) 176, 177
Lloyd Wright, Frank 137
JR Nikko Station 258
Local History Museum (Fukiya) 205

M

MacArthur, General Douglas 55
Madame Butterfly (Puccini) 236
Magome 136
Mahayana Buddhism 25
Maiko *see* Geisha
Mail 376
Maki Fumihiko
Spiral Building (Tokyo) 94
Mampuku-ji Temple (Uji City) 173
Mandala Live House (Tokyo) 105, 107
Manet, Edouard 66
Manga 21
Manshu-in Temple (Kyoto City) **172**
Man'yoshu 47
Maps
Central Honshu 124–5
climate 44–5
Fukuoka City Center 230
Hiroshima Peace Memorial Park 209
Ise Peninsula Tour 192
Japan at a Glance 120–21
Japan orientation 10–11
Kamakura 128–9
Kanazawa City Center 142–3
Kiso Valley Tour 136
Kobe City Center 199
Kume Island 247
Kyoto City 150–51
Kyoto City: Central shopping district and Gion 151
Kyoto City: Eastern Gion and the Higashiyama Street-by-Street 160–61
Kyoto City: Farther Afield 170
Kyoto City: Philosopher's Walk 164
Kyushu 226–7
Miyajima Island 210–11
Miyako Islands 247
Nagasaki City Center 234–5
Nara 184–5
Nikko 258
Northern Honshu 256–7
Okinawa archipelago 10
Okinawa Island 246–7
Onsen 347
Osaka City Center 195
prefectures of Japan 377
Maps (cont.)
Shikoku 216–7
Southeast and East Asia 11
Tokyo: at a Glance 58–9
Tokyo: Central Tokyo 61
Tokyo: East Shinjuku Street-by-Street 86–7
Tokyo: Farther Afield 96
Tokyo: Ginza Street-by-Street 62–3
Tokyo: Northern Tokyo 73
Tokyo: Shibuya Street-by-Street 92–3
Tokyo: Street Finder 108–117
Tokyo: West Shinjuku Street-by-Street 88–9
Tokyo: Western Tokyo 85
Western Honshu 182–3
Yaeyama Islands 247
Yokohama City Center 127
Markets 343
Ameyoko Market (Tokyo) **80**
food 309
in Kyoto 174–5
Nishiki Market Alley (Kyoto City) 174
in Tokyo 100
Tsukiji Fish Market (Tokyo) **64**
Martial arts **30–31, 350–51**
aikido 31, 351
books 401
dojos in Tokyo 105
judo 31, 350
K-1 351, 353
karate 31, 351
kendo 30, 31, 350
kyudo 30, 31
organizations 350, 351, 353
World Pancrase Create 351, 353
Marui (Young) Department Store (Tokyo) 93, 100, 103
Marunouchi District (Tokyo) **66**
Marunouchi Piccadilly 105, 107
Maruyama Okyo 219
Maruyama Park (Kyoto City) 156, 160
Maruzen
Kyoto City 174, 175
Tokyo 102, 103, 104, 107
Mashiko **266**
restaurant 338
Mashiko Reference Collection Museum 266
Matisse, Henri 81, 205
Matsue **206–7**
hotels 300
restaurants 332
Matsue Castle 207
Matsumoto **145**
hotel 296
restaurant 329
Matsumoto Castle 145
Matsumoto Folkcraft Museum 145
Matsuo Basho *see* Basho
Matsuri *see* Festivals
Matsushima **270**
Matsuya Department Stores 342
Tokyo 63, 100, 103
Matsuyama **220**
hotel 302
restaurants 335
Matsuyama Castle 220
Matsuzakaya Department Store (Tokyo) 101, 103
Medical facilities *see* Health
Meditation 25
at Eihei-ji Temple 144
at Engaku-ji Temple (Kamakura) 130
at Hokoku-ji Temple (Kamakura) 129
zazen sitting meditation 25, 130, 144
Meiji, Emperor 54
Meiji Mura 137, 348
Meiji Restoration 54
Meiji Seimei Building (Tokyo) 66
Meiji Shrine and Treasure House (Tokyo) **90**
Meimei-an Teahouse (Matsue) 207
Meoto Iwa rocks 192
Meriken Park (Kobe) 198–9
Metalwork 34
buying 345
ironware in Morioka 271
Metro (Kyoto City) 179
Mifune Matsuri (Kyoto City) 41
Mikimoto (Tokyo) 63, 101, 103
Mikimoto Pearl Island 192
Minami-Aoyama District (Tokyo) **94**
Minami-ike Shobuda iris garden (Tokyo) 90
Minami-za Theater (Kyoto City) 156, 178, 179
Minamoto family
Minamoto no Yoritomo 48
Minato Mirai 21 (Yokohama) 126, 349
Mingeikan *see* Japan Folk Craft Museum
Minka see Houses
Minochu (Kyoto City) 176, 177
Minowabashi (Tokyo) 97
Minsa fabric 253
Minshuku 291
Mishima Yukio
The Golden Pavilion 168
Mitsukoshi Department Stores 342
Ebisu (Tokyo) 99
Ginza (Tokyo) 63
Nihonbashi (Tokyo) 66, 103
Miyajima Island **210–11**
hotels 300
Kangensai Music Festival 41
map 210–211
restaurants 332–3
Miyake Issey *see* Issey Miyake
Miyako Islands **252–3**
hotel 305
map 247
Miyako-*jofu* fabric 252
Miyashita Obi (Tokyo) 101
Miyawake Baisen-an (Kyoto City) 177
Miyazaki 242
hotels 304
Miyazawa Kenji 270
Miyazawa Memorial Museum (Hamamaki) 271
Momoyama period 52
Money 372–3
banks 372
currency 372
customs information 361
paying in hotels 288
paying in restaurants 308–9
paying in shops 340–41
Mongol invasions 49, 225
Monorail systems 383
Monzen 144
Morel, Edmund 127
Mori Hanae *see* Hanae Mori
Mori Ogai
Vita Sexualis 213
Wild Geese, The 213
Mori Silver (Tokyo) 101
Morihisa Iron Studio (Morioka) 271
Morioka **271**
Chagu-chagu Umakko 41
hotel 306
restaurant 338
Morioka Castle 271
Morioka Hashimoto Art Museum 271
Morita Washi Wagami-no-mise (Kyoto City) 177
Moriyama Torao Workshop (Hirokawa) 232
Moronobu 81
Moto-Hakone 133

Motorbikes
renting 385
Mount Aso Volcanic Museum 239
Mountaineering 352
Mountains
Asahi 280
Aso **238–9**
Atago 171
Bandai 267
Daikanbo 238
Eniwa 279
Esan 278
Fuji **134–5**
Fuppushi 279
Gassan 268
Haguro 268
Hakodate 278
Hayachine 271
Hiei 170, 171, 172
Hotaka 144
Io 285
Iwaki 273
Iwate 271
Iwo 281
Japan Alps 144
Kanpu 272
Karakunidake 242
Kasayama 213
Komagatake 278
Komezuka 239
Koya **193**
Me-Akan 281
Misen 211
Mitake 132
Nakadake 238
Nantai 258, 259, 265
O-Akan 281
Omine-san 191
Onnebetsu 285
Ontake 136
Osorezan 273
Rausu 285
Rishiri 280
Rokko 199
Sakurajima 242, **243**
Sanjo-san 191
Shiretoko 285
Showa Shinzan 279
Takadake 239
Takao 132
Tarumae 279
Unzen 237
Usu 279
Yake 144
Yari 144
Yoshino 191
Yotei 278
Yudono 268
Yufudake 229
Mucha, Alphonse 197
Mukai Kyorai 171
Municipal History and Folklore Museum (Miyajima Island) 211
Municipal Museum (Hirosaki) 273
Municipal Museum (Tono) 271
Murakami-ju (Kyoto City) 176, 177
Murasaki Shikibu 48, 206
Murato Shuko 163
Murin-an (Kyoto City) 165
Muromachi period 49
Museums and Galleries (general)
admission fees 363
opening hours 362–3
Museums and Galleries (individual)
Aikawa Museum (Sado Island) 267
Ainu Museum (Sapporo) 279
Aizu Minzokukan Folk Museum (Inawashiro) 267
Art Museum (Kagoshima) 242
Asakura Museum (Tokyo) 80
Atomic Bomb Museum (Nagasaki) 237
Beer Museum Ebisu (Tokyo) 99

Museums and Galleries (cont.)
Bizen Pottery Traditional and Contemporary Art Museum (Inbe) 204
Bridgestone Museum of Art (Tokyo) 66
Chido Museum (Tsuruoka) 268
Daimyo Clock Museum (Tokyo) 80
Denshokan Museum (Kakunodate) 272
Doll House (Himeji) 203
Edo-Tokyo Museum (Tokyo) 98
Festival Float Hall (Takayama) 140
Fukuoka Asian Art Museum 231
Fukuoka City Museum 230
Goto Art Museum (Tokyo) **96**
Hakata Machiya Folklore Museum (Fukuoka) 231
Hakone Art Museum 132
Hakone Open-Air Museum 132
Hayashibara Museum of Art (Okayama) 204
Himeji City Museum of Literature 203
Hirata Kinenkan Museum (Takayama) 139
Hokusai-kan (Obuse) 145
Honda Museum (Kanazawa) 142
Hyogo Prefectural Museum of History (Himeji) 203
Iga Ninja Museum 191
Insho Domoto Museum (Kyoto City) **168**
Ishibashi Bunka Center (Kurume) 232
Ishii Tea Bowl Museum (Hagi) 213
Ishikawa Prefecture Art Museum (Kanazawa) 142
Ishikawa Prefecture Traditional Products and Crafts Museum (Kanazawa) 142
Iwakuni Historical Museum 212
Japan Folk Craft Museum (Tokyo) **96**
Japan Folklore Museum (Matsumoto) 145
Japan Rural Toy Museum (Kurashiki) 205
Japan Ukiyo-e Museum (Matsumoto) 145
Kamakura National Treasure House Museum 129
Kita Kyushu Municipal Art Museum (Kokura) 228
Kobe City Museum 198
Kobe Maritime Museum 199
Kumamoto Prefectural Art Museum 238
Kumamoto Traditional Crafts Center 238
Kumaya Art Museum (Hagi) 213
Kurashiki Archaeological Museum 205
Kurashiki Folk Art Museum 205
Kura-Zukuri Shiryokan (Takayama) 126
Kurume Regional Industry Promotion Center 232
Kyoto City Museum of Fine Arts 162
Kyoto National Museum **153**
Kyushu Ceramic Museum (Arita) 233
Kyushu History Museum (Dazaifu) 231
Liberty Osaka Museum 197
Lion Mask Museum (Takayama) 140
Local History Museum (Fukiya) 205
Mashiko Reference Collection Museum 266
Matsumoto Folkcraft Museum 145
Miyazawa Memorial Museum (Hamamaki) 271

Museums and Galleries (cont.)
Morioka Hashimoto Art Museum 271
Mount Aso Volcanic Museum 239
Municipal History and Folklore Museum (Miyajima Island) 211
Municipal Museum (Hirosaki) 273
Municipal Museum (Tono) 271
Museum of Contemporary Art (Hiroshima) 209
Museum of Contemporary Art (Tokyo) 94
Museum of Maritime Sciences (Tokyo) 99
Museum of Oriental Ceramics (Osaka) 195
Nara National Museum 184–5
National Museum of Japanese History 126
National Museum of Modern Art (Kyoto City) 162
National Museum of Modern Art (Tokyo) 68
National Museum of Western Art (Tokyo) 75
National Science Museum (Tokyo) 75
Natural Science Museum (Hakone) 133
Nezu Art Museum (Tokyo) 94
NYK Maritime Museum (Yokohama) 127
Ocha no Sato (Kanaya) 133
Ohara Museum of Art (Kurashiki) 205
Okayama Prefectural Museum of Art 204
Okinawa Prefectural Museum 248
Onarutokyo Memorial Hall (Shikoku) 219
Open-Air Museum (Shokawa Valley) 140
Orient Museum (Okayama) 204
Osaka City Museum 194
Ota Memorial Museum of Art (Tokyo) 91
Peace Memorial Museum (Hiroshima) 208–9
Peace Memorial Museum (Okinawa) 249
Reihokan (Mount Koya) 193
Saibu Gas Museum (Fukuoka) 230
Sakamoto Ryoma Museum (Kochi) 220
Sake-Brewing Museum (Kitakata) 266–7
Sapporo Beer Garden and Museum 279
Science and Technology Museum (Tokyo) 68
Shiki Masaoka Museum (Matsuyama) 220
Shikoku Mura Museum 218
Shin Yokohama Ramen Museum 127
Shiritsu Yaeyama Museum (Ishigaki Island) 253
Shitamachi Museum (Tokyo) **80**
Sueda Art Museum (Yufuin) 229
Sumo Museum (Tokyo) 98
Suntory Museum (Osaka) 197
Suntory Museum of Art (Tokyo) 95
Sword Museum (Tokyo) **89**
Taiji Whale Museum 193
Tanabe Art Museum (Matsue) 207
TEPCO Electric Energy Museum (Tokyo) 93
Tobacco and Salt Museum (Tokyo) 93
Tokugawa Art Museum (Nagoya) 137
Tokyo Metropolitan Art Museum 74
Tokyo Metropolitan Museum of Photography 99

Museums and Galleries (cont.)
Tokyo National Museum 59, **76–9**
Tosho-gu Treasure Hall and Museum of Art (Nikko) 259
Tsugaruhan Neputa Mura (Hirosaki) 273
Urushi Museum (Nikko) 259
Wax Museum of the Tale of the Heike (Takamatsu) 218
Yokohama Museum of Art 127
Yufuin Museum 229
Yushukan Museum (Tokyo) 68
Music
Kodo drumming group **267**
live venues in Tokyo 105, 107
taiko drumming 267
Tokyo Summer Festival 105, 107
Muso Soseki 129
Myoshin-ji Temple (Kyoto City) **169**

N

Nachi no Hi-Matsuri 41
Nachi Taisha Shrine 193
Nachi-no-taki waterfall 193
Nagano **145**
hotel 296
restaurants 329
Nagasaki **234–7**
hotels 304
influence of foreigners 234, **237**
Kunchi Matsuri 42
map **234–5**
restaurants 336–7
Nagashino, battle of 52
Nagata (Kyoto City) 175
Nagatoro 132
Nagoya **137**
hotel 296
Nagoya Festival 42
restaurants 329
Nagoya Castle 137
Naha City **248**
hotels 305
restaurant 337
Nai-en Garden (Tokyo) 90
Nakadomari (Kume Island) 252
Nakagusuku Castle Ruin **250**
Nakajima (Kyoto City) 175
Nakamise-dori (Tokyo) 82
shopping 101–4
Nakamura House **250**
Nakane Kinsaku 169
Nakanishi Toku Shoten (Kyoto City) 176, 177
Nakasendo post road 123, 136
Nakasone Toimiya 252
Nakatsuka (Tokyo) 102
Nakazato (Kume Island) 252
Naked Festival (Saidai-ji) 43
Nakijin Castle Ruin (Okinawa) 120, **251**
Namahage (Oga) 43
Names in Japan 367
Nametoko Gorge (Shikoku) 221
Namiyoke Inari Jinja (Tokyo) 64
Nanzen-ji Temple (Kyoto City) 164, **165**
Nara 13, 121, **184–9**
hotels 300
Kasuga Shrine Festival 40
Lantern Festival 43
Omizu-tori 38
On Matsuri 43
restaurants 333
Todai-ji Temple **186–7**
Yamayaki 43
Nara National Museum 184–5
Nara Park **184–5**
Narai 136
Naramachi District 185
Narita **126**
airport 378
Narita (cont.)
hotel 296
restaurant 329
Narita (Kyoto City) 176, 177
Narita Express 378
Naruto Whirlpools **219**
hotels 302
National Bunraku Theater (Osaka) 196
National Children's Castle (Tokyo) 94
National Film Center (Tokyo) 105
National Museum of Japanese History 126
National Museum of Modern Art (Kyoto City) 162
National Museum of Modern Art (Tokyo) 68
National Museum of Western Art (Tokyo) 75
National Noh Theater (Tokyo) 104, 107
National Parks
Akan **281**
Bandai-Asahi **267**
books 401
Chichibu-Tama **132**
Daisetsu-zan **280**
Ise-Shima 192
Japan Alps 144
Kirishima **242**
Kushiro Wetlands **284**
Nikko **265**
Onuma **278**
Rishiri-Rebun-Sarobetsu **280**
Shikotsu-Toya 121, **278–9**
Shiretoko **285**
Towada-Hachimantai **272**
Unzen-Amakusa 237
National Science Museum (Tokyo) 75
National Stadium (Tokyo) 106, 107
National Sumo Stadium (Tokyo) 31, **98**, 106, 107
National Theater (Tokyo) 104, 107
Natsume Soseki
Botchan 220
Natural Science Museum (Hakone) 133
Nature Conservation Society of Japan 353
Nebuta Matsuri (Aomori) 39, 42
Nemuro Peninsula **285**
Ne-ne no Michi (Kyoto City) 160
Neputa Matsuri (Hirosaki) 42
New National Theater (Tokyo) 105, 107
New Otani Hotel (Tokyo) 95
New Year's Day 43
parade (Tokyo) 43
Newspapers and magazines 374
Nezame-no-toko 136
Nezu Art Museum (Tokyo) 94
NHK Hall (Tokyo) 105, 107
Nichinan Coast **242**
Nichiren Sect Buddhism 269
Nichiren 267
Nightclubs
in Tokyo 106, 107
Nihon Buyo Kyokai (Tokyo) 105, 107
Nihon Minka-en 348, 349
Nihonbashi bridge (Tokyo) 66
Nihonbashi District (Tokyo) **66**
Nijo Castle (Kyoto City) **154–5**
Nikko 121, **258–65**
hotels 306
map 258
restaurant 338
Tosho-gu Fall Festival 42
Tosho-gu Grand Festival 41
Yayoi Matsuri 40
Nikko Botanical Gardens 259
Nikko Edo Village 348, 349
Nikko National Park **265**
Ninja **191**
Ninna-ji Temple (Kyoto City) **169**
Nio guardian statues 25
Nippara 132
Nippon Budokan (Tokyo) 68, 350, 353
Niseko Ski Resort **278**
Nishi Amane 213
Nishi Hongan-ji Temple (Kyoto City) **153**
Nishida Kitaro 164
Nishijima Umbrellas (Tokyo) 102
Nishiki Market Alley (Kyoto City) 174
Nishimura (Kyoto City) 177
Nishinokyo District (Nara) 187
Nishiumi Marine Park (Shikoku) 221
Noboribetsu 279, 347
Noboribetsu Date Jidai Mura 348, 349
Noboribetsu Marine Park Castle Nixe 349
Noh **32**
theaters in Kyoto 178, 179
theaters in Tokyo 104, 107
Yashima 218
Nomura House (Kanazawa) 142
Noodles
bars 311
dishes 314
types 317
see also Food and Drink and Restaurants
Northern Honshu **254–73**
climate 45
hotels **305–7**
map **256–7**
restaurants **337–9**
transportation 257
Northern Tokyo **72–83**
hotels **292–3**
maps 59, **73**
restaurants **325**
transportation 73
Noto Peninsula **144**
hotel 296
restaurant 329
NTT Intercommunication Center (Tokyo) 96, 102
Nunobiki Falls (Kobe) 199
NYK Maritime Museum (Yokohama) 127

O

O Island 252
Obi sashes 36, 157
shops in Tokyo 101
Obihiro 280
Obuse 145
Ocha no Sato (Kanaya) 133
Ochaya see Tea
Oda Nobunaga 49
birthplace 137
massacre at Enryaku-ji Temple 172–3
in samurai history 50
suicide 52
unification of Japan 52
Odori Park (Sapporo) 279
Oga Peninsula **272**
Namahage 43, 272
Ogi (Sado Island) 267
Ogimachi 140
Ogimi Mura (Okinawa) 251
Ohara District (Kyoto City) **173**
Ohara Magosaburo 205
Ohara Museum of Art (Kurashiki) 205
Ohori Park (Fukuoka) 231
Oigawa steam railroad 133
Oirase Gorge 272
Okamoto Taro 94
Okayama **204**
hotels 300–301
restaurants 333

Okayama Castle 204
Okayama Prefectural Museum of Art 204
Okazaki Area (Kyoto City) **162**
Okera Mairi Ceremony (Kyoto City) 43
Okinawa **244–53**
climate 44
hotels **305**
maps 10, 44, **246–7**
prefecture 377
restaurants **337**
transportation 247
Okinawa Battle Sites **249**
Okinawa Memorial Park **250**
Okinawa Prefectural Museum 248
Okochi Denjiro 170
Okochi Sanso Villa (Kyoto City) 170
Oku-Dogo Onsen (Matsuyama) 220
Okuni, Izumo no 33
Olympic Stadiums (Tokyo) 90
Olympics, Tokyo 55, 90
Omine-san 191
Omizu-tori (Nara) 38, 40
Omote-sando (Tokyo) 91
clothes shops 101, 104
On Air East (Tokyo) 105, 107
On Air West (Tokyo) 105, 107
On Matsuri (Nara) 43
Onarutokyo Memorial Hall (Shikoku) 219
Onin War 49, 149
Onsen (hot springs, general) 19, **346–7**
books 401
etiquette 346
map 347
types of *onsen* 346
Onsen (hot springs, individual)
Akan Kohan 281, 307
Arima 199, 347
Asahi-dake 280
Asama 145
Beppu **228–9**, 303, 347
Dogo 220, 347
Ebino Kogen Rotenburo 242, 347
Echigo Yuzawa 347
Goshogake 272
Hakone-Yumoto 132, 347
Hanamaki **270–71**, 305
Hayashida 242
Hoshi 347
Hottawa 347
Ibusuki 347
Izu 295
Jigokudani 19, 145, 347
Jozankei 279
Kamikita 306
Kamuiwakka 285
Katsuura 193, 347
Kawayu 281
Kinosaki 347
Kuroyu 347
Kusatsu 347
Narugo 347
Noboribetsu 279, 347
Odaru 347
Oku-Dogo (Matsuyama) 220
Osawa 347
Renge 347
Shikotsu Kohan 279
Shirahama 193, 347
Shirahone 347
Shuzenji 133, 347
Sounkyo 280
Spa World (Osaka) 196
Takamatsukuri 347
Takaragawa 347
Tenninkyo 280
Unzen Spa 237, 347
Utsukushigahara 145
Wakoto 281
Yufuin **229**, 347
Onsen (cont.)
Yumoto (Nikko) 265, 347
Yunishigawa 347
Yunokawa 278
Zao 347
Onta **232**
Onuma Quasi-National Park **278**
Open-Air Museum (Shokawa Valley) 140
Opening hours 362
banks 372
museums and galleries 362
post offices 376
shops 340
shrines 362
temples 362
Orient Museum (Okayama) 204
Oriental Bazaar (Tokyo) 91, 101, 103
Osaka **194–7**
cuisine 196
hotels 301
map **195**
restaurants 333–4
Tenjin Matsuri 41
Toka Ebisu Festival 43
Osaka Aquarium 197, 349
Osaka Castle 194
Osaka City Museum 194
Osaka Prefectural Gymnasium 350, 353
Oshidomari (Rishiri Island) 280
Ota Memorial Museum of Art (Tokyo) 91
Otoyo-jinja Shrine (Kyoto City) 164
Otsu 206
Owaku-dani (Hakone) 133
Oxygen bars 21
Oya Shobu (Tokyo) 102, 103
Oyakuen Herb Garden (Aizu-Wakamatsu) 266
Ozu **221**
hotel 302
restaurant 335

P

Pachinko **93**
Pacific Ring of Fire 13
Pacman 20
Pagodas 24
Daigo-ji Temple (Kyoto City) 173
Horyu-ji Temple **190**
Jojakko-ji Temple (Kyoto City) 171
Konpon Da-to (Mount Koya) 193
Goju-no-to (Miyajima Island) 210
Mount Haguro (Dewa Sanzan) 255, 268
Ninna-ji Temple (Kyoto City) 169
Senso-ji Temple (Tokyo) 83
Tojo Temple (Kyoto City) 152
Tosho-gu Shrine (Nikko) 261
in Ueno Park (Tokyo) 74
Yakushi-ji Temple (Nara) 187
Yasaka Pagoda (Kyoto City) 161
Painting 34
Kano School Painters **155**
nihonga painting 168
Palette Town (Tokyo) 99, 349
Panasonic Square (Osaka) 195
Paper *see Washi*
Paradise gardens 26
Parks
Arakawa Nature Park (Tokyo) 97
Arakawa Yuen Park (Tokyo) 97
Daisan Daiba Historic Park (Tokyo) 99
Glover Park (Nagasaki) 236
Goryokaku Park (Hakodate) 278
Hirosaki Park 273
Imperial Park (Kyoto City) **166**
Kikko Park (Iwakuni) 212
Kitanomaru Park (Tokyo) **68**
Maruyama Park (Kyoto City) 156, 160
Parks (cont.)
Meriken Park (Kobe) 198–9
Nara Park **184–5**
Odori Park (Sapporo) 279
Ohori Park (Fukuoka) 231
Peace Memorial Park (Hiroshima) **208–9**
Peace Park (Nagasaki) 120, 237
Ritsurin Park (Takamatsu) 218
Sapporo Art Park 279
Shiba Park (Tokyo) **65**
Ueno Park (Tokyo) 59, **74–5**
Uraku-en Park (Inuyama) 137
Wadakura Fountain Park Tokyo) 66
Yoyogi Park (Tokyo) **90–91**
see also Gardens, National Parks
Peace Memorial Museum (Hiroshima) 208–9
Peace Memorial Museum (Okinawa) 249
Peace Memorial Park (Hiroshima) **208–9**
Peace Park (Nagasaki) 120, 237
Pearl Harbor, attack on 55
Pentax Gallery (Tokyo) 106, 107
Perry, Commodore Matthew
arrival in Edo Bay 53
memorial on Okinawa 248
Personal Security 370–71
Petitjean, Bernard 236
Philosopher's Walk (Kyoto City) 121, **164**
Phrase Book **404–8**
Picasso, Pablo 66, 205
Pig & Whistle (Kyoto City) 179
Pilgrimages 25, **356**
33 Kannon temples 132, 173, 356
88-temple pilgrimage 120, **222–3**, 356
Mount Fuji **134–5**
Mount Koya **193**
Omuro 88-Temple pilgrimage 169
Pillow Book (Sei Shonagon) 48
Plus Minus Gallery (Tokyo) 102, 103
Pokémon 20
Politics 16
Pontocho Alley (Kyoto City) **156**
Pontocho Kaburenjo (Kyoto City) 178, 179
Prefectures 377
map 377
Printemps Department Store (Tokyo) 63
Public holidays 43
Puccini
Madame Butterfly 236
Pure Land Buddhism *see* Jodo Sect Buddhism
Putaro 272
Pyle, Ernie see Ernie Pyle Memorial

R

Radio 374
FM radio band 341
Railroads *see* Trains
Rainbow Bridge (Tokyo) 99
Rake Fair (Tokyo) 42
Ran (Kurosawa) 200
Rausu 285
Rebun Island 280
Regions of Japan 377
Reihokan (Mount Koya) 193
Reiun-in Subtemple (Kyoto City) 169
Religion 15
religious studies 356–7
see also Buddhism, Confucianism, Shinto
Rengeo-in Temple *see* Sanjusangen-do Temple
Renkodo (Kyoto City) 175
Renoir, Auguste 205

Restaurants **308–39**
aka-chochin 310
Asian restaurants 311
Central Honshu 327–30
chopsticks **312–13**
coffee shops 311
dress code 308
eating at a *ryokan* 291
etiquette **312–13**
fast food 309
Hokkaido 339
ippin-ryoriya 310
izakaya 310, 315
kaiseki 310
kappo 310
kissaten 311
koryoriya 310
kyo-ryoriya 310
Kyoto City 330–31
Kyushu 335–7
meals and meal times 308
nomiya 310
noodle bars 311
Northern Honshu 337–9
Okinawa 337
ordering 312
prices and paying 308–9
Reading the Menu **314–5**
reservations 308
ryotei 310
seating arrangements 312
Shikoku 334–5
shojin ryoriya 310
set dishes 308
specialty restaurants 311
sushi restaurants 310–11
Tokyo 324–7
Western Honshu 331–4
Western restaurants 311
see also Food and Drink
Rice
crackers **314**
dishes 314
eating 313
festivals 38, 41
growing 18
health risks 370
Richie, Donald
The Inland Sea 218
Rickshaws 385
Rikugi-en Garden (Tokyo) **97**
Rinno-ji Temple (Nikko) 258
Rishiri Island 280
Rishiri-Rebun-Sarobetsu National Park **280**
hotel 307
restaurant 339
Robots 20
Rock and Roll Museum (Tokyo) 91
Rokuon-ji *see* Kinkaku-ji Temple
Ronin
47 Ronin Incident 51, 99
Roofs
types 28
Roppongi District (Tokyo) **94–5**
live music venues 105, 107
nightclubs 106, 107
Rouault, Georges 66
Russo-Japanese War 54
Battle of the Sea of Japan 91
Ryonan-ji Temple (Kyoto City) 26, **168**
Ryogen-in Subtemple (Kyoto City) 167
Ryogoku District (Tokyo) **98**
Ryokan **290–91**
Ryotsu (Sado Island) 267
Ryukyu Islands *see* Okinawa
Ryusen dyeing 248, 251

S

Sado Island **267**
Sado Island (cont.)
hotel 306
restaurant 338
Saga City 233
Saga Diary (Basho) 171
Saga Pottery Towns Tour **233**
Sagano District (Kyoto City) **171**
Saibu Gas Museum (Fukuoka) 230
Saicho *see* Tendai Sect Buddhism
Saidai-ji Eyo Matsuri (Saidai-ji) 43
Saigo Takamori 50
statue (Tokyo) 75
suicide at Kagoshima 243
Saihatsuan Kaga Yuzen Silk Center (Kanazawa) 142
Sakamoto Ryoma 220
Sakamoto Ryoma Museum (Kochi) 220
Sake **323**
breweries in Kobe 199
Sake-Brewing Museum (Kitakata) 266–7
Sakuda Gold-Leaf Store (Kanazawa) 143
Sakura zenzen see Cherry blossom
Sakurajima Volcano **243**
Salarymen 368
Samurai **50–51**
Byakkotai (White Tigers) 266
San'ai Building (Tokyo) 60, 63
Sanbido (Tokyo) 102
Sanja Matsuri (Tokyo) 41
Sanjo-san 191
Sanjusangen-do Temple (Kyoto City) **152–3**
Sankei-en Garden (Yokohama) 127
Sanmon (gates) 25
Sannai-Maruyama (Aomori) 273
Sanno Matsuri (Tokyo) 41, 95
Sanoya (Tokyo) 101
Sanzen-in Temple (Kyoto City) 173
Sapporo **279**
hotels 307
restaurants 339
Snow Festival 43, **279**
Sapporo Art Park 279
Sapporo Beer Garden and Museum 279
Satsuma domain 242, 245
Science and Cultural Center for Children (Hiroshima) 209
Science and Technology Museum (Tokyo) 68
Screens
Namban (Suntory Museum of Art, Tokyo) 95
painted 34
Scuba diving
off Yaeyama Islands 253
Sei Shonagon 48
Seibu Department Store (Tokyo) 97, 100, 103
Seinan Rebellion 243
Seiryo-ji Temple (Kyoto City) 171
Seisonkaku Villa (Kanazawa) 142
Sekigahara, battle of (1600) 50–51
Sen no Rikyu 163, 167, 191
Senbazuru (Kawabata Yasunari) 130
Sendai **268**
hotel 306
restaurant 338
Sendai Tanabata 42
Sengaku-ji Temple and Museum (Tokyo) **99**
Sengoku Golf Course (Hakone) 351, 353
Senmaida 144
Senso-ji Temple (Tokyo) 24, 59, **82–3**
Hagoita-Ichi 43
Sanja Matsuri 41
Sensuikyo Gorge 239
Seppuku 50
Sesshu 34, 204, 212
Seto Ohashi Bridge 204, 217
Setouchi islets 243
Setsubun 43
Seven-Five-Three Children's Festival 42–3
Shamisen 143, 157
Sharaku 81, 91
Shiba Park (Tokyo) **65**
Shibuya (Tokyo) 58
Street-by-Street map **92–3**
Shichi-go-san 42–3
Shigemori Mirei 167
Shiki Masaoka 220
Shiki Masaoka Museum (Matsuyama) 220
Shikoku **214–23**
climate 44
hotels **302–3**
map **216–7**
region 377
restaurants 334–5
transportation 217
Shikoku Mura Museum 218
Shikotsu Kohan 279
Shikotsu-Toya National Park 121, **278–9**
Shima Geisha House (Kanazawa) 143
Shimabara Peninsula **237**
Shimoda 133
Shimogamo Shirine (Kyoto City) 166
Shimoji Island 253
Shimokita Peninsula **273**
Shin Edogawa Garden (Tokyo) 97
Shin Yakushi-ji Temple (Nara) 185
Shin Yokohama Ramen Museum 127
Shinbashi Enbujo Theater (Tokyo) 105, 107
Shingon Sect Buddhism 193, **269**
deities 223
Kukai 152, 193, 215, **222–3**
Shingu 193
Shinjuku (Tokyo) 20–21
see also East Shinjuku, West Shinjuku
Shinjuku Opera City Gallery (Tokyo) 102
Shinjuku Pit Inn 105, 107
Shinjuku Station 86, **89**
shopping 100
Shinkyo Bridge (Nikko) 258
Shinsendo Bookstore (Kyoto City) 178, 179
Shinto 15, **22–3**
architecture 22–3
ema boards 23
fertility 23
festivals 38–43
kami 22
legends 239
priesthood 22
organizations 256, 257
religious studies 256, 257
shimenawa ropes 22
see also Shrines
Shiogama 270
restaurant 338
Shirahama Onsen 193, 347
hotel 301
Shirakawa-go 140, 141
hotel 296
Shiretoko National Park **285**
Shiritsu Yaeyama Museum (Ishigaki Island) 253
Shisen-do Temple (Kyoto City) **172**
Shishigatani SABIE (Kyoto City) 179
Shitamachi 58, 73
Shitamachi Museum (Tokyo) **80**
Shitenno-ji Temple (Osaka) 196–7
Shizuoka **133**
hotel 296
restaurant 329
Shochu 242, 323
Shodo Shonin 258, 259

Shoes
etiquette 365
shops in Kyoto 176, 177
traditional 37
Shogun (James Clavell) 53, 133
Shoguns
Kamakura shogunate 48
Muromachi shogunate 49
Tokugawa shogunate 52–3
Shokawa Valley **140**
Doburoku Matsuri 42
gassho-zukuri houses **141**
hotel 296
Shopping **340–45**
arts and crafts centers 342–3
clothing sizes 341
discount stores 342
duty-free allowances 361
exporting large items 341
in Kyoto **174–7**
malls and arcades 342
opening hours 340
paying 340–41
prices and sales tax 340
rights and refunds 341
supermarkets 342
tax-free shopping 341
temple and shrine stalls 343, 345
in Tokyo **100–3**
What to Buy in Japan **344–5**
wrapping 343
Shoren-in Temple (Kyoto City) **162**
Shosei-en Garden (Kyoto City) 153
Shotoku, Prince
founding of Horyuji Temple 190
founding of Shitenno-ji Temple (Osaka) 196
promotion of Buddhism 24, 47
Showboat 5i (Tokyo) 106, 107
Shrines (general)
admission fees 362
architecture 22–3
etiquette 365
to Inari 22
opening hours 362
stalls at 343
Shrines (individual)
Ama no Iwato Jingu (Takachiho) 239
Asakusa Jinja (Tokyo) 83
Chinbei-donchi (Kume Island) 252
Confucian (Nagasaki) 236
Dazaifu Tenman-gu **231**
Dewa Sanzan 268
Fushimi **173**
Futara-san (Nikko) 259
Hachiman-gu (Kamakura) 128–9
Hanazono (Tokyo) 87
Harimizu Utaki (Miyako Island) 252
Hayachine (Tono) 271
Heian (Kyoto City) 162
Hie Jinja (Tokyo) 95
Itsukushima (Miyajima Island) 210
Izumo-Taisha 207
Kamigamo (Kyoto City) 166
Kamo (Kyoto City) **166**
Kanda Myojin (Tokyo) **69**
Kasuga Grand Shrine (Nara) 185
Keta Taisha (Hakui) 144
Kitano Tenman-gu Shrine (Kyoto City) **167**
Kumano Jinja (Kitakata) 267
Kunozan Tosho-gu (Shizuoka) 133
Kushida (Fukuoka) 231
Meiji (Tokyo) **90**
Nachi Taisha 193
Namiyoke Inari Jinja (Tokyo) 64
Osaki Hachiman (Sendai) 268
Otoyo-jinja (Kyoto City) 164
Oyama (Kanazawa) 142
Sengen Jinja (Fuji-Yoshida) 135
Shiogama 270
Shrines (cont.)
Shimogamo (Kyoto City) 166
Shinzan (Oga) 272
Shoin (Hagi) 213
Suiten-gu (Kurume) 232
Suiten-gu (Yanagawa) 232
Sumiyoshi (Fukuoka) 231
Suwa (Nagasaki) 235
Taga-jinja (Uwajima) 221
Taikodani Inari 213
Taiyuin-byo (Nikko) **264–5**
Takachiho Jinja 239
Takinoo (Nikko) 259
Tanuki (Badger) Shrine (Kyoto City) 156
Tatsumi Daimyo-jin (Kyoto City) 156
Togo (Tokyo) 91
Tosho-gu (Nikko) **260–63**
Toyokawa Inari (Tokyo) 95
Udo Jingu (Nichinan Coast) 242
Usa Jingu 228
Yasaka (Kyoto City) 156, 160
Yasukuni (Tokyo) **68**
Yoshino Mikumari 191
Zeni-Arai Benten (Kamakura) 130
Shugaku-in Imperial Villa (Kyoto City) **172**
Shugendo Sect Buddhism 268, **269**
yamabushi 268
Shukkei-en Garden (Hiroshima) 209
Shukunegi (Sado Island) 267
Shunkunitai 284
Shuri (Naha City) 248
Shuri Castle 248
Shuzenji 133, 347
Silver Pavilion *see* Ginkaku-ji
Sino-Japanese Wars 54, 55
Skiing 352
Skiing resorts
Higashi-Hachimantai 272
Niseko **278**
Skymark 379
Snow Festival (Sapporo) 43
Soccer 351, 353
J-League 17, 351, 353
in Tokyo 106, 107
World Cup 2002 17, 351
Social attitudes 364–7
business 368
to foreigners 366
group mentality 366
hierarchy 364
physical contact and sex 365
taboos 364
Sony Corporation 20
Sony Showroom (Tokyo) 62
Soseki *see* Zen Buddhism
Sosogi 144
Sounkyo 280
Sounkyo Gorge 280
Spa World (Osaka) 196
Space Invaders 20
Spectacles Bridge (Nagasaki) 235
Spiral Building (Tokyo) 94
Spiral Garden 102
Sports 17, **350–53**
books 401
venues in Tokyo 106, 107
see also Martial Arts, and under individual sports
Square Building (Tokyo) 95, 106
Birdland 105, 107
Star Festival 39, 41
Starck, Philippe 21
Stroll gardens 27
Stubbins, Hugh 126
Studio Alta (Tokyo) 86
Subway systems 382
Sueda Art Museum (Yufuin) 229
Sugamo Prison (Tokyo) 97
Suganuma 140
Sugawara Michizane 167, 231
Sugihara Chiune 137
Suizen-ji Garden (Kumamoto) 238
Sukeroku (Tokyo) 102
Sumida River Trip (Tokyo) **65**
Sumo 17, **30–31, 350**
ancient sumo ring 144
booking tickets 350
books 401
grand champions *(yokozuna)* 30
Japan Sumo Association 350, 353
origins 30
stables *(beya)* **98**, 106, 107, 350
tournaments (Tokyo) 106, 350
wrestlers 30, 98
Sunshine City (Tokyo) 97
Suntory Hall (Tokyo) 105, 107
Suntory Museum (Osaka) 197
Suntory Museum of Art (Tokyo) 95
Super Mario 20
Sushi and Sashimi **318–19**
see also Food and Drink and Restaurants
Suzuki Harunobu *see* Harunobu
Sweet Basil (Tokyo) 105, 107
Sword Museum (Tokyo) **89**
Swords 51

T

T-Zone (Tokyo) 101, 103
Tachikichi
Kyoto 176, 177
Tokyo 62, 102, 103
Taiho code 47
Taiji 193
Taiji Whale Museum 193
Taiko drumming 267
Taira family
Kenreimon-in 173
Tairo no Kiyomori 48
Taiso Yoshitoshi 81
print of Noh play 32
Taiyuin-byo Shrine (Nikko) **264–5**
Taizo-in Subtemple (Kyoto City) 169
Takachiho **239**
Takachiho Gorge 239
Takamatsu **218**
hotels 302–3
restaurants 335
Takamatsu Castle 218
Takamura Kotaro 272
Takane Jewelry (Tokyo) 101
Takao District (Kyoto City) **171**
Takarazuka 197
Grand Theater 197
Theater (Tokyo) 62, 105, 107
Takashimaya Department Stores 342
Kyoto 174, 175
Tokyo 100, 103
Takayama **138–40**
festival (matsuri) 38, 40, 42
hotels 296–7
restaurants 329
Takayama Jinya 140
Takeshita-dori (Tokyo) 91
Taketomi Island 253
hotel 305
restaurant 337
Takeuchi Seiho 173
Takinoo Shrine (Nikko) 259
Takumi (Tokyo) 102, 103
Tale of Genji (Murasaki Shikibu) **48**
scrolls by Fujiwara Takayoshi 96
scrolls in Nagoya 137
Tale of the Heike 49, 215
Tamagotchi 20
Tanabata Matsuri 39, 41
Tanabe Art Museum (Matsue) 207
Tanaka-ya (Kyoto City) 176, 177
Tange Kenzo 20–21
Akasaka Prince Hotel (Tokyo) 95
Cenotaph (Hiroshima) 208
Hanae Mori Building (Tokyo) 91

Tange Kenzo (cont.)
Olympic Stadiums (Tokyo) 90
Tokyo Metropolitan Government Offices 84, 88
Yokohama Museum of Art 127
Tanuki **311**
Tanuki (Badger) Shrine (Kyoto City) 156
Tatami mats 29
Tatsumi Daimyo-jin Shrine (Kyoto City) 156
Tatsuno Kingo 66
Tattoos *(irezumi)* 197
Taxes
airport 379
in hotels 288
in restaurants 309
in shops 340–41
Taxis 384
Tazuke (Kyoto City) 175
Tea **322**
ceremony **163**
etiquette 163
gardens 27
plantation (Kanaya) 133
shops in Kyoto 176, 177
utensils 163
Teahouses 163
ochaya 156, 157
Telephones 374–5
cards 374–5
directory enquiries 375
emergency numbers 371
information services 362, 363
international dialing codes 375
international calls 375
local calls 375
mobile telephones 375
public telephones 374
Teletourist Service 104, 107, 362, 363
Television 374
Temples (general)
admission fees 362
architecture 24–5
etiquette 365
opening hours 362
stalls at 343
staying in 291
Zen temple layout **131**
Temples (individual)
88-temple pilgrimage 120
Adashino Nenbutsu-ji (Kyoto City) 171
Asuka-dera (Asuka) 191
Benzaiten-do (Naha City) 248
Byodo-in (Uji City) 26, 173
Chikurin-in (Yoshino) 191
Chion-in (Kyoto City) **162**
Choju-ji (Hagi) 213
Chosho-ji (Hirosaki) 273
Churen-ji (Dewa Sanzan) 268
Chuson-ji (Hiraizumi) 270
Chuzen-ji (Nikko National Park) 265
Daigo-ji (Kyoto City) **173**
Daikaku-ji (Kyoto City) 171
Dainichi-bo (Dewa Sanzan) 268
Daisen-in (Kyoto City) 26, **166–7**
Daishin-in Subtemple (Kyoto City) 169
Daisho-in (Miyajima Island) 211
Daitoku-ji (Kyoto City) 163, **166–7**
Eihei-ji **144**
Eikan-do (Kyoto City) 164, 165
Engaku-ji (Kamakura) 130, 131
Enryaku-ji Temple (Kyoto City) **172–3**
Fuki-ji (Usa) 228
Futago-ji (Usa) 228
Ginkaku-ji (Kyoto City) 26, 164, **165**
Gio-ji (Kyoto City) 171
Hase-dera (Kamakura) 128

Temples (cont.)
Higashi Hongan-ji Temple (Kyoto City) **153**
Hofuku-ji (Hagi) 213
Hokoku-ji (Kamakura) 129
Honen-in (Kyoto City) 164
Horyu-ji **190**
Ishiyama-dera (Otsu) 206
Jakko-in (Kyoto City) 173
Jingo-ji (Kyoto City) 171
Joei-ji (Yamaguchi) 212
Joken-ji (Tono) 271
Jojakko-ji Temple (Kyoto City) 171
Jonen-ji (Hagi) 213
Kanchan-in (Tokyo) 80
Kantei-byo (Yokohama) 127
Kanzeon-ji (Dazaifu) 231
Keishun-in Subtemple (Kyoto City) 169
Kencho-ji (Kamakura) 130
Kinkaku-ji (Kyoto City) **168**
Kita-in (Kawagoe) 126
Kiyomizu-dera (Kyoto City) **162**
Kofuku-ji (Nagasaki) 235
Kofuku-ji (Nara) 184
Komyo Zen-ji (Dazaifu) 231
Konchi-in (Kyoto City) 165
Kongobu-ji (Mount Koya) 193
Koryu-ji (Kyoto City) **169**
Kotohira-gu 219
Koto-in Subtemple (Kyoto City) 167
Kozan-ji (Kyoto City) 171
Kurama-dera (Kyoto City) 171
Kyotoku-ji (Hagi) 213
Mampuku-ji (Uji City) 173
Manshu-in (Kyoto City) **172**
Meigetsu-in (Kamakura) 130
Motsu-ji (Hiraizumi) 270
Myohon-ji (Kamakura) 129
Myoryu-ji (Kanazawa) 143
Myoshin-ji Temple (Kyoto City) **169**
Nanzen-ji (Kyoto City) 164, **165**
Narita-san Shinsho-ji (Narita) 126
Ninna-ji (Kyoto City) **169**
Nishi Hongan-ji (Kyoto City) **153**
Onjo-ji (Otsu) 206
Reiun-in Subtemple (Kyoto City) 169
Rinno-ji (Nikko) 258
Ruriko-ji (Yamaguchi) 212
Ryoan-ji (Kyoto City) 26, **168**
Ryogen-in Subtemple (Kyoto City) 167
Sanjusangen-do (Kyoto City) **152–3**
Sanzen-in (Kyoto City) 173
Seiryo-ji (Kyoto City) 171
Sengaku-ji (Tokyo) **99**
Senso-ji (Tokyo) 24, 59, **82–3**
Shin Yakushi-ji (Nara) 185
Shisen-do (Kyoto City) **172**
Shitenno-ji (Osaka) 196–7
Shofuku-ji (Fukuoka) 231
Shoho-ji (Gifu) 137
Shoren-in (Kyoto City) **162**
Shoshazan Enkyo-ji (Himeji) 203
Sofuku-ji (Nagasaki) 235
Soji-ji (Monzen) 144
Sugimoto-dera (Kamakura) 129
Taizo-in Subtemple (Kyoto City) 169
Tenju-an (Kyoto City) 165
Tenkyu-in Subtemple (Kyoto City) 169
Tenno-ji (Tokyo) 80
Tenryu-ji (Kyoto City) 170
Todai-ji Temple (Nara) **186–7**
Toji (Kyoto City) **152**
Tokei-ji (Kamakura) 130
Toko-ji (Hagi) 213
Toshodai-ji (Nara) 187

Temples (cont.)
Yakushi-ji (Nara) 187
Zenko-ji (Nagano) 145
Zojo-ji (Tokyo) 65
Zuigan-ji 270
Zuiho-in Subtemple (Kyoto City) 167, 269
Zuisen-ji (Kamakura) 129
Tempozan Harbor Village (Osaka) 197
Tendai Sect Buddhism 228, **269**
Saicho 172
Tenjin Matsuri (Osaka) 41
Tenninkyo 280
Tenno-ji Temple (Tokyo) 80
Tenryu-ji Temple (Kyoto City) 170
TEPCO Electric Energy Museum (Tokyo) 93
Teramachi Club (Kyoto City) 175
Terauchi (Kyoto City) 177
Textiles 35
bashofu fabric 251
bingata dyeing 248, 251
buying 345
indigo 35
kasuri dyeing 35, 232, 251
for kimonos 36
Kumejima-*tsumugi* 252
minsa fabric 253
Miyako-*jofu* fabric 252
ryusen dyeing 248, 251
shops in Tokyo 101, 103
tsumugi silk 243
yuzen dyeing 35, 142
Theater (general)
contemporary 105
traditional **32–3**
see also Bunraku, Kabuki, Kyogen, Noh
Theaters (individual)
Gion Kobu Kaburenjo (Kyoto City) 156, 178, 179
Honma Noh Stage (Sado Island) 267
Imperial Theater (Tokyo) 66
Kabuki-za Theater (Tokyo) **64,** 104
Kamishichi-ken Kaburenjo (Kyoto City) 178, 179
Kanamaru-za (Kotohira) 219
Kanze Noh-gakudo (Tokyo) 104, 107
Kongo Nogakudo (Kyoto City) 178, 179
Kyoto Kanze Kaikan 178, 179
Minami-za Theater (Kyoto City) 156, 178, 179
National Bunraku Theater (Osaka) 196
National Noh Theater (Tokyo) 104, 107
National Theater (Tokyo) 104, 107
New National Theater (Tokyo) 105, 107
Nihon Buyo Kyokai (Tokyo) 105, 107
Shinbashi Enbujo Theater (Tokyo) 105, 107
Takarazuka Grand Theater 197
Takarazuka Theater (Tokyo) 62, 105, 107
Tokyo International Forum **67**
Uchiko-za Theater 221
Theme Parks **348–9**
Amazing Square (Tokyo) 348, 349
Dr. Jeekans (Tokyo) 348, 349
Festivalgate (Osaka) 196
Glucks Okoku (Hokkaido) 348, 349
Hakkeijima Sea Paradise (Yokohama) 349
Holland Village (Nagasaki) 237
Huis ten Bosch (Nagasaki) 237, 348
Joypolis (Tokyo) 349

Theme Parks (cont.)
Kamogawa Sea World 349
Kinugawa Western Mura 349
Kurashiki Tivoli Park 205, 348
Niigata Russian Village 348, 349
Nijinosato 348, 349
Noboribetsu Marine Park Castle Nixe 349
Okinawa Memorial Park **250**
Paradiso (Osaka) 349
Reoma World 348, 349
Sanrio Puroland 348, 349
Seagaia 349
Space World 349
Tazawako Swiss Village 348, 349
Tempozan Harbor Village (Osaka) 197
Tobu World Square 348, 349
Tokyo Disneyland 348, 349
Unesco Village 349
Yomiuri Land (Tokyo) 349
see also Historical parks
TIC *see* Tourist Information Centers
Ticket agencies
CN Playguide 104, 107, 178
Ticket PIA 104, 107, 178, 179
Ticket Saison 104, 107
Tiger Drinking Water (Kano Tanyu) 165
Time differences 363
Tipping 367
in restaurants 309
Tobacco and Salt Museum (Tokyo) 93
Tobu Department Store (Tokyo) 97
Todai-ji Temple (Nara) **186–7**
Togo Shrine (Tokyo) 91
Tohoku region 256–7, 377
Toi 133
Toilets 371
Tojiki Kaikan (Kyoto City) 176, 177
Toji Temple (Kyoto City) **152**
Tojo Hideki 68, 97
Toka Ebisu Festival (Osaka) 43
Tokaido post road 123
Seki-sho Barrier Gate 133
Tokiwada (Tokyo) 102
Tokonoma 29
Tokugawa Art Museum (Nagoya) 137
Tokugawa Iemitsu 258
mausoleum **264–5**
Tokugawa Ieyasu **261**
founds Kanei-ji temple (Tokyo) 74
founds Nijo Castle (Kyoto City) 154
mausoleum 258, **260–63**
named shogun 52
in samurai history 50
Tokushima **219**
Awa-Odori 42, 219
restaurant 335
Tokyo **56–117**
at a glance map 58–9
Central Tokyo **60–71**
entertainment **104–7**
Farther Afield **96–9**
Hanabi Taikai 41
history 58
hotels **292–4**
Northern Tokyo **72–83**
restaurants **324–7**
shopping **100–3**
Street Finder maps **108–17**
subway system 382, Back Endpaper
Tori-no-ichi 42
transportation 58
Western Tokyo **84–95**
see also Edo
Tokyo Big Sight 99
Tokyo Central Post Office 376
Tokyo Central Wholesale Market *see* Tsukiji Fish Market
Tokyo Classified 104, 374
Tokyo Day and Night 104
Tokyo Decks 99, 100
Tokyo Disneyland 348, 349
Tokyo Dome 106, 107
Tokyo International Exhibition Hall *see* Tokyo Big Sight
Tokyo International Film Festival 105, 107
Tokyo International Forum **67**
Tokyo Journal 104, 374
Tokyo Metropolitan Art Museum 74
Tokyo Metropolitan Government Offices 84, 88
Tokyo Metropolitan Museum of Photography 99
Tokyo National Museum 59 **76–9**
Gallery of Horyu-ji Treasures 77
Heiseikan building 79
Honkan building 76–7
shop 101
Toyokan building 78
Tokyo Opera City **96**
music venue 105
shopping 100, 102
Tokyo Station 66
shopping 100
Tokyo Stock Exchange 66
Tokyo Summer Festival 105, 107
Tokyo Tower **65**
Tokyu Hands Department Stores
Ikebukuro (Tokyo) 97, 100, 103
Shibuya (Tokyo) 92
Tolman Collection (Tokyo) 102
Tono **271**
hotel 306
restaurant 338
Torii (gates) 22
Great Torii (Miyajima Island) 210, **211**
Torii Kiyonaga 81
Torii Pass 136
Tori-no-ichi (Tokyo) 42
Toro ruins (Shizuoka) 133
Tosa fighting dogs 220
Tosa Token Center (Kochi) 220
Toshi-mashi-tei Garden (Yanagawa) 232
Tosho-gu Fall Festival (Nikko) 42
Tosho-gu Grand Festival (Nikko) 41
Tosho-gu Shrine (Nikko) **260–63**
Tosho-gu Treasure Hall and Museum of Art (Nikko) 259
Toshodai-ji Temple (Nara) 187
Tottori Sand Dunes **206**
Toulouse-Lautrec, Henri 197
Tourist Information Centers **362**
Kansai Airport 379
Kyoto Station 152, 179
Narita Airport 379
Sapporo International Communication Plaza 279
Tokyo International Forum 67
Tours 355
religious tours 357
Tours by car
Ise Peninsula Tour **192**
Kiso Valley Tour **136**
Saga Pottery Towns Tour **233**
Towada-Hachimantai National Park **272**
Tower Records (Tokyo) 93, 104, 107
Toyoda Aisan-do (Kyoto City) 176, 177
Toyokawa Inari Shrine (Tokyo) 95
Toyota cars
factory 137
Toyotomi Hideyoshi
birthplace 137
building of Osaka Castle 194
persecution of Christians 234
in samurai history 50
unification of Japan 52
Toys
buying 345
Trains 380–81
facilities 380–81
Green Windows 382
JR Pass 381
Oigawa steam railroad 133
Maglevs 197
rail network 380
rail passes 381
seat reservations 382
shinkansen 380
ticket machines 382
Torokko train 170
Travel **378–85**
air 378–9
bicycle 385
boat 379, 383
buses 383
car 384
Central Honshu 125
Hokkaido 276
Kyoto City 151
Kyushu 227
monorail 383
motorbike 385
Northern Honshu 257
Okinawa 247
rickshaw 385
Shikoku 217
subway 382
taxis 384
Tokyo 58
train 380–82
tram 383
Western Honshu 183
Travelers' checks 372
Tsugaruhan Neputa Mura (Hirosaki) 273
Tsujikura (Kyoto City) 176, 177
Tsukiji Fish Market (Tokyo) **64**
Tsukimochi-ya Naomasa (Kyoto City) 176, 177
Tsukuda island (Tokyo) 65
Tsumago 136
Tsumugi silk 243
Tsuruga Castle (Aizu-Wakamatsu) 266
Tsurui 284
Tsuruoka **268**
hotel 306
restaurant 338
Tsuwano **213**
hotels 301
restaurants 334
Tsuwano Castle 213
Tuna fish supplies **64**
Typhoons 370

U

Uchiko **221**
Uchiko-za Theater 221
Ueno Park, Tokyo 59, **74–5**
Uji City **173**
Ukiyo-e (woodblock prints) 17, **81**
buying 345
shops in Tokyo 68, 102, 103
see also Museums and Galleries
Unkei 171
Unzen Spa 237, 347
hotels 304
Unzen-Amakusa National Park 237
Uraku-en Park (Inuyama) 137
Urushi Museum (Nikko) 259
Uruwashi-ya (Kyoto City) 175
US-Japan Security Treaty 55
Usa **228**
Usokae (Dazaifu) 43
Usuki Stone Buddhas **229**
Utagawa Kuniyoshi 81
Utamaro, Kitagawa 81
Utoro 285
Utsukushigahara 145
Uwajima **221**
hotel 303

Uwajima (cont.)
restaurant 335
Uzahama (Okinawa) 251

V

Van Gogh, Vincent 81
Vegetarian food 309, 320
Zen 130
Vending machines **309**
Video
compatibility of systems 341
Viñoly, Rafael
Tokyo International Forum 21, **67**
Visas 360–61
working 369
Vita Sexualis (Mori Ogai) 213
Volcanoes 19
safety guidelines 370

W

Wadakura Fountain Park (Tokyo) 66
Wajima 144
Wakinosawa 273
Wako Department Store (Tokyo) 63, 342
Wakoto 281
Wanza Ariake Building (Tokyo) 99, 100
Waseda (Tokyo) 97
Washi (paper)
buying 344
shops in Kyoto 177
wrapping 343
Water-Drawing Festival (Nara) 40
Waters, Thomas 62
Watersports 352–3
Wave (Tokyo) 95
Wax Museum of the Tale of the Heike (Takamatsu) 218
Weaver Festival 39
Weddings
traditional 37
Welcome Cards 362
Welcome Inn Reservation Center 288
West Shinjuku (Tokyo) 58
Street-by-Street map **88–9**
Western Honshu **180–213**
climate 45
hotels **298–302**
map **182**
restaurants **331–4**
transportation 183
Western Tokyo **84–95**
hotels **293–4**
maps 58, **85**
restaurants **326–7**
transportation 85
Wild Geese, The (Mori Ogai) 213
Wildlife
books 401
brown bears 285
dolphins 285
eco-tourism 353
Iriomote wild cat 253
Japanese cormorants 285
Latham's snipe 278
minke whales 285
Wildlife (cont.)
Nature Conservation Society of Japan 353
porpoises 285
red fox 285
sea ducks 285
sea eagles 284, 285
sea hawks 253
short-tailed shearwaters 285
sika deer 285
spectacled guillemots 285
Steller's sea eagle 285
tancho (red-crowned crane) 284
white-tailed sea eagles 285
whooper swans 284
Wild Bird Society of Japan 353
Woman in the Dunes (Abe) 206
Women travelers 370
Woodblock prints *see Ukiyo-e*
Woodcraft 35
buying 344
kabazaiku woodwork 272
yosegi-zaiku woodwork **132**, 133
Working in Japan 368–9
World Cup 2002 *see* Soccer
World War II 54–5
Battle of Okinawa 245, **249**
bombing of Hiroshima **208**
bombing of Nagasaki 237
Imperial Navy Underground HQ **249**
kamikaze pilots 243
Okinawa Battle Sites **249**
Pearl Harbor, attack on 55
Wrapping 343

X

Xavier, Francis 242
founding of Jesuit mission 49
Xavier Memorial Chapel (Yamaguchi) 212

Y

Yaesu Station (Tokyo)
shopping 100
Yaeyama Islands **253**
map 247
Yajiyagama Cave (Kume Island) 252
Yakushi-ji Temple (Nara) 187
Yakuza **197**, 370
Yamagata (Dewa Sanzan)
hotel 307
restaurant 339
Yamagata Arimoto 165
Yamagiwa (Tokyo) 101, 103
Yamaguchi **212**
hotel 301
restaurant 334
Yamaguchi Seishijo Workshop (Yame) 232
Yamanote JR line (Tokyo) 58
Yamato 47, 181
Yamayaki (Nara) 43
Yanagawa **232**
restaurants 337
Yanagi Muneyoshi 96
Yanagisawa Yoshiyasu 97
Yanagita Kunio
Legends of Tono 271
Yanaka District (Tokyo) **80**
Yaotsu 137
Yasaka Shrine (Kyoto City) 156, 160
Yasukuni Shrine (Tokyo) **68**
Yayoi Matsuri (Nikko) 40
Yayoi period 47, 232
Yobuko 233
Yodobashi Camera (Tokyo) 101, 103
Yokohama **126–7**
hotels 297
map 127
restaurant 329–30
Yokohama Museum of Art 127
Yokoyama Taikan 259
Yonaguni Island 253
Yonaha Maehama Beach (Miyako Island) 253
Yosegi-zaiku woodwork *see* Woodcraft
Yosheido Gallery (Tokyo) 102, 103
Yoshida Shoin 213
Yoshijima Heritage House (Takayama) 138
Yoshimasa, shogun 165
Yoshino **191**
hotel 302
Yoshinogari Archaeological Site **232**, 233
Yoshitoku (Tokyo) 102, 103
Yoshiwara pleasure quarter (Tokyo) 82
Youth culture 95
Youth hostels 289
Yoyogi Park (Tokyo) **90–91**
Yufuin **229**, 347
hotel 305
Yufuin Museum 229
Yuki Matsuri (Sapporo) 43
Yukio Mishima *see* Mishima Yukio
Yunokawa 278
Yurikamome monorail (Tokyo) 99
Yushukan Museum (Tokyo) 68
Yuzen dyeing 35

Z

Zeami 32, 267
Zen Buddhism **269**
cuisine 130, 320
dry-landscape gardens 26, 269
Eisai 231
introduction from China 49
in Kamakura 130
layout of a Zen Buddhist temple **131**
Obaku Zen 269
Rinzai Zen 269
Soseki 168
Soto Zen 144, 269
religious studies 257
and the tea ceremony 163
see also Meditation, Temples
Zhu Shun Shui 69
Zojo-ji Temple (Tokyo) 65
Zuiho-in Subtemple (Kyoto City) 167, 269

Further Reading

Japanese names are given with family name last, as on book covers.

History

Everyday Life in Traditional Japan Charles J Dunn (Tuttle, 1972/1997)
Hiroshima John Hersey (Knopf/Penguin, 1985)
Japan: the Story of a Nation Edwin Reischauer (Tuttle, 1981)
Low City, High City: Tokyo from Edo to the Earthquake Edward Seidensticker (Knopf, 1983)
The Nobility of Failure: Tragic Heroes in the History of Japan Ivan Morris (Tuttle, 1982)
The Pacific War 1931-1945 Saburo Ienaga (Pantheon, 1978)
The Rise of Modern Japan W G Beasley (Weidenfeld and Nicolson, 1995)
A Short History of Japan W G Beasley (University of California Press, 1999)
Tokyo Rising: the City Since the Earthquake Edward Seidensticker (Knopf, 1990)
A Traveller's History of Japan Richard Tames (Windrush, 1993)
The World of the Shining Prince Ivan Morris (Penguin, 1964)

Society and Religion

The Chrysanthemum and the Sword Ruth Benedict (Routledge & Kegan Paul, 1967/Houghton Mifflin, 1989: first published 1946)
A First Zen Reader/A Second Zen Reader Trevor Leggett (Tuttle, 1960/1988)
Geisha Liza Dalby (University of California Press, reissued 1998)
Geisha Jodi Cobb (Knopf, 1997)
The Japanese Woman: Traditional Image and Changing Reality Sumiko Iwao (Harvard University Press, 1993)
Keiretsu: Inside the Hidden Japanese Conglomerates Kenichi Miyashita and David Russell (McGraw-Hill, 1996)
The Land of the Rising Yen George Mikes (Penguin, 1973)
Made in Japan: Akio Morita and Sony Akio Morita (Harper Collins, 1994/E P Dutton (1986)
Pink Samurai: an Erotic Exploration of Japanese Society Nicholas Bornoff (Grafton, 1991)
Religion in Japan ed. P F Kornicki and I J McMullen (Cambridge University Press, 1996)
The Way of Tea Rand Castile (Weatherhill, 1979)
Yakuza David Kaplan and Alec Dubro (Addison-Wesley, 1986)
Zen and Japanese Culture Daisetsu T Suzuki (Princeton University Press, 1970)

Japanese Arts

The Art of Japanese Gardens Herb Gustafson (David & Charles, 1999)
The Art of Zen Stephen Addiss (Harry Abrams, 1989)
Contemporary Japanese Architects Philip Jodido (Taschen, 1997)
Furo: the Japanese Bath Peter Grilli and Dana Levy (Kodansha, 1985)
How to Look at Japanese Art Stephen Addiss (Harry N Abrams Inc, 1996)
Japan Crafts Sourcebook Japan Craft Forum (Kodansha, 1996)
Japan 2000: Architecture and Design for the Japanese Public ed John Zukowsky (Prestel, 1998)
Japanese Art Joan Stanley-Baxter (Thames & Hudson, 1984)
Japanese Country Living Katoh & Kimura (Tuttle, 1993)
The Japanese Film Joseph L Anderson and Donald Richie (Princeton University Press, 1982)
The Japanese Print Hugo Munsterberg (Weatherhill, 1998
The Kabuki Handbook Aubrey and Giovanna Halford (Tuttle, 1990)
Matsuri: the World of Japanese Festivals Villar & Anderson (Shufunotomo, 1997)
Minka: the Quintessential Japanese House Kiyoshi Takai (Tuttle, 1998)
The Noh Plays of Japan Arthur Waley (Tuttle, 1976)
A Taste of Japan Donald Richie (Kodansha, 1985)
The Unknown Craftsman: A Japanese Insight into Beauty Soetsu Yanagi (Kodansha, 1989)
Vanishing Japan: Traditional Crafts & Culture Elizabeth Kiritani (Tuttle, 1995)
What Is Japanese Architecture? Kazuo Nishi and Kazuo Hozumi (Kodansha, 1985)

Sports & Outdoor Activities

A Birdwatcher's Guide to Japan Mark Brazil (Kodansha, 1987)
Grand Sumo Lora Sharnoff (Weatherhill, 1993)
A Guide to Japanese Hot Springs Anne Hotta with Yoko Ishiguro (Kodansha, 1986)
Hiking in Japan Paul Hunt (Kodansha, 1988)
Martial Arts & Sports in Japan (Japan Tourist Board, 1998)
National Parks of Japan Mary Sutherland and Dorothy Britton (Kodansha, 1981)

Travelogues and Memoirs

The Bells of Nagasaki Takashi Nagai (Kodansha, 1984: first published 1949)
From Sea to Sea Rudyard Kipling (Macmillan, 1908)
Glimpses of Unfamiliar Japan Lafcadio Hearn (Houghton Mifflin, 1894: first published 1903)
Home Life in Tokyo Jukichi Inouye (Routledge & Kegan Paul, 1985: first published 1910)
The Inland Sea Donald Richie (Century, 1971/1986)
Japanese Inn Oliver Statler (Picador, 1961/Tuttle, 1973)
Japanese Pilgrimage Oliver Statler (Picador/Morrow, 1983)
Kokoro: Hints and Echoes of Japanese Inner Life Lafcadio Hearn (Tuttle, 1972: first published 1896)
The Old Sow in the Back Room Harriet Sergeant (John Murray, 1994)
Pictures from the Water Trade John David Morley (Andre Deutsch, 1985)
The Railway Man Eric Lomax (Vintage, 1996)
The Roads to Sata: a 2000-Mile Walk through Japan Alan Booth (Weatherhill/Penguin, 1985)
Tales from the Burma Campaign 1942-1945 ed John Nunneley (Burma Campaign Fellowship Group, 1998)
Things Japanese Basil Hall Chamberlain (Tuttle, 1971: first published 1905)
Travelers' Tales Japan ed Donald W George and Amy Greinan Carlson (Travelers' Tales, 1999)
Unbeaten Tracks in Japan Isabella Bird (Virago, 1984: first published 1880)

Fiction

Anthology of Modern Japanese Literature Donald Keene (Tuttle, 1970)
An Artist of the Floating World Kazuo Ishiguro (Penguin, 1986)
Black Rain Masuji Ibuse (Kodansha, 1978)
Botchan Natsume Soseki (Tuttle, 1968)
The Counterfeiter and Other Stories Yasushi Inoue (Tuttle, 1965/Peter Owen 1989)
The Ginger Tree Oswald Wynd (Eland, 1977)
The Izu Dancer Yasunari Kawabata (Tuttle, 1954)
Kitchen Banana Yoshimoto (Faber & Faber, 1988)
The Legends of Tono Kunio Yanagita (Japan Foundation, 1975)
The Makioka Sisters Junichiro Tanizaki (Knopf, 1957)
Memoirs of a Geisha Arthur Golden (Chatto & Windus, 1997)
The Narrow Road to the Deep North Matsuo Basho (Penguin, 1966)
The Penguin Book of Japanese Verse (Penguin, 1998)
The Pillow Book of Sei Shonagon Sei Shonagon (Penguin, 1971)
Shogun James Clavell (Hodder & Stoughton, 1975)
Silence Shusako Endo (Penguin, 1988)
The Silent Cry Kenzaburo Oe (Serpent's Tail, 1988)
Snow Country Yasunari Kawabata (Vintage, 1996/1956)
The Tale of Genji Murasaki Shikibu (Penguin, 1981)
The Temple of the Golden Pavilion Yukio Mishima (Tuttle, 1958; Everyman 1956/1994)
Traveller's Literary Companion to Japan Harry Guest (In Print Publishing, 1994)

Acknowledgments

Blue Island Publishing would like to thank the following people at Dorling Kindersley:

Managing Editor
Anna Streiffert.

Managing Art Editor
Kate Poole.

Editorial Directors
Vivien Crump, Louise Bostock Lang.

Art Director
Gillian Allan.

Publisher
Douglas Amrine.

Production
Marie Ingledew, Michelle Thomas.

The Publishers would also like to thank the following people whose contributions and assistance have made the preparation of this book possible:

Main Contributors
John Benson lives in Kyoto and has written and edited many travel articles and website guides about Kyoto, Osaka, and other parts of Kansai.

Mark Brazil, a biologist, natural history and travel writer, and also film consultant, has lived for extended periods in Hokkaido and is a specialist in the natural history of the island.

Jon Burbank is a travel writer and photographer who lives in Chiba prefecture, to the east of Tokyo, with his family.

Angela Jeffs, a writer and editor, moved to Japan in 1986. She lives in Kanagawa prefecture, southwest of Tokyo.

Emi Kazuko is a writer and broadcaster who moved to London from Japan in the 1980s. She is the author of several books about the cuisine of her home country.

Stephen Mansfield is a travel writer and photographer based in Chiba prefecture, whose works about Japan and Asia have appeared in over 80 publications worldwide.

William F. Marsh, a versatile writer, editor, and filmmaker, sadly died in Tokyo while this book was in preparation.

Catherine Rubinstein is a London-based editor and writer who has lived and traveled for extended periods in Japan.

Jacqueline Ruyak is a travel writer who spends half of the year in the United States and the other half in a thatched farmhouse in the mountains of Northern Honshu.

Additional Contributors
Harry Cook, Brian Burke-Gaffney, Chie Furutani.

Design and Editorial Assistance
Amaia Allende, Annette Foo, Nicholas Inman, Anthony Limerick, Samuel Richardson, Lupus Sabene.

Special Assistance
David Hodgson at the Japan National Tourist Organization, the owners and chefs at Kiku Restaurant in London.

Artwork Reference
Photonica/Amana Images.

Additional Photography
Stephen Bere, Martin Plomer.

Photography Permissions
The Publishers thank all the temples, castles, museums, hotels, restaurants, shops, and other sights for their assistance and kind permission to photograph their establishments.

Picture Credits
t=top; tl=top left; tlc=top left center; tc=top center; trc=top right center; tr=top right; cla=center left above; ca=center above; cra=center right above; cl=center left; c=center; cr=center right; clb=center left below; cb=center below; crb=center right below; bl=bottom left; b=bottom; bc=bottom center; bcl=bottom center left; bcr=bottom center right; br=bottom right; d=detail.

The Frank Lloyd Wright Imperial Hotel has been produced with the permission of the copyright holder © ARS New York/DACS London 2000 348b.

The Publishers thank the following individuals, companies, and picture libraries for permission to reproduce their photographs:

AFP: Toshifumi Kitamura-STF 354t; Hwang Kwang 17t; Kauhiro-Nogi-STF 31cb; Ereiko Sugita-STF 55c; Yoshikazu Tsuno-STF 354b; Arcaid: Richard Bryant 1988/ Tadao Ando 21cb; Askaen Co Ltd: 190bl; Axiom: Steve J. Berbow 289b, Michael Coster 30–31, 30b, 163b; Jim Holmes 19tr, 30tl, 34cra, 371tl/crb, 104b,158-9, 365t; Paul Quayle 25tl, 31bl, 98t, 347t.

Dave Bartruff: 30tr, 31br, 33bc, 37b, 163t, 253t/c/b, 350b; Bridgeman Art Library, London, New York, and Paris: British Museum, London, Katsushika Hokusai (1760–1849) *Fuji in Clear Weather* from the series *36 Views of Mount Fuji* pub by Nishimura Eijudo in 1831, 53b; Fitzwilliam Museum, Cambridge, UK, Katsushika Hokusai (1760–1849) *Block Cutting and Printing Surimono*, 1825, 81b; Hermitage, St. Petersburg, Russia, *Fly Eating a Pear* 18th-19th century Japanese netsuke 34tl; Private Collection Ando or Utagawa Hiroshige (1797–1858) *Mountains and Coastline*, two views from *36 Views of Mount Fuji* pub by Kosheihi in 1853, 135c; Private Collection/

Bonhams *Satsuma Oviform Vase Decorated with Woman Playing the Samisen,* 19th century, 34br; Victoria and Albert Museum, London, Utagawa Kuniyoshi (1798–1861) *Mitsukini Defying the Skeleton Spectre* c.1845, 81crb; BRITISH AIKIDO FEDERATION 31bc; BRITISH LIBRARY: Maps Collection Maps 63140 (2) *Map of Yedo Japan*, 1704, 53c.

CHRISITE'S IMAGES: 34cla/cb, 35cl, 47t, 49t, 51cb; 53t, 81t/clb; CORBIS: 55t, 208bl, 249b, 356t; Asian Art and Archaeology Inc 32t, 50ca, 81cla; Morton Beebe S.F. 318tr; Bettmann 24tr; Horace Bristol 25bl; Burstein Collection 48ca; Ric Ergenbright 134tl; Eye Ubiquitous/John Dakers 38–9; Natalie Forbes 281b; Michael Freeman 41t; Historical Picture Archive 135b; Robbie Jack 32br; Kevin R. Morris 351b; Richard T. Nowitz 35br; Philadelphia Museum of Art 54t; Sakamoto Photo Research Lab 187tl; Liba Taylor 364c; Michael Yamashita 26tr, 31tr, 33c/bl/br, 39tr/39bl, 134b, 291b, 352b; DOUG CORRANCE: 24ca, 372c.

EVOLVER: 360c.

MICHAEL FREEMAN: 2-3, 19br, 122; FURUHATA BIJUTSU PRINTING COMPANY: Possesion of Rinno-ji Taiyuin-byo, Nikko, National Treasure, World Heritage 264ca; ZAIDANHOJIN FUSHIN-AN: 163cla.

GETTY ONE STONE: Thierry Cazabon 30cb; Paul Chesley 21tl, 370b; Charles Gupton 312t, 364b; Will and Deni McIntyre 14cr.

ROBERT HARDING PICTURE LIBRARY: Elly Beintema 364t; Nigel Blythe 15t, 29tl; C. Bowman 378b; Robert Francis 14b; Gavin Heller 14–7; Christopher Rennie 24–25c, 190tl, 383tr; Paul van Riel 382cl. NIGEL HICKS: 20ca, 23tl, 26br, 27tr/cra, 39cbr, 163crb, 280t, 358–9; HIKONE CASTLE MUSEUM: 50–1; GEOFF HOWARD: 20bl.

JAL AIRLINES: 378c; JNTO: 362t.

KOBE CITY MUSEUM: 50cb; KYORYOKUKAI CORP IN AID OF THE TOKYO NATIONAL MUSEUM: 48t, 49c, 59cl, 72, 76l/r, 77t/ca/cb, 78t/cr/bl/br, 79tl/tr/bl; Important Cultural Properties 46, 48cb, 77bl/bc/br, 78cl/bl, 79br.

NIJO CASTLE: 154t/b, 155tl/bl; MOH NISHIKAWA: 22–23c.

ORION PRESS: 41b; Angle Photo Library 284tl, 285c; Tori Endo 281t; Asao Fujita 284tr; Masami Goto 285b; Hirohito Hara 26cla; Jyunko Hirai 44t; Masaaki Horimachi 42t, 277b, 280, 285t; Yochi Kamihara 240–41, 244; Daimei Kato 37tr; Shoji Kato 39tl; Kitakanto Colour Agency 258b; Mitsutoshi Kimura 37tc; Fuji Kogei 36cla; Morita Collection 36t; Hideki Nawate 274; Nigata Photo Library 36cr; Yoshiharu Nuga 36clb; Minoru Okuda 45t; Akinari Okuyama 19tl/bl, 284b; Jiichi Omichi 163cra; Yoshikazu Onishi 252b; Sai 18c; Motonobu Sato 20–21; Shikoku Photo Service 219tl; Koichi Sudo 27tl; Hideaki Tanaka 36bl, 39cla, 199c; Nobuo Tanaka 28cb; Kosuke Takeuchi 38ca; Yoshio Tomii 43b; Tohoku Colour Agency 26cra; Eizo Toyoshima 37cr; Yoshimitsu Yagi 32c; Tomokazu Yamada 282–3; Yuzo Yamada 42b; Hiroyuki Yamaguchi 252t; Kenzo Yamamoto 27clb; Noriyuki Yoshida 12, 26bl, 28t, 36br, 37cl.

PHOTONICA: Amana Images/Seigo Matsuno 52t; /Ikuo Nonka 43t; /Hiroyoshi Terao 28bl; PICTOR: 38t, 55br; PRIVATE COLLECTION: 3i, 9i, 57, 119i, 287i, 359i.

REIMEIKAN COLLECTION, Kagoshima City: 50b; SIMON RICHMOND: 28br, 369c; BOARD OF TRUSTEES OF THE ROYAL ARMOURIES: Accession Number XXVIS.158–9 51t; Accession Number XXVIA.20 51ca; CATHERINE RUBENSTEIN: 131cr, 133t, 144t.

SHOGAKUKAN INC: publishers of *Big Comic Superior* illustration by Koyama Yuu, Ishikawa Yuugo, Hayakawa Shigei, layout by Norma Takashi & Kachidokii 21bl; SONY CONSUMER PRODUCTS: 20br; STOCKHOUSE, Hong Kong: 54c.

TELEGRAPH COLOUR LIBRARY: Tim Graham 350c, 370t; /Bavaria-Bidagentur 368t; Colorific/Jean Paul Nacivet 353t; Michael Yamashita 17c/b, 18br, 30ca, 163clb, 346c; 351t, 379b; Black Star/Patrick Morrow 275t, /Eiji Miyazawa 197bl/br; Matrix/Karen Kusmauski 322tr; /Japack Photolibrary 8–9; /FPG © Travelpix 279b; TREASURES FROM THE TOKUGAWA ART MUSEUM: 50–51b, 52t.

WERNER FORMAN ARCHIVE: 32bl/bcl/bcr, 33tr, 154ca, /Victoria and Albert Museum, London, 81car.

Front Endpaper: all special photography except MICHAEL FREEMAN Rcr; ORION PRESS: Yoichi Kamihara Ltl; Hideki Nawate Rtr; KYORYOKUKAI CORP IN AID OF THE TOKYO NATIONAL MUSEUM: Rbc.

Jacket: all special photography except front cover CORBIS: Jack Fields bc; Robert Holmes t; Richard T. Nowitz cra; PCTOR: cb.

Phrase Book

The Japanese language is related to Okinawan and is similar to Altaic languages such as Mongolian and Turkish. Written Japanese uses a combination of three scripts: Chinese ideograms, known as *kanji*, and two syllable-based alphabet systems known as *hiragana* and *katakana*. These two latter are similar, *katakana* functioning as italics are used in English. Traditionally, Japanese is written in vertical columns from top right to bottom left, though the Western system is increasingly used. There are several romanization systems; the Hepburn system is used in this guide. To simplify romanization, macrons (long marks over vowels to indicate longer pronunciation) have not been used. Japanese pronunciation is fairly straightforward, and many words are "Japanized" versions of Western words. This Phrase Book gives the English word or phrase, followed by the Japanese script, then the romanization, adapted to aid pronunciation.

Guidelines for Pronunciation

When reading the romanization, give the same emphasis to all syllables. The practice in English of giving one syllable greater stress may render a Japanese word incomprehensible.

Pronounce vowels as in these English words:

a	as the "u" in "cup"
e	as in "red"
i	as in "chief"
o	as in "solid"
u	as the "oo" in "cuckoo"

When two vowels are used together, give each letter an individual sound:

ai	as in "pine"
ae	as if written "ah-eh"
ei	as in "pay"

Consonants are pronounced as in English. The letter *g* is always hard as in "gate," and *j* is always soft as in "joke." *R* is pronounced something between *r* and *l*. *F* is sometimes pronounced as *h*. "*Si*" always becomes "*shi*," but some people pronounce "*shi*" as "*hi*." *V* in Western words (e.g., "video") becomes *b*. If followed by a consonant, *n* may be pronounced as either *n* or *m*.

All consonants except *n* are always either followed by a vowel or doubled; however, sometimes an *i* or *u* is barely pronounced. In this Phrase Book, to aid pronunciation, apostrophes are used where an *i* or *u* is barely pronounced within a word, and double consonants where this occurs at the end of a word.

Dialects

Standard Japanese is used and understood throughout Japan by people of all backgrounds. But on a colloquial level, there are significant differences in both pronunciation and vocabulary, even between the Tokyo and Osaka-Kyoto areas, and rural accents are very strong.

Polite Words and Phrases

There are several different levels of politeness in the Japanese language, according to status, age, and situation. In everyday conversation, politeness levels are simply a question of the length of verb endings (longer is more polite), but in formal conversation entirely different words *(keigo)* are used. As a visitor, you may find that people try to speak to you in formal language, but there is no need to use it yourself; the level given in this Phrase Book is neutral yet polite.

In an Emergency

Help!	たすけて！	Tas'kete!
Stop!	とめて！	Tomete!
Call a doctor!	医者をよんでください！	Isha o yonde kudasai!
Call an ambulance!	救急車をよんでください！	Kyukyusha o yonde kudasai!
Call the police!	警察をよんでください！	Keisatsu o yonde kudasai!
Fire!	火事！	Kaji!
Where is the hospital?	病院はどこにありますか？	Byoin wa doko ni arimass-ka?
police box	交番	koban

Communication Essentials

Yes/no.	はい／いいえ	Hai/ie.
… not …	･･･ない／ちがいます。	… nai/ chigaimass.
I don't know.	しりません。	Shirimasen.
Thank you.	ありがとう。	Arigato.
Thank you very much.	ありがとうございます。	Arigato gozaimass.
Thank you very much indeed.	どうもありがとうございます。	Domo arigato gozaimass.
Thanks (casual).	どうも。	Domo.
No, thank you.	結構です。ありがとう。	Kekko dess, arigato.
Please (offering).	どうぞ。	Dozo.
Please (asking).	おねがいします。	Onegai shimass.
Please (give me or do for me).	･･･ください。	… kudasai.
I don't understand.	わかりません。	Wakarimasen.
Do you speak English?	英語を話せますか？	Eigo o hanasemass-ka?
I can't speak Japanese.	日本語は話せません。	Nihongo wa hanasemasen.
Please speak more slowly.	もう少しゆっくり話してください。	Mo s'koshi yukkuri hanash'te kudasai.
Sorry/Excuse me!	すみません。	Sumimasen!
Could you help me please? (not emergency).	ちょっと手伝っていただけませんか？	Chotto tets'datte itadakemasen-ka?

Useful Phrases

My name is ….	わたしの名前は･･･です。	Watashi no namae wa … dess.
How do you do, pleased to meet you.	はじめまして、どうぞよろしく。	Hajime-mash'te, dozo yorosh'ku.
How are you?	お元気ですか？	Ogenki dess-ka?
Good morning.	おはようございます。	Ohayo gozaimass.
Good afternoon/ good day.	こんにちは。	Konnichiwa.
Good evening.	こんばんは。	Konbanwa.

Good night.	おやすみなさい。	Oyasumi nasai.
Good-bye.	さよなら。	Sayonara.
Take care.	気をつけて。	Ki o ts'kete.
Keep well (casual).	お元気で。	Ogenki de.
The same to you.	そちらも。	Kochira koso.
What is (this)?	(これは) 何ですか？	(Kore wa) nan dess-ka?
How do you use this?	これをどうやって使いますか？	Kore o doyatte ts'kaimass-ka?
Could I possibly have ...? (very polite)	…をいただけますか？	... o itadake-mass-ka?
Is there ... here?	ここに…がありますか？	Koko ni ... ga arimass-ka?
Where can I get ...?	…はどこにありますか？	... wa doko ni arimass-ka?
How much is it?	いくらですか？	Ikura dess-ka?
What time is ...?	…何時ですか？	... nan-ji dess-ka?
Cheers! (toast)	乾杯！	Kampai!
Where is the restroom/toilet?	お手洗い／おトイレはどこですか？	Otearai/otoire wa doko dess-ka?
Here's my business card.	名刺をどうぞ。	Meishi o dozo.

USEFUL WORDS

I	わたし	watashi
woman	女性	josei
man	男性	dansei
wife	奥さん	ok'san
husband	主人	shujin
daughter	むすめ	musume
son	むすこ	mus'ko
child	こども	kodomo
children	こどもたち	kodomo-tachi
businessman/woman	ビジネスマン／ウーマン	bijinessuman/wuman
student	学生	gakusei
Mr./Mrs./Ms. ...	…さん	...-san
big/small	大きい／小さい	okii/chiisai
hot/cold	暑い／寒い	atsui/samui
cold (to touch)	冷たい	tsumetai
warm	温かい	atatakai
good/not good/bad	いい／よくない／悪い	ii/yokunai/warui
enough	じゅうぶん／結構	jubun/kekko
free (no charge)	ただ／無料	tada/muryo
here	ここ	koko
there	あそこ	asoko
this	これ	kore
that (nearby)	それ	sore
that (far away)	あれ	are
what?	何？	nani?
when?	いつ？	itsu?
why?	なぜ？／どうして？	naze?/dosh'te?
where?	どこ？	doko?
who?	誰？	dare?
which way?	どちら？	dochira?

SIGNS

open	営業中	eigyo-chu
closed	休日	kyujitsu
entrance	入口	iriguchi
exit	出口	deguchi
danger	危険	kiken
emergency exit	非常口	hijo-guchi
information	案内	annai
restroom, toilet	お手洗い／手洗い／おトイレ／トイレ	otearai/tearai/otoire/toire
free (vacant)	空き	jiyu
men	男	otoko
women	女	onna

MONEY

Could you change this into yen please.	これを円に替えてください。	Kore o en ni kaete kudasai.
I'd like to cash these travelers' checks.	このトラベラーズチェックを現金にしたいです。	Kono toraberazu chekku o genkin ni shitai dess.
Do you take credit cards/travelers' checks?	クレジットカード／トラベラーズチェックで払えますか？	Kurejitto kado/toraberazu chekku de haraemass-ka?
bank	銀行	ginko
cash	現金	genkin
credit card	クレジットカード	kurejitto kado
currency exchange office	両替所	ryogaejo
dollars	ドル	doru
pounds	ポンド	pondo
yen	円	en

KEEPING IN TOUCH

Where is there a telephone?	電話はどこにありますか？	Denwa wa doko ni arimass-ka?
May I use your phone?	電話を使ってもいいですか？	Denwa o ts'katte mo ii dess-ka?
Hello, this is	もしもし、…です。	Moshi-moshi, ... dess.
I'd like to make an international call.	国際電話、お願いします。	Kokusai denwa, onegai shimass.
airmail	航空便	kokubin
e-mail	イーメール	i-meru
fax	ファクス	fak'su
postcard	ハガキ	hagaki
post office	郵便局	yubin-kyoku
stamp	切手	kitte
telephone booth	公衆電話	koshu denwa
telephone card	テレフォンカード	terefon kado

SHOPPING

Where can I buy ...?	…はどこで買えますか？	... wa doko de kaemass-ka?
How much does this cost?	いくらですか？	Ikura dess-ka?
I'm just looking.	見ているだけです。	Mite iru dake dess.
Do you have ...?	…ありますか？	... arimass-ka?
May I try this on?	着てみてもいいですか？	Kite mite mo ii dess-ka?
Please show me that.	それを見せてください。	Sore o misete kudasai.
Does it come in other colors?	他の色もありますか？	Hoka no iro mo arimass-ka?
black	黒	kuro
blue	青	ao
green	緑	midori
red	赤	aka
white	白	shiro
yellow	黄色	kiiro
cheap/expensive	安い／高い	yasui/takai
audio equipment	オーディオ製品	odio seihin
bookstore	本屋	hon-ya
boutique	ブティック	butik
clothes	洋服	yofuku
department store	デパート	depato
electrical store	電気屋	denki-ya
fish market	魚屋	sakana-ya
folk crafts	民芸品	mingei-hin
ladies' wear	婦人服	fujin fuku
local specialty	名物	meibutsu
market	市場	ichiba
menswear	紳士服	shinshi fuku
newsstand	新聞屋	shimbun-ya

pharmacist	薬屋	kusuri-ya
picture postcard	絵葉書	e-hagaki
sale	セール	seru
souvenir shop	お土産屋	omiyage-ya
supermarket	スーパー	supa
travel agent	旅行会社	ryoko-gaisha

Sightseeing

Where is ...?	・・・はどこですか？	... wa doko dess-ka?
How do I get to ...?	・・・へは、どうやっていったらいいですか？	... e wa doyatte ittara ii dess-ka?
Is it far?	遠いですか？	Toi dess-ka?
art gallery	美術館	bijutsukan
reservations desk	予約窓口	yoyaku madoguchi
bridge	橋	hashi/bashi
castle	城	shiro/jo
city	市	shi
city center	街の中心	machi no chushin
gardens	庭園／庭	tei-en/niwa
hot spring	温泉	onsen
information office	案内所	annaijo
island	島	shima/jima
monastery	修道院	shudo-in
mountain	山	yama/san
museum	博物館	hakubutsukan
palace	宮殿	kyuden
park	公園	koen
port	港	minato/ko
prefecture	県	ken
river	川	kawa/gawa
ruins	遺跡	iseki
shopping area	ショッピング街	shoppingu gai
shrine	神社／神宮／宮	jinja/jingu/gu
street	通り	tori/dori
temple	お寺／寺	otera/tera/dera/ji
tour, travel	旅行	ryoko
town	町	machi/cho
village	村	mura
ward	区	ku
zoo	動物園	dobutsu-en
north	北	kita/hoku
south	南	minami/nan
east	東	higashi/to
west	西	nishi/sei
left/right	左／右	hidari/migi
straight ahead	真っ直ぐ	mass-sugu
between	間に	aida ni
near/far	近い／遠い	chikai/toi
up/down	上／下	ue/sh'ta
new	新しい／新	atarashii/shin
old/former	古い／元	furui/moto
upper/lower	上／下	kami/shimo
middle/inner	中	naka
in	に／中に	ni/naka ni
in front of	前	mae

Getting Around

bicycle	自転車	jitensha
bus	バス	basu
car	車	kuruma
ferry	フェリー	feri
baggage room	手荷物一時預かり所	tenimotsu ichiji azukarijo
motorcycle	オートバイ	otobai
one-way ticket	片道切符	katamichi kippu
return ticket	往復切符	ofuku kippu
taxi	タクシー	takushi
ticket	切符	kippu
ticket office	切符売場	kippu uriba

Trains

What is the fare to ...?	・・・までいくらですか？	... made ikura dess-ka?
When does the train for... leave?	・・・行きの電車は、何時に出ますか？	... iki no densha wa nan-ji ni demass-ka?
How long does it take to get to ...?	・・・まで時間は、どのぐらいかかりますか？	... made jikan wa dono gurai kakarimass-ka?
A ticket to ..., please.	・・・行きの切符をください。	... yuki no kippu o kudasai.
Do I have to change?	乗り換えが必要ですか？	Norikae ga hitsuyo dess-ka?
I'd like to reserve a seat, please.	席を予約したいです。	Seki o yoyaku shitai dess.
Which platform for the train to ...?	・・・行きの電車は、何番ホームから出ますか？	... yuki no densha wa nanban homu kara demass-ka?
Which station is this?	この駅は、どこですか？	Kono eki wa doko dess-ka?
Is this the right train for ...?	・・・へは、この電車でいいですか？	... e wa kono densha de ii dess-ka?
bullet train	新幹線	shinkansen
express trains:		
"limited express" (fastest)	特急	tokkyu
"express" (second)	急行	kyuko
"rapid" (third)	快速	kaisoku
first-class	一等	itto
line	線	sen
local train	普通／各駅電車	futsu/kaku-eki-densha
platform	ホーム	homu
train station	駅	eki
reserved seat	指定席	shitei-seki
second-class	二等	nito
subway	地下鉄	chikatetsu
train	電車	densha
unreserved seat	自由席	jiyu-seki

Accommodations

Do you have any vacancies?	部屋がありますか？	Heya ga arimass-ka?
I have a reservation.	予約をしてあります。	Yoyaku o sh'te arimass.
I'd like a room with a bathroom.	お風呂つきの部屋、お願いします。	Ofuro-ts'ki no heya, onegai shimass.
What is the charge per night?	一泊いくらですか？	Ippaku ikura dess-ka?
Is tax included in the price?	税込みですか？	Zeikomi dess-ka?
Can I leave my luggage here for a little while?	荷物をちょっとここに預けてもいいですか？	Nimotsu o chotto koko ni azukete mo ii dess-ka?
air-conditioning	冷房／エアコン	reibo/eakon
bath	お風呂	ofuro
check-out	チェックアウト	chekku-auto
hair drier	ドライヤー	doraiya
hot (boiled) water	お湯	oyu
Japanese-style inn	旅館	ryokan
Japanese-style room	和室	wa-shitsu
key	鍵	kagi
front desk	フロント	furonto
single/twin room	シングル／ツイン	shinguru/tsuin

shower	シャワー	shyawa
Western-style hotel	ホテル	hoteru
Western-style room	洋室	yo-shitsu

Eating Out

A table for one/two/three, please.	一人／二人／三人、お願いします。	Hitori/futari/sannin, onegai shimass.
May I see the menu.	メニュー、お願いします。	Menyu, onegai shimass.
Is there a set menu?	定食がありますか？	Teishoku ga arimass-ka?
I'd like	私は･･･がいいです。	Watashi wa ... ga ii dess.
May I have one of those?	それをひとつ、お願いします。	Sore o hitotsu, onegai shimass.
I am a vegetarian.	私はベジタリアンです。	Watashi wa bejitarian dess.
Waiter/waitress!	ちょっとすみません。	Chotto sumimasen!
What would you recommend?	おすすめは何ですか？	Osusume wa nan dess-ka?
How do you eat this?	これはどうやって食べますか？	Kore wa doyatte tabemass-ka?
May we have the check please.	お勘定、お願いします。	Okanjo, onegai shimass.
May we have some more ...	もっと･･･、お願いします。	Motto ..., onegai shimass.
The meal was very good, thank you.	ごちそうさまでした、おいしかったです。	Gochiso-sama desh'ta, oishikatta dess.
assortment	盛りあわせ	moriawase
boxed meal	弁当	bento
breakfast	朝食	cho-shoku
buffet	バイキング	baikingu
delicious	おいしい	oishii
dinner	夕食	yu-shoku
to drink	飲む	nomu
a drink	飲みもの	nomimono
to eat	食べる	taberu
food	食べもの／ごはん	tabemono/gohan
full (stomach)	おなかがいっぱい	onaka ga ippai
hot/cold	熱い／冷たい	atsui/tsumetai
hungry	おなかがすいた	onaka ga suita
Japanese food	和食	wa-shoku
lunch	昼食	chu-shoku
set menu	セット／定食	setto (snack)/teishoku (meal)
spicy	辛い	karai
sweet, mild	甘い	amai
Western food	洋食	yo-shoku

Places to Eat

cafeteria/canteen	食堂	shokudo
Chinese restaurant	中華料理屋	chuka-ryori-ya
coffee shop	喫茶店	kissaten
local bar	飲み屋／居酒屋	nomiya/izakaya
noodle stall	ラーメン屋	ramen-ya
restaurant	レストラン／料理屋	resutoran/ryori-ya
sushi on a conveyor belt	回転寿司	kaiten-zushi
upscale restaurant	料亭	ryotei
upscale vegetarian restaurant	精進料理屋	shojin-ryori-ya

Foods *(see also Reading the Menu pp314–15)*

apple	りんご	ringo
bamboo shoots	たけのこ	takenoko
beancurd	とうふ	tofu
bean sprouts	もやし	moyashi
beans	豆	mame
beef	ビーフ／牛肉	bifu/gyuniku
beefburger	ハンバーグ	hanbagu
blowfish	ふぐ	fugu
bonito, tuna	かつお／ツナ	katsuo/tsuna
bread	パン	pan
butter	バター	bata
cake	ケーキ	keki
chicken	とり／鶏肉	tori/toriniku
confectionery	お菓子	okashi
crab	かに	kani
duck	あひる	ahiru
eel	うなぎ	unagi
egg	たまご	tamago
eggplant/aubergine	なす	nasu
fermented soybean paste	みそ	miso
fermented soybeans	納豆	natto
fish (raw)	さしみ	sashimi
fried tofu	油揚げ	abura-age
fruit	くだもの	kudamono
ginger	しょうが	shoga
hamburger	ハンバーガー	hanbaga
haute cuisine	会席	kaiseki
herring	ニシン	nishin
hors d'oeuvres	オードブル	odoburu
ice cream	アイスクリーム	aisu-kurimu
jam	ジャム	jamu
Japanese mushrooms	まつたけ／しいたけ／しめじ	mats'take/shiitake/shimeji
Japanese pear	なし	nashi
loach	どじょう	dojo
lobster	伊勢えび	ise-ebi
mackerel	さば	saba
mackerel pike	さんま	sanma
mandarin orange	みかん	mikan
meat	肉	niku
melon	メロン	meron
mountain vegetables	山菜	sansai
noodles:		
buckwheat	そば	soba
Chinese	ラーメン	ramen
wheatflour	うどん／そうめん	udon (fat)/somen (thin)
octopus	たこ	tako
omelet	オムレツ	omuretsu
oyster	カキ	kaki
peach	もも	momo
pepper	こしょう	kosho
persimmon	柿	kaki
pickles	つけもの	ts'kemono
pork	豚肉	butaniku
potato	いも	imo
rice:		
cooked	ごはん	gohan
uncooked	米	kome
rice crackers	おせんべい	osenbei
roast beef	ローストビーフ	rosutobifu
salad	サラダ	sarada
salmon	鮭	sake
salt	塩	shio
sandwich	サンドイッチ	sandoichi
sausage	ソーセージ	soseji
savory nibbles	おつまみ	otsumami
seaweed:		
dried	のり	nori
chewy	こんぶ	konbu

shrimp	えび	ebi
soup	汁／スープ	shiru/supu
soy sauce	しょうゆ	shoyu
spaghetti	スパゲティ	supageti
spinach	ほうれんそう	horenso
squid	いか	ika
steak	ステーキ	suteki
sugar	砂糖	sato
sushi (mixed)	五目寿司	gomoku-zushi
sweetfish/smelt	あゆ	ayu
sweet potato	さといも	sato imo
toast	トースト	tosuto
trout	鱒	masu
sea urchin	ウニ	uni
vegetables	野菜	yasai
watermelon	すいか	suika
wild boar	ぼたん／いのしし	botan/inoshishi

Drinks

beer	ビール	biru
coffee (hot)	ホットコーヒー	hotto-kohi
cola	コーラ	kora
green tea	お茶	ocha
iced coffee:		
black	アイスコーヒー	aisu-kohi
with milk	アイスオーレ	kafe-o-re
lemon tea	レモンティー	remon ti
milk	ミルク／牛乳	miruku/gyunyu
mineral water	ミネラルウォーター	mineraru uota
orange juice	オレンジジュース	orenji jusu
rice wine	酒	sake
(non-alcoholic)	（甘酒）	(ama-zake)
tea (Western-style)	紅茶	kocha
tea with milk	ミルクティー	miruku ti
water	水	mizu
whiskey	ウイスキー	uis'ki
wine	ワイン／ぶどう酒	wain/budoshu

Health

I don't feel well.	気分がよくないです。	Kibun ga yokunai dess.
I have a pain in …	…が痛いです。	… ga itai dess.
I'm allergic to …	…アレルギーです。	… arerugi dess.
asthma	喘息	zensoku
cough	せき	seki
dentist	歯医者	haisha
diabetes	糖尿病	tonyo-byo
diarrhea	下痢	geri
doctor	医者	isha
fever	熱	netsu
headache	頭痛	zutsuu
hospital	病院	byoin
medicine	薬	kusuri
Oriental medicine	漢方薬	kampo yaku
pharmacy	薬局	yakkyoku
prescription	処方箋	shohosen
stomachache	腹痛	fukutsu
toothache	歯が痛い	ha ga itai

Numbers

0	ゼロ	zero
1	一	ichi
2	二	ni
3	三	san
4	四	yon/shi
5	五	go
6	六	roku
7	七	nana/shichi
8	八	hachi
9	九	kyu
10	十	ju
11	十一	ju-ichi
12	十二	ju-ni
20	二十	ni-ju
21	二十一	ni-ju-ichi
22	二十二	ni-ju-ni
30	三十	san-ju
40	四十	yon-ju
100	百	hyaku
101	百一	hyaku-ichi
200	二百	ni-hyaku
300	三百	san-byaku
400	四百	yon-hyaku
500	五百	go-hyaku
600	六百	ro-ppyaku
700	七百	nana-hyaku
800	八百	ha-ppyaku
900	九百	kyu-hyaku
1,000	千	sen
1,001	千一	sen-ichi
2,000	二千	ni-sen
10,000	一万	ichi-man
20,000	二万	ni-man
100,000	十万	ju-man
1,000,000	百万	hyaku-man
123,456	十二万三千四百五十六	ju-ni-man-san-zen-yon-hyaku-go-ju-roku

Time

Monday	月曜日	getsu-yobi
Tuesday	火曜日	ka-yobi
Wednesday	水曜日	sui-yobi
Thursday	木曜日	moku-yobi
Friday	金曜日	kin-yobi
Saturday	土曜日	do-yobi
Sunday	日曜日	nichi-yobi
January	一月	ichi-gatsu
February	二月	ni-gatsu
March	三月	san-gatsu
April	四月	shi-gatsu
May	五月	go-gatsu
June	六月	roku-gatsu
July	七月	shichi-gatsu
August	八月	hachi-gatsu
September	九月	ku-gatsu
October	十月	ju-gatsu
November	十一月	ju-ichi-gatsu
December	十二月	ju-ni-gatsu
spring	春	haru
summer	夏	natsu
fall/autumn	秋	aki
winter	冬	fuyu
noon	正午	shogo
midnight	真夜中	mayonaka
today	今日	kyo
yesterday	昨日	kino
tomorrow	明日	ash'ta
this morning	今朝	kesa
this afternoon	今日の午後	kyo no gogo
this evening	今晩	konban
every day	毎日	mainichi
month	月	getsu/ts'ki
hour	時	ji
time/hour (duration)	時間	jikan
minute	分	pun/fun
this year	今年	kotoshi
last year	去年	kyonen
next year	来年	rainen
one year	一年	ichi-nen
late	遅い	osoi
early	早い	hayai
soon	すぐ	sugu